AMERICAN SHOWMAN

FILM AND CULTURE   *John Belton, Editor*

ROSS MELNICK

AMERICAN SHOWMAN

SAMUEL "ROXY" ROTHAFEL AND THE
BIRTH OF THE ENTERTAINMENT INDUSTRY, 1908–1935

COLUMBIA UNIVERSITY PRESS   *New York*

Columbia University Press
Publishers Since 1893
New York   Chichester, West Sussex

Library of Congress Cataloging-in-Publication Data
Melnick, Ross.
American showman : Samuel "Roxy" Rothafel and the birth of the entertainment industry,
1908–1935 / Ross Melnick.
p. cm. – (Film and culture)
Includes bibliographical references and index.
ISBN 978-0-231-15904-3 (cloth : alk. paper)
1. Rothafel, Samuel Lionel, 1881–1936. 2. Motion picture theater
owners—United States—Biography. 3. Radio broadcasters—United
States—Biography. 4. Businessmen—United States—Biography.
5. Motion picture industry—United States—History. 6. Motion picture
theaters—United States—History. I. Title.
PN1998.3.R68M45 2012
791.4302´32092—dc23
[B]
2011050324

References to Internet Web sites (URLs) were accurate at the time of writing. Neither the
author nor Columbia University Press is responsible for URLs that may have expired or
changed since the manuscript was prepared.

For my parents, who inspire me to write about the past, and
For my wife, Noa, who inspires me to dream about the future

CONTENTS

LIST OF ILLUSTRATIONS

(*following page 250*)

ACKNOWLEDGMENTS

This book began a decade ago in Jan-Christopher Horak's "American Silent Film" seminar at UCLA. So much has changed in my life since then, yet no matter where my career has taken me—to New York, Atlanta, or Michigan—the endless work on Roxy's career in film, broadcasting, and music has always been there. I'll miss the excitement, challenge, and consistency of that enterprise. I'll also miss Roxy and time traveling to the early twentieth century. After more than nine years, though, it's time to move on to other projects, but I'm not sure if I'll ever find another subject as captivating as this one. There's something intoxicating about Roxy's mix of artistry, idealism, and marketing.

This book would not have been possible without the support of my colleagues, friends, and family, Columbia University Press, and the many people who assisted me over the years.

I must first thank UCLA's Cinema and Media Studies program, including Nick Browne, Brian Clark, Teshome Gabriel, Jonathan Kuntz, Denise Mann, Kathleen McHugh, Chon Noriega, and Vivian Sobchack—an amazing group of scholars and friends. I wish I could share this book with Teshome and talk with him again outside, near Melnitz or Macgowan, where his spirit will linger forever.

In addition to those mentioned above, John Caldwell deserves not just my deep and abiding gratitude, but acknowledgment of the enormously important role he played in my critical thinking and development. John has always been a constant supporter, mentor, and friend. This book would not have been the same without him.

Janet Bergstrom's influence on *American Showman* was just as profound. I can scarcely remember a pivotal moment in this project's development that we did not discuss first before I began writing. In addition, much of my work on radio and convergence began with an article she edited and published in a 2005 issue of *Film History*. I cannot thank her enough for her support, her friendship, and for her interest in this project.

Steve Mamber, who guided this project at UCLA, deserves my unending appreciation for helping me through its completion and for spurring me on as its length and scope grew in unexpected ways. UCLA's CMS program was my home for many years and Steve always kept the door open and the fireplace lit.

Steve Ricci also had an enormous influence on this project and, specifically, on the formulation of the "unitary text." His friendship and support remain invaluable. I would also like to thank David Myers for his invaluable insights on this project. I was also thrilled to find Timothy Taylor at UCLA after completing the first draft of this work and I thank him profusely for providing me with several terrific discussions and the only copy of a Roxy broadcast I have ever heard.

I am also deeply grateful to my friends Eric Mack, Candace Moore, and Laurel Westrup who provided terrific feedback on this work as it developed. I also thank the rest of my cohort, Josh Amberg, Colin Gunckel, Sudeep Sharma, and Eric Vanstrom. I was very lucky to have such a talented group of scholars to learn from. Of the many additional friends who provided feedback and/or support, I must thank Vincent Brook, Emily Carman, Patrick Crowley, Dawn Fratini, Doron Galili, Jason Gendler, Ben Harris, Erin Hill, Jennifer Holt, Jennifer Moorman, Deron Overpeck, Scott Paulin, Miriam Posner, Mark Quigley, Mirasol Riojas, Mary Samuelson, Maria San Filippo, Eric Smoodin, Katherine Spring, Phil Wagner, Julia Wright, Michael Zoldessy, and Heidi Zwicker. Enormous gratitude to Rob King for his tireless enthusiasm and for being a truly fantastic editor and friend.

Perhaps no one deserves more credit for inspiring me to work on Roxy, though, than Chris Horak. I cannot thank him enough for his unwavering encouragement and support and for his friendship over the past decade. It's meant the world to me.

Tom Doherty has also been a tireless advocate over the past two decades and one of my best friends. This book is a testament to his work as my undergraduate mentor in the 1990s and his incomparable friendship ever since. He is one in a million. Thanks for everything, Tom.

I also thank Milton Moritz of NATO California-Nevada for his friendship and for his extensive knowledge of the history of film distribution and exhibition. Others who provided insight into the history of the exhibition business include Jim Amos, Alan Benjamin, Adam Bergerman, Edward Havens, Howard Haas, Janet Murray, Jim Rankin, Ken Roe, John Sittig, and John Spinello. Last, but certainly not least, are two wonderful friends and exhibition veterans, Andreas Fuchs and A. J. Roquevert.

I owe an enormous dept of gratitude to the Bill and Carol Fox Center for Humanistic Inquiry at Emory University for a postdoctoral fellowship during the 2010-2011 academic year that gave me the intellectual engagement and time to begin revising this book. I sincerely thank Sandra Blakely, Yayoi Everett, Amanda Golden, Amy Gansell, Davis Hankins, Emily Kader, Lori Leavell, and Carol Newsom for their invaluable feedback and constant support throughout the year. Enormous thanks to Deepika Bahri, Danielle Bobker, and Jeffrey Lesser for their warmth, enthusiasm, and always terrific counsel. Martine Brownley and Keith Anthony gave me a once-in-a-lifetime opportunity at the CHI and provided me with the time, space, and intellectual support to work on this book. At Emory, I also thank the incomparable Matthew Bernstein, whose guidance and support remain invaluable, as well as Annie Hall, Benny Hary, Karla Oeler, David Pratt, Michele Schreiber, James Steffen, Leslie Taylor, and Eddy Von Mueller for their friendship and their wisdom.

My wonderful colleagues at Oakland University have also provided me with the support to complete this book. Enormous gratitude to my Cinema Studies colleagues, Kyle Edwards and Hunter Vaughan, as well as my colleagues in the English Department, Robert Anderson, Gladys Cardiff, Jeffrey Chapman, Natalie Cole, Brian Connery, Annette Gilson, Kevin Grimm, Susan Hawkins, Niels Herold, Edward Hoeppner, Jeffrey Insko, Nancy Joseph, Andrea Knutson, Kevin Laam, Bailey McDaniel, and Kathleen Pfeiffer.

At Columbia University Press, I profusely thank Jennifer Crewe and John Belton for their tireless support and for enabling me to keep my vision of this book intact. I couldn't have found more supportive editors for *American Showman*. I must also thank Manisha Singh for her prodigious work on this book, Asya Graf for her assistance and enthusiasm, and Roy Thomas, who assuredly guided the manuscript from start to finish and was always there to keep the project moving forward. I also thank those invaluable peer reviewers who provided such terrific feedback and helped me to refine this work.

There are numerous librarians and archivists who made this book possible: Jeremy Megraw and the staff at the New York Public Library for the Performing

Arts; Marty Jacobs at the Museum of the City of New York; Brent T. Peterson, Executive Director of the Washington County Historical Society; Jana Armstead of the Ramsey County Historical Society; Ted Jackson at the Quigley Photographic Archive at Georgetown University; Jane Winton at the Boston Public Library; Paul Hogroian at the Library of Congress; Eva Tucholka at Culver Pictures; Eleanor McKeown at Lebrecht Music & Arts; Steve Wilson at the Harry Ransom Center; Ron Magliozzi at the Museum of Modern Art; John Kamins at *The Forest City News*; Lisa Kernan, Alan Michelson, and Diana King at the UCLA Arts Library; Sandra Joy Lee at the USC Warner Bros. Archives; Harry Miller and the staff of the Wisconsin Historical Society; Rochelle Slovin, Megan Forbes, Natalia Fidelholtz, and Dana Nemeth at Museum of the Moving Image; the staff at the Los Angeles Regional Family History Center; and the National Archives and Records Administration. Special thanks, as always, to Linda Mehr, Barbara Hall, Jenny Romero, Bob Dickson, and Galen Wilkes at the Margaret Herrick Library who continue to play an essential role in my work, and to Karen Noonan, Richard Sklenar, and Kathy McLeister at the Theatre Historical Society of America who provided essential assistance with images and such an invaluable service and organization.

Art Rothafel, Roxy's grandson, his wife Gigi, and daughters Chelsea and Roxanne, have been one of the most rewarding parts of this project. I first contacted Art in January 2003 and was delighted to learn that he lived about an hour from UCLA. I thank Art profusely for sharing his memories with me, a tape of his father talking about "the old days," and for trusting me to write whatever I wanted to about his grandfather—"warts and all" as I told him. I gained four wonderful friends through this project.

I must also thank Shmuel and Neta Bolozky profusely for their unwavering support over the past two decades and for their constant encouragement.

My brother Joshua has also watched this project unfold over the past decade and his support and patience always mean so much to me. I also cannot thank my parents enough for the enthusiasm and love they have always provided me. Throughout the life of this project, I spent countless hours on the phone with my father Ralph. He was always there to listen and to provide context for Roxy's place within American society and culture. I feel so blessed to have them all in my life.

Finally, I must thank my amazing wife Noa for her love, patience, and wisdom. It's hard to believe that it's been twenty-two years since we first met. Over that time, our hopes and dreams have changed considerably but our love for each other has not. In every way possible—logistical, emotional, and intellectual—Noa has supported this project and me. This book is for her.

AMERICAN SHOWMAN

INTRODUCTION

Samuel Rothafel was the father of present-day motion picture exhibition. . . . He created the presentation house, the picture stage show; he brought into movie theaters the big concert orchestras, the ballets, the concert and opera singers. Every important feature of motion picture presentation in the theater today was the inspiration of Roxy.
   —W. R. Wilkerson, *The Hollywood Reporter*, January 1936

No man has done more to make for the success of the radio in the family circle than has the well-known figure. . . . True, the radio made "Roxy," but "Roxy" has had much to do with the making of the radio.
   —*Woonsocket* (RI) *Call-Republican,* July 1925

Today the name [Roxy] means little, but a couple of decades ago almost every thing connected with that name made news.
   —Actor Pat O'Malley, 1957

Film historiography has often focused on production, stardom, and/or the intricate operations of the studio system—much of it to the exclusion of motion picture distribution and exhibition. *American Showman* analyzes the career of a single film exhibitor and radio broadcaster, Samuel Lionel "Roxy" Rothafel (1882–1936), between the years 1908 and 1935, in order to illuminate the work of a silent era "showman," the complex operations of an urban movie palace, and the multiple and interrelated venues created for film, music, and live performance on stage, on screen, and over the air. Whereas the film industry could debate which star or mogul held more sway during this period, for a quarter of a century no motion picture exhibitor had more industrial and cultural power or influence than Roxy. On radio, Roxy was also amongst the medium's most popular and innovative voices in the 1920s and 1930s, helping to determine early radio genres, formats, and broadcasting styles. His career not only illuminates the multifarious tasks of an urban movie palace exhibitor but Roxy's additional roles as a broadcaster, filmmaker, music director, stage producer, propagandist, newspaper columnist, and author demonstrate that exhibitors like Roxy were not bureaucratic functionaries but influential figures that can and should be analyzed for their own thematic and stylistic predilections and industrial, social, and cultural influence. This analysis also demonstrates the motion picture exhibitor's influence on spectatorship (both in film and live performances), narrative, and previously unexplored issues of authorship. Silent era exhibitors, in small and large venues, had tremendous agency over the texts they presented. In some cases, their preceding, intervening, and concluding music and live performances, and their editing of films, dramatically altered the narratives of the motion pictures they exhibited.

American Showman also situates the movie theater as one of the premiere venues for the physical and industrial nexus of early media convergence and examines how changes in film exhibition helped drive the entertainment industry's multimedia integration of motion pictures, broadcasting, and music publishing and recording. While convergence is a key component of contemporary discourses about media technology, power, stardom, and the utopian visions of tomorrow's entertainment possibilities, this first wave of media convergence remains vastly overlooked by comparison. This book historicizes the genesis of media convergence and locates Roxy's place and influence within this phenomenon in the 1920s and 1930s. From his earliest efforts, Roxy also emphasized the need to incorporate all of the "allied arts," including vaudeville, opera, ballet, film, classical music, and more in an effort to entertain audiences over the air and in the theaters he managed in Milwaukee, Minneapolis, New York City, Los Angeles, Philadelphia, and Washington, D.C. This integration subsequently helped break down the walls of these classed and disparate arenas and transformed them all into symbiotic elements of a convergent entertainment industry that benefited media companies, producers, and stars. Over time, Roxy and his on-air radio troupe known as "Roxy and His Gang" found success and celebrity from music publishing and recording, broadcasting, and motion pictures.

Broadcasting was initially perceived as a grave threat to the viability and dominance of motion pictures, but radio programs, stations, and networks eventually became key partners of the film industry and a crucial division and/or promotional association of any major entertainment media conglomerate. Roxy's early embrace and successful exploitation of this new medium—he was the first exhibitor to begin using broadcasting extensively as a promotional device—had a profound effect upon the film industry. Producers, studios, and exhibitors followed his example and reached out to radio listeners as a means to market films, theaters, and stars, as well as an eventual source of product extension, distribution, and revenue generation. In addition to this marriage between film and broadcasting, each medium's integration with the music publishing and recording industry expanded this growing convergence. These synergistic activities not only influenced the popularity of theme songs from motion pictures but cemented the need for aggregating film and music divisions within any major entertainment conglomerate.

Although substantial research has been conducted on Vitaphone and the production of early synchronous sound films in this format, research on Fox Movietone films between 1927 and 1929, the years in which Roxy and his musical director Erno Rapee scored a host of Fox films, remains scattered at best. This paucity of research has led to a lack of historical clarity about this period and the Roxy and Rapee–arranged scores for *Sunrise* (1927), *Four Sons* (1928), *Mother Machree* (1928), and other films by John Ford, Howard Hawks, Frank Borzage, and F. W. Murnau.[1] These soundtracks, often with sound effects and music assembled and arranged by Roxy and Rapee, and the theme songs generated for these motion pictures, typically written by Rapee and Lew Pollack, demonstrate the multiple channels of distribution for the Roxy Theatre orchestra in the late 1920s when the 110-piece symphony could be heard live in the 5,920-seat Roxy Theatre, nationally over the air on NBC-Blue, and in theaters around the world through Movietone. Rapee and Pollack's theme songs formed another important link between the film and music publishing and recording industries and were an important catalyst for the late 1920s theme song craze. The success of new synchronous sound films, and their music-related products such as records and sheet music, converted vertically integrated companies (with film production, distribution, and exhibition) into vertically *and horizontally* integrated media conglomerates (combining film, broadcasting, and music publishing and recording) that produced films and music that fed the demand for popular songs by music directors at radio stations and live orchestras as well as everyday consumers. Theme songs such as "Charmaine" and "Diane" sold millions of copies of sheet music and phonographs and led to an increasing reliance on ancillary revenues by film companies, as well as their subsequent purchase of music publishing firms. All of these synergistic practices influenced the demand for musicals such as *Fox Movietone Follies* (1929) and *Sunny Side Up* (1929), which generated new commercially extensible songs that were pre-sold to audiences over the radio and in live performance venues to sell sheet music, records, and movie theater tickets.

The film industry's need for ancillary revenue streams is typically analyzed in much later periods, such as the 1970s' high-concept blockbusters, but the endless loop between film, radio, and music began half a century earlier in the 1920s when companies like Radio Corporation of America (RCA) and Warner Bros. introduced the practice of one division of a media conglomerate's business working in tandem with another. These synergistic practices also extended the stardom of a growing list of performers like Roxy who found fame in broadcasting, film, and music publishing and recording. Along with the purchase of music publishing firms, all of these increasingly horizontally and vertically integrated entertainment conglomerates began investing in and working with radio stations and networks to promote and exploit their music catalogs, films, and theaters, thereby maximizing their products and stars.

In addition to music publishing (and in some cases recording) divisions, owning radio shows, stations, and networks became part of the media conglomerate strategy in the late 1920s. Paramount purchased station KNX and a 50 percent stake in CBS and established the *Paramount-Publix Hour* over William Paley's network.[2] RCA formed NBC-Red, NBC-Blue, and RKO, leading to the weekly *RKO-NBC Radio Hour*.[3] Warner Bros. also established stations WBPI and KFWB to promote company films, stars, and theaters and promoted their assets through the *Vitaphone Jubilee Hour*, which aired nationally on CBS.[4] Loew's purchased WHN to promote Loew's theaters and MGM films and benefited from Roxy's and, later, Major Bowes's weekly broadcasts from the 5,300-seat Capitol Theatre over NBC-Red. Fox theaters in New York, Philadelphia, and other cities transmitted entertainment from their theaters over the air, while exhibitors nationwide were broadcasting live from their stages and orchestra pits. The stardom of those who could capitalize on the growing opportunities for crossover entertainment included artists like Roxy Theatre organist Lew White, who performed live at the Roxy Theatre for audiences and over the air in his studio for NBC and who recorded popular songs for Brunswick Records.

In short, between 1922 and 1931, new radio and sound technologies helped convert the film industry into merely one part of a new and vast intertextual entertainment industry. While these technological developments are often situated within the "coming of sound" to motion pictures, this book takes a much wider view. This transformative moment was not simply the addition of new technologies to an existing medium and business but the beginning of the modern entertainment industry in which multinational media conglomerates developed brands and franchises that could exploit new revenue streams in order to maximize profits from content release "events" through soundtracks, feature films, live performances, print and other ephemera, as well as film and music recordings. This approach seeks to contextualize and situate much of this activity within the birth of media convergence and conglomeration and the activities of exhibition-related stars/moguls such as Roxy, Rapee, Lew White, David Mendoza, and Major Bowes, as well as executives such as Sam Warner, William Paley, and David Sarnoff.

Roxy's career as an exhibitor-broadcaster is emblematic of a generational cohort of which he was a leading, if now largely forgotten, member. As one of the few moguls who was both behind the scenes *and* publicly promoting his own brand image and stardom, Roxy's negotiation of his cultural and industrial status during an age of anti-immigrant and anti-Semitic attitudes tracks the social mobility which the entertainment industry has often afforded the "other" as audiences came to embrace the film, radio, and music worlds' leading members as a new form of American royalty. Roxy's personal narrative, his fame as an exhibitor and broadcaster, along with his military service before, during, and after World War I, served as crucial entry points for his embrace by religious, industrial, political, and cultural leaders and his engagement with such prominent figures as Hugo Münsterberg, Sarah Bernhardt, David Belasco, Otto Kahn, Theodore Dreiser, John D. Rockefeller, Constantin Stanislavski, Max Reinhardt, and Calvin Coolidge.

Stephen Whitfield writes that "The Jewish community has hardly been invulnerable to the pressures and interventions of the larger culture." However, he notes, "The creativity of American Jewry has also affected and altered that culture. Exchanging ideas and images with the larger culture in a network of reciprocity, Jews have borrowed freely but have also expanded the contours of that larger culture."[5] In order to understand the work of prominent American Jewish entertainers and entertainment executives like Roxy, Sid Grauman, William Paley, David Sarnoff, Sam Warner, Adolph Zukor, and innumerable others, it is important to trace the many ways in which film production and exhibition as well as broadcasting during this period appropriated existing forms of late-Victorian American culture and molded them into a new mass entertainment in movie theaters and broadcasting studios nationwide. Opera, for instance, once the domain of the upper classes, was increasingly welded onto elaborate motion picture theater programs and transmitted nationally to rural and urban audiences through broadcasting. Classical music, once requiring a Carnegie Hall ticket, was available at a Roxy theater throughout the silent and early sound film eras and featured some of the most talented musicians and conductors in the country. Making the movie palace a venue for the classes and the masses elevated the cultural status of motion pictures and created new audiences for mass entertainment products distributed by (often Jewish-run) companies such as Loew's, Paramount, Fox, and Warner Bros. The "larger culture" provided a road map for attaining cultural respectability, but Roxy hybridized established "high" cultural forms with "low" cultural products to create a new form of socially acceptable, mass entertainment on screen, on stage, and later, over the air. In "no other arena of entertainment," Steven Ross writes, were "high and low culture so closely intertwined."[6]

I situate all of this research not in "film history," but within the following fields of scholarship in media studies and historiography: the historical development of film exhibition between 1908 and 1935; the overlooked but crucial importance of analyzing the stardom and authorship of motion picture exhibitors; the film industry's role in World War I propaganda and its growing ties with Washington; the rise of broadcasting as a popular form of entertainment; and the role of technological and corporate convergence as a fundamental aspect of entertainment media (industry) history. Although a growing number of scholars recognize film exhibition's place within larger, convergent economic, technological, industrial, and entertainment configurations, an intertextual and *cross-media* approach to film, film exhibition, broadcasting, music, etc., is a central thrust of this book's methodology.

Beginning around 1911, the role of a motion picture exhibitor changed from that of a movie theater manager to a position somewhat akin to a theatrical producer/director. Exhibitors in large deluxe theaters were increasingly expected to manage scores of personnel; supervise or assemble the music for motion pictures; produce and/or book the theater's live stage shows; market the theater and its films to audiences and journalists; scout new talent (in the United States and overseas); book films from distributors; balance the complex requirements of a theater's financial operations; oversee the initial construction, maintenance, and/or refurbishment of the theater; liaise with the company's/circuit's central office (where necessary); and survey the latest technology, films, and entertainment to fit the needs and budgets of the theater and its constituency. In short, a movie palace exhibitor in the silent era was a tireless producer of live and filmed entertainment who oversaw a self-contained city of performers, employees, and customers for which no modern motion picture theater corollary exists.

In addition to these myriad tasks, by the 1920s, broadcasting, music publishing and recording, and other sources of revenue and brand extensions became key functions of some movie theater exhibitors, conductors, and performers. This growing media convergence, located at the site of motion picture exhibition, is a central concern of the second half of this book. This focus on media integration in the 1920s and 1930s follows a recent shift away from a strictly film or television historiographical model and into a wider field of media historiography. As Janet Staiger commented in 2004:

> Scholars need to stop thinking of film history as film history and start thinking more about media history. While I believe fully that the concept of media specificity exists, being sheltered by studying only film is to work

with blinders on. Film as a business and an art was never isolated from the other entertainments. . . . Researchers considering the business activities of the last thirty years tend to think of film as within larger media monopolies in a global circulation of product. This has always been the economic and political situation. Capital has been in a network of geopolitical relations, and film, in a multimedia environment.[7]

William Uricchio sees the current interest in media convergence as spurring a wider reexamination of media-specific histories. "Together, the efforts of historians to reconsider the taken-for-granted and the demands of the digital and convergent present have compelled a new view of media, one which benefits from considering other moments of media in transition."[8]

American Showman takes a multimedia approach, wherever applicable, to the study of silent and early sound film exhibition, broadcasting, live and recorded music, vaudeville, live performance, and all of the modes of entertainment mobilized by Roxy and those who worked for and with him. While this reformulation of film within wider industrial and discursive arenas is largely a new trend in media studies, it is *not* a new trend in terms of media practice.

Research and Sources

Research for this book was, at times, an enormous challenge. Roxy left no private papers, and the corporate records of all of his theaters, with the exception of Radio City Music Hall (which thrice denied access to their private archives), have long since disappeared. He was, however, extensively covered and interviewed over the course of his career. In addition to reviewing some correspondence in the NBC archives at the Wisconsin Historical Society and a select few other sources, reconstructing his career in film, music, and broadcasting required a painstaking review of trade journals from all three areas and popular press accounts that number well into the thousands, if not tens of thousands, and a constant need to read against the grain of so much spin from one of America's most talented publicists. Much of this research, therefore, was culled from very different kinds of sources: scrapbooks in the New York Public Library for the Performing Arts (Capitol Theatre and "Roxy and His Gang") and the Museum of the City of New York (Roxy Theatre); theater programs from the Roxy Theatre and Radio City Music Hall located in the New York Public Library for the Performing Arts; magazines, programs, letters, photographs, records, sheet music, promotional materials, and other ephemera purchased on eBay and through other sources; trade, fan, and popular journals; and a wide array of local, national, and international newspapers researched through microfilm and online. When I began this research in 2002, access to historical newspapers online was still limited. Over the past decade, companies such as ProQuest have made access to large city newspapers like the *New York Times*, *Los Angeles Times*, and *Washington Post* possible and searchable, even at three o'clock in the morning. In recent years, other services such as NewspaperArchive.com have enabled access to hundreds of small town newspapers across the United States. This made a considerable and invaluable contribution to my research. This local coverage throughout the country in places such as Sheboygan, Wisconsin, produced several important results: (1) Some New York–based columnists syndicated their writing in small town newspapers and thus this material is often unavailable to those merely searching the *New York Times* or other major metropolitan sources. (2) Access to these small town newspapers enabled me to track the regional popularity of "Roxy and His Gang," the proliferation of Roxy's brand name, and the speed with which Movietone and media convergence was accepted and normalized nationwide. (3) Finally, small town newspapers enable scholars to find wire service articles, photographs, advertisements, and other material deemed unimportant to those newspapers available through ProQuest and other "big city" sources. All of this material was central in understanding Roxy's career, his interest in film, radio, music, and early media convergence, and the formulation of what I call the "unitary text" of silent and early sound film exhibition.

THE UNITARY TEXT AND SILENT FILM EXHIBITION

The importance of the motion picture exhibitor is typically elided in contemporary discussions of authorship, narrative, censorship, and moving image archival practice. Despite a marked shift toward audiences, reception, and exhibition in film and television studies over the past two decades, especially in the analysis of small town theaters and city-specific studies, the impact of silent era exhibitors' frequent right to final cut and theater censorship practices is often ignored, while moving image archivists have often remained driven by two determinant goals in their restoration efforts: to reproduce the technical properties of a given film and/or to focus on the romantic notion of the author in determining original intent. While both can be crucial functions of a restorer's work, the motion picture exhibitor as one of the "authors" of a

given text has yet to be considered in any detailed context. But this individual
is a constituent, yet forgotten, part of the original experience of any silent
film, whose lasting influence can often be felt in the film's original musical
accompaniment, its resonant contemporary industrial and cultural impact,
and in some cases even its original narrative flow.

As Richard Koszarski and others have noted, the feature film was only one
part of "an evening's entertainment" during this period, and viewing it alone,
without considering its surrounding and intervening material, is to fail to
account for the "original experience." Not only did the surrounding program
give the experience a temporal uniqueness, Miriam Hansen argues, these live
performances were "essential" to the meaning of the moving images presented
and their effect upon audiences.[9] Koszarski adds that an important distinction
that has eluded much of the writing on moviegoing during this period is that
a silent era experience was "essentially a theater experience, not a film experience, calling into question the efficacy of the classical objective of a textu-
ally centered spectator."[10] These live events that surrounded the film, Hansen
writes, "lent the show the immediacy and singularity of a one-time performance, as opposed to an event that was repeated in more or less the same
fashion everywhere and whenever the films were shown. Hence, the meanings
transacted were contingent upon *local* conditions and constellations."[11]

This issue is important not only to post-1911 moviegoing, when live performance began to take on an increasingly prominent role in motion picture
theaters, but also for early cinema. Charles Musser has noted that exhibitors
exerted tremendous influence over the meaning of early silent films by their
careful arrangement of the overall program: the inclusion of framing stories,
lectures, voices heard before, during, and after a screening, and other interac-
tions with recorded media presented in nickelodeons, vaudeville houses, air-
domes, and other motion picture venues.[12] "The distinction between film and
program was a vague one in this period," Tom Gunning argues, "in which the
showman exhibitor asserted as much control over the final form of the film
projected as the production company that issued the individual bits of celluloid with which he worked."[13] Nicholas Hiley notes that scholars and archivists
of early British cinema have also trained their focus too heavily on film texts
outside of their economic, cultural, and industrial context:

The basis of [film] history is the individual film, and yet this approach is
misleading, for over the first 25 years of projected moving pictures, from
1895 to 1920, the individual film was of little significance. The basic unit
of exhibition was not the individual film but the programme, and the

commodity that most patrons wished to buy from the exhibitor was not access to an individual film, but time in the auditorium. Paradoxically, film historians now value these early films more highly than the people who originally paid to see them, and certainly more than the companies who originally produced them. . . . [H]istorians can learn more about the British film industry between 1895 and 1920 by studying the venues in which these films were exhibited, than by restoring these prints and projecting them according to their own personal tastes.[14]

David Robinson, recalling the "total experience" of viewing Kevin Brownlow's *Napoleon* screenings at Radio City Music Hall in 1980 with a live orchestra, argues that "to see a great silent film, in a lustrous print, with a symphonic live musical accompaniment, projected in a grand theater with a packed audience is an experience *de sui generis*. It is not like theater or ballet or film as we know it, but combines something of them all in a form that at its best can exert a unique power over the senses and the imagination."[15]

Transitional and Classical Era Silent Film Exhibition

"During the 1915–1928 period," a periodization that transcends the transitional period (1908–1917) and the "classical" or late silent era, Richard Koszarski notes, "the experience of viewing a film was far different from what it would be at any time before or since. Exhibitors considered themselves showmen, not film programmers. The feature motion picture was only one part of an evening's entertainment . . . [and while] exhibitors always hoped for a strong feature, they did not feel wholly dependent on that part of their show which arrived in a can. Nor were they above 'improving' their film subject by any means at their disposal."[16] The *Los Angeles Evening Express* argued in December 1919 that "Attendance at the presentation of a motion picture today is not merely the witnessing of the picture itself, but of hearing superb renditions of music, enjoying the wonderful beauty of interpretative dancing, and the marvelous lighting effects which convert the scenes on the film into a wonderland of delight."[17] Roxy noted, "The time is coming when the people will attend a picture presentation because it is in a wonderful theater. They will not attend the theater to see a picture show, but the picture will be an incidental on the program."[18] *Motion Picture News* highlighted, for instance, Roxy's presentation of *The Right to Happiness* (1919) at New York's Park Theatre:

When the film titles . . . are screened, the audience has [already] been treated to what is practically an opera and during its full fifteen minutes of presentation has been unconsciously tuned for enjoyment of the picture in a manner that could not have been accomplished in any other way. . . . If, therefore, "The Right to Happiness" is due for a long run in this theater as seems likely we believe that it is the prologue and stage setting as arranged by Mr. Rothapfel which will have a big influence in the film's success.[19]

Roxy was certainly not alone in marrying live performance with recorded media, with West Coast exhibitor Sidney Patrick Grauman offering his own elaborate stage prologues in Los Angeles that were specifically "devised to enhance the film that would follow," according to Steven Ross. In San Francisco, Jack Partington presented "Magic Flying Stages" that "lifted the grand symphony orchestra and gold-crusted organ consoles from the dark obscurity of the orchestra pit, and gave performers onstage a magic carpet to sing, dance, soar, sink, and vanish on." Ross adds that because of the period's incorporation of live performance in film exhibition, "There was no such thing as a 'typical' stage show" at a deluxe theater, but there was always a mélange of live performance and the projected reproduction of film art.[20] "Like many dimly remembered practices, early cinema's exhibition strategies have long seemed uniform in their otherness," Rick Altman adds. However, "listening more carefully to the diverse sounds associated with silent cinema, we grasp not only their variety but also the competing logics determining their development."[21] In short, Marcus Loew's famous dictum, "We sell tickets to theaters, not movies," epitomized the exhibiting ethos of the era.

Roxy's stage shows, musical accompaniment, and other live elements of the overall program were so influential that they were tracked weekly by the trade and popular press, sometimes in sections devoted only to his work as an exhibitor. In the late 1910s, "Seeing the Rialto with Rothapfel," "Rothapfel Tells of Advance on Weeklies," and "Rothapfel's Answers to Exhibitors" were three weekly articles in *Motion Picture News* alone. Together with wide coverage of his activities in New York and national newspapers, magazines, and trade journals, these articles were highly influential on domestic and international exhibitors.

During the 1910s, theaters emulating Roxy's urban palaces sprouted nationwide, with Regent, Strand, Rialto, and other theaters named after Roxy's movie houses opening across the country (and around the world). It was not just the names, sizes, and architectural styles of these theaters that were emulated but their operation as well. "If imitation is really the sincerest form of flattery, it is impossible to question the public appreciation of the Rothafel type of entertainment," journalist Golda Goldman commented in 1921. "Everything about it has been copied—the stage settings, orchestra, lighting effects, interpolation of ballet and concert numbers—all are to be found in two-hour program form in every up-to-date picture-house in the country."[22] Harold Franklin proudly noted the position of exhibitors during this period and their cultural and narrative arbitration of the motion picture: "The successful exhibitor," he told *Motion Picture News*, "has become as much a 'producer' of pictures as a manufacturer. The arrangement of the program, and the proper staging of the picture, is the one function that is entirely in the hands of the exhibitor."[23]

The adoption of these mixtures of live and filmed performances was not limited only to large, urban theaters. The interpolation of live and recorded media could be found from coast to coast and overseas, with the arrangement varying from city to city, town to town, theater to theater, and night to night. Gregory Waller, examining the 1920s from a small city (Lexington, KY) perspective, writes:

> When we take into account, as does Koszarski, not just the motion pictures screened but the whole "show," the multipart bill, the "balanced program," then moviegoing in this period looks far less homogenous. . . . There were, for instance, readily apparent differences between the Kentucky [Theatre]'s typical motion picture program and the Orpheum's feature-less bill. However, variety and heterogeneity were most strikingly and tellingly evident in the various ways motion pictures and live entertainment were combined in the city's theaters. . . . The Kentucky offered "acted prologues" for *The Thief of Baghdad* and *The Lost World* in 1925, yet this type of "multimedia performance" associated with large city picture palaces, was rarely seen in Lexington. Local residents were more likely to be entertained by a bill in which motion pictures were preceded by an organ solo, six acts of vodvil [*sic*], an orchestral concert, a stock company revue or melodrama, a touring jazz ensemble, a Charleston concert, or a marimba band."[24]

Yet despite this history, many film historians and archivists have focused almost exclusively on an ideal film text instead of placing a given film within a larger overall program. Audiences who attended a deluxe movie theater in the twenty years between 1911 and 1931 were routinely treated to a host of live and filmed programming, of which the feature film was merely one part of the entertainment. Deluxe theaters regularly offered a chorus, an orchestra of up to 110 members, a stage show featuring professionally trained ballet, modern and/or tap dancers, opera, classical music, short films, newsreels, travelogues/scenics, and, typically but not always, a feature-length film. To ensure the cohesion of the silent or early sound film era experience in many deluxe theaters, the stage show and prologue, as well as the other live entertainment, were often produced in accord with the aesthetic and/or thematic elements of the feature film.

Historians such as Waller have also demonstrated that these exhibition practices were carried on well past the demise of silent film, with stage, music, and screen variety a standard practice of exhibitors into the 1930s and beyond. (See, for instance, Gregory Waller's "Hillbilly Music and Will Rogers: Small Town Picture Shows in the 1930s.") Thomas Doherty's article "This Is Where We Came In: The Audible Screen and the Voluble Audience of Early Sound Cinema" confirms the agency of the 1930s exhibitor. "As the head cook," Doherty writes, "the individual theatre manager exercised a good deal of personal judgment over the composition and arrangement of the balanced programme."[25] Roxy's stage show for *Little Women* (1933), for example, reflected his enduring belief in the balanced program after the coming of sound and was billed by Radio City Music Hall as one that "surrounds" the film with a "beautiful atmospheric prologue."[26]

The Unitary Text vs. the Supertext

As our understanding of the narrative alterations and temporal specificities in silent and early sound film exhibition continues to grow, and as this phenomenon is increasingly theorized and documented, how can we better articulate this experience in stark contrast to contemporary motion picture exhibition? Nick Browne's concept of the "supertext" has previously been employed to articulate the importance of understanding the interstitial texts that precede, interrupt, and continue the televisual flow of a given program. In Browne's essay, "The Political Economy of the Television (Super) Text," he proposes a distinction between the all-encompassing "megatext," the supertext ("the particular program and all the introductory and interstitial material"), and the program proper (the featured show)—all of which could be appropriated to better understand the complex structure of an evening's entertainment during the silent era.[27]

If we were to use this methodology for silent and early sound film exhibition, the megatext of silent film exhibition would incorporate the architecture of the theater, the design and sensations of the lobby, the sights and sounds of the crowd, the pre-show music, and the aesthetics of the auditorium. As Roxy noted in 1932, "Theater entertainment, by my definition, takes place, not only on the stage, but at the box office, in the lobby, the foyer, the rest rooms, and the auditorium itself."[28] "The entire scheme," including lighting, settings, as well as short and feature-length films, "shall approximate one beautiful pictorial composition growing out of [a] harmony of ideas."[29] Edwin Schallert of the *Los Angeles Times* noted that Roxy's accompanying music and live presentations for *The Isle of Conquest* (1919) at the California Theatre "So carefully blended with the general mood of the story and its atmosphere . . . that the entire performance assumes a gradually heightened charm that leaves the spectator with senses pleasantly captivated." Roxy, he added, had "evolved a kaleidoscopic unity that is equally enriched with purpose and color."[30] The old exhibitor adage, "The show starts on the sidewalk," refers to the effort by more than a century of exhibitors to generate a sense of excitement from the first view of a theater's marquee and continuing throughout every facet of the moviegoing experience.

While the concept of the supertext is an attractive model for more clearly articulating the multifarious texts offered by silent cinema exhibition, the industrial and aesthetic differences between the often private televisual space of television programming and the coordinated public experience of silent film exhibition are far too great to enable the term's full employment here. Instead, I would like to mobilize the concept of a *unitary text* to better understand the meanings transacted during the live and filmed programming available to audiences during this period that had a tremendous influence on audience comprehension and on the original experience of any silent film. In Browne's formulation of television spectatorship, the supertext is comprised of many different texts of programming, interstitials, advertisements, etc. For silent film exhibition, the unitary text is a collective textual event, comprising all of the film, music, and live performance offered by a theater and often bracketed by breaks in the schedule (instead of television's flow). Constituent of a whole evening's entertainment, the unitary text is replete with synchronicity, interruption, alternation, and improvisation.[31] Rather than arguing for an "integrated text," or a "unified text," which would denote a purposeful and continual engagement between various forms of entertainment throughout a given performance, the term "unitary text" refers to a wide range of live performance and recorded media that *may* have been grouped thematically or aesthetically but were not necessarily similarly themed. And unlike the televisual supertext, which is comprised of often disconnected interruptions, commercials, promotions for other shows, etc., the unitary text of silent film exhibition was programmed by an exhibitor, not an advertising sales department, and was routinely but not always narratively or aesthetically linked.

While interstitial material has typically been accounted for in television and radio studies, film studies has often ignored the interstitial material of the unitary experience of (silent) film and has remained wedded to a single text analysis of a film's reception, endlessly bound to a production-oriented or auteurist vision of how films were exhibited in their original habitats. The original experience of a silent film is, however, of fundamental importance to understanding a given film's reception. The unitary text of a silent film's exhibition, unlike the television supertext, was often produced specifically in aesthetic and/or thematic relationship to the feature film, with dance, opera, and music produced in association with the film's themes and/or style.

AURA AND THE SILENT FILM EXPERIENCE

Given the irreproducibility of the original theatrical silent film experience, it is no wonder that Walter Benjamin spoke only of sound films in "The Work of Art in the Age of Mechanical Reproduction." This original experience, with its live performances and (sometimes improvised) musical accompaniment, is in fact largely irreproducible, like any live performance, based both on its unpredictability, its spontaneity, and the physiological realities of liveness. "Whether concerned with aesthetic, psychological or historical questions," Miriam Hansen writes, "all these texts contribute to a theory of experience in which the phenomenon Benjamin calls 'aura' plays a precarious yet indispensable part."[32] As Benjamin explains, "aura" is tied to the live actor's presence and, in his words, "there can be no replica of it," nor can there be a direct reproduction—only a partial reconstruction—of the original experience, whose aura vanishes at the end of each and every live performance.[33] While a silent film can be technically reproduced and exhibited, its original accompanying musical score cannot be if improvised, lost, or undocumented, along with any number of its live prologues or epilogues. After all, how does one *exactly* reproduce liveness? Or to paraphrase Heraclitus, "You could not step twice into the same river." Dudley Andrew posits that "We have [finally] come to recognize the multiple determinants of the film experience, and we doubt the ruling power of any single element, of the apparatus, for example, or even of the text. No longer can Metz's dream-screen be thought of as pure or essential. . . . Neither the producer, the text, the apparatus, nor the viewer is stable enough to hold us within a universal theory of the film experience."[34] In addition to the technical irreproducibility of the silent film experience, Janet Staiger adds that there are three additional categories of any public film experience that can never be duplicated: audience activity before, during, and after the event, those uncontrollable aspects of the unitary text of the original experience of an evening's entertainment.[35]

WHOSE CUT IS IT ANYWAY?

There is yet another concept rarely considered: Final cut, always assumed to be the domain of the director, producer, studio, or local censor, was often determined by exhibitors during the silent era. Some films were cut to better synthesize with music, some were edited for their content, while others were simply shortened to fit into the balanced program. In 1917, for instance, *The Easiest Way*'s premiere performance at the Rivoli Theatre showcased Roxy's version of the film, not the version distributed by producer Lewis J. Selznick. Roxy, who had seen Eugene Walter's original play on Broadway, objected to the film's new ending and reedited the print for his audience, returning the narrative to its original live theatrical form. Members of Selznick's company were shocked to see Roxy's changes on opening night, and Selznick strenuously objected to these edits. Roxy eventually restored some of the deleted scenes, but vehemently refused to show Selznick's new ending, reaffirming his claim to final cut.[36]

Throughout his career, Roxy asserted textual authority over any film that entered his theaters, all of which were personally screened and approved by him in advance. "I don't like to cut pictures as a rule," he noted in October 1918, "but occasionally it is necessary. Many pictures are spoiled by bad cutting and assembling. In my opinion a director should assemble his own picture. If he can't assemble, he can't direct." Roxy noted that he freely edited the newsreels, scenics, and short and feature films that passed through his cutting room. "As an outsider," he told *Variety*, "I feel that often a situation may be changed for the better, made more dramatic, better psychology interpolated by closing up a scene, the tempo improved, and so on."[37]

Nearly a decade later, this practice was still in effect and not just under Roxy's management. Eric T. Clarke, general manager of Rochester, New York's Eastman Theatre, and one of Roxy's more vocal critics, warned in 1927 that there was a growing "imitation of Roxy" with "All [the] deluxe theaters in New York liv[ing] on the remains of Rothafel's policies" and their subjugation of film as just one element of the unitary text. Clarke pointed to the example set by Roxy's exhibition of *What Price Glory* (1926) in August 1927 when he "slash[ed] away at the 11,960 feet" of film until it was shortened and fit within the overall program. "Rothafel," Clarke complained, "with his immense reputation can doubtless get away with it, for the public knows that he gives a show, and the public will come whatever the weakness of his feature picture."[38]

Roxy also edited footage from up to four different newsreel services to create his in-house newsreel program with titles such as "The Rialto Animated Pictorial" and then worked with his chief conductor to accompany the newly edited mélange with appropriate music. The original experience of newsreel exhibition and reception was, therefore, often determined not by the output of newsreel producers but typically by exhibitors in theaters across the country, who made their selections from the footage provided and then worked to edit their programs from all of the services from which they subscribed. These theater-specific newsreel compilations were often assembled with an eye (and ear) to the unitary text of the evening. Commercial exhibitors were often reluctant, for instance, to exhibit footage that would disrupt the atmosphere of a Harold Lloyd comedy and its surrounding program. The Roxy-Mastbaum in Philadelphia noted that for its amalgamated newsreel, "It is our desire to make this news pictorial entertaining and informative. We want to go on record in saying that we will not show morbid or what in our opinion are subjects of a depressing nature."[39] Those elements were simply cut from the program.

Roxy further demonstrated his authorial control over the motion pictures he exhibited when he edited and retitled films, such as Ernst Lubitsch's *Madame DuBarry* (1919) in 1920 at his 5,300-seat Capitol Theatre, then the largest motion picture theater in the country. First National had been unable to find a large theater willing to show the film due to its German origin and the industry's negative perception of costume dramas. Roxy, after viewing the film, immediately saw the intrinsic commercial and artistic value of the film, its star, and its director. He took the film into the editing suite, trimmed it from nine reels to six, worked with Katharine Hilliker to create new intertitles, and devised a new insert shot whereby a lit candle on a candelabrum was extinguished each time a main character died. The image of the candelabrum was then included in the new intertitles, and a new score arranged by Roxy and his musical director, Erno Rapee, was created.[40] Renamed *Passion* for its American distribution, the film was subsequently shown throughout the country following its much-lauded New York debut.[41]

The overnight success of the film no one wanted to exhibit paved the way for German films to enter the American market throughout the 1920s. One of the first of these new imports was *The Cabinet of Dr. Caligari* (*Das Cabinet des Dr. Caligari*, 1920), which Roxy also presented to his Capitol Theatre audiences. Instead of introducing the film with a stage show, Roxy commissioned a new prologue and epilogue for the film that recast the narrative in a far more conventional tone. The new epilogue concluded, for instance, that Francis was now "a prosperous jeweler in Edenwald, happily married, with a couple of healthy, normal children."[42] Mike Budd writes of these additions, "Questions are answered, homogeneity reinforced, the film adjusted for mass consumption."[43] The box office success of *Caligari* brought further acclaim to Roxy, and the scripts for the prologue and epilogue were reprinted in *Motion Picture News* so that other exhibitors could duplicate his presentation and the film's narrative alterations.[44]

Week after week from 1911 to the end of the silent era, Roxy was heralded for his achievements in producing live entertainment and musical accompaniment for the feature films he presented, often in aesthetic or thematic tandem to the motion picture. The *New York Times* praised his presentation of *The Old Homestead* (1922), for instance, writing that "With a reminiscent musical and dancing prologue, and a sympathetic musical accompaniment, S. L. Rothafel has materially increased the appeal of the picture."[45]

Interruption and the Unitary Text

Until now, I have largely described foregrounding or concluding narrative alterations, either in the exhibitor's editing of the feature film or through the interpolation of live performance. But in an era when there were few rules in silent film exhibition, and the intervention of live performance was not segregated outside the temporality of projected film, there were even more dramatic narrative interventions. For the Los Angeles premiere of *Soldiers of Fortune* (1919) at the California Theatre, Roxy devised a stage show that took place before and *during* the film. Prior to the film's projection, Roxy presented "an atmospheric prelude to the story [featuring] Sen[ñ]or and Sen[ñ]ora Espinosa in Spanish dances."[46] These "Characteristic Castilian Dancers" were joined by Manuela V. Budrow, "the Spanish Prima Donna," "Together With Her Chorus of Vocalists and Instrumentalists," and "Aided by [Carli] Elinor's California Concert Orchestra."[47] Next was Roxy's subsequent presentation of the feature film "that reached the heights of daring and originality," according to Henry Dougherty of the *Los Angeles Evening Express*:

> Twelve minutes after Allen Dwan's magnificent cinema spectacle, "Soldiers of Fortune," is under way, and after we have met his characters in the deserts of Arizona and later in the millionaire's ballroom in New York, the picture fades out and the stage is flooded with the glow of amber and gold. Out of the shadows come human beings, singing and dancing, and blending with the flood of color we hear dreamy melodies of South American music. The illusion lasts only a few minutes. The lights are dimmed, the melodies join their echoes and then the screen flashes back to us a panorama of a South American city. One seems to have stepped from the warm presence of real living people into their very own city as the characters of the play again are assembled and we find the locale transferred from gay old New York to the mining camps of the foothills of the Andes. The cut into the feature is a daring innovation, to say the least, but Mr. Rothapfel has done it successfully. The continuity of the story has not been interrupted but rather the action has been accelerated. Certainly the South American atmosphere introduced at this time prepares us better than any subtitle for our entrance with the characters of the play into that land of jealousies and revolutions.[48]

It would be hard to argue that this exhibition of *Soldiers of Fortune* would be the same as viewing the film at any other theater that did not incorporate these same elements. Roxy's Los Angeles presentation of *Soldiers of Fortune* was no aberration. Rick Altman notes that Roxy "often interrupted films for live musical interludes." For the presentation of Triangle's film *Peggy* (1916), for instance, Roxy stopped projecting the film when it cut from New York to Scotland, flooded the stage with light, and sent a bagpiper and a quartet singing "Loch Lomond" onto the stage. Once they finished performing, the film resumed once more.[49]

Walter Benjamin notes of these Brechtian moments that "Interruption is one of the fundamental methods of all form-giving. It reaches far beyond the domain of art. It is, to mention just one of its aspects, the origin of the quotation. Quoting a text implies interrupting its context."[50] For the unitary text, the context of the original experience is that which cannot be readily reproduced; it is that context that is amplified, altered, and complicated with each interruption, note of music, dancer, voice, song, or speech. It is this context—that of the unitary text which binds, surrounds, and intervenes in the presentation of a given film—whose aura cannot be duplicated through the projection of only those celluloid elements of an evening's entertainment. To understand the difference between the exhibition of *What Price Glory* at the Harris Theatre in 1926 and its exhibition at the Roxy Theatre in 1927, scholars, restorers, archivists, catalogers, etc., should seek out articles and reviews of a film's premiere performance, photographs of the stage shows presented along with the film(s) that day, the newsreels, scenics, or other short films that accompanied the film, and musical scores used for each performance. Only then can the unitary text be understood, recalled in the cataloging of a silent film, or detailed in an archive's program or a DVD's liner notes. A concerted effort to reproduce a film's original prologue/stage show can be a nearly impossible feat given the lack of extant scripts. However, its original corresponding cartoons, short subjects, newsreels, scenics, and other texts could theoretically be summoned to re-create, as much as possible, the original unitary text of a given film's exhibition during the silent era.

THE DIRECTOR/EXHIBITOR AND THE ORIGINAL EXPERIENCE

Having described the exhibitor's narrative alterations and/or additions through live performance, post-distribution editing, and live improvisation, we must turn to questions about a film whose stage prologue has been produced by the film's director. In 1919, D. W. Griffith staged his own nearly thirty-minute prologue for *The Greatest Thing in Life* (1918) at Clune's Auditorium in downtown Los Angeles. The opening night of the film was pronounced by *Motion Picture News* as truly "Griffithesque," reinforcing the surrounding program's integration with the feature film as produced and staged by the director. Its Los Angeles premiere (the film originally opened in Milwaukee) was "personally supervised by Mr. Griffith and his studio staff," *Motion Picture News* wrote, and was "preceded by an original prologue by Mr. Griffith, titled 'Voices,' which create[d] an atmosphere for the film." Louis Gottschalk composed the music for "Voices" and also arranged the musical accompaniment for the film, providing a tonal bridge between the live and recorded portions of the evening's entertainment.[51] The *Los Angeles Times* praised Griffith's prologue, writing that it was "one of the most beautiful and artistic spectacles of the sort that the stage has seen."[52] *The Greatest Thing in Life* remains a lost film, but if a print were found in the future, would the prologue be important for its contemporary exhibition or even mentioned in its DVD release? Once again, there is a demonstrable difference between the film's original experience in Milwaukee and its original experience in Los Angeles.

The Original Geographical Experience

Competing versions between a film's multiple "original" city-specific screenings is not an anomaly, especially in terms of musical accompaniment. Janet Bergstrom has written extensively about the premiere of *Sunrise* at the Times Square Theatre in New York, which contained the Rothafel-composed score for Fox Movietone prints, and *Sunrise*'s Los Angeles premiere at the Carthay Circle, which was presented with a live Carli Elinor score. There are, then, two different scores from two different composers. Which is the "original version" and what is the "original experience" of seeing (and hearing) *Sunrise*?[53]

Harry Pollard's *Uncle Tom's Cabin* (1927) opened on November 4, 1927, at the Central Theater in New York City at 141 minutes, with a score compiled by Hugo Riesenfeld and performed by a live orchestra and "an off-stage chorus of spiritual singers." For its original run, David Pierce notes that the theater's usherettes were even dressed in period costumes to enhance the unitary text for audiences. Nearly a year later, after screenings in Europe and around the United States, Universal released a new version of the film that was significantly trimmed to 114 minutes and, more importantly, contained a Movietone soundtrack by Roxy Theatre conductor Erno Rapee. The recording also included songs in full verse, human voices, and sound effects. For those theaters not equipped with Movietone capability, a cue sheet of music was compiled by James C. Bradford and distributed to exhibitors for their musicians. While there is more clearly an "original experience" here—namely the November 4, 1927, New York performance—even DVD distributors who specialize in silent film can obfuscate historical provenance. The 1999 Kino Video release advertised the DVD as "featuring the original orchestral score" on its front cover and listed under its special features the "original 1927 score by Erno Rapee" on its back cover. The Rapee score, of course, is not from 1927 at all, but from 1928, and the "original score" was assembled by Riesenfeld, not Rapee.[54]

In addition to varying local American versions of silent films, national and international versions created additional experiences and unitary texts, such as the regional specificities of *The Cabinet of Dr. Caligari* seen in Germany, the English-language version originally screened in New York with its Roxy-commissioned prologue and epilogue, and the same print without this surrounding material (and Roxy/Rapee music) shown in little cinemas throughout the 1920s (and beyond). Giorgio Bertellini writes of Enno Patalas's restoration of *Metropolis* (1927), for instance, and its complicated multinational palimpsest:

> Like Menard's rewriting of *Don Quixote,* the American version became another text, this time both philologically and culturally, fuelled by an interpretative apparatus which *literally* changed the body of the film. At this point, if we ask what is the sense of a project of restoring *Metropolis,* one may argue that the technical recovery of its *original edition* has to make clear that such "originality" or "authenticity" is not *Metropolis'* supertemporal essence. Rather, it is simply the semiotic verisimilitude of one of its German prints. . . . Thus, I would argue that "restoring *Metropolis*" means to establish complex and plurivocal transactions between the film text(s) and the cultural sites of their historical production and consumption.[55]

Bertellini's queries about *Metropolis*'s multiple contingent versions raise numerous questions about issues of local and historical reception that are not dissimilar to some of the same issues generated by an exhibitor's intervention in the original text and the very concept of the original experience. As Bertellini notes, "When we ask which is the most original and authentic version of *Metropolis,* we ask a philologic question and a cultural question. The former deals with issues of authorship, production circumstances, and textual evidence. The latter with transactions between film poetics and the cultural density of contingent historical receptions."[56] Jan-Christopher Horak, writing about *The Joyless Street* (*Die Freudlose Gasse,* 1925), adds:

> Future film historians when dealing with this or any other film are going to have to be much more exact in their definition of the text. They can no longer assume that the print they are viewing and analyzing is anything more than one possible text, making their reading only one of many possible readings. Just as philologists have long assumed that they must reveal the provenance of the literary text under discussion, so too must film historians spend much more time defining the exact characteristics of their particular texts.[57]

Paolo Cherchi Usai sees a temporal impossibility in re-creating this original experience due to the complexities of time and the unitary text: "When looking at a silent film being projected in a theater, or being analyzed at the viewing table, always remember that a different film was actually seen at the time of its commercial release . . . the equipment and the auditorium, the screen, the audience's psychological expectations, the cultural and economic conditions of the time cannot be reproduced nor recalled, even approximately."[58]

The silent era exhibitor, whose surrounding and intervening live performances, musical accompaniment, and other material framed, enhanced, subverted, complicated, and in many other ways altered the original meaning of the silent feature film, has not been properly understood within this context. In an academic era that takes the film audience and processes of consumption and reception into serious consideration, the exhibitor, with his/her cultural arbitration, is highly worthy not only of study but of assignment of authorship and consideration when attempting to account for the complexities of silent and early sound film exhibition and reception.

From 1908 to 1935, Roxy did not merely project motion pictures to audiences but presented unitary texts of which film was merely one (important) element. Understanding silent film era reception, and the industrial complexity of multimedia and multi-pronged entertainment at movie theaters nationwide, requires us to better understand how music, opera, ballet, newsreels, scenics, feature films, and other forms of live and recorded entertainment drew audiences to theaters and created habitual moviegoers who were often more attracted (at least initially) by the *experience* of "going to the movies" than by the feature films being presented.

For Roxy, the amalgamated unitary text extended well beyond film exhibition and formed the theoretical basis of his work in broadcasting as well. This intervention in the nascent field of radio and its programmatic forms led to his development of the variety show format, which he pioneered and promoted over the air.

CONCLUSION

American Showman examines the many changes in motion picture exhibition (and in broadcasting) during the silent and early sound film eras in order to analyze its influence on motion picture production, marketing, and distribution; the convergence of film, broadcasting, and music publishing and recording; and the ways in which film exhibition created a unitary text that was often the most important element in a movie theater's marketing and allure to audiences.

While many of Roxy's methods were copied and distilled by exhibitors in the United States, Canada, and Europe between 1908 and 1935, Roxy's career and celebrity should not be misunderstood as typical. Still, he was part of a distinct generational cohort that used motion pictures, music, broadcasting, and the development of a newly convergent and synergistic entertainment industry to expand their stardom and their careers in numerous fields. Roxy, along with Major Bowes, Erno Rapee, David Mendoza, and others, redrafted the idea of a film exhibitor or movie theater conductor. Media historians have for too long thought of silent and early sound film exhibition as merely the last stop on a film's journey from script to screen. Instead, *American Showman* demonstrates that deluxe movie theaters were places of production, as much as exhibition, of music, film, broadcasting, and live performance. Scholars of theater and performance, music, and cinema and media studies are only now beginning to find that more than three decades of ballet, classical music, opera, radio, newsreels, cartoons, travelogues, and feature films were produced wholly or in part inside these venues. Between 1908 and 1935, film exhibitors in deluxe theaters across the country were not merely movie theater managers and projectionists but music arrangers, theatrical producers, film editors, talent bookers, and film curators.

The exhibitor often most responsible for this vital but largely overlooked cultural and industrial transformation in the quarter century between 1910 and 1935 was Samuel "Roxy" Rothafel.

In addition to its focus on Roxy's extensive career in film exhibition, this book also examines his unique role during World War I as both an exhibitor and a producer of pro-war films and stage shows; his position as one of America's most popular and influential interwar broadcasters; his national stardom and its implications for Jewish visibility and assimilation; his work in converging film, broadcasting, and music publishing and recording; and, lastly, the importance of analyzing Samuel Rothafel within the "Roxy" phenomenon of the 1920s and 1930s in order to fully understand the career and influence of one of the nation's most prolific motion picture exhibitors and radio broadcasters.

PART ONE

ROXY AND SILENT FILM EXHIBITION

1. A NEW ART FOR A NEW ART FORM
ROXY AND THE DEVELOPMENT OF MOTION PICTURE EXHIBITION
(1908–1913)

If, when and as the Great American Novel is written Roxy will be the hero, and perhaps the whole cast. Roxy is so completely the personification of this curious America that he is both alarming and exciting to the observant mind.
—Terry Ramsaye, *Photoplay*, October 1927

Roxy was the first man to have the courage and finesse to elevate the exhibition of moving pictures beyond the store show level. He made the motion picture theatre the community art center and compelled public appreciation for their true artistic values.
—Carl Laemmle, January 1936

His story reflected a lot of the Jewish experience in America. The great urge to push in and to find one's place and then to assimilate into the culture. I mean, he wanted to assimilate like crazy.
—Irving Howe, discussing Leonard Zelig, in *Zelig* (1983)

The concept of a showman, in contrast to a movie theater manager, is not only lost on contemporary multiplex audiences but has also been scarcely analyzed by cultural and media historians. Nearly 120 years after the first public exhibition of motion pictures, there have been fewer than a dozen books published in the United States about individual film exhibitors. Ben Hall's *The Best Remaining Seats* (1961), Carrie Balaban's account of her father, Chicago exhibitor A. J. Balaban (*Continuous Performance*, 1964), Charles Beardsley's survey of Sid Grauman's career (*Hollywood's Master Showman*, 1983), and Charles Musser's examination of itinerant exhibitor Lyman Howe (*High Class Moving Pictures*, 1991) are among the only books published in the United States that focus on a single exhibitor's career and his or her contribution to the development of the art and industry of motion pictures. It is little wonder, then, given the contemporary critiques of motion picture exhibition and a continuing historiographical absence, that the very concept of a showman is still wrapped up in P. T. Barnum-esque clichés or confused with more automated multi/megaplex operators.

A focus on individual exhibitors is essential, though, in order to understand how these figures influenced American (and global) culture and how audiences were attracted to movies and movie theaters. Charles Musser writes in his examination of Lyman Howe's career that "a focus on exhibition lends itself to industrial history precisely because it must address the economic basis of the motion picture industry—the showman's ability to bring patrons through the front door."[1] In order to understand the artistic and managerial influences of showmen like Samuel Lionel Rothafel ("Roxy") and Sidney Patrick Grauman, one must analyze their construction of stardom, their ethnic heritage and cultural background, their facility with music, theater, film, and other performing arts, and the ways in which they motivated patrons to enter their "front door."

There were only three motion picture exhibitors during the silent and early sound film era who not only transformed exhibition in the United States but who also became well-known stars themselves: Roxy, Grauman, and Major (Edward) Bowes. There is much work to be done on Grauman's influence on motion picture exhibition and marketing and how Major Bowes, like Roxy, parlayed his position as managing director of the Capitol Theatre in New York into an enormously popular career in radio. For a quarter of a century, though, no motion picture showman on either side of the Atlantic was more prolific or influential than Roxy. While executives like Sam Katz and Harold Franklin perfected the chain-store management system on the business side of exhibiting, Roxy was the key purveyor of a new exhibition aesthetic that appropriated higher culture forms (legitimate theater, opera, ballet, and classical music) to attract middle-class and even upper-class audiences. Roxy's work in broadcasting and the development of a convergent entertainment industry was just as influential. He created a model for multimedia integration that was duplicated by nearly every major film studio, theater chain, and radio network in the 1920s.

This chapter does not seek to create a "great man" who worked outside of industrial constructs, commercial institutions, or economic models, or to generate a biographical study for the sake of narrative pleasure. It is important, though—crucial, in fact—to understand how the truths and fabrications Roxy told about his life were used extensively throughout his career in building a brand name that transcended film, music, and broadcasting, as well as his own social status and ethnic identity.

Not only was Roxy America's premier motion picture showman in the quarter century between 1910 and 1935 but also had an important role in transforming the art and technology of film exhibition, film music, broadcasting, and early media convergence (the industrial and technological integration of film, broadcasting, and music publishing and recording). Roxy scored motion pictures, produced enormous stage shows, managed many of

New York's most important movie houses, directed and/or edited propaganda films for the American war effort, edited newsreels and produced short and feature-length films, exhibited foreign, documentary, independent, and avant-garde films, and expanded the conception of mainstream, commercial cinema. He was also one of the chief creators of the radio variety program, he pioneered radio promotions and tours, and he helped establish the careers of innumerable radio, dance, and music stars such as Eugene Ormandy, Jan Peerce, James Melton, Erno Rapee, Lew White, Maria Gambarelli, and the Rockettes. Each of his theaters and radio performances contained his signature style and personality. In short, he was a showman, but that title denoted very different proclivities for Roxy, Grauman, and Bowes.

Roxy's motivation for all of these activities was both professional and personal—a categorical distinction that Roxy did not always make. In order to understand how he marketed motion pictures, motion picture exhibition, broadcasting, music, *and* his own personality and stardom, it is imperative to examine the very private Samuel Rothafel before he became the very public film and broadcasting icon named "Roxy." "His life history is like a story in fiction," a *Springfield News* journalist noted without a hint of irony in 1925.[2] The newspaper was unaware of how true that statement really was. Despite Roxy's later proclamations, he was not an American-born Horatio Alger character. His background, instead, had far more in common with another now consecrated American folk hero: the European Jewish immigrant movie mogul. It is imperative, therefore, to place Roxy and his work within the context of the times in which he lived and the immigrant Jewish experience in late-nineteenth-century America.

THE WANDERING JEW

"It is quite unlikely that any day in my life was or will be as important as July 9, 1882," Roxy would recall more than thirty years later, already conflating his personal and professional existence. "That was my birthday and necessarily marks the beginning of my career."[3] Little else of Roxy's background is very easy to discern, though hundreds, if not thousands, of short biographies were printed in newspapers and magazines over his lifetime, each parroting the skeletal details he provided. Nor is much about his family's background any clearer. Roxy's father, Gustav Rothapfel (Roxy changed his last name to Rothafel in 1920), a twenty-four-year-old shoe cobbler, and Rosalie Schwerzens, three years his junior (and later known by a host of names, including Rosalia,

Cecelia, and Celia) appear to have married in Germany in 1879.[4] Three years later, their first son, Samuel, was born, possibly in Bromberg, Germany (now Bydgoszcz, Poland), followed by another child, Max, in 1885.[5] Whether it was the pressure of supporting a wife and children on a shoe cobbler's earnings—Roxy noted that his father was of "German peasant stock"[6]—or merely a decision to follow the latest wave of Jewish immigration to America, Gustav appears to have immigrated to the United States in September 1885 on his own aboard the steamship *Katie* from Hamburg, Germany, to New York.[7] On May 11, 1886, Rosalie, Samuel, and Max Rothapfel boarded the steamship *Rugia* in Hamburg and sailed to New York,[8] arriving on May 24, 1886.[9] It is unclear, however, whether Gustav was waiting for them in New York or if the three made their way directly to the logging town of Stillwater, Minnesota, where they later settled.

Stillwater

Stillwater was developed in the mid-nineteenth century, carved out of the newly settled Minnesota Territory. By 1849, it was among the area's most important centers, with a population of 609—one-eighth of the population of the entire territory. Over the next twenty-five years, and especially after the Civil War and the arrival of the railroad, Stillwater became central to the state's logging industry. Thousands poured in to the area to clear the forests while others created businesses to cater to them. Earlier wooden-frame structures were quickly replaced with buildings made of brick and stone. The three-story, 1,217-seat Grand Opera House, opened in May 1881, was among the most lavish of these new structures and appealed to the city's growing desire for culture and entertainment.[10] Roxy began attending the theater as early as 1889, watching an operetta that "even then entranced him."[11]

Newly minted fortunes were already being made and the city was now one of three in Minnesota with a prominent Jewish population.[12] "Shaking off the makeshift look of her youth," Patricia Johnson writes, "Stillwater came of age in the most lavish attire lumbermen could afford."[13] Stillwater residents wore the finest shoes and repaired those they owned in order to demonstrate their newfound wealth and sense of accomplishment. A young shoemaker named Gustav Rothapfel opened his first store in downtown Stillwater at 117 S. Main Street, a short walk from the family's new home at 307 N. Main Street, two blocks from the St. Croix River, Minnesota's natural border with Wisconsin.[14] Gustav's store would have catered to the need for spiked shoes for lumberjacks and more elegant and casual footwear for "urban" dwellers. Gustav, ensconced in the town with a business and a family, formally declared his intent to become a naturalized citizen before a Washington County District Court clerk on October 18, 1886.[15] Gustav and Rosalie wasted little time in conceiving another child, and just over nine months after her arrival in the United States, Rosalie (now listed as "Lizzie" on the child's birth certificate) gave birth to Anne Rothapfel on February 8, 1887.[16] Another son (name unknown) followed a year and a half later on July 15, 1888.[17] Roxy was now the eldest of four siblings.

"The most pleasant days of my life were spent in Stillwater," Roxy remembered nearly four decades later."[18] Ever the showman (or opportunist), Roxy later claimed that he charged his "troupe of juvenile playmates" a penny for tours of neighboring villages.[19] "As a youngster," he added, "I was like most others of the day and of the environs of Stillwater—given to a certain amount of mischief. An occasional broken window as the result of an improperly aimed bit of snowball or the report of a bit of sharp-pointed hardware having been placed upon someone's chair was always sure to bring down the paternal ire upon my head."[20] Roxy also shined shoes, sold newspapers, and "borrowed" apples from a local grocery store.[21] Childhood friends would later recall a "barefooted, overalled boy," while merchants remembered his antics "grab[bing] the shoulders of the wooden Indian on Main Street" and then swinging himself "until driven off."[22]

Stillwater was at its peak by 1890, with 450 million feet of lumber cut down and shipped that year and a booming population that had now reached 18,000.[23] The Rothapfels were moving as well, two blocks west to 231 S. 2nd Street with Gustav's shoe store migrating to 110 S. 2nd Street, next door to John Splan's barber shop.[24] It is here that Gustav's outspoken nature, which his son Samuel inherited, was captured by a local newspaper. *The Messenger* observed that Gustav was a boisterous man with a heavy German accent and alternately referred to him as "a descendant of Abraham, as his features plainly indicate," an "Israelite," and, worse still, "the little Jew." *The Messenger* reported that sometime in May 1890 Gustav "invested a dollar in a Louisiana lottery ticket in the hope of winning a prize that would help defray the expenses of maintaining his family and providing nurses, medicines and delicacies for his invalid wife." Barber John Splan entered Gustav's shoe shop "for the purpose of having a little fun at the expense of the Israelite" and provoked an unwelcome result.

> With an air intended to convey the impression that Rothappel [*sic*] had drawn a valuable prize, which he (Splan) was trying to obtain by superior shrewdness and cunning for a fraction of its value, Splan accosted the

little Jew with "Well how much will you take for your lottery ticket? I'll give you two dollars for it." He increased his offer until he had laid down $30 in front of the humble shoemaker. "Vell, I dakes it!" at this point exclaimed the Crispin knight. But before the words had escaped his mouth he had his broad hand on the bills, which he placed in his pocket, shoving the ticket over toward the barber. Splan had a momentary feeling that the joke hadn't turned out just as he had planned it. . . . For the time being he entertained considerable animosity toward Jew shoemakers. He invoked the aid of the law, but could get no satisfaction, there being nothing to show that Rothappel had committed any offense, having simply sold something for an agreed price.

After paying off some business expenses, Gustav spent the remaining money on "medicines, etc., for his wife and children."[25]

By 1893, Gustav had moved his shop back to 231 S. Main Street, while the family also moved back to their first Stillwater residence at 307 N. Main Street.[26] It is hard to see this latter move as one of economic progress. Gustav's antics made the local newspaper again that year, this time in the May 31 issue of the *Stillwater Daily Gazette*. A local man, John O'Shaughnessy, approached Gustav and asked him how much his business was worth. He responded "at least 'ein thousand tollars.'" O'Shaughnessy, unbeknownst to Gustav, was the town's assessor, and the shoe cobbler's bluster put him in a tough spot. He was immediately assessed $700 in taxes and responded, according to the newspaper's transliteration, "Taxes! mein Gott: me pay taxes! Vy I haf nodings here to pay for. Absolutely noding. I couldn't gif this blace away if I vanted to."[27] It seems reasonable to assume that Gustav's business was not flourishing given the family's move back to their original 1886 dwelling. In addition, the Splan incident had spoken to Gustav's expense of caring for his "invalid wife" and children. There may have been other family issues not reported. The couple's third son appears to have died, been sent away, or been institutionalized between his birth on July 15, 1888, and the 1900 census, in which his name is absent.[28] The couple's second daughter, Tina, was born on April 30, 1894, but died on May 9. The cause of death was listed as "Non Viability."[29] Roxy never spoke of either child in print.

New York

Perhaps it was a desire to be among people with backgrounds more similar to theirs, an effort to escape Stillwater's harsh winters, a need to erase the bad memories of Tina's death (and perhaps of their youngest son as well), or the hope of Rosalie's recovery closer to New York's medical community that prompted a move to Brooklyn's growing Jewish hub in 1896.[30] "I'll never forget the thrill I used to get whenever I heard the first strains of a band in the distance," Roxy recalled four decades later of his affection for the sound and spectacle of Stillwater's parades. "We moved to Brooklyn when I was still in short pants, and I went to P.S. 90. My deepest impressions, of course, were of the immensity of the metropolis and its surge of life. But what pleased me most was that there were bigger and better parades, more bands."[31]

By then, Roxy was fourteen years old and had little job prospects or money. "After quite a search," he remembered,

> I was able to persuade John B. Collins, who was then in business on 14th Street, that I would be a valuable asset to his business as a cash boy. Perhaps he was impressed by my earnestness, for he agreed to hire me at the grand and glorious salary of $2 a week. After the first week, however, he showed signs of impatience. The end of the second week found me with my second $2 but without a job. During the next year or so I landed, and lost, one job after another. I cannot blame those good but gossiping persons who came to regard me as the family black sheep and ne'er-do-well.[32]

Roxy next became a copy boy at a newspaper,[33] and then a traveling bookseller, where he became "a most unwelcome visitor at many homes." He later recalled that "This kind of thing discouraged me greatly."[34] Roxy subsequently began hanging "around street corners, getting into trouble," and, according to journalist Louis Sobol, "bringing worry and despair to his father":

> One night, the boy didn't come home. Goaded beyond endurance, his father threw him out the next day, left him to shift for himself. For the next six years he was a little roustabout, a dirty, roving vagabond. Now he was a theater usher. Now an errand boy. Then a runner for a newspaper. Next a helper in a pool room. He never kept a job more than a few months. Invariably, a quarrel with the boss ended his promising career. Of course the neighbors were right. He was headed for the reformatory. There was no doubt that he'd come to no good end.[35]

Despite these claims of homelessness—and that Gustav had chased him out of the house—there is no evidence to support this narrative.[36] Instead, according to the 1900 U.S. Census, an eighteen-year-old Roxy was a "laborer," still living at home at 916 Rogers Avenue in Brooklyn with Gustav and Rosalie, his brother Max, now a fifteen-year-old office boy, and his sister Annie, thirteen.[37] Samuel Rothapfel did not appear to be "a dirty, roving vagabond," but he was a nameless nobody in a teeming city of millions. He had joined the hordes of New York City immigrants scraping together a meager existence, searching for something that a man with dreams but little education or training could accomplish.

New York had not cured Rosalie of whatever ailed her either. Dr. Adolph Lundquist began treating her on November 30, 1901, and soon placed her in the New York Polyclinic Medical School and Hospital, a facility staffed by volunteer doctors and student nurses who cared for a wide range of the city's poor. She was reportedly suffering from cholelithiasis (the presence of gallstones in the gallbladder), which had induced bronchopneumonia. Lundquist tended to her for the last time on December 7, 1901, and by 4:30 the next morning, Rosalie had suffocated and died. She was identified as Celia on her death certificate and buried on December 10 in Washington Cemetery, a Jewish cemetery roughly three miles from the Rothapfel home.[38] Roxy had lost his "greatest friend."[39] The Rothapfel family quickly broke apart following her burial.

Recruiting Rothapfel

Roxy's enlistment in the United States Marine Corps five months later, on May 24, 1902, may be attributable to Rosalie's death. Now almost twenty years old and with no discernible career path, Roxy hoped that the Marines would give him structure, standing, and a new set of skills. "I found it difficult to reconcile my ideas of what life should be, with life as I found it," he later wrote. "Like many another discouraged youth who finds it hard to make an honest living and has no particular trade or talent to fall back on, I joined the Marines."[40] As a private, his monthly pay was small but dependable, roughly $13. He spent a week at the Brooklyn Navy Yard's Marine barracks before being transferred to the Charlestown Navy Yard, just north of Boston.[41] By October 6, 1902, Roxy was serving on the USS *Bancroft*, an 1892-built steel gunboat sailing for duty out of San Juan, Puerto Rico, mainly to patrol the waters throughout the West Indies. Roxy would call the 190-foot-long *Bancroft* and the city of San Juan home for the next two and a half years, often serving as a "mail orderly."[42]

Roxy's service records are mostly unremarkable, but his reputation for total discipline during his theatrical career makes his few service infractions noteworthy. Within his first five hours of training, Roxy had already been thrown in the guardhouse for fighting.[43] In December 1903, he was "deprived of liberty" for ten days and reduced one rank.[44] Three months later, in March 1904, Roxy was cited again, this time for not properly stowing his hammock.[45] This latter infraction was not damaging enough, though, to keep him from a promotion to the rank of corporal on April 2, 1904.[46] Roxy proudly remarked that he was "the third Jewish boy in this branch of the service to achieve this distinction."[47] Despite his new rank, it did not take long for Roxy to find trouble again. After being promoted to captain's orderly on the *Bancroft*, Roxy was charged with "gross neglect of duty" three months later. He was deprived of liberty on shore for ten days.[48] For the remainder of his time aboard the *Bancroft*, however, Corporal Rothapfel followed the rules.

Life for the Rothapfel family back in Brooklyn meanwhile moved on without him.[49] Gustav opened a new cigar store inside a small, two-story wood-frame house that he shared with Orland Way, a carpenter, and H. P. Holm, a painter and decorator.[50] With his wife deceased, his eldest son in the Marines, and his youngest son Max pursuing an increasingly lucrative career as a cocoa trader, Gustav's life had changed dramatically. At the age of 19, Max was already sailing to Port-au-Prince, Haiti, in April 1904, and filing for a passport to travel out of the country for up to two years. Pursuing vastly different careers, Samuel and Max may well have passed one another on different ships in those southern waters.[51]

In early March 1905, Roxy was transferred to the Marine barracks at Fort Jefferson in Dry Tortugas, Florida.[52] By the end of June, Roxy began moving from one site to the next as a full-time recruiter for the Marine Corps. From Florida he went to the Norfolk, Virginia, Navy Yard in July, to Pittsburgh, Pennsylvania, in August, and returned to the Norfolk barracks in September.[53] Chief Quartermaster Clerk Charles Wiedemann, who was stationed at Norfolk with Roxy at the time, would later remember the young corporal as "a man one would like to have for a friend and shipmate, a good boy and soldier."[54] In October 1905, after several months of signing new recruits up and down the East Coast, Roxy was discharged from the Marine Corps.[55]

Despite the glorious tales he would later tell of his military career, there were no battles listed in his records, and definitely no participation in the Boxer Rebellion, which had ended in September 1901, more than half a year before he entered the service. Over the years, though, the skilled publicist would drum up that story whenever it could be useful, and it can be found in innumerable biographies written about him over the past century. As early as 1911, only six years after his discharge, Roxy was already spreading this heroic mythology. "He served about six years," James McQuade would write in the *Moving Picture World,* "during which time he held many responsible positions and having been in action on several different occasions."[56] So ubiquitous had the tale of Roxy's exploits become that, in 1925, the Marine Corps journal, *The Leatherneck,* characterized Roxy "as a fighting, smashing Leatherneck," who once had battled the enemy "before the walls of Peking during the Boxer uprising."[57] But the truth was different. Instead of the "smashing Leatherneck," the "six years" of service, or any of the other fictions he perpetuated, Roxy had served the military for three and a half rather uneventful years. Yet it proved to be a crucially formative time as the lessons learned in the Marines were many. His punishments taught him discipline, his promotion to corporal gave him his first taste of success, and, most importantly, his role as a recruiter sharpened his promotional, sales, and people skills. Each of these would play a key role in his theatrical career. "Those years were the most valuable training I've ever had," Roxy would later remark, "and for me they took the place of a college education."[58] He wrote to other Marines in *The Leatherneck* twenty years after his tour of duty:

> The Marine Corps Institute does not carry courses in the theatrical profession which is my business, but it does instruct in things that no business can succeed without: Management, Personnel Organization, Banking and Business Law, Bookkeeping and Business Forms, English and Bookkeeping, Complete Commercial, Shipping and Distributing, and the Advertising Courses. I recommend these for the consideration of any ambitious man who wants to prepare himself for higher usefulness in life.[59]

In Roxy's mind, the military had enlisted an unformed post-adolescent and churned out a budding businessman. He added in 1923:

> The years of my enlistment were among the best years of my life. I met other young men from every walk of life and profited by my contact with them. My duties took me to all parts of the world and my vision was broadened as only travel can broaden one. The discipline, exercise and training were entirely different from anything I had previously experienced. It quickened my actions, sharpened my wits, and provided me with a feeling of independence and self-confidence I had not known before.[60]

Still, after his discharge, he was back to where he had been before his enlistment, selling John Lawson Stoddard's multivolume books on global

geography and cultures, *John L. Stoddard's Lectures*, door-to-door.[61] The following year, Roxy moved to Northampton, Massachusetts, roughly twenty
miles north of the growing city of Springfield. There are few details available
about this period of his life, but two items stand out: Roxy worked as a clerk at
"The Hampton" hotel and served as an umpire for "the greatest of all" baseball
games between the town's doctors and lawyers on August 17, 1906.[62] Roxy
only stayed in Northampton for a year (or less), but his experience there with
hotels and baseball would serve him well in the years that followed.

CARBONDALE

By 1907, Roxy had left New England and began selling insurance in the "coal
fields of Pennsylvania."[63] The insurance company, "impressed by his methods,"
had sent him there "to build up their clientele in new fields."[64] He was now
twenty-five years old and had moved to the small city of Carbondale, Pennsylvania, nineteen miles northeast of Scranton. "There's an aroma of peace
and comfort in Carbondale," William Henry Feeney wrote in the *Carbondale
Leader* that year, and yet,

> Carbondale is thriving. Here is the steady growth that means progress,
> prosperity for the manufacturer and merchant and an honest dollar for
> all who toil. The men and women of this 20,000 city are a folk good to see
> with visiting eyes. Our northern Pennsylvania young man is no delicate
> youth. He gets his inheritance of brawn from the pioneers of the coal
> regions. . . . Carbondale is essentially a residence of deeply religious folk.
> From the old, old man waiting at the church door with that deep quiet
> faith in his calm old eyes to the ordinarily riotous youngsters with the
> reverence of youth, the populace strikes one as having, despite the cares
> and vexations of modern life, kept faith with their early precepts. . . . Car-
> bondale is a good place to live in, a good place to come back to, a good
> place to do a reasonable business, a place to save money, a good place to
> spend declining years. A good city at any stage of the game.[65]

Roxy's arrival in Carbondale coincided with its Jewish community's coming
of age as it began constructing the town's first synagogue on September 15
of that year. The three-story building was designed to serve the needs of the
city's twenty-five Jewish families and those Jews living in more isolated towns
such as Forest City.[66] Carbondale likely appealed to Roxy's small-town, folksy

nature, perhaps echoing happier times in Stillwater and his own working-class roots, while offering him some connection to the ethnic community whose background he shared. If it was indeed "a good city at any stage of the game," then Roxy's humble beginnings fit right in.

Roxy held a series of jobs in Carbondale, including book salesman and insurance manager, but his most prominent was that of pitcher for the city's baseball team.[67] Roxy, who had been dubbed "Sodawater" during his Marine days in Puerto Rico because he never consumed alcohol, was also "known as one of the most ardent baseball fiends that ever hit the island" after discovering the game while on shore leave. "After that," a *Boston Traveler* columnist later wrote, "his only desire" was a "request for a transfer to shore duty" in order to play baseball on the Marine team. Roxy later described himself as the "Babe Ruth of the old Porto Rico baseball team."[68]

If he had been a great player, though, his skills had waned in the intervening years. Roxy appeared in the Carbondale team's box score for the first time on July 25, 1907, in a losing game described as an "an awful slaughter from the very first."[69] On September 1, Roxy pitched against a team from the neighboring town of Forest City five miles away. *The Forest City News* (*TFCN*) characterized the contest as "undoubtedly the most interesting game of the season," mostly because Roxy was shelled during "a grand batting rally in the last inning." *TFCN* quipped that "Rothaphel [*sic*], the spit-ball performer, was on the mount [*sic*] for Carbondale, but his twisters availed nothing against the slugging frenzy of 'Slim' Cavanaugh's wielders of the willow." All told, Roxy hit a batter, struck out seven, and collected zero hits out of four times at the plate.[70] Roxy pitched again a few days later and was shelled once more by the Forest City team. By then, the nickname that would one day brand his international fame was already in use.[71] "Just to show that they meant business," *TFCN* wrote, "poor 'Rocksie' was jumped on at the start and when the side was retired, Forest City had the prosperous looking lead of three runs. . . . The second inning looked more dismal to Carbondale than the storm cloud that hung in the southern sky. The ball was driven here, there, and all over the field and when the round was ended Forest City had chalked up to its credit eight additional runs, making a total of eleven. . . . This inning saw the finish of Rothaphel [*sic*] in the box."[72] Carbondale selected a different pitcher for the next game, and Forest City was held to just one run and beat its rival.[73] Roxy's career as a baseball player was over.

The following spring, in 1908, Roxy hung up his pitcher's glove and became the manager of the Carbondale Baseball Association.[74] This new role tested and honed his ability to organize, maneuver, and manage a business and its personnel. Roxy also became involved in a variety of local events. "Always active and enthusiastic," *TFCN* observed four decades later, Roxy "participated in a local minstrel show and a drill, under his direction, was the hit of the show, giving the first hint of his ability as a show man."[75] It was "my first experience in showmanship," Roxy later recalled. "I staged a minstrel [show] for the St. Aloysius Society of the Knights of Columbus at Carbondale, Pa. A vaudeville circuit offered engagements for a tour, but the non-professional cast couldn't accept."[76] Journalist Mary Jacobs stated that Roxy "coached the men, doped out the stage lighting effects, planned the costumes, [and] chose the skits." Roxy later claimed that vaudeville impresario Sylvester Poli was visiting Carbondale that evening and was "so impressed" that he offered Roxy and his first gang of performers $2,000 per week to tour. (This figure seems ridiculously embellished.) The "mostly" family men could not afford to give up their jobs—whatever the rate—especially during the national economic crisis that began in 1907.[77]

Forest City

Roxy also used his baseball notoriety to become the district organizer of the Red Cross Protective Society, and when he traveled to Forest City on May 26, 1908, the local newspaper took note of his visit.[78] The town, roughly seven miles from Carbondale, was originally known as Pentecost. The population grew after a railroad linked Carbondale to the network of towns dotting Susquehanna County.[79] Primarily a lumber town, coal was discovered in 1871.[80] The ability to ship coal from the area gave rise to a mini-boomtown by the late 1870s. The area's first store opened in 1875. Six years later, the first hotel, the Fleming House, appeared on Main Street.[81]

In 1886, just as Rosalie, Samuel, and Max Rothapfel were arriving from Germany, Julius Freedman immigrated to the United States with his wife, Lena, and daughters Rosa and Tillie.[82] Their eldest son, Samuel, was born in New York in 1889, and by the time their third daughter, Sarah, was born three years later, the Austrian-Jewish family had settled in Pennsylvania.[83] By March 31, 1898, Julius Freedman had raised enough money to become the owner and operator of Forest City's Fleming House, one of the town's most important establishments. It was subsequently renamed the Freedman House.[84]

The hotel/saloon was not without competition for the town's 4,279 residents and those coming to visit Forest City.[85] The Muchitz Hotel, owned and operated by Martin Muchitz, replaced the Davis House after it burned down on May 1, 1899, opening its doors on January 22, 1902.[86] A 1907 ad for the Muchitz Hotel noted its "Fine Table Board, Light, warm and airy rooms. Terms reasonable. Country and Transient Trade Especially Solicited."[87] The Freedman House countered with its own marketing: "Centrally located on Main Street. RATE $2.00 A DAY. . . . Electric Lights. Well Heated. Commercial Trade Solicited. Bar Stocked with Choicest Wines and Liquors. Fell Beer on Tap. LUNCH COUNTER."[88]

By the time Roxy first visited Forest City, Julius Freedman was the town's most prominent Jew. In addition to his ownership of one of its premier lodging facilities, with its operation as a dining and drinking establishment as well, Julius was also active in local politics, serving as one of the vice presidents of the Forest City Taft and Sherman Republican campaign club.[89] Roxy would later note that Julius Freedman was "the mayor, store-dealer, postmaster, saloon keeper, and policeman of the community."[90] He was also one of the initial stockholders of the town's First National Bank and its first depositor.[91]

Julius and Lena's children were not a group of homebodies either. Rather, like other Jews living in rural areas, they encouraged their daughters and sons to move out into the world. Between 1907 and 1908, Pearl was a teacher at the Carbondale Commercial Institute, Sarah attended Scranton Business College, and Samuel studied pharmacy until 1909, when he entered the Medico Chirurgical College of Philadelphia (which later merged with the University of Pennsylvania). (Jennie Freedman would later attend Syracuse University.)[92] Despite their busy schedules, Pearl and Sarah, together with their older sisters, Rosa and Tillie, routinely spent time with friends in New York, Wilkes-Barre, Scranton, and smaller hamlets in the area.[93] (For the Freedmans, religious services would require travel to the new synagogue in Carbondale, though High Holy Day services were held in Forest City at the Odd Fellows hall building.)[94] Indeed, with Julius's rise in stature, and his family's numerous, if still modest, accomplishments, *TFCN* often provided weekly accounts of the family's comings and goings.

Apocryphal stories have appeared in innumerable (short) biographies about how Roxy met Rosa Freedman and began working at the Freedman House. Most tales, including one told by Forest City native and silent-film actor Pat O'Malley, claim that their chance occurrence took place inside the tavern of the Freedman House after a baseball game.[95] Roxy, though, recalled three decades later that their meeting took place because of his sales job. As an insurance salesman, he was going house to house in Forest City one day with "Door upon door . . . slammed in my face." He finally arrived at the Freedmans' home. "A young, slim, dark-haired girl opened the door," he remembered. "[Y]ou'll have to see Daddy for that," she told him. "He's post-master, you know." Rosa invited him inside while Roxy waited for Julius to come home for lunch. The "postmaster" refused to buy any insurance, but Roxy's interest in Rosa encouraged him to move to Forest City where he "wore a groove into the wooden steps leading to the Freedman porch."[96] Roxy and Rosa had much in common: both immigrated to America at an early age and grew up Jewish in predominantly working-class, Christian small towns.

Julius required Roxy to work behind the bar at the Freedman House, serv-ing food and ale to the town's grizzled miners, in order to court his daugh-ter.[97] "You work behind my bar for a year and I'll see how you stack up as a husband," Julius told the nomadic Roxy. "Her parents," he noted, "would not let her marry a traveling man."[98] Roxy was already familiar with working in a hotel after his experience at The Hampton in Massachusetts two years earlier. "The customers were tough coal miners, so he knew that job would test my mettle," Roxy later recalled. "I worked the year out and won my bride. There were plenty of scraps, but, after seven years in the Marines, I was a pretty good scrapper."[99]

Family Theatre, Forest City, PA

By the time Roxy moved to Forest City in May 1908, it was a city ripe for the taking. In a short article titled, "A Few Things We Need," from a May 1907 issue of the city's *The Shoppers' Guide* (a flyer produced twice a month and dis-tributed to every house in Forest City and nearby Vandling), the editors ob-served that the town needed a "shake-up" and was "growing grey-haired in her youth."[100] Adding to those woes, Forest City's Opera House was demolished in late 1907 and the loss of the venue, which had opened just fifteen years earlier, was deemed a "serious loss to the town . . . affect[ing] every resident. Those who wish to see a dramatic performance must journey to Carbondale. Probably next to the churches and the local newspaper," *TFCN* argued, "an opera house plays a greater part in the general life of the community than any other institution."[101] A "nickelet" (movie theater) operated by a "couple of men" from Columbia County also failed to attract an audience.[102] The city was growing in size, but its place as an entertainment and cultural hub for area residents would have to await the perceptive vision of its newest resident.

The Freedman House, along with his relationship to Rosa Freedman, had given Roxy the stability he had been looking for, but he still felt unful-filled. "After leaving the U.S. Marine Service," he later stated, "the very idea of 'service' was uppermost in my mind. I wanted to live my life so that it would be of as much value to as many of my fellowmen as possible."[103] With an empty backroom in the Freedman House available, Roxy dreamed of a public entertainment venue for all of Forest City that would fulfill his dream of "service" and create a job that would satisfy his financial and emotional needs. After all, he later recalled, he was badly in need of "some pin money in addition to [his] regular salary" behind the bar.[104]

Film was not central to his vision. Instead of a "nickelet," Roxy hoped to create a mixed-use vaudeville theater and roller-skating rink. Roxy told *TFCN* in early November 1908:

Yes I am turning the hall into a theatre and rink. . . . Both forms of amusement will be conducted on the highest principles and any lady or child can come and be entertained without the least fear of embarrassment. There will be no rowdyism or indecency tolerated and the offender will be punished severely and forever barred from entering the place. I have arranged with booking agencies for the very best talent and only such as will entertain any member of the family, in fact I have decided to call it "The Family Theatre." The hall is going to be one of the most comfortable little theatres.[105]

Motion Picture News recalled in 1914 the space that later became the Family Theatre:

"The dance hall," a title that remained as its last claim to civilization, and conferred upon it by a few whose memory of earlier days had clung as a solace, had long been crammed with kegs, chairs minus legs and arms, glass smashed to bits through slipping from uncertain fingers in the adjoining room, musty carpets and matting, and an odor. This last was not exactly an odor. It was a plague, communicated to every board and remnant of shoddy furnishings housed in the room. It suggested a blended mixture of liquor-soaked carpets, moss, frowsy wallpaper and moisture-rotted wood. Into this uninviting place walked a resolute man who wanted to become an exhibitor.[106]

Roxy had a few short weeks to turn the dank space into a profitable entertainment venue.

Roxy's new theater/rink was named the "Family," joining other similarly named venues in Carbondale and Wilkes-Barre that were part of a growing attempt to attract women and children to vaudeville and movie houses.[107] The floors were re-laid, the walls were covered with matting, and the dingy alley behind the Freedman House, which served as the de facto lobby of the theater, was illuminated with bare lights.[108] It was enough in 1908, at least, for a nickel ticket. The hall, *TFCN* noted when the work was completed, was "transformed into a place of great beauty and will be a revelation to those who see it for the first time." Even at this early stage, the newspaper wrote that "No expense has been spared to improve the interior."[109]

On Monday, December 21, 1908, Roxy opened the Family Theatre, "the new pleasure resort," according to *TFCN*, with its first three days dedicated to roller-skating.[110] "A large number of young people enjoyed the glide on rollers," the newspaper reported. And in a sign that roller-skating was meant to be a permanent fixture of the Family Theatre's entertainment, Roxy immediately ordered more ball-bearing skates for his customers.[111]

Three days later, on Christmas Eve 1908, the Family Theatre premiered a mix of vaudeville and motion pictures.[112] Roxy spoke glowingly of the remodeled space in *TFCN* at the time, but his memory nearly a decade later was that the Family was an "old dump of a hall behind the barroom" with "250 undertaker's chairs, an old Power No. 4 Machine, a screen made from an old bed sheet, and a second-hand piano."[113] His first night offered a "Grand Opening in Vaudeville," featuring daytime showings at 2:00 and 3:30 and evening performances at 7:30 and 9:00. The program began with an "overature" [*sic*] by Professor James Curry at the piano, followed by a "cameragraph" and then the Beverly Brothers performing "The Gentleman and the Coon," described as a "refined Talking and Singing Act." Next on the program were "illustrated songs," the Petersen Trio in another "Refined Musical Act," followed by a "Special Engagement of the Famous Rossleys—Jack and Marie, Direct from the Keith and Procter [*sic*] Circuit in the Screamingly Funny Sketch, 'The Scotch Tourists.'" Roxy presented a "Special Added Feature," a reel of highlights from the recent World Series between the Chicago Cubs and the Detroit Tigers. The film, Roxy remarked, was shown for the "first time in this section [of the state] at popular prices." Many future elements of a Roxy show were already on display: the mixture of live and filmed performances, an attention to music, and uniformed ushers who, according to advertisements, "will assist you and show you every courtesy."[114]

The Family Theatre's contrast to the "big city" entertainment in Carbondale and its appeal to all classes came the next day when *Madame Butterfly* opened at Carbondale's Grand Opera House. Street cars shuttled residents from out of town (including those from Forest City) to the theater, where an orchestra

of thirty musicians and a theater company of seventy-five entertained holiday crowds. Unlike the Family's ten-cent admission, the cost of tickets at the
Grand ranged from fifty cents to two dollars.[115] The resources of the Grand
probably did not hurt the Family's attendance, as its lower ticket prices (and
geographical proximity) assured it of a different kind of audience. "The Family Theatre is demonstrating that there was an opening in this place for an
amusement place where people could go and enjoy an hour's entertainment at
a nominal price," *TFCN* wrote, "and Manager Rothapfel is to be congratulated
on seeing the opportunity and taking hold of it. His cosy [*sic*] little theatre has
been well patronized every evening since the opening and the patrons have
been given a program that was clean, clever and pleasing." Roxy, the budding
marketer and showman, had already won over the local newspaper staff, a
strategy he would employ for the rest of his career. *TFCN* suggested that readers "look over" the week's program listed in the Family Theatre's advertisement and "make up your mind to go."[116]

The Family's second program, following another three days of roller-skating, began on New Year's Eve and was entirely new. Roxy featured Jack Rossley
again in a new farce, "A Dollar for a Kiss," along with "New Acts! New Songs!
New Pictures!" But of all of the features of the week, Roxy made "The World
Series" film the featured attraction. "This is by far the greatest picture ever
shown here and was secured at great expense," the theater's advertisement in
TFCN noted, adding that it "Positively will appear at each performance."[117] It
was already evident that film (and in this case nonfiction film) was the draw
for many. Motion pictures "struck my imagination very forcefully" Roxy recalled nearly two decades later. "I saw in them something which would relieve
the tension of the American business man."[118]

In 1917, Roxy looked back upon those early days with more than a touch
of nostalgia for what had been lost in the frenzied years that followed:

> I used to get up in the morning at daybreak, and go out and paint my own
> signs on paper that I procured from the printing office—ordinary one-
> sheets of different colors—and I became quite adept with the brush. I used
> to arrange my music for the orchestra, which consisted of a piano player,
> and then I went up and cleaned my machine. When I had everything
> spick-and-span, I cleaned the theater, met the train in the afternoon, got
> my films, looked them over, and saw that the patches were in good shape.
> Then I was ready to make my announcement from the back of the little
> balcony, where the people had to turn around in their seats to hear me.
> Gee, those were the good old days.[119]

Roxy's recollection outlines his early management practices: his arrangement of the music for accompaniment, his review of every film he booked, and his opening remarks before their presentation. His lectures and other introductions not only revealed a keen desire to contextualize his filmic offerings, which he would later produce through stage shows and other presentations, but also demonstrated his desire to become the star of his own theater. His introductions were an extension of his need to offer a show *and* to be its showman.

The Family Theatre's (largely Polish and Slovak)[120] crowd was Roxy's first listening audience. As such, they were expected to remain in rapt attention. "There was a night, early in the movement," the *American Hebrew* later recalled, "when the audience, used to the cheap melodies of the tin-pan piano, jeered and hissed the rendition of a fine musical number. [Roxy] came out and offered to return the admission price to those who wished to leave. No one moved. The experience was never repeated."[121] Roxy sought throughout his career to regiment the behavior of those who worked for him and those whom he entertained. Ever the perfectionist, everything needed to be on his terms.

His supervision of all tasks, from marketing to maintenance, would also remain a constant throughout his career. Roxy was known to clean up after his employees and chastise them for their apparent lack of care. *Motion Picture News* recalled one such incident at the Family Theatre:

> Two men, employed jointly as ushers and cleaners, fulfilled the former duty with the audience, but in a spirit of independence, failed in the latter. An angry but determined employer arrived early the next morning. There were the same muddy tracks on the floor that had been left the previous night by rain-soaked shoes; the usual adornment of peanut shells, empty candy bags, a stray handkerchief or hair pin. There was no waiting, no hesitation. . . . Into a small storeroom plunged the proprietor, and a minute later he emerged armed, with a pair of overalls, a mop, pail and a plentiful supply of soap. Down on his hands and knees he went, and fairly drove that scrubbing brush into the floor by his energy. Then came the mopping, the dusting of the chairs, and an hour later, spattered with dirty water, his face dripping perspiration, he completed the task. That night two new ushers helped him greet the patrons, but the theatre was spotlessly clean, and the proprietor had lived up to his standard.[122]

Roxy often retold these kinds of stories about his meager beginnings at the Family Theatre. Heavily clichéd and overly heroic, Roxy recalled in 1917, for instance, how he had once battled a severe storm to secure a Vitagraph print for the day's performance. "I walked from Forest City to Carbondale in a blinding snowstorm, a distance of seven miles each way, so that I would not disappoint my patrons," he told *Moving Picture World* in 1917.[123]

As he would for most of his career, Roxy reportedly worked up to eighteen hours per day at the Family, "perfecting his system of management" and "experimenting for better projection" while growing his patronage. Still, "Things didn't go with a whoop from the start," *Motion Picture News* recalled nearly five years later, with "many chairs . . . vacant six nights a week":

> Many of the miners were foreigners, and these silent, hard-handed men, understanding little of America and its ways and somewhat prone to suspicion of their neighbors' intent, were loath to mingle with the strangers. . . . So they came, slowly at first, and then in increased numbers, when they found the theatre spotlessly clean, the air sweet and pure, the pictures of the kind that appealed most strongly to their pleasure-loving and highly impressionable natures, the manager courteous and always smiling. They understood that smile, whether or not they grasped the meaning of the kindly spoken 'good evening,' and the pleasant 'good night.' They felt that they were welcome, and that here was one who allowed no one to laugh and ridicule their quaint manner of dress and the odd little topknots of hair affected by their women. The patronage grew greater as weeks passed. The man who wanted to become an exhibitor had achieved the first little corner of his ambition. He had established a theatre that gave every indication of becoming a permanent institution in the community.[124]

Motion Picture News recalled that the Family, like other nickelodeons, offered new immigrants a chance to learn about domestic customs and ideology in a safe environment for new Americans. "It required months . . . for me to sense out their desire to learn," Roxy later recalled. "They spoke no word of their appreciation. Sometimes they laughed. Exceptional comedies provoked them to such mirth that chairs were broken in their momentary hysteria. They swarmed to the theatre in crowds when the posters told them, in the only language they could understand—pictures—that blood and thunder would prevail at night."[125]

As the new year of 1909 began, Roxy continued to offer roller-skating on Monday through Wednesday nights and motion pictures and vaudeville for ten cents to capacity crowds on Thursdays through Saturdays.[126] Mary Jacobs expressed that the Family gave its patrons "a chance to see the strange, ever-beckoning land of adventure; to see how other people, free of the taint of coal-encrusted mines, lived. . . . They even began to dress up for the movies, as they did for church. To them, Roxy, who had made this possible, became a personage, someone to be respected."[127]

With the Family a success, and her father having no more objections to their courtship, Samuel Rothapfel and Rosa Freedman applied for a marriage license on January 26, 1909, and married in early February.[128] Roxy's growing position in Forest City was noted in the above-the-fold, front-page column in *TFCN* dedicated to their wedding in which "the community was deeply interested." The nuptials took place in the parlor of the Freedman House and were conducted by Rabbi Eben of Scranton's Linden Street Temple. Only relatives were on hand; whether Gustav, Max, or Annie made the trip is unknown. Roxy and Rosa honeymooned in Philadelphia and New York City. It is possible that Rosa may have met her in-laws at that time. Their vacation was short, though, perhaps because of the need to return to Forest City and manage the theater. By February 10, the couple returned home and took up residence in the Freedman House.[129]

The Family Theatre's fortunes rose that month, aided by a recent remodeling of the theater[130] and changes in the streetcar schedule to and from Carbondale. Trains that ran at half-hour intervals throughout the afternoon and evening, shuttling Forest City's residents to their neighboring town's Grand Opera House and to its Family and Dreamland theaters, now ran only once per hour, making trips out of Forest City harder for townsfolk to plan.[131] Procrastinating residents or those whose schedules did not match may have begun to see the Family Theatre as an even more attractive option.

The reputation of the theater also grew during its first few months in operation. By mid-March, Roxy claimed that the Family was "arous[ing] the admiration of every picture operator in the valley," especially as the live acts began to decrease and the number of films he booked rose in concert with the demand for new motion pictures. "We are showing from 2 to 3 reels of pictures at each performance," Roxy mentioned in a March 11, 1909, advertisement, "and we show nothing but first class films 4 and 5 subjects and an Illustrated Song for . . . 5c."[132] This attention to newspaper advertising was one of Roxy's innovations and primary methods of competing with another Forest City nickelodeon, the Lyric, which did not advertise in *TFCN*.

As films grew in importance, Roxy shifted the first night of motion picture programming to Wednesday instead of Thursday to take advantage of the growing crowds.[133] He also cut his overhead in order to alternate his schedule with more elaborate (and expensive) films, which largely ended the practice of hiring visiting performers. Locals Lillian Jones and Mabel Rennie were now, respectively, the Family Theatre's primary vocal and piano accompanists. By the last week in March, Roxy was able to feature a different film each day: Film Import and Trading Company's *Circumstantial Evidence* (1909) and Siegmund Lubin's split reel, *An Honest Newsboy's Reward* (1908) and *Two Little Dogs* (1908) were shown on Thursday alongside other shorts; three "special subjects" appeared on Friday; and on Saturday, there were four films, including Vitagraph's *The Chorus Girl* (1908) and *Rustic Heroine* (1908). Roxy proudly concluded the week's *TFCN* ad with a challenge to the competition, in town and elsewhere: "We are giving you a bigger and better show for 5 cents than you can get even in Scranton." Roxy added in large face, bold type: "We Lead and the Rest Follow."[134] Motion pictures quickly overtook what was left of the roller-skating business at the Family. By April 8, Roxy expanded film exhibition to seven days a week and announced that "Roller Skating has been discontinued until next fall." It would never return.[135]

For Roxy, each moment of success seemed temporary. "[B]ig audiences" attended the theater during its first six months, he recalled in 1934, but the crowds soon began to dwindle as the novelty wore off. "I knew that something had to be done," Roxy remembered,[136] and he began experimenting with a variety of ideas, including perfuming the auditorium during a screening of the Pasadena Rose Festival. Roxy recalled the effort five years later:

> I looked at the pictures and noticed that the prevailing flower was the rose. I bought an ounce of rose perfume dipped them in tiny paper streamers and as soon as we set the fans going we let the currents of the air blow the streamers all about the theater. I noticed that the audience looked very closely at the picture when the scent made itself felt. One young lady stopped me on going out and said: "Why, Mr. Rothapfel, those rose pictures look so natural I honestly thought I could smell the perfume of the rose."[137]

Roxy claimed it was his "first real attempt at showmanship."[138] "The projector was crude, the screen billowy and the lights poor," Roxy recalled eighteen years later, but the Family proved to be a "laboratory of my dreams, enabling me to try out, in very primitive ways, some of the ideas I had."[139] Another innovation was a crude lighting setup that enabled ambient colors to be reflected throughout the auditorium and upon the screen at the commencement and finale of every show.[140] Roxy also created and operated an electric switchboard in the projection booth to signal pianist Mabel Rennie to change the mood of the music through a series of colored lights.[141] This setup was certainly *not* typical for an exhibitor–pianist relationship during this period. Exhibitors might dictate the tone and style/theme of the music during pre-show meetings, but few directed the theater's music in this way. (Roxy would later eschew this method by insisting on rehearsals.)

In late April, he made several upgrades to the theater, including the addition of a new frontage with three hundred colored lights and a new patch of grass which led from the front of the Freedman House to the back of the building where the Family Theatre entrance was located.[142] Inside, baritone Edgar Sullivan replaced Lillian Jones in mid-May as the theater's singer of illustrated songs.[143] Roxy, feeling self-congratulatory and no longer in need of describing his film listings—as if the "Family" branding were sufficient—simply advertised, in a rather linguistically Jewish manner, "WHAT'S THE USE–YOU KNOW–EVERY EVENING–5c."[144]

In June, the Lyric, Forest City's other movie house, buckled under the competition. Unlike the Family, it had failed to run a single advertisement in *TFCN* as the two theaters competed head-to-head.[145] At a time of increasing popularity for motion picture exhibition, as evidenced by the growing number of reels shown at the Family Theatre and by the opening of a second "nickelet" in nearby Montrose a month earlier, the Lyric had stagnated and died.[146] The use of newspaper advertising was a key part of the Family's marketing and separated it from the now-defunct Lyric. It was highly unusual for a nickelodeon to advertise so heavily in 1909 and to provide such detail. Roxy's advertisements were not addenda to the Freedman House's notices, but appeared separately and prominently. Never more than one-eighth of a page, their prominence, repetition, and language were all noteworthy for Forest City and for the period. Vaudeville and legitimate theaters were frequent advertisers in the nation's newspapers in 1909; the Family was just as bold.

Samuel and Rosa Rothapfel celebrated the Family's success by moving out of the Freedman House and into the Bloxham building on North Main Street.[147] (Family Theatre pianist Mabel Rennie shared the space with them as a boarder.)[148] The couple's newfound independence required a steady stream of income. Many theaters closed during the summer months, owing to the heat and humidity inside these buildings. Roxy was determined, though, to make moviegoing a year-round activity in Forest City. Unlike the Family Theatre in Carbondale, and so many other movie houses of the era, the Family Theatre did not close during the summer of 1909. "It matters not how Hot the weather is—Come to the Family," the theater's July 8 ad urged its readers. "We cool our place with 8 large fans, two ventilators and 11 windows."[149]

The ability to remain open during the summer not only generated increased revenue but also helped to alter the area's perception that moviegoing was a seasonal recreation. The gamble worked. With little competition, the Family Theatre reported sold-out crowds in mid-July for its exhibition of the D. W. Griffith film, *A Baby's Shoe* (1909).[150] On July 29, Roxy boasted that "THERE ARE FEW people in this town who have not witnessed our Performance."[151] Moviegoing for Roxy was a twelve-month business.

Roxy's reputation began to extend beyond the small hamlet of Forest City, and a steady stream of visitors from various exchange houses began to arrive. By late July, Roxy was "recognized as one of the expert operators of this state," and he had become an advisor to the Pittsburg Calcium Light and Film's eastern branch.[152] (Originally known as the Pittsburg Calcium Light Company, their Motion Picture Department distributed song slides, "picture machines and all kinds of films, foreign and domestic.")[153] The PCLF job would be the first of many consulting positions. "Experts come here day after day to see our machine and our pictures," a Family Theatre advertisement noted, "and all proclaim it the best they have ever seen."[154] Another ad stated that Forest City residents should come to the Family Theatre, "The theatre that is considered by experts to be the highest type of its kind in any town. . . ."[155]

The Family churned on during the summer, offering up programs that would become hallmarks of Roxy's pro-American, pro-military exhibitions. In mid-August, he booked a double bill of Vitagraph's *Washington Under the British Flag* (1909) and *Washington Under the American Flag* (1909) and used the films as teaching tools, encouraging audiences to see "The two greatest patriotic films ever printed." Roxy added that "Every school child should see these great pictures."[156] His appeal to families had begun. If the Family could become a place for men *and* women and children, it would become more than an entertainment venue; it would become an irreplaceable cultural and community center. This would achieve his financial and philosophical goals. By early September, Roxy began debuting Saturday matinees, some of which were programmed for broader, pedagogical goals. These reels, he promised, would feature "travel, history, educational and natural history subjects, intermingled with clean comedy and other special features such as lectures upon different countries. This entertainment is built solely for children and ladies and the same high class performance as characterizes the theatre will be given."[157] *TFCN*, predictably, backed Roxy's efforts: "This is a good move and should be well patronized especially by the school children."[158] Cultural uplift through motion pictures backed by a leading voice in the community—Roxy's exhibition strategy was in place.

The theater was making money, but Roxy wanted to augment his revenue and the number of women attending the Family. He invented a new process—"daylight pictures"—that enabled him to project motion pictures inside a completely illuminated theater.[159] This would not only provide a new marketing gimmick but assure (female) audiences that all other patrons would be visible. It was certainly a Roxy-esque novelty—inventive, yet not groundbreaking, and highly lauded. The first advertisement for the process appeared in *TFCN* on September 9 under the headline "LIGHT": "The management of The Family has so far improved and perfected the projection of motion pictures upon canvass [*sic*] that it is no longer necessary that the audience sit in darkness to witness the action of the performance. A soft light that is in harmony with the nature of the entertainment fills the room and adds to the comfort of the patrons of the theatre."[160] Daylight pictures would become a hallmark of Roxy's early career and part of his appeal to families.

THE PASSION PLAY

On October 21, he unveiled a new, more elaborate program than he had offered before, with *The Passion Play* (1904) as its centerpiece. Family Theatre patrons were charged ten cents (instead of five) for *The Passion Play* in order to see and hear four soloists, "a well-drilled choir," and an organist. Roxy announced that he had "spared no expense or effort to make this an event worth remembering."[161] This special exhibition offered a first glimpse of what Roxy would develop and market in the years to come: an elaborate presentation of film and live performance that catered to the classes and the masses. It also foreshadowed his use of religious occasions and themes to attract seasonal audiences to celebrate religious holidays and customs in a multicultural and distinctly secular space. Churches and synagogues would commemorate Christmas and Passover through prayer and ritual; Roxy would commemorate the same holidays through music, film, and live performance. In this way, the movie house cemented its place as a cultural center and an important part of any community, while Roxy the Jew became a key provider of Christian celebrations.

The presentation of *The Passion Play* also outlined how tightly Roxy controlled all aspects of theatrical exhibition, especially the soundscape over which he presided. For each of his two nightly shows, Roxy "respectfully request[ed]" that audiences "come early enough as we will close the doors and keep them closed until the performance is over. Absolute quiet is imperative, and would therefore suggest the babies in arms be left at home." Roxy had begun to rearticulate the role of an exhibitor from one who "showed" movies to one who included work as a sound designer and not merely a musical accompanist. Control of all aural components of the show, from that produced by his musicians to that produced by the crowd, was essential. This is, of course, a rather radical departure from our contemporary understanding of the role of a motion picture exhibitor. But Roxy was adamant about his need to produce a picture, sound, and experience that was, in theory, the same for each audience member. This control more closely appropriated the operation of a legitimate theater, like the Grand Opera House in Carbondale, than a theater like the Family. Roxy also challenged the continuous performance model at the theaters he operated. Showtimes were regimented. *TFCN* recognized the change, and gushed profusely about the quality of the show:

> Never in the history of Forest City, has such an elaborate or productive play been staged as that given at the Family Theatre. . . . It was a record breaking crowd that witnessed the Passion play, the premier of all moving pictures, and was executed to the queens [*sic*] taste. . . . The chorus of singers in addition to four talented soloists was especially good, with renditions on the organ by Miss Rennie and chimes on phonograph helped to make up one of the best entertainments ever put before the public. Forest City is to be congratulated in having a man of such artistic taste in entertaining the public with such classical pictures.[162]

It is certainly worth noting Roxy's use of a phonograph player during this performance, already blending live entertainment with visual and aural media.

Roxy was honest about his growing interest in films with "strong moral lessons." It was "quite by accident," Roxy later recalled, that the film exchange began sending him a series of more dramatic films with his usual order of comedies. Among the new lot was a film that captured the capitalistic dream of new American immigrants, and he took note of its effect on his patrons:

> They were quiet when these were shown, but their faces were serious and their eyes puzzled when they left the theatre. The screen characters, beginning, in the first hundred feet, in the guise of laborers, and ending, after the usual phenomenal triumphs of the hero and heroine, in a dazzle of riches and refinement, struck home more deeply than I imagined. The pictures were showing this crude, uneducated, people a broader vista of

possibilities. They were awakening a latent desire to progress, to improve their positions in life. Ambition was being aroused in these stolid forms, and some day it would become manifest.

Roxy requested more of these types of films, which also encouraged those in the town's upper echelon to attend the Family. "The moral dramas, the scenics and industrials had found a market in this out-of-the-way community," Roxy remembered.

> A better class of people, meaning Americans in business there, came to the theatre, very few in numbers at first, but later as often and as numerously as the foreigners. At last I had stumbled upon a great secret. Not only did the foreign element seek knowledge and incentive to ambition, but business men, women of social standing, and boys and girls of education as well.[163]

From that point on, at the Family and throughout his career, Roxy emphasized the strategic importance of exhibiting middlebrow educational and religious-themed films that would fit the needs of his multi-class audience, many of whom shared similar origins and/or aspirations.

Roxy's first child, Arthur, was born a few days after *The Passion Play's* successful opening. *TFCN* stated that Roxy would "start right in imparting the secrets of the motion picture machine to 'Roxie' junior."[164] For the better part of a year, Roxy's personal life had remained unreported. Since his honeymoon, nearly all references to Roxy had been related to the Family Theatre. The announcement of his son's birth was a rare interjection of the personal into what would largely remain a private domain throughout his life. Samuel Lionel Rothapfel would slowly and carefully evolve into an almost mythic, living caricature named Roxy. He would obfuscate and/or exaggerate his past, keep all elements of his contemporary personal life hidden from view, and would rarely speak of Rosa or his child(ren) to the press. His brother and sister were never discussed and his father and deceased mother were mentioned only in retrospective biographies. A new Roxy would quietly replace the Samuel Rothapfel that residents of Carbondale and Forest City grew to admire as the first decade of the twentieth century drew to a close. This new modern Roxy was not a "salt-of-the-earth" man looking to succeed. He would become, instead, a self-appointed cultural Prometheus, bringing music, art, film, education, and culture to people he felt were much like his old self. Roxy wanted to help those like Sam Rothapfel who, because of their station in life, had not been exposed to art, music, and culture. With his role as an exhibitor of an integrated media and performing arts center, he would stretch their nickels, dimes, and, later, quarters to create a Carnegie Hall and Metropolitan Opera House for the masses.

After *The Passion Play*, films based on the works of Tolstoy and other "great writers" were shown at the Family Theatre to "audiences that appreciate and are interested in these works that are classics. They are educational and tend to the uplift of the community. What you see at The Family is always strictly moral and refined," a November 4 ad stated. "The same high class performance every evening."[165] And when the Family showed a filmed adaptation of *Oliver Twist* (1909) the following week,[166] *TFCN* effusively commented that "It seems there is no limit to the excellence of these performances. We go there and say to ourselves, 'well this would be hard to beat' but we come the next time and behold some thing new stares us in the face and we are again wondering where the end will be."[167] These kinds of reviews—and his own interminable drive—led Roxy to try and exceed his previous performance for the rest of his career. Each week had to be better, larger, more complex, and more lauded than the week before. It became the driving force behind his creative strategies. The music, he reasoned, must be improved. He lured Irma Walter, "the young virtuoso" violinist, to the Family for a long stay upon her return from Brussels where she had been studying at the Royal Conservatory.[168] And to ensure that every performance was flawless and better than the last, Roxy insisted on a "strenuous" four-hour rehearsal every afternoon for both his staff and musicians. Few movie theaters (if any) in the nation required such efforts in 1909, but it was the beginning of a new strategy aimed at total control. "Each artist is drilled in their respective line by the efficient manager Mr. Rothapfel as they would be in any of the New York theatres," *TFCN* reported.[169] With its attention to the arts, and not just film, Roxy reasoned, a coal miner could become a music lover and a bartender (like Roxy) a film exhibitor. In his mind, everyone and anyone could be Roxy. After all, Samuel Rothapfel already was.

In December, Roxy began a ritual that would last throughout his career (and leave one of his most indelible marks on American popular culture): his decades-long tradition of producing shows for the Christmas holiday. His special attention on Christmas began in a small way at the Family Theatre and concluded with the United States' most famous and popular Christmas spectacular at Radio City Music Hall a quarter of a century later. In 1909, his "Christmas Attractions" were a bit more meager, though, and included "selected films," "special music," and "special songs." But they were no less significant to his Christian audiences or more highly touted in his advertise-ments and programming.[170]

To cap off a triumphant year, Inspector O'Grady of the Underwriters As-sociation of America visited the theater in December 1909 and concluded that the Family was "one of the safest, most commodious, best ventilated and up-to-date theatres in the State, a model of perfection."[171] "Bring the Children," the Family Theatre's final advertisement of 1909 advised—and they did.[172]

BEYOND THE FAMILY

Forest City's population had grown more than 25 percent in the decade since 1900, and, by 1910, 5,749 people called the little town their home, includ-ing the small but growing Jewish community.[173] In addition to the Rothap-fels and the Freedmans, Jewish names and businesses could increasingly be found among the city's retailers and on the pages of *TFCN*, with Cohen Bros.' clothing store and Feldman's shoe store in full swing as the second decade opened.[174] And when Rosh Hashanah came later that year, *TFCN* would note that "some of our leading stores were closed from sundown on Monday until Wednesday evening."[175]

But few businesses, Jewish or otherwise, were doing as well by early 1910 as the Freedman House and its Family Theatre. With a potential market of only 7,000 people (including those from surrounding villages), the Family Theatre was selling a thousand tickets a day.[176] Small-town success was no longer enough for Roxy, though. He had already hosted industry guests and other business visitors during 1909, but the frequency of these visits acceler-ated in 1910. *TFCN* proudly noted that Roxy was not only a local sensation but that his management and technical skills were also recognized throughout the industry. Roxy had begun to market Roxy.

> It will be surprising to people of Forest City to know that the talented young manager of the Family Theatre is recognized as being the most ex-pert operator in this section of the country today. Experts from New York and Philadelphia have visited this popular little theatre during the last week and pronounced it one [of] the best equipped in the country. His machine is a wonder of excellence, employing some of the best features in the moving picture world and some which are exclusively his own. His talent, that is, artistes Mabel Rennie pianist, Irma Walter, violinist and Thos. H. Earl, baritone singer, are the best to be found anywhere.[177]

Roxy was also marketing daylight pictures to his frequent visitors and the promise that they too could exhibit movies in a lit auditorium. A demonstration of his "invention" during the week of January 10, 1910, for instance, was received with "great enthusiasm" and "heartily applauded."[178]

Inevitably, the Family Theatre's success and its "New Way" brought duplication and competition. In late January 1910, Martin Muchitz, following the model of the Freedman House, opened the Grand Theatre for motion pictures and vaudeville inside his hotel in a space once known as Muchitz Hall.[179] TFCN offered the new theater little praise, though, reporting its arrival with much less fanfare than it gave to the Family Theatre's opening in 1908. In fact, during the Grand's first week, the newspaper made a special point to shower Roxy with accolades, perhaps owing to their advertising customer's loyalty. "The ad. of the Family theatre last week in some manner explains why that popular little theatre has been so successful." the newspaper wrote. "We doubt very much if there are many young men with more real advertising ability than the young manager of 'The Family.' His work and signs are clever. In asking him recently to what he owed his success, he replied: 'Tell 'em what you have, on the outside, and make good on the inside.'"[180] TFCN's article was rather self-serving and perhaps intended to goad Muchitz's Grand Theatre to place more ads of its own in the News. Still, the comment makes evident that even at this early stage Roxy recognized the important part marketing played in his success. It had already helped the Family run the Lyric into the ground and was essential to combat new competition.

The National Stage

The opening of the Grand may have presented a new reason for Roxy to begin expanding his business horizons. The Family Theatre was certainly a success, but what more could he accomplish there? With this in mind, Roxy traveled to a New York motion picture exhibitors conference on January 22, 1910, accompanied by the manager of the Wilkes-Barre branch of the General Film Company. It was an event that, unbeknownst to Roxy, would transform his life and career.[181] The conference revealed, in Roxy's judgment, an exhibition industry in disarray: naive, unformed, and without the many high standards of practice he imagined "big city" exhibitors had already established. "While in New York," Roxy told his Forest City patrons upon his return,

I took particular pains to see the performances there in places where they charged from 5 to 15 cents admission. I was accompanied by some of the biggest men in the motion picture business. I can truthfully say that you are seeing right here in this little town a picture performance that is far superior to anything in New York at the prices quoted above. I can not tell you how proud I felt to know that we were ahead of these people who live in the biggest city in our country.[182]

Roxy had imagined an industry of lions, but, in his view, they were a collection of lambs.

He walked around the convention, introduced himself to new colleagues, and offered his theories of exhibition. His public pronouncements attracted the watchful eyes of the *Moving Picture World*, whose editors acted as if they had been searching for a messiah. "If there is one thing more than another that makes us grateful for having been the guest of the exchange men at the convention in the Hotel Imperial," the *World* noted in February 1910, "it is that it gave us the opportunity of becoming personally acquainted with the ideal exhibitor."[183] The journal's James Chalmers approached Roxy and asked if he would be interested in writing a column.[184]

PROSELYTIZING FOR *MOVING PICTURE WORLD*

Roxy's first offering challenged an industry that he believed had yet to understand its purpose. "Now, my brother exhibitors and operators, I do not wish to be held up as an authority, nor do I say that I am absolutely correct, but what I am about to impart to you has been the result of many days of hard work and the expenditure of a considerable amount of money," he wrote.

> Motion pictures are no longer a fad—they are here to stay, and are sure to become the greatest source of amusement in this country. The day of the ignorant exhibitor with his side-show methods is a thing of the past, and the public now demand an intelligent interpretation of these pictures and the conducting of these theaters in a more businesslike and artistic manner, and if you expect to remain in this business and reap a reasonable amount of profit therefrom you will have to join the ranks of the higher class exhibitors who are sure to spring up every day, or else you will fall by the wayside. The secret of the successful motion picture theater of the future will be the ability of the management to make the people forget that

they are witnessing a motion picture, to make them forget that they only paid you five or ten cents to witness the performance.[185]

Roxy's column was reprinted in *TFCN* on February 17.[186] He now had two distinct audiences: his Family Theatre patrons in Forest City and the growing film (exhibition) industry. This would become another hallmark of his career: shepherding one or two theaters locally, while also promoting himself and his work (inter)nationally.

Roxy remodeled the Family Theatre auditorium in March, adding five hundred new opera chairs and "the installation of a patent coolor [*sic*] for the purpose of supplying cold air from a natural ice house, all through the hot weather."[187] As he would often in his career, he also began consulting other businesses on the side. He continued to work for the Pittsburg Calcium Light and Film Company and traveled to Montrose during the week of March 21 to install a new projector in that city's Family Theatre.[188]

In late March, Roxy closed his own Family for further renovations.[189] The Family's temporary closure may have unexpectedly aided the competing Grand Theatre's fortunes. During the Family's renovations, the Grand announced that it was now enjoying sellout crowds.[190] Muchitz and Edward McCrew, who managed the Grand, also began following Roxy's model by placing advertisements in *TFCN* each week as the Family remained closed during construction. Both theaters placed advertisements in the April 7, 1910, issue of *TFCN* and emphasized their differing strategies regarding the Motion Picture Patents Company. The Grand Theatre proudly announced that it was showing four reels provided by an independent service "beyond Trust control," while the Family Theatre stated that "WE use licensed service only and have always used it and always expect to. We have built up our business on it, and you know what to expect when you see it. YOU TAKE NO CHANCE."[191] For Roxy, a film's license from the MPPC demonstrated its industrial and legal approval. It was further proof that the Family was a mainstream organization showing socially (and industrially) acceptable films. Rather than seeing the Trust, as Laemmle and Fox did, as a collusive business in restraint of free trade, Roxy used his theater's association with the MPPC as evidence that he was a legitimate business and businessman. Roxy was proud to note that the Family was now showing "licensed service" films even before their debut in the far larger city of Scranton (population 129,867 in 1910).[192]

Roxy's second article for *Moving Picture World* was published on April 9, and he chastised the industry even more than before. Commenting that it was a "deplorable fact that fifty per cent of the motion picture theaters of to-day are very badly managed," Roxy remarked that in most theaters, "Practically no attention is given to detail, and without detail you never have a first-class performance." He reminded exhibitors to be showmen, not just managers or projectionists, and emphasized the use of psychology:

> A very important item to be considered in careful management is the arrangement of programs. By this I mean the order in which the respective reels and songs are run. The first thing to be considered is that the performance shall have a beginning and an ending. It should he arranged, as far as possible, to offer a complete and consecutive presentation, just as though the patrons were watching a dramatic or any other performance. The present day helter-skelter methods of many exhibitors sends their audiences away in a bewildered and dissatisfied frame of mind, without any very clear idea of just what they have seen. If the programs are arranged with care and worked up to the psychological point, the audiences will go away contented and carry with them a definite recollection of the entertainment. They would come again and again, and that is what every successful manager desires to create, a steady patronage that will allow him to build up an average that will hold day in and day out regardless of conditions.

Roxy further emphasized music and "a careful rehearsal of your show" more than anything else:

> After all is in readiness, the music chosen for the respective reels, and reels having been inspected, take a seat in your theater and view your performance from a critical standpoint. Make note of things that you do not like and, if possible, correct them on the spot. Do not let it proceed until you are satisfied that it is all right, and when you are, O.K. it, and you may rest assured that if the performance pleases you it will invariably please your patrons.

Roxy also repeated a lesson he had learned from his time in the Marines. "Do not tolerate familiarity in your employees," he warned, "as this will surely destroy their respect for you in the end and make system impossible."[193] Music, rehearsals, and regiment were the Roxy way.

The Family Theatre reopened on May 9 to the unqualified praise of its leading advocate, *TFCN*, which declared the revamped theater a "decided success."[194] Frank Devlin, manager of theaters in Carbondale and Wilkes-Barre, complimented Roxy: "I have seen all the pictures around these parts, in the larger cities, too, but there are none to compare with that shown in the Family Theatre at Forest City. They are without question the finest I have ever seen and are as near perfect as I believe it possible to make them."[195] Three months later (in mid-August), Roxy began managing the Family Theatre in Carbondale in place of Devlin—the first of many times Roxy managed two theaters simultaneously. " 'Roxie,' has gained a considerable reputation in the motion picture business," *TFCN* reported, using his increasingly well-known nickname, "and he will give the pioneer city [Carbondale] a 'classy' entertainment; you can depend on that."[196]

Daylight Pictures and Points East

Roxy's management of the Forest City Family continued in the months ahead. On October 13, he announced that daylight pictures had finally been "perfected" to his specifications and satisfaction. "After experimenting for over a year," Roxy mentioned in the Family's advertisement, "I offer for your approval the absolutely flickerless picture and guarantee that they will not even tire the most sensitive eyes. The theatre at all times hereafter will have enough light to see everything and everyone in the entire audience"—a particular concern for women and those who worried about the composition of motion picture audiences—"but not enough to effect the projection in the least—in fact it will improve it."[197] The rollout of daylight pictures was a fitting end to Roxy's Forest City career as "some western parties" (perhaps the Pittsburg Calcium and Light Company) lured him away from Susquehanna County. Roxy would never return to Forest City for anything more than a visit. In his absence, Rosa Rothapfel managed the Family Theatre, while John Coveleski, who had been with theater for years, took over its technical operation.[198]

In November, Roxy was hired as motion picture consultant to the Benjamin F. Keith vaudeville circuit on the advice of John Dougherty, manager of Keith's Bijou Theatre in Philadelphia.[199] Roxy was brought to Keith's through Charles J. Kraus, a local booking agent of the United Booking Offices. The new Motion Photoplane Company was organized in New York under the direction of UBO's J. J. Murdock, and Roxy reportedly signed a $5,000, three-year contract with the new company.[200] Roxy unveiled the "Photoplane" process at Keith's Bijou and at another Keith's theater on Chestnut Street in Philadelphia in November 1910. (Roxy's penchant for creative storytelling was already evident in the *Philadelphia Inquirer*'s short biography, which noted that the exhibitor was "a graduate of the University of Wisconsin.")[201] *Variety* observed that, "The process throws a remarkably clear, smooth and sharp picture." By January 1911, the process had been installed in theaters in Philadelphia, Cleveland, Indianapolis, Cincinnati, Columbus, Detroit, New York, and Washington, DC. A Photoplane advertisement in *Variety* told exhibitors that "pictures will stand out five hundred per cent stronger" through the use of the process. In addition, this would mean "No Darkened House! No Complaints From Civic Bodies! No Room for the Eye Specialist to Rant!"[202]

Roxy's success with daylight pictures in other cities was used for good promotional effect back in Forest City as the Family Theatre announced that films were now being shown "Family Theatre Style" at Keith's Fifth Avenue Theatre in New York.[203] *TFCN* boasted that "The process [daylight pictures] which the moving picture authorities throughout the country regard as a marvel, was evolved here and the Family Theatre was the first theatre in the United States to show moving pictures with the lights turned on."[204] Roxy's daylight pictures were given a host of new names as "the process" moved across the country, including "photoplane" and "light house projection." By year's end, Roxy would install it in the Keith Hippodrome in Cleveland and in the circuit's Indianapolis theater.[205]

Roxy also landed a deal with United Booking Offices to tour the country improving projection at their many theaters[206] and added another circuit to his list with the installation of daylight pictures at Poli's Theatre in Hartford, Connecticut, part of Sylvester Poli's vaudeville circuit,[207] and at the Nickel in Manchester, New Hampshire, and other venues.[208]

Roxy's and daylight pictures' success was in stark contrast to the fortunes of the Family Theatre. By 1911, despite its recent renovations, crowds had become increasingly sparse. Along with motion pictures, the Family tried booking other attractions, including a pow-wow on February 27 hosted by the Neponset tribe and the Pocahontas Council.[209] A week later, the Family closed temporarily.[210] A once thriving theater that had drawn visitors from across the state was now just another struggling nickelodeon. After traversing North America installing daylight pictures from California to Canada, Roxy returned to Forest City in mid-March in an attempt to revive the venue that had launched his career. Renovated for a third time, he reopened the Family under his direction on March 20, though he would not stay long in Forest City.[211]

Days after Roxy's brief visit to Forest City, he was back in New York, installing daylight motion pictures in Manhattan's New York Theatre for William Fox.[212] Loew's Herald Square Theatre in Manhattan may have also featured the process. A 1911 photograph shows its rooftop sign advertising "Daylight Photo Plays," while a billboard notes that its "10 c Daylight Photo Plays" were "Shown Here First On A Silver Sheet."[213] In a fairly short amount of time, some of the most important vaudeville and motion picture theater magnates—Benjamin Keith, William Fox, and Sylvester Poli (and possibly Marcus Loew)—had embraced Roxy's daylight pictures.

But what exactly was the daylight pictures process? During its earlier, late-1910 installation in Cleveland, Roxy had told a reporter that he held "no patents on this device, for what I have done is simply to apply certain laws regulating the projection of the light's rays in a way of my own. What I have accomplished is by means of very powerful lenses, a new way of directing them on the screen, and then a chemical application to the screen that absorbs the light so that instead of the light hitting the screen as a ball would a brick wall it is absorbed and all the rays like those you see around a street light at night are brought to the center." Roxy's explanation, in addition to being vague and wordy, also seems to make little sense. In low-light situations, it is actually better to have a screen *reflect* light rather than to *absorb* it. (Hence Loew's "Silver Sheet" and the need for reflective screens.) Roxy, though, was always a better marketer than a scientist. He noted that each room that installed daylight pictures "requires a different treatment of all these elements. My protection lies in knowing how to do that."[214] In other words, Roxy would have to consult every venue in which his process was installed, thus making money on the sale of the system and ensuring that only he could properly implement the process.

Roxy managed to sell exclusive rights to his invention to the Orpheum circuit, although other theaters would continue to use his technology anyway. At its Los Angeles debut, the process was dubbed "Orpheum Daylight Motion Pictures," a "Novelty of the Age."[215] "Until you've seen it in fact, you can't just comprehend how such a thing can be," the *Los Angeles Times* hyped. "Yet the try-out late Saturday afternoon, before a number of newspaper men, was an entire success."

Roxy's daylight pictures, upon further inspection, appears to be a mixture of technical prowess, industry ignorance, and well-sold hocus-pocus. Roxy, "a German now resident in New York," the *Los Angeles Times* noted, claimed to have spent ten years developing "his chemical mechanism." For its science, Roxy relied on his experience in the Marines and his time at the Florida barracks. "The preparation upon which Rothapfel covers his screens is related to luminous paint," the *Times* wrote in another long-winded explanation, "but is unlike any luminous paint on the market. The principal ingredient is a chemical substance found in the Dry Tortugas" derived from a "microscopic creature whose corpse makes the breakers of our summer sea shore blaze with greenish fire on dark evenings. The lens concentrates the light in a fashion all its own." With little that could not be copied, Roxy was justifiably worried that his system would be duplicated. He would never allow others to install the device, even after licensing it to the Orpheum circuit. When it needed to be installed at an Orpheum theater in Winnipeg, for instance, Roxy traveled north. "The miracle is in the preparation of the screen, and the construction and composition of the ions," the *Times* attempted to explain. "The screen Rothapfel prepares himself secretly." After every performance at the Los Angeles Orpheum, the daylight pictures lens was removed, brought to a safe, and guarded by Emil Girard, "Grand Chief Interpreter" of the Orpheum staff, now dubbed the "Lord High Custodian of the Lens." The *Times* added that what information Roxy did impart to the theater's projectionist was only enough for him to operate the system—not to steal it.[216] In the end, there seemed little science to the system but a lot of successful marketing and bluster.

A bill requiring the use of daylight pictures for all movie houses in California helped boost the system even further when it was introduced in the California legislature by state Senator Ed K. Strobridge and "fathered" by Assemblyman A. A. Rogers. The proposed law required using Roxy's technology so that theaters would at all times be sufficiently lit to allow patrons to clearly distinguish the features of other attendees. Packaged with a group of measures, including a curfew for minors and the prohibition of "immoral and crime depicting plays," the bill's primary purpose was to patrol the social behavior of the movie house rather than to endorse the technology. The bill was eventually passed by both houses.[217] The publicity surrounding this legislation may have helped ticket sales, and when the new Orpheum Theatre opened in Los Angeles in June, daylight pictures were a featured attraction.[218] It was so great a draw, in fact, that the Orpheum continued to advertise the use of this "technology" well into the following month.[219]

Roxy had built his early reputation largely on the careful selection of film, music, and live performance at the Family Theatre. But he was now becoming better known for his technical acumen and salesmanship than for his managerial skill and showmanship. It would be an odd detour, in retrospect, though certainly not the last time new technology would transform his career. In the months to come, more daylight screens would pop up around the country, including an installation at the 5,000-seat Madison Square Garden Theatre in late May 1911, making it, for a very brief moment, the largest movie house in the world.[220]

Of course, not everyone was amazed by Roxy's new process—least of all America's increasingly skilled projectionists (and especially those who supported the Herbst full-light process instead). *Moving Picture World* commented that daylight pictures at the B. F. Keith Theatre in Boston, for instance, produced a picture that "lacked sharpness and intensity," adding that "a light auditorium hardly compensates for the lack of these features."[221] Exhibitor Charles E. Schneider of the Nelson Theatre in Springfield, Massachusetts, argued that at most daylight pictures were basically accomplished "with more light going through the film" coupled with "masking around the screen. The Rothapfel system," he told the *World*, "employs a black border around the actual picture; and to whatever extent this may result in betterment of the picture or better lighting of the auditorium it is entitled to full credit. Every practical operator, however, knows that the 'proper wiring' in this case means simply more amperes at the arc and consequent bigger bill for current to secure stronger projection upon the screen and overcome the house lights; and, stripped of all misleading discussion, the Rothapfel system deals primarily and, so far as any innovation is concerned, wholly with the screen."[222] Still, daylight pictures proved to be a brief marketing and exhibition sensation, and one of the primary keys to Roxy's early success. Exhibitors were drawn to the system to lure in audiences who had been told that watching motion pictures could damage their eyes or that, with the lights off, theaters might be unsafe for women and children.

Alhambra Theatre, Milwaukee, WI

Scholars have often focused their attention on the social composition of motion picture theaters in the United States during the first decade of the twentieth century, yet there remains a dearth of in-depth analysis demonstrating how theaters of the early 1910s countered reformers' complaints during this period and began routinely drawing members of the middle and upper classes. Roxy's work in the Midwest between 1911 and 1913 demonstrates how he ensured that his theaters were embraced by self-appointed social and cultural guardians and ushered in a new era of social acceptance for motion pictures and motion picture theaters at a time when the industry desperately needed political, religious, moral, and legal approval.

Though the year 1913 is often recalled as the moment when audiences began embracing American and European multi-reel films in upscale venues, middle- and upper-class audiences were already patronizing deluxe film-only theaters in the Midwest by 1911 due to a new breed of movie theater that catered to literary, stage, and biblical adaptations. Theaters like the Alhambra in Milwaukee and the Lyric in Minneapolis not only programmed multireel films based on well-known novels, plays, and biblical narratives but also added live performance and classical music to lure in a multi-class patronage. By understanding how these two theaters were programmed by Roxy—and how he reached out to clergy, politicians, business leaders, women, men, and children—we can better understand how these theaters created fertile venues for feature-length films. It was the Midwest, not New York, that was at the vanguard of film exhibition in 1911. Roxy is best known for his work in New York, but his career was established closer to his boyhood home in Minnesota.

Roxy's work with daylight pictures was profitable for his wallet and his reputation, but he was looking for a greater challenge and a return to theater management. His opportunity came that spring when he was hired by Herman Fehr to resurrect the Alhambra Theatre in Milwaukee, which was normally closed or half empty during the summer months, when the oppressive heat kept audiences away. Roxy took over the 3,000-seat legitimate theater and installed film as the primary entertainment, making it the largest motion picture theater in America at the time.[223]

Roxy, Rosa, and Arthur arrived in Milwaukee in late May, living in the Aberdeen Hotel seven blocks away from the theater.[224] The Alhambra's live performance-only days ended on June 1, 1911, with a final appearance by Sarah Bernhardt during her tour of the United States.[225] Roxy reportedly went to see Bernhardt's play "and went around to talk to her," he recalled in 1923. "The celebrated actress heard his story with keen interest and predicted a great future for him."[226]

He immediately hired a new staff of ushers, replaced the carpets and draperies, and added a nursery to take care of children—an initiative to bring in and curry favor with women. Roxy also marketed film's ability to provide education, culture, and uplift through advertisements aimed at the general public and in letters he sent to one thousand of the city's most prominent residents offering free tickets to see *La Caduta di Troia* (*The Fall of Troy*, 1910).[227] Much of what he had learned in Forest City was repeated in Milwaukee. Admission prices were reduced to a dime for adults and a nickel for "kidlets," daylight pictures were highlighted as a technical marvel, and only "licensed" pictures were shown.[228] In a move that would be duplicated in other Roxy houses, he also covered over the orchestra pit and placed an expanded orchestra, directed by Fred Brunkhorst, on one side of the stage while adding the Nonparell [sic] quartet and a group of soloists to the other. By moving the orchestra from the pit to the stage, Roxy foregrounded the importance of music, visually and aurally binding it to the films presented. The enormous stage also housed a grand piano and an organ, which were used until the orchestra and soloists began their work at 3:30 P.M. The debut of Roxy's "motion pictures de luxe" immediately won the support of the local press, altering popular opinions in the city about the social and entertainment value of motion pictures. The *Milwaukee Daily News*, for instance, noted how the revived theater gave residents "something new in the way of amusement." The films were of "an exceptional character," the *News* added, "while the stage setting for the pictures and the musical numbers provided are far out of the ordinary."[229]

Roxy's well-coordinated publicity campaign featured his photograph in the *Milwaukee Free Press* and the *Sunday Sentinel*.[230] He also distributed prepackaged editorial copy and press releases, many of which were reprinted almost verbatim and appeared in nearly identical articles in both the *Milwaukee Daily News* and the *Milwaukee Free Press*,[231] while the theater's taglines read, "Motion Pictures De Luxe at the Alhambra / Milwaukee's Coolest Theater / Latest Pictures–Best Music / Wonderful Boy Soloist / Never Dark–Always Light."[232]

The Alhambra's success was instantaneous. Four days after it opened, the *Daily News* reported that audiences were filling "the lower floor and overflow into the balcony at each performance."[233] Not only were the audiences large, they were also filled with new motion picture converts.[234] The *Milwaukee Daily News* reported on June 16 that "People who never went to motion picture theaters are going regularly to the Alhambra, where the motion pictures de luxe are proving the summer amusement sensation of the city. The use of the daylight system, the many innovations, the music, the courtesy of the attendants and the general air of refinement offer a pleasing hour and a half of entertainment."[235] Motion picture–only venues had been scantily attended by many members of the upper and middle classes, but with the adoption of the medium at one of the city's largest and most prestigious theaters, the Alhambra's shows were "adding hundreds daily to the roll of motion picture patrons." The success of the theater's new programming surprised even Roxy, who had intended to use only the orchestra level for nightly performances. However, with the consistently large crowds, the balcony was opened to the public.[236] "Nothing in the summer amusement line," the *Sunday Sentinel* mentioned, "has been so instantaneously successful in years as the motion pictures de luxe at the Alhambra theater."[237]

Only weeks after opening, the *Sunday Sentinel* reported that Roxy had by then drawn visitors from across the state and from other parts of the country:

"Managers of exchanges and exhibitors from all over this section are coming to Milwaukee, to see what they say is the classiest and most up to date presentation of animated photography."[238] By successfully introducing "high-class" motion pictures into the ornate theater, Roxy had "broke[n] all records for that house," and, according to *The Green Book Magazine*, "turned a white elephant of a dramatic theatre into one of the most successful picture houses in America."[239] The Alhambra's success was bittersweet for *Moving Picture World,* which lauded the theater, yet lamented, "Here we are in New York City, which is claimed to be America's foremost city, yet we do not have an all-picture show put on in the style that is done at the Alhambra. We are living in hope that some day a New York exhibitor will rise to this opportunity, meanwhile we compliment Milwaukee in setting the pace."[240] The Saxe Amusement Enterprises recognized the value Roxy had created and contracted with the Shubert Theatrical Company to take over the lease and management of the Alhambra. The deal was struck at the end of July, with the handoff taking place on August 20. Thomas Saxe announced that the theater would now become a movie house year-round. Herman Fehr had leased the theater for the previous seventeen years, but was outbid by Thomas and John Saxe.[241]

Fehr, instead, signed a new agreement with Lee Shubert to sublease the Lyric in Minneapolis for $14,000 for the year beginning that September.[242] Fehr's managerial choice for the Lyric was easy: Roxy. He had already seen his work at the Alhambra, which had also been a former legitimate Shubert venue. The Alhambra had been a complete success; Fehr could only wonder what he and Roxy might be able to accomplish in a city devoid of Saxe Amusement Enterprises and other competition. Minneapolis, unlike Milwaukee, had few large movie houses.

The Deluxe Motion Picture Theatre Comes of Age, Lyric, Minneapolis, MN

The trip to the Twin Cities was something of a homecoming for Roxy. After a seventeen-year absence, he was now roughly thirty miles from Stillwater. He made the trip alone, though, as Rosa and Arthur returned to Forest City to be with her ailing father.[243] Rosa was also familiar with Roxy's pattern during the first weeks at a new theater, with its tireless days and endless nights. There was no need to travel to a new city just to sit in a hotel room.

Even before he took over the reins of the Lyric in Minneapolis, Roxy picked up a little side work at a small nickelodeon, the Colonial Theatre (known as the Crystal Theatre until 1911), in the neighboring city of St. Paul.[244] Roxy paid a fifty-dollar license fee to the city of St. Paul as the "proprietor of [the] motion picture show at Number 446 Wabasha Street."[245] Giving this new venue his usual adornments, he drafted an orchestra and a group of vocalists, hired a staff of female ushers, and, as part of his well-tested strategy of rebuffing reformers' complaints and currying favor with family-minded patrons, added a matron to care for the children.[246] If the theater was truly a Roxy-run house and not just a brief consulting gig—and *Motography* claimed that he *was* managing it—it certainly did not act like one. The Colonial placed only one advertisement in the *St. Paul Pioneer-Press,* on September 3. The theater promoted its "Refined Daylight Motion Pictures" and its "large orchestra and splendid singers."[247] Days later, Roxy was gone.

Martin Miller Marks has accurately observed that for much of the next twenty years "every new stage in Rothapfel's career eclipsed the one before."[248] Yet Minneapolis would prove to be an unexpected challenge. Opened in 1885 as the Hennepin Theatre for live performances, the theater became known as the Lyceum in 1905 and was remodeled and renamed the Lyric in 1908. Three years later, in September 1911, Roxy reopened the Lyric for the season, hoping to replicate the Alhambra's success with film rather than dramatic plays.[249]

Minneapolis would not succumb as easily as had Milwaukee. Motion pictures had already offended local reformers, while the city's legislators looked upon movie theaters as dangerous fire hazards—or worse. "Everyone was antagonistic to pictures," Roxy would later recall of his early days in Minneapolis, including the clergy, police, merchants, and the city's educators:

> My first task was to find the reason for this dislike. After days of questioning, after being openly insulted for my interest in pictures, and many discouragements from every side, I found that Minneapolis had been flooded with sensational, objectionable film, and that a wave of protest and indignation had followed. The parasites who seek "easy money" with no thought of the future had descended upon the city, reaped a harvest by catering to the baser natures, and then fled, leaving in their wake a seething cauldron of outraged dignity, shattered ideals, religious uprisings and moral protests. . . . The theatre was opened with a program of morally enlightening pictures. I was obliged to adopt this policy and stick to it tenaciously.[250]

For its reopening on September 18, 1911, Roxy installed a $2,500 pipe organ, a concert grand piano, and the all-women Fadette Orchestra of Boston.

He also presented a variety of soloists along with the newly formed Lyric Quartet.[251] The opening bill featured the films *Sight Seeing in Boston, The Voyageur, The Ruling Passion, Captain Kate,* and *The Runaway Leopard* (ca. 1911).[252] All of this was provided for a ticket price of between 10 and 20 cents at the 1,700-seat theater—roughly the same cost as the city's cheaper nickel and dime houses and dramatically lower than the Lyric's prices when operated as a legitimate theater.[253] Roxy's new staff included footmen, pages, matrons, and female ushers who courteously assisted all patrons during the four daily hour-and-a-half shows.[254] Roxy refurbished the Lyric Theatre as well, elaborately decorating the stage and screen. And with uneven projection in theaters across the city (and throughout the country), the Lyric's daylight pictures were now intended to encourage repeat attendance, attract women, and boost perceptions. Elsewhere, palms, flowers, and an electric fountain prominently graced the entryway.[255]

"The two large audiences that thronged into the Lyric last night gasped a little in astonishment at the changes that have been wrought in the once familiar playhouse," the *Minneapolis Journal* added after its opening-night premiere. "The process of rearranging the theater to make it the home of 'motion pictures de luxe' has resulted in a brilliant success. The arrangement of the stage, the light effects and the refurbishing in evidence everywhere combine in what may be described as an artistic triumph."[256] Several Minneapolis newspapers quickly repeated Roxy's claims that the Lyric was now the "finest picture show in America."[257]

Roxy was discerning in his selection of films, viewing each one in advance before agreeing to its exhibition. This, too, was a departure, signaling that exhibitors should be programmers and exhibitors and not just projectionists and bookers. Four reels were chosen for each performance from a selection of scenics, travelogues, educational pictures, dramatic stories, historical films, and comedies.[258] Roxy determined the music that accompanied each of the films he selected and exerted authorial control over the films as well, spending hours editing them, and, in some cases, eliminating scenes whole cloth.[259] Celluloid shipped to Roxy, in his mind, was merely a rough draft; once it arrived, he would begin his work, seeing himself as every film's final editor. Nor was his control over the live performances at the Lyric any less stringent, insisting upon daily rehearsals for his musicians, dancers, and other performers to ensure consistency in both quality and content.[260]

His staff, like that at any Roxy theater, was given a military-style inspection each day, with the ringing of a gong in the Lyric's foyer (an instrument that would become iconic in the hands of Roxy's future boss Major Bowes) summoning his troops to line up for review. Corporal Rothapfel would then inspect every seam, glove, cap, collar, hem, head, and fingernail, making certain that his employees were ready to receive their patrons.[261] After the review, two bells sounded and the staff scurried to their posts. The ringing of three bells opened the Lyric for business, leaving Roxy with the task of keeping his troops looking as fresh and tidy throughout the day as they had at 9:59 A.M.[262] This was still not typical of 1911-era movie houses, but was an attempt to incorporate the high standards of legitimate theaters into this new entertainment world, an effort for which Roxy's previous military training proved essential.

Roxy's staff also knew exactly what to expect in preparation for the programmatic changeover each Monday and Thursday. With everyone present, Roxy would be seated on the stage next to his stenographer and, facing the screen, would signal the projectionist to begin the new film's screening. An endless stream of ideas about mood, themes, pieces of music, places to cut, moments to emphasize, and the like would bellow forth. Before the film was over, Roxy was already calling out to his staff what music would be used and what, how, and where music and sound effects should be employed. Viewing Roxy's frenzied performance art in which he continually tossed about the names of familiar music titles while feverishly watching a feature film, travelogue, newsreel, or short, James McQuade wondered, as so many would, how Roxy was able to have command over so extensive a body of work without any formal training. "It is strange that Mr. Rothapfel should state that he does not know a note of music, except by ear, yet he has the scores of every light opera and musical comedy at his command, and can draw on grand opera and on the symphonies to assist him in playing the pictures. In addition, he is familiar with the popular lyrics of many countries." McQuade reported as well that Roxy was already fashioning himself a relief conductor, wielding the baton whenever needed. "He gets at the very soul of a score," McQuade added, "and brings out its beauty, or its weirdness, with the skill of a master." All of these aural accoutrements, Roxy told him, were used in service of heightening each "psychological point in the story."[263]

Roxy began his community building efforts in late September by presenting a screening of the film *The Star Spangled Banner* (1911) to the Boy Scouts. Roxy, who was hailed by the press as "a champion of the Boy Scout movement," addressed the crowd on the subject of signaling, drawing from his own Marine Corps experience.[264] Thus, an appeal to children was part of the Lyric's approach. "Probably never in the amusement history of Minneapolis has an enterprise made such a marked impression as has the Pictures de Luxe

at this theater," the *Minneapolis Tribune* commented. "Mr. Rothapfel's 'The
Star Spangled Banner' last week" was "one of the finest things ever produced
here on any stage."[265]

Roxy also reached out to and joined the city's businessman's club and
hosted the annual "Elks' Night" at the Lyric.[266] He made sure that his theater's
charitable efforts were well publicized in local newspapers.[267] *Moving Picture
World* journalist James McQuade observed that Roxy's efforts were "so keenly
appreciated by prominent people in that city, that club members, both ladies
and gentlemen, are exerting their influence to support him, and other people
of influence go to the expense of printing circular letters and mailing them to
acquaintances and business men."[268]

With the promise of filmic material suitable for middle-class audiences in
an increasingly socially acceptable venue, many of Minneapolis's once reluctant citizens were transformed into Lyric patrons. "Best of all," the *Tribune*
added, "parents feel certain that the entire atmosphere . . . will be clean."[269]
Motion Picture News wrote that "clergymen had gone again and again to the
theatre, and always there greeted them the same clean, healthy atmosphere,
both on the screen and in the physical appearance of the house."[270] As Rever-
end James W. Cool wrote to Roxy, "A man who will brave the chance of losing
money rather than pander to the lower tastes should receive the support of
every citizen interested in the welfare of humanity."[271]

Roxy further appealed to the city's clergy with an elaborate exhibition of
The Passion Play—his Christmas pageant for 1911—that was exhibited four
times a day between December 18 and Christmas.[272] Mimicking the format of
opera houses and legitimate theaters, he closed the doors at the beginning of
each show[273] and, as Robert Grau noted, was "uncompromising in demanding that the same rules that prevail for grand opera (in seating the audience at
the start of the show and forbidding an exodus while the curtain is up) must
be observed."[274] The feature film was accompanied by "Holy City" and other
melodies, which bellowed from the organ and were performed by twenty boy
vocalists as well as the Lyric's in-house musicians and singers.[275]

The 1,700-seat theater was repeatedly sold out during that week and had to
turn away many seeking tickets. Roxy remarked that the exhibition had "done
more to gain him a prominent place in picturedom than any other presentation."[276] By cementing the Lyric's relationship to Christmas, Roxy had proven
the movie house to be a worthy secular institution capable of honoring the
traditional and the sacred. For Roxy the Jew, it demonstrated once more that
the audience for what others pejoratively characterized as the "dirty movies"
could be expanded greatly if it provided meaningful entertainment and uplift

in keeping with mainstream Christian life and values. This was a lesson he would long remember and later employ at theaters such as Radio City Music Hall, where his Christmas pageants continue more than 75 years after his death.

The success of *The Passion Play* in 1911 served an industrial purpose as well—it was Roxy's retaliatory strike against any concerns about the morality and, more importantly, the safety of movie theaters. Only a month earlier, the city's most influential newspaper, the *Tribune*, had attacked all forty-seven motion picture theaters in Minneapolis as unsafe. In fact, only one, the Elite, had been declared a fire hazard by the city.[277] Extravaganzas like *The Passion Play* enabled Roxy to demonstrate the quality of his musicians, his interest in cultural and spiritual uplift, and his ability to attract the middle- and upper-class audiences he needed to make the Lyric, and motion pictures, a cross-cultural and multi-class form of entertainment. It both separated the Lyric from other movie houses in the city, while elevating those same theaters by generic association. To close the Lyric now, after *The Passion Play*'s success, would be the equivalent of closing a secular cathedral.

Roxy left little to chance, though, and soon invited Minneapolis's fire chief and a group of firemen to be his guests at a special screening of images of the New York City Fire Department a few weeks later.[278] The following month, the fire marshal, along with the city building inspector and the city electrician, sent a signed report to the *Tribune* arguing that the city's theaters were "safe and sanitary, and as well safeguarded against panic and fire as any class of public buildings in the city."[279] "I would advise any exhibitor to mix freely in local affairs," Roxy would later remark. "It is a wonderful power for good."[280]

Roxy's next move was to raise the theater's status by increasing the Lyric's ticket prices, further separating it again from Minneapolis's smaller movie houses. Although matinees were still ten cents, evening prices were increased to twenty cents for the ground floor and twenty-five cents for box seats—a signal to the middle and upper classes that securing premium seats at the city's largest movie theater was now a privileged activity.[281] These tickets had an exclusivity of both price and location that made them attractive to those who needed to demonstrate their affluence and position in society. Sitting in a box seat at the Lyric quickly became a form of social plumage—something that had been previously unheard of in Minneapolis.

One of Roxy's more esteemed box seat patrons, who made "regular weekly visits," was a 41-year-old Swedish immigrant, Governor Adolph Olson Eberhart. The governor may have found in motion pictures, and in Roxy's presentation thereof, the same cultural uplift and advocacy of Americanization and assimilation that appealed to the Lyric's growing, multi-ethnic audience.[282] Roxy wrote to the governor on January 6, 1912, inviting him to see a newsreel of the governor's trip east, alongside the presentation of William Selig's film, *Cinderella* (1912).[283] The governor accepted the invitation and the Lyric's organist serenaded him with a song written in his honor.[284] Roxy's campaign to convert legislators into moviegoers was part of his efforts against local censorship and other related concerns then being discussed in the state legislature.[285] Eberhart was so taken with the Lyric and motion pictures that he was chosen as a keynote speaker at the first convention of the Motion Picture Exhibitors League of Minnesota.[286]

It had taken just four months to make the Lyric and its motion pictures a cultural institution in Minneapolis. The success of *The Passion Play* and films such as *Cinderella*, as well as the scenics, educational films, and travelogues he presented, had brought the theater and Roxy acclaim with the region's reformers, clergy, politicians, educators, and businessmen and -women.

The cultivation of the city's female population, though, was perhaps the most important victory for Roxy, as it assured the theater a growing audience of women *and* children. The following letter, published in the *Minneapolis Tribune* from a female patron of the Lyric, demonstrates the rapid change in viewpoint: "For one hour and a half one can be very much benefited and rested," Mrs. J. K. mentioned. "The pictures on the screen are delightfully free from coarse suggestions. The songs and music are elevating. One is never afraid something is coming next to disgust you either in seeing or hearing. The Bible scenes and history of the same are surprising, and certainly an education for people who cannot understand the Bible by reading. . . . Parents and children will do well to patronize this theater."[287]

Despite all of these apparent successes, Roxy abruptly announced his departure from the Lyric, effective April 29, 1912. No explanation was given for the decision when *Moving Picture World* reported the precipitous news and the "Regret over Manager Rothapfel's departure from the scene of his brilliant success in Minneapolis." By then, the "cultured" women of Minneapolis, members of the Thursday Study Club, the Authors' Study Club, the Pathfinders, the Prospect Park Study Club, the Utopian Club, and the Shakespeare Club, had all changed their view of motion pictures during his tenure at the Lyric. *Moving Picture World* reported that "A party of about one hundred women, representing several of the women's clubs of the city, attended the matinee at the Lyric Theater this afternoon as a mark of appreciation of Mr. Rothapfel's efforts to give to the public a good clean show, presenting pictures both entertaining and instructive."[288]

ROXY COMES AND GOES

On May 6, 1912, the employees of the Lyric honored Roxy with a farewell banquet.[289] Several days later, Roxy headed to Chicago to present the American debut of the Selig Polyscope Company's film, *The Coming of Columbus*. Selig also entrusted Roxy to arrange the film's musical accompaniment.[290] Roxy invited the trade press, Chicago's clergy, the Knights of Columbus, and the board of education to the opening, after which he advertised that *The Coming of Columbus* was "Endorsed by Educators Pulpit Press Historians and Public."[291] The film's subsequent run at the Lyric in Chicago generated "tremendous business."[292] When Selig distributed the film around the country with Roxy's score,[293] "Crowded houses were the rule everywhere."[294]

Roxy was commissioned by J. J. and Lee Shubert to become the general manager of their new chain of motion picture theaters. These were to include Roxy's own former house, the Lyric in Minneapolis, another Lyric in Chicago, the Boyd Opera House in Omaha, the Garrick in St. Louis, the Grand in Atlanta, and other Shubert theaters in St. Paul, Kansas City, and St. Joseph, Missouri. The plan was for all of these theaters to begin showing motion pictures under Roxy's direction to expand the Shubert movie theater chain to more than two dozen.[295]

Roxy's work at reviving the Lyric in Chicago was the first exploratory step in this effort.[296] Prior to his arrival, the Shuberts had leased the theater at a cost of $1,500 per week, but were accruing a mere $375 for their motion picture performances. They handed the troubled venue to Roxy. Even despite his impressive track record, *Motography* expressed an early "fear [that] Mr. Rothapfel has chosen an unfortunate location for his project in Chicago."[297] The Lyric, according to Jerry Stagg, "was a jinx house for J. J. The theater had two entrances, both of them, as Jake once said, carefully hidden from anybody who was looking for them."[298]

Patronage at the Lyric, which reopened on June 9, was still unsatisfactory.[299] From a meager $350 per week, Roxy was able to double the theater's receipts, but the $800 weekly shortfall was unacceptable to the Shuberts. Roxy had spared no expense to earn that $700, leaving the Shuberts with an even greater net loss, on top of which Roxy's salary was $100 per week. Shubert sent numerous telegrams to Roxy expressing his concern over rising operating costs, including a bill for the theater's palms. Roxy responded by redoubling his efforts, and by the third week, had brought the theater's weekly gross to $1,300.[300] With the Lyric still experiencing a net loss, Roxy announced on August 23 that prices had been reduced with "NO SEATS HIGHER THAN

TEN CENTS." The theater now offered showtimes continuously from 11:00
A.M. to 11:00 P.M. These tactics failed as well and the Shuberts removed Roxy
from the Lyric. Jerry Stagg writes that J. J. Shubert attempted to salvage the
Lyric, but his own strategies came to a similar end. Without Roxy, he lost even
more money, and ultimately subleased the theater to a vaudeville company
that managed to make it a success.[301]

After the debacle in Chicago, the Shuberts moved Roxy to their Boyd
Opera House in Omaha in late June where he installed his "De Luxe Pictures." The repertoire included daylight pictures, a large orchestra, as well as
cabaret and opera singers. A new ventilating system at the theater promised
to lower the summer temperature by forty degrees and enable the theater
to attract much better patronage during the torrid summer months.[302] Less
than a month later, the last Boyd's advertisement with "De Luxe Pictures"
for ten cents for adults and five cents for children appeared on July 14 in the
Omaha World-Herald.[303] Despite the usual assortment of orchestral accompaniment and well-manicured staff, Roxy was dismissed again. "You are fired,"
Shubert reportedly wired Roxy. "Go back to Minneapolis and take the God-
damned palms with you."[304] *Moving Picture World* tended to the wounds of its
fallen angel. "It must be said, in justice to Mr. Rothapfel, that he received very
shabby treatment at the hands of the Shuberts, both at the Lyric here, and at
the Boyd, Omaha," the journal commented in July 1912. "They expected him
to turn large legitimate houses in one week into successful picture theaters."[305]
A victim of his own meticulously crafted reputation, Roxy was unfairly expected to work one-week miracles. He had done so in Milwaukee, but even
the Lyric in Minneapolis, by Roxy's own account, had taken time to cultivate.
Motion pictures were not wholly embraced in Chicago, or anywhere for that
matter. If Roxy had had the time to curry favor with reformers, civic groups,
politicians, clergy, and his usual gaggle of supporters, his efforts at the Lyric
in Chicago and at the Boyd in Omaha might have been different. In fact, if
the theaters had been a quick success for the impatient Shuberts, the company might have plunged further into motion picture exhibition. Instead, the
brothers returned to a largely legitimate theater business model and made
investments in companies like Loew's, but had no large-scale operation of
deluxe motion picture houses.[306]

In mid-July 1912, the growing Saxe circuit in the northern Midwest hired
Roxy to direct the chain. The company had already benefited from his work,
having taken over the Alhambra after his departure the previous year. The
appointment would also enable Saxe to use Roxy to run their newest acquisition: the Lyric in Minneapolis. The Saxe circuit spent a considerable amount

to upgrade the Lyric, constructing a new façade and lobby, redecorating the theater, and installing "special stage settings." To make the Lyric turn a profit, Saxe needed Roxy "to give the presentations of pictures for which his name has become famous."[307] Frank L. Hough, Jr., traveling in July on behalf of the Edison kinetoscope department, "was impressed by the hearty and enthusiastic welcome given to S. L. Rothapfel" when he returned to the Lyric.[308] It is unknown when exactly Roxy arrived, but the *Minneapolis Journal* noted on July 7 that the theater had now "taken on a new lease of life."[309] Advertised as "Saxe's Lyric," and claiming to be "America's Finest Picture Performance," it was noted to once again be under the "Direction of Mr. Rothapfel" by July 14—the last day of "De Luxe Pictures" at the Boyd in Omaha.[310] Roxy began speaking directly to his Minneapolis patrons through local newspapers and advertisements, reestablishing his personal connection.[311] Roxy the showman and public relations force had returned to form.

Of all of the elaborate presentations Roxy presented at the Lyric in the second half of 1912, none seemed to be as lauded as the unitary text for *Queen Elizabeth* (*Les Amours de la Reine Elisabeth*, 1912) with Sarah Bernhardt in the lead role. Despite the heavy cost, Roxy refused to raise ticket prices and pledged to accept the financial loss as a show of his "appreciation of the public's generous patronage." For this special performance, he once again augmented his coterie of singers and musicians. Reasserting his role as exhibitor and sound designer, Roxy sought to maintain a high-class, adult atmosphere without the sounds of children. (No children's tickets were sold for the performance.)[312] It is unclear whether Roxy did this solely to chill the soundscape of the theater, removing the crying of babies or the higher-pitched voices of children, or whether he was also installing a makeshift rating system. At a time when he and other exhibitors were still cultivating a family audience of women and children, the prohibition of children at an increasing number of films was striking. The appraisal of the audience and the city's cultural critics "marked the turning point in my career," Roxy recalled eleven years later, "for this picture and its presentation" (which the *Minneapolis Journal* remarked "created such furore [*sic*]") "secured national recognition for me." The film would also help launch the career of its distributor, Adolph Zukor, who would play a part in Roxy's final years.[313]

By 1913, the Lyric's mix of religious, literary, stage, and other adaptations, its educational, scenic, and news films, along with its augmented orchestra, chorus, and highly trained staff—all of which received strong newspaper coverage and the aid of a well-managed advertising campaign—helped substantially to make motion pictures an acceptable public amusement in

Minneapolis. After a lengthy period of renewed reformist scorn that had followed his earlier departure, residents were once again flocking to the theater
to see films. One study conducted by the *Minneapolis Tribune* reported that
out of 10,000 local families in the survey, 6,653 were going to the movies. In
addition, one-third of these moviegoers attended at least once per week, with
each of the 6,653 families spending roughly $7.50 per year. Sixty percent of
those attending were adults, while 40 percent were children—proving the success of the Family Theatre model in which all age groups were sharing in the
experience.[314] Moviegoing in Minneapolis, in part due to Roxy's influence, had
become an activity that was far less constrained by class, gender, age, ethnicity,
or religion, though racial boundaries continued. The success of high-class, deluxe theaters like the Lyric and the Alhambra were certainly part of the reason.

As head of exhibition for the Saxe circuit, Roxy had primarily remained in
Minneapolis upon his return to the Lyric. Still, he would occasionally travel
to other Saxe houses to punch up their presentations. For the American premiere of Film D'Art's *Romeo e Giulietta* (1912), Roxy returned to the Alhambra in Milwaukee where he oversaw the creation of a new score for the film
and costumed its singers in thematic garb. Roxy then brought the film to Minneapolis's Lyric, where it received similar staging, including an "augmented
orchestra" of musicians playing the same score written for the Milwaukee
premiere. This intercircuit transfer, under Roxy's management, extended beyond films and their scores. Long before Balaban and Katz had copied the
vaudeville circuit's practice of rotating live talent from one of its theaters to
the next, the Saxe company had begun to move their musicians, such as the
Lyric Quartet from Minneapolis and perhaps other personnel, from theater
to theater.[315]

In February 1913, Roxy reported that Saxe's flagship Lyric, with its newly
renovated façade and interior, now decorated in the French Renaissance style,
was playing to "capacity at all times, regardless of weather conditions." James
McQuade observed that official endorsements of the theater by the governor, "clergy of all denominations," the board of education, women's clubs, and
"prominent educators" had been framed and hung in the lobby. "The Lyric
today is just such an institution as I once dreamed of having," Roxy proudly
stated, "and it is patronized substantially. It is not alone an artistic success, but
a financial one as well."[316]

Roxy continued to count on the goodwill and publicity generated by religious-themed films in the months that followed, unveiling his Easter celebration for April 21–23, 1913, which included the presentation of Kalem's
From the Manger to the Cross (1912). Roxy invited the city's clergy to a private

screening to engender their support and promotion of the film on the Lyric's behalf.[317] Rev. Ulysses S. Villars, pastor of the Prospect Park Methodist Episcopal Church, wrote to Roxy after attending the advanced screening of the film:

> As you know, we were enthusiastic over the "Passion Play," but to my mind there is no comparison to be made between the two. I have great confidence in your judgment and "good taste," but I confess I was not prepared for such a reverent, sympathetic and appreciative presentation of the life of Our Savior as is shown in these pictures. I wish I could be as sure of the good effect of the sermons we preach as I am of this remarkable production. As I have opportunity I am urging my friends to attend, for all, clergy or laity, must be impressed and inspired by it. . . . I feel that you have added greatly to the debt the people of this city owe you.[318]

It had now been more than three years since his presentation of *The Passion Play* at the Family Theatre in Forest City, but many of the same methods were employed.[319] "During the De Luxe presentations, immediately upon commencing the performance, the doors will be closed and no one will be allowed to enter until the following performance," Roxy announced before its exhibition. "This is imperative for the success of the presentation."[320] James McQuade reported that Roxy was "highly pleased at the way in which the audiences complied with this [current] request, and many present congratulated him on the great benefits resulting there from, there being nothing to distract the attention of those present from the pictures and the accompanying music."[321] After a prelude arranged by the Lyric's organist, the film was shown to the accompaniment of "Adeste Fideles," "The Palms," and "Calvary." "Manager Rothapfel, who is not infrequently called 'The Belasco of Moving Picture Presentations,' has outdone his own record in the production of the Kalem film," the *Minneapolis Journal* mentioned. "Here is a new passion play for the moving picture public, as reverent as Oberammergau [*sic*] and more beautifully and accurately imagined. This film should not be missed. It marks the top notch of moving picturedom."[322] The presentation was in "such irreproachable good taste," the *Journal* added, "that the Lyric is apparently transformed for the nonce into a great cathedral."[323] Because of its success, and with "requests pour[ing] in from all sides for its re-presentation," the film was shown once more between April 28 and April 30 to "overflowing houses." Roxy relaxed his restrictions on young attendees, but still prohibited any "Children in Arms."[324]

Not long after the success of *From the Manger to the Cross*, Roxy followed up with another literary adaptation, *The Prisoner of Zenda* (1913). To create "atmosphere," Roxy dressed his vocalists, members of the orchestra, and the staff stationed in front of the theater (a mix of aesthetic extension and marketing ballyhoo) in replicated costumes from the film. Governor Eberhart brought his staff for the event, and the Lyric was patronized by "a notable gathering" of prominent members of the social, business, and educational community.[325] Audiences such as these had grown accustomed to and appreciative of Roxy's presentation style, with his framing and enhancing of motion pictures with similarly themed costumes and decorations that draped the theater in the thematic and aesthetic elements of a given film. In addition, his aural and visual interventions *during* the presentation of silent motion pictures, for instance, were becoming increasingly commonplace and normalized by their frequency. Motion picture audiences in Minneapolis, Milwaukee, and wherever Roxy had had an impact slowly became accustomed to his method of turning film exhibition into a much larger enterprise than just the projection of celluloid and musical accompaniment. Entertainment at a deluxe movie house was increasingly becoming a multi-platform synergy of live and recorded entertainment that comprised a much more complex narrative and phenomenological experience.

The rest of the summer of 1913 proved to be a fairly quiet one for Roxy professionally. The Lyric ably filled its seats, garnered additional praise, and cemented its place in the city's cultural landscape. Roxy, as the city's foremost exhibitor, was appointed by the Minnesota Exhibitors' League to be a delegate to the National Convention of the Motion Picture Exhibitors League in early July 1913.[326] The Lyric's stability also enabled Roxy to spend a few days away from the theater with his newest child, Beta Cecelia Rothapfel, born June 26, 1913.[327] The good times at their home at 1915 Aldrich Avenue South in Minneapolis were short lived, though, as always.

Roxy returned from his brief paternity leave to discover that not everyone at Saxe was enamored with his management style. That August, Roxy decided to leave the Lyric for the second and last time.[328] His tenure came to an end with little explanation from Saxe or from Roxy. He had arrived in September 1911 and was leaving exactly two years later, having transformed the Lyric from a mildly successful legitimate venue into arguably the most lauded motion picture house in the United States, second perhaps only to the Alhambra, which he had also resurrected. In transforming the Lyric, Roxy had rebranded motion pictures as middle-class, if not high-class, entertainment. Few in Minneapolis now routinely stayed away from deluxe motion picture theaters, thanks in part to his aggressive public relations skills; his efforts at community outreach; his broad use of religious, stage, and literary adaptations; and his employment of classical music for his organist, orchestra, and chorus. Roxy had been elected an honorary member of the University Club and gained admission to the Civic and Commerce League. According to *Motion Picture News*, he was now "a recognized figure in local affairs."

> By persistent effort, and bulldog tenacity, he fought for recognition until finally his theatre, his pictures, and his whole business was endorsed by every welfare organization in the city, and by several notable state officials who had taken an active part in the censoring of pictures. But more im-portant than his financial success, he had convinced these societies that there was no need for censorship. The right kind of policy, adapted to the needs and wishes of the community, and not to the whims and fancies of himself as an individual, had won out.[329]

Roxy's efforts to generate public support for what he was creating at the Lyric between 1911 and 1913 would foreshadow the work of film exhibitors, producers, and distributors throughout the 1910s to craft a new identity for the cinema, one that would be fully realized during World War I when movie houses were deemed "an essential business" by the United States government. The movie theater, no longer seen by elites as a venue solely for the promo-tion of vice and sin, would become a popular, if still contested, public sphere where audiences engaged the content on the screen and each other. Socialist or capitalist, CEO or laborer, the movie house would seemingly become a venue for all.

The Lyric is almost entirely forgotten today—even in Minneapolis—and typically glossed over in contrast to Roxy's later work. But his efforts there and in Milwaukee demonstrate that the gentrification of the movie house was often less architectural than it was social and cultural. Roxy's Alhambra and Lyric established new venues for multi-reel films and classical music. These film-only theaters (not vaudeville and film houses) formed a burgeoning net-work of deluxe motion picture venues that began changing the way film was exhibited and perceived in cities across the United States. New York's Regent and Strand theaters would later expand and more soundly promote their own innovations, but it was Roxy's pivotal work in the Midwest between 1911 and 1913 that created the model for the next two decades of American and even global deluxe film exhibition.

Roxy was now thirty-one years old and unemployed for the first time in half a decade, but his career had only just begun.

2. BROADWAY MELODY
ROXY AND THE DELUXE THEATER MOVEMENT
(1913–1917)

If every exhibitor in the country could be invisible and could see Mr. Rothapfel as he goes over the first show, there would be an awakening among the showmen of the country that would accomplish marvels.

—*Motion Picture News*, December 29, 1917

The period between 1908 and 1913, the first half of what some film historians have dubbed the "Transitional Era" (1908–1917), was a period of gradual but profound change in the motion picture industry, from film exhibition's transition from nickelodeons like the Family Theatre to deluxe theaters like the Lyric in Minneapolis, to developmental changes in narrative filmmaking and the importation and production of new multi-reel, feature-length films.[1] These films, often based on literary or stage classics, lured in middle- and upper-class audiences who were attracted to the opulent settings and mixed entertainment offerings at deluxe theaters opening across the country. The success of venues such as the Alhambra in Milwaukee and the Lyric in Minneapolis inspired producers like Adolph Zukor to imagine a new kind of theater and a new expanded audience for motion pictures. The larger and more opulent the setting, the more once skeptical women, politicians, clergy, and other social guardians began to embrace these theaters. Roxy had already convinced a varied demographic in Milwaukee and Minneapolis that motion pictures in the 1910s would chart a different cultural and industrial course than before.

REGENT THEATRE, NEW YORK, NY

In the early 1910s, New York City had large theaters (with 1,000 to 3,000 seats) exhibiting film, many built by Marcus Loew's or William Fox's growing chains, but they were typically combination vaudeville-movie houses. These theaters provided a panoply of entertainment at an affordable price, but they were not necessarily created to showcase motion pictures exclusively. Loew, for instance, programmed each of his theaters to correspond to the class and taste of the theater's surrounding neighborhood. Some of his theaters hardly exhibited films at all, while others, based on popularity, barely employed vaudeville. As he famously said, "We sell tickets to theaters, not movies." The photoplay, to paraphase *Hamlet*, was not necessarily "the thing."

During the summer of 1912, when Roxy was moving from the Lyric in Minneapolis to the Lyric in Chicago to Boyd's in Omaha and then back again to the Lyric in Minneapolis, construction had begun on a new deluxe movie theater in the upper Manhattan neighborhood of Harlem that would capital-ize on the growing desire for highbrow films in high-class settings. The Regent Theatre, built at an estimated cost of $600,000, was set to become the first *purpose-built* deluxe motion picture theater in the United States.[2] Whereas the Milwaukee Alhambra and the Minneapolis Lyric were converted into deluxe motion picture theaters in 1911, they had been adapted for that purpose, hav-ing originally been designed for live entertainment. The new Regent Theatre, though, was the first large, upscale theater designed expressly for the exhibi-tion of film and built to capitalize on the success of those Midwestern venues, the growth of motion picture audiences, and the popularity of increasingly complex motion pictures. Construction of the elaborate Regent would take just over half a year—a far cry from the nickelodeon era where store show theaters could be built in a matter of weeks.

As 1913 arrived, many in the motion picture industry sensed that it was the temporal beginning of something new. The previous decade's moments of dis-covery were in the past. New moments and epiphanies were certainly to come, but with the MPPC waning, the number of feature-length films growing, the appearance of new deluxe movie houses, and the ethnic transformation of its leadership, the industry had changed and matured into a more solid and multivalent business. The year 1913, David Robinson writes, was "a revolution in the cinema, the watershed between the tentative years and the modern cin-ema industry as we know it. For the public at large, perception of the movies had subtly shifted from the almost clandestine backstreet nickelodeon era to a new glamour, reflected by James Hill's celebratory piano suite, 'La Cinema.'"[3]

By then, the success of motion pictures and motion picture theaters was already having a dramatic effect on vaudeville and legitimate theater. Prolific stage producer and soon to be motion picture producer Daniel Frohman told *Variety* that, "the movies ha[d] emptied the galleries of the regular theatres of the country."[4] The year also brought a renewed industrial (and press) focus back to exhibition in New York. The industry's "city on the hill" would soon shift from the Alhambra and the Lyric in the Midwest to the Regent Theatre in New York City.

Despite our contemporary understanding of its importance, though, the Regent caused little stir when the 1,900-seat theater opened for "straight motion-picture performances" with "no vaudeville" on February 8, 1913. "The performances will consist of the best pictures and a programme of music," the *New York Dramatic Mirror* wrote at its opening. "Next to the pictures, the music will be a feature." A $15,000 organ was installed for Arthur Depew, former organist of the famous 1904 Wanamaker Organ at Wanamaker's Department Store in Philadelphia, while an eight-piece orchestra directed by Conrad Koschat accompanied "some of the best operatic and concert singers" in the city.[5] The theater "may be classed among the most refined and uplifting in New York City," the *Moving Picture News* wrote after its debut. Reflecting its ambitions, prices were well above the humdrum motion picture houses in neighboring areas, with a vaudeville-esque scale of twenty-five, thirty-five, and fifty cents.[6]

When the Regent opened, no motion picture–only theater in the city could match it. Loew and Fox continued to operate large combination vaudeville-movie houses in the boroughs and neighborhoods throughout the city. But none—including Loew's $400,000 National Theatre in the Bronx, the circuit's first deluxe theater, with room for 2,397 patrons—was strictly a motion picture house like the Alhambra in Milwaukee or the Lyric in Minneapolis, instead offering a mix of vaudeville performances and motion pictures.

The fact that the Regent was purpose-built for motion pictures, not as a combination house, is what has rendered it important in the retrospective gaze of historians. As a venue, the Regent was spacious but certainly not the largest theater of its era. It was, in fact, smaller than the Alhambra in Milwaukee. The theater was situated far away from the entertainment hubs of Herald Square and more than seventy blocks north of Times Square. The Regent was also unremarkable for the size of its orchestra, smaller even than the twelve-piece orchestra at the outdoor Skydome Theatre in Springfield, Missouri.[7] It is largely in retrospect, then, that the Regent's importance can be appreciated, viewed as significant by historians because it was the country's first purpose-built deluxe motion picture theater—not because its operation, size, or accoutrements were in any real way innovative, at least at its start.

The Regent was not an overwhelming financial success and went largely unnoticed in a sprawling city teeming with movie houses, both big and small, and with even larger vaudeville and legitimate theaters. Harlem was home to vaudeville and burlesque theaters and to much smaller movie houses. The Regent's opening, though, was a direct challenge to B. F. Keith's Alhambra Theatre. The struggling vaudeville house did not need additional challenges. The Alhambra, located between 125th and 126th Streets and Seventh Avenue, ten blocks due north from the Regent, had been run as a "big time" vaudeville theater with decreasing success by mid-1913. That August, *Variety* announced that the admission scale of the Alhambra had been reduced to one akin to "pop vaudeville." Performances would now run at ten, fifteen, and twenty-five cents for matinees—even lower than the Regent's ticket prices—and fifteen to seventy-five cents at night.[8] The change in pricing did little to effect any real financial change. During the normally popular Labor Day holiday, the theater "should have turned 'em away," *Variety* reported. "But it didn't. There were many vacant seats downstairs."[9]

By early October 1913, the theater had turned pathetic, imploring its audience to help build atmosphere through their own participatory engagement. "Don't be afraid to laugh or applaud if you find a point that pleases you," a Keith program mentioned at the time. *Variety* was stunned by the shameless pleading. "Can you beat it?" the trade journal chided. "Unable to give a whole show, the Keith program makers are calling on 'their' audiences to help."[10] By early November, *Variety* reported that the Alhambra was receiving only "slight attention from the Harlemites."[11] It was amid this lackluster competition that Roxy arrived in New York, able to take full advantage of the Regent's faltering neighbor.

It was not a direct route to New York, however. With Roxy's reign at the Lyric in Minneapolis ending in mid-August 1913, Rosa, Arthur, and Beta left the city and arrived once more in Forest City.[12] Roxy, according to one published report, was staying behind in Minneapolis to build a new 3,200-seat motion picture theater at 8th Street and Hennepin Avenue next to the Lyric. The theater would have been the largest movie theater in the country at the time and a challenge to the Lyric, the Alhambra in Milwaukee, and the new Regent in Manhattan. The $300,000 theater was scheduled to open in the spring of 1914 with a large lobby and foyer, quarters for the eighteen-piece orchestra (more than double the size of the Regent's orchestra), and a children's playroom that would have furthered Roxy's efforts to bring the whole family to motion picture houses (yet making them quiet enough for adult audiences to enjoy). Roxy also planned a local newsreel service that would provide almost immediate access to the city's news by using "a special automobile with a camera, and an operator who will rush to the scene of every accident."[13] For reasons unknown, the theater was never built. It would be another month before news of Roxy's whereabouts and of his next project would surface. There was no record of his arriving in Forest City to join his family in the town's newspaper or of his involvement in the new theater that Julius Freedman was planning with the architecture firm of Davey & Crothers in October 1913 to replace the worn-out Family Theatre.[14]

Terry Ramsaye notes that Roxy had instead come to New York at the request of Marcus Loew to manage one or more of his theaters.[15] Loew, in addition to his many other vaudeville and movie houses, had recently opened the Loew's Avenue B that January (built on the site of his childhood tenement in Manhattan's Lower East Side), the 3,200-seat Loew's Orpheum for movies and vaudeville at 86th Street and Third Avenue in Manhattan, and the 1,910-seat Loew's Spooner in Brooklyn. He had also taken a new lease on the Broadway Theatre at 41st Street and Broadway in Manhattan, and announced the construction of two more 2,000-plus seat venues in the city.[16] There were certainly plenty of Loew's theaters that needed experienced showmen, a commodity not as easy to find in 1913 as it would be a decade later. When Roxy arrived at the appointment, Ramsaye recalled thirteen years later, Loew, who would be fondly remembered as one of the gentler personalities in the exhibition sector, was "giving somebody pieces of his mind," and Roxy sat anxiously listening to "large jagged chunks of the conversation." In the middle of Loew's tantrum, Roxy "reached for his hat, and left."[17] "I didn't have the heart to wait," Roxy remembered over a decade later. "I decided that if Mr. Loew had a job for me it would be better to let him keep it for a while."[18] As Roxy recalled, he walked out of Loew's Theatrical Enterprises' offices and in a tidy—perhaps too tidy—coincidence, immediately ran into two men "who had just procured the Regent Theater" from Biograph founder Henry Marvin, and they asked Roxy "to come up and take it."[19] *Variety* reported on October 17 that the Photoplay Theatres Company, whose managing director was Samuel Rothapfel, had secured a five-year lease of the Regent Theatre in New York City.[20]

The move to New York from Minneapolis was another homecoming for Roxy, bringing him a subway ride away from his father, brother, and sister for the first time in over a decade. Most importantly, Roxy was in the growing media center of the nation. Having used public relations successfully in the

Midwest, Roxy may have been excited by the idea of broadcasting his message of film (and music) populism through the thousands of print journalists in Manhattan.

Heaven Up in Harlem

Harlem was seemingly a perfect fit for Roxy in 1913, with its large population of both German (like Roxy) and East European Jews.[21] Journalist Therese Rose Nagel would remark a decade later that at the Regent Roxy "first made his attempt to try to give the common herd soft music, soft lights and better motion pictures. This he attempted where he knew he would appeal to Jewish audiences, for he knew that the Jews were a music loving race."[22] As with most lower- to middle-class Jewish communities of the era, motion pictures had by now become a popular attraction, but they still remained an affront to the Orthodox Jewish immigrants of the area.[23] Still, much of the Jewish population was just the right kind of patron for Roxy. These residents were upwardly mobile, desirous of art, culture, and music, unable to attend Carnegie Hall on a regular basis, and able to be convinced that motion picture presentations could be an extension and amalgamation of literature, theater, dance, photography, and music. A perfect Roxy patron in 1913 was an individual who could afford a seat in his theater and could scarcely afford to miss it. Roxy may have appealed to the elites of American society to approve of his cultural "mish mosh," but his bread and butter would always be the army of janitors, factory workers, tailors, shopkeepers, and others who toiled with their hands. It was they who would most appreciate his films and music and the work of his ushers, bathroom attendants, and other service touches throughout the theater.

In 1910, *Moving Picture World* had asked:

> Must New York always lag behind in the progress of the moving picture industry? . . . New York City with its five hundred or so moving picture houses does not boast one worthy of the name of "picture palace." . . . All the great cities of the Union have their picture palaces represented from time to time in our pages. When we illustrate these fine picture theaters we do so with something like a feeling of shame that the Empire City of the East, should have to stand behind her sister cities in other parts of the country and be content with such band-box looking places. . . . Who will take the lead in altering this stupid state of things, so that New York may come into its own?[24]

A year later, *Moving Picture World* had again wrote, "There are so few moving picture houses here [in Manhattan] which attract the most desirable classes."[25] The Regent had been built to satisfy this want. But while it had the size of Minneapolis's Lyric, it had not drawn the same volume or class of audience. After signing the lease, Roxy quickly went to work to redress the house, Lyricizing it with many of the same touches. Journalists would soon highlight its new marble facing, its glass canopy over the sidewalk, and the hundreds of electric lights that now illuminated the theater.[26] W. Stephen Bush lavished praise on Roxy's removal of the dreaded "posteritis" as well with "No three sheets exuding blood, and no six sheets picturing murder."[27] *Motion Picture News* parroted this assessment. "The success of Mr. Rothapfel," the journal argued, "knocks to pieces the argument of certain exhibitors who claim that a show must be advertised with an overdose of ugly and sensational posters."[28]

Admission prices were lowered to fifteen cents for the orchestra, with boxes and loge seats costing twenty-five cents, in order to attract a full house. Matinee prices were even lower at ten cents throughout the theater, except for the boxes.[29] By lowering his prices, Roxy had enabled the Regent to undercut the Alhambra's financial advantage and attract more patrons. Roxy believed empirically that motion picture exhibition was a volume business, and he had always preferred to have more patrons paying less than fewer patrons paying more. Regent patrons now received much for their nickels and dimes, with each Roxy program offering five reels of "first run and one day old" licensed pictures (as Roxy remained a Trust advocate). To encourage repeat patronage, the program was changed each Monday, Thursday, and Saturday, at least initially. Inside the theater, the Regent was outfitted in Roxy's design aesthetic, with the same kind of indirect lighting system that he had installed throughout the Lyric's public spaces.[30] The Regent, though not a new theater, was reborn in price, aesthetics, and policy under Roxy's management.

The gala premiere of the newly revamped Regent was an uncontested hit. "T'was a magic wand that S. L. Rothapfel waved o'er the Regent," *Motography* wrote.

> From the courtesy of the ushers to the selection of the musical numbers, from the choice and placing of flowers to the ways and means of ventilation, the hand and mind of Mr. Rothapfel are seen. It was no idle fancy that conceived and bestowed upon him the title "Belasco of motion pictures." In the art of planning and making for a theater beautiful, he has no peer; he is the master in his chosen line. . . . If you are of New York and haven't as yet dropped into the Regent, take the first opportunity and

the subway's Lenox local and do so. And by all means, wait around a few minutes and get a glimpse of the man who has made the theater more than worthy of the title "de luxe." He may be directing the orchestra.[31]

In addition to the programming, service, and interior design of the theater, Roxy remained equally concerned with technical matters. Instead of placing the projector(s) in abandoned balconies or on the side of the theater, as it had been when the Regent opened, thereby distorting the picture, he helped make the Regent's presentation the best in the city by moving the projectors down to the orchestra level. More than seventy blocks away from Times Square, the Regent's technical prowess easily outshone the newly reopened Vitagraph (formerly Criterion) and Hippodrome theaters, among its other metropolitan rivals.[32]

What seemed to set the Regent apart from other venues, perhaps even more than its service and decorative upgrades, were its music and overall presentation—the highlights of any Roxy show. "With the idea that music could be made to fill a most important place in his scheme of entertainment," Gordon Whyte of *The Metronome* recalled fifteen years later, "Roxy cast around for a conductor for his orchestra. He needed a man who knew the classic repertoire and had no sniffish ideas about popular music. It was Roxy's idea that all music should be used, so long as it fitted into his scheme of things. Necessarily, he needed a conductor of wide tastes and few fixed ideas."[33] The answer was band leader Carl Edouarde. Edouarde, originally a violinist, was trained at the famed Royal Conservatory of Music in Leipzig, Germany. By 1908, Edouarde had become the director of Knapp's New York State First Regiment Band and was already considered "one of the foremost musicians and band directors in this country."[34] As a "band" and not an "orchestra" that performed in armories and other locations like the Belasco Theatre in New York, a disdain for middlebrow entertainment (and audiences) was not apparent.[35] Rosa Rothapfel had attended one of Edouarde's concerts, and when Roxy took hold of the Regent and began looking for a conductor, she mentioned his name. Roxy sent for Edouarde and convinced him to join the Regent and lead its fifteen-piece orchestra.[36]

When it reopened, the Regent featured a new "visible" and "white-mittened orchestra" that nearly doubled in size from the original eight to fifteen, with Carl Edouarde conducting his musicians and "incidental songsters" playing along to the motion pictures presented.[37] Of the assembled orchestra, Roxy, not Edouarde, boasted that he had picked "every man Jack of them," asserting his sense of taste and musical judgment.[38] Roxy emphasized the place of music at the Regent by moving the orchestra to the center of the stage. Directly in front of the orchestra was a small fountain, which, like other Roxy venues, displayed a variety of colored lights "that blend into one another."[39] Vocalists were also housed in carefully chosen surroundings, spotlighted in "leafy bowers" on each side of the proscenium.[40]

Rehearsals at the Regent were, as always in Roxy's theaters, lengthy and continuous. Edouarde and Roxy worked tirelessly to add music to each new short, newsreel, and feature. "For the first time in this country I was made aware of the possibilities of the music," W. Stephen Bush wrote. "The movements of the orchestra all through the evening were of extraordinary ease and smoothness, no doubt due to careful and painstaking rehearsals. What can be done with the right music was most plainly demonstrated in a two-reel Vitagraph [*The War Makers*], most fittingly chosen for such a glorious motion picture celebration."[41] The *New York Dramatic Mirror*'s review was similarly glowing about the Regent's musical accompaniment:

> It is the old saying that "Fine feathers, make fine birds." Take the picture by itself and it comes to us a little bare, a delight to the eye alone. Surround it by pretty finishings, beautiful decorations, and fine music, and the picture is raised to the same high plain as its surrounding, and not only the eye, but also the ear is pleased; two senses instead of one are entertained at one and the same time. These are the means by which he has popularized the moving picture drama among the better educated people of the neighborhood.[42]

Bush added to the saccharine praise the Regent engendered:

> Such theaters as the Regent are what we all hope for. They are the best friends the motion picture industry has. It is well to set them on a hill that they may be see[n] and imitated. They are bulwarks in the fight against the corruption of public taste. . . . We will all go back to the Regent, and we are glad to know where to conduct the next stranger who asks us to take him to the best motion picture house in the city.[43]

It took Roxy less than one week to convince the trade press that his revamped theater was New York's gold standard. "Without a doubt the Regent Theater is the best picture house in New York City," *Moving Picture World* added the following month. "New York City has been waiting for just such an establishment and Mr. Rothapfel is the man to give it to us."[44]

The innovations at the Regent (which were extensions of his earlier work at the Lyric) quickly became more than just a local story, especially after extensive coverage in film trade journals. With his additional proximity to New York's leading newspapers and journalists writing for nationally distributed and syndicated newspapers and magazines, Roxy's newest accolades spread quickly. The theater's name began being appropriated by new venues across the country and, soon, around the world. For the remainder of Roxy's career, the names of theaters he managed were given to innumerable venues in the United States and elsewhere. Roxy's national influence was also aided by admonitions from Bush and other journalists to small- and big-city exhibitors to pay attention to and duplicate his practices.[45] Less than a year later, for instance, *Green Book Magazine* stated, "He came to the Regent and there made innovations which have become, some of them at least, so much a general practice in the different motion picture theatres that it has already been forgotten that any one man thought of them."[46] With the Regent an instant success, and numerous signs that this would not be a repeat of Roxy's disastrous Shubert adventures in Chicago and Omaha, Rosa arrived in Manhattan along with Arthur and Beta in late November 1913.[47] The Rothapfels had arrived in New York.

Roxy continued to spend much of his time focusing on the Regent's musical accompaniment in the weeks that followed. *Motion Picture News* remarked that the time Edouarde and Roxy spent assembling the scores for each picture was already earning dividends. A *News* journalist mentioned after seeing their presentation of *Last Days of Pompeii* (1913) that the Regent's union of music and motion pictures seemed like "a prerequisite to the picture, that to an educated audience the two should, and must hereafter, go together."[48] In addition to music, Roxy also employed carefully chosen sound effects to be used throughout the picture. *Moving Picture World* claimed that these were "so realistic that it was almost continually applauded."[49] He also turned to an old Forest City trick, diffusing the smell of burning sulfur into the auditorium during the eruption of Mount Vesuvius.[50] The whole presentation brought "tremendous business," *Moving Picture World* reported, as audiences "really went into ecstacies [*sic*] of delight over the show."[51] *Motion Picture News* called the presentation of the George Kleine–distributed film, "A remarkable incident in the history of the motion picture," and added that, "it served very clearly, to the writer, to portend for the first time the theatrical future of the picture. In short, it was little less than a revelation."[52] As word of these presentations spread, the *World* reported that "The class of people patronizing the Regent" began to be "of the more intellectual order: appreciative to a considerable degree."[53] *Motion Picture News* added, in a foreshadowing comment, "The audience, it should be noted, was of the kind found in the best playhouses. Judged by their decorum and sincere appreciation, they might have been at the opera."[54]

One of those who attended the Regent was David Belasco, the prolific stage writer, director, producer, and theater owner and operator who had been the inspiration for Roxy's other nickname, "the Belasco of motion pictures." Roxy, then, could only have blushed when Belasco viewed his presentation of *Last Days of Pompeii* and remarked that it was "one of the best things I have ever seen."[55] Belasco returned again to see Roxy present *A Good Little Devil* (1914) (in which Belasco appears) and subsequently created a public relations event that signified Roxy's entrance into middlebrow respectability and Belasco's own abrupt shift toward motion pictures. The two, along with a gathering of celebrities and reporters, met at Belasco's office on 44th Street in a well-orchestrated photo opportunity.[56]

By the end of the year, the Regent was an industry phenomenon and the most popular motion picture–only theater in the city. William Fox would recall in 1927 that he ordered his staff to go to the Regent in 1913 in an effort to duplicate Roxy's efforts. He and his employees visited the Regent for five successive days to study his methods but were never "able to imitate him."[57] "Those who are dubious as to the success of a big exclusive house in New York City should pay a visit to the Regent Theater," *Moving Picture World* remarked in January 1914 "where their dubiousness will undergo a complete change."[58]

Quo Vadis?

Roxy produced a number of widely publicized cultural extravaganzas during this period, but few could trump the applause he received for his presentation of Cines's *Quo Vadis?* (1913). Roxy had seen the film half a year earlier at the McVickers Theatre in Chicago, but he had yet to exhibit it at either the Lyric or Regent.[59] Roxy would often book the first run of many feature films, but his presentation of *Quo Vadis?* demonstrated that he was unafraid to exhibit films that had been seen elsewhere before, even half a year earlier. "[I]f the current releases do not suit me, I prefer to repeat with some previous success," he remarked in early 1914. "The first-run pictures are the bane of a picture man's existence," Roxy continued in a surprising admission, noting that these films offered little time for his lengthy preparations.[60]

Rehearsals for the presentation were, as always, grueling as Roxy attempted to outdo the McVickers performance he had witnessed. At a rehearsal attended by *Moving Picture World*'s W. Stephen Bush before the film opened, Roxy was horrified that the film was being projected "out of frame." "The effect on Rothapfel was electric," Bush reported, in a scene that would be replayed a thousand times over the length of Roxy's career. "He leaped into the air and came down accompanied by a shower of polite profanity." After stopping himself, "his portly form" stood inside the auditorium "quivering with repressed rage." Bush had thought to say something to Roxy, "But a careful survey of Rothapfel as he stood before me, still trembling and darting wrath from his eyes, made me change my mind."[61]

Roxy moved on to the rest of the presentation, with two assistants taking down copious notes at every moment using a small spotlight for illumination. His assistants recorded the precise length of each piece of music and its synchronicity with the picture. "They see to it that the cues are properly distributed and properly followed," Bush added. Roxy's frenetic energy was spent over the hours rehearsing, as he "constantly distribut[ed] himself all over the theater," jumping on stage to tell Edouarde that there was "too much brass in this last piece," and then having a lengthy conversation with the stagehands. Still, he was not without some semblance of benevolence once rehearsals were over, readily admitting that his lack of musical knowledge and skill at properly synchronizing the music to the picture, and at relaying that information to the orchestra, made him dependent upon Carl Edouarde, "who bosses the music," Bush noted, and about whose work Roxy could not "say enough in praise."[62]

When the rehearsals were finally completed to his satisfaction, Roxy was ready to reveal his presentation of *Quo Vadis?* After an "awe-inspiring prelude" featuring music from numerous composers, the film's presentation began in complete darkness. A single spotlight then shown on two seats in one of the upper boxes where a boy and an elderly man, William Calhoun, were playing the part of "learner and listener." The boy asked the man about the meaning of *Quo Vadis?*[63] Calhoun spoke briefly about how Henry Sienkiewicz, the author of the original novel, obtained his idea for the story and then relayed a brief outline of the film. This setup was not only a theatrical device but a psychological one as well. "Here a great problem is solved," Bush wrote. "The audience is educated without having its ignorance obtruded upon itself. . . . This neat device of Rothapfel secures him at once the good will of his audience, and puts them in pleasant humor." As soon as Calhoun finished his lecture, the curtain lifted, the singers on each side of the stage began to sing, and the orchestra, garlanded in flowers, was revealed.[64] The overture was performed and followed by what Roxy dubbed "the 'Aida' tubas." Finally, the film began.[65]

Roxy's multi-sensory presentation was used to its fullest extent with the score accompanied by carefully placed "shouts and shrieks" and "the sounds of the frenzied assemblage," according to a *Moving Picture World* account. Roxy appealed not only to the eyes and ears but to the nostrils as well with "the burning of incense which pervaded the atmosphere of the auditorium at all times."[66] Roxy claimed to have "intensified the atmosphere a hundred-fold" with his use of smell.[67] All of these effects, the *World* commented, "made one feel as though he were back in the years in which the action of the play is laid—66 to 68 A.D." The film was presented in three sections, with Calhoun lecturing before each one. *Quo Vadis?* was exhibited four times per day between Monday, January 26, and Saturday, January 31, at the Regent, with two performances accompanied by pipe organ and the others given a full orchestral treatment.[68]

Reviews of the *Quo Vadis?* shows were glowing. "The artistic manner in which S. L. Rothapfel presented the Cines version of 'Quo Vadis?' marks an advance in picture exhibition," *Moving Picture World* commented.[69] The presentation was deemed so remarkable by the journal that it devoted extensive articles to the film's rehearsal and its presentation in the first two February editions. Though the film had already been exhibited at the Astor Theatre in New York during the spring and summer of 1913, and elsewhere around the country during the year, often with "special music arranged and composed for the performance," according to *Moving Picture World*, it was Roxy's presentation of the film that received by far the most ink.[70]

This development raises an important industrial and historiographical issue: it was not necessarily because of the quality of Roxy's scores, however highly regarded, that they were used or at least somewhat imitated in other theaters. Rather, it may well be because of their wide acclaim in trade and popular journals that they were extensively used during this period (and recalled by music and film historians). With journalists consistently advocating the Roxy method to musicians, conductors, and organists around the country, Roxy's brand name and management and presentation style became increasingly well known and imitated. This inevitably led to some following his musical cues and suggestions in their own scoring of motion pictures. Roxy was "an informal demonstrator," Rick Altman notes, "of the industry's hopes and aspirations for film accompaniment."[71] In an era when "There seem[ed] to be no end of interest taken in just how the pictures are developed, and particularly how the music for them is selected, arranged, fitted, timed and played,"

L. L. Mayhew would later report in *The Metronome* that Roxy's methods had a wide influence, thanks to an unending amount of trade press coverage and industry adulation.[72]

STRAND THEATRE, NEW YORK, NY

Roxy, regardless of the success of *Quo Vadis?* and the crowds filling the Regent, was on the move just weeks after taking over the Harlem theater. In early December, after viewing his elaborate presentation, a *Motion Picture News* writer told Roxy that "such a production should be on Broadway at much higher prices." He responded quickly: "It will."[73] Less than two months after he took over the Regent, the nomadic exhibitor received an offer from the Mitchel Mark Realty Company to manage a new motion picture theater opening not in faraway Harlem but near Times Square at 47th Street and Broadway.

Over a year earlier, in October 1912, Max Spiegel had taken his idea for a new theater to Mitchel H. Mark, who along with his partners and Spiegel incorporated a new company and leased the highly desirable 47th Street property that December. Thomas W. Lamb, the de facto house architect for Marcus Loew who had also designed the Regent (with George M. Keister), was hired to design the new Strand Theatre and the building that would house offices and a roof garden along with the new 3,500-seat theater. The plans were accepted in May 1913, and Cramp & Company broke ground on its construction on July 11.[74]

The Strand was originally imagined to be a new home for "big musical productions at popular prices," but the success of motion pictures, and specifically that of Roxy and the Regent, changed the Mark Company's mind.[75] Still, many suggested that while motion pictures would open the Strand, it would only be a seasonal fad and the theater "would take on a legitimate attraction by next season, probably musical comedy."[76] The Mark Company also needed some reassurance that its management and presentations would approach the level of the Regent, if not surpass it. In short, they needed Roxy. After all, much of New York's society crowd shared the same opinion as Hugo Münsterberg, who mentioned in 1914 he "had never seen a real photoplay" and "felt it as undignified for a Harvard Professor to attend a moving-picture show."[77]

To lure Roxy away from the Regent, where he had intended to spend the next five years, he was given "the highest salary ever paid to the manager of a theater of any kind," according to the *New York Dramatic Mirror*.[78] With a magnificent new structure housed within the burgeoning heart of New York's entertainment scene near Times Square, *Motion Picture News* stated that the opening of the Strand as a movie house would place the theater in the best position "in the entire world in which to test the real value of motion pictures."[79] The new endeavor would become the largest motion picture theater in the United States, surpassing even the Alhambra in Milwaukee and the American Theatre in Salt Lake City, both of which contained *only* 3,000 seats.[80]

Expectations for the Regent were meager compared with those for the new Strand. Rather than taking over an underperforming deluxe house in an uptown neighborhood, the opening of the Strand was being keenly observed by legions in motion pictures, vaudeville, and the legitimate stage. Its failure could mean the end of motion pictures at the Strand and a warning to other investors and exhibitors to keep out of the Times Square area. Success, however, would ignite an industry that was already succeeding in attracting middle- and upper-class crowds in New York and elsewhere and making increasingly bold proclamations.

Six months after he left the Lyric in Minneapolis, the vaudeville, legitimate theater, and film industries were all focused upon Roxy. He needed to surpass his recent success at the Regent and perhaps even his own expectations. The Strand would become a canary in the cinematic coal mine. If it succeeded, Times Square would become a new haven for motion pictures. If it failed, Roxy's reputation and the estimation of motion pictures's commercial value would suffer.

Roxy Sails to Europe

Roxy was looking for talent and inspiration for the Strand and he imagined that European cinemas would provide the best opportunities for new employees and new ideas. The United States was still seen by many in 1914 as provincial and uncultured—the runaway child of mannered European parents. Surely it was in Europe, Roxy reasoned, that great music and musicians could be found, even in movie houses. He sailed on February 3, 1914, to "observe methods of presentation" there and "to acquire ideas for the Broadway house."[81] Over the next three weeks, he visited movie theaters in London, Paris, Berlin, Rome, and other major European cities while meeting with many distributors, exhibitors, and journalists.[82]

Roxy sailed home from Cherbourg, France, on February 25 aboard the SS *Kaiser Wilhelm II*. He arrived in New York on March 4, a month after he departed, thoroughly dissatisfied with his trip.[83] "We have nothing to learn," Roxy said dismissively upon his return. "As far as projection goes, we are away [*sic*] ahead of Europe. Their handling of the light problem is atrocious, even in some of their so-called best theaters."[84] He added, "One year ago we were several years behind Europe in the way of picture theatres. To-day we are several years ahead." Roxy, still pushing his daylight pictures system in his own theaters and to others, complained, "All the European houses are pitch dark while the pictures are being shown." Few if any had heard of daylight pictures nor did they understand why any exhibitor would want to employ it. "Another curious fact," *Motion Picture News* wrote, "was that many of the largest theatres on the Continent were operated with but one projection machine," thus preventing the continuous flow of narrative due to reel changes.[85]

"The European house may, on the whole, be better, but we have houses on this side that far surpass their best in the matter of music," he told *Moving Picture World*. He reported seeing only two pipe organs in use during the entire trip and he assailed the use of sound effects that were "generally carelessly and poorly used." While French and English cinemas were lightly praised, though not exalted, he pointedly critiqued the cinemas of his motherland—Germany. There, he told *Moving Picture World*, "The business is being ruined through excessive censorship. It has come to pass in Germany where only comedies are allowed; the police scissor the life out of every drama."[86] In addition to their generic preferences, few films that were not made in Germany were even permitted to be shown. "In spite of our present local censorship troubles [in America]," he added, "we have a paradise in this country." The theaters themselves were observed with equal scorn. Of the famous Kammerlichtspiel in Berlin, Roxy was equally dismissive. The interior decorations of the theater, he concluded, were "loud and gloriously vulgar."[87] "I cannot explain why the people in Europe who earn far less money than we do are willing and able to spend so much money for amusements," he remarked to *Moving Picture World*. "Everywhere the European prices are much higher than ours and some of these expensive shows are hideously bad. I refer in particular to an evening I spent at the Plasticon in Paris, where I paid five francs to see a show that was hardly worth a nickel."[88]

BACK TO THE STRAND

By the time Roxy returned to New York, much of the Strand's construction and interior layout was already completed. Thomas Lamb's auditorium design was part of a revolution in theater architecture, much of which had been a result of film exhibition economics. While the Strand was constructed with a large lobby and foyer, a legitimate-theater attribute that was now being appropriated for deluxe movie houses, Lamb's design eschewed one of the more typical aspects to be found in legit theaters: a second balcony. "The economy of cinematograph productions makes it possible to provide seats on the orchestra floor and in the balcony at a price so low that the physical effort of climbing to a second balcony would not compensate for the reduced cost of the seat," *American Architect* explained. "Thus, in a few short years, has a single mechanical invention occasioned a great change in a type of building which was the development of two thousand years."[89] Still, despite this social egalitarianism, the Strand's ticket prices were not uniform. While the orchestra and balcony offered tickets ranging from ten to twenty-five cents, box and loge seats—whose social and physical exclusion from the main body of the audience was part of their draw—cost fifty cents at the theater's opening.[90] (After the theater opened, Roxy created another exclusive section by charging fifty cents for the first fifteen rows of the theater, closer to the musicians and the stage. To keep the mythology of a democratic temple alive, he did not advertise the increased price in this section.)[91] There may have been a democratic appeal (and rhetoric) to the movie house as a place for all, but the divisions of class still remained. The realities of the day trump our gauzy memories.

Lamb's inclusion of a second-floor promenade (on the balcony level) that enabled patrons to mingle during intermissions and engage in other social activities normally associated with the area's legit theaters was perhaps even more important in luring middle- and upper-middle-class audiences to the Strand. "Looking up, one is greeted with a surprise, for a mezzanine promenade, on the style of the theaters of the Continent, extends along the width of the theater," the *New York Dramatic Mirror* observed. "This provides a rest-place during the Intermissions, and also an opportunity to meet your friends."[92] The *New York Times* added that "the mezzanine promenade" was an "innovation" that "adds a social feature to the theatre that enables the patrons to meet and converse during the intermissions,"[93] while W. Stephen Bush commented that, "promenading around the loop in the intermissions will be one of the popular things at the Strand."[94]

In keeping with the new cantilever-inspired theaters of the period, there were no posts, pillars, beams, or other obstructions anywhere in the auditorium. Nothing was added in the Strand that would detract from patrons' sightlines or comfort. Ample space (for 1914) was also provided between rows, and the American Seating Company chairs were reported to be "the most luxurious to be found in any theatre on Broadway."[95] Roxy also installed lighting effects that would simulate sunlight, moonlight, or starlight to complement the mood of the film and/or live presentation. Most importantly, Roxy again employed two Simplex projectors instead of one to make reel changeovers seamless.[96] The narrative would not be broken by technical limitations.

Edouarde's orchestra was placed in full view of the audience, with the now-routine adornment of ferns and flowers surrounding them. A fountain was also placed on the stage in between the orchestra and the audience. "The motto of the theatre," *Motion Picture News* mentioned, "is to have 'photo-play features' blended with the very finest music."[97] To fulfill this promise, three organs were installed at the back of the stage and "experts on acoustics" were hired to arrange and place the organs "in such a way as to get every bit of real music to the ear of the audience."[98] As the Strand's inaugural program proclaimed, "The presentation of photoplays will have all the advantages and aid that money and science can provide."[99]

When it opened, eighty-four full-time employees operated the theater.[100] Roxy's ushers, the Strand's inaugural program boasted, were once again "trained to receive audiences with almost military respect and discipline."[101] The *Blue Book* noted that Roxy's Marine training was being put to use. "Military discipline rules," the journal stated, and to maintain this sense of perfection, there is "a drill after each performance." In addition, "Ushers are instructed in the science of handling crowds. Subordinates have a military salute for their superiors. A gesture means one order, a snap of the fingers another."[102] Ushers also performed a "courtesy drill" every Sunday morning and a fire drill at the end of every night.[103] Roxy ran the theater like the USS *Bancroft* and, just as he did at the Family, made sure to get to know as many of his patrons as possible. "We make it a point, even here in New York, to learn the names of steady and distinguished patrons of whom we have many," he told W. Stephen Bush. "These patrons are always addressed by name and carefully catered to. Hence that feeling of loyalty among patrons here. Whenever an usher in any way learns the name of a patron he is supposed to report it at the office and in his treatment thereafter we are able to sound the pleasing personal note."[104]

Not least of the Strand's new hires was its publicity manager, Arthur Warde, whom Roxy lured away from George Kleine's company.[105] Ever conscious of the need to out-market his competitors, for the remainder of his career Roxy would see this as a key position in any theater he managed. As the Strand's publicist, Warde would inevitably become Roxy's press agent as well, a role all of his publicity managers took on as part of their duties. Warde helped oversee the swarm of journalists who visited the theater before, during, and after its April 11 premiere. With Warde and Roxy ginning up coverage in the trade and popular press, W. Stephen Bush was one of many who sensed the Strand's importance to the industry. "It does indeed mean something to the art and industry at large," Bush wrote shortly before its debut, "that a group of men of affairs have erected such a costly monument of their faith in the future of motion pictures."[106]

The Strand's gala opening drew a capacity, multi-class crowd and even members of high society. What seemed to astonish journalists the most about the theater, more than its elegant design and size, was the composition of its opening-night audience. Dressed in evening wear for the debut, they looked remarkably different from the moviegoing audiences at the nickelodeons of the Lower East Side or even the movie houses of Harlem or the Bronx. Victor Watson remarked in the *New York American* that,

> Going to the new Strand Theatre last night was very much like going to a Presidential reception, a first night at the opera or the opening of the horse show. It seemed like everyone in town had simultaneously arrived at the conclusion that a visit to the magnificent new movie playhouse was necessary. . . . I must confess that when I saw the wonderful audience last night in all its costly togs, the one thought that came to my mind was that if anyone had told me two years ago that the time would come when the finest-looking people in town would be going to the biggest and newest theatre on Broadway for the purpose of seeing motion pictures I would have sent them down to visit my friend, Dr. Minas Gregory at Bellevue Hospital. The doctor runs the city's bughouse.[107]

Bush described a similar scene of the Strand's frenzied debut and its fashionable attendees:

> A little after seven o'clock the management had to put huge signs on the sidewalk before the theater announcing that every seat in the vast theater had been sold and that even "standing room only" was but a hope. A long procession of handsome autos passed slowly but steadily in front of the attractive entrance and each car discharged its passengers, most of them in evening dress. The whole aspect of things was far more suggestive of a night at the opera than a motion picture entertainment. By eight o'clock the big theater was filled to its utmost capacity. Groups of

prosperous-looking theatergoers gathered about the entrance and the lobbies, voicing well-bred disappointment at being unable to share in the glories of the first night. . . . The quality of audiences at motion picture entertainments has been improving, as everybody knows, for the last three or four years, but the demonstration of the fact was never made more complete, than Saturday night.[108]

The cost of Roxy's expensive new theater and its live presentations seemed to prove the concept.

In addition to the fashionable elite of New York City, Roxy had begun winning over the same types of political figures as he had at the Lyric in Minneapolis, including Fire Commissioner Adamson, who was a first-night attendee. Roxy's audience was also filled with motion picture and legitimate theater impresarios. Bush described the night's audience as a veritable "Who's Who in [Film and Theater] Society" including William Selig, the producer of the theater's first feature film, *The Spoilers* (1914), Daniel Frohman, Adolph Zukor, George M. Cohan, Samuel H. Harris, and William Farnum, the star of *The Spoilers*, who was seated in a box seat near the screen.[109] Commensurate with their turn to motion pictures, the appearance by Frohman and others was as much a symbol of the Strand's success as it was a statement about the cultural, social, and industrial status of motion pictures by April 1914. The *New York Times* remarked that the gala opening and early reception of the theater was indeed a shock to the consecrated system of New York amusements. For the newspaper, the appearance of the Strand amid the myriad venues for live theater was akin to "walking along the streets of a placid Canadian town to find old churches converted to motion picture uses and placarded in front with all manner of lurid posters. In terms of shock to Broadway, it is an even more striking and impressive thing to see this newest of theatres, luxurious, spacious, and costly, throw open its doors with a flourish of trumpets as a home of the movies. For the Strand is interesting and important as a straw showing which way the wind blows—and how hard it is blowing."[110]

While the structure and the composition of the crowd were widely praised by the press, the opening program was equally lauded. As the audience sat in semi-darkness, their "whispered impatience" was broken by the sounds of heavy artillery that immediately silenced the crowd and gave way to the Strand orchestra's stirring rendition of the national anthem accompanying Edison's *The Birth of the Star Spangled Banner* (1914), foregrounding Roxy's and the industry's patriotism to its new society crowd.[111] The second half of the program consisted entirely of Roxy's exhibition of *The Spoilers*.[112] "It was a happy idea of the management to put the picture on without any break whatever," Bush wrote, commenting on the multiple Simplex projectors that allowed for continuous exhibition without pausing for reel changes:

> "The Spoilers" as a novel is one of those books that we like to read to the end if possible. . . . Breaks and pauses in a running visualization of the novel would be even less welcome than interruptions in the reading. That the audience was well pleased with this new wrinkle was plain. It absorbed the story without an effort and its interest never lagged—at 11:30 we were more interested in the fate of Glenister and all the rest than at 9:15, though we had been looking intently at the screen for more than two hours.[113]

Variety reported "very big" business on its first day (Sunday); in fact, the Strand played to capacity audiences until that Wednesday, with every evening performance turning away a thousand people hoping to get inside. *The Spoilers* and the surrounding entertainment proved so popular that it was held over for another week. First-week figures were projected to be $9,000 in ticket sales, double the expenses of rent and theater operation.[114] When *Brewster's Millions* (1914) began showing at the Strand on April 26, 1914, similar throngs attended.[115]

The opening of the Manhattan Strand was part of a new multiple-area strategy for the Mark Company, Edward Spiegel, and their associates. New deluxe Strand theaters opened soon after the Manhattan venue in Newark, New Jersey, on May 2, 1914, and in Brooklyn as the first steps in a planned theater chain.[116] The Manhattan Strand, though, remained the flagship operation, with Roxy as its chief spokesman and media darling. He had conducted so many interviews and distributed so many press releases in the previous two months that he had already become well known for his marketing bluster and publicity skills. Thus, it was little surprise that when an elaborate burglary took place at the Strand in mid-May, the New York police quickly assumed it was a hoax designed to drum up even more publicity for the city's newest and most popular movie house. Roxy signed an affidavit with the police that insisted the heist was not a publicity stunt.[117] By then, the Strand didn't need it.

In late May, with the Strand's acclaim at fever pitch, Roxy demonstrated a personal, though privately guarded, note by projecting footage of the Vaterland's ship arriving in New York from Hamburg, Germany.[118] The screening may have been mere coincidence, but if Roxy was aware of his country of origin, the obsessively careful exhibitor would have known that it was the anniversary of his voyage to America twenty-eight years earlier in May 1886. By then, once poor Jewish exhibitors like Roxy were coming into their own, with elaborate theaters built by Marcus Loew and William Fox filling the boroughs of New York City.[119] Loew's good friend and the co-founder of the People's Vaudeville Company (later known as Loew's) was actor David Warfield, born David Wohlfeld to an Orthodox Jewish family in San Francisco. Warfield, along with fellow Jews Charles Frohman and David Belasco, were regular patrons at the Strand, as was Oscar Hammerstein, who attended every new performance in 1914.[120]

In June 1914, Roxy was invited to speak at an exhibitors' convention in New York. Four years after his first trip from Forest City to a similar gathering, he sat at the speakers table with John Bunny, J. Stuart Blackton, Upton Sinclair, J. C. Graham, Jesse Lasky, and Frohman, among others.[121] His presence among them was recognition by his peers of Roxy's growing influence. The erudite Roxy, with his mix of Midwestern charm and immigrant New York Jewish moxie, was an ideal and enthusiastic spokesman for a generation of exhibitors. "Don't give the public what it wants," Roxy was often quoted as saying, "but what you think it wants."[122] He expanded on that theme to *Green Book Magazine* that August when he remarked,

> I don't like to be following in everyone's footsteps. I don't like to do things the way everyone else does them. All one hears about the theatres is the ever-lasting cry of the managers that they are looking for "what the people want." That idea is fundamentally and disastrously wrong. The people themselves don't know what they want. They want to be entertained, that is all, and they properly leave it to the men who make a business of entertaining to do the thinking about what is the thing to offer. Don't give the people what they want—give them something better than they expect. . . . The idea of doing better than the other fellow is the secret of all success.[123]

This methodology was about more than just greenbacks for Roxy: the desire for cultural uplift was as strong as ever. "Teach the public, but teach it subtly," he said that summer. "Don't insult it by calling it ignorant."[124] Rather than looking down on the public like a progressive reformer who wanted to clean up the morass, Roxy saw hordes of people like himself who needed only music, film, and other forms of art and culture to become as successful and as educated. He believed fully and without question that America had given the huddled masses of the world a level playing field and that the Strand's job was to tastefully and entertainingly deliver a university's education for the price of a movie ticket.[125]

Roxy's lineup of clean, educational films was part of this ethos and strategy. *Motion Picture News* noted that a typical program at the Strand included "a feature melodrama, a Keystone comedy, and two interesting educationals—all interspersed with excellent musical features. Here is a complete appeal—to the entire public." The *News* added that Roxy's recent exhibition of two Éclair educational films, *Lake Como* (*Sul Lago di Como,* 1913) and *Caddis Flies* (ca. 1914) were not only finding appreciative audiences and "applause" but that other exhibitors who attended the Strand booked these films based on their audience reaction.[126] The Strand quickly became an important film venue—perhaps the most important venue—by mid-1914, capable of making or breaking a film. The idea of a shop window theater (a term that had not yet been employed) was being created in which a prominent movie house in a major city served to demonstrate to exhibitors inside and outside that municipality how and what to present to an audience. In a few short months, the Regent was largely forgotten as the Strand's programming and success took center stage.

The Strand and Its Music

One of the central attractions of the Strand was its music. The Strand orchestra was so widely lauded under Edouarde's direction that many cited it as much as the building or the films as their reason for attending. The music received rave reviews from the trade press and newspapers such as the *New York American,* whose music critic (whom Robert Grau dubbed the "dean of musical critics") gave Roxy and his musical corps tremendously high marks.[127] "The first thing you know," *Green Book Magazine* told Roxy, "people will be coming to your theatre to hear your orchestra and not to see your pictures."[128]

Roxy began to expand his conception of musical accompaniment at the Strand, working with Edouarde to "consciously or unconsciously" realize "the producer's ideals." Roxy noted:

I know that I utter the sentiments of all my brother exhibitors when I say that this task is a very hard one most of the time. After all, we are working with the thoughts and ideas of somebody else. These thoughts and ideas are frozen on the film; they are not flexible or plastic. The best then that we can do is to interpret what the director intended to convey, to emphasize and amplify his meaning. I try to read the mind not only of the director, but of the scenario writer as well, and I follow the actors very closely. Only in this way is it possible to do full justice to the combined efforts of the men in the studio.[129]

He explained his methodology further to *The Metronome*, an important music journal that now began to take music for motion pictures—and Roxy—much more seriously:

> I make the picture interpret the music, and the music interpret the picture. Music, to my mind, is just as important as the picture. I admit that I cannot read a single note, but my memory is excellent, and I have another gift—call it intuition if you will—which for this particular purpose is absolutely essential and invaluable. . . . Just as soon as I have selected, trimmed, and fitted the music to a film, I can in my mind, see the entire picture from start to finish by simply hearing the orchestra play.

Roxy relied on this gift for aural memory and remarked that he was "familiar with every strain that I can possibly use out of grand opera. I am more than well acquainted with all the light operas. I have heard many of them and used them in our theatre."[130]

Rehearsals were increased exponentially at the Strand to ensure that the sounds in Roxy's head matched those that reached his audience's ears. The projectionist, organist, singers, and the entire orchestra attended these rehearsals.[131] Robert Grau added that this level of preparation was still unheard of for the era. "If any local management 'rehearsed the films' with full orchestral and organ accompaniment before Rothapfel did," Grau wrote, "my attention was never directed toward the innovation."[132] One reporter who witnessed these rehearsals mentioned that preparation for a Strand performance was "the most painstaking thing in the world."[133] Roxy also took up the baton again at the Strand, conducting some of the orchestral rehearsals and occasional public performances. "Watching him at such moments from the wings it is easy to get the right perspective of his passionate love and study of music," Bush wrote.[134]

Roxy's influence on musical accompaniment grew exponentially during this period as he seemed to be approached on the subject more than any other figure. Roxy emphasized the psychological aspects of his methods in an early September 1914 issue of *Reel Life*:

> To begin with we always select a theme, it may be some little aria, or a little andante movement or perhaps a march, but we always get a theme,

then we counterpoint with several different melodies or a situation and we keep working to the psychological point in the picture. Our overtures, as a rule, are used to create the atmosphere for the picture in which the theme of course is predominant."[135]

Sometimes, of course, a motion picture required two themes, such as in the Strand's presentation of *Wrath of the Gods* (1914). The basic theme was Christianity and Buddhism, Roxy observed, and the musical accompaniment needed a specially written score "entwining a little Japanese melody into the more simple strain of Adeste Fideles."[136]

During its first year, Roxy seemed to add a new singer every week, such as tenor Frank Coombs,[137] or a musician like pianist Joseph Littau, who left the Regent to rejoin Roxy by September 1914.[138] Roxy did not want seasoned musicians but younger artists whose temperament and excitement mimicked his own. "I prefer young men and women who can be more easily molded and in whom the fire of enthusiasm burns most brightly," he told Bush.

The kind of musicians I want to keep away from is the man who tries to subordinate the pictures to the music. After all, the pictures must always remain the groundwork of our entertainment, and it just jars me when I hear an orchestra hammer away all through a picture with but small regard for the action on the screen. When a musician begins to think that the people come mainly to hear the music and that the pictures are but an incident, he has outlived his usefulness with me.[139]

The unitary text, as before, remained of utmost importance to Roxy. Motion pictures, no matter their importance or distributor, remained only one part of a blended program of which music played an integral but often secondary role—at least for now.

THE STRAND'S INFLUENCE

Over the next year, the Strand began increasing the amount of live entertainment it offered, with ballet, operettas, and a variety of music, both vocal and orchestral. The new mixture of film, music, and live entertainment was quickly duplicated around the country in other deluxe theaters. "The writer has been in most of the principal motion picture houses of the East," W. Stephen Bush remarked in June 1915 and "there is no question that the inspiration for improved methods of presentation has come from the example of [Roxy]. This refers to everything, from the balancing of the program to the minutest details of projection."[140] That same month, William Johnston of *Motion Picture News* remarked that the Roxy method had been adopted in deluxe theaters across the country and the unitary text had now become an important method of presenting live and filmed entertainment. "The Strand style of program, now so popular in the larger theatres, is formed like the make-up of a popular magazine," Johnston noted. "The instantaneous, and striking success of this style of program is due to it's [*sic*] broad appeal—its appeal to people, very largely, who never before went to see motion pictures. And so we shall have new program successes, not by following narrowly the prescribed standards of the legitimate and especially the vaudeville field, but by broadening the picture to include the successful phases of a much greater world of entertainment."[141]

Another journalist would later add, "Throughout this country and even in Europe the Strand Theatre idea has proven highly profitable, so profitable in fact, that every new moving picture house built in recent years in any city or town has been [organized like] the Strand," which had now "become established as an American institution which almost every visitor to New York considered it his duty to see."[142] By 1920, the influence of the theater was still unparalleled. Journalist Golda Goldman noted that the success of the Strand had made Roxy the key figure in altering and determining the direction of high-class motion picture exhibition for the next decade. "If imitation is really the sincerest form of flattery," she wrote in the *American Hebrew*, "it is impossible to question the public appreciation of the Rothafel type of entertainment. Strand Theatres, theatres a la Strand, have appeared in every town. Everything about it has been copied—the stage settings, orchestra, lighting effects, interpolation of ballet and concert numbers—all are to be found in two-hour program form in every up-to-date picture-house in the country."[143] The Strand chartered a new course that did not call for motion pictures alone but was an amalgam of early-twentieth-century forms of live and recorded entertainment.

The success of the Strand had achieved its desired effect for the industry as well. By proving that motion pictures could hold their own along Broadway, an area that had been the almost exclusive locale of legitimate theater and vaudeville, it gave hope and direction to motion picture exhibitors, seasoned and new, across the nation. Throughout 1914, there were innumerable conversions of old opera houses, vaudeville theaters, and legitimate theaters into motion picture houses. That summer, for instance, six Chicago legit theaters planned to switch to motion pictures.[144] The Strand had proved that movie theaters, not just mixed vaudeville-movie houses like those operated by Loew and Fox, could command the same or more dollars as vaudeville. This change, Robert Grau granted, was largely due to the "influence of Rothapfel." Left out of much of the hype about a Strand program, though, was the production cost—roughly three to four times the overhead of a small venue from the previous decade. Exhibitors following the Roxy model had to balance their production costs with their elevated ticket prices, ensuring that they charged enough to make a profit but not too much to scare off the working class.[145]

The timing of the Strand's success was fortuitous as well for producers like Adolph Zukor and Jesse Lasky, who championed the feature-length film over the one-reel show. Zukor, through his company Famous Players, argued that by creating feature-length films, the medium could be used not only to entertain but to move and uplift audiences while also elevating motion pictures to the level of other art forms (and generate more revenue). With theaters like the Strand bringing music to the masses and introducing ballet, opera, and other previously unavailable forms of culture to even the poorest citizens of New York, the notion of motion pictures as art fit perfectly with the ideology of exhibitors like Roxy, who saw the movies as great social equalizers and the movie house as a temple for all of the "allied arts" and classes. Aside from these cultural points, the fact that thousands of dollars were being spent each week at the Strand and Regent in New York, the Lyric in Minneapolis, and the Alhambra in Milwaukee, to name but a few of the era's deluxe motion picture theaters, helped spur the production of films that could satisfy these multi-class venues. The feature films of the era, both imported and domestic, were often dressed up as high-class entertainment; movies and moviegoing were becoming legitimate social and cultural attractions.

ROXY AND AUDIENCE SURVEILLANCE

Roxy's attention to the social and cultural effects of film (and music) was part of his developing theories about motion pictures, audiences, and exhibition, all of which were spurred as much by his attention to presentation as by his interest in crowd—not mob—psychology. Given his experience over the past five and a half years, Roxy had begun to develop theoretical suppositions about audience behavior, gleaned through years of trial and error and, most intriguingly, through audience surveillance and response. Years before Hollywood began analyzing its public, George Gallup began polling movie audiences, and Margaret Thorp and others began studying them, Roxy crafted his own system to ensure repeat attendance. "It is the exhibitor's business to entertain them and find out what they want or better still give them what they are sure to like without trying to poll them on the subject," Roxy stated in December 1914. "I know what my audience wants because I have spent hours and hours watching them from a little vantage point in this theatre. No one knows where this vantage point is, but it enables me to watch the faces of the men and women and children who compose my audience. I have seen how, during certain pictures, their faces were drawn tensely, how immovable they sat and how at the same time they enjoyed what they saw." Roxy also approached audience members directly and was known to occasionally invite them to his office to gauge their opinions of the film, the music, and the show as a whole. But he remained coy in these conversations, prying their convictions from them casually. "I never ask any spectator directly what he or she thinks," Roxy mentioned. "I mingle with my audience in various ways and wait for an opinion that utters itself voluntarily without promptings of any kind. These unsolicited opinions may not always be to the exhibitors' liking, but in many cases they have a great, constructive value to the progressive exhibitor. Such opinions often may enlighten him upon facts of which he was theretofore in ignorance."[146] Roxy's qualitative analysis predates the ethnographic research film producers and filmmakers have routinely sought over the past century.

Roxy drew from his own experiences as a poor German-Jewish immigrant in Minnesota and New York, his efforts recruiting young men into the Marine Corps, selling books and insurance door to door, and all of the successes and failures he had produced as an exhibitor since 1908. Having worked as a salesman and a recruiter, Roxy knew how to read an audience individually and as a collective whole. It was the subtlety of his salesmanship, though, providing a variety of entertainment in association with motion pictures, that did not condescendingly contextualize its importance to his mass audience and made it so alluring to those who had never been exposed to ballet, opera, or classical music.

As the Strand's coffers and seats remained filled during 1914, Roxy felt justified in his pronouncements about audience research, his use of lay theory, and his nuts and bolts industrial stratagems. Mingling amid the massive crowds each night and beaming with pride as his theater and his name were splashed across the city's newspapers and the industry's trade journals, there was virtually no criticism of his methods printed or another formidable exhibitor to challenge his beliefs. W. Stephen Bush and other journalists extolled his methods, and Roxy became entrenched in his own ideas and attached to the feedback loop from his patrons. "I get hundreds of letters from patrons every week," Roxy explained, "some making suggestions, some just criticising [sic]. I welcome these letters and answer every one provided it is signed." With these letters providing even more insight into his audiences, their age, gender, ethnicity, class, education level, etc., he began to see his role not only as a benevolent puppet master but as a kind of father figure to a new generation of entertainment seekers. Playwright and producer Winthrop Ames, for instance, a frequent patron of the Strand, confirmed Roxy's greatest hopes that his presentations were making audiences happier after each performance. "My audience is with me always," Roxy remarked to Bush.

> I feel that in many respects the exhibitor must act as the trustee and the plenipotentiary of his audience. Take the selection of pictures for one thing. He must look at the pictures he intends to put on his program with the eyes of his audience, but how can he do it without knowing his audience and knowing it intimately? Hence the necessity for the constant study of the audience. . . . I know better than any one else just what my audience wants and I am particularly aware of what they do not want. No exhibitor has learned even the rudiments of his profession if he has no strong and definite feelings on this subject.[147]

In addition to his views on audiences, Roxy was also developing his own theories of how motion pictures worked and how to amplify certain effects to heighten their realism. "I find that the darkening of the house during a tense dramatic scene, the brightening of the house during a comedy never fails in psychological effect," he said in November 1914, directing exhibitors to "Plunge your house into entire darkness while the people on screen are passing through a tunnel." Roxy added that he wanted "everybody to be transported, as it were, into the picture. This always reacts upon the audience and increases its own [in]tensity and its own appreciation of realism."[148] Roxy's appeal to realism (and psychology) included opening the Strand's door and letting cold air rush into the auditorium during a film in which the "audience was cold with horror."[149] Roxy made other observations: he argued against the use of flashbacks, but for the use of close-ups whose "intimate view . . . of the actor's features" was "better to register a certain emotion." He argued as well that the "better production" should reduce pantomime and exaggerated expressions; actors, he noted, should instead demonstrate their emotions "by the merest gesture; the imagination of the audience will do the rest."[150] This set of criteria was used to substantiate Roxy's need to "correct" the films he presented by altering them in the Strand's editing room. Sometimes, though, Roxy remarked, "[T]he blemish on the picture is incurable," and no amount of editing could save it. In other cases, Roxy added instead of subtracted, introducing "details forgotten by the director."[151] Roxy was already asserting a measure of authorial control and his own right to final cut.

Rothapfel and Münsterberg

Roxy's audience research and his thoughts on film and narrative coincided with theoretical writings about film by Vachel Lindsay and Hugo Münsterberg. Like Roxy, Lindsay and Münsterberg were also trying to understand the machinations of film and its effect upon audiences. While their goals were not commercial, the work of early film theorists and early film exhibitors interested in this subject certainly overlapped temporally.

Roxy was one of the "Zeligs" of early-twentieth-century media, at the physical, industrial, or technological crossroads of some of its most transitional moments for a quarter century. Perhaps, then, it should come as no surprise to find that the Strand was among the crucial stops made by Hugo Münsterberg as he began to study motion pictures and their effect upon audiences. Allan Langdale notes that "Some time in 1914, for some inexplicable reason—but perhaps for mere escapism or out of curiosity—a likely despairing Hugo Münsterberg [upset over his career] went to a moving picture for the first time in his life."[152] Münsterberg's subsequent visit to the Strand, unlike his "inexplicable" first visit to a movie house, was, Roxy later noted, "for the same reason that all people come, for amusement, rest, relaxation." And when the show was over, Roxy recalled years later, Münsterberg "had apparently got what he had come for and he wanted to know how the wheels back-stage, mental and emotional, went round." The Harvard professor walked backstage to Roxy's office "quite unannounced" late one afternoon. Roxy remembered their meeting with great pride nearly two decades later:

> We talked for a long time, forgetting hours and food and appointments. His interest in me lay in the fact that what he was studying in theory, the mass mind and mass emotions, I was working out quite unconsciously on the broad laboratory of the stage. Perhaps it is essential that all showmen be psychologists. It is certainly important that a showman—I use the word in its broadest sense—be in continual harmony with the heart and mind of the times. The good showman feels the pulse of today's

heartbeats and can, like a good physician, prognosticate the change that may come tomorrow.[153]

That their meeting seems to have been productive, cordial, and lengthy may surprise some. Frank Landy, for instance, notes that Münsterberg was often difficult in person and his "pro-German attitudes and behavior were compounded by his personal style." Yet, it may have been for that very reason that the visit was so amicable. Landy notes that Münsterberg "was condescending to all but Germans."[154] Roxy was perfectly suited for an audience with the professor as the two actually had much in common: they were both German-Jewish immigrants (Münsterberg had converted to Christianity years earlier, probably for professional reasons) and equally strong-willed. Münsterberg's childhood was no more glamorous than Roxy's—Moritz Münsterberg had been a lumber merchant, while Gustav Rothapfel sold shoes to lumberjacks. In a strange coincidence, Moritz was also first married to a woman named Rosalie, who had also passed away at a young age, and then to another woman named Anna (the same names as Gustav's two wives and in the same order).[155]

While these personal details may or may not have been shared that evening at the Strand (though they certainly informed their personalities and tastes), both were deeply interested in questions of psychology, culture, and Kultur, and saw film not as a commercial device alone but as a distinctive and new art. Beyond their biographical similarities, Roxy and Münsterberg may have been united in their relative professional solitude as well. Both were at the vanguard of their place within film history, with Roxy the most public spokesman of film exhibition and Münsterberg soon to be a leading voice in film theory/psychology. As such, their pronouncements were bold and largely unaccompanied by other voices. The trades had not yet exalted other individual exhibitors like they had Roxy, with the much more press-shy Marcus Loew and William Fox quieter in their personal coverage (although their corporations received a good deal of press) and Sid Grauman's stardom still a few years away. Among those writing about film, Vachel Lindsay had begun his own work, and others had begun to write about film and its effects upon society as well, but few had already put into words a cohesive theoretical doctrine about how film worked (upon an audience). Sitting in the Strand that evening, these two seemingly disparate individuals may have felt like homesteaders after the Oklahoma Land Run tending to their respective chunks of mental real estate. Or perhaps they felt more like explorers on the moon. Whatever they may have felt, it seems that both men came away impressed by the other. Before he left that night, Münsterberg reportedly dubbed Roxy "the world's most natural psychologist."[156] *The Theatre* confirmed in 1916 that it was "Mr. Rothapfel [who] perceived the natural connection between music and pictures, an alliance recently recognized by no less an authority than Hugo Münsterberg."[157]

At the Strand and Elsewhere

As Roxy's reputation continued to grow among those within the film industry, he quickly became the go-to exhibitor for staging the premiere screenings of films at nearby legitimate theaters, a growing trend in 1914. In November, Samuel Goldwyn and the Jesse L. Lasky Feature Play Company hired Roxy to present the premiere of Cecil B. DeMille's *Rose of the Rancho* (1914) not at the Strand, where it would move not long after its premiere, but at the Belasco Theatre on November 15. Roxy was charged with presenting the film to a crowd that included William Randolph Hearst, Otto Kahn, David Belasco, Daniel Frohman, Adolph Zukor, Mary Pickford, and Marcus Loew, among other notable guests. The evening was as much a confirmation of the rise of the motion pictures, now housed within one of Manhattan's more fashionable legitimate theaters, as it was a coming-out party for Roxy, whose presentation was lauded. The evening had another benefit as it put him in direct contact with Otto Kahn and other important figures—ties that would be developed over the next few years. *Moving Picture World* lavished praise on their favorite son, remarking that the live prelude he produced for the film was one of "magnificence."[158] The evening was a success. Lasky and Belasco visited Roxy at the Strand on November 29, where the film was now playing, and presented him with a commemorative silver cup as a token of their appreciation.[159] Fresh off that success, Roxy capped off the year by staging the premiere of Famous Players' new eight-reel film, *The Eternal City* (1915) at the Lyceum Theatre, another legitimate house, on Sunday, December 27.[160]

By the end of 1914, the success of Manhattan's new Strand Theatre was emblematic of the national growth of deluxe motion picture theaters.[161] "For the comfortable housing of this newer and greater audience there have sprung up all over the country—from Broadway to Vancouver—large and beautiful edifices, devoted wholly to motion pictures," *Moving Picture World* wrote. "Never in the entire history of the amusement business has there been a building era so remarkable in every way. The better picture, the better class of patrons, the better theatre—these are the developments of the year past, in so remarkable a degree that 1914 will remain a red letter year in the history of the industry."[162] *Photoplay* remarked that the theater's new fifty-piece Strand Concert Orchestra was now the largest theater orchestra in the United States "excepting, of course, institutions where grand opera is presented."[163] The year 1913 is often regarded as the beginning of the deluxe motion picture theater era, particularly because of the opening of the Regent in Manhattan, but 1914 spawned a fleet of new deluxe houses to be built across the country in the years that followed. Many of these new theaters took the Strand's increasingly famous moniker to borrow some of the luster and esteem established by Roxy in his new Broadway venue.

Between 1905, when the Times Building was erected in what had been known as Longacre Square, and 1915, Times Square had become (according to the *New York Times*) "the theatrical centre [*sic*] of the world. There are more theatres in this section of New York," the newspaper reported, "than in any other city in the world."[164] It was against this backdrop that the Strand had succeeded beyond all expectations. The Mark interests did not convert the theater into a once-rumored home for musical comedy or for any other live performances. Instead, the Strand would remain a motion picture theater for the next seventy-three years. *Photoplay Magazine*, reveling in the Strand's early success, reminded its readers that Mitchel Mark had been called "a silly meddler in metropolitan amusement affairs; one who would speedily and laughably go the way of other meddlers."[165] The Strand had instead proved the viability of deluxe motion picture theaters in the Times Square area. Roxy was soon shuttled by the Mark Company to Syracuse, New York, to open the newest link in the Mark Strand Theatre Company's chain, the 2,000-seat Strand, on March 17, 1915. The *Times* was happy to report that the sister Strand would "follow the same policy of motion pictures and music" as the original in Manhattan.[166]

The Manhattan Strand celebrated a banner anniversary on April 11, 1915, with raw statistics revealing the breadth of its success.[167] Since its debut, the theater had hosted an average of 12,000 patrons per day and a total patronage of 4,380,000 for the year, "almost equalling [*sic*] the entire population of New York City," one journalist wrote.[168] It wasn't just the size of the crowds at the Strand that was newsworthy but their composition. *The Metronome* observed:

> Mr. Rothapfel knows through personal experience that the most intelligent and cultured class will patronize the movie theatre providing it meets their requirements. Moreover, this has been proven at the Strand, with hundreds of automobiles depositing their passengers at the entrance and with evening performances that show what no other moving picture

house has ever shown—a liberal sprinkling of ladies and gentlemen in evening dress. In speaking of the particular field of motion picture enterprises, Mr. Rothapfel looms up as a figure of remarkable prominence. As a producer he has no equal.[169]

Roxy reflected on his success at the Regent and Strand theaters in January 1915: "My own experience in New York has been most wonderful," he told W. Stephen Bush. "I came here an absolute stranger. Men who had spent their lives in the show business freely predicted my utter failure. I encountered most bitter opposition, for which I could discern no rational motive."[170] A little more than a year after arriving in New York, Roxy had few doubters left to convince. *National Magazine* observed that Roxy's success was not contested: "He came, he saw and he conquered Broadway, and inside of six years has leaped from obscurity to prominence. The people no longer stutter and stammer in trying to pronounce his name—for young Rothapfel has already carved out for himself an enduring fame as the most successful moving picture maestro of America."[171]

The success of the Strand and other new motion picture theaters near Times Square, such as the Vitagraph, heralded the beginning of the industry's invasion of formerly legitimate spaces and encouraged others to buy, build, or lease exclusive showcase, "first-run" theaters in or around the Times Square area. Hosting the premiere of a film within blocks of the growing media in the area was a surefire way of guaranteeing coverage by the motion picture trade journals and the popular press. The importance of a "Broadway" run was already evident in and outside New York by mid-1915. The Eau Claire, Wisconsin, *Sunday Leader*, for instance, noted that the New York Strand's anniversary presentation of the film *Snobs* (1915) had bestowed great importance on the film merely by being chosen for exhibition there, and thus made it a must-see for the citizens of Eau Claire three months later. The fact that the film played "this most important of all picture playhouses," the newspaper stated, "stamps it as a production of extraordinary importance and as a comedy presentation without a peer." Such a recommendation now prompted immediate attention by patrons, journalists, and other exhibitors.[172]

Adolph Zukor led a group of investors including Daniel Frohman and Edwin S. Porter to lease the Broadway Theatre from Stanley Mastbaum through the Waybroad Film Company and "devote the theater exclusively to the exploitation of the greatest film productions in the world." Roxy, who had already put over successful premieres for Famous Players, was chosen by Zukor to select the "best and most suitable music" for each production to be played by a large symphony orchestra and led by a "conductor of national repute." The Broadway reopened on February 20 with *The Eternal City*.[173] The new Famous Players theater, coupled with Vitagraph's new showplace, signaled the escalating vertical integration of the American film industry. Producer Lewis J. Selznick dubbed the Strand one of "the Two Premier Theatres of America," alongside the 5,000-seat Hippodrome nearby on 42nd Street and Sixth Avenue.[174] The owners of the Hippodrome, the Shuberts, reportedly flirted with motion picture theater operation once more and approached the man they had tossed out of their organization three years earlier—Roxy—to be the colossal theater's general manager. Roxy refused.[175]

In the coming months, despite these outside tasks and other attempts to lure him away, Roxy's focus remained on the Strand. His workaholic nature was evident: "The fact is when I leave the office I am always anxious to get back," Roxy remarked in January 1915, "the work draws me, I do not try to resist."[176] Roxy's assistant mentioned that his employer "worked for fifteen hours at a stretch with nothing but a sandwich."[177] "I adore my work," Roxy expressed. "I want my children to follow me. I would not have them enter any other profession. I want my boy to continue my work after me."[178] With his breakneck pace, it would have been hard for Roxy to know what young Arthur Rothapfel would have wanted out of life. Roxy was rarely home for more than a quick meal and an occasional slumber. As his son Arthur recalled roughly three-quarters of a century later, Roxy "was not a particularly good family man as such. He didn't dote on his children." Arthur and Beta often received more cash than attention. "He gave us everything we wanted," Arthur Rothafel recalled, but "we were our mother's children."[179]

In previous years, work had been Roxy's mistress. Now he had become a "bigamist." With its stable of box office "girls," young male ushers, and others under his tutelage, Roxy created a second family at each theater he managed. Live theater staffs often changed with each passing show; Roxy's theaters would create more permanent "families" that worked and often stayed together for years, traveling with him from theater to theater throughout his career. Even at this early stage, there was already a "Roxy and His Gang."

ROXY AND THE COMMUNITY

With his private time increasingly scant, Roxy's second family included all of his employees and seemingly every patron. At the Strand, Roxy created a safe space for women amid the bustle of the city. Under the "patronage of Fifth

Avenue's society women," Roxy created a noontime "dansant" for working girls, "a working girls' 'cafeteria'" that served over 1,500 young women every day, and an emergency hospital for Strand employees and the women who found a midday home there.[180] When Roxy heard about eastside children going hungry, he immediately sprang to action and instilled his version of *tikkun olam* ("repair the world") at the Strand.[181] Prior to several performances at noon, Roxy began opening early for shows whose proceeds went directly to these children. "The modern exhibitor must share in the civic life of his community," Roxy said, extending his community-building efforts that dated back to his days as a Red Cross organizer in Carbondale. "He is the most powerful factor for good or evil." W. Stephen Bush described the Strand's charitable effort:

> It costs but ten cents to buy one of these tickets, but you can give as much more as you like and few I imagine will claim to be exempt from paying more. Not only does the purchaser see a show which is easily worth a dollar, but he is buying a decent breakfast for little boys and girls who would otherwise go hungry. . . . It is hard to see what prestige and what popularity our premier exhibitor has thus conferred not alone upon the Strand, but upon the cause of motion pictures generally. After this splendid feat in the name of Humanity and of the Motion Picture we are, I suppose, quite willing to listen to Rothapfel's opinion on the exhibitor as a factor in the civic life of his city. The press of the city has taken up his cause and is giving it unstinted publicity. The Board of Education is heartily co-operating with him, the whole city is interested.[182]

Cultivating the support of the Board of Education and the popular press was nothing new for Roxy, but it served to heighten his message that motion pictures and motion picture theaters could and would be moral institutions, especially at deluxe houses that presented film, live performance, and music in addition to charity. *National Magazine* added that the Lyric strategy was in full bloom as Roxy "counts among his intimate friends Catholic priests and several prominent clergymen, for he appreciates the depth and power of true religious devotion" and "won for him the hearty support of people who are not ordinarily patrons of theaters."[183]

It would be naïve to analyze Roxy's generosity isolated from its strategic value. While his charity to women and children was certainly befitting the gentleman and Marine Roxy perceived himself to be, it was also an extension of his appeal to families, social reformers, politicians, and, above all, the clergy. This effort to feed Manhattan's eastside children was certainly born out of both generosity and strategy. "Before you can expect the teachers and the ministers and the press to join hands with you," he mentioned, "you must 'show them.'" And after this plan to feed the city's poorest children was successfully put into effect, Roxy noted a clergyman's recent visit to the Strand with pride. "Mr. Rothapfel," he remarked, "your theater is at this moment doing more good in the city of New York than any single church or school or library that I know of." Roxy was certainly proud of the Strand's generosity, but he was even more excited about the value it had brought to his theater and to his profession:

> It is and surely ought to be a source of pleasure to all of us exhibitors to know that even the greatest and most widely circulated periodicals are now not only interested, but very friendly though but a year or so ago they were letting no chance escape to hit at the picture. Look, too, what the change has been in the attitude of the clergy. Now if we were able to do big things for our communities in spite of this powerful opposition what will we not be able to do with all these vital forces of the community arrayed solidly with us? Our interest in the civic life of the communities in which we live ought to be stimulated by these two facts: The motion picture has become by far the most important factor in entertaining the great multitudes; it opens up avenues of civic usefulness which were absolutely unknown to the theater of old. . . . With this spirit of building on deep foundations there is no obstacle which the exhibitor cannot overcome.[184]

For his next bit of *tzedakah* (charity), Roxy donated a film projector to the Sing Sing Brotherhood (at the infamous Sing Sing prison in Ossining, New York) and traveled upstate with his chief operator to install the machine. From that point forward, Roxy routinely sent films for the inmates' entertainment.[185] Film, in Roxy's mind, was an imperative and shared commodity.

RIALTO THEATRE, NEW YORK, NY

The Shuberts had been unable to lure Roxy away from the Strand, but deeper pockets finally prevailed. By the end of May 1915, news reached as far away as Indianapolis that Roxy was leaving the Strand for a new project at "the Corner" of Times Square.[186] O. O. McIntyre's syndicated column "Sketches of Little New York" claimed that Roxy "resigned in a huff," though no evidence was offered to support this assertion.[187] Hammerstein's Victoria, at 42nd Street and Seventh Avenue, was the latest victim of the growth of motion pictures and motion picture theaters in the area. Unlike the Vitagraph, Broadway, and other converted legitimate theaters, the Victoria would not be renovated for motion picture use, but torn down instead to make way for a 2,500-seat deluxe movie theater.[188]

At the start of Roxy's last rehearsal at the Strand on May 29, every employee in the building appeared on stage and presented Roxy with five large silver vases linked by silver chains and filled with roses. Roxy was treated to a loud cheer, and Carl Edouarde led the orchestra as they played "He's a Jolly Good Fellow" and "Auld Lang Syne."[189] B. A. Rolfe took over the management of the Strand Theatre on June 6, 1915. Five blocks away, Roxy told the *New York Times* that even more than the Regent and Strand, the new Rialto Theatre would be known "far and wide."[190] The *Times* reported that the owners of the $600,000 Rialto Theatre Corporation, New York bankers Felix Kahn of Kuhn, Loeb & Co. (brother of the more famous financier and Metropolitan Opera benefactor Otto Kahn, whom Roxy had met at the premiere of *Rose of the Rancho* over seven months earlier) and Crawford Livingston had insured the life of their chief representative—Roxy—for $250,000 through the Equitable Life Assurance Company (with Kahn and Livingston the sole benefactors).[191] Roxy was no longer an employee of a given theater but a listed asset and a brand name. If he died working long hours at the Rialto, Rosa would not receive a penny. Roxy's life now belonged to his employers. Kahn and Livingston gave Roxy "an absolutely free hand in the carrying out of his unique ideas," *Motion Picture News* reported, loosening constraints he had felt under other bosses. Roxy's ego was also on the rise. "I believe I can say that I have lifted motion picture presentation to a higher plane," he told the *News*, "and the Rialto is to be the apogee of my efforts. I am going to do things at the Rialto as yet undreamed of, and . . . [it] will be the most conspicuously beautiful structure outside and inside in America. . . . That I have been able in seven years to graduate from a small mining town to my own theatre in New York gives me the right to believe in my own theories."[192]

Roxy announced that the Rialto would offer a thirty-six-piece orchestra under the direction of Hugo Riesenfeld, former concertmaster and director of Hammerstein's Opera Company—the same organization Roxy was supplanting by demolishing the old Victoria.[193] Born in Vienna in 1889, Riesenfeld made his way to America in 1907. By February 1908, he was performing at the Manhattan Opera House and serving as concertmaster.[194] By the end of 1908, Riesenfeld joined the faculty of the National Conservatory of Music of

America in New York City.[195] In 1911, he became conductor at the Chestnut Street Opera House in Philadelphia.[196] By 1915, Riesenfeld was an accomplished conductor with a solid pedigree and experience arranging music for a variety of forms—exactly the kind of résumé Roxy had sought in Carl Edouarde for the Regent.

THE TOAST OF BROADWAY

The demolition of the Victoria to make way for the Rialto was widely hailed within the film industry. A venue built for movies would now occupy the figurative and literal hub of entertainment in America's largest and most important city. It was not only Roxy who had succeeded beyond all expectations by mid-1915 but the motion picture industry as well. Friends and colleagues held a gala celebration for Roxy at the Hotel Astor on June 24, 1915. *Moving Picture World* dubbed it "The 'social event' of the season in motion picture circles." Thirty-one of the industry's most important executives, producers, and other individuals were on hand to fete Roxy, including the Rialto's backers, Felix Kahn and Crawford Livingston, as well as Daniel Frohman, Edwin Thanhouser, William Fox, Winfield Sheehan, Samuel Goldfish (Goldwyn), and Lewis J. Selznick. Siegmund Lubin, Joseph Kennedy, William A. Brady, and others sent words of praise in their absence. At the conclusion of the dinner, the toastmaster commented upon the intricate ways in which Roxy's "high-class" exhibition had laid the groundwork for feature-length, "high-class" films:

> The man whom we seek to honor tonight has created a new form of entertainment. When recently I spoke from the stage of The Strand, gazing into a sea of faces marked with intelligence and culture, when I saw before me an audience such as might well have graced grand opera, I realized to the fullest what work Mr. Rothapfel had accomplished. You are here tonight because you feel that this man has opened the doors to the temple of quality. He has encouraged the producer with high ambitions and corresponding ability. He has set an example; yes, he has founded a school of exhibition, which will stimulate high-class productions. We cannot at this time have the full perspective of the man and his work; that is reserved to a later generation; but we have seen enough of the practical fruits of his work to feel impelled to honor him for what he has done. He has served the whole industry as no man has ever served it before.[197]

Frohman, Fox, and Selznick toasted Roxy next, as did James D. Williams, who described Roxy as a man "who made poor pictures good and good pictures better."[198]

ROXY HOSTS ADDITIONAL PREMIERES

While Roxy waited for the Rialto project to move forward, he resumed his work staging trade and public premieres of (and supplying scores for) new motion pictures from a variety of distributors. Throughout the summer, as plans for the Rialto developed, he served as business manager for the Academy of Music on 14th Street in Manhattan.[199] On September 6, Roxy presented the trade screening of Equitable Motion Picture Corporation's new film *Trilby* (1915) at the 44 Street Theatre.[200] The film's music was performed by a selected orchestra of fifty musicians under the direction of Roxy's new sidekick, Hugo Riesenfeld, who had helped him assemble the overture and incidental music. Roxy and Riesenfeld's score was subsequently used by a host of other exhibitors and conductors—a trend that would continue in the decade to follow.[201]

The Battle Cry of Peace (1915), a film made against the backdrop of World War I, was shown to a private, invited audience in August 1915, but for its public debut the Vitagraph Company called on Roxy to "stage" the film and arrange accompanying music. The company's flagship Vitagraph Theatre closed for two days in September to allow Roxy to redecorate the theater and prime it for the film's premiere run with tickets ranging from twenty-five cents to two dollars.[202] Roxy's influence on the film's exhibition elsewhere was noticed again in the ensuing months in the *Sandusky* (Ohio) *Star Journal* and the *Sheboygan* (Wisconsin) *Press* in January and February 1916, respectively. In each obviously canned piece the following words were printed: "The musical and orchestral effects for the picture were arranged by S. L. Rothapfel, the man who opened the Strand theater in New York and who is admittedly the greatest motion picture orchestration expert in America."[203] While it is always hard (if not typically impossible) to note whether cue sheets and/or sheet music provided by the distributor were used, the promotion of Roxy's musical score at least suggests there was an effort by Vitagraph to push exhibitors to use his score.

Of all of Roxy's special presentations that fall, none was more elaborate than his presentation of *Carmen* (1915) on October 1, 1915, at Boston's Symphony Hall. Like *Battle Cry*, *Carmen* had also been shown to a "select crowd in Hollywood" before its public debut. The film's star, Geraldine Farrar, requested that the film's public premiere be held in her hometown of Boston.[204] A "capacity crowd" turned out for the premiere, and Jesse Lasky and director Cecil B. DeMille used the screening as a testing site, listening to the audience reaction during the evening through a telephone connection from Boston to the Lasky studio in Hollywood. The *Christian Science Monitor* remarked that Roxy and Riesenfeld synchronized the score with various themes from the opera, but took them to task for opening the film with a "medley of national airs," an "impropriety" the newspaper could not overlook. "This is not a period when nationalism should be emphasized," the *Monitor* commented, "and a motion picture program should perhaps never be a medium through which such emphasis is laid."[205]

Rothapfel-Mutual Tour Begins

By late September, Kahn and Livingston were still convinced that the Rialto would be ready for its November opening, but there would soon be a mountain of evidence to the contrary. Roxy had taken an $85,000 annual lease on the property for nine years and hired Thomas Lamb to design the new movie house.[206] Roxy, though, may have sensed the overly ambitious prognostications from the construction company he employed at the outset and had cleverly signed a contract that required the theater to be fully completed by November 1 or a $1,000 per day penalty would be exacted. The original design for the Rialto called for much of the original Victoria to be stripped down to its bare walls and then a new house built from the foundations. However, following that demolition, the city's Building Department condemned the remaining walls, requiring the complete razing of the building and a new project started from scratch. Coupled with new building and fire laws in place by 1915, the cost of the Rialto began skyrocketing, forcing construction to cease.[207] When it finally resumed, Roxy seemed unfazed by the turmoil, fully expecting the November 1 opening day to arrive without a hitch. By the time he returned from Boston at the end of September, however, it was obvious that the Rialto would not be opening in November or anytime in 1915.

Terry Ramsaye, then Mutual Film Corporation's publicity and advertising director, "had a brief talk with the impatient Roxy and immediately set about inventing methods of getting him elsewhere." Roxy was an extreme workaholic and the idling months would have driven him, Kahn and Livingston, and everyone else mad. Ramsaye's scheme to use Roxy to promote Mutual Film product was a coup for the company in that it secured the services of one of the industry's leading voices and enabled Roxy to forget that he was without a theater to manage for the first time in more than four years. Ramsaye recalled that the result of this brainstorm "was the then widely and expensively proclaimed Rotha[p]fel-Mutual tour, a hippodroming of the United States with exhibitor luncheons and dinners in the key cities, for the intended scheme of having Roxy tell them how to play Mutual pictures." In October and November 1915, the tour covered twenty-eight cities in twenty-nine days.[208] If Roxy was a local celebrity in New York before the Ramsaye tour, he quickly became a national figure in motion picture circles.

The tour began on October 21 in Philadelphia before moving on to Washington, D.C., and Atlanta.[209] New Orleans was next, followed by a trip to Dallas on October 29 where a banquet in his honor was held at the city's Oriental Hotel.[210] In Los Angeles, Roxy's sixth stop on the tour, local representatives of the Mutual Film Corporation hosted a lunch for one hundred exhibitors at Christopher's restaurant at 741 South Broadway in Roxy's honor.[211] In Salt Lake City on November 10, the local Mutual Film branch manager, W. P. Moran, hosted a regional banquet with roughly 275 Utah and Idaho exhibitors so they could meet the visitor. After the banquet, Roxy and those assembled went to the American Theater to see one of the nation's largest movie houses and the pride of Utah's exhibition industry.[212] The "directing genius," the *Salt Lake Tribune* reported, told exhibitors to once again "use [their] heads." The *Tribune* pointed out that Roxy had been a trendsetter in the management of theater personnel, teaching his ushers to say "thank you" and "that no matter what happens, the patron is always right." Roxy was also very specific about gender roles: "When a patron comes to my theater, he buys his ticket from a charming young woman. No beauty, you understand, who wears jewelry and chews gum."[213] After Salt Lake City, Roxy moved on to Denver, Kansas City,[214] Milwaukee,[215] Indianapolis,[216] Cincinnati, Detroit, Cleveland, Pittsburgh, Buffalo, and Boston, where the tour finally ended on November 27.[217] The tour was an enormous success for Roxy, who had been well paid for his trouble and added to his growing fame and esteem. "He covered [the country] handily," Terry Ramsaye recalled twenty-four years later. "The Mutual was somewhat better known ... and Roxy, making the show very much his own, was a national figure on new important terms."[218]

Despite his new nationwide esteem, there was always one city seemingly unimpressed by anything Roxy did: Chicago. The city that had been inhospitable to him in 1912 at the Lyric remained so three years later. The *Chicago Daily Tribune* remarked a year after his visit during the Rothapfel-Mutual tour:

> S. L. Rothapfel is as thorough a New Yorker as ever came from Oklahoma. He goes into ecstasies over little old Broadway just as a southerner from Bismarck, N. D. applauds "Dixie." Mr. Rothapfel came down to look over things here on earth a year or so ago and visited Chicago. He was going to tip us off to a few things we ought to have out here, such as street cars, napkins, and quill toothpicks, and was so profoundly overcome with the discovery that we had installed these conveniences in advance of him that he went home to dear old (not Oklahoma) Broadway.

Although the exhibitors in Chicago had "chided Mr. Rothapfel in a jovial way" upon his visit there, the *Tribune*'s sarcastic comments were a reminder that Roxy was often treading the fine line between dispensing advice and dogmatic lecturing.[219]

KNICKERBOCKER THEATRE, NEW YORK, NY

Roxy received a more steady commission while waiting (impatiently) for the Rialto to open. The Triangle Film Corporation hired him to manage the company's recently subleased Knickerbocker Theatre at 38th Street and Broadway in Manhattan, four blocks away from the Rialto construction site. Triangle had subleased a number of theaters throughout the United States for first-run venues for new Triangle product in 1915 with the Knickerbocker serving as the flagship theater for the company (and thus receiving the lion's share of industry and press attention). The upscale venue charged up to two dollars per ticket in order to attract upper-class patrons to their more lofty (highbrow) films. Despite the extremely high ticket prices for a movie house, the theater generated only $1,800 per week in gross income for Triangle by December 1915.[220]

On January 5, 1916, Triangle announced that Roxy had been hired to take over the underperforming theater.[221] *Motion Picture News* noted that because he was known "to exhibitors all over the country, following his great tour of last fall," he was an ideal choice for Triangle to send a message to the industry about its efficacy in film exhibition. "We have invited Mr. Rothapfel to take the management of the Knickerbocker in order that we may have the benefit of his experience in making the house a true model Triangle theatre," Harry

Aitken, president of the Triangle Film Corporation, remarked. This "will show the motion picture managers throughout the country just what can be done in the proper presentation of those plays and in the management of theatres. We feel that in having the co-operation of Mr. Rothapfel we will accomplish that."[222] Aitken reportedly gave Roxy one basic order: "Turn a profit."[223] Roxy's contract with Triangle also included an agreement to exhibit Triangle films exclusively at the Rialto when the venue finally opened. "Both places, however, will be run simultaneously with the Triangle program," Roxy told *Motion Picture News*, "but I will see to it that they do not conflict, or be placed in the position of cutting each other's throats."[224]

When the Knickerbocker reopened on January 15, after closing for a week-long renovation,[225] the length of each program was cut nearly in half, from up to fourteen to a mere seven reels. Some of the theater's ticket prices remained at two dollars, "merely to fulfill the terms of the lease," but most seats now ranged from twenty-five to fifty cents for continuous shows that began at noon and lasted past midnight. (There was a service advantage to paying the higher ticket price—two-dollar patrons were able to reserve their seats in advance without having to wait in line, an amenity for the theater's wealthier clientele.)[226] In addition to Triangle films and Hearst-Vitagraph newsreels, Roxy also created his own newsreel service by hiring an automobile, a driver, and "a squad of snap-shotters" led by H. S. Martin, formerly a photographer from the *New York Evening Sun*, to film local events as they happened. The footage was then shown exclusively at the Knickerbocker less than twenty-four hours later.[227] (Roxy's newsreel hounds once again complicate the inaccurate notion that an industrial wall has always divided those who produce motion pictures from those who exhibit them.)

The theater reopened with *Peggy* (1916), a Thomas Ince film starring Billie Burke, alongside a Keystone short, *Because He Loved Her* (1916), a Hearst-Vitagraph News pictorial, and a travelogue, *Rivers of France* (ca. 1916). It may have been an upscale Triangle theater, but the unitary text was a typical Roxy evening with a short and feature film, newsreel, travelogue, and live performances: a dance by Hilda Biyar and a song by Ruth Freeman. "When Rothapfel took hold he still retained Triangle as the piece de resistance, the really nourishing course of the feast, but he added a lot of appetizers," W. Stephen Bush mentioned.[228] Roxy attracted his usual coterie of admirers for the theater's (re)opening night, including Billie Burke, Mary Pickford, Allan Dwan, Adolph Zukor, Al Jolson, Harry and Roy Aitken, Charles Kessel, and Robert Goelet, the owner of the Knickerbocker Theatre. The Knickerbocker was now steeped in the Roxy brand. "Mr. Rothapfel's method of direction was noticeable in respect to every detail of the program's presentation," the *Motion Picture News* wrote. "The music in its entirety was exceedingly well arranged and adapted for the pictures. The ushers had been visibly drilled along the manager's particular lines. A finger to the cap and a 'Thank You' were never forgotten."[229] If audiences weren't aware that Roxy was now managing the Knickerbocker, he made sure to remind them in the next day's advertisement:

> [T]he interested crowds that jammed into the redecorated—and revised—Knickerbocker Theatre found a magically new and attractive atmosphere, an exhilarating atmosphere. It was all new, from street door to stage. S. L. Rothapfel had remade it in a week for the second edition of Triangle productions. There was a feeling by everyone that they were glad to be there, glad to see "Peggy," glad to hear the new music, the new singers. There was a new feeling in the air, a vitalising [*sic*], entertaining feeling, an intimate feeling of being a part of a huge and delightful success. . . . Everybody was happy, everybody satisfied, as you will be when you go—and go you will, because you won't be able to stay away.[230]

Everybody, though, was not happy; Robert Goelet, the theater's owner, was livid about the new management's policy. Goelet quickly dragged Klaw & Erlanger and Hayman Frohman, the lessees of the theater, and sublessee Harry Aitken into court in an attempt to stop them from exhibiting "the Rothapfel brand of entertainment," which did not charge two dollars for all tickets and thereby, in Goelet's estimation, diminished the rental value of his theater. Goelet also asserted that the Knickerbocker's continuous performances, in stark contrast to the theater's previous mode of exhibition and its quiet intervals between showtimes, made the theater a "second-class" venue.[231] The *New York Times* argued that the case was not a mere contractual suit. In an era in which motion pictures were fighting for legitimacy in the Times Square area and in the public sphere, the newspaper argued that the outcome would denote the "exact status of the movies" legally and culturally and have a truly lasting impact on the film industry.[232] With the stakes high for Triangle and other companies, Rob King notes that Aitken secured nine affidavits "in defense of Rothapfel's credentials" and submitted them to the court.[233] So many affidavits were offered for the defense, in fact, that Goelet had to ask for a postponement to rebut.[234] By February 21, a little over a month after Roxy's reopening, the case was over. Justice Cohalan of the New York Supreme Court refused to grant an injunction that would restrain Triangle from exhibiting films in the "Rothapfel" way. In fact, the *New York Times* noted, "The court said that the coming of moving pictures into the theatrical field had changed the theatrical business to such an extent that high-grade pictures interspersed with musical numbers did not affect the character and standing of a first-class theatre."[235] In a sense, the proliferation of the unitary text had shielded the Knickerbocker from claims that the theater was now being run like a movie house; instead, it was being operated as a mixed entertainment venue that appealed to the middle and upper classes. The court victory was another marker in the changing perceptions of motion pictures and the theaters that exhibited them.

The theater was earning larger grosses under Roxy's management, but it was still not a net moneymaker given Roxy's increased production costs.[236] Triangle, though, reasonably satisfied by the theater's growing revenue and Roxy's positive press coverage, sent him to Chicago to perform a similar makeover at the company's newly leased Colonial Theatre. The theater, which had hosted *The Birth of a Nation*'s (1915) "phenomenal" Chicago run, was leased for a year, with Roxy engaged to run the house for "at least" six weeks. Like its sister theater in Manhattan, the Knickerbocker, the Colonial sold most tickets at popular prices—ten, twenty-five, and fifty cents—reflecting the new Roxy-ized Triangle policy. Roxy refashioned the theater, installing a large electric sign in front, a new Minusa Cine screen, two new Simplex projectors, and a $3,500 stage setting to frame the motion pictures he exhibited.[237] "[T]he Western home of the *Triangle films*" now boasted a twenty-five-piece orchestra, initially conducted by Roxy, performing music he assembled.[238] Its invitation-only premiere brought out many socially prominent patrons who were saluted, thanked, and handed a program "by one of the three negroes in Hindu garb," the *Motion Picture News* reported in the language of the era. "The head usher, dressed in a military uniform decorated with gold triangles," saluted patrons again, directed them to a specific aisle, and thanked them for their attendance. From there, patrons were saluted and thanked once more, this time by the aisle usher.[239]

Roxy returned to Manhattan in early March. Instead of managing the Colonial for six weeks, he guided the theater for roughly six days. In his place, Roxy installed Alfred De Manby, who had worked for him at the Knickerbocker, to present "Real Roxy Shows" at the Colonial.[240] Roxy, the *Middletown* (New York) *Daily Times-Press* reported, had now "cease[d] commuting between the two cities until the premier of the Rialto Theatre."[241] By April 24, Triangle films ceased at the Colonial and the *Chicago Daily Tribune* used the news to take one more swipe at Roxy: "So passeth the shadow of Mr. Rothapfel, who came hence from the bright places of Manhattan to bring us the exhibitorial light—and found us already illuminated and sadly unappreciative of further candle power."[242] Roxy would never manage another theater in Chicago. When "a business meeting of the big noises in reeldom" was later held at the Hotel Sherman there in mid-July 1916 and Roxy was asked to appear, he sent a telegram of regret instead: "Doctor advises me bad for my health to come to Chicago."[243]

There were also others (in addition to Chicago's press) not easily seduced by Roxy's resume or by his charm. Hugo Münsterberg may have treated Roxy with sincere respect, but for many others, motion pictures and the men and women behind them were still outsiders. Roxy could send his children to boarding schools and mix in higher social circles, but to many, like Theodore Dreiser, Roxy and his cultural and industrial cohort would never be more than well-dressed shams. "At 5 I shave and dress and go to S. L. Rothapfel's for dinner," Dreiser writes. "He is a clever Jew who has become managing director of three great movie houses in New York."

> We go across to the Rialto, where I meet Rothapfel again. Plainly I have made a great impression on him for some reason. He is ridiculously impressed. He has some surgeon from the navy there, also his brother, and we pick up a Mr. Jacobs at the Friars Club. Get in his auto and ride to 450 Riverside Drive. That apartment! And his wife! Former kikes all, raised to ridiculous heights by wealth. He wants to play the pianola! Some owner of the Universal Film, a director whom I have never seen, and others. We talk of gambling, cargoes, life in the navy. I must say that Rothapfel in his way shows more tact than any. After dinner more friends—a sister-in-law, aged 19, and very pretty. The men start a gambling game, $1 ante, out of which I stay. A typical American parlor evening—puritanism, until all are thawed out and sure of their ground, then an eager seeking for freedom and pleasure! What a trashy land![244]

The Rialto Opens

The Rialto was nearly completed upon Roxy's return from Chicago. "The enterprise is another instance of so-called 'Wall Street money' entering the movie field," the *Lincoln* (Nebraska) *Daily Star* wrote of Kahn and Livingston's investment. "The theatre depends for its life, however, on the genius of S. L. Rothapfel,"[245] who was now being paid $10,000 per year to manage the theater.[246] Roxy sent out the usual invitations for the Rialto's gala premiere to the political and cultural elite of New York and to the major players in the entertainment industry. Roxy wrote to George Kleine that one month before its opening the demand for seats was already enormous.[247] *Wid's* added that the premiere "will probably be a case of everyone who . . . is anyone in the film game being on hand."[248]

The Rialto Theatre finally opened on April 22, 1916 (five months late), with the Triangle-distributed film *The Good Bad-Man* (1916), starring Douglas Fairbanks and directed by Allan Dwan.[249] Journalists observed once more that Roxy's selection of the film provided it instant status as his reputation as an industry tastemaker grew.[250] Music for the opening number was "suggested and arranged by S. L. Rothapfel and Hugo Riesenfeld." Putting his stamp on all aspects of the show, titles for the Rialto Topical Digest were noted to have been created by Emil Chautard and the omnipresent Roxy.[251] The showman also claimed credit for one-half of the United States patent for the Rialto's signature swirled electric sign.[252]

The Rialto's chief innovation, according to its publicity, was that it was to be a pure deluxe motion picture venue built without a stage, intended to further divorce motion pictures from vaudeville. *Motion Picture News* stated, despite this claim, that there was certainly "enough of a stage to accommodate not only the large chorus, but to provide room for dancers." The *News* reported that live performance was "kept short" at its premiere in keeping "within its character of [a] photoplay house."[253] (The Rialto would become well known for its live performances, despite its early rhetoric.) The theater boasted the largest organ ever installed in a theater until then, as well as a forty-piece orchestra decked out in "fine velvet and silk costume." The "program boys" (ushers) were dressed in "oriental costumes," while the ticket takers were, in harmony with the unitary text, outfitted in a "frock-cut coat harmonizing with the settings of the theatre."[254] Roxy clung to the "gang" he had created since the Regent, bringing union projectionists Lester and Ivan Bowen to the Rialto to ensure its technical proficiency. Both had worked for him at the Strand, while Ivan had worked at the Liberty Theatre during its historic exhibition of *The Birth of a Nation* and with Roxy at the Knickerbocker.[255]

The much hyped opening did not fail to disappoint gathered journalists. The theater was so packed with people, famous and otherwise, that "The performance was delayed to allow the crowds to surge around the house and inspect its arrangements." The Rialto Theatre's entertainment officially began "with a blare of trumpets" followed by a "preponderance of brass, backed by a large chorus pouring forth its greeting" as the audience "rose to its feet and applauded enthusiastically." The musical prelude was topped off by the new tune "Rialto March," written for the occasion by A. Holzman. (In a clever bit of merchandising, the "Rialto March" was copyrighted, published, and sold to sheet music consumers with a photograph of Roxy and Norden's electric sign on its cover.) When the "March" was completed, Hugo Riesenfeld leapt up the steps to the Rialto's small stage, reached behind the maroon curtain and pulled out Roxy, who bowed before his cheering audience. After the two men left the stage, the Bowens projected the "Rialto Topical Digest," Roxy's amalgamation of current news, followed by two solos by Mary Ball and then a classical dance by Pauline McCorkle and Violet Marcellus. Roxy alternated between live and recorded entertainment all night, with travelogues to follow before a violin solo by S. Fidelman. Roxy then unveiled the five-reel film, *The Good Bad-Man*. A baritone solo by Alfred de Manby and a song by the theater's male quartet came next before the evening came to a close with the two-reel Keystone comedy, *The Other Man* (1916).[256]

Even magazines like *The Theatre* that had previously shunned motion pictures covered the event. Lynne Denig wrote in the journal that the Rialto's premiere was indeed "An event of moment in the amusement life of New York."[257] *Wid's* estimation, with that journal's typical sobriety, evoked Roxy's nickname in one of its earliest mentions in print:

> Well, the Rialto is open. It was a big night and everybody who is anybody in the film business was on hand. At least, it looked like they were all there, because there were distinguished guests in every row. The house is certainly a beauty. It is not the biggest theatre in the city, but Roxie can certainly be very proud of it, and truly, it is a "temple of the motion picture." The program for the opening night was an unusually fine one, and knowing Roxie's ability to pick good stuff, I would say that the Rialto is sure to be a big success. The location is undoubtedly the best in the world, because he has the best corner in New York, and a wonderful sign to attract any strangers to the "Gay White Way" who may not know where the Rialto is located.[258]

The opening of each New York theater—the Regent, Strand, Knickerbocker, and Rialto—and each film premiere he staged evoked the same congratulatory excess. In an era known for its lack of journalistic restraint, it is hard to determine how impressive these events may have been. As a body of press coverage, though, they certainly attest to Roxy's status and notoriety.

Roxy's management style, like his press coverage, had not changed much from theater to theater. He still painstakingly reviewed every film he exhibited, despite his contract with Triangle. When he booked Charlie Chaplin's film *Police* (1916) a month later, for instance, he "made no exception to his custom of insisting upon a film inspection before signing," despite the actor's growing popularity.[259] His methods for musical accompaniment and rehearsals also remained the same. *Motion Picture News* described the process of scoring, editing, and staging a film at the Rialto during this period: "Friday night we sat with Mr. Rothapfel, Dr. Reisenfeld [*sic*] and other members of the musical board of the Rialto and witnessed the selection of the music. The picture is started, a musician at the piano plays the airs suggested by Mr. Rothapfel, who stops the operator every few moments to make changes in the music, to suggest effects here and there."[260] The following night (Saturday), Roxy selected and edited together all of the footage he had received from various services for the Rialto Animated Pictorial. He then edited the travelogues and scenics.[261] After two days of editing and scoring all of the films (and live performances), Roxy woke up on Sunday morning, arrived at the theater, and began choosing the lighting and other visual and sensory effects for the entire program.[262]

The Rialto was yet another critical success, and, satisfied by his efforts there, Roxy wasted little time in shedding the Knickerbocker albatross. He announced less than a week after the Rialto opened that he could not give adequate attention to the Knickerbocker because of his new time commitments at "the Corner." With that, the Knickerbocker abruptly closed on April 29,[263] five days after the Colonial in Chicago had also dropped its Triangle exclusivity.[264]

CIRCLE THEATRE, INDIANAPOLIS, IN

The early summer months were successful ones for the Rialto, but Roxy was rarely content with only one project. The owners of the new 3,000-seat Circle Theatre in Indianapolis enlisted his services to consult on the deluxe motion picture theater's operation and management and to supervise its opening on August 30, 1916. Roxy was named to the board of directors of the Circle Theater Company, no doubt receiving financial compensation as a member of the board and as a consultant.[265]

His first trip to Indianapolis took place in early July, just over two months after the opening of the Rialto, and he returned again the following month for the Circle's grand opening.[266] The theater was originally slated to exhibit Triangle films, perhaps the reason Roxy was connected to its operation in the first place, but there was no mention of Triangle when it debuted as the largest movie house in Indiana (and one of the largest in North America).[267]

The Circle replicated the Rialto's lighting and decorative scheme, and an early advertisement noted Roxy's installation of "Scientific color lighting throughout the house, an innovation in the West, [that] will reflect the mood of the moment."[268]

The theater, like all Roxy houses, put an emphasis on film *and* music.[269] "Soloists of repute, singers with a popular appeal, will add variety to each entertainment," a Circle advertisement boasted, while highlighting its diversity of film programming: "The most noted photoplayers, the most elaborate photodramas, the liveliest comedy productions, the most wide awake picture news service and the most interesting and instructive educational subjects have been definitely arranged for."[270] The *Star* remarked that soloists would be booked to play the Circle Theatre through an exchange system with other large "photo-theaters, including the Rialto of New York," suggesting a Balaban & Katz–esque operation where talent would be booked, presumably by Roxy, and then shuttled between theaters.[271] The rest of the theater's operation was Roxy-esque: eighteen ushers were hired "under the direction of Capt. W. C. Wulff and trained in everything that an usher should know by Herman Knicke," a former employee of Roxy's Rialto in New York. Roxy also captured motion picture footage of the ushers working, for a film that was to be screened at every performance with the accompanying words, "Yours for service."[272]

By the day of its opening, August 30, all 2,200 advanced tickets had been sold with an additional 800 held out for latecomers.[273] The Circle's newspaper advertisements prominently stated that the premiere would be "Under the Personal Direction of Mr. S. L. Rothappel [*sic*] of the Rialto Theatre of New York."[274] The entertainment began at 8:00 P.M. with dedicatory addresses by A. G. Ruddell, president of the Indianapolis Chamber of Commerce, and the city's mayor.[275] These proclamations were followed by an "elaborate" musical program performed by an orchestra of twenty musicians and an organist.[276] Eduardo Ciannelli, a Neapolitan baritone who remained at the theater for the next two weeks, sang an aria from *Pagliacci*, while the "Méditation" from *Thaïs* (a typical Roxy selection) was performed by the orchestra under the direction of H. L. Spitalmy.[277] After the premiere performance, the mayor hosted an after-party in the theater's honor.[278] Deluxe motion picture exhibition had come to Indianapolis. The *Star* lavished praise on this new "model" theater (and its new advertising client), consecrating it as an acceptable mainstream attraction worthy of replication: "The Circle Theater, as its name implies, is the beginning and the end of beauty, luxury and attention to every detail that lift 'going to the movies' far above the usual idle time-killers and places it in the front rank of entertainments."[279] The *Star* added the following day that, "No one feature plays a bigger part in the life of the city of Indianapolis than the playhouse, and this is the most beautiful and complete of them all."[280]

Roxy did not stay long in Indianapolis that September, returning to New York only days after shepherding the Circle Theatre to a successful debut.[281] It is unclear how or if he remained tethered to the Circle in the years to come. He would note three years later that "At one time I also had a circuit [of theaters] about Indianapolis, but I have never regarded the circuit plan as a good idea because you cannot lend to it the personal touch."[282]

One hundred and thirty miles away from Manhattan—and perhaps even further from Roxy's thoughts—his first theater, the Family, also reopened on September 17 with the town's other celebrity, film actor Pat O'Malley, in attendance.[283] Instead of revisiting his past, Roxy was looking ahead. On November 2, the *New York Times* published confirmation of a palatial new Roxy-managed theater near the Rialto.[284] The new theater, the Rivoli, was financed once again by "Downtown" (Wall Street) money and set to rival any movie house in the area.[285]

FINAL CUT / *THE EASIEST WAY*

Despite strategizing for the new Rivoli, there was plenty of work still to be done at the Rialto. Roxy's first task was to wrest control of the theater's bookings away from his troublesome contract with Triangle in early December 1916.[286] Now, instead of booking a new Triangle film, Roxy selected the independent film *The Witching Hour* (1916). The film's exhibition was a signature Roxy production with an appeal to at least three senses: sight, sound, and smell. In addition to the music and colored lighting system that changed to "suggest the mood reflected by the unfolding plot," Roxy diffused a healthy dose of mignonette perfume through the theater's ventilation when the words "the delicate odor of mignonette, the ghost of a dead and gone bouquet" appeared on the screen.[287] In addition to their focus on sight and smell, Roxy and Riesenfeld continued to churn out accompanying film scores that were used across the country. Their score for Vitagraph's *The Girl Philippa* (1916), for instance, was used by theaters such as the Queen Theatre in Brownsville, Texas.[288] How many others may have employed this score is unknown.

Roxy's influence on the narrative and setting for the feature films he presented through accompanying music, lighting, scent, and other forms of live entertainment excludes another factor that has rarely been considered. Final cut, always assumed to be the domain of the director, producer, or distributor, was often determined by exhibitors during the silent era, in small towns where distributors were physically absent or ignored these activities, or in large cities like New York where independent exhibitors like Roxy held tremendous sway.

Eugene Walter's play *The Easiest Way* was performed at the Shubert Theatre in Minneapolis in the summer of 1913 when Roxy was still manager of the Lyric.[289] Four years later, it had become a Lewis J. Selznick–produced film and was booked by Roxy for the Rialto. Despite his selection, Roxy wasn't pleased with the film's new ending. Roxy had seen Walter's original play during its New York Broadway run and objected to Selznick's alteration. When the film arrived at the Rialto, Roxy edited the final reel, returning the narrative to its original theatrical flow. "Mr. Rothapfel knows something about art, too," the *New York Times* commented about the episode, "and although the apocryphal scenes were duly furnished him by the producers he lopped them off at the first showing yesterday and ended the picture as the play had." Members of Selznick's company who were in attendance were shocked to see Roxy's changes on opening night, and Selznick voiced his strong objections to Roxy. (Eugene Walter, who was a frequent patron at the Rialto, claimed not to care about Roxy's alterations or the ones made by Selznick.) Roxy eventually agreed to restore some of the deleted scenes, either out of deference to the man who had hosted an industry dinner in his honor two years earlier or to maintain good business relations, but he vehemently refused to reinsert Selznick's new ending, reaffirming his claim to final cut. "[S]ome of the deleted scenes were restored," the *Times* wrote, but Roxy "was adamant against the restoration of the deathbed repentance."[290]

These kinds of unilateral decisions were admired by some and hated by others. *Photoplay* wrote that Roxy was no longer "a universally popular fellow, in spite of the fact that he is New York's foremost exhibitor, and probably the most spectacular success of his kind in the world. Other exhibitors—to put it in their words—think Rothapfel is a nut." Still, the Rialto was a success and as the journal later mentioned, "Rothapfel's accomplishments have justified most of his stunts." His editorial decisions frustrated producers like Selznick, but booking a film at the Rialto was a coveted spot. At the Rialto and other Roxy houses, film was presented the Roxy way or else. "The producers used to think him a crazy egotist who criticized their films and tore them to pieces to satisfy his own vanity," the magazine continued.[291] Roxy countered that editing a film was a reluctant but central part of an exhibitor's work. "I don't like to cut pictures as a rule, but occasionally it is necessary," he later stated. "In my opinion a director should assemble his own picture. If he can't assemble,

he can't direct." Still, he argued, "As an outsider I feel that often a situation
may be changed for the better, made more dramatic, better psychology interpolated by closing up a scene, the tempo improved, and so on."[292] Though it
seems unfathomable today in an era in which domestic distributors strictly
forbid such editorial practices, the silent era exhibitor, not the producer, director, or distributor, was often the final arbiter of a film's narrative. And with
the preceding, intervening, and surrounding nature of the unitary text, the
short and feature films presented at deluxe motion picture theaters should
be understood as only one of the ingredients, blended together with many
others, that were framed and edited in ways screenwriters and directors may
never have intended.

First and National

In April 1917, Roxy found an even larger enterprise in which to exert his
authority. Two weeks after he had chopped up *The Easiest Way* (1917) to Selznick's consternation, Roxy was named president of the new First National
Exhibitors' Circuit, Inc.—an amalgamated group of exhibitors pushing back
against the growing power of Triangle, Paramount, and other distributors—
which hoped to not only pool their resources but also finance motion pictures
to fill their schedules instead of relying solely on the growing power of a few
expensive and increasingly dominant distributors.[293] Roxy had reached a new
zenith. By then, the Rothapfel name had not only become synonymous with
deluxe film exhibition, and thus his ascendancy to the president of the new
exhibition company, it was also synonymous with the most highbrow form of
motion picture entertainment. "The greatest advertisement your picture can
get is that it played my Theatre," he told actor Pat O'Malley.[294]

As his prestige grew, theaters continued to seek him out to stage premieres
and other events. In July 1917, for instance, the Saenger Company hired Roxy
to stage the first performance at the new Strand in New Orleans on August 4
and its debut film, *Wild and Woolly* (1917), starring Douglas Fairbanks. *Moving Picture World* reported that "Even the orchestra was under the personal
direction of the New York exhibitor."[295] Roxy's paid invitation was intended
to confer status upon the theater, and he delivered to the *New Orleans Times-
Picayune*: "You may say for me, and emphasize it, that there is no other theater that I have seen outside of New York that will compare with this one in
elegance of design and treatment in its furnishings. . . . I have been present
and assisted at the opening of many theaters in various parts of the country,

and I can truthfully say that I have never seen one that will equal the Strand in all of its appointments."[296] "[A]t last," Roxy told *Moving Picture World*, "the South has a real photoplay theater."[297]

Roxy's publicity machinery kicked into high gear, and he continued to promote his theater *and* his brand. Columnist Harriette Underhill noted, "Interviewing Samuel Rothapfel has been done before. In fact, every one does it nowadays. It is not a difficult thing to do, for Mr. Rothapfel is not averse to talking about himself, and you don't have to worm it out of him, either. . . . [P]eople like to have him do it. He is good copy."[298] His career accomplishments and his widespread publicity turned Roxy into film exhibition's first national star. Proof of the ubiquity of the Rothapfel name in and out of motion picture circles came when George Jean Nathan wrote about his "Musings on the Moving Pictures" in the April 1917 issue of *Vanity Fair*, dubbing the article "The Philosopher in the Rothapfel Orchard"—even though Roxy was not once mentioned in the two-page piece.[299]

Roxy and His Musicians

The Rothapfel name had become synonymous with film, but it was becoming just as well known for his use of music in accompanying motion pictures. The *Lincoln* (Nebraska) *Sunday Star* wrote on September 2, 1917, for instance:

> More and more are the managers of the larger motion picture theatres coming to an appreciation of the part that music plays in the popularity of this theatre, and today it is no unusual thing to have skilled orchestras of from ten to thirty musicians devoting their entire time to the work of rounding up and practicing appropriate music for the performances of an evening. The pioneer in this field is without question S. L. Rothapfel, the owner of the Rialto theatre in New York. It is now a well-known fact that Hugo Reisenfeld [*sic*], the leader of the Rialto orchestra draws a salary equal to that given but few of the grand opera directors. As a result of this the people at large are getting more, and learning to expect more, in the way of good music.[300]

Motion Picture News sprinkled its pages with similar accolades. "We believe that the music at the Rialto has done more than any one thing to bring pictures to a higher standard," the trade journal mentioned, "and that Rothapfel has done more than any group of men in the industry to give the presentations a substreme [*sic*] appeal."[301]

Roxy consistently demonstrated his desire but also his lack of expert skill in conducting the orchestras he managed. When Hugo Riesenfeld needed a day off (his boss apparently did not require one), Roxy did not hire a short-term replacement. Instead, he took over as conductor for two weeks.[302] When Riesenfeld had surgery in late October, Roxy conducted the now fifty-piece orchestra again and continued scoring the Rialto's films without the help of his Austrian maestro.[303] These were, of course, the sort of activities that heightened his reputation (and his megalomania), a benefit that paid off in even more press coverage. *New York Tribune* columnist Harriette Underhill wrote in 1918, "Every one knows, too, that Samuel Rothapfel can get out and lead the Rialto orchestra—yes, lead, not follow it—when he cannot read a note of music, and that he knows more about lighting and color combinations and their effect on the senses than most any one else in the world."[304]

His musical staff included members who would over time become some of the most esteemed movie palace conductors of the era, among them Erno Rapee and Nat Finston.[305] Rapee had a background similar to Riesenfeld. Born in Budapest, Hungary, on June 4, 1891, he graduated from the Budapest Conservatory in 1909 with a gold medal as a pianist and a composer. He later worked as a conductor in Europe, including a stint as an assistant to symphonic and operatic conductor Ernest von Schuch at the Dresden Opera House.[306] His piano concerto was also reportedly performed by the Philharmonic Orchestra of Vienna.[307] Rapee arrived in the United States in Hoboken, New Jersey, on October 8, 1912, with twenty dollars. His first position was as a pianist at the Monopol Restaurant at Second Avenue and 9th Street in Manhattan, making twenty-five dollars a week.[308] He next joined the Hungarian Opera Company as musical director. It was with this company, before a performance at Webster Hall, that he wrote much of the melody for perhaps his most famous song, "Charmaine," which would become one of the most popular tunes of the late 1920s and the theme song for *What Price Glory?* (1926).[309] He followed these performances with a tour of Mexico, South America, and the United States.[310] By December 1916, he was playing piano for Elmer Hoelzle at the Aeolian Hall in New York City.[311] A few months later, he made his way to the Rialto and joined one of the most talented corps of movie theater musicians ever assembled.[312] Rapee would eventually share conducting duties with Riesenfeld at the Rialto and later at the Rivoli.[313]

Despite Rapee's quick ascension, only Riesenfeld was allowed to share even some of the spotlight with Roxy. Mouthpiece for himself, mouthpiece for the

Rialto, and mouthpiece for the industry, there was no other exhibitor who had generated half the acclaim as Roxy by 1917. Whereas producers, distributors, stars, and even directors could argue over their respective clout, Roxy had no discernible rival as an exhibitor. Fox and Loew were building empires and brand names, not personal reputations, and they were always more mogul than showman. Sid Grauman was 2,500 miles and a few years away from the same kind of acclaim. Balaban & Katz were just getting underway in Chicago, while Harold Franklin was marking time in Buffalo. Those who had succeeded Roxy at the Regent and Strand were doing well, but their names and personalities were largely unheralded. How many B. A. Rolfe profiles appeared in the New York newspapers and industry trade journals? Even when Riesenfeld and Rapee reached the apex of their careers, their press coverage was still paltry in comparison. The coverage awarded to Roxy proved beyond a doubt that publicity and marketing were the new hallmarks of a successful career as an exhibitor. To reach the top, movie theater managers now had to think like showmen and market themselves like movie stars. Roxy was certainly talented, but he was also a gifted publicist who understood the press's desire for new theaters, new innovations, star-studded events, and a host of other firsts. Rolfe was the manager of yesterday's theater.

"Seeing the Rialto with Rothapfel"

By October 1917, Roxy's name was more prominent than ever before. *Motion Picture News* began a new weekly column devoted entirely to his work of presenting, scoring, and editing motion pictures, and producing the music and live performances that comprised each unitary text. The first installment of "Seeing the Rialto with Rothapfel" revealed some of Roxy's stratagems: that Roxy "spent nights inspecting pictures," that he reviewed "fifteen or twenty reels from which to select the Rialto Animated Weekly" and spent "hours going over all the weeklies and culling the most interesting features," that "Mr. Rothapfel is his own sternest critic," and that his assistants "think that the director of the Rialto is 'too fussy' about these little things." "Seeing the Rialto" also revealed another aspect of Roxy's career: he not only edited, scored, and exhibited films but also produced and directed them. Roxy, for instance, got a "'scoop' on the world" when he traveled to West Point in October and shot footage of the Japanese commission visiting the cadets. The film was then exhibited at the Rialto.[314]

An almost sickly sweet adulation of Roxy's work appeared in each week's installment of "Seeing the Rialto with Rothapfel." The *News*, genuflecting in front of their idol, wrote in the first installment:

> Seeing a "moving picture show" is one thing; seeing the Rialto show is quite another, and seeing the Rialto with Rothapfel brings one in the closest possible focus with the perfection that may be wrought by the exhibitor. If every exhibitor in the country could "See the Rialto with Rothapfel" there would be a revolution in motion pictures. They cannot, so we are going to bring you as close to this wonderful man of ideas and accomplishments here each week.[315]

The feature was instantly popular, as mail poured in to the trade journal (and to the Rialto Theatre) from around the country. "Even far away Japan is interested in what the big New York theatre is doing," the *News* noted, as Roxy received a postcard from theater manager F. Horibe of the Movie Show in Yokohama, asking for a copy of a Rialto program. "If a showman in Yokohama can get benefit out of these articles," the journal remarked, "the American exhibitor ought to get very much more."[316] This press coverage, not surprisingly, only begat more as Roxy's commitments to *Motion Picture News* increased. "One of the penalties Mr. Rothapfel pays for his prominence in the theatrical world," the *News* wrote, "is the receipt of hundreds of queer letters from queer people wanting queer things."[317] Horibe's request and the questions of countless other exhibitors prompted the trade journal to start yet another weekly feature, "Rothapfel's Answers to Exhibitors," in which the "World's Greatest Exhibitor" would "Answer Questions on Showmanship Through the News." "You all know who Rothapfel is," an advertisement for the new weekly feature remarked:

> You know what he has done for theatre after theatre. You all know the wonderful strides ahead that he has taken with the Rialto. And in a very short time you are going to see the Rivoli presenting to the world radical and wonderful developments in the exhibition of the motion picture. Mr. Rothapfel is an exhibitor pure and simple. He has won his own way in the cinema world. He has blazed the way for others to follow. He is today the most independent exhibitor in the world. He can dictate, if need be. *And with all his big undertakings commanding his time, there is no exhibitor more interested in his fellow showmen than he. It is purely out of that unselfish interest he has agreed to answer questions for the exhibitors of*

the country on the problems of presenting their pictures. You can have the benefit of his amazing experiences, his wonderful skill and his brilliant ideas without a cent of cost to you. It would be impossible for you to set out and buy this expert advice. You could not get Mr. Rothapfel to stop his work and give you the benefit of his experience with your problems in any other way.[318]

Roxy could not have asked for better publicity.

RIVOLI, NEW YORK, NY

By the end of 1917, the Rialto was still attracting nearly 10,000 patrons per day, an enormous number for a theater that seated 2,500.[319] Still, Roxy was not satisfied. When the *News* complimented him on a recent show, noting that it had "surpasse[d] anything that ha[d] before been done in a motion picture theatre," Roxy was dismissive. "Wait until the Rivoli opens," he said, "and I will show you something real."[320]

All year he had been planning the construction, design, and operation of his new and even more opulent movie house, whose name was derived from Paris's Rue de Rivoli, which connects the Musée du Louvre (pictures) with the Paris Opéra (music). Instead of the Rialto, which was just a "rebuilt theatre" in Roxy's view, the Rivoli would be, according to *Theatre Magazine*, "the realization of those dreams, a perfect home for the form of amusement which has come to be known as 'The Rothapfel Idea.'"[321] The Rivoli would, of course, have an even larger orchestra of sixty pieces, besting the Rialto and the Strand, a chorus of twenty-five, and a seat count of 2,500, giving Roxy 5,000 seats to fill each week in two theaters. The Rivoli was fully conceived as a sister theater to Roxy's other venue. While the Rialto was dubbed the "Temple of the Motion Picture," the Rivoli's new subheading would be "The Triumph of the Motion Picture."[322] Roxy imagined that the 110 musicians from both theaters would perform together weekly at the Rivoli as the Rothapfel Symphony Orchestra.[323] Roxy would note that through his new orchestras, and the replication of his musical accompaniment practices and standards throughout the country, "The motion picture has done much more for music than ever music could do for the motion picture. The motion picture has brought music to the masses."[324]

When the Rivoli finally opened, Roxy wielded unparalleled power as an exhibitor. The former Marine would soon use that position, and the size and scope of his two audiences, to generate support, enlistment, and revenue for America's fight in World War I. His weekly press coverage in trade journals and newspapers around the country would similarly be exploited to spread a message of national solidarity and militarism, while Roxy's unitary texts would become increasingly bold in their patriotic and militaristic fervor. The period between the end of 1917 and 1918 would herald in more press adulation for Roxy, a new theater, and a new relationship with national political and military leaders. A decade earlier he had been an itinerant insurance salesman in the hills of Pennsylvania. In the coming months, George Creel and the Committee on Public Information would employ Roxy to promote the American war effort.

Motion pictures were no longer merely diversionary entertainment, but an art form whose intersection with other forms of culture would change the perceptions about those who produced, exhibited, and watched them. They would, through Roxy, begin to provide an avenue for social and political engagement and advancement. Through the success of the Strand, Rialto, and Rivoli theaters, deluxe film exhibition—celebrated earlier in the Midwest and in Harlem—invaded Times Square and captured the national attention and imagination.

3. THE MOVIE HOUSE AS RECRUITING CENTER
ROXY, WORLD WAR I DOCUMENTARIES, AND
THE ENGINEERING OF CONSENT
(1917–1918)

You owe it as a duty to use your theatre in every way possible to aid the nation in making war with a full heart.
  —"Seeing the Rialto with Rothapfel," *Motion Picture News*, Oct. 20, 1917

The United States' entrance into World War I on April 6, 1917, would have far-reaching effects on the film industry and on the consecration of the movie house as a community (and propaganda) center. When the "Great War" began, there was little cooperation between Washington and the commercial film industry, still largely based in New York. However, by the end of the war, one figure above all others—Roxy—would begin to link these two disparate centers in a tenuous but inextricable partnership that has remained ever since. His work producing and exhibiting propaganda films during World War I helped link the predominately American-born, Protestant establishment in Washington with a small coterie of Jews and immigrants in New York who had begun to dominate American film exhibition, production, and distribution by 1917.

Roxy utilized his power and prestige within the film industry, as well as the captive audiences at his Rialto and Rivoli theaters, to increase military enlistment and patriotic fervor among the hundreds of thousands, if not millions, who attended his shows and read his pronouncements in industry trade journals and daily newspapers. His career took on a new dimension during this period as he directed and edited two documentaries for the Marine Corps and assembled (edited) one of three official feature-length compilation documentary films for the American government's Committee on Public Information. These films were distributed to theaters nationwide (and overseas) and were presented by Roxy at the Rialto and Rivoli alongside pro-war newsreels and patriotic stage shows that transformed him into one of the most influential American film propagandists of the era.

In order to situate Roxy within the complex legal, industrial, political, and social context of the period, and to understand his cooperation with the government to engender pro-war sentiments and encourage military enlistment, it is necessary to locate the motion picture industry within the social and political realities of life in the United States between 1914 and 1918. "Up until the end of 1916," Andrew Kelly writes, "prominent film makers attempted to persuade Americans to support President Wilson's non-intervention policy" by producing a number of influential films "which kept the neutrality flame bright." The National Board of Censorship (Review) of Motion Pictures enforced this attitude, requesting, for instance, that American newsreels with war footage display the following message before any screening: "In accordance with President Wilson's proclamation of neutrality, patrons will please refrain from expressions of partisanship during this picture." Fiction films also strenuously avoided the appearance of being partial to either side. There were some exceptions, of course, such as a *Chicago Tribune*–produced, pro-German documentary, *The German Side of War* (ca. 1915), which attracted 150,000 patrons during its first three weeks alone.[1] But these were rare throughout the war's early phase.

By 1917, after three years of global conflict, the American government's position shifted from neutrality to preparedness as it continued to supply its allies overseas. Support for America's turn away from isolationism had not been unanimous, even within Congress, and the decision to officially enter World War I was equally contested. Debate about President Woodrow Wilson's proclamation of war in early April raged on for thirteen hours in the Senate and even longer in the House of Representatives. But on April 6, 1917, the war was approved by the legislative branch and declared against Germany.[2]

Looming doubt in Washington about support for the war among German- and Irish-Americans was immediate, as was a deep suspicion about the loyalties of America's millions of new immigrants.[3] Nor were these newly hyphenated Americans the only ones who fell under an ever-watchful eye. George Creel, head of what James Mock and Cedric Larson later dubbed "America's first propaganda ministry"[4]—the Committee on Public Information—recalled the impetus for the creation of the CPI thirty years later: "The sentiment of the West was still isolationist; the Northwest buzzed with talk of a 'rich man's war' waged to salvage Wall Street loans; men and women of Irish stock were 'neutral,' not caring who whipped England, and in every state demagogues raved against 'warmongers.'[5] Michael McCarthy notes that the Division of Work with the Foreign Born, another governmental body, was tasked to "ensure the loyalty of 'hyphenated' Americans."[6] The anti-war movement of the era also stood in the way of a national consensus. This movement, Andrew Kelly writes, "was supported and often led by socialists, radicals and feminists and was a key component of the progressive tradition in American politics up to 1916."[7] "How could the national emergency be met without national unity?" George Creel later remarked, "The printed word, the spoken word, motion pictures, the telegraph, the wireless, cables, posters, signboards, and every possible media should be used to drive home the justice of America's cause."[8]

In order to pacify all of these groups, and bring them into accord with the new war effort, the government needed to address each of these increasingly vocal communities, while cloaking its foreign policy decisions within the rubrics of freedom, democracy, and, above all, patriotism. "It is our opinion that the two functions—censorship and publicity—can be joined in honesty and with profit," Creel wrote to the secretaries of State, War, and Navy on April 13, 1917.[9] The following day, Woodrow Wilson signed an executive order formally establishing the Committee on Public Information to not only promote the war through propaganda but to censor any and all public dissent in books, magazines, newspapers, and other media.[10] Creel and the CPI would publish 75 million pamphlets, 6,000 press releases, and 14,000 drawings for the war effort. The organization also printed the *Official Bulletin*, distributed to every American military camp in the world and to the nation's 54,000 post offices. Children were targeted as well, with the bi-monthly *National Service Bulletin* sent to 600,000 schools.[11]

The motion picture industry, in keeping with the CPI's mission and messaging, quickly enacted its own self-censorship, with the *Exhibitor's Trade Review* summing up this new edict in its April 21, 1917, issue. "There is no time now to discuss a producer's abstract right to make and market any kind of picture he pleases," the trade journal argued. "Probably he possesses that right. But public right takes precedence over any private right, especially in time of war."[12] Adolph Zukor and other industry leaders rationalized their lack of agency during this period by noting the ultimate benefit it would bring to the industry's business prospects. Though they could no longer effectively market anti-war films or films advocating neutrality, Zukor found a silver lining in Paramount's diminished artistic freedoms. "When the war is over," he remarked, "and the country again filled with gladness, it will be a difficult matter to wean patrons from the theaters that established a clientele during the dark hour when entertainment was not merely a pleasure but a necessity."[13] The film industry, for the first time in its history, was under a national order of (self-) censorship.

Chicagoan Donald Ryerson sought to exploit the film industry's submissiveness and approached Creel with the idea of placing patriotic speakers in movie theaters across the country where immigrants, women, socialists, Jews, Germans, Russians, and Irish-Americans, as well as a host of other groups under suspicion could easily be found and influenced.[14] These speakers would deliver overt messages of patriotism, anti-German rhetoric, and direct appeals for fundraising, enlistment, and faith in Wilson's foreign policy. Creel immediately backed the effort, creating "the Four Minute Men," an allusion to the Minutemen of the American Revolution, as well as the amount of time (four minutes) they were granted to speak between reel changes. The CPI described the government's vocal foot soldiers as "a specialized publicity service giving four-minute talks by local volunteers, introduced by a standard introduction slide furnished by the government, in the intermission at motion picture theaters in accordance with a single standard plan throughout the country." Additional speakers were conscripted to reach out to women's and children's groups, while a new Church Department was established to send even more local volunteers to proselytize at churches, synagogues, and Sunday schools.[15]

More than 75,000 volunteer speakers would deliver a total of 755,190 speeches to nearly 315 million listeners across the country. (These numbers were probably conservative.) The government would later argue that because of the "considerable number of communities" that gave incomplete or no reports at all, the audience for these speakers was probably closer to 400 million.[16] The success of these speakers lay in the CPI's modus operandi in which no other voices were allowed to compete with the Four Minute Men. Wherever they appeared, these speakers demanded absolute exclusivity—and reported the unwillingness of exhibitors and others to accept that arrangement.

Still not satisfied, the CPI looked elsewhere for more ways to engineer a consensus of militarism and nationalism that it hoped would strip away ethnic, racial, class, gender, and social differences. The CPI had already identified effective ways to reach these disparate groups at the nation's movie theaters through the Four Minute Men, but what about the rest of the motion picture program? How could they influence that material as well? How could they convert the movie house—a secular community center in the days before radio that brought together all segments of the population, where the rich supposedly rubbed elbows with the poor, and every nationality, religion, gender, and ethnic group could conceivably be found—into a satellite arm of the CPI's wishes?[17] On September 25, 1917, the CPI formerly inaugurated a new Division of Films under presidential order—an acknowledgment of the growing role of motion pictures and motion picture theaters in American society and their ability to sway public opinion. The Division of Films's first act was to begin the production, distribution, and exhibition of official (mostly nonfiction) war films. The Division argued that it was the duty of average Americans to see these films and an obligation by local exhibitors to present them.[18]

Creel selected *Hearst's Magazine* advertising manager Charles Hart, and not a film industry veteran, to oversee the CPI's new film division. By Hart's own account, he "knew nothing about films" but "was chosen for the post because I obviously had an independent attitude, and not being commercially interested in films could not be accused of having an axe to grind."[19] Hart, like Creel, seemed to trust no one within the film industry and sought to "have the government itself present the pictures," thereby bypassing the disproportionately Jewish and immigrant film moguls, executives, and exhibitors as the CPI, George Creel would later note, "went into the motion-picture business as a producer and exhibitor."[20] Dennis Sullivan, Clare de Lissa Berg, Chester Campbell, William Rose, Dean Matthews, William Grant, Rufus Steele, T. S. Barrett, Marcus Beeman, E. M. Anderson, George Bowles, and Robert Rinehart served under Hart.[21] "It is evident," *Moving Picture World* complained at the time, "that the Government and its auxiliary agencies have gone into motion picture production, distribution, and exhibition with a minimum of counsel from the wise heads of the industry and the maximum of direction by those unacquainted with the films."[22] "The motion picture industry was anxious to help," Jack Warner would later argue, "but because the government controlled the entire war film production program, there were no great inspirational pictures made."[23]

Still, a tenuous working agreement did begin between Washington and the film industry. A War Co-operation Committee was established in July 1917 to ensure that the film industry complied with the government's new strategy of promotion and censorship. Roxy was among those called to service by the government and appointed to assist the Department of the Interior, alongside Richard A. Rowland of Metro Pictures.[24] Exhibitors, too, were eager to assist. Leslie Midkiff DeBauche argues that this form of "practical patriotism" was typical, with the film industry excited by "an opportunity to help disseminate government propaganda while at the same time improv[ing] its image with those who might wish to interfere in its business affairs."[25] She notes that "the-ater managers allied themselves with the war effort in visible ways designed to attract trade and to build the base of their regular clientele. . . . In the short term, these tactics helped exhibitors to fill the seats in their theaters; the long term hope was that they would function strategically and help to institutional-ize the theater within the community."[26]

Another reason for the industry's compliance was the threat of closure as a "nonessential" industry that, it could be claimed, sapped resources from the war effort. The issuance of such a judgment would, of course, have been highly subjective, but it was a serious and looming threat nonetheless for an industry dominated by Jews during an era of intense anti-Semitism and popu-lated with immigrants at a time rife with xenophobia. Herbert Hoover, then with the United States Food Administration (and later an intimate friend of Louis B. Mayer), was one of several who came to the industry's defense. He stated that because of the film industry's efforts in lending the screen (and movie theater stages) to government propaganda, "at the present moment there is no necessity to close the moving pictures as non-essentials. . . . They are educational and they have great value from a moral point of view. War does not imply the abolition of recreation so long as it is not wasteful of natu-ral resources." Secretary of the Treasury William McAdoo also mentioned that movie theaters had become beneficial propaganda centers: "The majority of the moving picture theatres of the country have placed themselves unreserv-edly at the disposal of the Government for the furtherance of Liberty Loan, War Savings, and other Government movements, and deserve the thanks of the country for their patriotic attitude. I should look upon it as a misfortune if moving pictures or other clean forms of amusement in America should be abolished." And then there were other officials, like Harry A. Garfield, son of former President James Garfield, who served as head of the Federal Fuel Administration during World War I, whose approval of movies and movie theaters as government propaganda instruments was far less subtle. "So far as I have any personal conviction in the matter," he wrote to George Creel, "I am frank to say that I consider the motion picture, properly controlled, as having distinct educational value, and as well being a legitimate amusement which I see no present need of the government curtailing."[27] The message was clear (and Garfield's letter was reprinted in *Motion Picture News*): as long as the film industry followed the wishes of the government, it would remain in business. Anything less could mean an immediate shutdown.

Although DeBauche is correct in her assertion that the industry was mo-tivated by these commercial self-interests and the threat of closure by the government as a nonessential industry, there was more at stake than just wartime profits and post-war benefits. Issues related to culture, ethnicity, religion, assimilation, and class were ultimately bound up in the World War I activities of the industry's War Cooperating Committee, which included many Jews (and immigrants) such as William Fox, Adolph Zukor, Lewis Selznick, Jesse Lasky, Joseph Schenck, Marcus Loew, and Carl Laemmle. This was a moment to prove that the industry's executives and exhibitors were 100% American.

Samuel Rothapfel had, on paper, one of the most suspicious of backgrounds for the CPI—he was an immigrant with a German surname. While Roxy's younger brother Max never shielded his German-born status on census and other official documents, Roxy had always hidden his immigrant roots by listing Stillwater, Minnesota, as his birthplace.[28] If his Germanic origins had been known, it might have cast considerable suspicion.[29] Roxy had earned a national platform, though, thanks to his unequalled career in film exhibition and, more importantly, was one of the very few motion picture executives who had also served in the military.

Roxy now became an unabashed propagandist for the war effort. When the United States entered the conflict the following year and the CPI's Division of Films began churning out its *Official War Review*, Roxy signed up immediately. Beginning with between 6,000 and 8,000 feet of footage each week supplied by the CPI and other newsreel services, Roxy and his staff trimmed the Rialto Animated Pictorial down to between 2,500 and 3,000 feet of carefully composed reels that would "appear in the right psychological order."[30] He used the extensive press coverage he received in *Motion Picture News* each week (see Chapter 2) to advocate for the use of wartime newsreels that followed his narrative structure, beginning with

marching troops or some subject that will immediately enthuse the audience and then follow in sequence, such as the troops arriving at camp, their embarkation on transports, their arrival in France, then intimate scenes showing them in their billets or on the front line. You see this gives you a sequel and will hold the interest of the audience for about ten to fifteen minutes. . . .Then we start another sequel—it might be concerning activities at home, such as conservation, war activities, etc. This, of course, has a relation to the first unit, then we continue with war work, women's activities, such as the Red Cross, war charities, etc. After that comes the foreign element which of course includes all our Allies. . . . Last of all we generally wait for the Punch.[31]

To secure the desired emotional response to the climax—what Roxy referred to as the "Punch"—he employed the same theatrical and presentation tools he had developed over the past decade, relying heavily on music to conjure emotion. In one newsreel presentation, he used two projectors to overlay scenes from *Joan the Woman* (1916) with newsreel footage of French troops marching amid the ruins. "The music that we used for this subject was the 'Allegro Movement' from Robespierre Overture, by Littolf, and as Joan appeared we raised our trumpets high and started the chorus of the 'Marseillaise' which took the people right out of their seats," Roxy recalled. "The applause lasted nearly a minute and a half after the picture had closed and didn't cease for a moment but instead grew louder and louder and held up our performance."[32]

Roxy also added sound effects to newsreel images of big guns firing, advising exhibitors to use "a simultaneous crash of cymbals and then a rumble on the organ with the biggest pipes we have."[33] More than effects, though, it was music that "really lifted the war film," David Mould notes.[34] Roxy replaced Germanic music with largely American compositions and told the nation's exhibitors in *Motion Picture News* (and other journals) to use wartime tunes such as "My Dough Boy," "Keep the Home Fires Burning," and "Good Bye Broadway, Hello France."[35] When Allied armies were shown on screen, Roxy advised the use of their respective national anthems.[36] So many requests for patriotic, American music had already been made by May 1917, just one month after the American entry into the war, that the Rialto needed to hire two additional trumpeters.[37] At the Rialto, *Motion Picture News* commented, "you are led to the spiritual plane where you do not force yourself to applause to show that you are a good American, but where you are carried away on the tide of sentiment."[38]

The rising popularity of American music was an outgrowth of the nation's virulent anti-German sentiment that caused once-popular German music and musicians to quickly fall out of favor. The Metropolitan Opera programmed no German operas during the 1917–1918 seasons and dismissed five of their German opera singers in December 1917.[39] "A gathering storm has been observed for some time," *Musical Courier* wrote that November, "closing about the heads of unnaturalized musicians of German birth and with Teutonic affiliations and sympathies."[40]

Against this nationalistic backdrop, movie house conductors/composers like Hugo Riesenfeld, Roxy's Vienna-born conductor, immediately arranged patriotic American music for the Rialto's newsreels, stage shows, and feature films. "The war will awaken the real American spirit—our best democratic instincts—and that will surely be reflected in our musical life," Riesenfeld remarked in February 1918. "Good music will move the masses as never before."[41] The Rialto's appeal to patriotism was typified in its use of "Onward Christian Soldiers" as a musical backdrop to a Red Cross parade in the "Rialto Animated Magazine" in mid-October 1917. *Motion Picture News* remarked that the combination generated thunderous applause:

> How many managers through the country would think of this musical selection in connection with this news scene? All over the U. S. A. the orchestra will be playing martial music well enough, but when you come to think of it there is only one air that really fits the picture, and that was "Onward Christian Soldiers." We were present Saturday evening when Mr. Rothapfel was spending several hours going over various news reels which he inspects in making up his week. The moment that the first of the pictures of the parade were shown he turned to Dr. Riesenfeld and suggested the air. . . . Here is the thing that makes Rothapfel the master. These ideas come to him on the jump; he doesn't have to "study" over them.

The trade journal added that this was but one example among many of the Rialto's approach. While music was typically used to gin emotions, Roxy's use of sound effects could also be used for similar effect during the same presentation.

> To-day, with this country in the war, and most of the subjects bearing more or less on the great fight, the news section of the program is one of the most important parts. Rothapfel put over another one in the closing part of this Animated Magazine picture showing young American aviators in training. These are really remarkable pictures, taken from one of the airships. There wasn't any music at all with this, only the effect of the whirring motors and the splash as the planes hit the water, or the murmur as they rose into the air. The audience sat spellbound through this part of the picture and then burst into applause, and in every handclap one could almost hear the cry of admiration for the young men who are to win battles for Democracy in the clouds. . . . It's not the cheap sort of ballyhoo patriotism, either. It perfects unison of the picture and the music that stirs the better things in every heart. We'd hate to think how a friend of the Kaiser felt after sitting through a Rathapfel [*sic*] presentation.[42]

Roxy, always conscious of the psychological effect of music on his audience, selected the popular standard "Over There" to accompany one week's "Rialto

Animated Magazine" featuring American troops in France. "The effect of the good-by to the first troops and the others already 'over there,'" *Motion Picture News* reported, "was so striking as to come home quickly to every one."[43]

In mid-November 1917, Roxy contributed once again to the war effort by leading the "Our Boys in France Tobacco Fund," donating five percent of the Rialto's gross receipts to the fund and urging others to do the same in a letter to exhibitors published in *Motion Picture News*: "Write today to Our Boys in France Tobacco Fund notifying them that you will do this. Our fighting men somewhere in France will know and will not forget. Do your bit." He also sent a letter to "every known exhibitor in the country" urging them to follow suit.[44] First National Exhibitors Circuit, of which Roxy had recently been appointed president, immediately backed the effort.[45] The *Motion Picture News*, using a more forceful approach, chastised exhibitors who did not fall in line. "You are not going to war," the trade journal wrote. "The men who are need all the comforts you can give them. Help them get cigarettes. That is your patriotic duty. . . . Don't be a slacker!"[46]

Week after week, the trade journals spoke of Roxy's influence on the industry and its efforts to support the war. The *News* commended his innumerable efforts to raise funds, enlistment, and patriotism in his theaters, writing that "Rothapfel is performing a service to the nation in his spurs to patriotism. If we had iron crosses and medals of the Legion of Honor and the like his breast should be heavy with them."[47] The journal added a month later that,

> [A]nyone who does not leave the [Rialto] theatre at least a more active American in the cause of his country certainly lacks the red corpuscles in his blood. To tax a theatre that is doing what the Rialto is doing is injustice; better had the Government pay such a motion picture house a bonus. And every one of you can aid your country along the same line—all can contribute something to the national cause through your screen and your music. And you can do it with the feeling that you are giving the public just what it wants—if you show the pictures in that spirit that warms the heart—and not in the spirit of exploitation. Rothapfel does not advertise his patriotism: the Rialto reveals it.[48]

The laudatory praise was relentless and served to goad others into following Roxy's example. "When the medals are pinned on, there will be several exhibitors in these United States who will step forward to hear their names praised as 'princes,' 'bricks' and other things which in America denote titles of the highest sort," the *News* added.[49]

Roxy's work, and that of exhibitors across the country, quickly conferred a new national status on motion pictures and motion picture theaters. A *Chicago Tribune* editorial stated, for instance, that "The moving picture theaters are becoming community centers of patriotism. The producers are turning out films reflecting the American war spirit, and the majority of the theater owners have devoted a part of each program to pictures and slides calculated to arouse support of the Government."[50] The presentation of war-related newsreels, of course, was only one part of a Roxy theater's overall program. Stage shows often incorporating active soldiers were another popular attraction at Roxy's wartime venues.

THE RIVOLI OPENS

In addition to his day-to-day management of the Rialto, which included all of the work editing and scoring motion pictures and producing the live entertainment presented there, Roxy was also overseeing the construction and development of his newest theater: the 2,000-seat Rivoli at 49th Street and Broadway in Manhattan. With its premiere on December 28, 1917, Roxy now managed two of the most important movie theaters in the country. Its opening was also a historiographical bookmark, coming at the end of the so-called "transitional era" which some film historians mark as beginning in 1908, the year Roxy's own career began at the Family Theatre in Forest City, Pennsylvania, and ending in 1917 with the growth of the vertically integrated film industry.[51] The opening of the Rivoli, the newest deluxe theater, marked a fitting end to the period.

Roxy used the Rivoli's debut to give a visual and aural expression to his pro-American zeal. The first portion of the theater's opening program was given over to a massive stage show titled "The Victory of Democracy," which consisted of a series of recitations with music, a chorus of thirty voices, and stage performers "giving a history of freedom in the U.S.," according to a *Variety* reviewer.[52] The journal estimated the stage show's running time at twenty-three minutes, but *Motion Picture News* placed it closer to seventeen minutes, shortened from its originally conceived thirty-minute length.[53] "The Victory of Democracy" was "conceived, planned and produced" by Roxy and consisted of eight episodes: "The Pilgrims," "The Minute Men," "Bunker Hill," "The First Stars and Stripes in Battle," "The Star Spangled Banner," "The Battle Hymn of the Republic," "Lincoln at Gettysburg," and "Pershing in France."[54] The pageant concluded with the chorus singing: "The Liberty Legions sweep on through the sea/While over them flutters the Flag of the Free/Our millions united have answered the call/ For the rights of the world and Freedom of all."[55] Roxy used rifles loaned by the United States Navy to add an air of authenticity to the spectacle.[56]

The *Exhibitor's Trade Review* wrote that the opening was "one of the most pretentious affairs that have occurred in local theatricals in many months. Everyone connected with the motion picture industry in New York City, several from out of town and many public officials were among the first night audience."[57] Roxy invited President Wilson to the opening ("HOPING AGAINST HOPE THAT HIS EXCELLENCY WILL ATTEND"), setting aside a private box for what he dubbed in a telegram sent to Creel, "THE GREATEST EVENT IN THE HISTORY OF NEW YORK THEATRICALS."[58] The war, however, kept Wilson tethered to Washington, D. C. The president sent foreign policy advisor Edward "Colonel" House as his official representative.[59]

The Unbeliever (1918)

The Rivoli, like the Rialto, was a venue for Roxy's unique mix of propaganda, sentimentality, and entertainment. The theater's presentation of *The Unbeliever* (1918), for instance, a film "Produced in Co-operation with the U.S. Marine Corps"[60]—an alliance that apparently annoyed the CPI, which was not consulted for its approval—employed much of Roxy's skill assembling musical scores, editing films, and presenting them.[61] Roxy edited and retitled the film for its New York debut—a typical but often overlooked part of his work in the 1910s and 1920s—for which distributor George Kleine paid him $1,000.[62] Roxy later stated that his revision of the Alan Crosland–directed film was deemed "very satisfactory from all points of view."[63] Roxy's legendary sentimentality was on full display during rehearsals in which he was "overcome by tears when the Marine Corps colors were brought on the stage" and then "sobbed audibly through the reading of 'Semper Fidelis' by Forrest Robinson."[64]

Marine Corps General Barnett appeared on the film's opening night along with "a squad of marines under Corporal Sammy Nolan, [and] a well-known bugler . . . stationed at the theatre."[65] In addition, the film "was introduced by the appearance of a squad of marines from a nearby station."[66] *Motion Picture News* lauded the performance, calling it "Unquestionably the most striking presentation ever given a motion picture. It was a splendid opportunity and Mr. Rothapfel showed his genius to the fullest and employed all of the wonderful effects that were at his command to create the most striking scenes that probably have ever been witnessed in a motion picture theatre." The trade journal reminded readers:

> You probably know that before the beginning of his business career he was a member of the U. S. Marines. . . . That was one of the reasons why he was able to obtain a large detachment of marines for the whole week at the Rivoli. Another reason was that the Government has recognized the splendid propaganda for patriotism that Mr. Rothapfel has done at his theatres and knew that in the presentation of this picture he would arouse the enthusiasm for this branch of the service as it probably never had been aroused in a theatre. . . . There have been some wonderful demonstrations of patriotism in the New York theatres, but we have never seen anything like this one.[67]

Roxy, always convinced of the purity of the causes he championed, explained his efforts in his weekly column to exhibitors, advising them to treat their flag and country with reverence:

> This week we are co-operating with the Marine Corps, and, while we are presenting a picture which is purely propaganda, still [the presentation] is in good taste. . . . Using the national anthem indiscriminately—merely for cheap advertising purposes—shouting from the housetops—is not good taste. Indeed, it is almost desecrative. Love, reverence, respect for the colors and the national anthem are to be held sacred. Our national symbols ought not be cheapened or debased by crude commercialism. . . . Propaganda work at all times is a thing not to be desired. Frankly, I abhor it, except where the best interests of our country are connected—and then it is to be used in the very best taste possible. . . . Don't rave about your patriotism. Don't advertise that you *are* playing the anthem, but do it because you *want* to do it.[68]

While his influence during this period remains hard to measure quantitatively, one aspect, at least, of Roxy's prologue was duplicated elsewhere for the film. When *The Unbeliever* was later presented in Chicago, active Marines appeared in the live prologue.[69]

LIEUTENANT ROTHAPFEL

Roxy was, by now, the most vocal and important proponent of propaganda in the motion picture industry. He was also, columnist Harriette Underhill wrote in the *New York Tribune*, "the man who has done such great things in the motion picture world that he has a whole continent talking about him."[70] On March 18, 1918, three weeks after his presentation of *The Unbeliever*, Roxy reenlisted in the class 4C reserves of the Marine Corps as a first sergeant and was assigned to recruiting duty, a task he had last performed officially in Norfolk, Virginia, in 1905. He was placed under the command of Major Parker, head of the Marine Corps Publicity Bureau, and tasked to "give his attention in the distribution of motion pictures."[71] He was discharged on April 2 and appointed second lieutenant on April 3. *The Recruiters' Bulletin* wrote that he would subsequently "superintend the work of making movies for the Publicity Bureau" and was "planning some special features that will be filmed by the Bureau photographers in the near future."[72] Other duties included staging military-themed events, including a personal appearance in full Marine uniform at a Liberty Bond rally at the Rivoli, helping to raise $34,900.[73] Roxy also later served as director of the Moving Picture Bureau of the National Publicity Committee, working to support the United War Work Campaign.[74]

Roxy, now officially serving the U.S. government, announced that he had reached an agreement with Otto Kahn, chairman of the board of the Metropolitan Opera, to lease the prestigious Metropolitan Opera House for the exhibition of British, French, and American war films to raise money for the military campaign. Kahn, brother of Rialto co-owner Felix Kahn, had achieved an elevated social position in New York thanks to a highly successful career on Wall Street. The financier offered little resistance to Roxy's idea, allowing, for the moment, motion pictures to enter a top society venue formerly off limits to film. Kahn, the *New York Times* noted, was won over by the "patriotic purpose of showing war films" and the revenue it would generate for the government through the added war tax placed on ticket sales.[75] The board of directors of the Metropolitan Opera, though, had a change of heart, noting that it had only agreed to allow Roxy's exhibition of D. W. Griffith's film *Hearts of the World* (1918) and no other motion pictures. When that film's American release was delayed until May 1918 due to its English premiere, the opera house was already booked for the season and the board cancelled the plan outright, using the scheduling conflict as a convenient escape clause.[76]

FLYING WITH THE MARINES (1918) / DEVIL DOGS (1918)

Roxy's skills and his military background were instead put to other uses. A month later, Roxy and five other "official Marine Corps movie men" sailed

from New York to Paris Island, South Carolina, and Miami, Florida, to supervise the filming of a new documentary, *Flying with the Marines* (1918).[77]
(Wire services, reporting what sounds like typical Roxy-esque publicity, noted
that Roxy spotted a German U-boat off the coast of South Carolina while
sailing to Key West aboard the *Comal*.)[78] To shoot the Marine Corps aviation
film, two motion picture and three still cameras were used to expose roughly
15,000 feet of film and to take hundreds of still images.[79] Footage captured by
Quartermaster Sergeants John M. La Mond and Freeman H. Owens under
Roxy's direction featured Marine Corps pilots flying, diving, and performing
maneuvers in a show of strength and preparedness for battle. La Mond shot
his footage inside an airplane while performing loops, tail spins, and nose
dives. The three-reel film was then edited by Roxy, who was also in charge
of its publicity campaign in New York.[80] The *Times* reported that "Advance
notices describe the pictures, which were made under Mr. Rothapfel's supervision at Miami, as the most thrilling of their kind ever shown."[81] The film was
"Mr. Rothapfel's personal production," the newspaper added in asserting his
authorial control, "having been made under his direction at aviation camps
in the South and arranged and edited by him."[82]

After post-production work was completed on *Flying with the Marines*,
Roxy traveled to Marine Corps camps at Paris Island and Quantico, Virginia,
to direct a second squad of cameramen shooting Marine Corps training footage for another documentary he directed and edited, *Devil Dogs* (1918).[83] The
film, the *New York Times* wrote, showed Marines "being trained and drilled
for just such work as those in France are now doing." When the film debuted
at the Rialto on June 9, 1918, it was accompanied by "a timely program" that
featured Greek Evans singing "The Americans Come" "in a costume and setting suggestive of France." The film, when exhibited by Roxy, was reportedly
"received with enthusiastic applause."[84]

Two weeks later, Roxy's *Flying with the Marines*, "made and released in
conformity with the regulations of the War Department and the Committee
on Public Information," was given an opening week run at Roxy's posh Rivoli
theater on June 23, 1918.[85] Heywood Broun reported in the *New York Tribune*
that, "at the Rivoli, O. Henry's saccharine little story 'Sisters of the Golden
Circle' is distinctly secondary to the film called Flying with the Marines.'"[86]
The Rivoli gave *Flying with the Marines* top billing in all caps, above all other
attractions.[87] Roxy announced that it would be "Marine Week at the Rivoli,"
with *Flying with the Marines* and other aviation films screened together with
personal appearances by "Marines from Brooklyn and Philadelphia, accompanied by one of the bands of their corps, [who] will be on duty at the theatre

every day."[88] Throughout the war, Roxy and other exhibitors would match filmic depictions of World War I and military training with live servicemen in his theaters, coupling the silent and cinematic soldiers on screen with their corporeal representations on stage and in the lobby. Marines were both matinee idols and everyday Joes—exemplary to an audience watching them on screen, but human enough that any patron could also become a "devil dog."

The reviews for *Flying with the Marines* boosted Roxy's new profile as a film editor and director. "No such spectacular pictures of flying have been shown before," Heywood Broun commented. "The film is beautiful as well as exciting. In the field of pure action the motion picture has never done anything more praiseworthy than 'Flying with the Marines.' "[89] Broun's opinion did not waver and he praised the film the following month, commenting that it was both "a model for American war films" and "by far the most thrilling war picture."[90] *Moving Picture World* also heralded it as "an epoch in aviation photography,"[91] while the *New York Times* worshipped at Roxy's altar:

> What stage or book or poem, for example, can bring airplanes with such a great part of their fascination to people all over the world as does S. L. Rothapfel's "Flying With The Marines"! What journeys one may take to strange lands, to beautiful places, to centres of life—via the screen! . . . What an impression of the war in its actuality and its meaning motion pictures can give, and what an invaluable record of the war they are making for posterity! . . . What possibilities has the screen in the entertainment of spectators in theatres, in the instruction of children in schools, in the spread of knowledge and culture, in supplementing telephone, telegraph, and transportation in bringing together the peoples of the world! Its opportunities are literally immeasurable—and in consequences, its responsibility is tremendous.[92]

Stephen Pendo notes that the film "was certainly intended to 'sell' Marine aviation," and did so stealthily with a modicum of overt propaganda fed to the public as mere actuality.[93] In addition to its theatrical distribution, the United States Marine Corps Publicity Bureau also used the film as a morale booster and training film.[94]

The retrospective importance of these and other nonfiction films has long been overlooked. The war not only generated a large volume of propaganda motion pictures, fictional and nonfictional, but created a growing critical, industrial, and popular appetite for all types of documentaries. Between 1917 and 1918, the popularity of nonfiction films rose with both audiences and critics, and the genre was increasingly being distinguished from "photoplays" because of their (supposedly) nonfictional characteristics. The *New York Times* mentioned that the production and exhibition of Roxy's documentaries were among many at the time that celebrated the sensationalistic aspects of world events and cultures:

> Encouraged (thank heaven!) by his success in the venture of featuring "Flying with the Marines," a pictorial from unusual life, instead of a photoplay, S. L. Rothapfel will present "Among the Cannibal Isles" at the top of his program at the Rivoli this week, the remainder of the bill being made up of music and short film subjects, including the Official War Review and the animated news. In selecting as his feature such a film as, judging from advanced notices, Martin Johnson's seems to be, Mr. Rothapfel, as maintained in these columns before, is promoting the highest development of the motion picture by giving it a chance in its most promising field.[95]

The *Times* added that audiences watching the innumerable documentaries and newsreels presented at the Rivoli and Rialto "will realize that Mr. Rothapfel has once more got away from monotonous movie routine and given them a chance to see something that raises the motion picture beyond the reach of those who would keep it trash."[96] The *Times*' and other publications' middlebrow valorizations of colonial fantasies such as *Among the Cannibal Isles of the South Pacific* (1918) and propagandistic pageantry like *Flying with the Marines* were an important development that helped usher in the production and exhibition of other feature-length nonfiction films such as *Nanook of the North* (1922) and *Grass* (1925) in the decade that followed. (It is worth noting that Roxy would help catapult *Nanook* into the mainstream four years later.)

Roxy and the Four Minute Men

Coupled with his reenlistment in the Marine Corps, Roxy could not have been blamed for feeling comfortable even in a time of fear, xenophobia, and censorship. Yet perhaps he had forgotten his religious and ethnic background. He would soon learn that no one in those charged times was above the fray—anyone could be caught up in the red-baiting and fear-mongering of the period. Anti-war and anti-government rhetoric was not only treated with scorn but with the threat of imprisonment. Foreign-born musicians and other artists had already been arrested and placed in internment camps. Dennis J. Sullivan of the CPI was perhaps the most blunt about the CPI's public threats against exhibitors who did not comply with government demands. He told the *New York Tribune*, while "laughing at the recollection," that an exhibitor had come to his office and was uninterested in booking the CPI's official films. He asked the exhibitor, "Don't you know . . . that it is your duty to show these pictures in your theatre?" Sullivan recalled that the man "shrugged his shoulders and muttered: 'Show me where I can make as much money as I can out of Charlie Chaplin and I'll take it.' So I let him go, and in a few minutes he came rushing back and said: 'Say, mister, I'll take that picture. You must think I'm a Hun.' And he insisted on paying a great deal more for it than I was asking him. Either his conscience got to working or he began to think about those internment camps."[97] Pro-war compliance was demanded, not requested.

Four days before his successful exhibition of *Devil Dogs*, on June 5, 1918, Joseph B. Thomas of the New York Division of Four Minute Men notified Roxy that he would be sending Dr. David H. Holmes to speak at the Rialto on June 12, followed by an appearance at the Rivoli on June 13. In his letter to Roxy, Thomas wrote, "Now that the drives are over and life is running along as usual, we will again resume sending some of 'President Wilson's Propagandists,' as the Germans call them, to your houses . . . giving you a week's notice as usual."[98] Roxy was either too busy preparing for the exhibition of his first documentary or he simply ignored Thomas because of his own growing commercial and artistic distaste for the Four Minute Men and their intrusion into his programming.[99] Instead of responding quickly to Thomas's letter, Roxy let it go unanswered. On June 11, Thomas wrote Roxy again, accusing him of ignoring his first communication and demanding to know why the Four Minute Men were not being allowed to speak at his theaters. Thomas remarked, with little subtlety, that theater managers everywhere were allowing his group to speak, except for those, he wrote, "with clearly marked bolsheviki characteristics." His letter took on an even more menacing tone when he questioned Roxy's patriotism and loyalty, writing that the lecture to be presented by the Four Minute Men that week "cannot possibly annoy anyone except possibly those whose Americanism may be under suspicion." Finally, Thomas brought his provocative communiqué to its inevitable conclusion, expressing in one sentence the implicit threat that pervaded the industry's fears—especially in light of Robert Goldstein's imprisonment for producing the "treasonous" film *The Spirit of '76* (1917) and the deportation and internment of foreigners. Thomas reminded Roxy that his words and deeds were under constant surveillance, as were those of other exhibitors in a position of cultural power.

"Washington requires weekly reports from us as to the attitude of New York managers," Thomas wrote, "and will no doubt be surprised if I am forced to report my present understanding of your unwillingness to co-operate."[100]

Roxy was enraged. He and Thomas engaged in a series of acrimonious phone calls in which Roxy stated that Thomas's behavior was "most dictatorial and if, I may say so, very discourteous." He quickly fired off two letters, the first to Thomas and the second to George Creel, his powerful ally in Washington.[101] Thomas's bullying tactics would probably have been met with submission by any other exhibitor than Roxy. However, he managed the two most powerful theaters in New York City, and his presentation of pro-war, patriotic documentaries, newsreels, feature films, music, and stage shows, in addition to his work as a propaganda filmmaker for the government, placed him in a position of strength that no other exhibitor (or motion picture industry executive) held. Roxy, instead of cowering, was defiant. "I am compelled to ask you not to send any speakers either to the Rialto or to the Rivoli until such time as I have taken up the question at issue with our attorneys," he wrote to Thomas and added:

No one, I am sure, will ever accuse us here of being un-American or of not doing everything in our power to help the government. The results of our co-operation [with the Four Minute Men] during the Liberty Loan and Red Cross drives are a matter of record and are most gratifying, both as to the Rialto and the Rivoli. . . . All of us here are doing everything in our power to help the government in every possible way. Nevertheless, we feel that those two drives hurt the attendance at both theatres to such an extent that instead of being in a condition of absolute prosperity, as they were before the drives began, they are now struggling for existence. It is not that the management is personally opposed to having your men speak here but when they do speak the people who make up our audiences simply stay away. . . . If I could grant your request, and thought it would do any good, I would do so, even at the risk of sacrificing still more patronage and running the two houses at an absolute loss, but that in turn would involve a direct loss to the government which you do not seem to take into consideration. When business is poor the government suffers proportionately through loss of the revenue derived from the war tax on tickets. That revenue is of greater value, in our opinion, than anything which can be gained by having some speaker try to drive home points to an audience which has paid us money to be entertained. I have no moral right to do anything else but entertain them unless I can introduce propaganda in an entertaining way, which everyone will admit we are doing with marked success.[102]

Roxy argued further that Thomas's challenge to his allegiance was an outrageous slap and had ignored both his devotion as a civilian and as an enlisted man. "I surely cannot be accused of being pro-German or of being in sympathy with the unspeakable Hun," he cautioned Thomas. "If need be I would gladly give up my life in our country's cause. I am at the command of the Marine Corps, to be sent anywhere they like at any time and I am ready to go." He remained adamant that the Four Minute Men could not return to his theaters. "I am not giving you my opinion of this matter alone," he advised Thomas, "but have taken up the question from many angles and it is unanimously agreed that I would be making a grave mistake at this time if I allowed any more speakers to speak from my stages."[103] Roxy may have been an important propagandist of the era, but he was also a businessman and this type of proselytizing was bad for business.

Roxy next fired off a letter to George Creel, pleading to be relieved of any obligation to allow the Four Minute Men to speak at his theaters. He complained that while some of the speakers were well educated, "others were so illiterate and used such bad taste and were so undignified that it was pitiful. The class and reputation and dignity of these two theaters must be upheld," Roxy argued, however divided he may have felt between his responsibilities as a theater employee and as an enlisted Marine. "If we are compelled to allow speakers in our theatres despite the fact that in my opinion the amount of good that might be done will be greatly offset by the loss to the government in money," Roxy wrote, "why 'Kismet'—I will do my best, but not until I am ordered to do so will I allow it."[104] Creel responded to Roxy two weeks later with a deferential letter. He wrote that he would send William McCormick Blair, then national head of the Four Minute Men, to New York to speak with Roxy personally in an attempt to come to some accord. That Creel, then one of the most powerful men in the nation, head of America's propaganda machine, and a close political ally of the president, deferred to Roxy's judgment on what was best for his theaters spoke to his growing political and cultural stature. Roxy, despite his background was still a powerful ally in the fight to build (and maintain) a national consensus for the war and for Wilson's policies among the multiple class, ethnic, racial, and religious groups who regularly attended his theaters. "I do not wish to work the slightest inconvenience to you," Creel wrote, carefully trying not to upset his New York ambassador, ". . . so I beg that you will talk the matter over frankly and fully with Mr. Blair."[105]

The Thomas/Rothapfel matter was never publicly reported and has remained an unexcavated episode in the history of the CPI. Joseph Thomas's chilling language, full of red-baiting and implicit and explicit threats, provides an important look at the coercive power of a national propaganda initiative and reemphasizes how, despite Roxy's (unique) ability to push back against Thomas's demands, no one was truly above suspicion—even a Marine Corps lieutenant and one of the nation's most accomplished propagandists. Throughout the war, suspicions existed between the government and the heads of the American film industry, creating rifts that would not be healed until World War II when the Office of War Information commissioned films from Frank Capra, William Wyler, Walt Disney, John Ford, John Huston, and others.[106] "Hyphenated Americans" like Roxy always seemed to be under suspicion during times of internal and external strife. Yet it was Roxy's unique military background among the other New York Jewish moguls, as well as his artistic prowess, his influence among the industry, and his sizable immigrant and native audiences of all classes that made him the ideal choice for the production and exhibition of fiction and nonfiction war films and afforded him the political protection of George Creel and the CPI. Because of this stature, the battle between Roxy and Thomas, which would most likely have taken a different course for any other exhibitor, was short-lived and quickly forgotten.

PERSHING'S CRUSADERS (1918) / AMERICA'S ANSWER (1918)

With the government's trust in him assured, the CPI looked to Roxy to edit, direct, and/or exhibit additional films. In early 1918, the Division of Films produced its first feature-length compilation documentary, *Pershing's Crusaders* (1918), edited by Herbert C. Hoagland.[107] The film premiered in Cincinnati on April 29, 1918, before securing exhibition at New York's Lyric Theatre on May 21.[108] Advertisements for the film were provocative, with some invoking images of the Crusades depicting American soldiers with a cross on their chest on the battlefield.[109] Other advertisements touted the film's visceral qualities and its ability to reproduce images directly from the battlefield. "Parents can see their boys, girls their sweethearts, children their fathers, all helping to win this great war," read one advertisement in the *New York Times*.[110] President Wilson was also part of the marketing campaign as he urged Americans to see the film.[111] One hundred and twelve prints were struck and shown at 3,352 theaters nationwide by 1919, earning $181,741.69.[112] Craig Campbell argues that its box office receipts might have been even higher, but in its laudable efforts to create a strong, desegregated, and unified nation, the film's inclusion of African-American troops may have hurt its performance in the "patriotic south."[113]

The government's next compilation documentary, *America's Answer* (1918), shifted its focus "more toward overseas activities" than *Pershing's Crusaders*, Michael Isenberg notes, "with the usual scenes of marching, reviews, and drills. The entire film was an assemblage of vignettes on soldiering; it said little about the nature, aims, or causes of the war. Labor again was courted."[114] The film also depicted the work of labor in ship building, images of government and military leaders, and activity behind the front lines in France.[115] Its action footage was advertised in *Moving Picture World* as "filmed at the gates of hell and brought back through submarine-infested waters."[116] To secure all of this footage, CPI's second "official war film" may have featured several sequences from Roxy's film, *Flying with the Marines*. The film was edited by Ray Hall, who would intersect with Roxy nearly a decade later, and M. L. Ginouris and was assembled from 50,000 feet of film into an eight-reel film.[117]

Though *Pershing's Crusaders* was well-timed to appeal to audiences hungry for moving-image representation of the overseas war, and the desire by exhibitors to appropriate this content for profit and community-building, the exhibition strategy set by the CPI in which these films were distributed (initially) in house by the Division of Films was ill-conceived. For its next production, *America's Answer*, new Congressional legislation forced the committee to work more closely with motion picture industry distributors and exhibitors to ensure maximum attendance nationwide.[118] To enact this plan and ensure a financial and critical success for the new film, Creel and Charles Hart turned to their New York proxy, Lieutenant Samuel Rothapfel, for help.[119] The presentation of these films in New York and other big cities was still under the coordinated auspices of the CPI (the film's distribution in smaller cities and towns was now on a rental basis), but its new association with more established motion picture exhibitors, according to Creel, "was given the utmost care." These "official showings" needed "an impressiveness that would lift them out of the class of ordinary motion-picture productions in the minds of the public," Creel would later recall. Roxy, thus, "gave us his own aid and that of his experts in the matter of scenic accessories, orchestra, and incidental music."[120]

America's Answer opened in New York at the George M. Cohan Theatre on July 29, 1918, and was presented by Roxy who, according to the *New York Times*, was in charge of musical, lighting, and scenic effects for the exhibition of the film.[121] Roxy, the *Times* said, "prepared a patriotic setting . . . and arranged a tableau vivant entitled, 'Columbia' that remained clear in the mind after the last of the motion picture had been shown." Charles Hart spoke before the screening, and, adding to the night's importance, Creel delivered an address during the intermission that "explained the purpose of the film, and urged Americans over here to make supreme and unselfish efforts in support of their own on the other side."[122]

Roxy subsequently took the film and its entire presentation on the road, presenting the film to President Wilson and other high-ranking officials in Washington, D.C. Roxy wired Creel before his visit seeking governmental coordination:

AM MAKING ARRANGEMENTS TO PRESENT PERSONALLY AMERICAS ANSWER FOR YOU TO PRESIDENT AND CABINET ON MONDAY BUT AM SENDING MY OWN STAFF AND EQUIPMENT READY FOR OPENING ON SUNDAY AS PER YOUR WIRE. . . . CAN I RESPECTFULLY REQUEST THAT YOU TAKE CARE OF MARINE CORPS GENERAL STAFF ON MONDAY EVENING WILL CONSIDER THIS A GREAT FAVOR AND WILL HELP ME IN OBTAINING MARINES FROM WASHINGTON BARRACKS FOR TABLEAU [the stage show].[123]

Roxy had been a rural barkeeper just ten years earlier; now he was presenting government sanctioned propaganda to the president of the United States and his cabinet.

While the CPI gently urged Americans to support the film, its appeal to exhibitors became increasingly aggressive. David Mould notes that the Division of Films, through advertisements in the trade press, "made it clear to exhibitors that it would be unpatriotic to refuse" to exhibit *America's Answer*. Nor was its showing supposed to be a calculated business decision. One advertisement placed in *Motion Picture News* addressed those in the film industry who sought to profit "over here" by what footage had been shot "over there." "Our Government requests that you run these live pictures of our own sons, brothers and friends," the advertisement advised its readers. "[Y]ou are asked not to haggle and barter and hold off, but to be personally as anxious to exhibit them as our intrepid soldiers are to establish democracy with the blood of their stalwart bodies."[124] Hall's film, despite Roxy's well-publicized presentations, its marketing, and its more standard distribution strategy, did not fare that well. *America's Answer* screened in fewer theaters (3,026) than *Pershing's Crusaders* and earned only $3,000 more.[125] One of the reasons for its lack of appeal may have been its timing; as the film was completing its tour of American theaters throughout the late summer and early fall, the Allied victory was nearly complete.

The CPI, despite the Allies' continued strategic victories, pressed on with its campaigns, as did Roxy, dutifully screening the Fourth Liberty Loan films before an invited audience at the Rivoli in mid-September under the direction of the Liberty Loan Committee. The theater was "donated by Lieutenant Samuel Rothapfel, U. S. M. C," *Variety* reported, while the film's national distribution was handled by the National Committee of the Motion Picture Industry, which was chaired by Adolph Zukor in association with the Treasury Department. This symbiotic arrangement was more evidence of the growing cooperation between the film industry and the government.[126] The war granted certain industry figures like Zukor prestige and, later, access to government officials and business leaders who were looking for the film industry to gain political, industrial, social, and cultural legitimacy before beginning to invest. This kind of investment in the immediate post-war years would transform Paramount and Loew's, for instance, into vertically integrated, multinational, and, later, multimedia corporations.

UNDER FOUR FLAGS (1918)

Creel offered Roxy an even more pivotal opportunity to produce, edit, and direct the CPI's last feature-length compilation documentary, *Under Four Flags* (1918). Throughout October and early November 1918, Roxy assembled the footage necessary to craft his epic two-hour film that would utilize the editing skills he had honed making Marine Corps pictures, compiling weekly newsreels at his theaters, and editing the work of other filmmakers for exhibition. Footage shot in France, Belgium, and Italy by the United States Signal Corps, Navy, and Allied cameramen comprised the bulk of its source material.[127] Roxy enlisted (or was forced to accept) Kenneth C. Beaton's work on the film's titles—the same man who had written the intertitles for the previous two CPI feature films.[128] The film was nearing its final edit when the armistice was signed on November 11, 1918, and the war was over, forcing a dramatic change in the film's editing and its overall messaging. Roxy quickly retitled and reedited the film with changes made to reflect the war's end and the Allies' success.[129]

When it was finally released, *Under Four Flags* contained seven episodes: the first, according to *Variety*, depicted "French refugees fleeing from the

German invaders, the conference at Versailles, embarkation of American troops, [and] an attack by an enemy submarine on our troopships." The second featured "the disembarkation, intensive training, [and] propaganda celebration of the American troops after the engagement at Belleau Woods." Episode three captured "the battle of Chateau Thierry," episode four featured Marshall Haig on the British front, episode five contained footage of "Italian forces on the Piave," and the sixth episode featured "the battle of St. Miblel—the first engagement of the Americans as a complete division, under command of American general officers." The film concluded with "views of the celebration in New York on receipt of news of the armistice."[130] *Motion Picture News* commented that the stars were "Generals Foch, Haig, Diaz and Pershing—the support is the united armies of France, the British Empire, Italy and the United States—the best cast ever assembled for a motion picture!"[131]

The reviews for *Under Four Flags* were generally positive, with a number of journalists commenting on the film's ability to deliver the grittiness and raw emotions conjured by war. (Harriette Underhill was one of the few who mentioned that *Under Four Flags* was "not quite as good as 'America's Answer.'")[132] While *Pershing's Crusaders* had used some faked footage—not yet a controversial practice—Roxy's film was heralded for its use of real shots in an era when staged war footage was easy to come by. "These pictures have the mark of realism on them," *Moving Picture World* stated, "for those who know the difference between the genuine article and its imitation."[133] The *New York Times* added that the film offered many scenes that "seem[ed] to often surpass anything of the kind seen before in its power to thrill."[134] Dubbed a "work of art" by the *Times*, *Under Four Flags* reportedly met "the requirements of the moment, anticipating the mood of its spectators, quickening their emotions, and offering them opportunity for unrestrained expression of their feelings after the war."[135]

Another *Times* article pointed to the film's possibilities in encouraging more filming of "real life": "What Mr. Rothapfel has done under difficulties is highly worth while in itself," the newspaper added, "but its great importance is in pointing a way in which the screen can be developed in its own artistic field."[136] The film and other World War I documentaries helped usher in a greater appreciation of nonfiction on the part of motion picture critics, audiences, and exhibitors. Roxy would become a champion of the documentary form in the 1920s, pioneering the use of nonfiction and avant-garde films as stand-alone entertainment or as backdrops for his dramatic stage presentations. But it is his role in directing, editing, producing, accompanying, and exhibiting state-sponsored documentary films during World War I that has remained one of the least examined aspects of his multi-pronged career.

Under Four Flags was, of course, neither marketed as a "documentary," a term John Grierson and others had not yet popularized, an extended newsreel, or as an actuality, but instead as a " 'fact' picture." "Put on this 'fact' picture about the war," one advertisement for the film heralded, "and regard the public as *victors*, not *combatants*, in giving them information."[137] To further advertise what would be the last CPI feature film, a squadron of military airplanes flew over New York City dropping posters announcing the simultaneous screenings of the film at the Rialto and Rivoli theaters beginning November 17, 1918, the first (and perhaps only) time the two theaters had ever shown the same feature film at the same time.[138] Despite a steady rain that fell throughout opening day at the Rivoli and Rialto, the much publicized film drew "remarkable" crowds.[139] Each day of its opening-week exhibition was dedicated to a different group: Sunday was Allies' night; Monday, French night; Tuesday, British night; Wednesday, Italian night; Thursday, Belgian night; Friday, American night; and Saturday was Red Cross day. Seats for the Friday afternoon showings of *Under Four Flags* were available at no cost to wounded veterans from any branch of the military, who were invited to be "the guests of Mr. Rothapfel and Charles S. Hart."[140]

The film remained at the Rivoli after its first week run, while the Rialto opened a new feature film, Samuel Goldwyn's *Too Fat to Fight* (1918). Here, too, Roxy played a role in the film's production as a technical supervisor for its battle scenes shot in Fort Lee, New Jersey. Real Marines portrayed the troops in the trenches, with Roxy directing their actions for the camera.[141] "Everyone knows that [Roxy] has a mighty good idea of what pictures should be," *Motion Picture News* reported at the time. "So Director Hobart Henley, who is responsible for the excellent production, turned over to him the making of the night trench scenes and the result has been some of the most vivid work that the screen has ever seen."[142]

Roxy's multiple skill sets had never been more utilized or pronounced than in late November 1918. In addition to his presentations of *Too Fat to Fight* at the Rialto, a film he helped create, and *Under Four Flags* at the Rivoli, a film he had assembled and exhibited with music he had also arranged, he took up the baton at the Rivoli and conducted the theater's orchestra.[143] The *New York Times*, in reviewing his dexterity with the management, presentation, and production of film, as well as the arrangement and conducting of its music, commented, "When one sees the theatre's managing director so competent with the baton he gets some insight into why so many things are done artistically at the Rivoli and Rialto. It is evident that Mr. Rothapfel is not just a manager with only business sense."[144]

It is important to reconsider the Rivoli and Rialto during 1917 and 1918 as something other than traditional movie houses. With Marines stationed at theater entrances and on stage for live presentations, patriotic music, pro-American newsreels, short films, and feature-length nonfiction and fiction films, Liberty Bond rallies, speeches by the Four Minute Men, and other appeals, the Rivoli and Rialto, like other World War I movie houses, were propaganda centers that have no contemporary rival in their holistic approach to pro-war influence. In an age before radio and television, these movie houses were essential to the war effort and to indoctrinating thousands of New Yorkers from all ethnic, religious, and demographic groups. The Rivoli and Rialto were central hubs of propaganda and military recruiting in New York City. The Rivoli, specifically, *Motion Picture News* commented in early 1919, had "done its part in winning the war. It is here that the greater number of war features have been shown and the propaganda patriotism has been carried to its fullest limit. Not only that, but, together with the Rialto, it has played a big part in the Liberty Loans, Red Cross, and other drives."[145] The exhibition of *Under Four Flags* was merely the culmination of a year-long effort to convert patrons into soldiers and/or military benefactors.

After *Under Four Flag*'s successful debut in New York, the film was road-showed around the country. Its national distribution was preceded by advanced publicity and the production of several hundred twenty-four-sheet, three-sheet, and one-sheet posters, along with thousands of window cards displayed throughout the nation. Regional invitations were sent to local dignitaries, and representatives of the French, British, and Italian High Commissions attended various screenings. In Washington, D. C., the president and members of his cabinet, as well as congressional leaders and scores of other public officials, screened the film, with their attendance exploited in national advertising. After all, if the president had time to see the film, couldn't *you* find a few hours to support your government by viewing it? There were also "department-store window and hotel-lobby displays, street-car cards, and banners and newspaper space donated by local advertisers," Creel later reported. In addition, under the Division of Films's Marcus Beeman, the campaign was further backed in each locality by "personal interviews with representatives, officials, and leading citizens, clubs, societies and organizations, including large industrial plants and firms. Churches, schools, chambers of commerce, political and social clubs, Young Men's Christian Association, Red Cross, Liberty Loan, and fraternal organizations were among those included in the lists."[146]

Like the Four Minute Men certificates that conferred the status of patriot to the rewarded—and suspicion to the excluded—additional certificates were given to theaters that played *Under Four Flags* and other government-produced films.[147] The CPI further lured exhibitors (while chiding others) by printing a "Roll of Honor" that listed theaters exhibiting its official films.[148]

With the war now over, the CPI's address to the industry for *Under Four Flags* was more subtle than its campaign for *America's Answer* had been, this time using the words of prominent exhibitors, rather than the more intimidating tone it previously employed across the country, to attract others to show the film. "The exhibitor who overlooks booking these remarkable government pictures makes the biggest mistake of his life," Harry Crandall of the Metropolitan Theatre in Washington, D.C., was quoted in one advertisement, "because he not alone co-operates with his Government, but he does a business at his boxoffice which will make him wish for a Government picture every day, if he could get it." Frank Buhler of the Stanley Theatre in Philadelphia remarked, " 'Under Four Flags' was conceded by the newspapers to be the best war picture ever produced. Patrons were lavish in their praise and patronage. I am sure the Division of Films will have very little trouble in placing this picture in the representative theatres throughout the United States." The Circle Theatre in Indianapolis, which opened in 1916 under Roxy's supervision (and where he may have maintained a financial interest), commented, "The picture itself is an artistic achievement that merits the unanimous praise it has received on all sides."[149] The managing director of the Circle would later report that *Under Four Flags* had outperformed any other war film shown at his theater.[150] Roxy, never hesitant to self-promote, dubbed his own film "the greatest war picture that has ever been produced":

> In booking the new official war picture, I have not considered the financial side at all, but desire to cooperate with the Committee on Public Information and its Division of Films to give the public the greatest war picture that has ever been produced. I intend to contribute my time and the services of my staff . . . to assist the Division of Films and its producing department to prepare a pictorialization of America's participation in the war, in conjunction with the Allies, that will not only be splendidly effective from the standpoint of the camera art, but which will also register events that will live through all history.[151]

Roxy was quoted in another advertisement labeling his documentary "perhaps the most important picture of the Great War."[152]

Despite all of this hoopla, *Under Four Flags*, like *America's Answer*, was also an economic victim of timing. "Peace," *Variety* wrote in late November 1918, "has caused a great change in the taste of the public for amusement. . . . It was inevitable that a number of war plays, playing to good business, should see a shrinking of patronage."[153] *Too Fat to Fight* had similar problems as well. The film, *Variety* noted, "should have been exhibited long before peace was even considered. It is purely propaganda material and of a kind which has not the slightest point at this time when the problem is how best to get our men home."[154] By the time the post-war Creel Report was submitted in 1919, only seventy-three prints of *Under Four Flags* had been made and shown in 716 theaters, earning $63,946.48, roughly a third of what the previous CPI war films had garnered (excluding receipts from North Dakota, California, and Michigan, where distribution was handled by state agencies). While there were still 1,104 theaters scheduled to play the film at the time of the report, it seemed clear that the CPI's film propaganda was no longer finding the same level of interest in a war-weary nation looking for physical, psychological, and emotional healing.[155]

Under Four Flags's waning status foreshadowed the end of the Division of Films and the CPI.[156] Following the end of hostilities, nations began burying their dead and preparing for life after an unprecedented conflict whose brutality would become well known in the years that followed. American war films, filled with cheer for the victory of democracy, also began finding inhospitable audiences overseas after the armistice of November 1918, depriving the CPI of any significant revenue that could be generated through international distribution. Great Britain, for instance, immediately halted the importation of any American pictures "that even suggest propaganda," *Variety* mentioned in mid-December.[157] CPI films quickly lost their foreign markets, and domestically Americans were just as eager to move on with more diversionary fare, or at least a more distanced and nuanced commentary on the war. *Under Four Flags* instead found an afterlife as an educational film for thousands of school children. The *New York Tribune* reported in February 1919, that "many prominent educators have adopted the idea of securing the film for exhibition in the schools."[158]

The CPI's efforts during World War I were not soon forgotten by the public, journalists, novelists, artists, and by those caught up in the nationalistic frenzy. Its reputation has only withered in the century since its inception. For Roxy, like many of his generation, World War I had a profound, if quiet, effect that would remain with him throughout his life. He expressed, nearly two decades later, that his work during World War I was "a chapter I'd just as soon skip." Roxy recalled seeing wounded veterans in subsequent years and "The suffering I saw then prompted me later to do all I could to see that veterans' hospitals were equipped with radio sets, a blessing to the sick and the shut-in."[159] Roxy still remained ever the dutiful Marine after the war, continuing to appear in magazines across the country in his Marine Corps uniform during the 1920s, practicing drills with other reservists, and extolling the virtues of military training and Marine service, both in his theaters and for general life skills.[160] As *The Leatherneck* wrote in 1925, he was "a good example of the old adage, 'Once a Marine, always a Marine.'"[161] Throughout the two decades after the war, he was among the most frequent visitors to the Marine Corps' chief convalescent center, Walter Reed Hospital, visiting the wounded and raising tens of thousands of dollars for veterans through fundraisers at his theaters and through personal appearances. "The sight of these men," a journalist reported, "hopelessly maimed in the World war, went so deeply into Roxy's heart" that he worked tirelessly over the next decade to secure radios for every wounded Marine in a veteran's hospital.[162]

This charity work would remain a lifelong effort for Roxy, part duty as a Marine and part obligation for being one of the most influential propagandists in New York during this period. Roxy was, in fact, the crucial early bridge between the motion picture industry and the political elite—fostering the growing relationship between the film industry and Washington that continues today in its frictional yet symbiotic state. His legacy in directing, editing, and scoring propaganda films and coupling them with pro-war stage shows and music at his Rivoli and Rialto theaters is an enormously important segment of his career. It both exemplified the power of the unitary text to convey aesthetic and thematic meaning through film and live performance and demonstrated the multiple opportunities available to exhibitors like Roxy at the end of the transitional era, as the film industry's ties to political and corporate power continued to coalesce in new and unexpected ways.

4. "THE MAN WHO GAVE THE MOVIES A COLLEGE EDUCATION"
ROXY, RAPEE, AND MOTION PICTURES AT THE CAPITOL THEATRE
(1919–1922)

"[Roxy] had a rare ability for personal advertisement."[1]
—Messmore Kendall, Capitol Theatre owner, 1946

Roxy's propaganda work during World War I, in which he directed, edited, consulted, scored, and/or exhibited a wide range of war-themed fiction and nonfiction films, and produced related stage shows and other patriotic drives, established his political power and his growing bona fides as a filmmaker, editor, and cultural tastemaker. Coupled with the extensive coverage he was granted in *Motion Picture News* and other trade journals, Roxy's confidence had grown exponentially.

The year 1919, though, despite all of its postwar promise for Roxy, would become the most difficult of his early career, full of new challenges, failures, and some successes. The growing vertical integration of the American film industry, and the influx of tens of millions of dollars of capital by investment banks and firms, had already begun to change the nature of exhibition as theaters like the Rivoli and Rialto sought alliances with powerful distributors like Paramount to ensure the flow of top-shelf product and stars. There were also new opportunities for the nation's exhibitors and for those, like Roxy, who could navigate the complex political and industrial matrix that had begun to network Washington, D.C., with New York and Los Angeles.

Roxy had now been with the Rialto for two and a half years, his longest stint yet at any venue, and had grown impatient with exhibition. In mid-December 1918, shortly after the release of *Under Four Flags* and *Too Fat to Fight*, Roxy took a working vacation and traveled the country with Samuel Goldwyn (then Goldfish). They stopped in Seattle and then San Francisco where Roxy and Goldwyn advised the Tivoli Theatre on its "plans for a radical reconstruction of the interior" along with "a new lighting scheme."[2] When the two arrived in Los Angeles, Douglas Fairbanks posed with Roxy for publicity shots.[3] Roxy also visited Thomas Ince at his studio in Culver City.[4] Roxy and Goldwyn, while touring other studios and meeting with the expatriate industry now growing in the west, professed their disappointment with the artistic stagnation of the industry both in terms of film production and exhibition. Roxy saw little innovation on the part of industry leaders, a sentiment he observed among a group of theater owners who held a dinner in his and Goldwyn's honor in Los Angeles. The film industry was in a "rut," he added and so too, in his estimation, was his own career.[5]

Roxy began to ponder the immense number of opportunities in Europe for film exhibitors and film distributors in a postwar market battered by economic and logistical difficulties. Roxy planned to build new theaters in London and Paris along the same lines as the Rialto and Rivoli and "expect[ed] to make a great deal of money over there, because the cost of exhibition is not nearly so high as here." Roxy added, presciently, only a month after the Armistice: "There is no doubt American films will be more popular even than before the war, and there is no doubt that the thousands of photoplays now reposing on the shelves of American producers will be eagerly welcomed by the peoples of other countries."[6]

His postwar reputation, like his expectations, remained astronomically high. The *New York Clipper*, for instance, included "Sam Rothapfel's rep as a showman" in its list of "Things Worth Having" in mid-January 1919.[7] By then, *Motion Picture News* wrote, Roxy was "probably known to more people than any person connected with the industry."[8] He had already begun using his clout to butt heads with anyone who disagreed with him. His increasingly dictatorial manner at the Rialto and Rivoli theaters, though, had created some internal strife, much of it unbeknownst to Roxy who assumed, as always, that he was beloved by all. When he found out from the director of the Strand Theatre, Howard Edel, that some members of the Rivoli and Rialto staff had not spoken "very well of him," he immediately ordered all of his senior staff to report to his office. He then put them all through a "third degree examination" to find out the source of the complaints—and the source of the leak—to no avail.[9]

He also clashed with J. D. Williams of First National and subsequently resigned his position.[10] Roxy's worst battle, though, even beyond his argument with Joseph Thomas of the Four Minute Men, may have been with Richard Rowland of Metro Pictures. Although the two had served together on the War Co-operation Committee assisting the Department of the Interior,[11] a "lively argument" ensued when Rowland insinuated that the Rialto and Rivoli's recent arrangement with Paramount Pictures made Adolph Zukor Roxy's new boss—a charge that incensed the independent Roxy as it insinuated that he had lost control of his decision-making in booking films.[12]

When Roxy finally returned from his trip out west, he was also peppered with questions from his Rialto and Rivoli employers about a number of phone calls he had made to the nearby Havre deGrace racetrack. With internal and external critiques of his management rising, Roxy decided to make a complete break from the area of the business he had built to such acclaim over the past decade. Noting his exhaustion with the daily grind of managing theaters after ten years in exhibition, he abruptly resigned his position as manager of the Rivoli and Rialto in January 1919.[13] The news startled an industry that continued to look to him for leadership. There was barely a deluxe movie house in the Times Square area that had not been managed by Roxy at one time or another (or had been leased for one of his many premieres on behalf of Paramount and other distributors). In film trade journals and in local newspapers, Roxy was the unparalleled leader in the area of motion picture theater management. The *New York Times* commented upon his resignation, "New York has him, more than any other man, to thank for the presentation of motion pictures in a way attractive to persons of taste and intelligence."[14] In the area of film exhibition, there was Samuel Rothapfel and then there was everyone else.

Roxy's close friends argued that instead of the racetrack dispute, his resignation was the result of belt-tightening by the theaters' owners who had grown weary of Roxy's spending habits with ever-larger orchestras, more elaborate stage settings, and spending, spending, spending on anything and everything to make the Rialto and Rivoli second only to each other. Roxy was tired of all the penny-pinching, his associates noted, and felt "handicapped by purely business reasons." Roxy was a bit more vague, however: "I am leaving this connection to take up the preliminaries in a project of significance and with a greater claim upon my attention, the nature of which I cannot discuss in detail at this time," he told *Motion Picture News*. "The organization which I have built will go on with the work. I shall always feel a deep personal interest in the welfare of these theatres which I have fathered on Broadway."[15]

There were many directions Roxy's life and career could have taken in 1919: working exclusively for the Marines, managing a new theater, taking a new executive role at one of the growing number of film companies, or perhaps entering a new field entirely. News of his departure caused the rumor mill to spin out yarns. Several reports (and denials) claimed Roxy was joining Goldwyn Pictures as general director of productions in mid-January 1919. Yet another rumor situated Roxy in London, building "a huge cinema" in Piccadilly Circus financed by Jacob Wertheimer, with Roxy supposedly leaving for Europe in February.[16] *Motion Picture News* reported the same rumor as well, adding that "those closest to him believe that the next of his activities will be in London or Paris, or both, where he has for some time had a desire to conduct motion pictures on the same scale, or greater, than at the two New York houses."[17] (Roxy's links to a new London cinema project would be repeated for the next fifteen years with at least half a dozen possible scenarios and backers. None of them ever came to pass.)

Beyond the organizational disputes with the Rialto and Rivoli owners, Roxy was also looking for a way to express himself further as an artist, a title he was not shy about claiming. Through his earlier work for the Committee on Public Information and on other films over the past decade, Roxy had become notorious for inserting himself into the production and post-production process. He had already reedited *The Easiest Way* (without Lewis Selznick's knowledge) and *The Unbeliever* (at the request of George Kleine), directed a troop sequence for *Too Fat to Fight*, and bullied J. Stuart Blackton into letting him take over directing a scene in Vitagraph's *The Courage of Silence* (1917).[18] Roxy sought an opportunity to expand his work in filmmaking. In October 1918, he wrote, "Someday, perhaps in the near future I may try my hand at producing. . . . I honestly believe I can make a success because I will employ the same fundamental principles in producing as I do in presenting motion pictures."[19] In mid-January 1919, *Variety* reported that Roxy had left New York again for California to direct a new film starring Elaine Hammerstein and produced by Harry Rapf. Nothing, however, seemed to come from the project.[20]

Still, Roxy was undeterred. His success with *Devil Dogs, Flying with the Marines, The Courage of Silence, Too Fat to Fight, Under Four Flags*, and other films he had edited with and without a distributor's consent had convinced him to follow many of the other moguls such as Mayer, Fox, and Laemmle, who had long ago moved from film exhibition to film production and distribution. He also remained, according to *Motion Picture News*, "available for brief stretches to any theatre owner who desires the benefit of his 'on-the-ground' advice."[21] Roxy also toyed with the idea of becoming vertically integrated by making and distributing films. "There is no law, you know," he told *Moving Picture World* in February 1919, "to prevent me from having a theatre of my own on Broadway."[22]

ROTHAPFEL UNIT PROGRAMME (1919)

In mid-February, Roxy formed a new $150,000 company with Frank G. Hall, head of the Independent Sales Corporation, known as the Rothapfel Pictures Corporation, located at 130 West 46th Street in Manhattan.[23] Roxy was president of the company, with Hall serving as vice president. Roxy no longer had an employer. The company, Roxy and Hall announced, was established to produce the *Rothapfel Unit Programme* (1919), an entire evening's worth of films—a prepackaged unitary text—for any theater. The canned selection of films included an overture, "The Rothapfel Unit of 1919," arranged by Roxy and his former musical director Hugo Riesenfeld; *The Last Hour*, a visualization of Massenet's *Élégie*; a scenic picture, *The Wood of Fair Water*, which was intended to complete a magazine or newsreel supplied by the theater; another short, *A Thought of Equity*; a short comedy, *Wild Flowers*, whose story was developed by Roxy; and a feature film, *False Gods*, written by E. Lloyd Sheldon and directed by the relatively unseasoned Wally Van.[24] The inspiration for Roxy's packaging of a filmed unitary text for exhibitors who wanted a Roxy-style program, but did not want to spend Roxy-sized dollars, came from his trip with Goldwyn. "[The new project] is the result of keeping my eyes open while traveling about the country and visiting the different picture houses," Roxy told *Moving Picture World*. "I found that all exhibitors were not so situated that they could put together a perfectly balanced bill, with music cues, light plots and every detail of presentation worked out in a thoroughly artistic and showmanship manner. With my complete 'unit programs' at his disposal all an exhibitor will have to do is attend to the ordinary running of his house."[25] Roxy saw these films as a constituent part of a unit, a collection of linked films, rather than modular segments. Like Raymond Williams's concept of "flow," theaters booking the *Rothapfel Unit Programme* became networks for the syndication of Roxy's "evening's entertainment" in which one entertainment unit flowed into the next. His interpolation of live performance and recorded media had always worked this way; the *Programme* remediated this kind of performance and packaged it for national distribution.

Expectations for Roxy's new venture were incredibly high, just as Hall and Roxy had hoped. The president of the Women's Forum wrote Roxy that "All women interested in the real uplift and advancement of a great art will wish you Godspeed, knowing that you are sure to meet all your expectations in the future, as you have done in the past."[26] Roxy, in turn, promised to do no less than raise the level of cinematic artistry through his *Programmes*. "I shall make features that will embody a new form of construction—a step forward in the art. My comedies will also have new ideas. I shall select the stories, engage the actors and superintend the entire production of the pictures."[27]

In March, the Rothapfel Pictures Corporation announced that it would produce six *Rothapfel Unit Programmes* each year, all featuring a "dramatic feature picture, a comedy, scenic and news or magazine films, together with complete musical scores, lighting effects, incidental numbers" and more.[28] By mid-April, Hall and Roxy began running weekly advertisements in film trade journals with Frank Hall writing to "The Exhibitors of America" that "Judging from the finished subjects I have seen, it may truly be said that the *Rothapfel Unit Programme* will prove beyond all question the Highest Class Entertainment in the World."[29] Proclamations like these were ultimately counterproductive and raised unreasonable expectations for Roxy's first effort. The choice of relatively unknown actors and the unproven Wally Van to direct the *Programme*'s first feature film, *False Gods*, also seems, in retrospect, to have been a questionable move. The choice of Van, in fact, remains one of the least explicable decisions of Roxy's career.

The *Rothapfel Unit Programme* was given an enormous amount of marketing and distribution support. Predating David O. Selznick's landmark campaign for *Duel in the Sun* (1946) by nearly three decades, Hall and Roxy devised a saturation booking and marketing strategy through which they would distribute the *Programme* day and date in as many North American cities as possible. By April 19, the Rothapfel Pictures Corporation announced that the *Programme* would be unveiled in forty-five theaters on the same date, a new booking record and one that *Motion Picture News* stated could attract three to four million patrons in its first week alone.[30] Roxy and Hall stated that the campaign was "of gigantic proportions [in which] we are doing things on perhaps the largest scale ever attempted in the history of the theatrical business."[31] Billboard ads were placed throughout the country and exploitation (promotional) materials were distributed to exhibitors wherever the film was booked.[32] Buoyed by all of the pre-release hype, Roxy began planning eight additional *Programmes*.[33]

The American trade screening for the first *Rothapfel Unit Programme* on May 9, 1919, attracted nearly two thousand exhibitors, critics, and other journalists from all over the country to cram into the Rialto.[34] That evening, a dinner was held at the Hotel Astor in Roxy's honor with representatives of nearly every film trade journal in attendance, as were a host of other journalists who covered the industry, such as Louella Parsons (then the motion picture editor of the *Morning Telegraph*).[35] The marketing effort helped sell the *Programme*'s foreign rights to Robertson-Cole and generated a "vast sum" for Roxy and Hall.[36] To lure additional exhibitors, the *Programme*'s May 24 advertisement included three pages of exhibitor and press comments extolling the *Programme*'s virtues. Sylvester Rawling of the *New York Evening World* wrote that "Rothapfel has done for the Movies what Wagner did for Opera; he has co-ordinated the Arts into one harmonious whole."[37] The *New Rochelle Daily Star* called the program "the biggest entertainment idea ever launched in America,"[38] while S. Jay Kaufman remarked that "Mr. Rothapfel has done a big work for the movie theatre which hasn't a Rothapfel at its head."[39] The *New York Globe* was perhaps the most bombastic, commenting that the *Programme* "marks the most interesting departure from screen precedent since the days when this same Samuel Rothapfel turned the old time 'nickelodeon' into the institutions we now know as the Rivoli[,] Rialto, and Strand."[40]

Judging by those three quotes alone, one might have guessed that the *Rothapfel Unit Programme* would be universally lauded. This was not the case. The majority of the *Programme*'s trade reviews were lukewarm. *Moving Picture World*, which had helped launch Roxy's career nearly a decade earlier, concluded that "Its most impressive feature is the promise it gives of what may be accomplished in this direction."[41] Praise for the *Programme* was often confined to the comedy, *Wild Flowers*, the only film in the *Programme* whose story line Roxy developed. The feature film, *False Gods*, in contrast, turned out to be a flop and it ultimately sank the *Programme*. Hall and Roxy purchased six pages of advertising space in several trade papers and filled it with well-chosen blurbs from critics. There was little else they could do.

On May 25, Frank Hall announced that the Park Theatre, which had just concluded an eight-month run of opera performances, would be leased as a showcase house for the *Programme*(s). Roxy was signed to be its new manager for this release and for other Independent Sales Corporation films for the foreseeable future.[42] Landing Roxy's management skills and the coterie of talent he attracted for his company's releases was a coup for Hall, but the Park Theatre would turn out to be purgatory for Roxy.[43]

Hall and Roxy's saturation marketing and distribution plan also left them in an ironic quandary. If they could distribute the *Programme* to the entire nation at the same time, how could Roxy's presentation be distinctive at the Park Theatre? Roxy's need to outdo the competition belied the great fallacy of the *Programme* itself—that it was indeed a turnkey exhibition solution. Roxy exhibited the same group of films at the Park as his competition, but the unitary text—its surrounding live performances and the musicianship of his new concert orchestra at the Park—would inevitably separate it from the *Programme*'s exhibition at Loew's and other theaters. "S. L. Rothapfel's

Complete Show Idea" at the Park included Adolph Bolm's "Miniature Ballet," with scenery designed by longtime Roxy collaborator John Wenger and music by Victor Herbert.[44]

Roxy's surrounding entertainment at the Park, and that of other theaters exhibiting the *Programme*, could not save it. The *New York Times* review was blunt:

> The first Rothapfel Unit Program was disappointing. Of this there can be no doubt, and the fact should be frankly admitted. Those familiar with Mr. Rothapfel's achievements as managing director of the Strand, Rialto, and Rivoli, and with something of his ideas about the photoplay, had let themselves expect great things—even from the former exhibitor's first effort as a producer. And they were disappointed.[45]

The *Chicago Daily Tribune*, Roxy's longtime detractor, was merciless. "If the program shown yesterday was a fair sample," a *Tribune* journalist wrote, "I should say that Mr. Rothapfel had better confine his attention to the business of exhibiting."[46]

Roxy was eager to move on to the second *Programme*. He quickly announced that he had "practically all details completed for the commencement of the second Unit which is scheduled for release some time in the fall."[47] As the weeks went by, however, no filming began and no advertising space was booked. The *Rothapfel Unit Programme*, supposedly the first of many to come, would be the only one made and the last film Roxy would ever produce.

From 1908 to 1918, Roxy had experienced nearly continuous success. In just a few short months, he would almost drift into relative obscurity. Roxy was stuck in a contract as the manager of the Park Theatre, located at Columbus Circle, seventeen blocks north of the Rialto. It might as well have been Siberia—or Forest City, Pennsylvania. In one bold stroke, Roxy had spent much of the cultural and industrial capital he had built up over the past decade on the *Programme* and now had little to show for it. Instead of being heralded as the next great producer like Goldwyn or Selznick, Roxy had failed in spectacular fashion. Like his idol, Napoleon, he was alone on Elba—or in this case, the entertainment island that was the Park Theatre. The *Programme* was a career misstep. In the weeks that followed, exhibitors, unhappy with its financial results, began dumping it. By July 1919, the *Rothapfel Unit Programme* had been broken apart at numerous theaters. At Loew's Metropolitan in Brooklyn, for instance, only *False Gods* (and not the rest of the *Programme*) was screened as a double bill with " 'Resista,' The 98 lb. Girl No Man Can Lift."[48]

Roxy began looking for new projects and an escape plan. In August, he was reported to be heading up the new National Academy of Motion Pictures in Rochester, New York, for George Eastman. The theater would reportedly seat 3,500 and house an orchestra of one hundred.[49] But the project was still months away from anything concrete.[50]

For the next few months at the Park, Roxy was barely mentioned in the New York newspapers or in the film trades. He was also no longer the primary exhibitor attracting media attention, even by the *Motion Picture News*. Buffalo showman Harold Franklin was given a full-page study in the September 27, 1919, issue of the journal to discuss recent trends in motion picture exhibition.[51] That same issue featured an extensive treatment of a recent Sid Grauman prologue and stage setting.[52] Hugo Riesenfeld's successful management of the Rialto and Rivoli also made Roxy's name harder and harder to find in print from mid- to late 1919.

Roxy's elaborate prologue for *The Right to Happiness* (1919) finally earned him a modicum of press with featured articles in both the *New York Times* and *Motion Picture News*. Still, the *Times* mentioned that his scenic and live prologue were "entirely too elaborate for the picture,"[53] though *Motion Picture News* was more than satisfied that their idol had returned to form. The *News* devoted an entire page to Roxy's work and remarked that nearly a year after the end of the war Roxy was still screening films that were "undeniably propaganda." The *News* also mentioned how much had changed in the short time since Roxy left the Rialto and Rivoli only eight months earlier:

> Artistic presentation of feature pictures, especially in the matter of elaborate prologues and stage setting have to all intents and purposes reached a much higher stage of development in the West than in the East with New York very badly in the rear ranks for the most part in the latter connection, so it is with considerable local pride that we seize on the presentation of the "Right to Happiness" at the Park theatre, New York, as an opportunity to tell of a stage setting and prologue, the creation of S. L. Rothapfel, which rivals if not surpasses those of Los Angeles.[54]

Out west, Sid Grauman's Million Dollar Theatre—and to a lesser extent Fred Miller's new California Theatre—in Los Angeles had begun staging elaborate prologues that captured the attention of the trade journals which had been New York–centric. Chiefly known as a new center for motion picture production, California was slowly becoming a vaunted hub of motion picture exhibition as well with theaters and exhibitors that rivaled Chicago and even New York City.

While the *Rothapfel Unit Programme*—and its disconnected films—was still playing in smaller cities and towns around the country, including the Show Shop in Middletown, the Palace in Olean, and the Auditorium in Kingston, New York, Roxy left the Park Theatre for good in late September and formed a new company, the S. L. Rothapfel Corporation, with a valuation of $550,000.[55] He was rumored to be headed to Paris for negotiations—possibly to build a theater there. Instead, he was headed back to California and a head-to-head competition with his rival in prologues and film exhibition, Sidney Patrick Grauman.[56]

CALIFORNIA THEATRE, LOS ANGELES, CA

Samuel Goldwyn's 1919 was far more successful than Roxy's, though no less stressful. That summer, Goldwyn had refinanced his company with separate $125,000 investments from Lee and J. J. Shubert, Sam H. Harris, and Al Woods. Goldwyn continued to cultivate additional investments from Joseph Godsol and others that would help him expand his studio and its slate of films.[57] By the end of the 1910s, securing theaters for these films was paramount. When, in the fall of 1919, Goldwyn Pictures Corporation began expanding its growing circuit of theaters across the country, Samuel Goldwyn needed a figurehead who could oversee the chain. Roxy's trip across the country with Goldwyn ten months earlier had afforded both the opportunity to learn each other's thoughts and proclivities. Goldwyn needed Roxy and Roxy certainly needed Goldwyn. Roxy left the Park Theatre behind (and the bitter memories of his *Programme* experience) and was named "national director of moving picture presentation" for Goldwyn Pictures.[58]

Roxy's previous visit to California had coincided with the opening of Fred Miller's California Theatre in downtown Los Angeles on Christmas Eve 1918.[59] Miller and managing director Harry Leonhardt were given high marks for their elaborate stage and film presentations, but it was conductor Carli Elinor's work that later drew the lion's share of acclaim by fall 1919.[60] *Motion Picture News* cited Elinor's music at the California and Sid Grauman's prologues at the nearby Million Dollar Theatre (which had opened on February 1, 1918) as yet another sign that Los Angeles was becoming a new center of elaborate film presentation.[61]

The attention placed on these two theaters and the importance of having an exclusive first-run venue in downtown Los Angeles were not lost on Goldwyn. He began negotiating to purchase the California Theatre from Miller in

September and completed the transaction on October 28, 1919. He immediately commissioned Roxy to enhance the theater's presentation standards and management.[62] The California, the *Los Angeles Evening-Express* wrote, would now have "a famous theater manager at its helm, a man whose knowledge and artistic genius has made him a world famous figure in the world of motion pictures."[63] Roxy closed the venue on November 3 for five days to augment the theater's orchestra to forty musicians, now the largest theater orchestra on the West Coast, and make "many improvements." Elinor remained as the theater's conductor, working with Roxy to score each picture.[64]

The California Theatre reopened on November 7, 1919, with Goldwyn's *Flame of the Desert* (1919).[65] The *Los Angeles Times* remarked that the opening performance "justified the promises and [Roxy's] own long experience in the important picture houses of New York."[66] The *Los Angeles Examiner* was similarly approving, mentioning that "In sending Samuel L. Rothapfel, noted New York exhibitor, here to effect the reorganization of the theater and its demonstrative effects, Samuel Goldwyn has paid high compliment to the taste of Los Angeles."[67] Henry Doughtery was similarly effusive, writing that he "heard nothing but praise on every hand" at the opening, "a gala event in the theatrical history of Los Angeles. . . . We came out of the theater with a feeling that a new spirit—a new genius—something different had invaded the Los Angeles theatrical firmament."[68] In the coming days, the *Examiner* reported that the theater continued playing to "immense audiences" who were "loud in their praise of every feature."[69] For the moment, at least, the California Theatre, not Grauman's Million Dollar, had attracted the Los Angeles spotlight. Weeks later, the *Evening Express* remarked that the California was still garnering the city's accolades and Roxy was "entitled to the splendid response the public is giving in appreciation of the wonderful program that is being daily presented under his direction."[70]

Grauman did not stand pat, though, and continued to churn out ever more elaborate prologues. *Motion Picture News* wrote in its December 6, 1919, issue that his "A Tour Through Grauman's" show, a stage spectacular that highlighted the theater's organ, ushers, electricians, and other personnel and equipment, was "the most interesting special program number since the opening of the house." The show was designed to both entertain audiences and highlight the attributes of the venue.[71] Grauman also seemed to chide Roxy's efforts to uplift and/or teach his audience. "I am of the opinion that most of us are still children and regard the universe as a playground," Grauman told the *Evening Express*. "I would never try to teach a child calculus or [feed] strong meat to a baby."[72] He added a few weeks later, "It is not my desire to take issue with any exhibitor, either in Los Angeles or elsewhere. These are merely my ideas, and that's the end of it."[73] The *Atlanta Constitution* commented that with Roxy and Grauman outdoing themselves and each other, "A novel duel" was being "fought" that had begun to interest the "picture theater men all over the country. . . . The contest has even got to the betting stage, local film people having laid wagers on their favorite to outdo his rival."[74] It was the first time Roxy had worked in a city with true competition for public and critical favor, and the challenge seemed to spur both exhibitors.

Roxy's presentation of Allan Dwan's *Soldiers of Fortune* (1919) in early December was both a new weapon in this conscious or unconscious battle for local and national favor and one of the most important examples of the interventions inherent in a Roxy unitary text. The elaborate stage show began before the projection of the film *and* interrupted the screening. Prior to the film's projection, "an atmospheric prelude to the story" was presented featuring "Senor and Senora Espinosa in Spanish dances."[75] These "Characteristic Castilian Dancers" were joined by Manuela V. Budrow, "the Spanish Prima Donna," "Together with Her Chorus of Vocalists and Instrumentalists," and "Aided by [Carli] Elinor's California Concert Orchestra."[76] Henry Dougherty of the *Evening Express* described Roxy's programs as "original and sometimes daring in [their] conception of pictures presentation . . . springing new innovations and surprising the public as well as competitors." But Roxy's presentation of *Soldiers of Fortune*, even more than before, Dougherty argued, "reached the heights of daring and originality":

> Twelve minutes after Allen Dwan's magnificent cinema spectacle, "Soldiers of Fortune," is under way, and after we have met his characters in the deserts of Arizona and later in the millionaire's ballroom in New York, the picture fades out and the stage is flooded with the glow of amber and gold. Out of the shadows come human beings, singing and dancing, and blending with the flood of color we hear dreamy melodies of South American music. The illusion lasts only a few minutes. The lights are dimmed, the melodies join their echoes and then the screen flashes back to us a panorama of a South American city. One seems to have stepped from the warm presence of real living people into their very own city as the characters of the play again are assembled and we find the locale transferred from gay old New York to the mining camps of the foothills of the Andes. The cut into the feature is a daring innovation, to say the least, but Mr. Rothapfel has done it successfully. The continuity of the story has not been interrupted but rather the action has been accelerated. Certainly the

South American atmosphere introduced at this time prepares us better than any subtitle for our entrance with the characters of the play into that land of jealousies and revolutions.[77]

Roxy had not presented a film surrounded by atmosphere but had made the film only part of the evening's unitary text. By not privileging the film more than the live performances, he was able to interrupt its flow with music and dance to create one (largely) harmonious whole. "The time is coming when the people will attend a picture presentation because it is in a wonderful theater," Roxy remarked to the *Evening Express*. "They will not attend the theater to see a picture show, but the picture will be an incidental on the program."[78]

By the end of 1919, Roxy was in familiar territory—presenting films at an important first-run, urban venue and courting the press for constant attention and adulation. The *Evening Express* stated, for instance, that Roxy's work, and specifically his presentation of *Blind Husbands* (1919), represented "advance steps in motion picture entertainment" and gave Roxy, the *Los Angeles Record* wrote, "another artistic triumph."[79] Many accounts of Roxy's career skip over his time at the California Theatre, but it was the opportunity that rehabilitated his career and image. Roxy did not intend it to be a short-lived experience either and may have wanted to make Los Angeles home. "It is the most wonderful climate in the world," he told the *Evening Express*, "and once you get a taste of it you do not want to go back to New York or anywhere else in the east."[80]

If it was sunshine Roxy was after, though, the radiant glow was wasted on him. When not working tirelessly at the theater, he was drumming up new business for Goldwyn. In early January, Roxy and [F. J.] Joe Godsol traveled to San Francisco, most likely to scout for new theaters and/or supervise those affiliated with the company, returning in time to see the world premiere of Goldwyn's latest release, *The Cup of Fury* (1920).[81] Roxy's elaborate presentation of that film, which began on January 4, 1920, featured an atmospheric prelude, six additional presentations of live and recorded entertainment, and an interpretative dance by a then little-known member of the Denishawn dance company, Martha Graham.[82] While the *Evening Express* commented that Roxy's presentation "promises to even outdo anything before attempted by him,"[83] the *Los Angeles Times* wrote that with the exception of Graham's "fire dance," the bill's quantity of entertainment was its biggest selling point.[84] Graham remained at the theater for the debut of yet another Douglas Fairbanks film, *When the Clouds Roll By* (1919), the following week.[85]

The Cup of Fury was Roxy's Los Angeles swan song (part of the reason he may have put so much effort into the show and returned in time for its debut).

Goldwyn was satisfied with Roxy's work at the California and wanted him to perform similar tasks throughout the country at other Goldwyn houses.[86] Roxy was subsequently named general director of exhibition and began to oversee Goldwyn's expanding chain of theaters as the company sought to widen its circuit throughout the country as Paramount, First National, and Loew's continued their growth.[87]

By January 25, Roxy had already made his way to Goldwyn-affiliated houses in St. Louis, Chicago, and "other cities in the Middle West," according to *Moving Picture World*. Roxy set up temporary headquarters in Chicago and was reunited with his old friend James McQuade who was still covering the region for *Moving Picture World*. Roxy took a swipe at those like Riesenfeld and especially Grauman (without naming them) who were starting to claim some of the limelight, telling McQuade that "motion picture presentation has been at a standstill for the past year"—in other words, ever since he had left the Rialto and Rivoli.[88] Those venues, despite their importance, were slowly becoming yesterday's news in New York after the opening of the new 5,300-seat Capitol Theatre in October 1919.

CAPITOL THEATRE, NEW YORK, NY

In 1916, Messmore Kendall, a prominent lawyer, real estate investor, financier, author, and producer, met "Major" Edward Bowes, a real estate investor, through Crosby Gaige of the entertainment firm Selwyn and Company.[89] Selwyn hoped to operate two new theaters north of Times Square and asked Kendall to finance the construction and then lease the theaters to Selwyn. The future site of the Capitol Theatre housed a saloon, blacksmith shops, a filling station, and a livery stable. The property was close to the Times Square area, though, and a subway station was about to open at the corner of 50th Street and Seventh Avenue one block away, which could deliver patrons from across the city. It seemed like a good long-term investment to Kendall.[90] Through his Moredall Realty Corporation, he leased a significant swath of property at 50th Street and Broadway for twenty-one years at $100,000 per annum to build a new office building and two motion picture theaters. One new movie house was slated to fill 3,800 seats with motion pictures at "popular prices," while the other 2,500-seat theater would showcase "special film productions of high class."[91]

Kendall traveled to San Francisco and Los Angeles in January 1917 at the request of Harry Aitken of Triangle Pictures. He visited the company's studio in Culver City for several days and was smitten with the film business and the financial possibilities for his new enterprise. He immediately wired Bowes to change their plans and decided to build one massive theater (instead of two) with 5,000 seats and a skating rink on the roof.[92] Thomas Lamb, who had built nearly all of New York's most prominent deluxe movie theaters, including the Regent, Strand, Rialto, and Rivoli, was commissioned to design the Capitol, although the credit for the auditorium, according to Kendall, should actually be given to C. A. Sandbloom, who worked in Lamb's office.[93]

The Capitol Theatre was not backed by members of the film industry or by the growing number of large investment firms financing the industry's expansion and vertical integration.[94] The theater's board of directors included no Wall Street financiers or film executives, despite Kendall's relationship with Selwyn and Company.[95] Kendall, buoyed by Triangle's high-class aspirations, envisioned the Capitol Theatre as a venue that would elevate and profit from "refined" motion pictures. He lured Bowes away from the Selwyn organization by naming him managing director of the theater with an annual salary of $25,000.[96] Bowes carried out Kendall's vision and wrote in an open letter to the public printed shortly before the theater's opening, "There is much gossip abroad concerning the tremendous size of the new Capitol Theatre. Size means nothing unless justified by attractiveness. Good taste is the foundation upon which the Capitol Theatre is [built]."[97] The Capitol's printed programs were dressed up to look like Broadway playbills (not deluxe movie theater programs like those at the Rivoli or Rialto), with illustrated covers and messaging more in line with the tastes of polite society. The Capitol's early programs also treated audiences as guests rather than as customers or patrons. Even more than Triangle's (failed) operation of the Knickerbocker Theatre, the Capitol Theatre under Kendall and Bowes was intended to be a motion picture theater for the classes. Instead of using long box office lines as part of the theater's marketing, for instance, Bowes instituted a policy whereby tickets were sold by mail and picked up at the theater. The Capitol's box office and mail-order service sold all of its seats up to eight weeks in advance. This strategy may have enticed those unwilling to stand in line, but it removed one of the most important aspects of urban moviegoing in the years before multiplexes and Internet ticketing—the visual spectacle of a long line and its conferral of status upon a film's and/or a theater's importance to passersby.

Lengthy delays due to material shortages during World War I, several worker strikes, various logistical difficulties, and the sheer size of the project slowed construction well beyond its planned opening. It took more than two and a half years to build the Capitol Theatre between the time Kendall signed

the lease for the property and its official opening on October 24, 1919.[98] Before its debut, some were already skeptical about its viability as a venue for
motion pictures. Theatrical producer Morris Gest remarked to Kendall that
"If it doesn't go over, as it probably won't because you amateurs cannot make
a success of as gigantic a theatre as this, don't worry, I will be here to take it
over and make it a go."[99] Bowes's job was to add an air of confident legitimacy
to an enterprise that had little film industry backing and just as little support
from Wall Street.

Major Bowes was a solid publicist—though not of Roxy or even Grauman
proportions—and he had a very press-worthy object to sell: the largest motion picture theater in the United States. If the Capitol had been a 2,500-seat
theater, it would hardly have merited the attention it soon received. Its sheer
expanse captured the imagination of New York audiences and the attention
of trade and newspaper journalists eager to see if, in fact, 5,300 New Yorkers
would fill its seats. "[E]very newspaper in the United States commented on the
size and splendor of the institution," *Motion Picture News* mentioned upon its
opening.[100] The Capitol boasted a seventy-piece orchestra led by Arthur Pryor,
an art department led by John Wenger, elaborate stage productions by Ned
Wayburn, a large ensemble of live performers, and a motion picture department directed by Henry "Hy" Mayer, a former *New York Times* cartoonist and
filmmaker.[101]

The opening four-hour program consisted of an eclectic mix of film (newsreels, short films, and *His Majesty, the American* [1919]), organ and orchestral
music, and live performances. A young Mae West was featured, with Wayburn, formerly Florenz Ziegfeld's assistant and a prolific choreographer of the
early 20th century, producing all of the live entertainment. Among the other
artists selected for the "Demi-Tasse Revue" was a "slight, rosy-cheeked, black-
haired boy" who played two of his unpublished works. The "boy" was George
Gershwin, who performed "Come to the Moon" (with lyrics co-written by
Wayburn) and Gershwin's soon-to-be-classic "Swanee," performed for the first
time in public and accompanied by a bevy of dancers.[102]

Morris Gest's prediction that Kendall and Bowes were in over their heads
was half right. Despite their business acumen, they *were* relative "amateurs"
at running such an enormous theater. Motion pictures were still as big a draw
as ever but perhaps not at the prices Bowes and Kendall wanted to charge.
Even with Bowes's artful direction of the Capitol and the talented Wayburn
choreographing such elaborate shows, the Capitol's first eight months were financially difficult. Bowes's effort to create a high-class motion picture theater,
like Triangle's Knickerbocker Theatre several years earlier, was hampered in

part by his insistence on comparatively high ticket prices that made it difficult
to fill 5,300 seats several times a day—especially with the Strand, Rivoli, and
Rialto still attracting patrons at more desirable locations with lower prices.
The structure of the Capitol would have worked far better for a theater half
the size and with half the overhead.

The Capitol Theatre's financial difficulties presented an opportunity Samuel
Goldwyn could exploit. He hoped to further expand his theatrical empire and
establish a New York showcase, staking his claim as a vertically integrated film
company alongside Loew's (which had recently purchased Metro Pictures),
Paramount, Fox, and First National. He and his backers, including Joe Godsol, chairman of the executive committee of Goldwyn Pictures Corporation,
and Lee Shubert (who was also a major investor in Loew's, Inc.), had been
interested in leasing Manhattan's Astor Theatre. Instead, they purchased a
controlling interest in the Capitol in May 1920. Goldwyn wanted the theater
to be the showcase for Goldwyn Pictures, but Godsol colluded with Shubert
to block that plan. The Capitol would have first crack at the Goldwyn lineup,
but neither of the two men wanted to stake their theater investment on the
company's films alone.[103] The theater would serve its investors first and Goldwyn's expansion plans second.

The reconstituted board also wanted a fresh infusion of ideas and a showman whose decision-making would not be questioned by the industry, press,
or Samuel Goldwyn. There was only one man suited for the role who was
also capable of keeping the peace with the feisty Goldwyn: his friend Samuel
Rothapfel. Roxy was the ideal choice to be the new director of presentations in
part because Joe Godsol and (especially) Lee Shubert knew that Roxy would
do whatever he wanted, regardless of his loyalty to Goldwyn.[104] Roxy, in his
own mind, reported to no one.

Major Bowes had run the Capitol admirably but not profitably. To make
way for Roxy, he was relieved of his day-to-day duties at the Capitol and
placated with a new, more impressive title, vice president of the Goldwyn
Pictures Corporation, overseeing all of the circuit's theatrical operations, virtually swapping roles with Roxy. Despite the change, though, Bowes was given
far less authority than his new title would otherwise suggest.[105] Bowes was still
listed as the theater's managing director but had unofficially become, according to historian Gertrude Jobes, the "vice-president-in-charge-of-nothing."[106]
Bowes became part of a long industry tradition of failing upward and was paid
an additional $25,000 per year for his new position.[107]

Roxy was also given a salary that "took away his breath" and he was instructed to immediately fill the theater with patrons.[108] The Capitol announced

in a May 30 advertisement that Roxy would soon "present the unique form of motion picture-musical entertainment he devised and upon which his world-fame rests."[109] He built a new stage for the enlarged orchestra and chorus, improving their visibility and sound, an enhancement commented on by "every newspaper in New York," according to *Motion Picture News*. A new lighting scheme was installed throughout the auditorium, replicating his lighting designs at the Rialto and Rivoli several blocks away.[110]

Nat Finston was hired as the theater's chief conductor and music director, William Axt and Joseph Klein served as assistant musical directors, John Wenger continued to provide the background settings for Roxy's expanded stage shows, and Alexander Oumansky became master of ballet, among a host of other personnel who would contribute to the Capitol's resurgence.[111]

The heads of many Capitol Theatre departments were much like Roxy, immigrants who had embraced their adopted country. Oumansky emigrated from the Ukraine in 1911, where he had been raised with famed pianist and composer Leo Ornstein and had become well known as a member of the Ballets Russe under Vaslav Nijinsky.[112] He previously served as the ballet master at the Metropolitan Opera House.[113] His prima ballerina, Maria Gambarelli, was also an immigrant from Northern Italy. Her blond hair and blue eyes prompted one journalist to remark, "She doesn't look the least bit Italian, as we think of the race." She had begun dancing at age seven and was trained by Madame Cavalazzi, ballet mistress at the Metropolitan Opera House, whom she would later recall struck her in the leg with a baton whenever she missed a step. After a year at the Met, she was engaged by Anna Pavlova and danced with her at the Hippodrome in New York before going on tour with a variety of performers, including Theodore Kosloff and Ed Wynn.[114] She later appeared in a wide array of New York venues.[115] Roxy saw her in 1920 on a scouting trip to the Lexington Opera House while preparing to reopen the Capitol.[116] Gamby, as she would become famously known in the 1920s, and dancer Doris Niles quickly became two of the theater's most popular attractions. The assembled corps of musicians, conductors, dancers, and choreographers was a principal reason for the Capitol's success in the latter half of 1920. Film would certainly be a draw, but Roxy reveled in the size, budget, and grandeur of his latest sandbox. Gamby also shared her employer's interest in cultural uplift. As she told the *New York Times* nearly seventy years later, "During my time, even if I danced in movie theaters, I made people, the everyday public, love the dance. We taught them about ballet."[117]

Roxy officially took over the Capitol's presentations on June 4, 1920, reducing the top admission price to $1.10. With terrific resources at his disposal, he set out to expand the partnership between music, motion pictures, and the performing arts. "[T]he Capitol streamlined its presentation policy . . . when S. L. Rothapfel was brought in," Richard Koszarski notes,[118] focusing on fewer and smaller acts than Wayburn's "Revues." "The elaborate operatic numbers of the former régime have been given up" in favor of a "'typical' Rothapfel program," the *New York Times* reported, featuring "shorter and smaller musical and dancing numbers, similar to those seen at the other motion picture houses on Broadway." Roxy also reduced the show's running times from three hours to two, generating more showtimes at "materially lowered" prices rather than fewer shows at higher prices. He also canceled Bowes's reserved seating policy, forcing audiences to stand in line while also encouraging more drop-in traffic.[119]

(Re)opening night on June 4 was a typical Roxy affair. Although the theater had already been open for more than seven months, Roxy's return to New York was attended by "probably the largest audience that ever witnessed a motion picture offering in a theatre," the *Motion Picture News* reported. Its 5,300 seats were filled with a "distinguished audience" of the "best known men and women of the stage and screen" who gave forth a "riot of applause" for each live act and film Roxy offered.[120]

Roxy's first months at the Capitol were a complete turnaround. Even Messmore Kendall was forced to admit that the Capitol "prospered under Roxy."[121] By the end of the summer, the press re-anointed Roxy as the top film exhibitor in the country. When *Photoplay* featured eight of the industry's leading players for a September 1920 article, Samuel Rothapfel, "in other words 'Roxy,'" was featured.[122] And despite the economic recession, *Wid's* wrote that since Roxy had taken over the Capitol he had "Made history there. And keeping it up. Even during the slump."[123]

The theater's first anniversary in October 1920 was a showcase for all of Roxy's newly assembled talent. The theater had reopened in June with Nathaniel Finston as musical director, but former Rialto and Rivoli musician/conductor Erno Rapee, who had left the Rivoli in November 1919 and served as musical director for the stage production of *Lassie* at the Nora Bayes Theatre in New York from April to August 1920, was now conductor of the Capitol Theatre orchestra, with William Axt serving as assistant music director.[124] Alexander Oumansky continued to direct the ballet with Maria "Gamby" Gambarelli at the lead. Hy Mayer's travelogues were still featured and John Wenger's stage settings framed the entertainment.[125] The Capitol's team was firmly in place.

In the fall of 1920, the Friars and a host of celebrities described as a "Who's Who in Filmdom," including Charlie Chaplin, Raymond Hitchcock, Pearl

White, William Farnum, and Lillian Gish, feted Roxy during their second annual "Motion Picture Night."[126] George Kleine wrote Roxy a few months later, congratulating him "upon the commanding position which [the Capitol] has taken among the theatres of the world. It is my belief that it is the most conspicuous success in the film universe."[127]

Roxy and the German Invasion

Roxy exerted his creative freedom at the Capitol Theatre to broaden his audience's artistic exposure by bringing some of the most lauded German films to the United States, lending his prestige and reputation to them and thereby giving them greater prominence and commercial viability. It is highly probable, for instance, that without Roxy's intervention and presentation, Ernst Lubitsch's *Madame DuBarry/Passion* (1919) might never have received a New York audience—or an opportunity to break through the unofficial American boycott of German goods, including motion pictures, that continued well into 1920.

First National, after acquiring the American rights to Lubitsch's film, was unable to find a New York theater willing to show it. The anti-German sentiment in America, even two years after the cessation of the war, coupled with the public's disinterest in costume dramas, forced the company to miss its target New York release date of October 4, 1920. Even the company's New York showcase house, the Strand, refused to exhibit the film.[128] The *New York Times*' October 24, 1920, edition devoted a lengthy paragraph to a new film made in "Northern Germany" but did not give its name or where it could be seen. The source of the new film had previously been the subject of rumor, which the *Times* now reveled in divulging.[129] *Motion Picture News* commented that it was "the first film of any pretensions to be imported from Europe since the war, and in it the film industry in this country will find the answer" as to whether there would be a postwar market for German films.[130] *Madame DuBarry*, though, continued to languish in American obscurity that fall. The film was finally given a short run in Philadelphia on November 11, 1920, and another booking in Paterson, New Jersey—both in cities with large German populations—in an effort to drum up business, gauge the public's reaction, and entice a New York theater.[131]

The trade journals lauded the film, but still no New York exhibitor had yet shown an interest. Roxy, however, enthusiastically agreed to exhibit it after a screening.[132] He still felt changes would be necessary, though, to win its acceptance. He trimmed the film from nine reels to six, created new intertitles with Katharine Hilliker (who would become preeminent in that role in the 1920s), and devised an insert shot whereby a lit candle on a candelabrum was extinguished each time a main character died. The candelabrum was then included in the design of the new intertitles and a new score, jointly devised by Roxy and Erno Rapee, accompanied the film.[133]

The film's exhibition at the Capitol grew more problematic, though. In early December, the German minister of finance and economics ordered German police to bar any theater from exhibiting American films.[134] First National now had to worry about the film's prospects with American exhibitors who might consider booking the film unpatriotic. A spectacular opening at the Capitol Theatre was perhaps the film's only chance to reach national acclaim and convince other exhibitors of its artistic value *and* commercial viability. If a 5,300-seat theater managed by a Marine reservist and former American propagandist (who had recently dropped the German "p" from his last name) could play the film with success amid the lingering anti-German sentiment, then surely a 250-seat house would not have to worry about similar issues.[135]

Roxy's conversion of *Madame DuBarry* to *Passion*, its extensive edits, and Hilliker's new intertitles, were heartily welcomed by New York audiences and critics.[136] The *New York Times* remarked that his version of the film "may be written down as one of the pre-eminent pictures of the day."[137] Roxy supervised the research and selection of music from the Louis XV period and compiled it with Rapee into an appropriate overture.[138] Alexander Oumansky produced a ballet built on the themes and style of the film and John Wenger designed appropriately thematic sets.[139] The blending of the overture, prologue, feature film, and other attractions created a harmonious unitary text, what *Motion Picture News* deemed "a comprehensive and colorful whole."[140]

Roxy's advance publicity for the film's exhibition and the critical raves raised expectations. There were so many patrons who attempted to get into the theater on the film's opening night that officers from the 47th Street police station were called to manage the crowds and "keep peace."[141] "After the opening performance at the Capitol Sunday, Broadway rang with Rothafel's praises, it being stated that he had given 'Passion' the master presentation of all times in the history of picture exhibiting," *Variety* wrote. "The keen sense of values of S. L. Rothafel, manager of the Capitol, must be credited with having picked the pictorial plum of the year."[142] A *Variety* reviewer remarked that the film "jammed the Capitol theatre, drew long and hearty applause, was cut with rare skill and moved through two hours speedily, holding the interest" of the audience.[143] The Capitol Theatre was frequently sold out during

Passion's two-week run, attracting 94,501 patrons in its first week (and a total of 175,000), breaking all box office records at that time and paving the way for German films to be imported into the United States.[144] "The film that nobody had wanted," Scott Eyman writes, "whose distributors were so unsure of it that they virtually abdicated responsibility for its presentation to the exhibitor, had conquered New York."[145]

Passion was immediately booked for exhibition around the country, *Moving Picture World* reported by early January 1921, in order to meet "the hordes that have crowded into theatres in this country" to see it.[146] In Los Angeles, the Kinema theater smashed all previous records for attendance there with 40,000 viewing *Passion* in its first week alone before being held over due to the demand. "Seldom in the history of local motion-picture presentations has a production caused a like amount of enthusiastic comment," the *Los Angeles Times* wrote.[147] Similar reports were filed by theaters in Atlanta (Criterion), Cincinnati (Walnut), Raleigh (Superba), and Olean, New York (Haven).[148] Roxy's work editing and exhibiting *Passion* had a lasting impact on the prospects for Ernst Lubitsch, Pola Negri, and German films, but Roxy remembered it later as a turning point for . . . Roxy. He boasted twelve years later, still proud that he alone had seen the film's intrinsic value:

> Usually I guess right about pictures. No, I don't know how; just the feel of it, I guess. Probably you don't remember when I brought "Passion" to the Capitol Theater? No? Well, it was a German film that had been kicking about for months. I saw something in it, had it cut and edited. I devised that three-candle idea, with the candles burning lower and lower, and one flickering out each time a principal character died. That made a great hit.[149]

In 1935, a full fifteen years after the film's release, its success was still noteworthy. The *West Australian*, a Perth-based newspaper, recalled *Passion*'s American debut as the catalyst for Lubitsch's states-side success. The film "that nobody wanted except S. L. Rothafel" made "money previously unheard of in the industry," the newspaper reminded readers, and "lifted all concerned to screen fame."[150]

Passion was such a "phenomenal success," Julie Hubbert writes in a 2005 *Musical Quarterly* article, "Modernism at the Movies," "that its record-breaking profits inspired the Goldwyn company to import another German film that had recently played to great popular and critical success in Germany," *Das Cabinet des Dr. Caligari* (*The Cabinet of Dr. Caligari*, 1920).[151] Roxy described the Robert Wiene–directed film as "remarkable in many respects" and one that "introduces an absolutely new innovation in motion picture production."[152] Roxy had no hesitation in exhibiting his employer's newest release. He wrote to audiences in a *New York Times* advertisement two weeks before its debut at the Capitol that "Those who are truly interested in the unfolding of new possibilities in the art of motion pictures will observe in this photoplay a quality which so far has not been attained in screen productions."[153] *The Metronome* reported that the film "utilize[ed] the principles of modern art" in which "the standards of art and production, which have hitherto been considered inflexible, can be discarded for a form of impressionism that creates and intensifies the mood and theme of the changing action."[154] Roxy commented presciently on the day of its American premiere at the Capitol on April 3, 1921, that *The Cabinet of Dr. Caligari* would "create a sensation in America."[155]

Instead of framing the film's aesthetic and/or thematic elements through music and dance, Roxy wrote a spoken-word prologue and epilogue that recast the film in a more conventional manner. The unitary text thus homogenized the film's jagged eccentricities by altering the film's narrative. With Francis now "a prosperous jeweler in Holstenwall," as the stage epilogue concluded, Roxy's alterations made the narrative, which began on the stage, continued on film, and concluded before Capitol patrons with another stage performance, more "suitable for American audiences," with "a happy ending for those who demand them," the *New York Times* commented.[156] Mike Budd notes how the new Roxy-scripted material for *The Cabinet of Dr. Caligari* smoothed out the film's edgier subject matter with "Questions . . . answered, homogeneity reinforced, [and] the film adjusted for mass consumption."[157] The Roxy-generated prologue and epilogue were judged by *Motion Picture News* to be so effective that the entire script was reprinted in the trade journal, which ensured its subsequent use throughout the country.[158] (Kristin Thompson argues, however, that the ubiquity of this usage remains in dispute since the film had barely been exhibited around the country by then to merit such a claim.)[159]

The narrative alterations may have been in line with already conventional American notions of "happy endings," but the music used throughout the film's accompaniment was not assembled to comfort the ears of New York audiences more familiar with Strauss than Stravinsky. Roxy used the music of the "most ultramodern and controversial composers," Julie Hubbert notes, including Schoenberg, Stravinsky, Prokofiev,[160] and other modern composers, to strike a balance between this new sanitized narrative and the film's inherent psychological tensions, striking visuals, and disturbing themes. "Mr. Rapee and I felt that the orthodox thing would not do," Roxy explained to *Musical America*.

A film conceived along revolutionary lines called for a score faithfully synchronized in mood and development. We took psychology into reckoning—the psychology of the audience no less than of the play. In the phantasmagorical scheme of "Dr. Caligari" people move and live in a world out of joint. . . . The key principle of this sprawling architecture and wild terrain is distortion. With that steadily in mind we built up the score. . . . We assembled our themes, assigned characteristic ideas to the principals of the play, and then proceeded to *distort* the music. The music had, as it were, to be made eligible for citizenship in a nightmare country. The score is built up on the leitmotif system; quite in the Wagnerian manner. . . . These main ideas appear singly or together, whole or in part, as the psychology of the tale demands. The scoring is not that of the original, but has been done here and is contrived to emphasize the *macabre*.[161]

Roxy was modest in his estimation of their work. "I think I may confidently and justly say that the whole represents the most daring musical achievement in the history of the American motion-picture theater," he told *Musical America*. "Musically no less than pictorially it opens up a virgin country."[162]

Julie Hubbert writes that although the Roxy-Rapee score has long been highlighted by Thompson, Budd, and other scholars, it may actually have had even more importance than previously stated, especially with American audiences still starved for European music during the postwar ban on German art, cinema, and culture.[163] Hubbert writes that because of the absence of much of Schoenberg's and Stravinsky's work in American concert halls, the assembled Roxy-Rapee score gave many audiences their first taste of these composers and the music that would soon be popularized nationwide.

In the sense that their music itself was almost unknown to U.S. audiences, the score did not so much lend an understanding of modernism as it *anticipated* the establishment of European musical modernism in U.S. concert halls. The film did not so much borrow from the music a sense of modernism as it helped form that definition of modernism. The only observation perhaps more significant than the fact that Rothafel and Rapee brought Stravinsky and Schoenberg to the movie theater, and to 70,000 New York moviegoers no less, is that they did it before [Leopold] Stokowski and [Edgard] Varèse brought Stravinsky's and Schoenberg's most significant works to U.S. audiences. [Roxy and Rapee] brought European modernism to an audience the size and scope of which these two composers would never see in the concert hall.[164]

Hugo Riesenfeld would note in 1926 that most silent films scored before and after *Caligari* drew on earlier works instead of contemporary modernist and/ or popular music. But Roxy and Rapee's work on *Caligari* was daring on a host of levels—artistically, commercially, and politically. "No score that has been written for the cinema," Riesenfeld argued at the time, "has the distinction of this production in its truly contemporary feeling or unity of form." The score for *The Cabinet of Dr. Caligari* was innovative and more contemporary than most, but unlike other musical scores that used a contemporary tune like "Over There" as a leitmotif, Roxy and Rapee built their musical cues and associations for the film with music unknown to almost everyone in attendance and with music that had not yet proven its commercial or even critical value in the United States.[165]

The music's inherent modernism may have had much to do with the film's success at the Capitol, and *Caligari's* financial and critical reception helped create an even larger audience for German and "expressionist" films in America. Over 70,000 patrons saw the film at the Capitol during its one-week run.[166] Given the film's national reception and its continuous showings in little cinemas and other theaters during and after the 1920s, Roxy's claim of having a special sense about film may indeed have had some merit. (Six years later Roxy would prove his foresight regarding German films yet again, declaring *Sunrise* to be "the greatest motion picture that I have ever seen"—nearly five months before it was released to the public.)[167]

High praise for his programming ability came even from those who roundly attacked the bulk of theater owners who were now, whether they assumed that position or not, serving as cultural gatekeepers and tastemakers for the nation's moviegoers. Kenneth Macgowan wrote in a 1921 *North American Review* screed that, "Of all the personal ineptitudes of the screen, none is more powerfully sinister than the exhibitor, the man who owns and manages the theatres where the photoplays meet their public. It is the exhibitor, ignorant and naive when he is not vicious and corrupt, that accents and perpetuates every fault, banality, and vice of the photoplay producers." By then, however, Macgowan began to recognize that there were "geniuses of a sort among the exhibitors . . . who have seen the possibilities in salesmanship that this new entertainment presents—men like Rothapfel, Riesenfeld, Grauman."[168] Roxy ("the name by which everyone is coming to address him" *Zit's* mentioned in May 1921)[169] was now dubbed "the man who gave the movies a college education" by journalist Golda Goldman in the *American Hebrew*.[170]

Roxy was certainly willing to buck conventions in booking motion pictures, but his business sense was still conservative, despite his faith in films like *Passion* and *Caligari*. Roxy often relied on earlier, evergreen successes to balance out these more risky selections. In May 1921, for instance, Roxy dusted off *The Birth of a Nation* (1915) and presented it with a new score that he and Rapee devised. It was performed by the Capitol's then eighty-piece orchestra.[171] The *Evening Journal* commented that the film's "revival at the Capitol is memorable, for it combines a great story with a musical accompaniment that lifts it to the highest plane."[172]

The exhibition of *Birth* was not without controversy, though, and highlights both Roxy's continued editing of the feature films he exhibited and his unwillingness to bow under any pressure from outside or inside the Capitol Theatre. Melvyn Stokes writes that after Roxy announced his upcoming presentation of the controversial film, Walter F. White, the assistant secretary of the NAACP, wrote to Roxy asking him to cancel the film's exhibition. Roxy replied that he had already removed some of the film's objectionable scenes and sought to allay White's fears that the film's screening would generate hatred toward African-Americans. In the end, Roxy was insistent that the "master picture" should still be shown. The NAACP appealed to New York City officials to intervene on the organization's behalf, but the group was rebuffed as the city cited a lack of jurisdiction. Although many former servicemen and service women protested the film's screening during the week of May 8, 1921, their veteran status was apparently not enough to sway Roxy's head or heart.[173] When he was asked some months later about his favorite virtue, he uttered one word without irony or hesitation: tolerance.[174]

ROXY AND REHEARSALS

Preparations for each week's shows were increasingly complex, taxing the physical strength of anyone involved in the creative end of the Capitol's operation. On Monday and Tuesday nights, after the last patrons had left the building and until two or three in the morning each night, Roxy and his assistant Tommy Dowd screened short subjects for possible inclusion. Between 10,000 and 15,000 feet of film was reviewed each week in order to find twelve minutes of usable footage. On Tuesdays, Roxy also organized a meeting of the theater's department heads to discuss the upcoming program. The meetings, according to Walter Eberhardt of *Filmplay Journal*, were "very informal and every one has a right to a free and frank expression of opinion." Eberhardt noted that after Roxy had chosen a specific piece of music for the overture, Rapee and Axt rehearsed the chosen piece with the orchestra.

Alexander Oumansky then choreographed and arranged the ballet sequence in harmony with the music.[175]

Roxy and Rapee spent Wednesday and Thursday evenings scoring the feature film. The two men, along with William Axt and other members of the music department, gathered in the theater's twenty by forty–foot projection room and stared at the small screen. A piano was placed at the back of the room where shelves filled with sheet music lined both walls. Roxy and Rapee sat at a desk facing the screen.[176] The film was projected for the assembled group, but frequently stopped "on a second's notice" and then restarted, "the whole tedious process repeated *ad lib.* until the picture has been gone over perhaps four times. During all the time Mr. Rothafel and his aid[e]s are jotting down selections to be used at each cue, marking the cue and the number of bars to be played for each selection."[177] Roxy and Rapee had a wealth of musical choices with the Capitol music library then housing nearly 33,000 orchestrations and 15,000 catalogued selections by more than 1,500 different composers from "every music publisher throughout the country." The collection also included 1,200 original manuscripts by Rapee as well as Axt, Mendoza, and other Capitol staff, as well as "symphonic scores, operas, chamber music, popular overtures, light operas, musical comedies, folk dances, choral music, classic lieder, popular ballads, and folk songs." The library was staffed by a head librarian, an assistant, and six copyists.[178]

After the appropriate music was selected for the short and feature films that week, as well as the overture and ballet, Friday night's task was dedicated to assembling the newsreel from the new footage from Fox, International, Kinograms, Pathé, and Selznick.[179] Roxy did not take his own notes during the newsreel screenings but squawked his directions to Tommy Dowd and the projectionist about what to play back, keep, or cut. By the end of the evening, 6,000 feet of film had been whittled down to 1,400 feet of news coverage and edited together to form part of the unitary text.[180] "Cut that scene Tommy. . . . Take that long shot of the troops," he called out the night Robert Undegraff from *Physical Culture* showed up to witness the Capitol's extensive weekly preparations. To understand how the newsreel comprised such an important part of the unitary text, and how the unitary text imposed its creative limitations over the entire evening's entertainment, one needs to pay even more attention to what Roxy cut out rather than what he chose to include. "Cut the Chinese famine scene entirely," he told Dowd that evening. "I'm not going to throw misery on the screen . . . I want a bill of *joy.*" The sight of starving Chinese men, women, and children would have (apparently) disrupted the psychological and emotional tone of the overall show. Roxy then started over from scratch. Twenty minutes later he handed Dowd four pages of notes with little white space left. "That'll make your fourteen hundred feet, Tommy."[181]

By the time the newsreel selection was completed, it was nearly midnight. But Dowd's night was far from over. He immediately went to work cutting out the unwanted footage and splicing together the segments Roxy selected. "Now we'll take a little breathing spell while they're piecing the film together," Roxy told Undegraff. "Then we'll do the most interesting part. You see," Roxy said as if it were nine in the morning, "we've only just begun." When the new reel was created, Roxy worked with one of the theater's conductors to provide an accompanying score for the footage. Roxy then made further cuts to the footage to fit the scenes to the music (and vice versa). Undegraff asked Roxy if the late schedule was typical. Yes, Roxy said, "We have to stick at it until it is *finished*, no matter how late it keeps us." By 2:30 A.M., Roxy finally finished for the night and headed home, eager for the next morning's work.[182]

The next evening (Saturday), after the last show was over, Roxy began lighting the stage and auditorium for each sequence of the overall program—the overture, ballet, short and feature films, etc. To accomplish this task quickly, a telephone was wired directly to the lighting and switchboard operators and Roxy called each one of them feverishly during the late evening to infuse sections of the stage with different colored lights.[183] Roxy was still tinkering and barking at 3:00 A.M., but he had long since dropped the telephone in exchange for a more efficient megaphone. Finally, a half hour later, Roxy was done and he left the Capitol before 4:00 A.M. Instead of going home to Rosa, though, he headed out to a restaurant with the reporter from *Physical Culture*.[184] He returned to the Capitol a few hours later for the final dress rehearsal that took place every Sunday morning at 10:00 A.M. Even then, Roxy was still tinkering, cutting, and adding to the live and filmed performances. During the morning's last-minute ballet rehearsals, he was still changing the show to inspire the right kind of attitude and feeling in his patrons. "Just a change of expression," Eberhardt wrote, "the intensity of a spotlight, a shifting of position—all playing their part in the science of audience psychology." During the week in which Walter Eberhardt of *Filmplay Journal* was on hand, Roxy was still trimming the newsreels during the final rehearsal as well. The entire session finally finished at 12:30 P.M. that Sunday when audiences were already lined up down the block to see the new Capitol show.[185]

Some films called for even more rehearsals than Eberhardt described. Roxy had ordered four rehearsals for the "ultramodern" score for *The Cabinet of Dr. Caligari*, not the usual two, to ensure that the orchestra was ready for their performances. "The extra two rehearsals it required . . . created a significant strain on the already tightly scheduled and overworked orchestra, making them rehearse into the early morning hours not just for two nights, but for the better part of a week," Julie Hubbert notes. "And because the orchestra players needed to be compensated financially for the extra rehearsals, the score also taxed the theater's music budget by doubling its average weekly expenditures."[186]

The breakneck pace of the Capitol and its long hours are hard to fathom— not only for the length of each day, which was considerable, but the fact that each week was as long as the next and Roxy and his employees, rarely, if ever, took a day off. "My work is almost an obsession with me," he remarked to Frank Crane of the *Globe*. "I cannot eat or sleep or shave or walk without thinking of it."[187] Robert Undegraff added that the only way to see and under-stand Roxy's work schedule was to "forget all about sleep." Roxy, he observed, "produces in one week a show that most theatrical managers would consider required from three to six weeks to create and put on, and he does it *every week in the year!*"[188] Today, Roxy would be considered a workaholic, but in a period of expansive economic growth and heady capitalist sentiment, Roxy seemed to be an inspiration to journalists, not a cautionary tale. Instead of his workload and obsession being viewed as a possible detriment to his psycho-logical and physical well-being, his ability to work continuously was consid-ered inspiring by magazines like *Physical Culture* (a popular health and fitness magazine of the era). The journal's coverage of Roxy demonstrated both his wide appeal to the popular press and the exemplary (and self-destructive) nature of his work habits. *Variety* would later report that some Capitol em-ployees felt that Roxy was a "slave driving" taskmaster due to the length and rigor of his rehearsals and his demands on theater employees—though few, if any, journalists put those sentiments into print at the time.[189]

Owing in part to the physical nature of the work, Roxy routinely hired ush-ers, musicians, and even his senior staff based as much on their age as their experience. "I prefer young people because they haven't the smug attitude of self-satisfaction that belongs to the professional of long experience," he ex-plained to the *Evening Mail*. "They have the inspiration of youth."[190] With so many exhibitors, musicians, and conductors in the field first serving in movie houses under Roxy, he had become something of a kingmaker, a talent scout, and an inevitable step along the way for many, including Eugene Ormandy. Ormandy was born in Budapest on November 18, 1899, and was, accord-ing to David Ewen, "a child prodigy." After performing throughout Europe, Ormandy arrived in the United States "penniless." "One day he was standing on the corner of 50th Street and Broadway with only five cents in his pocket," Ewen writes, and ran into "an acquaintance from Budapest" who gave him a loan and suggested he seek out another Hungarian: Erno Rapee. Ormandy was hired as a violinst and "in a week's time" became the concertmaster. When David Mendoza was sick one day, Ormandy took over as conductor. He remained one of the principal conductors of the theater for the next seven and a half years before leaving in 1929 for a lucrative career as a guest conductor and with the Philadelphia Orchestra.[191]

Roxy also created a school of theater management at the Capitol. "Among the subjects to be taught," a journalist mentioned, "are the psychology of entertainment, program building, color and lighting, coordination of music and picture, editing of film units, scoring of pictures, scenic investiture, and management of a theater."[192] The Capitol was a theater management and music factory, producing entertainment and future industry leaders.

NANOOK OF BROADWAY

By June 1922, Roxy had been with the Capitol for two highly successful years, establishing a proven track record for the theater and reestablishing his own credibility as the nation's most prolific and influential exhibitor. Roxy's booking of the film *The Crossroads of New York* (1922), for instance, was cited as proof of the film's merits by the *Los Angeles Times* in early June, some 2,500 miles away from the Capitol Theatre.[193] The *New York Morning Telegraph* mentioned that same week that Roxy was once again "looked upon as the leading exponent and the originator of this country's favorite entertainment [deluxe moviegoing]. There have been many who have followed in his footsteps, but none that have been able to keep pace with his untiring progressiveness and his keen ability to build what is new."[194]

Roxy celebrated his two-year anniversary at the Capitol with an elaborate seven-unit presentation of the Goldwyn film *Golden Dreams* (1922) and by taking a fishing trip with E. F. Warner, publisher of *Field & Stream*. Roxy, who had taken only three vacation days in the previous two years, traveled to St. Albans, Vermont, to steal a few quiet moments.[195] He was tired but typically resolute. "It's quite a grind working seven days a week the year round," he quoted, "and yet I wouldn't give it up for all the fish in the sea."[196] Though Roxy was physically away from the Capitol, the venue was not far from his thoughts. He took along a motion picture cameraman to capture his fishing adventure and "bring back evidence of the anglers' prowess" for a later program at the Capitol.[197]

The idea of visible evidence had, of course, been paramount to a Roxy show from its earliest Forest City origins. Actualities, newsreels, and short documentaries had all been part of his repertoire for nearly fifteen years. His desire to capture and project the "real"—whether World War I battle footage, wild animals in Africa, or European vistas—was sated weeks before his fishing trip when Roxy had seen something new. It was a feature-length documentary that could be used for more than just a visual backdrop for his live performers or stripped of its narrative to create a travelogue. Instead, this was a nonfiction film that could stand alone as the featured attraction for the entire week: Robert Flaherty's *Nanook of the North* (1922).

Flaherty had already had enough trouble finding a distributor for the film—both Paramount and First National passed before Pathé agreed to distribute it—but finding an exhibitor for the film would be difficult.[198] Feature-length documentaries as the premiere attraction, rather than as an additional part of the unitary text, were not typical. Pathé suggested that the film would be more suitable to exhibitors if it were chopped into smaller parts and sold as educational shorts. Over time, though, as several others saw the film at Pathé's projection room, the excitement about *Nanook* grew. Pathé decided to keep the film intact and try to book it at a Broadway house. "The problem then," Robert Flaherty recalled nearly three decades later, "was to get one of the big theatres to show it. Now the biggest theatre in New York then was the Capitol, run by a great film exhibitor, Roxy." Pathé had an "in" as the sister of the company's publicity head was a "great friend of Roxy's," Flaherty mentioned. The plan to seduce/induce Roxy to present it involved a collaborative scheme. "[W]e knew very well that to show it to Roxy cold was to invite failure," Flaherty remembered. Pathé was confident that it could be sold to Roxy, but executives commented that "We'll have to salt it." Flaherty recalled the plan in which Roxy's friend was implicated:

> So it was arranged to show it first to her and some of her friends and tell them where to applaud through the picture, and then they would come along to the showing to Roxy in his very elaborate projection-room at the Capitol. We also told them never to talk directly to Roxy about the film but to talk to each other across him as if he were not in the room. Well, by the time the film was over, Roxy was tearing his hair. He used such words as "epic," "masterpiece" and the like. He booked it.[199]

Roxy had already helped set the course for German films in America for the 1920s. His acceptance of *Nanook of the North* was about to have a similar effect on nonfiction films.

Roxy's excitement did not waver in the days leading up to the film's debut at the Capitol. "I consider 'Nanook of the North' so out of the ordinary," Roxy stated before its premiere, "so distinctive and original, and so rich in other elements entering into an unusually fine picture, that I feel no doubt of its welcome by Capitol patrons."[200] In fact, he noted, "I consider 'Nanook of the North' the greatest sensation of the season. It ranks as one of the four most distinctive pictures I have ever run at the Capitol Theatre."[201]

The unitary text of *Nanook of the North* was certainly not confined to the live and filmic entertainment. Audiences were immersed in the aesthetic of the film as soon as they entered the Capitol Theatre's lobby, where deerskin coats and "Eskimo wearing apparel" were hung on the walls along with a dogsled with whips and spears.[202] The lobby was turned into a "veritable museum," *Exhibitors Herald* commented, with "actual implements and utensils, for hunting and domestic life" displayed along with (supposedly) Nanook's "skin-covered 'Kayak' or boat, his dog-drawn sled, snow shoes, harpoons, fishing tackle, dog harness, seal-skin waterproof boots, and costumes for himself and the women and children, besides knives made of walrus ivory, stone lamps and pots used in the 'Igloo.'"[203] Arctic iconography and Eskimo fetishizing extended beyond the walls of the theater as well. Window displays of Eskimo Pies were featured in tie-ins with a number of retailers in the blocks surrounding the Capitol during the week of the film's run, while books focused on the "Far North" were featured at Putnam's Book Store nearby.[204]

Roxy treated the premiere of *Nanook of the North* as an important event and he sent the following note to journalists across the city emphasizing its "real drama" and its "reality":

> So much that is ordinary comes from the mill of picture-making, that when something different and unusual is produced we feel we are justified in calling it to your attention. . . . You will notice an absence of drawing-room drama, of the "eternal triangle" and "emoting," but you will feel the real drama of human beings in the eternal conflict with natural elements, and the thrilling reality of the snowlands. "Nanook of the North" will take you far from the beaten track and it may be that the box office will suffer thereby. Be that as it may, we feel that so unusual, distinctive, and beautiful a production justifies our sponsorship and merits the attention of all who are interested in the welfare of the screen.[205]

"Leaders of New York society," drawn out by the extensive publicity and promotional campaign, arrived for its debut "in large numbers" and others "prominently associated with exploitation and all forms of life were on hand for the first performance," *Exhibitors Herald* wrote. "Many members of local geographical and regional clubs were also interested in attending."[206]

Expectations for the film, and its possible effect on screen content and studio decision-making, were high. Some critics remarked that *Nanook* and other nonfiction films could become a new, high-class alternative. The *Morning Telegraph* wrote that the film "is one of those unusual features so original in theme and treatment that it makes one wonder why so many direc[t]ors cling to hackneyed plots and settings."[207] Another journalist commented that Roxy should be congratulated "for his public recognition of so amazing and unique a picture."[208]

The film opened on June 11, 1922, and tallied $43,000 at the box office during its weeklong run at the Capitol.[209] While the figure was slightly underwhelming, it is important to note that nearly all of the theaters near Times Square suffered declines that week because of the intense summer temperatures, which were "partially to blame for the sour grosses across Broadway," according to one report.[210] It might have been a disappointment for a new Chaplin film, but it was an important marker that feature-length nonfiction films could be the featured attraction at the nation's largest theater. For Roxy, it was another effort to expand the scope of entertainment available to his patrons and central to his argument that film was indeed art.

The success of *Passion*, *Caligari*, and *Nanook*, to name but three of the lauded films that premiered at the Capitol during this period, burnished Roxy's reputation as an important tastemaker. The *New York American*, for example, noted his extended cultural and professional influence in bringing such films to the Capitol's audience:

Within the last year Mr. Rothafel has introduced such notable films as "Passion," "Nanook of the North," "The Cabinet of Dr. Caligari," "The Silent Call," "The Glorious Adventure," "My Country" and others, each of which was the pioneer film in a new school of picture production. These films, several of them, were refused by exhibitors generally, either because it was not thought a propitious moment to risk offering novelties, or because the films were not suited to American audiences. "Passion" was entirely reassembled by Rothafel. For two months he worked, the motion picture editors for the film, for New York audiences. For this patience and perspicacity little credit is given by the average picture reporter. Fortunately, the public has a longer memory for those who have the courage to open new vistas of beauty to its long suffering eyes. . . . No creative artist has ever made more persistent and intelligent effort to raise the standard of his art, to improve it, and to get it before the public than S. L. Rothafel has striven for the motion picture. He has blazed the trails, and to him have fallen the proverbial difficulties of the pioneer.[211]

Between 1920 and 1922, the Capitol Theatre became the most lauded theater in the United States due to its enormous size and, more importantly, Roxy's selection of feature films and their accompanying elaborate presentations. Roxy's bold choice to exhibit German films after World War I—despite his own anti-German propaganda work during the war—enabled their acceptance by film exhibitors throughout the 1920s. His presentation of *Nanook of the North* was equally important, giving the film a Broadway debut and the largest possible audience for a first-run release of a feature-length nonfiction film. These three motion pictures—*Passion, Caligari,* and *Nanook*—are canonical today, but were highly risky upon their release. Their exhibition at the Capitol Theatre in New York had an enormous impact on their success, the careers of Ernst Lubitsch, Pola Negri, and Robert Flaherty, and on the commercial and critical acceptance of Weimar cinema and feature-length documentaries. Together, they boosted Roxy's reputation and his growing stardom amongst industry players, newspaper and trade journalists, and everyday moviegoers.

PART TWO

ROXY AND THE EMERGENCE OF CONVERGENCE

5. A CAPITOL IDEA
ROXY AND THE BIRTH OF MEDIA CONVERGENCE
(1922–1925)

Roxy was born in the first pink blush of radio's morning. Before that he was S. L. Rothafel. Then came this new force. They placed a microphone before his lips, he spoke into it, and his words clutched a million hearts though the miles between were many.
—*American Business Magazine*, 1925

Only in an age of radio and of broadcasting is such a phenomenon as "Roxy" possible.
—*Boston Herald*, April 1925

He was the phenomenon of the '20s. We think that, at that time, he was as well known as Lindbergh. It's really quite astonishing.
—Susan Sontag, discussing Leonard Zelig, in *Zelig* (1983)

Film exhibition in the postwar period ushered in larger orchestras, more elaborate stage shows, and a growing acceptance, fostered in part by Roxy, of foreign, documentary, and avant-garde films. It was also a period of great technological advancement—of new synchronous sound formats developed by Lee DeForest and Western Electric, and, through the use of some of those same patents, the development of sound amplification and wireless transmission. In the coming decade, Roxy would harness his growing political and cultural might and a host of new technologies to become not only the most famous film exhibitor in the United States but one of the most famous entertainers in North America.

ROXY AND THE RADIO

The first radio broadcast took place exactly two years before Roxy's first motion picture–vaudeville show at the Family Theatre, on Christmas Eve 1906. Amateur experiments to broadcast voice and music over the air continued during the next decade but came to a halt during World War I when broadcasting and telegraphy were commandeered by the American war effort. After the end of the war, amateur broadcasts revived around the United States, creating a small but growing number of (often male) radio producers and listeners. Early sets were purchased for their technical capabilities and not for their aesthetic value. Many listened through headsets rather than speakers, creating an intimacy between broadcaster and listener that, by proxy, limited radio as a familial attraction.

The first commercial broadcasting station, KDKA in Pittsburgh, made its first broadcast on November 2, 1920. After premiering with presidential election returns, the station relied on musical programs to maintain listeners and build interest in the station.[1] Radio was imagined by some as a democratic tool, linking citizens to culture, social engagement, religion, and information through new technology. Others saw dollar signs through the sale of radio equipment and the development of new patents and technology. Broadcasting power was often low at the beginning, but the small number of early stations enabled radio-set consumers to tune in broadcasts from both close and far distances. By 1921, there were roughly 50,000 radio sets in the United States.[2] One year later, following the launch of new stations across the country—largely in the Midwest and East Coast—that number had skyrocketed to 1,500,000.[3] Sixty million dollars worth of radio receiving equipment was sold in 1922, and new magazines geared to consumers such as *Radio Digest*, *Radio World*, and *Radio Broadcast* were feeding the public's appetite for news about radio's latest technology, equipment, shows, and burgeoning stars.[4] By November 1922, well over 500 stations were airing programs coast to coast.[5]

The American Telephone and Telegraph Company (AT&T) capitalized on this desire for live home entertainment and the technology it required by monetizing radio broadcasts through advertising. Until that time, radio programming was typically provided as a free service with future profit and organizational models yet to be determined. On August 16, 1922, AT&T launched WEAF as "the world's first toll broadcasting station."[6] Twelve days later, WEAF earned its first $100 from an apartment complex advertising for prospective tenants.[7]

The success of early broadcasting did not escape Roxy's attention. From his first days in entertainment in 1908, he had often used the latest technology as part of his arsenal for entertainment and publicity, tinkering with daylight projection, employing phonograph players, and consistently acquiring and developing new lighting and projection equipment. "I believed in the ultimate destiny of radio," he told *Radio Guide* without a hint of doubt more than a decade later. "I did foresee that some day radio would be hailed as one of the greatest contributions to civilization and the arts. For this reason I allied myself to it. I mentally vivisected its tendencies, its limitations, its strength, and its weakness, and after making my analysis I gambled everything on my decision."[8] While Roxy likened himself to a radio pioneer, his first efforts with "wireless" came about because of AT&T and not because of his supposedly visionary prescience. Nor was he the first exhibitor to use radio to broadcast music and other performances from a theater. On February 20, 1922, for instance, a broadcast of orchestral and vocal numbers from the Kinema Theater in Los Angeles was sent from the venue's "wireless station" to the Electric Club listening in at a banquet held at the Alexandria.[9] Roxy's subsequent use of radio to promote his theater was not his true innovation—it was the form of his broadcasts, his cultivation of personality, and his public appeal that diverged markedly from WEAF and many other broadcasters of the era.

The Capitol Theatre was ideally suited to become a venue for radio broadcasting. From its inception, radio historian William Peck Banning writes, the Capitol was famous for its acoustics.

> [T]elephone engineers engaged in the development of public-address systems were exceedingly anxious to use the auditorium for more extensive tests than were possible in the Western Electric laboratory. When it was suggested to Mr. Rothafel that he discard his megaphone at rehearsals and conserve his energy by using instead a microphone, an amplifier, and a loud speaker he was frankly skeptical but consented to try the apparatus. Its usefulness was, of course, apparent at the first demonstration, and the delighted director gave the engineers permission to utilize an off-stage dressing room for their testing equipment, and to install microphones at various places on the theatre's great proscenium arch to pick up the music of the Capitol's large and distinguished orchestra.[10]

With the theater fully wired not only to amplify sound but to transmit it as well, George F. McClelland, program director of WEAF, approached Roxy with the idea of broadcasting the musical portions of the Capitol Theatre show that preceded or accompanied the short and feature films he exhibited.[11] The integration of radio at the Capitol, rather than being an ingenious Roxy brainstorm, actually came about because of AT&T. It was another example of an opportunity for Roxy that was available because of his management of New York's largest movie house.

The Capitol orchestra's performance during the week of November 19, 1922, was part of its new series, "Impressions of Great Composers," that sought to provide audiences with "the representative works that have endeared the great masters to the music-loving public." Roxy's first thought was Richard Strauss and he planned to highlight Wagner, Tchaikovsky, Verdi, and Brahms, among others, in future performances. The focus of the first week's musical offerings, instead, was Strauss's symphonic poem "Ein Heldenleben" ("A Hero's Life"). The Capitol Theatre stated that it was the first time the work was performed in any theater.[12] Jack Banner later noted that Roxy chose the piece for broadcasting "because of its especially adaptable tonal qualities."[13]

On November 19, workers suspended several microphones from the ceiling of the Capitol Theatre, just above the orchestra.[14] AT&T acoustical engineer Frederick W. M'Kown then worked with Roxy and the Capitol orchestra to broadcast their performance.[15] Roxy "gave the signal to conductor Erno Rapee which sent the first bars of the beautiful melody crashing out through space," Banner wrote.[16] It was the first broadcast in radio history to emanate from the stage of a theater, rather than from an orchestra pit, a fairly dubious distinction that was parroted endlessly despite its relative insignificance.[17] If this was a historic occasion, it was certainly not treated that way by local newspapers, perhaps because of the Kinema's and other theaters' efforts. The *New York Times*, for instance, devoted only one sentence in their November 24, 1922, "Music Notes" column: "Strauss's 'Heldenleben' has been heard by 73,000 patrons this week at the Capitol Theatre, and by probably 600,000 more by radio."[18] That number may have been even larger. "[D]espite the limited extent of the broadcasting and receiving equipment of the day," Banner recalled, "clear reception was reported throughout the eastern seaboard, ranging as far south as Mississippi and as far north as Canada!" Roxy's first broadcast was international. The next morning, according to oft-repeated lore, several thousand letters arrived at the Capitol Theatre "commenting on the general excellence of the program."[19]

Although these broadcasts were to be tests for AT&T, WEAF, and the Capitol Theatre, in typical Roxy fashion, he reoriented the focus of these weekly broadcasts to himself with his legendary sentimentalism. "My friends call me by my nickname, Roxy," he told an early audience, "and when you write you can call me that, too, if you want to!"[20] Perhaps most popular was his chatty greeting, "Hello, everybody!" and his sign-off each Sunday night, a secular benediction that became a household phrase across the country: "Good night, pleasant dreams, God bless you." Roxy later revealed that the sign-off had been a spontaneous gesture and one that had left him uncomfortable until an unnamed radio executive implored him to repeat it the following week, noting "that God-bless-you stuff was great, just the kind of hokum people eat up. It's in!"[21] The connection he instantly established with his unseen audience was evident in one of the letters that arrived shortly after his first broadcast. A Boston woman wrote, "Your 'God bless you' was a benediction. Your voice helped me to think that I was blessed. I felt as if in you I had found an intimate friend."[22] That connection became a hallmark of Roxy's on-air personality and something that broadcasters have tried to emulate ever since. The inclusion of personal messages and elements of his "personality" in his broadcasts was in direct contrast to every other WEAF broadcaster in 1922.

Roxy was paid no salary by WEAF or AT&T, and the Sunday evening broadcasts were intended purely as a promotional tool for the theater.[23] But, Daniel Okrent writes, "[W]hen the lines the next morning reached halfway down the block, four abreast," as radio listeners wanted to see the theater and the orchestra that had produced the over-the-air music and the host (Roxy) who had presented this entertainment, "the radio advertisement was on its way to commercial beatification." The country's leading exhibitor had harnessed broadcasting to give him and the Capitol a national voice. The era of film and radio working in harmony had begun. The Capitol's broadcasts were "radio's first genuine hit," Okrent writes, and Roxy's initial shows were heard across the United States, well into Canada and Cuba, and on ships at sea that picked up the broadcast.[24]

The timing of Roxy's newly won public prominence in and out of New York coincided with lists that placed him among only four personalities (along with D. W. Griffith, Charlie Chaplin, and Adolph Zukor) who were named by both *Motion Picture News* and a separate list created by Terry Ramsaye as the "twelve greatest" in the motion picture industry at the end of 1922.[25] Roxy had already created a Rothafel brand, but he would soon replace his surname with a nickname that was easy to remember and hard to forget: "Roxy." Even today, the name is global, though few are aware of its etymological origin.

It is important to refute, once again, the notion that Roxy was alone in broadcasting a performance from a movie theater at the time. Two days after Roxy's first Capitol Theatre broadcast, Sid Grauman transmitted a *Robin Hood* concert from his Egyptian Theatre in Hollywood over Los Angeles radio station KHJ.[26] Grauman's broadcasting efforts were sporadic and localized, however. Roxy, in contrast, was quick to ingratiate himself into the burgeoning radio field and popularize the Capitol name nationwide.[27] Over the next two months, the Capitol Theatre broadcasts could be heard at various times on Sunday nights by tuning in to WEAF.[28] On January 14, 1923, for instance, "Music from the Capitol Theatre" could be heard over WEAF from 9:15 to 10:00 P.M.[29] Two weeks later, the show began at 7:55 P.M. and lasted until 9:00 P.M. and, like Grauman's November 1922 broadcast, included "selections from the opera 'Robin Hood.'"[30]

Over their first few months, Roxy transformed the broadcasts from a transmission of the Capitol orchestra's music into a multi-tiered variety show, one of the first of its kind on radio. Roxy adapted the vaudeville/variety format for radio and helped consecrate the genre at the genesis of national broadcasting. As Jack Banner would later recall, Roxy "searched his files and his memory for artists whose voices would register well over the tricky microphone." After "endless tryouts," he selected many of the Capitol's performers including "Gladys Rice, a young coloratura soprano; 'Wee Willie' Robyn, tenor; Douglas Stanbury, baritone; Celia Branz, contralto; Joseph Stopak, violinist; Phil Ohman and Victor Arden, pianists; Frank Moulan, comedian; Florence Mulholland, contralto; Beatrice Belkin, soprano; and Maria Gambarelli, singer and dancer."[31] He "soon turned the broadcast into 'Roxy and His Gang,' " Messmore Kendall wrote, "with an occasional reference to the theatre."[32] In January, to accommodate his troupe of performers, Roxy began construction on a new broadcasting studio inside the Capitol Theatre. It was used for the first time on February 4, 1923. Roxy was no longer promoting only the theater's live performances on the air, but his "Gang" of Capitol dancers, singers, and musicians and a few outside players whose on-air performances were heard only by those listening at home.[33] The Capitol Theatre now had two audiences: one physical and local and another invisible and international.

ROXY TRAVELS TO EUROPE

One day after the Gang's first broadcast from the new Capitol Theatre broadcasting studio, Roxy sailed for England. He would often travel to Europe during the 1920s for inspiration, to cull talent from local movie theaters, opera houses, and music halls, and, while there, to spread his prophecies and advice to anyone who would listen. He also badly needed a break, having last taken a vacation during his fishing trip to Vermont nine months earlier. *The Sun* remarked that most would have shied away from traveling the choppy seas and "February gales" of the Atlantic Ocean, but not the former Marine.[34] In a fitting touch that either played as a salute to their leader or as a testament to his own workaholic nature, the Capitol Theatre orchestra broadcasted Roxy's favorite overture which he tuned in through a radio in his stateroom on the SS *Berengaria*.[35] Listening to his orchestra over the radio playing expressly for him as the ship glided through the Atlantic, it is hard not to imagine Roxy feeling a deep sense of accomplishment. Roxy's (brand) name had been synonymous with film and film exhibition; now, radio captivated his and the country's attention and imagination.

Roxy's filmic and broadcasting accomplishments made news on both sides of the Atlantic well before his visit. The January 29, 1923, edition of London's *Evening Standard* commented, for instance, that Roxy was "the first film exhibitor to conceive the idea of broadcasting his programme by wireless . . . patrons who are unable to attend the theatre to see the films can enjoy the music in their own homes."[36] *The Film Renter & Moving Picture News* noted that he was "easily the foremost showman of our time," while *The Bioscope* welcomed Roxy to England as the "Industry's Greatest Showman" and a "genius." *The Bioscope* added that his visit was slated to be "one of outstanding interest to all sides of the British industry."[37] News of Roxy's imminent arrival was also published in Liverpool, Birmingham, Sheffield, and Westminster newspapers, among others, including the *South Wales Echo,* which referred to him as the "U.S. Film King."[38] The *Liverpool Courier* generously added that "Almost every new idea introduced into kinema theatres has had its origins in his brain."[39]

Upon Roxy's arrival, the London and Home Counties branch of the Cinematograph Exhibitors Association held a luncheon for 150 in his honor at the Trocadero Restaurant in Piccadilly Circus.[40] The audience comprised "every man of note in the Industry" including "All the most important members of the C.E.A. general council . . . and practically every renter [exhibitor]."[41] At the event, Roxy urged exhibitors to use psychology to understand their patrons and to uplift them. The *Kinematograph Weekly* was impressed that Roxy had convinced "even conservative British exhibitors" to use "sound theory" over the gut instincts of the "showman"—a reversal of more conventional industry philosophy.[42] *The Film Renter & Moving Picture News* certainly enabled his influence on English exhibitors, pushing them to "Go Thou and Do Likewise," as one article about Roxy's visit was titled. "Take a lesson from the greatest showman in America," the journal wrote, "and study your audience."[43] *The Motion Picture Studio* was even more pointed. The journal praised Roxy for noting that "The mistake of the exhibitor all over the world is that he underestimates the intelligence of his audience," and added, "We should like to see these flaming letters over every exhibitor's desk in the kingdom."[44] *Motion Picture News* commented that "his recent entry into London was similar to Caesar's triumphal entry into Rome after his Alps campaign."[45]

From London, Roxy traveled next to the Regent Theatre in Brighton where Walter Wanger, who was then the manager of the Regent before heading to America and a long career as an executive and producer, held a dinner in his honor.[46] The train ride, which shepherded "all the notables of the English film world" to Brighton, was an event in itself. On board, the train featured a host of dishes dedicated to Roxy, including "Délice à la Roxy," "Saumon Poché Rothafel Presentation," "Pommes Godsol" (for Goldwyn executive Joe Godsol), and "Pêches à la Capitol."[47] When he finally arrived in Brighton, Roxy was highly impressed by Wanger's management and hospitality, dubbing the Regent "magnificent"—rare praise for a British cinema by an American.[48] In all, *The Sun* reported, "the reception given to Mr. Rothafel was one of the warmest in the history of British film circles and everything was done to make the foremost of American exhibitors to feel at home."[49] Roxy left Southampton, England, on February 10 and arrived in New York on February 18.[50] The net result of the trip is unclear, but his reputation in England was certainly enhanced. Roxy's foreign tour also led to coverage by journalists in other parts of the British Empire. The *Western Argus*'s (Kalgoorie, WA) "Special Representative" in London noted in April 1923 that Roxy was "the greatest intellectual force in the American industry" and was "known as the 'Moses' of the cinema world."[51]

Roxy Returns to Radio

After Roxy's return to New York, his radio program's popularity grew. He even arrived just in time to go on the air that night. After all, no time was wasted in a Rothafel day. Roxy also resumed his work accompanying, with Rapee's assistance, the films presented at the Capitol. For Goldwyn's *Souls for Sale* (1923), Roxy wrote a theme song for the film that was sung by Evelyn Herbert, Betsy Ayres, and James Parker Coombs in a prelude before the film's exhibition.[52]

Roxy traveled to Rochester, New York's newly opened 3,094-seat Eastman Theatre a few days after returning from Europe. Once rumored as a possible director of the theater, Roxy was glowing in his praise of the new venue. "I am thoroughly acquainted with every motion picture house of importance in both this country and Europe," he told the *Rochester Herald*, "and without exception the Eastman Theatre, in point of beauty, good taste, refinement and artistic appointments, leads them all; in fact, there is nothing like it in the world."[53] Roxy may have had a motive in his flattery, having recently been hired by George Eastman for $50,000 to begin supervising the theater's presentations on May 1, 1923, and to hire new artists for the Eastman. The arrangement called for Roxy to finish his work for the Capitol each week by Sunday night and then take a late-night train to Rochester, over 300 miles from Manhattan. He would then direct the Eastman Theatre's presentations on Monday (his one night off from the Capitol) and return by train to New York City late that night. The plan was feasible because the Eastman Theatre would present whatever film(s) the Capitol had shown a week earlier (and thus Roxy already had a clear idea of what live and musical accompaniment should be used by the seventy-five-piece orchestra). Roxy, the *New York Clipper* reported, would also choose the theater's on-site, day-to-day director.[54]

The Eastman Theatre was just one of many distractions from the daily tasks at the Capitol. None, however, was as alluring to Roxy as the opportunities presented by broadcasting. By mid-1923, Roxy had become entranced by radio and its ability to reach millions simultaneously. Each two-hour show at the Capitol could only reach 5,300 patrons; Roxy's radio show could already reach a million listeners or more.

Audiences seemed enamored with the new troupe he dubbed "Roxy and His Gang." "The Capitol Theatre needs no introduction" the *Atlantic City Gazette Review* noted in mid-April 1923, when its music is "broadcasted to the world. In the hotels and cabarets of Atlantic City as well as in hundreds of homes Mr. Rothapfel's [sic] weekly offering is eagerly awaited."[55] This poem, from Mary Burns in May 1923, demonstrates how Roxy had already made several of his artists beloved radio stars after only six months on the air:

On Sunday night 'tis our delight, To listen for your voice;
For then we know we'll be entranced, By all your artists' choice.
There's Betsy with her southern drawl, And with her giggle dear,
And Evelyn whose wondrous voice, Can bring a smile or tear.
And Bunchuk with his 'cello grand, Whose playing leaves us mute,
And all the others in your band, Including Edna—cute.
We'd like to have their pictures; You promised one, you know,
So will you kindly send it, To the name you see below?
Now, while we love the programme, Which we receive by proxy,
We know the man behind it, Is a fellow known as Roxy.
Comparisons are odious, But all must realize
That the programme from the Capitol, Should really take the prize.[56]

Radio Digest, noting his place among families across the country, commented in early June that "Many people accustomed to go out for dinner Sunday evening, now wait for the announcement in Mr. Rothafel's inimitable manner of the Capitol's musical programs, which are uniformly the finest series of concerts offered either on the air or in the concert hall."[57] In just over six months, Roxy's Sunday night broadcasts had already become appointment listening and had begun, like other beloved radio programs, to restructure familial activities and expectations.

Each week Roxy connected with fans and thus became more invaluable to the program and the theater. He was building patronage for the Capitol and for his own personal leverage. He was soon rewarded with a salary increase from his Capitol managers from $52,000 to $65,000 per year.[58] The raise was clearly aimed at keeping him happy and firmly entrenched at the Capitol. (Given his record of nomadic employment, this was always a concern for Roxy's employers.)

Perhaps the most critical question to be asked of Roxy's radio success—and the one that journalists, industry executives, and exhibitors most often argued over at the time—was what tangible result Roxy's radio program had on theater attendance, both positively for the Capitol and, perhaps, negatively for other theaters. Were patrons staying home to listen to the radio? Roxy argued that the Capitol broadcasts actually *added* $5,000 per week to the Capitol's box office. "The financial receipts of the Capitol have gone up by thousands a week since we started in broadcasting our program here on Sunday evenings," he said in August 1923. "The radio has brought the Capitol Theater into the family life of America. It has brought me into the homes of my Public. We are in touch."[59] The *Exhibitor's Trade Review* added, "Thousands of [radio fans] attend his Capitol Theatre simply because he has 'sold' them his personality over the air route. Their first thought in selecting a showhouse is 'Let's go to "Roxy's" theatre.' "[60] Michele Hilmes notes that Roxy and His Gang was a gateway show for many and one of two "groundbreaking programs . . . that deployed what Warren Susman identifies as the 'Culture of Personality' to introduce the expanded and newly constituted listening public to the experience of radio."[61]

Roxy's ideology for his radio program was much the same as his Capitol Theatre live performances: to entertain the masses with fine music while using the airwaves to create a new, more intimate connection with radio listeners through his amiable style. As always, Roxy fashioned himself as a champion of the middle and lower classes who he felt were no less deserving of high culture. Many contemporary press accounts noted that he was also a healer, able to inspire, console, and embolden the weak. Numerous articles detailed sickly listeners, young and old, living only to hear Roxy's voice, while accompanying letters to newspapers and others sent to Roxy reinforced the notion that he was working for a higher, nobler purpose than just to promote the Capitol. "I have never been to your theatre," one woman wrote in 1923, "because I am an invalid but they are going to put me in [a] taxi now and take me down to your theatre because I have enjoyed your broadcasting."[62] The *Evening-World* reported that "Another enthusiast is a ninety-seven-year old lady, an invalid who has not walked since 1917. As soon as the weather permits, she says she is coming[,] she is going to get a taxi and come up to see the theatre, where she can watch the performance for herself from a wheelchair."[63] Roxy was understandably moved by the results of his show.[64] "We were inspired," he said, "by the thought that we could make life more livable and bright for those shut-ins who for one reason or another could not leave their homes, who, in a word, are deprived of those pleasures which we so freely enjoy and frequently fail to appreciate."[65] For Roxy, no group of "shut-ins" received more attention than disabled veterans, who in the following years would become a focal point of his fundraising.

His radio program continued to be a crucial part of the Capitol's ever-growing success, with broadcasts from Roxy and His Gang encouraging more and more listeners to patronize the theater. *Exhibitor's Trade Review* noted that by May 1923 the Capitol had already received "thousands of letters" which "actually state that the writer, although never before in this theatre has been converted into a steady patron . . . direct evidence of the possibilities of radio broadcasting as a means of bringing new people into the theatre and making new friends for it and the motion picture."[66] *Wireless Age* quoted another man who said he had never been to the Capitol before building a radio set at home and hearing Roxy's broadcasting. Since then, he had already visited the Capitol five times.[67]

Audiences looking for members of the Gang at the Capitol weren't disappointed. In addition to individual performances by Gambarelli et al., Roxy frequently presented his radio troupe as a unit of his show. In July 1923, for instance, he presented the second edition of "In Our Broadcasting Studio" that introduced "some of the Capitol Theatre artists who broadcast through Station W. E. A. F.," including William Axt, Betsy Ayres, Douglas Stanbury, William Robyn, Yasha Bunchuk, Eugene Ormandy, and others known to listening audiences at home.[68] In the coming months and years, the titles of his live presentations would better harmonize with the name of the group as "Roxy's Gang" segments were sometimes offered at the Capitol Theatre four times per day.[69]

Roxy's success with radio did not quell the film industry's concern about radio, though. While some journals were sold on the influence of his radio show on the Capitol's box office, the issue was still hotly debated throughout 1923, even by Roxy. Although he had noted in May that his "experience thus far is that [his radio listeners] do come and that they have increased the business at this theatre,"[70] he hedged that statement somewhat the following month in *Wireless Age*:

> It is impossible to determine whether it has increased the attendance or not. That takes care of itself. But I have noticed this: it has a psychological effect. It makes the theater audiences much more cordial. Their applause is warmer. You can feel it quite decidedly, especially when some artist comes on whom they have learned to know by radio. . . . Broadcasting gives us a personality.[71]

By April 1923, after moving time slots and expanding his radio program's length, the format of the program was finally set. Instead of the broadcast conforming to the schedule of the motion picture theater, Roxy reorganized his Sunday evening shows at the Capitol to conform to his radio broadcasts—an important distinction and deviation. Capitol Theatre audiences on Sunday nights were now strictly regimented for the benefit of Roxy's invisible radio listeners. At 7:20 P.M., Roxy gave "introductory remarks" to the evening's broadcast. From a microphone placed near the stage, he described in detail what Capitol Theatre audiences were about to witness. Ten minutes later, the Capitol Grand Orchestra, conducted by Erno Rapee, played for both live and radio audiences. At 7:42, radio audiences listened in to the "incidental music" for the Capitol News[reel] program. At 7:50, the Capitol Theatre featured artists such as James Coombs and Willie Robyn performing on stage at the Capitol (they could also be heard over the radio).[72] Roxy was never far from the microphone and frequently described over the air the images of the newsreels and other short films audiences saw at the Capitol Theatre.[73]

While the first half of the show was heard by Roxy's live audience and by listeners at home, from 8:05 to 9:00, Roxy and His Gang (and other invited artists) moved from the Capitol Theatre stage to the broadcasting studio. Rapee remained downstairs to conduct the orchestra for the feature film.[74] William Axt, who was named director of radio activities of the Capitol Theatre in May 1923, conducted the musicians in the studio.[75] *Hostess Magazine* provided a more detailed description of the studio broadcast sessions and the buzz of activity that took place after the musical performance downstairs:

> By 8 o'clock the private office and connecting halls are teeming with artists and their moral supporters; powdered and bewigged singers and players

who have just performed in the stage below appear in flushed excitement; cello and violin cases hobnob in empty corners and there is an atmosphere of contagious exhilaration. With a nod to his artists, "Roxy" steps into the broadcasting room down the hall, followed by a troop of giggling, serious, blase [*sic*] and thrilled performers. Grateful chairs cuddle close to the walls, a solemn silence is maintained to the accompaniment of sly winks, many gestures and an incessant coming and going of important looking persons who carry messages on yellow pads and phone caps on their ears. So, Mr. Smith of Sheridan, Wyoming and Mr. Tone's of Portland, Oregon, when you hear Station WEAF on Sunday night, just close your eyes and picture a grey curtained room atop the Capitol Theatre where earnest efforts are being made to give you the best in music.[76]

The importance of inviting magazines like *Hostess* to watch a Roxy broadcast was in its ability to bring a visual corollary to the disembodied voices audiences had grown accustomed to.

Just as Roxy sought control of all aspects of the Capitol's lighting design to affect the mood and psychology of his audiences during the presentation of live shows and films, he sought to do the same for his radio audiences. During the broadcast, he would often request that his listeners dim their lights (or extinguish them completely) in order to focus on a melody such as "Love's Old Sweet Song" performed by Betsy Ayres in the Capitol studio. In this way, *Radio Digest* noted, Roxy brought "his own lighting effects into their homes" and many listeners "wrote in to say that they had followed this suggestion with telling effect."[77] Another week he instructed his audiences to "Turn out the lights, now, folks and we'll let you hear 'Meditation.'" When "one of his 'gang' . . . sweetens the air with the strains of that soft music," journalist Mary Radcliffe noted, "mother and father and those of the upcoming generation sit in darkness and listen."[78] Another newspaper's account reflects how many had followed his advice in lighting:

No one, so far, has employed the personal note of radio as well as "Roxy." To the thousands who sat in the semi-gloom of dimmed lights or low-burning logs last night and heard the concluding part of his program—a series of sentiment-provoking ballads, the Capitol Theater studio was not a hundred or a thousand miles away. It was just past the half closed doors in the adjoining room, and "Roxy" and the gang were sitting also quiet in the semi-gloom, dreaming and echoing their dreams in song. It was a device worthy of a Barnum turned Barrie.[79]

Roxy and His Gang audiences were not addressed as listeners but as friends. The broadcasting studio was not spoken of as a place far away but one connected, seemingly next door, through radio. A friendly, genial host, nicknamed artists who spoke or performed directly for audiences at home, and a direct appeal to light one's home like the Capitol Theatre studio were all devices aimed at making the radio show seem less like a performance over the air than an intimate gathering of friends.

BANKING ON CONVERGENCE

With Sunday nights across the country occupied by Roxy and His Gang for millions of houses, apartments, town halls, radio stores, and other venues, Roxy, Rapee, and Axt worked to expand their growing multimedia empire. This was part of Roxy's extensive promotional efforts on behalf of the Capitol and a way to capitalize on the troupe's newfound stardom. Erno Rapee had already reached a modicum of fame within the music and film industries by the time he joined the Capitol in 1920. He had managed to leverage his success at the Rivoli, for instance, with work for Duo-Art playing tunes for player-piano rolls such as "Some Other Girl."[80] The work he performed accompanying motion pictures at the Capitol and conducting its large and accomplished orchestra brought increased recognition between 1920 and 1923. He was praised for his score for William Fox's *The Queen of Sheba* (1921)[81] and later for Fox's *Iron Horse* (1925).[82] He performed similar work for Fox when his score for *If Winter Comes* (1923) was used in theaters across the country. Rapee's name and music were a central part of the film's advertising in the *Davenport* (Iowa) *Democrat and Leader*, for instance, reinforcing his own ability to build a brand name for himself—even in Roxy's considerable shadow.[83]

Because of Rapee's work scoring motion pictures for a variety of films and distributors in and out of the Capitol, as well as the work of Roxy, Axt, and Mendoza, "hundreds" of exhibitors, *Dance Review* reported, routinely asked for their cue sheets, scores, and selections for the same films when they debuted elsewhere. The largest music publishers of the era took note of the demand and offered Rapee and Axt contracts to commercialize their work for distribution. The two settled on an exclusive three-year contract with publisher Richmond-Robbins for all of their compositions. Three new series of sheet music were published following the deal in March 1923, including "The Capitol Photoplay Series."[84]

Rapee and the Capitol Grand Orchestra added music recording to their endeavors as well. In February 1923, Brunswick Records released the first of several Capitol Grand Orchestra performances to consumers, its first a recording of Grieg's "Peer Gynt Suite,"[85] followed by records featuring "Orpheus in Hades Overture," "In a Monastery Garden," and "Cavalleria Rusticana." The Capitol Theatre (brand) name, known in print and over the radio to a nation of music lovers, was now used to sell Brunswick's latest offerings. The company placed advertisements nationwide to sell the record, noting that the music was "Played by the CAPITOL GRAND ORCHESTRA, Erno Rapee, Conductor. . . . Conceded by many critics to be the finest symphony orchestra in any theatre in the world."[86] A Brunswick advertisement in the *Los Angeles Times* proudly noted that the Capitol's musical organization was "now an exclusive Brunswick orchestra."[87] With music publishing and recording, broadcasting, and motion pictures under one roof, the Capitol became the first movie theater to fully embrace the possibility of early media convergence. Roxy, who had always embraced the latest technology, and Rapee were at the forefront of a new movement to break down the walls that separated the disparate fields of music, broadcasting, theater, and film and bring them all together for entertainment, culture, and profit in public spaces and private venues.

Roxy's convergent success with radio (and the Capitol's efforts in music publishing and recording) proved too tempting for his rivals to ignore. Manhattan's 3,500-seat Strand Theatre, one of Roxy's many former deluxe houses, announced in June 1923 that it would begin broadcasting its stage programs and music over the air. Loew's quickly followed, buying New York radio station WHN as a vehicle for promoting the company's Metro Pictures films and Loew's theaters, while promoting the entertainment available at its flagship Loew's State in Times Square.[88]

William Fox sought not only to duplicate Roxy's methods but to procure one of his key players. He had already been employing Erno Rapee to create scores for some of his films, and now he hired him away from the Capitol and made him the managing director of the new 2,423-seat Fox Theatre in Philadelphia, which like the Strand, Loew's State, and Capitol theaters in New York also became a venue for media convergence. Rapee subsequently conducted the theater's fifty-five-member orchestra and initiated the theater's broadcasting efforts over station WOO on November 26, 1923.[89] The theater's broadcast, like others of the era, extended far beyond the Philadelphia area.[90] (William Axt and David Mendoza subsequently assumed primary conducting and arranging duties at the Capitol.)

In the coming months, Harold Franklin, then head of Famous Players-Lasky, joined Fox, Loew's, and other independent exhibitors (such as Kansas City's Liberty Theatre) in advising his circuit's theater managers to use radio tie-ins to boost attendance.[91] "There are several [more] theatres in the United States," *Exhibitor's Trade Review* wrote, "that are using every effort to tie in to their enterprises the far-reaching wireless."[92] Roxy came up with a self-serving solution for smaller houses that could not afford to broadcast their own performances: he suggested they pick up his program over the air and amplify the broadcast through their speakers, thereby using the Capitol Theatre music "in lieu of the regular house orchestra."[93]

Roxy was also heartened by the industry's imitations. "Any attempt to stop [radio] would be like trying to push back the Atlantic Ocean," he told the *New York Times* in June 1924. "It is true that people may stay at home to listen in, but this only makes them all the more eager to see the entertainment. They want to see the things they hear."[94] The Capitol Theatre program featuring Roxy and His Gang now reached an estimated five million listeners every Sunday.[95] Nearly 25,000 letters arrived at the Capitol each week from fans all across North America and Cuba,[96] along with postcards, telegrams, "flowers, fruit, fish, garters, books, a painting, 141 newly composed ballads, seven original cartoons, an Airedale terrier, a police dog, 328 postcards from listeners on vacation sending a note to their 'friend,' letters from 17 couples on their honeymoons, and a great deal more."[97]

B. P. Schulberg shrugged off any concern over Roxy's and other broadcasts' collective effect on theaters. "It is ridiculous," he told *Exhibitor's Trade Review*, "to suppose that a medium so totally different in its appeal will make any inroads whatever on attendance."[98] Independent exhibitors like Sydney Lust and William Brandt, though, were alarmed. "The radio is decreasing the patronage of the movies," Lust noted.

As an illustration, at my home I have installed a very fine radio set and on Sunday evenings when Roxy is broadcasting, my wife and a party of friends sit around and listen in, where heretofore they would go to the movies.... While it may not decrease the patronage of the first run houses or the downtown houses, the community houses are suffering. You understand that I have asked a number of exhibitors who conduct community houses and this is also their version of the question. The radio may help the Capitol in New York, since they broadcast their program and at the same time advertise their theater, but this does not help the residential exhibitor.[99]

Zittel, of *Zit's Daily*, also warned Roxy and Loew that they would be "sorry" for giving away their programs for free. "When the aerial picture machine [television] is perfected," he presciently noted, "everybody will wake up."[100] While the *Morning Telegraph* reported that "Debate [was] hot and heavy in many quarters over the effect of the radio on the attendance of motion picture theatres and the relative value of the same as a publicity promoter for the houses,"[101] *Variety* studied its "figures and facts" and concluded that radio was indeed a danger to moviegoing and movie theaters.[102] Roxy challenged Lust and other radio opponents within the film industry by arguing "that the motion picture is in a peculiarly favorable position with respect to broadcasting. Its chief form of entertainment, the picture, can not be transmitted through the air—yet—and if people who hear the Radio concert like them in Radio form they must actually attend the theater to get the picture." Roxy argued further that stars would not necessarily be lost to radio either, noting in February 1924 that he had invited John Barrymore to join the Gang on the air during a recent broadcast and that Barrymore had "trembled like a leaf." He added that despite his great professional respect for Charlie Chaplin's films, the actor was also a "bust" on the radio.[103]

Journalists did not necessarily buy this replacement theory either. Evelyn Lanzius of *Radio Digest* argued that audiences knew that in terms of phenomenological excitement and aural fidelity, and in order to see the visuals they were missing at home, it was "an indubitable fact" that "thousands of Radiophans attend the theatre to get the original music and to see the performers who have been broadcasting."[104] *Exhibitor's Trade Review* also contradicted Lust by noting that radio was capable of producing tremendous results for individual films, such as Roxy's proclamation to his radio listeners on WEAF and six allied (or "networked") radio stations that the film *Black Cyclone* (1925) was "the best picture that he had seen in five years." The trade journal reasoned that his broadcast approval of the film was "expected to have a great effect in winning enlarged audiences everywhere for this picture."[105]

By the end of 1923, Roxy's radio audience continued to grow beyond those able to pick up WEAF's broadcast when the show began being "relayed" and broadcast to thirteen stations across North America (including Toronto).[106] In January 1924, that coverage grew further when WEAF announced an expansion of its wavelength in order to reach California and the rest of the West Coast.[107] "Of those who sit in California, Florida or Missouri and turn their radio dials till the wee early hours," *Hostess Magazine* noted that month, ". . . everyone knows 'Roxy', that is, everyone of the several millions who 'listen in' on the

Capitol Theatre's music program broadcasted every Sunday night."[108] Roxy was a national phenomenon and star.

In addition to drumming up box office for the New York theater, Roxy and His Gang aided the growing number of radio manufacturers that hoped for one or more shows that could drive a multi-class desire for radio ownership. The *Evening-World* noted, for instance, that their broadcasts had quickly "struck the chord of intimacy that has revolutionized radio entertainment and made it a feature of home life."[109] Another journalist added that "Thousands of old ladies and gents, young men and maidens meek, squat about the family neutrodyne each Sunday evening, listening to the aerial japing of the fellow and the chanting of big entertainers of the great Capitol movie theater, New York."[110] Radio retailers also took advantage of their stardom; one store advertised radios and Roxy's show as a cure for the question of "How to Keep Your Wife Quiet." The advertisement quoted a letter from a listener to Roxy that claimed that the Capitol Theatre radio program was "the only thing I have ever discovered that keeps my wife quiet for one whole hour."[111] Roxy also cited evidence of their influence on radio purchases. "I have received some very complimentary letters," he remarked in October 1923, "which indicate quite clearly that we of the Capitol have been responsible for the installation of receiving sets in many home[s] where they had not been considered previously."[112]

By 1924, a radio in the home had become a status symbol, an entry point into the middle class. This kind of social capital became increasingly important as the country grew more entertainment obsessed, easily able to identify movie, theater, sports, and now radio stars, as evidenced by an advertisement for Haynes-Griffin radios with the headline "Get Acquainted with Roxy." The ad's copy captured what others would later call the "water-cooler" effect of national broadcasting.

> Everyone you meet Monday morning will ask you this question—"What did you think of Roxy and the Gang last night?" Then they'll start to tell you that they were listening in their own homes to the finest musical program they ever heard. If you want to join the thousands of Radio Fans who "listen in" every Sunday night on Roxy and the Gang do as they have done and get yourself on EASY PAYMENTS.[113]

Roxy and His Gang was no longer just a better time listening to the radio, but now a seemingly integral part of a better life.

The national reputation of the Capitol Theatre and its radio broadcasts did have its organizational drawbacks—over time, more and more of the Capitol's department heads were lured away by higher salaries and positions. Albert Kaufman, managing director of Grauman's downtown Los Angeles theaters, hired Alexander Oumansky in February 1924 to take charge of the live performances in those theaters.[114] Maria Gambarelli, who had been named ballet mistress of the Capitol in March 1923, took over after his departure.[115] "Gamby" now had a dozen women, many "older and larger than herself," under her authority as prima ballerina and ballet mistress.[116] By January 1924, thanks to her on-air and in-person appearances, Gambarelli had become a full-fledged radio star with photographs and articles about her rise to fame appearing in newspapers across the country.[117] Her fans now included celebrities such as John Barrymore, who made regular visits to the Capitol to watch her perform.[118]

On the Road

As Roxy and His Gang's fame grew in large cities and small towns across the country, theaters and audiences up and down the Atlantic seaboard began asking for selected members and the entire Gang to appear in person.[119] Over time some members of the Gang such as Betsy Ayres were loaned out to other venues.[120] Jack Banner noted that during 1923 and 1924, out-of-towners vacationing in New York kept flocking into the theater begging Roxy to take his Gang on tour so that their townsfolk might be able to see the Gang in action. Many of these requests came from Roxy's favorite charity group, "shut-in veterans in the various government hospitals."[121]

The Gang made their first appearance outside the Capitol at the Lyric Theatre in Hackensack, New Jersey, in early February 1924, performing a concert for their fans.[122] Later that month, Ayres and another Gang artist, Florence Mulholland, performed in Washington, D.C., at the annual mid-winter dinner of the Washington Board of Trade. The dinner's 600 invited guests included congressmen, senators, and members of President Calvin Coolidge's cabinet, who, the *New York Review* noted, "have heard these artists broadcast over the radio from the Capitol."[123] Willie Robyn also traveled to Washington, D.C. at the same time, appearing at the Rialto Theatre there in mid-February, pleasing the city's "radiacs," according to the *Washington Post*.[124] A few weeks later, Maria Gambarelli and members of the Capitol Ballet Corps performed at the Stanley Theatre in Philadelphia.[125] For the moment, the Gang's personal appearances were sporadic and were sometimes merely personal, rather than group, occasions.

In early March, Roxy and the entire Gang made another trek together, visiting Ossining, New York's famous Sing Sing prison where Roxy had donated projection equipment and his time several years earlier. The prison's Mutual Welfare League sponsored the trip in which Roxy and His Gang put on a "de luxe performance" of motion pictures complete with music, "ballet, singers, and lighting effects" for the prisoners.[126] A *New York American* journalist noted that "there ha[d] been many presentations of motion pictures" at the prison since Roxy's first visit there and came away "impressed with the good behavior of the audience."[127] All of these appearances spread the name and reputation of the Capitol Theatre and its artists—publicity that would soon benefit everyone involved.

After Sing Sing, Roxy announced that the Gang would launch a full-scale promotional tour. "It's all right to be a success in your own home town," he remarked about the impetus to go on the road, "but the way to really get a line on yourself is to try your talents out somewhere else. . . . Then you know just where you stand."[128] While press tours are a natural component of entertainment promotion today, the idea of a radio star (let alone a theater manager) touring at the time was novel. Five days after Sing Sing, the Gang commenced a ten-day tour of the Northeast and mid-Atlantic states, with stops in Philadelphia, Baltimore, Washington, D.C., "and some of the smaller cities in Pennsylvania." The plan was perhaps inspired by the recent tours of a number of recording artists who sought to drum up interest in their records. According to *Times Square Daily*, however, Roxy's tour "appear[ed] to be the first radio crew to make a tour that called for appearances in legitimate theatres." In addition to bringing new audiences to their radio show, the newspaper saw the move as an "exploitation stunt for the Capitol."[129] Roxy took twenty-four members of the Gang, including Betsy Ayres, Maria Gambarelli, David Mendoza, Eugene Ormandy, Yasha Bunchuk, William Axt, Douglas Stanbury, Gladys Rice, Willie Robyn, members of the Capitol orchestra's string section, and "some of the principal members of the ballet corps."[130]

The group expected a turnout in each city, but the reaction was overwhelming. When they arrived by train in Providence on March 16 they were mobbed by 60,000 fans, necessitating "police interference" to disperse the horde.[131] "Talk about the circus coming to town," the *Morning Telegraph* wrote. "The whole gosh darned populace turned out to see what Roxy and his Gang were like in the flesh."[132] Roxy was astonished by the crowds that greeted them and the familiarity they had engendered through radio:

[W]e found that everybody knew us. Our public acquaintance began with the sleeping car porter. He addressed a half dozen of our performers by name just as intimately as though they had been friends for years. When we got to Providence the word of our coming had preceded us. I never had such an experience. . . . Everywhere we went in Providence, people seemed to know us, first names and all. We were scheduled to appear there in a large store. When the time came a crowd filled the streets for blocks, everybody from mothers with baby carriages to staid business men. And they had such a welcome for us that we felt as if each one was our personal friend. It was a touching thing; it made us realize that we had a great responsibility to the public; that we must do better than ever before if we possibly could. The esteem of those good people was the finest tribute any of us ever had.[133]

Roxy and His Gang gave two days of afternoon and evening performances on March 16 and 17 at Providence's 2,500-seat Majestic Theatre to raise funds for the Palestine Temple of Shriners. AT&T worked with WJAR, "the Outlet Company of Providence," to broadcast the concert through New York and Washington, D.C. stations WEAF and WCAP, respectively, relaying the audio by telephone.[134]

The Gang traveled next to Boston where the crowds were just as large. AT&T, which had sent executives along with Roxy to facilitate the tour and survey the effect of on-site promotion, estimated that 50,000 people turned out to see Roxy and His Gang arrive by train, even though no performance was scheduled or given. "Perspiring women carrying babies, men, the young and the aged, crowded their way before the artists," observed an internal report sent to AT&T manager of broadcasting Jon Holman. "Woman after woman came to Mr. Rothafel and said that he could not appreciate what they had gone through for the privilege of seeing him, but you had only to look at them to gain an idea."[135]

The Capitol in the Capitol

In the nation's capitol, where the *Washington Post* noted that the Gang "need no introduction to radio enthusiasts in the eastern section of the country," they were greeted with a similar reception.[136] A mob of 35,000 people swarmed the train station hoping to get a peek at their radio idols. "Why, I never had an idea that we were so well known," Roxy noted. "It's remarkable how interested every one is in the personality of the people he hears over the radio."[137] Their show at Poli's Theatre in Washington, D.C. on March 18 sold out immediately.

Crowds to buy tickets were so large and unwieldy that "police reserves were called out" to handle the throng. All of the proceeds, as usual, benefited local military hospitals and soldiers' funds.[138] Due to the demand, Roxy and His Gang extended their stay and tickets were sold for another performance on March 19.

In addition to their concerts, the Gang visited Walter Reed Hospital and performed for injured veterans. "The sight of these men, hopelessly maimed in the World war," a journalist later noted, "went so deeply into Roxy's heart that he said, 'these men must have a radio set by their beds if I can possibly help them get it."[139] Jack Banner recalled the performance a decade later "for the benefit of the war-crippled lads":

> Here Roxy realized more than ever the powerful influence radio was beginning to exert on the masses. The eager attentiveness and the enthusiasm of the hopelessly crippled soldiers left an indelible print on his memory. At the same time he realized the crying need of headphones for the boys in the hospitals. A large horn, shaped like the old gramophone amplifier, provided the only means of program receptions, Roxy was touched and decided to do something for the boys. After the concert he gathered several of the Cabinet members together, and the upshot of the following discussion was that he agreed to take his gang on a noncommercial tour, the proceeds to go into a fund with which to purchase headpieces for every bed in every government hospital.[140]

A reception was held at the Wardman Park Hotel on the night of March 18 with all of the proceeds given to soldiers' funds. General John A. Lejeune and Secretary of War John Weeks also attended. Roxy's reputation, his work for the CPI during WWI, the radio show's popularity, and the benevolent nature of their concerts engendered numerous offers of assistance and support from "heads of Government departments, the Navy Band, the Army Band and the Marine Band."[141] The performances at Poli's Theatre on March 18 and 19 raised $8,600 for injured veterans.[142] In honor of their generosity, President Calvin and Grace Coolidge invited Roxy and His Gang to the White House.[143] From purgatory at the Park Theatre in 1919 to a presidential reception in 1924: much had changed in those five years.

AT&T employee A. V. Llufrio noted that "the success of the trip far exceeded the expectations of everyone," and he predicted that "Roxie's [sic] Gang will have a much larger Radio audience then ever before."[144] The tour's success made the case for similar promotional efforts for other personalities looking to boost their radio audience and prestige. "Radio will do—has already done—more for [Roxy] than his picture work could ever accomplish," a journalist noted at the time. "At the present rate it is only a question of a short time until he becomes President, and broadcasts handshakes from the executive offices each Wednesday sharp."[145] Beneath this throwaway sentiment—and its foreshadowing of Franklin Roosevelt's "Fireside Chats"—was a realization that celebrity could translate into industrial and political power. That power enabled Roxy to manage the Capitol as he liked, run his radio program as he saw fit, and bring music (and banter) to the masses without fear of cancellation. By April 1924, the size of the Gang and their musical ambitions were no longer suitable for their makeshift studio. A newly constructed studio was installed at the Capitol that could more easily accommodate the growing numbers of the Gang and afford more programmatic flexibility and space.[146]

In the ensuing months, Roxy continued his fundraising on and off the air.[147] Their Washington concerts, for instance, had benefited Roxy's favorite audience, disabled veterans at Walter Reed Hospital and Mount Alto. The proceeds had been used in part to buy radios for the wounded veterans who in turn dubbed their new listening devices their "Roxys."[148] By mid-April 1924, Roxy's radio fund for wounded servicemen had already raised $20,000, and the fund planned to use that sum to buy radio sets for more than 4,000 veterans.[149] "Roxy, with the pleasing voice, now sending out a word of cheer to his disabled buddies," a letter from a 16-year-old fan to the *Washington Post* noted the following year, "has done more for our bed-ridden boys than all the doctors in the world can hope to do. He has made them take a new lease on life by working with his heart and soul to install radios at their bedsides."[150]

In order to raise even more money for the fund (and other charities), Roxy and His Gang went on another, smaller tour shortly after their Sunday night broadcast on April 20, traveling to Suffern, New York; Rutherford, New Jersey; Brattleboro, Vermont; and Fall River, Attleboro, and New Bedford, Massachusetts.[151] After returning for their April 27 broadcast, the Gang gave a three-hour benefit concert two days later at the Elks Auditorium in Elizabeth, New Jersey.[152]

It is not an outlandish question to wonder who exactly was planning all aspects of the Capitol's presentation during Roxy's repeated absences when the Gang toured. Even though Roxy often returned on the weekends for rehearsals and other preparations, it is reasonable to assume that during some weeks he and Gamby were less involved than others in the Capitol's live presentations. As a journalist from *New York American* noted without a hint of irony, "[W]hen he is not busy with the radio he manages the Capitol Theatre."[153]

HIGHS AND LOEW'S

Because of his most recent tour, Roxy was also scarcely present to notice the organizational shifts taking place within Goldwyn Pictures. On April 17, 1924, Loew's, Inc., formally acquired Goldwyn Pictures and Louis B. Mayer Productions for $65 million and merged them with Metro Pictures to create Metro-Goldwyn. One of Roxy's chief exhibition rivals (with several nearby theaters) had now become a corporate cousin. Loew's, Inc., now controlled or was affiliated with five hundred theaters nationwide, including the Capitol Theatre in New York and other former Goldwyn houses, as well as venues formerly part of the Ascher (Midwest), Bishop Cass (Rockies), and Miller Amusement Company (California) circuits.[154] The Capitol Theatre would now share its flagship status in the Loew's circuit with the Loew's State a few blocks south in Times Square.

The Loew's, Inc., acquisition of the Capitol also meant that WHN and Roxy's broadcasts over WEAF were no longer in corporate competition. Each program afforded Marcus Loew and Nicholas Schenck an opportunity to profit from each theater's convergent activities. The acquisition of the Capitol was not an insignificant pickup in the deal for Goldwyn Pictures and its assets; the takeover meant that all of the Capitol's artists, including its musicians, conductors, and its director of presentations, Roxy, were now under Loew's/MGM control. Major Bowes, William Axt, and David Mendoza, for instance, would later play important roles in the presentation and, with Axt and Mendoza, in the scoring of MGM films such as *The Big Parade* (1925). Major Bowes, who had traveled to Europe in 1924 to finalize plans for the filming of *Ben-Hur* (1925) as vice president of Goldwyn-Cosmopolitan, was now made a vice president of Loew's, Inc.[155]

The fact that Roxy was now an everyday employee of Loew's struck him "as an amusing coincidence." Eleven years earlier (in 1913) he had waited outside Marcus Loew's office in vain for an interview. Roxy noted that he had "decided that if Mr. Loew had a job for me it would be better to let him keep it for a while. He did," Roxy added, "for a good many years. But I have it at last."[156] Roxy had already performed sporadic work for Loew's even before the merger. In January 1923, he had scored the premiere presentation of Metro Pictures' *Hearts Aflame* (1923) in Newburgh, New York.[157] The following year, two months before the Loew's-Goldwyn merger, Metro hired Roxy to stage the prologue and exhibition of their latest film, *Thy Name Is Woman* (1924), at the Lyric Theatre.[158] Now that he was employed by Loew's, these kinds of arrangements would be far easier for the vertically integrated company.

In early May 1924, the Gang resumed their appearances in cities across the region, including return engagements at the Lafayette Theatre in Suffern, New York, on May 6 and the Rivoli Theatre in Rutherford, New Jersey, on May 8.[159] Roxy and His Gang would continue to tour throughout 1924, raising $70,000 for the radio fund by mid-June thanks to additional concerts.[160] Jack Banner noted that the tour was managed by the American Legion and supported by the press. "Wherever the gang appeared," Banner noted, "Washington, Boston, Philadelphia and various other principal cities—vast throngs greeted the troopers. Every auditorium was packed to capacity, with the result that in a comparatively short time every service man's cot was equipped with a set of headphones. Roxy was astounded at the phenomenal success of the tour. The new art was progressing faster than he had realized."[161] The national media support paid dividends for his radio show, while the goodwill he engendered through his support of injured veterans cemented his reputation as a patriotic American. "How noble a thing of this kind is," *American Organist* commented on his and the Gang's work, "compared to the thievery of the Senate and Congress that [had recently] passed the elect-me-again bonus."[162]

Roxy and the Cult of Personality

Radio Broadcast took stock of Roxy's radio accomplishments in July 1924. "His efforts, and the efforts of his company, have caught the public fancy," James C. Young wrote, "in a more pronounced way for a longer period than the efforts of any other group or individual."[163] The *Caldwell News* added:

> Among commuters, in the office, on the trolley, on the scaffold and in the shop, the commonest question Monday morning was "Did you tune in to 'Roxie' last night?" The tremendous welcome, evidenced by the thousands of letters showered upon Mr. Rothafel this week, shows what a dominating personality one man can become by means of the radio. Better known and better loved than any man in the public eye for the past decade— actor, statesman or writer—"Roxie" is not known even by sight by one per cent of his admirers.[164]

So what made Roxy and His Gang such a popular program? Personality and style were the most common answers for how a theater manager from New York could quickly become one of the most famous personalities on the air. Before Roxy, the majority of New York announcers were automatons, recounting what music or information they were presenting as energetically as one might read a city directory. WEAF, for instance, wanted personalities that would only reflect its burgeoning brand image as a business advertiser's station. Because of its popularity, though, Roxy's program was absolved of this dictate. "The new interest in personality," Warren Susman writes, "both the unique qualities of an individual and the performing self that attracts others— was not limited to self-help authors in this period. It extended to participants in the high culture as well." The ability to market oneself as a discernible brand was now seen by many as the difference between success and failure.[165] For Roxy, he worked to ensure that Roxy the brand was indistinguishable from Rothafel the man. One was corporeal, the other ethereal. Both had their value and place and benefited the other.

Radio producer and journalist Nellie Revell would later write that it was Roxy's straightforward nature that captivated audiences and made Roxy and His Gang approachable by tearing down the walls that divided Americans by money, class, and privilege.[166] "He was nobody's son-in-law," Dr. Frank L. Crane added. "He was not a protégé of Jake and Lee [Shubert]. Neither J. P. Morgan nor Roosevelt nor Boss Murphy took him up. And you needn't look around further for some sinister explanation of his success. He made good. That's all. That's why he came to this cold, cruel city and ate it up."[167]

Roxy was, of course, not just a regional hit in the Northeast. "His fame is country-wide," another journalist noted. "Folks away down South love him for the kindliness which seems to be his method and manner."[168] "Everybody wants to know what it is—this personality that is winning radio fame as 'Roxie,'" a New Bedford, Massachusetts, newspaper commented at the time. "We'll warrant that he is not all temperamental Jewish blood. There must be a drop of New England that makes his whole world of the radio kin."[169] Whether it was New England, the South, or the Midwest, every region of the country seemed to claim him as a native son. He seemed to be everything to every- one. While there was little New England in Roxy, his immigrant past, his childhood in Minnesota and Brooklyn, his service in the Marines, his work as a military recruiter, and his days as a baseball player, traveling bookseller, hotel clerk, insurance salesman, barkeeper, and film exhibitor had made him keenly aware of the world outside the privileged gates of the Ivy League and the boardrooms of America's largest corporations. He was folksy and very much an American, yet his expressiveness and his moxie were typical traits of late-nineteenth-century immigrant Jews. Instead of being alien, though, they seemed more American to audiences than any other voice on the air. Unbeknownst to AT&T, farmers in Iowa, coal miners in Pennsylvania, and store clerks in Georgia had more in common with a Jew like Roxy than a well-bred Wall Streeter. On Sunday nights, after church or a restful day with the family, many Americans were coming home (and staying there) for Roxy's evening of entertainment. For an hour and a half, millions of radio listeners, young and old, waited for Roxy to welcome his friends to the Capitol before treating them to music, comedy, and banter that was both technologically and stylistically new and yet comfortingly conservative in its tone.

America's favorite radio troupe was also a perfect reflection of the changing demographics of the nation. Roxy was an immigrant from Germany; Gambarelli had emigrated from Italy; Stanbury was from Canada; cellist Yasha Bunchuk was born in Kharkov, Russia; and even the American-sounding Willie Robyn was from Pasiene, Latvia.[170] This group, loved by Americans across the country, was filled with foreigners—a symbolic retort to the rampant xenophobia of the era.

Not all journalists were enamored by Roxy's infusion of so much "personality" into his shows, however. A columnist from the *New York Tribune*, who had weeks earlier praised Roxy and his broadcasts, later critiqued his broadcasting style and even questioned his sincerity and authenticity. "Roxie [*sic*]," the *Tribune* column began, "we have been thinking about you a great deal lately. . . . 'Are you too informal?' . . . Do you 'stutter' naturally, Roxie? Are you simple minded? Is there a 'radio Roxie' and just an 'everyday Roxie' or are you one and the same person?"[171] Roxy's sometimes halting on-air manner, which was anything but stentorian, was caused, he claimed, by "feeling" and "perpetual stage fright."[172] Roxy did not respond to the column, but a fan wrote to the *Tribune* in his defense. "You are a fickle person . . . you whack at him straight from the shoulder, even to the stuttering, which, of course, must be natural. No man would stutter if he could avoid it. I never saw Roxie, I don't even know what his real name is, but I and many others much prefer his style to the 'icy formality' which most announcers fall back on, and I should think you would, too." The *Tribune* columnist replied that it had given the matter serious thought and had printed the remarks only because Roxy was "radio's greatest impresario."[173]

Mary Radcliffe recounted the ways in which Roxy and His Gang had ingratiated themselves into American homes and popular culture:

The voice with the personality—sincere, kindly, filled with humor and philosophy, which places a hand under the downcast heart and restores one's faith in simple brotherhood, old-fashioned goodness, active kindliness—that's "Roxy of the Radio." "Who is Roxy?" That's the question which

thousands of radio fans throughout the East are asking. For "Roxy" has
become a household word, and his Christmas cards are still being delivered from all sections of the Atlantic Seaboard. . . . Roxy has done something for the radio which is unique. When he comes into the library of
the Four Hundred, the kitchen of the farm house, the parlor of the small
apartment, the living room of the large one, he creates atmosphere by the
vibrations of his voice. He is regarded today as the outstanding man in
the radio world, broadcasting waves of humor, faith and fellowship every
time he opens his mouth.

Roxy, Radcliffe surmised, had struck a chord with rural and urban Americans
who approached the Roaring Twenties with both excitement about new technologies (such as radio) as well as apprehension about the future in the wake
of World War I and the recent recession. The pace of American life, especially in urban areas, had quickened, with free-market capitalism spurring the
growth of cities across America. And everywhere one looked, music, talk, and
entertainment could be found, not just in vaudeville and movie theaters but
through radio sets that were perfuming the air in private and public spaces
nationwide. "Do you who are quite grown up and have children remember
those days some twenty years ago when an evening of fun consisted of a group
about the family piano singing the old songs, an evening when even the voice
with a crack was very welcome?" Radcliffe asked. "Well, Roxy has restored
that evening of innocent enjoyment to thousands of homes. And those who
remain home from church to hear him might do something far, far worse."[174]
In houses, apartment buildings, hospitals, hotels, and numerous other spaces
where Americans gathered in the 1920s, Roxy and His Gang was appointment
listening—a weekly visit from a group of friends with Roxy serving as a quasi-
father figure to millions. In that way, he and the Gang were the perfect pro-
moters of WEAF, the Capitol Theatre, and all of the records, sheet music, cue
sheets, and personal appearances they spawned. They were friendly, warm,
familiar voices emanating out of a technologically new apparatus.

ROXY VS. AT&T

AT&T had given Roxy's style and informality a free pass since the show's
inception in large part because of the attention and audience he brought to
the station. Roxy appreciated the stylistic freedom he had been given, and he
rewarded AT&T for their loyalty with his own. David Sarnoff, vice president

of RCA, had offered Roxy a position as musical director for a proposed group of eight "super-power" stations in December 1924, but Roxy shrugged off the opportunity, telling Sarnoff he intended to stay with AT&T and WEAF.[175]

With hundreds of thousands of letters (and other items) trucked in to the Capitol Theatre every year, full of praise and gratitude, there were, from all accounts, very few that contained the slightest bit of scorn for the program. AT&T was certainly aware of the massive public acclaim for Roxy and his radio program, yet they seemed to have been alarmed by a single letter from Jere J. O'Connor sent to AT&T president Walter S. Gifford on January 26, 1925. In his culturally provocative note, O'Connor wrote about Roxy's radio program:

> Cannot something be done to improve the broadcasting through WEAF Sunday night? I refer solely to the Muscovite from 51st Street [the location of the Capitol Theatre]. All through this running fire of objectionable cheap facetious comment, with its halting and stammering, is discernible the tactics of the little man elbowing his way forward. The Sunday night hour has become a medium of personal advertising. . . . If broadcasting does not sink to the level of the dirty movies, it will only be because Christianity will not permit it.[176]

O'Connor had asked AT&T's elite to rein in their folksy, Jewish announcer, with a little red-baiting thrown in for good measure. The letter cries out for "Christianity" to save radio from the "dirty movies," known even then as a disproportionately Jewish business, and remarks that broadcasting, with personalities like Roxy, could just as easily sink into similar hands.

Whether this letter was the impetus for what followed—AT&T's censorship of Roxy and their insistence that his broadcasts become more formal— is unknown. Letters found in the NBC Company records do suggest that the letter had an immediate impact on the views of AT&T, Western Electric, and WEAF on Roxy's broadcasts. A note from J. A. Holman, broadcasting manager of WEAF, to AT&T vice president William Harkness noted that due to the "attached letter of Jere J. O'Connor . . . arrangements have been made for Mr. Rothafel to confine his announcing to the requirements of good taste and dignity."[177] Holman also wrote back to O'Connor asking to speak to him by phone "with respect to the action that I have taken on your letter."[178] The two men spoke on January 28 and O'Connor then wrote to AT&T president Walter S. Gifford, remarking that Holman's actions regarding Roxy's broadcast were "interesting," "enlightening," and "entirely satisfactory." O'Connor concluded by thanking Gifford and Holman for their "prompt action in this manner."[179]

That a letter that appealed to "Christianity" to save broadcasting would raise alarm at AT&T and Western Electric is not entirely surprising. In his years of contentious dealings with David Sarnoff, Walter Gifford remarked in 1923 that his rival was both "abrasive" and, perhaps even worse, Jewish.[180] Harry Warner, per Cass Warner Sperling and Scott Eyman, reportedly commented that John Otterson, general manager of Western Electric, which operated WEAF, was an avid anti-Semite.[181] Historian Evan Schwartz writes that, under Gifford's watch, AT&T was a "domain of discreet anti-Semitism. The company certainly didn't permit blacks, women, and most ethnic immigrants to join its executive ranks, but it seemed especially wary of Jews."[182] The problem was far more systemic than just with Gifford or Otterson. "[N]owhere did the behavior of existing elites establish the tone for an entire community more than in the business world," Daniel Okrent writes. "You didn't have to dislike Jews or think them inferior (although there were plenty who did both); you just had to regard them, and treat them, as the Other."[183] AT&T had crawled into bed with Roxy out of industrial necessity, but that partnership did not prevent Gifford, Otterson, and other AT&T executives from throwing their weight around—especially when asked to save radio from the same people who produced and exhibited the "dirty movies."

Michele Hilmes offers another contributing theory regarding Roxy's subsequent censoring—that Roxy's stature was beginning to overshadow that of WEAF. "Roxy's personal popularity," she notes, "although useful in drawing an audience to WEAF's nascent network efforts, had increased to such a degree—while representing certain less-desirable qualities—that Rothafel threatened to overwhelm WEAF's identity with his own." Furthermore, his " 'folksy,' sentimental style [was] ill-befitting WEAF's image as a business advertisers' station."[184]

Whatever the cause, two days after O'Connor's letter, Roxy told a crowd gathered at the Newark Armory that AT&T had ordered a change in the nature of his program and particularly his style of announcing. Roxy was ordered to conform, the *Boston Globe* reported, and "conduct himself after the fashion of the usual Sabbath announcer."[185] Fans immediately began to write plaintive letters to AT&T. J. J. Frish of the Peoples Finance Service Company, for instance, wrote, "If you take 'Roxy' from the Capital [*sic*] Gang, you take the soul out of the rose. . . . He has brought comfort where others have failed, he has put faith in God and Man, where Churches and Organizations have failed."[186] Frish's statements that Roxy had succeeded where clergy had not might have only added to the company's displeasure of his increasing public acclaim and raised other troubling issues.

Roxy immediately devised a plan to use his public stature to fight back against his increasingly dictatorial partners at WEAF, Western Electric, and AT&T. Instead of merely toning down his next broadcast, he took WEAF's mandate to its most absurd conclusion and spoke in virtual monotone throughout the February 1, 1925, show and did not bother to infuse it with any of his usual joy and effusiveness. "We never went on the air as we did Sunday night," Roxy told the *Brooklyn Daily Eagle* after the broadcast. "The American audience, I think, wants informality and good taste and camaraderie. The gang and I are heart-broken."[187]

The effect on the show was obvious to executives at the station. J. A. Holman sent an angry note to Capitol Theatre managing director Major Bowes, chastising him for allowing Roxy to "sulk" during the broadcast and saying that Roxy's overtly stiff announcing was not appreciated. "We do not feel that Mr. Rothafel handled the situation fairly. Further, we feel that he deliberately overdid the dignity phase in his announcements and that it was apparent from his manner that he was desirous of calling particular attention to the fact that he was being restricted with the view of stimulating a reaction based on emotion and not on logic."[188] The folly of AT&T and WEAF's reasoning is obvious. In giving Roxy a platform on the air, they wanted to benefit from his popularity but were stunned that he would use it in what they felt was a "private" matter. Broadcasting, much to WEAF's seeming amazement, had brought on a new age in which broadcasters and media personalities could take their issues and grievances directly to the public. Roxy was certainly not one to work things out privately in an executive office. Radio had given him a national voice, and he was fully and happily prepared to use it.

AT&T was not the only one who noticed the marked change in Roxy's broadcast. Journalists began peppering WEAF with questions about what had happened to the show that was beloved by millions. Besieged with questions, Holman told the *Brooklyn Daily Eagle* that Roxy had not been censored but was asked to be "more dignified." "Not stiff and unnatural, you know, but a little less breezy. We feel that audiences prefer more dignified announcements. We have often told Roxy about it.'" AT&T also refused to flinch. "If Roxy changed his style last night, that was up to him," William Harkness, vice president of AT&T, told the newspaper after the February 1 broadcast. "We have always had certain rules, and we want them lived up to by those using our station. I don't want to get into a discussion of whether he always has obeyed these rules. That is a matter simply between the telephone company and Mr. Rothafel."[189]

The truth, despite AT&T's public pronouncements, was that it was not a private matter. Headlines like the *Daily Mirror*'s ("'Roxy' Gets Spanking") soon spread across the country, and the public quickly joined the press's outrage. Ernest Clark, a Manhattan listener, sent the following letter about AT&T to the *Brooklyn Daily Eagle*:

> Roxy has become a national institution, a factor in recreating the American Sunday night home gathering. . . . If the statement made by The Brooklyn Daily Eagle tonight that the difference in his manner . . . was due to your dictation [AT&T] . . . [then] you have proved yourselves unworthy of the trust the public has given you and your station should be subjected to Government control to prevent the use of private ownership of a public utility to forwarding exclusively private interests.[190]

In Worcester, where Roxy and His Gang had visited to great acclaim, several ministers leapt to his aid as well. In one of several letters printed in the *Worcester Evening Gazette*, Rev. Dr. William S. Mitchell declared, "The things Roxy says are clean things and fine things. I confess, he's quite got to me. There is something infinitely friendly in his 'Good night, God bless you, pleasant dreams.' I am one preacher, at least, who appreciates this opportunity to hear good music in a friendly atmosphere, when I am back home Sunday night, after a hard day's work."[191] Radio columnist Aunt Enna added that in censoring Roxy and having him skip his secular benedictions, the move had done more harm to AT&T and Christianity than it had to Roxy:

> Somebody may think this is a way to drive men to church. Somebody is fast on center; this is the way to keep men away from church. We would rather hear Roxy's "Good night, pleasant dreams, God bless you!," than some religious dissertations. . . . We like our telephone service—sometimes—but when the outfit we buy it from begins to meddle with what we have been foolish enough to think as our Sunday liberty, we can't say we are going to throw any somersaults of joy over it. . . . We wonder if Mister Harkness knows that it was this same Roxy who made WEAF what it is today.[192]

At a time when policymakers were deciding how to regulate broadcasting and how much control corporations should have in limiting free speech over their

stations and their burgeoning networks, the entire affair was shortsighted—
especially given Roxy's immense popularity.

The *Providence News* also attacked AT&T and printed forms in the newspaper that readers could sign, cut out, and send directly to the telephone company.
"Give 'Roxy' His Freedom" the form's headline read. "Take Off That Gag, Un-
muzzle The 'Air'!" The form continued: "The Providence News urges its readers
who depend on the radio for Sunday night entertainments to sign this blank as
a form of protest against the action of the owners of the broadcasting stations
through which he sends his program."[193] In the two days that followed Roxy's
sullen broadcast and the ensuing public controversy, over 265,000 letters and
telegrams of protest were reportedly sent.[194] AT&T immediately buckled to public pressure. "We are not going to censor him," Harkness remarked disingenu-
ously. "WEAF is glad to have people put personality into the programs."[195] Roxy
was elated. The public right, at least for the moment, had won out.

Taking a Toll on AT&T

For Roxy, the battle against AT&T's censorship was more evidence that he
had become a celebrated national figure, a man who could summon the will
of the public, journalists, and the clergy. For AT&T and WEAF, though, it was
a giant black eye.

Over the years, Roxy had hosted radio shows and live events that included
politicians from the Wilson, Harding, and Coolidge administrations and
many top military and political figures.[196] Perhaps Harkness had not remembered Roxy's recent visit to the White House, his embrace by many other
politicians, and his widespread popularity in Washington both personally and
for his work on behalf of injured veterans. "Congress was on the verge, the
very verge, in fact, of ordering a congressional investigation of the incident,"
the *Evening Star* reported.

> The boys in the hospitals were ready to quit cots and crutches and go to
> war again in defense of "Roxie." Each one was planning to take the matter
> up with "his" congressman. . . . Only a complete surrender by WEAF in
> the face of an overwhelming bombardment kept Congress from acting or
> attempting to act.[197]

Roxy's work for the CPI during WWI and on behalf of the war's injured veterans had made him nearly bulletproof. Roxy's radio audience, his Marine

service, and his film and radio industry adulation all created a unique persona that was very nearly above reproach in the mid-1920s. Even a corporation convinced of its own upper-crust certitude should have understood that.

Many now viewed the victory over AT&T as a symbol of the power of the individual over corporate interests. "Never before in this land of the free were so many letters written in a good cause as swamped the headquarters of the American Telephone and Telegraph Company in behalf of Roxy and the Gang," the *Hackensack Republican* opined.[198] Another journalist remarked that "The big, flaming, important thing is this: No company or institution or person is greater than the public it serves."[199] The battle between AT&T and Roxy had reasserted, for a brief time anyway, the power of audiences over the interests of increasingly powerful broadcasting companies. For his part, Roxy quickly worked to smooth over the relationship between AT&T and WEAF and the public in the weeks that followed the much publicized incident.[200] In less than two weeks after the controversy began, the power balance had entirely shifted.

Roxy and Religion

Roxy had mollified most of his critics, but there remained a small undercurrent of cultural and/or religious friction. Not everyone was in love with the prominent New York Jew who was already being dubbed a radio "idol"[201] and was such a favorite of radio listeners on the Sabbath. (Roxy's religion was certainly not a secret and led to at least one newspaper accidentally calling him "S. L. Rosenthal.")[202] Will E. Smith was one of those who questioned the appropriateness of Roxy's work on Sundays, in his *Washington Star* column on February 24. However, just like AT&T, Smith quickly felt the retort of Roxy's Capitol-area fans with a "score of letters" flooding the newspaper in response. "What the world needs most is more 'Roxies' to spread 'good cheer' and make us think of better things and less of the narrow-minded, straight-laced, Puritanical thinking people who want to shut off everything but Christ and church on Sunday," one letter noted. "The church has ever tried to make men good through fear; 'Roxie' is doing the same work by making men appreciate their duty toward other men. That is good work—work we can all do regardless of race or creed. God bless 'Roxie' and may his tribe increase."[203]

Smith's attack was not alone. While Protestant clergy had come out strongly in favor of Roxy's Sunday evening broadcasts, he seemed to have irked some Catholics with the popularity of his Sunday broadcasts and, more importantly, through his famous secular benediction and sign-off: "Good night, pleasant dreams, God bless you." An editorial in the *Providence Visitor*, the official Catholic newspaper of Rhode Island, denounced Roxy in what one journalist called "the first editorial denouncement of the radio entertainer ever printed" and one that reflected the "Antagonism by the Catholic Church toward Roxy." The editorial, which was approved by William A. Hickey, bishop of the Diocese of Providence, asked:

> May we hope to be pardoned for expressing a very personal opinion of America's wishy-washy, goody-goody man, one Roxy? In things that are blatant and banal he is the supreme offender. How can a man be expected to sleep nights having listened to his foolish sentimentality? How on earth is it possible for anyone to stomach Roxy's idiotic blessings and benedictions? We always see Roxy the *alert business man* [my emphasis] behind his words. We have tried our best to throw the mantle of charity over this piously-inclined entertainer, but we never turn from the radio without a picture of Roxy's leer.[204]

Each time someone spoke out against Roxy's appearance on Sundays, other voices came to his defense. It was the national media, once again, who suggested that something sinister was behind this animosity. "When an idle muser in type aims a squirt of nasty ink at Roxy, we usually get pretty well boiled up over it," *Popular Radio* wrote, before venturing further:

> As might be expected from most religious bigots, it seems that the ordained have a monopoly on blessings and benedictions and that should anyone outside God's hand picked followers communicate an honest blessing to his fellow men, he must be a shameless hypocrite and a soothsayer. Just remember this, because if you have not got a holy license to wish a friend well, you must be purveying your kindness for business reasons. That the writer of this malicious item never turns from the radio "without a picture of Roxy's leer" admits very little for so pious a gentleman. Where is his tolerance, his professed Christianity?[205]

Whether the "alert business man" comment in the *Providence Visitor* was a typical anti-Semitic reference to a Jewish desire for money or simply a statement that Roxy's friendliness was an act to gain popularity is not clear. But there was definitely a connection being drawn that his secular blessings might be inappropriate for so secular a figure (and a Jewish one at that). Yet, while

Roxy had offended Jere J. O'Connor, the *Providence Visitor*, and others with his Sunday broadcasts, other (often Protestant) clergy, like Rev. Robert Mac-Donald, pastor of the Plymouth (Massachusetts) Congregational church, praised him and his broadcast and approved of its consumption by religious audiences. "Roxy's Sunday night broadcast by radio can be listened to without twinge or conscience by a Christian," MacDonald declared, "for I listen to it and I am supposed to be a Christian."[206] Listeners who could not travel for organized prayer also hailed the program. *The American Magazine*'s Mary Mullett wrote that she had "met a dear old lady, eighty-six years old, who says that Roxy and his gang are the greatest blessing God ever gave to old ladies who can't go to church."[207] Broadcasters and movie stars had become a new source of American adulation. A personality as beloved as Roxy, insulated from scorn through his charitable work, could not be as easily dismissed as unholy or impure.

After his victory over AT&T, along with the recent embrace by members of the media and some of the clergy, could any Jew in America rival his esteem in the American national consciousness? There were at that time few Americans, Jew or non-Jew, who held a higher place in the moral leadership of the country. The acceptance of Roxy, a secular Jew, by many Christians was an important foreshadowing of how prominent Jews in entertainment would become socially acceptable figures through an informal appeal to the heart and mind and, of course, through their popularity as entertainers. This march was not entirely vertical, but the climb for Jewish entertainers would be among the most important factors in the group's acceptance and assimilation into mainstream American society. As Roxy's voice traveled to farmlands, rural towns, and remote areas of the country, he was often the first Jew many had "met." Through his broadcasts, he made himself and his motley crew of immigrants accepted and even beloved by millions. His voice and brand name were so prominent by 1925 that he was the ideal choice to be appointed president of the newly formed Radio Announcers of America.[208]

ON THE ROAD AGAIN

Roxy and His Gang embarked on yet another tour in March 1925, capitalizing on their growing acclaim (and the publicity generated by the AT&T fiasco). The Gang arrived first in Providence on March 2 and this time "Mrs. Roxy" (Rosa) came along as well and was introduced to the crowd at a gala dinner held at Rhodes on the Pawtuxet in Cranston.[209] Two days later, the Gang performed at a charity concert at the Manhattan Opera House to help build a camp for "crippled children" under the auspices of the New York Rotary Club.[210] The following day, Roxy and his Gang arrived in Baltimore to perform at the Lyric.[211] "Every occupation and profession was represented" at the concert, the *Baltimore Post* reported, and the crowd included "every possible section of Baltimore."[212] After the shows were completed, Roxy stopped by station WFBR that evening and served as guest announcer for the local Baltimore station.[213]

Roxy saved the most important stop for last. To thank and solidify the locus of his political power, Roxy and His Gang traveled to Washington, D.C., by arrangement of the National Press Club. On March 6 and 7, 1925, Roxy and His Gang gave several concerts at the 6,000-seat Washington Auditorium. Veterans who were given radios thanks to the Roxy Radio Fund were invited as guests of the Press Club. The concerts also coincided with inaugural week and were intended to take advantage of the throng of citizens from across the country who planned to be there for the festivities. Ticket prices ranged from fifty cents to $2.20, depending on the seat and time of the performance. Newly elected President Calvin Coolidge and his wife Grace, Vice President Charles Dawes, along with Coolidge's entire cabinet, attended Roxy and His Gang's concert, along with other "high government officials and their ladies" who were invited as guests of the National Press Club.[214] Six thousand fans also crammed into the building for the first performance. In addition to the Gang, Roxy brought along the entire thirty-five-piece Capitol Broadcasting Orchestra.[215] The shows sold out rapidly, with only standing room available by the time the Gang arrived in Washington.[216] The "idols of the ether," the *Washington Star* reported, turned "the new Washington Auditorium into a radiance of syncopation for the benefit of the National Press Club. If the President ever had a more enjoyable evening at a public entertainment it is not on record. He smiled often, and even went a bit further and laughed when the 'gang' began cuttin' up."[217] The next day, the Gang was welcomed again to the White House by the President and First Lady.[218] AT&T had had no idea what or who they were dealing with.

Roxy Expands His Reach

Roxy's and the Capitol Theatre's convergent activities expanded even more that month when Roxy launched a new phase of his career by co-authoring a book, *Broadcasting: Its New Day*, with Raymond Yates. The book, which analyzes the past, present, and future of radio, was released on March 15, 1925, and published by the Century Company.[219]

Days later, Roxy announced that he would reach even more of his fan base through print in a new daily column, "Hello Everybody!" syndicated across the country in newspapers such as the *New York Daily News*, *Providence News*, *Baltimore Sun*, *Chicago Daily Tribune,* and *Boston Traveler* Monday through Saturday.[220] Roxy argued that by writing his daily column, he would now be able to "broadcast" to his audience seven days a week.[221] The *Providence News* noted in announcing the column that Roxy "is the man who has made about twenty million friends by just talking to a little black disc every Sunday night."[222] "Here I am," Roxy wrote in his first "broadcast." "This is my first appearance as a regular columnist. Many of you have asked me to talk to you on the air more than once a week. Because I cannot do this, I am going to talk to you in this column of the Boston Traveler six days a week and I will be with you on the radio Sunday nights as usual."[223]

Through his broadcasts, his personal appearances, his book, and his column, Roxy had become a multimedia star. His voice was so well known, for instance, that when he went into a shoe shop in Manhattan, the clerk instantly recognized his intonation and remarked, "I know your voice. You're Roxy!" He had a similar experience outside of New York when he hailed a cab. The driver recognized him and remarked, "Sure, jump in, Roxy," and then refused to accept his money for the fare.[224] That same month, a new women's shoe line named for Roxy (predating the current sportswear line "Roxy" by roughly seventy-five years) was unveiled. "The vamps and quarters are covered with radio stripes," the *Newsburyport News-Herald* reported of its design.[225]

Roxy and His Gang continued touring over the next few months, appearing in Providence, Rhode Island, as well as Worcester, Lowell, Attleboro, and Boston, Massachusetts. Their visit to Boston was once again greeted with tremendous fanfare. A special detail of police officers was provided for Roxy,[226] while a grand parade snaked through the streets of the city in tribute to him and the Gang. "His coming was like that of a conquering hero," the *Boston Traveler* noted.

> Two great lanes of cheering humanity flanked his triumphant entry into the South station, which he entered at the head of his famous "gang". . . . They greeted Roxy as an old comrade-in-arms, and escorted him as he moved toward the train shed gates and the eager crowds waiting beyond.

At the head of the crowd that flanked either side of the lane kept open by a cordon of police were two ranks of marines, standing at attention. They came to a snappy salute as Roxy passed.[227]

Roxy and His Gang performed for four thousand fans at the Brooklyn Academy of Music on April 30 before embarking on another tour in early May around New England.[228] To ensure attendance, even at ticket prices that ranged to upwards of $2.50 per ticket, Roxy added the following notice to the Gang's advertisements: "There Will Be No BROADCASTOING [sic] of These Concerts."[229]

His fundraising for radios for injured servicemen was completed (for the moment) by April 1925 when their tour came to an end. "To-day," Roxy proudly noted, "there isn't a single military bed in a United States military hospital unequipped with radio."[230] The fund was such a success that after every bed was outfitted in the country, $85,000 was still left over. The excess funds were turned over to the American Legion to benefit the wounded soldiers for the remainder of their lives.[231] The National Sojourners, a Masonic organization comprised of Army, Navy, and Marine Corps officers, hosted a testimonial dinner for 700 in Roxy's honor to thank him for his work on the campaign.[232] General John Lejeune and a host of high-ranking military officials paid tributes in speeches. The Gang and the Navy Yard Band provided entertainment and the entire affair was broadcast over the air.[233] Everything, it seemed, could be repurposed for radio.

FILM AND RADIO IN 1925

Roxy was still director of presentations at the Capitol Theatre, but he spent a growing portion of his time on broadcasting and promoting the Gang, not on film exhibition. Amidst the accolades, the tributes, and the tours, Roxy made a shocking statement to anyone who had followed his sixteen-year career as an exhibitor. "If I had to give up the Capitol or the radio, I'd give up the Capitol," he told the Theatre Assembly gathered at the Hotel Astor in Manhattan. "I'd rather be what Roxy represents than be the richest man in the world. . . . Everything else is an also ran to me now. It has become the one great developing work of my life. Instead of the theatre, it is the radio." His broadcasts— thanks to the AT&T dustup, his live appearances, and his new column—now reached approximately eight million listeners every week, an increase of three million in less than a year's time.[234] His radio success had now obfuscated the original source of his fame. "I am also in the picture business," Roxy was forced to remind journalists from time to time.[235]

The "picture business" by 1925, in large part due to Roxy's success, had seismically shifted its philosophy toward broadcasting. While some exhibitors still complained that radio was hurting their businesses, an ever-growing number of theaters, especially larger first-run movie houses in major metropolitan areas, had harnessed radio's marketing power and followed Roxy's model. The Chicago-based Balaban & Katz circuit, for instance, created its own radio division to broadcast concerts from the circuit's flagship Chicago Theatre and from its McVickers and Riviera houses over four local Chicago radio stations.[236] "By November 1924," Douglas Gomery writes, "all of Broadway's major motion picture theaters had followed Roxy's lead and were broadcasting their stage shows."[237] In Brooklyn, the Mark Strand Theatre joined its sister venue in Manhattan, broadcasting its own live entertainment over WNYC, while Richard A. Rowland, then general manager of First National Pictures, conceded that strategic cooperation between the two media was now imperative.[238]

The Warner brothers—especially Sam Warner—were perhaps the most vocal motion picture advocates of radio at the time besides Roxy. Sam Warner, through his contact with Western Electric, purchased the necessary equipment to build the studio's own radio station on their Hollywood lot, KFWB, which opened in March 1925. According to Hilmes (and Scott Eyman), Warner Bros. used the station to promote their films and their stars, "borrowing techniques from an even earlier radio innovator, Samuel Rothapfel [sic]."[239] (In Los Angeles, Carli Elinor "and his brilliant concert orchestra" also began broadcasting from the city's Loew's State through KFWB.)[240] Harry Warner began advocating that the industry create its own radio network to promote the industry's films and stars, although he found little interest in the idea.[241] Warner admonished those who felt that the company's broadcasts might hurt exhibitors and cited Roxy and the other New York theaters' use of radio as a means to promote their venues.

> Does anyone suggest that the Capitol Theater in New York has been hurt by the broadcasting of "Roxy and His Gang," or the Strand by [Joseph Plunkett's] "The Plunketeers" or the Rialto and Piccadilly by the radio entertainment of those theaters? . . . My contention is that the producers can do for the whole industry, including the exhibitor, what Rothafel,

Plunkett, Riesenfeld, Ochs and other big-town exhibitors are now doing
for their respective theaters: what we are attempting to do for the West
Coast with our new broadcasting station, KFWB, at our Hollywood studio, and what Balaban and Katz and other big booking combines, who
control chains of theaters, are about to do.[242]

Warner Bros. would later create an East Coast station, WBPI, in New York in
1926, while Sam Warner, à la Roxy's East Coast jaunts, would take "a portable
transmitting device and 'studio' on a cross-country tour," according to Hilmes,
"broadcasting on KFWB's bandwidth from theaters showing Warner films."[243]
Roxy's influence on Warner Bros. and other vertically integrated companies
would continue in the years ahead.

Roxy's use of radio was also replicated by theaters overseas. In 1923, for example, the Capitol in Cardiff, England, claimed daily broadcasts of its live performances.[244] By the end of December 1926, *The Bioscope* would report that
eleven different London cinemas, including that city's own Capitol, Rivoli, and
Rialto cinemas, had already begun broadcasting their cinema orchestras and
other entertainment. Outside the city, the Walpole Cinema in Ealing and "a
number of houses in the provinces" had already provided "regular broadcasting entertainments."[245] The following year, the Astoria cinema began broadcasting twice a week.[246]

Roxy Leaves the Capitol

The *New York Herald Tribune* had asked Roxy in June 1924 if he had any
plans to leave the Capitol Theatre. "When I do," he told the newspaper, "it
will be [for] a theater of my own."[247] Investor Herbert Lubin eyed a group of
old car barns at 50th Street and Seventh Avenue and envisioned an enormous
new theater that would supplant the Capitol as the city's largest and most
important film venue. Unlike Messmore Kendall, though, he and his fellow
investors did not try to launch their plan without Roxy. Lubin was quite aware
that Roxy was the only man whose name and brand image could help secure
the millions in financing required to build an enormous movie palace in the
increasingly expensive 1920s.[248]

On June 3, 1925, the *New York Times'* front page announced that Roxy,
after five years at the Capitol Theatre, was leaving for a new project a block
away. Roxy was given absolutely free rein by Lubin in terms of management

and a full hand in designing the theater from top to bottom. Broadcasting would, of course, play an even larger role in his new theater as its live and filmed entertainment.[249] News of Roxy's departure was carried in newspapers across the country, such as the *Lima News* in Lima, Ohio, which made Roxy's departure from the Capitol a front-page story.[250] The new project struck the imagination of journalists with its claim of 6,100 seats—the largest movie theater in the world. The *Chicago Tribune* was proud to note that local architect Walter Ahlschlager was given the commission to design the structure.[251]

Film historians routinely note that the Roxy Theatre was named for him because of Roxy's success as an exhibitor, but it should be clear by now that hiring Roxy and naming the theater for him were based just as much on the value of his famous nickname and his success over the airwaves—perhaps even more so.[252] That Roxy would have been hired for this new theatrical enterprise without his radio success is certainly possible; that it would have still been named for him is highly doubtful. His was now an American brand name as recognizable as Ford or Coca-Cola, signifying a particular kind of entertainment to moviegoers and a nation of radio listeners. "Where a corporation built the Paramount," the *New Yorker* later noted, "a personality built the Roxy." Roxy himself added, "The name of the theater is dearer by far than the name I was born with."[253] He added that the radio microphone he dubbed "Mike" was "probably the most valued and indispensable friend in my long career. Without him, we could never have had our theatre." Roxy paid homage to the role broadcasting had played in his success and the role it would play at his new theater by imbuing the buttons on Roxy Theatre usher uniforms with a microphone design.[254]

Roxy and His Gang (as currently assembled) took one final tour as members of the Capitol in early July, traveling to Toronto, where the *Toronto Daily Star* estimated a million Canadians were already avid listeners. The Gang was welcomed during a reception in their honor at the parliamentary buildings by acting Prime Minister O. R. Henry.[255] Roxy subsequently announced a new campaign to raise money to supply radios to Canada's war wounded.[256] He and the Gang then broadcasted a show over CFCA and CHNC that could be heard across the northeast.[257] The Gang stayed nearly three weeks in Ontario, touring the province where they "saw Indians and lots of wonderful scenery" and visited Lake Nipigon for fishing. Roxy maintained his usual broadcasting schedule by returning to Toronto each Sunday during their visit, where government officials allowed him to use a room in a parliamentary building for his weekly North American broadcast.[258] Their trip was frequently chaperoned by government officials who made sure their adventure was carefree; even their train service was supervised by the Canadian government.[259]

When they returned to New York, Roxy was finally ready to say good-bye to the Capitol, his theater family, and his invisible family over the air. His final broadcast from the Capitol Theatre on July 26 was a tearful one for Roxy as Major Bowes took over broadcasting duties. Bowes began the final show by introducing Roxy to his radio audience. Roxy stepped in front of the microphone and remarked, "I am not going to say good bye, but only au revoir. I have worked three years here—seven days a week. And now I am tired. I want to take a rest."[260] Bowes, who had learned a few tricks from Roxy over the years, laced his first broadcast with his own well-spun sentimentality. "Now, with a sob in our hearts," he told his first radio audience, "we will endeavor to make merry again." Roxy couldn't bear to watch. "Before anyone had time to know what he was about Roxy slipped through the studio door," the *Herald Tribune* reported. "Say goodbye to them for me," Roxy told Bowes, "I can't."[261] "True, the radio made 'Roxy,'" the *Woonsocket Call-Republican* noted after Roxy departed the Capitol broadcasting studio for the last time, "but 'Roxy' has had much to do with the making of the radio. . . . Sunday nights, in many an American home, will not be the same without him."[262]

Most of the Gang remained, for the moment, at the Capitol under Bowes's radio and stage direction. It is scarcely remembered today that Major Bowes, who would become one of the most prolific (and wealthy) broadcasters between 1925 and 1945, may not have entered the field of broadcasting if not for his takeover of the Capitol Theatre radio program. He "will be a popular announcer, we are quite sure," the *Brooklyn Daily Times* noted after Bowes's first radio effort. "His voice is even and firm, his enunciation clear. . . . we think we liked that."[263] Over time, he became a new Sunday favorite for millions. Not everyone gravitated to him immediately, though, and Bowes was forced to admit that not all of the letters he received shortly after taking over the radio reins were positive. Some listeners had written negatively of his "cold-blooded" and "unsympathetic" announcing. Journalists also wanted him to be less of an announcer and more of a personality and a friend.[264] They wanted him to be more like Roxy.

Roxy had finally found his niche as an exhibitor/entertainer/broadcaster and fully embraced media convergence, in which his broadcasting efforts at the Capitol created new possibilities for film and theatrical promotion, music publishing and recording, and newspaper and book publishing. He had also, once again, redefined the role of an urban movie palace exhibitor to incorporate new marketing, technological, and industrial synergies. In the coming years, Roxy, Erno Rapee, William Axt, David Mendoza, Major Bowes, and others who had worked for or with him would expand these possibilities even more. The industrial and technological walls that divided film, music, and broadcasting would soon be removed by multimedia artists like Roxy and by companies like RCA that could harness radio, television, film, and music to create a new convergent entertainment industry and reach audiences in both public and private spaces.

FIGURE 1. The Freedman House in Forest City, Pennsylvania, as it appeared on March 2, 1915. Note the sign for the "Family Theatre" (partially obscured) on the right side of the image. (*Courtesy Billy Rose Theatre Division, New York Public Library for the Performing Arts; Astor, Lenox, and Tilden Foundations*)

FIGURE 2. The elaborate framing of motion pictures (the motion picture screen) at the Alhambra Theatre, Milwaukee (ca. 1911).

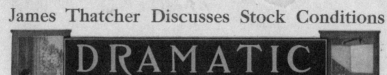

James Thatcher Discusses Stock Conditions

The Possibilities of Short Film Features

FIGURE 3. Roxy on the cover of the April 21, 1917, issue of *Dramatic Mirror* magazine. (*Author's collection*)

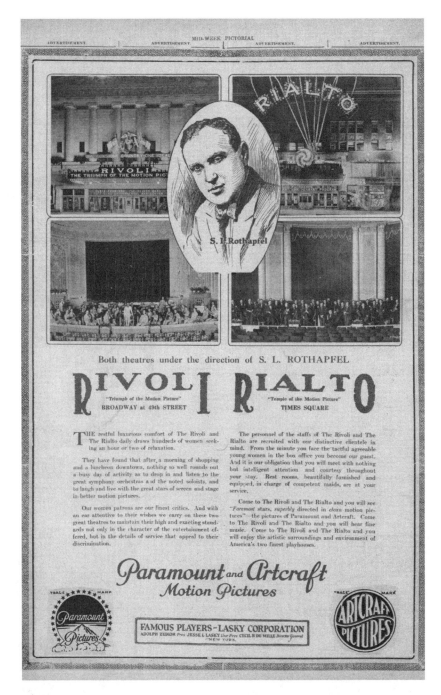

FIGURE 4. Advertisement promoting the music of the Rialto and Rivoli theaters (*Mid-Week Pictorial*, ca. 1918). (*Author's collection*)

FIGURE 5. Maria Gambarelli and other Capitol Theatre performers. (*Author's collection*)

FIGURE 6. Roxy seated in the Capitol Theatre using a Western Electric microphone (ca. 1923). (*Courtesy Morris Rosenfeld/Prints and Photographs Division, Library of Congress, LC-USZ62-43436*)

FIGURE 7. Early postcard featuring the Capitol Theatre broadcasting Gang, including Roxy, Eugene Ormandy, and William Axt. (*Author's collection*)

FIGURE 8. Roxy and His Gang at Walter Reed General Hospital (March 19, 1924). (*Courtesy National Photo Company Collection, Prints and Photographs Division, Library of Congress, LC-DIG-npcc-10796*)

FIGURE 9. Roxy, backed by a military band, at Union Station, Washington, D.C., March 18, 1924. (*Courtesy National Photo Company Collection, Prints and Photographs Division, Library of Congress, LC-DIG-npcc-10803*)

FIGURE 11. Roxy at Union Station, Washington, D.C., March 6, 1925. (*Courtesy National Photo Company Collection, Prints and Photographs Division, Library of Congress, LC-DIG-npcc-26876*)

FIGURE 10. (FACING PAGE) Roxy at the White House, Washington, D.C., March 20, 1924. (*Courtesy National Photo Company Collection, Prints and Photographs Division, Library of Congress, LC-DIG-npcc-10804*)

FIGURE 12. Sheet music for "Humanity's Friend" and "Good Night (Pleasant Dreams) God Bless You," by George Spink (ca. 1925). (*Author's collection*)

FIGURE 13. Roxy sailing on one of his many trips to and from Europe. (*Author's collection*)

Hello Everybody

Roxy & his Gang

The Greatest Popular Entertainment in the World

SAVOY THEATRE
Asbury Park

2 Performances Thurs., February 18th
MATINEE and EVENING

FIGURE 14. Cover of a Roxy and His Gang program from an appearance at the Savoy Theatre in Asbury Park, New Jersey, on February 18, 1926. The back cover of the program advertises "Roxy's New Home"— the Roxy Theatre—which was scheduled to open later that year. (*Author's collection*)

FIGURE 16. (FACING PAGE) "Roxy Medal Award for Movies," "S. L. Rothafel, presented with a silver placque [*sic*] by Erno Rapee on behalf of the theatre organization in recognition of his achievement in creating the world's greatest amusement enterprise in the theatre bearing his name" (ca. 1927). (*Courtesy Harold Stein/Quigley Photographic Archive, Georgetown University Library Special Collections Research Center, Washington, D.C.*)

FIGURE 15. Samuel "Roxy" Rothafel: the theatrical field general in his war room. (*Courtesy Ben M. Hall Collection, Theatre Historical Society*)

FIGURE 17. Lew White and the Roxy Theatre featured on the cover of White's curated collection of sheet music for organ or piano. Robbins Photoplay Series, No. 20 (ca. 1927). (*Author's collection*)

FIGURE 18. Roxy broadcasting. (*Courtesy Ben M. Hall Collection, Theatre Historical Society*)

FAMOUS RADIO BROADCASTERS

"ROXY'S GANG"

Broadcasting From The Roxy Theatre, New York

JOHN J. KEATING EDWIN ZIMMERMAN JOHN YOUNG GEORGE REARDON FREDK. THOMAS BERNARD P. AROHS LEO RUSSOTTO DOUGLAS B. MURRAY LEW WHITE JOSEPH STOPAK
ADELAIDE De LOCA HAROLD KRAVITT HELEN ARDELLE ALDO BOMONTE "BOMBY" DOUGLAS STANBURY MILDRED HUNT "ROXY" GLADYS RICE ERNO RAPEE MILTON CROSS VIOLA PHILO YASHA BUNCHUK JOSEPH LI
HARRY BREUER CHARLES PREVIN DOROTHY MILLER FREDERICK FRADKIN BEATRICE BELKIN HENRY NOSCO

FIGURE 19. Roxy and His Gang at the Roxy Theatre. The Gang now featured artists such as Yasha Bunchuk, Charles Previn, Erno Rapee, Douglas Stanbury, and Joseph Littau. (*Author's collection*)

FIGURE 20. Ferde Grofé, George Gershwin, Roxy, and Paul Whiteman at the Roxy Theatre, New York (ca. 1930). (*Courtesy Lebrecht Music and Arts*)

FIGURE 21. Stage show featuring the Roxyettes at the Roxy Theatre (ca. 1930). (*Courtesy Billy Rose Theatre Division, New York Public Library for the Performing Arts; Astor, Lenox, and Tilden Foundations*)

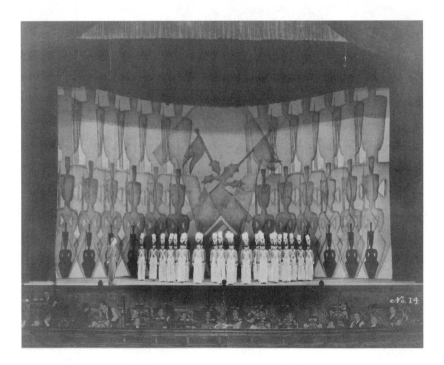

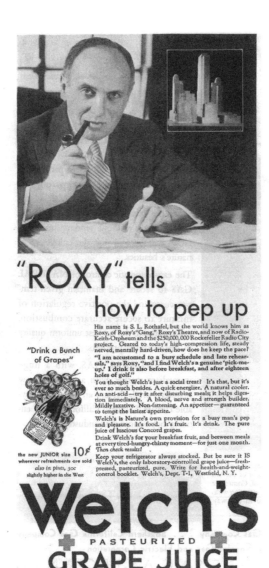

FIGURE 23. Welch's Grape Juice advertisement featuring Roxy (Time, June 1, 1931). (*Author's collection*)

FIGURE 22. (FACING PAGE) "Parade of the Wooden Soldiers" at the Roxy Theatre's Christmas Revue featuring the Roxyettes. (*Courtesy Ben M. Hall Collection, Theatre Historical Society*)

FIGURE 24. George McClelland (left), vice president and general manager of NBC, Major Bowes (*center*), head of the Capitol Theatre broadcasts, and Roxy, "who needs no introduction" according to the caption on the back of this November 1931 photograph. "These three pioneers of radio were heard on the gala program emanating from the Capitol Theatre Studio on the occasion of its 9th anniversary last Friday— the Capitol first going on the air November 19, 1922, the first theatre to broadcast a regular program." (*Author's collection*)

FIGURE 25. Montage of audiences at Radio City Music Hall (ca. August 17, 1933). (*Author's collection*)

FIGURE 26. Rudy Vallee, James Melton, and Roxy at Jack Dempsey's restaurant, celebrating Melton's new film, *Stars Over Broadway* (1935). Melton was a longtime member of the Gang. This is one of the last photographs of Roxy, taken in late November 1935, less than two months before his death on January 13, 1936. (*Author's collection*)

FIGURE 27. Roxy in his favorite pose—at the NBC microphone. (*Author's collection*)

6. "IT'S THE ROXY AND I'M ROXY"
BUILDING THE BRAND AND THE ROXY THEATRE
(1925–1927)

"The radio made Roxy, as Roxy helped to make the radio. It made him, in fact, America's greatest showman. His name became a household word."
—Jack Jamison, *Radio Guide*, April 1936[1]

Back in the dim days when the speaking stage was of some importance they used to call Mary Pickford "the Bernhardt of the screen" and Rothafel was "the Belasco of the movies." Now the screen is dominant as a field of fame and one word—"Roxy"—says it all. . . . Broadway is his.
—Terry Ramsaye, *Photoplay*, October 1927

Roxy talks very little about the cinema. He is much fonder of the radio.
—The *New Yorker*, May 28, 1927

The Capitol Theatre had been the epicenter of the film–radio movement in the early to mid-1920s and a key catalyst for the film industry's use of broadcasting for the promotion of motion pictures, stars, and theaters. Roxy's latest project, the 5,920-seat Roxy Theatre, was intended to become a new locus of media convergence where film, music, and broadcasting would promote individual films, songs, writers, and stars. In order to understand the many ways in which the Roxy Theatre was not just a movie palace but also a broadcasting and sound recording studio, symphony hall, motion picture theater, and theatrical venue, it is necessary to trace the development of the theater (and Roxy's brand name) between 1925 and 1927. The theater's unparalleled capabilities and media attention would spur new corporate alliances and competition and later become an integral part of Fox's distribution and exhibition chain.

By July 19, 1925, Roxy, Arthur H. Sawyer and Herbert Lubin, president of Associated Pictures Corporation, "completed preliminary arrangements for the construction of six huge motion picture theatres in New York City" that were part of a planned Roxy circuit. By then, the famous showman was broadcasting to eight million loyal listeners over WEAF every week.[2] Roxy's radio prominence was expected to help fill each theater's seats. "He probably addresses more people in a year than any human being in the entire history of the world ever did before," the *Detroit News* noted at the time.[3] The *Woonsocket Call-Republican* summed up his status by 1925:

> A few years ago S. L. Rothafel was known to a comparatively few people outside of New York, where he was connected with a great moving picture theater. Today, "Roxy," as he has come to be known, is a National character. . . . What child is there, what crippled soldier is there, who does not know of "Roxy"? . . . Not in our recollection has one man been so responsible for a quiet Sunday evening in American homes each week as has S. L. Rothafel. . . . No man has done more to make for the success of the radio in the family circle than has the well known figure. He is known and loved by old and young far and wide. . . . True, the radio made "Roxy," but he "Roxy" has much to do with the making of the radio.[4]

Imbuing the new theater with the name "Roxy" was not a token gesture on the part of Sawyer and Lubin or an egotistical demand of their new showman. Instead, it was a prudent business decision, aligning the theater with a brand name known to millions. If fans wanted to see their radio idols (Roxy and His Gang), they would have to travel to New York and visit Roxy at the Roxy. Roxy allied name recognition and broadcasting with a physical venue decades before Walt Disney built a theme park in Anaheim, California. A nation of devoted radio listeners could now visit the physical structure where their favorite stars appeared on stage. Upon its opening, the Roxy Theatre would become one of the most popular tourist destinations in New York.

By the mid-1920s, a movie palace manager was required to understand and/or assemble musical compositions for a symphony orchestra; be able to choose feature films, newsreels, scenics, and other films, arrange them in sequential order, and edit them when necessary; synthesize ballet, dance, vaudeville, and other live performance in order to harmonize an evening's entertainment; and profitably serve as a marketing manager and publicist who understood how to work with newspapers, local retailers, chambers of commerce, women's societies, and, now, radio stations to promote a theater and its upcoming films. The mid- to late-1920s movie palace was a city within a city that produced fantasy for audiences but behind the scenes was equal parts factory and performance venue. The Roxy, for instance, employed 584 people at its opening.[5]

Walter W. Ahlschlager, a prominent Chicago architect, was chosen to design the new Roxy Theatre and the smaller theaters being built for the Roxy circuit.[6] Roxy headed to Chicago in August 1925 to meet with Ahlschlager. By then, the flagship Roxy was rumored to cost $7 million.[7] Construction was set to begin on the showcase theater on September 15, 1925, with October 1926 as a goal for its opening.[8]

Roxy headed to Europe in September to "take a rest" and "tour the old world."[9] He sailed from New York on September 5, 1925, aboard the *Leviathan* with Arthur Sawyer and production designer Clark Robinson, ostensibly to scout talent in Europe.[10] There may have been additional reasons for visiting.

THE RAPEE OF EUROPA

No movie palace conductor in 1925, except perhaps Hugo Riesenfeld, was more prolific or sought after than Erno Rapee. He had been the conductor of the 5,300-seat Capitol Theatre in New York until November 1923 when he became manager and conductor of the Fox Theatre in Philadelphia. Rapee's reputation, like Roxy's, was international and both men were well known to executives at the German film company, Universum Film Aktiengesellschaft (Ufa). Rapee had worked with Roxy on the music for both *Passion* and *The Cabinet of Dr. Caligari* during their celebrated American premieres. Rapee had achieved further acclaim through his scoring work for Fox, his recent book and music publishing, and his reputation on both sides of the Atlantic among musicians and music directors.

It is not surprising, therefore, that Ufa would hire him in August 1925 to come to Berlin and oversee the management, conducting, and music direction of the Ufa-Palast am Zoo, the country's most prestigious cinema. Ufa, *The Metronome* reported, "engaged Erno Rapee to present their programs in the American way." The company promised Rapee one of the largest theater orchestras ever established—eighty-five musicians—and he "accepted with alacrity."[11] Rapee was only one part of the package. Ufa also hired Alexander Oumansky, former head of ballet at the Capitol Theatre under Roxy, to import the movie theater stage show.[12]

Upon their arrival in Berlin, Rapee and Oumansky were focused on the reopening of the Ufa-Palast am Zoo on September 25, 1925. Roxy also sailed for Europe in time to arrive in Berlin and assist his former employees.[13] Rumors circulating in Germany and England noted that Roxy was paid $3,000 a week to help supervise the opening of the theater. He flatly denied such reports.[14] "The most notable trade visitor of this week has doubtless been S. Rothafel, the famous American showman, generally called 'Roxy,'" "Red" reported in

The Bioscope. "He has been here for four or five days" and "has given quite a lot of time to inspecting the reconstruction of the 'Ufa Palast.'"[15]

The reopening night was everything Ufa, Rapee, and Oumansky could have hoped for. The elaborate orchestra, the inclusion of a new jazz band, an organ and organist, the renovation of the theater, its upgrade in interior lighting, and its new American management were inspired by the Capitol in New York and the Fox in Philadelphia. Rapee's musical accompaniment and Oumansky's stage shows successfully brought American presentation to Germany. "[F]or the first time in Germany a combination of symphony concert, ballet and film was offered," the *New York Times* wrote. "The Americanization of the theatre's methods of presentation has been carried out by its new directors" and "The Ufa Palast has been rebuilt according to American ideas."[16] Roxy observed that in all of Europe it was only at the Ufa-Palast am Zoo "that he saw a show which might be favourably compared with American big city standards."[17]

Ufa not only entrusted its most important cinema to Rapee but also commissioned him to arrange music for a number of Ufa productions in his role as senior music director for the company.[18] Rapee remained at the Ufa-Palast am Zoo for nearly one year, departing on July 27, 1926, after presiding over the debut of the company's newest flagship cinema, the Gloria-Palast in Berlin. "[T]he occasion of his farewell performance is one that will long be remembered in Berlin," *The Metronome* reported. "The audience was wildly enthusiastic and at the close of the performance shouted for him to 'come back soon.'"[19] The *New York Times* reported that Rapee left Berlin to the sounds of a "long and enthusiastic ovation" at his farewell performance; his presentation methods would now be continued by new management at both theaters.[20] Siegfried Kracauer, writing in 1926 of Ufa and Berlin's post-Rapee era, remarked that moviegoing and the city had been changed forever:

> The large picture houses in Berlin are palaces of distraction; to call them *movie theaters (Kinos)* would be disrespectful. The latter are still abundant only in Old-Berlin and in the suburbs where they serve neighborhood audiences, and even there they are in declining number. . . . it is the picture palaces, those optical fairylands, which are shaping the face of Berlin. The Ufa palaces—above all the one at the Zoo . . . enjoy sellouts day after day. The newly-built Gloria-Palast proves that the style initiated by these palaces is still developing in the same direction. . . . Gone is the time when films were allowed to run one after another each with a corresponding musical accompaniment. The major theaters at least have adopted the

American style of a self-contained show which integrates the film as part of a larger whole.[21]

The *Wall Street Journal* also commented on the changes in German presentation standards:

> For the first time in Germany the opening of a cinema had the dignity and importance of a dramatic premiere. In keeping with the caliber of its audience, the "movie" offered a new standard of motion picture presentation. A well manned symphony orchestra accompanied the film showing, ballet and soloists provided a supplemental program. The movie as a high class entertainment had arrived.[22]

Erno Rapee was not shy about claiming his influence on German film exhibition. He wrote in *Variety* on June 8, 1927, that the transformation of European movie palaces

> reached its climax with the Americanization of the big German Theatre chain, the Ufa, in 1925. Under American influence, and American capital, its houses were remodeled and enlarged and in the largest house an orchestra of 85 was installed and stage attractions presented, which equalled [*sic*] anything shown in America in size as well as quality. . . . [T]his American type of entertainment, the backbone of which I consider the large and well trained orchestra, has won out and is today the customary way picture theatres are being run.[23]

As important as Roxy, Rapee, and Oumansky were in delivering German films to American audiences with *Passion* and *The Cabinet of Dr. Caligari*, they were just as essential to the cultural and industrial influence of American moviegoing practices upon Germany.

ROXY RETURNS TO RADIO

While Rapee was in Germany working for Ufa, Roxy was in New York maintaining his image and celebrity. Before he left for Europe, Roxy had negotiated a new agreement with NBC, even without a theater to promote or a discernible "Gang" to draw upon. Jon Holman of WEAF wrote to Edgar Bloom of AT&T urging the company to maintain their association with Roxy. "It is the consensus of opinion that Mr. Rothafel has the money and ability to provide the finest program broadcast," Holman wrote Bloom on August 19. "Other stations are inviting him. It is in our interest to retain him." AT&T agreed to carry Roxy's new radio show, in whatever form it entailed, from October 1925 to October 1926, when the Roxy Theatre was scheduled to open.[24]

Roxy went back on the air for weekly broadcasts beginning October 30, 1925, on WEAF.[25] Some of his old Gang was still employed at the Capitol, but Roxy was able to pry Maria Gambarelli, Douglas Stanbury, James Coombs, Frank Moulan, Florence Mulholland, and a few others loose for his new program.[26] (Tommy Dowd, dancer Doris Niles, and longtime publicist Martha Wilchinski, for instance, did not join the new Gang, preferring instead to stay at the Capitol.)[27] Instead of Sunday nights—now the domain of Major Bowes and his Capitol radio show—Roxy and his "new gang" began broadcasting on WEAF from 9:00 to 10:00 on Friday nights instead, with the show transmitted across a chain of nine stations including WWJ in Detroit and KSD in St. Louis.[28]

These new broadcasts were essential to Lubin and Sawyer's plans to keep Roxy visible as the theater began selling stock to cover its mounting costs. In addition to hooking additional large investors, they also increased their campaign to lure small investors to buy shares in Roxy's new entertainment center. Stock was sold over the air and in print using his radio fame and theatrical track record as bait. A November 1925 advertisement for the Roxy Theatres Corporation noted that "ROXY Will Soon Talk to You *from* His Own Great Theatre!" and included a personal appeal from Roxy to prospective investors:

> The Roxy Theatre is not to be my theatre only. I don't want it to be a one-man affair. I want you all in on it. I want you to come in as my partners—you, the motion picture and the radio public. The plan is completely financed, of course, but I wish as many of my friends as possible to be stockholders with me in the Roxy Theatre. I want all of you who have followed me in my theatre career and all of you who have formed my great unseen audience on the air, to join me in the final ownership of the Roxy Theatre. I want us all to be one big Gang together, running our own big theatre.

Roxy promised his fans/prospective stockholders that when it came to the new Roxy Theatre, "If we've left out anything, it's because it hasn't been invented yet."[29]

Class A (Preferred) stock was sold for forty dollars per share—a hefty sum for the period.[30] The value of the Roxy Theatre was estimated at ten million dollars.[31]

Subsequent advertisements for Roxy Theatres Corporation stock were placed in newspapers in areas where Roxy and His Gang had visited in the past, such as Bridgeport and Hartford, Connecticut.[32] The *New Yorker* later referred to the Roxy Theatre as the "temple of many stockholders,"[33] while Upton Sinclair remarked that its marketing as the world's "grandest motion picture theater" hooked "thirteen thousand people, mostly workers, [who] took Roxy's word for it and bought stock in the enterprise."[34]

Roxy also drummed up additional publicity for his radio show and "to promote stock selling for the current proposition," when he and the Gang embarked on a new ten-city tour to "make personal connections with local business men" and visit all of the major stations that aired his weekly (typically Friday night) broadcasts.[35] Four thousand individual investors eventually purchased stock in the theater prior to its opening.[36]

Over the next several months, Roxy and his Gang continued to tour, promoting his new theatrical venture while raising money in Washington, D.C., for the benefit of a hospital for tuberculosis patients in Albuquerque, New Mexico, and appearing at Trenton, New Jersey's Crescent Temple for that city's Young Men's Hebrew Association in January, continuing his aid to Jewish charities and benevolent associations.[37]

In December 1925, the American Motion Picture Association chose its twelve "Immortals," the "most representative men who stand as the ideals in the progress, growth, and expansion of the industry." The group included Adolph Zukor, Will Hays, Marcus Loew, D. W. Griffith, Carl Laemmle, William Fox, and Roxy.[38] He remained dominant in broadcasting as well. In February 1926, Roxy was voted the most popular radio entertainer by the readers of *Radio World*.[39]

For years, Roxy's recommendations on air and in print had boosted the box office potential of innumerable films. Thus it was a coup for Fox News service to be given the first film contract for the theater in February 1926, a fact William Fox exploited in advertisements and trade articles.[40] Roxy's marketable name and voice were also being mobilized for the sale of other new products. Roxy appeared in a full-page advertisement for the latest edition of F. H. Richardson's book *Handbook of Projection* in February and in March his face appeared in advertisements for Arch Preserver shoes with the headline, "Roxy takes 18,908 steps every day."[41] Hawking shoes was a new conferral of status for the son of an immigrant shoe cobbler.

Roxy took a break from his radio show to focus more of his attention on the theater and announced after his February 24 broadcast that he would not be back on the air until the Roxy Theatre was ready to open. Still, whether it was the need to increase Roxy Theatres Corporation stock sales, fundraise for charities, or his unending need to connect with his fans, Roxy's live appearances did not cease. He performed in March with the Gang at venues such as the Arcadia Ball Room in Bridgeport, Connecticut, and at the Newton Theatre in Newton, New Jersey, giving the latter movie house audience a two-and-a-half-hour performance.[42]

While Roxy blamed his departure from the air on his need to focus all of his time and attention on the construction of the new theater, Roxy's doctor had ordered him to take six weeks' complete rest for an unspecified reason. Roxy and Rosa left for California on March 18, 1926, to get away from New York and his workaholic endeavors. The estimated date of the Roxy opening was now moved back to December. The trip, despite doctor's orders, was not entirely a vacation as Adolph Zukor, Carl Laemmle, William Fox, Winfield Sheehan, Richard Rowland, and Samuel Katz were all in Los Angeles meeting with their studio heads and staying at the Ambassador Hotel along with Roxy.[43]

Roxy's departure to Los Angeles was his first time away from radio audiences since November 1922, but he found other ways to stay visible. In May 1926, *McClure's* magazine announced that Roxy would launch the magazine's new radio section with a story about the behind-the-scenes (and false) relationship between Douglas Stanbury and Maria Gambarelli.[44] Roxy could also be seen on screen in a series of one-reel shorts that were filmed during his trip with the Gang to Ottawa in the summer of 1925. The films were made under Canadian government auspices and then reedited by William Brotherhood for mass distribution. The first short featured Roxy "broadcasting from the wilds" of Canada. "He then takes you for a trip," *Motion Pictures Today* noted, "and gives you a wonderfully interesting time." Other reels, "Sportsman's Dream," "Rushing Waters," and "Shadowland," showcased members of his famous radio troupe.[45]

Roxy worked feverishly over the next few months to populate the small city needed to operate a 5,920-seat movie palace during the late silent era. He hired H. Maurice Jacquet and then Charles Previn as two of his conductors in October 1926.[46] Previn, *The Metronome* noted, was "one of the best known of the younger Americans" and had "an enviable reputation in this country." He previously served as the general musical director of the Klaw and Erlanger enterprises and then became the musical director for film exhibitors Charles, Spyros, and George Skouras of Skouras Bros. Enterprises, supervising the music for the Missouri and Ambassador theaters in St. Louis.[47] He also served as conductor of the St. Louis Municipal Opera Company.[48]

The attention to music was unparalleled at the Roxy Theatre. Along with the acquisition of Victor Herbert's music library, Roxy would eventually hire four of the most capable conductors in the nation for his 110-piece symphony orchestra. No Roxy theater before or after would boast the size or scale of its musical endeavors.[49]

Fox, Roxy, Rapee, and the Eucharistic Congress

One name remained conspicuously absent from the new Roxy Theatre: Erno Rapee. Rapee had sailed back to the United States in August 1926 without an offer from Roxy. The two had not officially worked together since 1923, when Rapee left the Capitol to manage the Fox Theatre in Philadelphia and conduct its orchestra. Still, theirs had been an inspired collaboration, producing scores for films such as *Passion, Over the Hill* (1920), *Robin Hood* (1922), *Monte Cristo* (1922), *Nero* (1922), *If Winter Comes, The Queen of Sheba,* and *A Connecticut Yankee at King Arthur's Court* (1923).[50] Roxy seemed to prefer new blood for his newest theater.

Rapee's work with Roxy and for Ufa, his industry-standard book *The Encyclopedia of Music for Pictures* (1925), and his work producing cue sheets and scores for other films which were "in extensive use by every first class cinema theatre," according to *The Metronome*, led to a new contract with Carl Fischer, Inc., to prepare twenty-four "adaptations and arrangements of works by master composers, both classic and modern, for use with photoplays." Rapee was also signed to the company's famous Playhouse Series, along with composers such as Victor Herbert and Frederick Stahlberg.[51] Rapee was not the first movie house conductor/composer to receive a contract from a music publishing company but part of a new trend. The Carl Fischer contract gave Rapee the financial flexibility to act as a journeyman conductor, arranger, and composer.

In October 1926, William Fox opened a new 3,873-seat, $1.2 million theater, the Academy of Music, near Union Square in Manhattan, across from the site of the old Academy of Music.[52] The new Academy was now the flagship theater of the Fox circuit, according to *Motion Picture News*, part of a new building campaign by the company.[53] Fox asked Rapee to be guest conductor for the theater's premiere performance, at which *The Family Upstairs* (1926) and "an elaborate surrounding program" were the featured attractions.[54] Rapee then stayed on as the musical director of the Academy of Music through at least November.[55]

Fox's relationship with Roxy and Rapee would bring the two together again for an audacious effort that demonstrated the power of Fox's newsreel division, the indexical value of nonfiction film, and the cultural worth of motion pictures. In 1926, Roxy and Rapee exhibited Fox's twenty-camera coverage of the 28th International Eucharistic Congress in Chicago, "a world gathering of the Roman Catholic faithful," which took place between June 20 and June 24. International Newsreel also had access to the event, but Fox, under Winfield Sheehan's stewardship, "bankroll[ed] a feature-length documentary of the Eucharistic Congress," and, according to Thomas Doherty, donated "exclusive copyright and all profits from the film to the Catholic Church." Ray L. Hall was assigned to supervise a team of twenty cameramen to record the events "from send-off in Rome to fade-out in Chicago."[56]

How Roxy became attached to this project remains unclear, though he had a number of connections with multiple parties that helped bring *Eucharistic Congress* (1926) to the screen. There is certainly enough circumstantial evidence, for instance, that Roxy and Hall were acquainted. Hall had been the editor of the CPI's Official War Reviews during World War I when Hall had also compiled and edited *America's Answer* (1918). The film may have used segments from Roxy's film *Flying with the Marines*. *America's Answer* was also scored and presented in New York and Washington, D.C. by Roxy, possibly putting Hall and Roxy in direct contact.[57] Roxy's own compilation documentary for the CPI, *Under Four Flags*, was also culled, in part, from the newsreels Hall had produced. There is no direct evidence, though, that the two met during the war, even if they were certainly familiar with one another's work by mid-1918.

If they had not met in 1918, then they certainly had by 1926. Hall penned a lengthy article for *The Independent* ("Seeing Is Believing") in September 1926 in which he spoke at length about the CPI, propaganda, and motion pictures. He wrote that some exhibitors were reluctant to show controversial subject matter in newsreels and recalled a meeting "in S. L. Rothapfel's office" and "in his projection room" where the two men discussed footage of Vladimir Lenin's funeral. (Roxy refused to show it.) Hall may have been one of the voices who suggested that Fox employ Roxy for the premiere of *Eucharistic Congress* at [Al] Jolson's 59th Street Theatre in Manhattan.[58]

Other voices may have contributed to the selection as well. Martin Quigley, editor and publisher of *Exhibitors Herald*, who had brokered the deal between Fox and the Catholic Church,[59] was certainly aware of Roxy's unparalleled status within the industry. If Allene Talmey's 1927 account is to be believed, however, the decision to commission Roxy to stage the presentation of the film was not made by Hall, Fox, Quigley, or any other film industry player, but supposedly requested by George Cardinal Mundelein, archbishop of Chicago.[60]

The choice was certainly not perfunctory, despite his reputation and his work exhibiting feature-length documentaries like *America's Answer*, *Under Four Flags*, and, more recently, *Nanook of the North* at the Capitol Theatre. Roxy's relationship with some of the nation's Catholics had certainly been mixed. For nearly two decades, he had been a strong believer in celebrating Christian holidays and customs, especially as they enhanced the unitary text of his presentations and the coffers of his theaters. Beginning with the Family Theatre in Forest City, Pennsylvania, Roxy had often presented filmed versions of the Passion Play and added hymns and other religious matter to his shows during the Easter, Christmas, and New Year's holidays. While Protestant clergy and parishioners seemed to love Roxy and his radio benediction, "Good night, pleasant dreams, God bless you," the phrase and his personality had run afoul of some Catholic radio listeners during his Sunday evening broadcasts from 1922 to 1925. His work on behalf of orphans, veterans, the impoverished, and many other charities had, however, produced a figurative armor that was not easily pierced. A good example of the kind of approbation he received could be found in an April 1926 account of his work for the YMCA in Elizabeth, New Jersey. The *Elizabeth Times* noted his popular acclaim and his generosity to Christian causes, despite his religious and ethnic background:

> "Roxy" is a big man in the theatre, in the movie world, in music, and he is "Roxy the First," king of the air, for millions have worshipped at the shrine of "Roxy" and his "Gang" for the weekly radio concerts. . . . But aside from "Roxy's" success in business, he is of big caliber, yet simplicity is his outstanding characteristic. . . . And that is why "Roxy" cancelled some business engagements, away out in California, so he could start home a day earlier and be on hand to help give the Y. M. C. A. drive in Elizabeth, New Jersey, the KIND OF A START it needs, the kind of a start it DESERVES. "Roxy"—Samuel A. [*sic*] Rothafel—is a Jew. The drive is for $500,000 for a Young Men's CHRISTIAN Association building in Elizabeth. What cares "Roxy" whether it is Jew or Christian, Protestant or Catholic. All he cares about the drive is that it is for the purpose of building a BIGGER and BETTER CLUB HOUSE for the boys and young men of Elizabeth.[61]

Roxy was perceived by many as a showman, a veteran, an all-American Horatio Alger, and a righteous Jew.

His exhibition of the eight-reel, ninety-six-minute *Eucharistic Congress* at Jolson's Theatre was another form of charity that ultimately served to build goodwill for the Roxy name, benefiting the showman and his new enterprise.

Roxy was paid nothing for his work presenting the film, giving "his time and energy to the cause without charge," according to *Motion Picture News*.[62] He supervised the premiere of the film on November 8, 1926, and staged its "striking" prologue that, Doherty notes, "dramatized the birth of the baby Jesus of Bethlehem" and added to the evening's religious unitary text.[63]

Roxy also supervised the scoring of the film with Rapee, bringing the two together again for the first time in more than a year. Otto A. Singenberger, musical director of the St. Mary-on-the-Lake Seminary in Mundelheim, Illinois—who had directed the children's choir at the Eucharistic Congress in Chicago—also "cooperated with Erno Rapee on the musical score," according to *Motion Picture News*. The music "was strikingly effective," the trade journal noted, and "had the audience humming throughout the show."[64]

Will Hays singled out the collaboration between Jews, Catholics, and Protestants to stage the film during his introduction before a packed audience of 1,770. He was followed by Monsignor C. J. Quille, secretary general of the Eucharistic Congress, who noted that Roxy was a Jew and so were many of those in his hand-picked orchestra performing in the nativity-inspired stage show.[65]

The significance of *Eucharistic Congress* is at least threefold. First, its significance as the first feature-length filmed documentation of a live event cannot be understated, foreshadowing the birth of other such documentaries in the 1930s, including, most notoriously, Leni Riefenstahl's *Triumph of the Will* (*Triumph des Willens*, 1935) and *Olympia* (*Olympische Spiele*, 1938). It also foreshadowed the growing ties between the Catholic Church and the American film industry. Finally, *Eucharistic Congress* was the first union of Fox, Roxy, and Rapee. Roxy and Rapee's successful work on the film would serve as a dry run for their later efforts and may have spurred Fox's desire to bring Roxy into the company's fold. When Fox later had the opportunity to place Roxy and Rapee under his aegis, he didn't need to wonder what their union might produce; he had already seen what they could accomplish with a film Doherty notes was "as tedious as a droning homily."[66]

FOX, RAPEE, AND ROXY

Rapee continued to work for Fox after *Eucharistic Congress* and was commissioned to assemble a new score (and write new music) for the East Coast premiere of Raoul Walsh's film *What Price Glory* (1926), at the Harris Theatre on November 23, 1926.[67] Rapee's score contained approximately 168 different pieces, with some newly composed by Rapee. *Motion Picture News* granted "great praise" to Rapee and commented that the film's music "match[ed] every nuance and shade of the picture's sweep and by-play."[68]

The *News* missed the most important feature of Rapee's work on *What Price Glory*, though: the creation of a new theme song, "Charmaine," and its use as a leitmotif throughout the film. The song was new to Harris Theatre audiences, but its melody was actually composed thirteen years earlier when Rapee was conductor of the Hungarian Opera Company and performing at New York's Webster Hall.[69] Perhaps due to the short window Rapee had to come up with a score for the film, he recycled an old tune he had generated during his first years in America. Rapee then teamed up with lyricist Lew Pollack to add words to Rapee's melody for the love theme for Dolores del Rio's character Charmaine de la Cognac in order to make it popular and saleable to radio listeners, nightclub crooners, and family sing-alongs.[70] *Musical Courier's* Josephine Vila noted that the song "quite haunts one with its simplicity and method."[71] Lea Jacobs writes that the song still holds much of its power: "I defy anyone who has heard the recording of [organist] Gaylord Carter playing it on the Wurlitzer to keep a dry eye."[72]

Rapee and Pollack, despite Rapee's contract with Carl Fischer, Inc., published "Charmaine" through Sherman, Clay & Co. The song would become a massive hit over the next three years, selling roughly two million copies by mid-1929.[73] Rapee would later use the success of "Charmaine" to substantiate his claim as the "originator of the film theme song."[74] William Johnston remarked that the success of the film and its music was not only important for Fox's standing in the industry but perhaps even more so for Rapee, who had been away from Broadway for three years in Philadelphia and then Berlin. His return to New York, Johnston concluded, was now an unquestioned success.[75] A panoply of political and theatrical figures, including Mayor James Walker, Joseph Plunkett, Florenz Ziegfeld, Allan Dwan, Hugo Riesenfeld, Adolph Zukor, Jesse Lasky, Gloria Swanson, William Fox, and Winfield Sheehan were on hand for *What Price Glory's* Broadway debut and Rapee's return to the Times Square area.[76]

One other name in attendance was perhaps even more conspicuous: S. L. Rothafel, who was still filling out his musical staff for the Roxy Theatre.[77] Shortly after the Harris Theatre premiere of *What Price Glory*, Roxy hired Rapee and Frederick Stahlberg to be the final two of four conductors at the Roxy Theatre.[78] *The Metronome* noted that each of the four men would "perform their duties on an equal basis" with Roxy rotating each conductor to "focus attention on their respective merits."[79] Roxy posited that the theater would not only be the largest movie palace in America but one of the most important music venues in the world.

In August 1926, Rapee had returned from Germany as a freelance conductor/ composer. Less than six months later, he had secured long-term contracts with one of the largest music publishers, the largest motion picture theater in the United States, and with Fox Films as it began assembling a roster of exhibition and music talent that matched its stable of elite European and American directors such as Walsh, Dwan, Howard Hawks, John Ford, Frank Borzage, and F. W. Murnau.[80]

Fox was still without a flagship theater along Broadway and without a circuit leader like Paramount's Harold Franklin or Loew's' Nicholas Schenck. Getting the Roxy Theatre would solve both problems at once. "The rumor that William Fox is going to be interested in the new Roxy (50th street) persists despite denials," *Variety* noted in late December 1926. While Herbert Lubin continued to assert that the Roxy Theatre (and the others in the circuit) would remain independent, Fox was angling behind the scenes to take over the Roxy in a "deal with the bankers," according to *Variety*. Courtland Smith, a former associate of Will Hays, handled negotiations. Fox was still unable to purchase a controlling interest in the theater by early 1927, but Smith was able to at least secure exhibition for ten Fox films at the Roxy for 1927—whenever the enormous theater finally opened. (The December 1926 premiere date had long since been revealed as a fantasy.)[81]

Fox was still on the outside of Broadway looking in, forced to rent the Harris Theatre and other smaller houses for his films' Broadway runs. While Paramount had just opened its new 3,664-seat showplace in Times Square on November 19, 1926,[82] and Loew's/MGM continued to benefit from its Capitol and Loew's State theaters (as well as others), Fox was still small-time in New York City's entertainment hub. Roxy's contract for Fox News and his booking of ten Fox feature films did not change any of that. If Fox wanted to be as powerful a vertically integrated film company as Paramount or Loew's, it would need a theater that represented that dominion. The Academy of Music, while opulent for 1927, might as well have been located in Poughkeepsie.

THE ROXY THEATRE TAKES SHAPE

The Roxy Theatre was already months late and well over budget by January 1927. That did not dissuade Lubin and other investors from forming a new company, the Roxy Circuit, Inc., capitalized at $150 million and incorporated for the purposes of creating a new chain of theaters in the greater New York area. The Roxy Circuit planned to acquire the Roxy Theatre, the new Roxy Mansion at 58th Street and Lexington Avenue on the Upper East Side of Manhattan, and the future Roxy's Midway on the Upper West Side. The *New York Times* reported that Roxy would serve as "Director General of the new enterprise," while William E. Atkinson, formerly vice president and general manager of MGM, became the Roxy Circuit's general manager. Ahlschlager was conscripted to build all of "the theatres under Roxy's control" to create a measure of architectural uniformity.[83]

Roxy finally moved into the Roxy Theatre on January 5, 1927, determined to meet his new March deadline. Temporary offices were situated in the theater's dressing rooms while Roxy, chief executives, and other members of the personnel and publicity departments waited for their permanent offices to be finished.[84] Lubin and Sawyer may have been worried about the ever-growing cost overruns and construction delays, but Roxy seemed to revel in the chaos. He arrived at the theater in his town car every day, ready to assess the progress of construction and marvel at what he had wrought. "Under lathings," Allene Talmey recalled, "through all the roar of hammers, over planks and plaster moldings, he crawled to steep himself in his pleasure. He scrambled to the rim of the auditorium, to the great stage where he could admire the orchestra's spaciousness."[85] And when he tired of the din of the construction, he escaped from the dust and noise to his Steinway Hall studio and office at 383 Madison Avenue.[86] To Lubin and Sawyer, the Roxy Theatre was a $10 million gamble, an unaffiliated movie palace in an era of chain management. To Roxy, it was a monument to his career and a site for the industry's convergent entertainment possibilities. Roxy spent each day imperially deciding on everything from carpet samples to paint tones to seat ends.[87]

Allene Talmey and numerous journalists of the era noted that these and other flourishes were the physical embodiment of a marketing and egocentric metaphor—that the Roxy, Talmey noted, was "Built on the foundation of the personality of Samuel Rothafel."[88] Roxy publicity materials transmitted this message to journalists. "A tremendous asset of the Roxy Theatre is the fact that it is essentially a theatre built on a personality," Roxy Theatre press notes stated:

If you want to know the secret of S. L. Rothafel's outstanding position as a master showman, here it is. He envelops the theatre in his personality. The inanimate structure of steel and stone becomes the visible reflection of the spirit of the man who dominates it. He breathes the breath of life into it. Here is no cold monument reflecting the mechanical atmosphere of an efficient business organization. It is a living temple of the ideals, hopes and ambitions of its presiding genius.[89]

The cult of personality built a temple for Roxy's millions of worshippers.

Journalists from *The Metronome, Variety*, and other trade and popular journals were given an all-access pass to his in-progress colossus in order to show off the theater's progress after months of delays. The calm, jovial demeanor Roxy projected to outsiders belied his internal temperature as the months wore on. When *The Metronome* visited, journalist Gordon Whyte found Roxy angered that a model of the curtain for the new Roxy Theatre had become tangled during a presentation. If it happened on opening night, he told his employees, "I'll murder you."[90] When Roxy wasn't showing signs of stress and impatience, he transmitted a deep sense of fatigue, even to visiting journalists. "Once as ebullient and 'wise' as any young press agent he had become sober and silent," *Personality* remembered a year after the Roxy's debut. "From a Broadway promoter had evolved a capitalist as calm as a Wall Street banker."[91] The experience of building the Roxy, Carl Helm wrote in the journal, was enormously difficult. Roxy told the Cheese Club a few months before the Roxy Theatre opened, "Nobody human knows what I have been through in these past two years—the doubts that have assailed me, the lack of sympathy and support I have encountered. At this moment I think of the nights I have gone home to my room and sat there alone, thinking that it all was too much for one person to hear. I tell you truthfully that I would not go through it again if you paved Broadway with gold from the Battery to the Bronx. On the other hand, I would not give up that experience, as hard as it was, for that pile of gold."[92]

Whatever his anxiety, stress, or fatigue, Roxy's focus was unwavering and a tightly wound sense of perfectionism enveloped the building; employees of the Roxy Theatre were not just highly drilled personnel as they had been at the Capitol, Rivoli, or Strand theaters but were now expected to be flawless workers who served as emissaries of Roxy's personality. "They are not merely efficient automatons," Jack Alicoate wrote in *Film Daily*'s dedicatory program. "They are Mr. Rothafel's personal representatives acting as individual hosts to carry the spirit of friendliness to every guest that enters."[93]

Nowhere was this ethos more rigorously enforced than in Roxy's strict standards for the 125 men who comprised the Roxy Theatre usher corps.[94] While his army of ushers was intended to act like Roxy, they were certainly *not* supposed to look like him. At the theater's outset, Roxy sought "one hundred college boys" who were "polite and well bred."[95] "Take a letter," he barked to his secretary in January 1927. "Want college students, must be tall and blonde with straight noses. Send letter to City College of New York."[96] The *Sioux City* (Iowa) *Citizen*, knowing that in the 1920s City College was filled with Jews often unable to enter more exclusive universities that still practiced openly anti-Semitic acceptance policies, quipped, "Perhaps you do not know the City College of New York?"[97] Roxy had noted a decade earlier, for instance, that "No beetle-browed doorman with a cultivated Bowery slang will ever work in any theater which I am asked to manage."[98] Like the plethora of Eastern European Jewish movie moguls pushing anglicized stars in front of the camera, Roxy hustled his casting call of white perfection to the front of the house to serve as the public face of a very international and multi-ethnic theater.

Applicants for the highly sought-after position were assembled from colleges across New York and were judged on appearance and cleanliness and given a medical and dental examination by the house physician.[99] (The Roxy Theatre hospital, which was free of charge to employees and patrons, was staffed by a physician from Mount Sinai Hospital.)[100] Once hired, the ushers were trained on a military schedule by two ex-Marine sergeants. In addition to microphone buttons signaling the theater's integration with broadcasting, the usher uniforms had a quasi-military appearance designed by Roxy based on "ideas picked up in various universities and military academies during his recent trip to Europe."[101] Each man was given two sets of uniforms—one for the afternoon and another for the evening. The ushers were inspected by the chief of their usher division throughout the day, and showers were required between performances to ensure cleanliness at all times. A gymnasium was constructed for the staff in order to complete their training.[102] "Here is the university from which will graduate future theater managers to spread the Roxy system of friendliness and personality throughout the land," Jack Alicoate noted.[103] Cole Porter would make these dapper young men the symbols of youth and efficiency in his song "You're the Top," from his 1934 musical *Anything Goes*: "You're the steppes of Russia, / You're the pants / On a Roxy usher."[104] The Roxy was intended to be the absolute last word in size, scale, and detail. "I'll make a bet that in my time or yours you are never going to see this theatre equaled," Roxy declared to the *New York Times* in late February.[105] He uttered something similar before opening or managing every new theater, but Roxy never felt any hubris in making this prognostication, even if it was almost always refuted by his next effort.

Between January and late February, Roxy continued to pluck talent from around the globe for his new theater. He dragged Leo Staats, former master of ballet of the National Opera of Paris, to the States for his ballet corps. (Staats had also produced works at the Cigale, La Scala, Casino de Paris, and Folies Bergères.) Staats, who had just choreographed Roger Ducasse's three-act ballet *Orphée*, arrived in New York during the first week of February.[106] Roxy also hired Leon Leonidoff, the ballet master at the Uptown and Glaser theaters in Toronto and a principal at a ballet school in the city.[107] Both men supervised a ballet corps of fifty, including Maria Gambarelli (and later famed Russian dancer and choreographer Léonide Massine).[108] "[W]e have the largest organized ballet in the country," Roxy boasted at the time.[109]

Roxy hired Clark Robinson, a holdover from the Capitol Theatre, for the Roxy's art direction. Robinson had first worked as the "architectural director" for D. W. Griffith on *Way Down East* (1920) before designing sets for Famous Players-Lasky and Distinctive Pictures. During the period between Roxy's departure from the Capitol and 1927, the *Telegraph* noted that Robinson had "made the sets for many of the Broadway successes" and taught scenic design at the John Murray Anderson–Robert Milton School of Theater and Dance.[110]

Another of D. W. Griffith's former employees, Arthur J. Smith, was chosen for the Roxy Theatre's projection booth, the most modern in the industry, with six Simplex projectors and six high-intensity color flood lights. Smith, who had been chief projectionist at the Capitol Theatre between 1920 and 1927 and had "been in charge of practically every new Broadway motion picture theatre on its opening night," was given a similar post at the Roxy. Roxy and Smith, *Motion Picture News* remarked, were "instrumental for the development of many lighting and projection features now in general use".[111] When the Roxy Theatre finally opened, Smith oversaw a platoon of sixteen projectionists.[112]

Every technical aspect of the Roxy was intended to be the newest, largest, or some other superlative that proclaimed it the "last word" in exhibition. Although its screen was only forty-four feet wide, small for a theater as gargantuan as the Roxy, it was twice the size of the screen at the new Paramount and supposedly the largest screen in any movie theater in the world.[113] Roxy also employed a 128-foot cyclorama, which served as a backdrop for stage acts and other live performances. Spyros Skouras, touring the Roxy before it opened, was stunned by the enormity of the machine and the theater. "Even the ancient Greeks would have cause to be jealous of you," he told Roxy.[114] The theater's stage switchboard was also the largest in the world for any theater, requiring the equivalent electricity of 2,000 homes.[115]

The theater's aural capabilities were just as impressive. The Roxy was outfitted with three enormous Kimball organs and wired for Vitaphone sound amplification, one of the first in the nation to install Warner Bros.' synchronous sound technology. "And if you want to hear the real Tchaikovsky '1812,'" Roxy noted, "we will give it to you with the real chimes. There are twenty-one great chimes that are 110 feet up in the building and they can be heard from outside as well as inside the structure."[116] To fill the auditorium with sound, a chorus of 110 voices matched an orchestra of 110 members.[117] The Roxy Theatre was certainly not intended for subtlety. Its music library contained 10,000 numbers and 50,000 orchestrations, easily able to take advantage of the raw power of its orchestral and vocal performers. It was, according to *The Leatherneck*, "the largest music library in the world."[118] Three music librarians, led by Al Gaber, manned the shelves and cabinets, able to spit out stock tunes for action sequences, love scenes, or music for any other theme.[119] A sound effects room was constructed that was "arranged to operate with the orchestration"—something that would come in handy as synchronous sound recording became part of the Roxy Theatre orchestra's repertoire.[120] Otto Kahn was so impressed by the artistic capabilities of the new theater that he invited Roxy to become a member of the advisory board for the new Metropolitan Opera House.[121]

On February 25, Roxy hosted another press tour and announced the Roxy Theatre's official opening date: March 11, 1927.[122] The six-story building now contained private screening rooms, dressing rooms, "clubrooms," a gymnasium, handball courts, and full shower facilities.[123] Roxy added that construction of Roxy's Mansion, the next theater in the chain, would begin on March 1, 1927.[124] Roxy's Midway, located on Broadway between 74th and 75th Street, would be next. Films shown at the Roxy would not necessarily rotate around the circuit, but live shows produced at the flagship theater were intended to move from one Roxy house to the next as a unit, thereby maximizing the investment of time and money in scenic design and rehearsals.[125] S. Jay Kaufman, blurring the line between praise and worship, remarked that he knew of "no greater contribution to civilization than a chain of theatres along Roxy lines."[126]

It is easy to see how Roxy and his cohort may have become swept up in their own hype. To remind him of where he came from and how far he had traveled, Roxy hung a framed copy of the first Family Theatre program from December 1908 in his new Roxy Theatre office.[127] The contrast was staggering: his new theater had nearly twenty-five times the capacity of his first movie house in Forest City. Less than twenty years earlier, he was serving beer and films to a small town in the snow. Now, through radio and the Roxy Theatre, he was serving millions every week and had become a household name and brand.

RADIO AND THE ROXY THEATRE

The broadcasting industry had reorganized and consolidated during Roxy's nearly yearlong absence from the air. RCA had purchased WEAF from AT&T in 1926 and the station became part of the new NBC-Red network. RCA's WJZ was now part of the company's other network, NBC-Blue. Major Bowes and the Capitol Theatre "Family" continued broadcasting over WEAF on the NBC-Red network, so Roxy's new contract moved him onto NBC's Blue network when he went back on the air in March, just days before the opening of the Roxy Theatre.[128]

The Roxy may have been principally a movie house, but public spaces in the theater (and some of the private ones as well) were wired for home audiences to listen in. "From the very beginning," Jack Banner observed in *Radio Guide*, "it was Roxy's idea to make the theater a combination of movie house and radio broadcasting studio." Microphones were placed in the Roxy Theatre stage footlights, backstage, in the orchestra pit, on the balcony, and in the wings to capture the direct and ambient sounds of the performers *and* the audience. The broadcasting soundscape as picked up inside the auditorium was intended, as much as possible in 1927, to imbue each broadcast with the sense of *being* in the theater. "This indeed was a far hail from the crude equipment that had been installed in the Capitol Theater on that epochal day in 1922," Banner observed.[129]

Upstairs, no expense was spared to build Roxy and His Gang's new broadcasting studio as well as an adjoining studio to broadcast organist Lew White's performances on one of the three Kimball organs. The Roxy Theatre studio seated sixty musicians and was the first to be built in a theater by acoustical engineers for broadcasting.[130] The studio was equipped with sixteen microphones, "fourteen of which could be operated at one time, though as a general rule three microphones sufficed for each broadcast—one for the orchestra, one for the chorus and one for Roxy."[131]

The building was brand new, the technology upgraded, but the entertainment was much the same as it had been at the Capitol. Even Roxy's new Gang looked a lot like his old troupe. "Many old favorites and some new faces" was how Jack Alicoate described the gaggle of veterans like Maria Gambarelli, Gladys Rice, Frank Moulan, Douglas Stanbury, Florence Mulholland, Daddy Jim Coombs, Harold Van Duzee, and a few newcomers like whistler Mickey McKee and Beatrice Belkin.[132] Newspapers across the country promoted the return of America's favorite variety hour—though that title was now being challenged by Major Bowes's increasingly popular broadcasts. The *Hartford*

Courant commented on March 6 that Roxy and His Gang still "gripped the hearts and the affections of millions of people all over the country. 'Roxy' appeals to the masses: to the fundamental emotions evoking tears and laughter. A smile for everybody, a jovial remark, and what counts most, real entertainment by artists, who pour their souls into their music, spells the secret of his success."[133]

Roxy and His Gang's first broadcast over WJZ and the NBC-Blue network took place on Monday, March 7, at 7:00 P.M. and lasted until 8:30 P.M.[134] Roxy also appealed to long-distance fans, those so-called DX'ers, who found him over the southern-division chain by tuning their radios repeatedly to catch him, even if only faintly.[135] "My, but I'm nervous," Roxy began the broadcast, reestablishing his folksy yet vulnerable connection with radio listeners throughout North America. Roxy did not forget the true aim of the show, though, promoting the debut of his new theater. "I'm hopping around like a grasshopper getting things fixed up, but everything's all right and will be ready for Friday night," he told his unseen audience.[136] Will H. Smith, the *Atlanta Constitution* radio columnist, wrote that "It was a typical 'Roxy' program and sounded much like the good old hours he used to stage before the mike from WEAF."[137] Roxy held the baton for most of the broadcast and argued that it was a shame audiences could only *hear* the broadcast and not have a chance to see what went on in the studio. "Those who watched the opening performance of 'Roxy and His Gang' last Monday night easily realized that the radio audience would have enjoyed a much greater treat had television been a reality," the *New York Times* noted.[138]

Roxy's return to radio was a national success, and NBC-Blue now had an anchor program for its Monday night schedule. The *Toronto Daily Star* commented that New Yorkers were not the primary audience for Roxy's radio show by then, although they comprised an important part of his listening audience and theater patronage. Instead, the Roxy Theatre would rely not only on the habitual, local patron but on the innumerable number of tourists who would make the Roxy a required stop on any trip to New York. "Roxy broadcasts for advertisement," the newspaper noted. "Thus, his theatre is known in Tucson, Arizona; and when Tucson goes to Broadway its first objective at a dollar a seat is Roxy's to see the man whose voice and musical programs have been heard, talked about and written about in letters to Roxy among his two million letters on file."[139] "I haven't seen your new theatre yet," one Pennsylvanian man wrote to Roxy shortly after the theater opened, "but I certainly shall see it upon my next trip to New York." A young girl from Pittsburgh wrote to Roxy, "My sister and I have been invited to spend the week-end in New York and the biggest thing we want to do is to visit your theatre." The infirm were also mustering their strength to visit his theater to make tangible the voice that emanated from the 50th Street broadcast studio. One man wrote to Roxy that his wife was an invalid and although they were unable to get around much, "we have hopes in the near future to get over to New York to spend at least a night so that we may see your wonderful theatre and see and hear the Gang that we love so well."[140] Roxy Theatre advertisements abetted this desire, including copy that read, "No visitors to New York will have seen the greatest wonder of the city until they have seen the Roxy."[141] The *Musical Courier* wrote that the Roxy "undoubtedly is 'one of the things to see' in New York,"[142] Through his broadcasts, Roxy added an unknown number of theater patrons comprised of tourists desperate to see the building that housed their radio friends and provided their Monday night entertainment.

NBC thus sewed up connections with the two largest movie houses in the country, the Capitol and the Roxy, and exhibitors and radio stations took notice of these strengthening bonds between movie houses and radio stations and networks. "The Roxy Theater proved to be the renaissance of the radio industry," Jack Banner noted retrospectively:

No longer were artistic noses held high when the subject of broadcasting was mentioned. The glamorous personalities of the stage, screen and operatic worlds fought for radio contracts and appearances. Radio, indeed, became the Mecca and goal of the royal families of the make-believe worlds.[143]

For many of the vertically integrated film companies, the opening of the Roxy Theatre brought a new sense of urgency for media and industrial convergence. As Michele Hilmes argues, "The year 1927 marked the high point of film industry attempts to expand into radio broadcasting,"[144] an expansion which *Moving Picture World* traced directly to the opening of the Roxy Theatre. In a front-page article titled "Broadcasting War Looms," journalist Merritt Crawford remarked:

Radio now looms as a big factor in the theatre war precipitated on Broadway by the opening of the Roxy. Reports were current late this week that several of the big theatre-owning companies, anticipating the competition which the Roxy's opening would inaugurate, some months ago formed a working combination to underwrite a radio station of their own . . . [where] they could broadcast programs at will boosting their own pictures and theatres. The idea, it was said, was to put on the air programs of such high quality as to offset, as far as possible, the popularity of Roxy's radio entertainers and minimize the advertising value of his tie-up with WJZ and some nineteen other stations networking the country.[145]

The opening of the Roxy spurred a wave of broadcasting synergies. In Chicago, for instance, Warner Bros. began broadcasting weekly news about its films and stars every Monday evening for an hour over station WBBM.[146] The city's Chicago Theatre, controlled by the Balaban & Katz circuit, announced that it had also started a new radio station the same week that the Roxy Theatre opened.[147] To broadcast B&K's talent, in addition to broadcasting stage shows from the Oriental and Chicago theaters, a new studio was constructed on the seventh floor of the Chicago Theatre building.[148]

Roxy Theatre, New York, NY

By 1927, film was less important to Roxy than the overall show. In his mind, the unitary text could enhance any film and was the theater's chief attraction. Few, for example, attended the Roxy's first week to see Gloria Swanson's latest United Artists film, *The Love of Sunya* (1927). Roxy paid the distributor $50,000 for the rental—$15,000 more than the Strand's bid[149]—but *Sunya* may not have been Roxy's first choice for the theater's debut. Roxy's predilection for German films had not waned in the years since his heralded presentations of *Passion* and *Caligari,* and he offered Ufa $100,000 for the exhibition rights to *Metropolis* (1927), whose set he had visited during a trip to Germany.[150] Even after Paramount had secured the film for its own Rialto Theatre, Roxy remained hopeful that he could throw enough money at the film to lure it away from the growing Paramount-Ufa-Metro-Goldwyn-Mayer (Parufamet) relationship.[151] An independent exhibitor in 1927, though, even the most powerful one, could not trump the buying power and strategic relationships fostered by multinational and vertically integrated conglomerates like Paramount and Loew's. The Roxy Theatre would have to feast on a diet of United Artists, Warner Bros., Fox, Universal, FBO, and other "independent" films. The selection of *The Love of Sunya* was no doubt more important to Swanson and United Artists than it was to Roxy; when *Sunya* was shown at Poli's Majestic Theatre in Bridgeport, Connecticut, the following month, it was advertised in the *Bridgeport Telegram* as "The picture selected to open the ten million dollar Roxy Theatre."[152] A *Toronto Daily Star* advertisement similarly noted that the film was "The Picture Chosen to Open the Roxy, the World's Largest Theatre."[153]

Anticipation for the theater's opening night was palpable among Roxy employees and patrons as well as journalists and industry competitors. Twenty-six thousand applications were sent in by moviegoers hoping for their March 11 golden ticket. Only six thousand were able to gain admittance, with another thirteen thousand crushing the doors of the Roxy Theatre, clamoring for a glimpse of the new theater and the celebrity crowd who attended the premiere. Sixty policemen did their best to keep the crowd at bay.[154] Carl Helm noted that despite the ability to gouge even more patrons, "a good number of the seats that would have sold $50 apiece were set aside for the veterans, who came with their nurses."[155] "Cabinet officials, U.S. senators, state governors, army and navy officials, and notables of New York life were [also] in attendance," Motion Picture News observed, "testifying to the importance of the event as a national affair."[156] Will Hays, Charlie Chaplin, Harold Lloyd, Irving Berlin, Joseph Schenck, Richard Rowland, and Jesse Lasky were also expected to be on hand for what the New Yorker called "The super-super-opening of the new Roxy Theatre."[157] In a tidy bit of chauvinism that defined the era's journalism, Moving Picture World remarked, "Everyone who was anyone in the picture world was there with his wife."[158] Major General John A. Lejeune and Florenz Ziegfeld were also in attendance. Even J. J. and Lee Shubert were on hand to witness their former employee's latest opening.[159] "Thousands of curious onlookers packed the surrounding streets, taxing police efforts to the utmost," Motion Picture News wrote. "The house had been sold out weeks before, but many last minute efforts were made to obtain seats. As high as $100 per pair was offered, but those lucky enough to obtain seats were not interested in disposing of them."[160]

All four conductors were to play a role in the premiere performance, but after a last-minute clash with Rapee, Previn, and Jacquet, Fredrick Stahlberg stormed out of the Roxy Theatre and never came back. Erno Rapee was immediately elevated to the position of music director, with Previn and Jacquet serving under him.[161] The clash turned out to be a lucky break for Roxy as Rapee's lead replicated his early Capitol Theatre arrangement and afforded him one less paycheck to dole out.

The backstage drama had little to do with the show's excessive delay, though. The crowd of thousands, gawking at the enormity of the theater's rotunda and its auditorium, was still milling around well past 8:20. Backstage, the hundreds of performers were also still being corralled. The whole lumbering production did not get under way until nine o'clock.[162]

The evening began with a grand organ concert before Stephen Wright read the theater's religious-themed invocation: "Ye Portals bright, high and majestic, open to our gaze the path to wonderland, and show us the realm where fantasy reigns, where romance, where adventure flourish. Let Ev'ry day's toil be forgotten under thy sheltering roof, oh glorious, mighty hall—thy magic and charm unite us all to worship at beauty's throne."[163] It was a far cry from the *Eucharistic Congress* premiere, which had worshipped God instead of a radio idol.

"A Symphonic Tone Poem" conceived by H. Maurice Jacquet and conducted by the three remaining conductors followed the invocation. The printed program described the "poem" as "a tonal description of the events surrounding the writing of 'The Star Spangled Banner.' " Next came "A Floral Fantasy," featuring Maria Gambarelli and the Roxy Ballet Corps, choreographed by Leo Staats, "le Maître de Ballet," and Leon Leonidoff, associate ballet master. Finally, a bit of celluloid was sprinkled into the mix. Roxy offered his audience "Film Greetings"[164] that demonstrated the showman's political heft with the International News Reel featuring words of support from President Coolidge, the Secretary of the Navy, and on the Democratic and local side, New York governor and soon-to-be presidential candidate Al Smith.[165]

"A Fantasy of the South," featuring the Roxy Chorus and Ensemble, with Charles Previn serving as choral master, continued the evening. Baritone Julius Bledsoe sang "Swanee River," followed by "The Southern Rhapsody" with a vocal arrangement by Erno Rapee. To create a dynamic visual effect, a Trans-Lux transparent screen, illuminated through the company's rear projection system, framed the vocal performances with appropriately themed images. The "Roxy Pictorial Review," the house's cobbled-together program of world events, then preceded the first presentation of Irving Berlin's "A Russian Lullaby," sung by Gang members Gladys Rice and Douglas Stanbury, backed by the Roxy Chorus.[166]

The next selection was an important one for the era. Having contracted with Warner Bros. to outfit the Roxy Theatre with Vitaphone projectors and sound amplification, Roxy offered a "Vitaphone Presentation" with selections from Bizet's *Carmen*. *Musical Courier*, in a report that should have pleased the Warners, noted that the short was one of the most successful bills of the program.[167] The Metropolitan Opera Chorus and Ballet backed soloists Giovanni Martinelli and Jeanne Gordon on the accompanying Vitaphone-recorded music which, according to the Roxy program, was conducted by Erno Rapee.[168] Where or when this recording may have taken place is a mystery, but if Rapee did in fact conduct the music for the Vitaphone film, it would suggest even more breadth to his impressive résumé.

Roxy kept up his interpolation of film and live performances with a live prologue before the exhibition of *The Love of Sunya*.[169] Although prologues had "practically vanished" in many other Broadway palaces by 1927, the *Motion Picture News* observed, Roxy still relied heavily on their ability to frame a film and attract audiences regardless of the feature. Roxy's entertainment offerings were conservative by design, virtually unchanged from his work at the Capitol. He still believed strongly in a unitary text that blended live and filmed entertainment, even though other exhibitors like Major Bowes were removing their stage shows.[170]

The screening of *The Love of Sunya* completed the evening's entertainment. The *New Yorker* wrote that the show's mixture of Americana, quasi-religious reverence, and entertainment was full of "allegory, patriotism, symphony, clairvoyance, grand opera, terpsichore, and Mayor Walker. The whole show was typical Rothafelian."[171] Dozens of journalists from across the country threw out their usual hosannas, and the whole event fit the late-1920s narrative of progress—economic, technological, social, and otherwise. *The Leatherneck*, the Marine Corps journal, reported that "New York City dressed up in high hat and evening gown and turned out thousands strong on the night of March 11 to welcome and attend the opening of Major S. L. Rothafel, U. S. M. C. R. [and] Roxy Theatre, the world's largest and most elaborate theatre in the world."[172] *Moving Picture World* added to the adulation that greeted its debut, writing that the Roxy's opening night "was a brilliant program, approved by an equally brilliant audience and the applause was generous in the extreme of each offering. It was a wonderful night for Roxy, for he had arrived at the summit of his one-time ambition to present his own ideas in his own idea of what a theatre should be."[173] The Roxy represented much of what journalists seemed to cherish before October 1929: spectacle.

Roxy's allusions to religious edifices and practices, from his "Let there be light!" proclamations to the massive size of the auditorium meant to render audiences awestruck as one might be in a cathedral, were not lost on the press. (*Theatre Magazine* would later call the Roxy Theatre a "cinemagogue.")[174] "Now that New York has three cathedrals, St. Patrick's, St. John's, and Roxy's, we can look for the canonization of the latter almost any day now," *Moving Picture World* quipped. "Meanwhile Cardinal Hayes and Bishop Manning will have to look to their laurels. Both get on the first pages of the dailies almost as often as Roxy, but we bet his cathedral will have the attendance record for all that."[175] The *New Yorker* later wrote that "if this is the Jehovah of the movies, this man with the sensitive, smiling eyes, and the obvious, honest sentiments of Stillwater, Minnesota, then it is a decent, a creative, and a jovial Jehovah."[176] Perhaps after presenting *Eucharistic Congress* a few months earlier, no one seemed to mind Roxy's challenge to neighboring religious institutions for Sunday audiences. Bishop Rothafel (with his "Cathedral of the Motion Picture") was never afraid to use overtly religious themes in his messaging. "They say the age of miracles is dead," he humbly noted in 1926 of his new cathedral to worship movies, radio, music, and live performance. "It isn't at all. This is the miracle."[177]

The critical acclaim and public support conferred status once more upon the last exhibitor who needed it. During its first two days open to the public, Saturday and Sunday, March 12 and March 13, the Roxy Theatre earned $50,000 in gross receipts,[178] with 51,513 patrons attending.[179] By the end of its first week, the Roxy had already grossed more than $125,000, "a world's record likely to stand for years to come," *Motion Picture News* noted, with more than 157,000 tickets sold.[180] (That record would fall just weeks later.) Overseas, considerable attention was also paid to the theater. "The Roxy proves beyond doubt that no theatre can be bigger than the personality behind it," *The Bioscope* commented in early April 1927. "£23,000 is the yearly turnover of many important English cinemas. Roxy and his theatre took it in six-sevenths of a week."[181]

Although few realized it at the time, two and a half years before the October 1929 stock market crash, the opening of the 5,920-seat theater was the pinnacle of the movie palace era.[182] With its cavernous auditorium and rotunda, its battalion of well-drilled ushers, its ever-expanding stage shows, and its 110-piece orchestra and 110-member chorus, the Roxy exemplified the excess that defined the era's movie palaces and the growing ties between America's premier stages—one live and cinematic, and the other floating through the air and into millions of homes. Karen Bramson wrote in the Parisian *Comoedia*, "Roxy is a monument. An American monument. It is the pyramid of Cheops, dreamed of and realized on Broadway. It is the Colosseum [*sic*] of the Roman Empire translated into America in the year 1927 A.D."[183] Roxy's pride was evident: "It's the Roxy and I'm Roxy," he noted at the time. "I'd rather be Roxy than John D. Rockefeller or Henry Ford."[184] Producers and distributors, eager for his stamp of approval and for the advertising leverage his nationwide broadcast provided, clamored for the opportunity to launch their films at the country's newest and largest movie palace.

By mid-March, Adolph Zukor's Paramount Theatre in Times Square, with roughly half the seat capacity, was already an afterthought—yesterday's news—only five months after its debut. On radio and in the augmentation of theater orchestras, usher corps, and live performers, exhibitors and broadcasters scrambled to match Roxy and the Roxy. *Motion Picture News* summed up the impact the theater had made after only a few weeks:

> A lot of people figured, prior to the premiere, that the advent of the Roxy would not cut much ice. But the other Broadway houses braced themselves for the shock, elaborated their shows, made additions to personnel, and indicated in several other ways that they were ready for the competition. In its first week, the Roxy grossed approximately $127,000 out of a total of about $500,000 for all picture Broadway, counting roadshows at legitimate theatres, as well as the regular film houses. At the same time, careful figuring shows that every theatre, except one, fell off at the box-office, the total drop for all being around $20,000 compared with the week prior to the Roxy opening.[185]

The Paramount, Loew's State, and the Capitol, to name but a few, would remain flush with audiences over the next few years, but they had all lost a little luster as a result of the Roxy's opening. Older houses like the Strand, Rialto, and Rivoli would modernize in the coming years, but all were vestiges of the past, banking on their association with larger film concerns for first-run appeal and steady, if unexciting, patronage. For now, at least, the Roxy Theatre was the new center of attention.

WHAT PRICE ROXY

In early 1925, William Fox had surveyed the Broadway area for a location for a new movie palace for Fox films. "[T]he place I had picked out as the site for these structures was that on which the old car barns stood, bounded by Sixth and Seventh Avenues and Fiftieth and Fifty-first Streets," William Fox recalled two years later, "and that I had heard that $5,000,000 would buy the land." Fox had instructed a Mr. Kempner, who was handling Fox's real estate investments at the time, to purchase the property one block away from the Capitol Theatre. "Mr. Kempner cautioned me that while I might be quite right as to the value of the land, he thought that I had better get appraisals from experts." The "experts" Fox hired valued the land at well below $5 million so Fox dropped the idea and waited for a more attractive price. By July 1925, Fox discovered that Lubin, Sawyer, and Roxy had purchased the land and were planning to build a new theater (the Roxy) and a hotel (the Taft) on the property. "By that time that plot was worth about three times what I had said I would pay for it," Fox later lamented. "Now I have made up my mind that never again shall any one talk me out of doing what I feel impelled to do."[186] It is worth pondering whether this event may have factored into the many impulsive decisions Fox would make over the next decade.

In early 1926, Fox approached Lubin, possibly without Roxy's knowledge, to negotiate a deal whereby Fox would gain control of the land and the theater.[187] Fox was not the only suitor, however. By the time he began organizing the *Eucharistic Congress* premiere, putting Roxy and Rapee together for a brief reunion, Fox's offer had escalated and trumped other possible investors. "I've been pretty certain during the last six months," he noted in late March 1927, "of being the lucky person."[188]

The theater had additional importance for Fox. A film's outcome at the Roxy would soon have ample influence over its success elsewhere, especially in the eyes of the press. "We take New York's verdict for almost everything," the *Toronto Daily Star* commented. "Pictures are no exception. If a film has a long New York run it is regarded as a good Canadian investment, which it usually is. . . . If Roxy plays a picture to twenty-one times 6,000 people in a week at his eight-million-dollar house, Toronto should except [*sic*] it as a good picture. For profit, yes."[189]

On March 24, 1927, Fox announced an agreement with Lubin and Sawyer to acquire a controlling interest in the Roxy Theatre and the burgeoning Roxy circuit. Fox noted the purchase price of the theater was "$15,000,000 and more."[190] (It is unknown what Lubin and Sawyer received for selling their stake in the theater, but two years later Fox still owed Lubin $5.6 million.)[191] The *Miami Herald* and *Motion Picture News* both claimed that the purchase price was actually $20 million.[192] The Fox Theatre Corp. gained control of seventy-five percent of Roxy Circuit, Inc., which in turn controlled fifty-one percent of the common stock of Roxy Theatres Corp. The Roxy was projected to earn nearly two and a half million dollars a year for Fox, enabling the company to immediately realize earnings despite the expensive initial investment.[193]

There was far more to the acquisition than just the theater; Fox wanted the man who was running it. Fox had watched Roxy's career closely over the years and keenly remembered his first New York effort at the Regent Theatre in 1913. "He is the greatest genius of motion picture presentation," Fox told the *New York Times*. "He is to our theatres what Max Reinhardt is to Germany."[194] Fox added that the purchase of the Roxy Theatre and the employment of the industry's most lauded exhibitor was "the supreme achievement" of his life.[195]

Fox was clear that "What interests me more than the Roxy Theater is getting the services of Roxy, whom I consider the greatest showman in the world today." In one expensive move, Fox could now lay claim to the largest theater in the world and the employment of an exhibitor admired on two continents. He told *New York World* that "he regarded the acquisition of [Roxy's] personality as a bigger thing than the acquiring of the theatre itself."[196]

The Roxy Theatre purchase was central to Fox's effort to become the dominant player in the motion picture industry. Fox, as he had in hiring top directors like F. W. Murnau, reasoned that talent acquisition was one of the central keys to this success. Fox wanted Roxy to not only manage the 50th Street movie palace but enhance the current and future Fox theaters in his growing exhibition chain. Of course, the acquisition also secured even more control over Erno Rapee, who already had a contract with Fox. Fox could now claim to the employment of the country's most successful motion picture exhibitor and its most prolific music director and movie theater conductor. The two men most responsible for the presentation and scoring of *Eucharistic Congress* were now in place.

Fox had bought something else—brand equity—and he boasted to the *New York Times* that the purchase had secured the name and services of Roxy, who had "become a world figure through his radio broadcasts."[197] The Roxy and Fox brands were now inextricably linked for ten million NBC-Blue listeners across the United States. Newspapers across the country also reported that Roxy and the Roxy were now part of the Fox Film Corporation.

Fox was elated, but Roxy was not. Roxy had left the Capitol in part because it was owned by a vertically integrated company that might meddle in his selection of films and in his management style. Roxy had had free rein at the Roxy and did not have to seek Lubin's or Sawyer's permission for budgetary or artistic decisions. After the Fox purchase, Roxy now had a corporate overseer that was likely to make decisions that were best for the company rather than necessarily best for the theater. "Can't you imagine Fox with a fat cigar in his kisser walking into the Roxy and after lamping the 100-piece orchestra telling Roxy: 'Cut 50 men out of that band—tell the others to play louder,' " one insider commented to *Variety*.[198] Whether it was the prospect of a dictatorial boss, the secrecy of the negotiations, or a squabble over the finances involved in the deal, *Variety* reported that Lubin and Roxy "had some healthy words over the outcome."[199] Roxy spun the acquisition as an addition rather than a reduction in control:

> This affiliation brings to us the forceful personality of William Fox, one of the pioneers of the industry. I have known Mr. Fox intimately for 15 years,

and have admired his great fearlessness, his vision and his great success in building his corporation to rank as one of the great forces in the motion picture industry. He seeks an ideal which he sees exemplified in the theatre which we have the honor to direct, and I have a feeling of great security and assurance, not alone because of his advice, counsel and guidance which he is so fitted to impart, but also because of the knowledge that the affiliation will give him an impetus to produce films of a quality to merit presentation in the theatre that we so proudly call "The Cathedral of the Motion Picture." I am very happy indeed and am sure that the success of our enterprise is assured.[200]

Roxy worked out one important concession from Fox—that no Fox films would be booked into the Roxy Theatre unless Roxy was "desirous of playing them."[201] Fox executive John Zanft moved his office to the Roxy Theatre and began booking films for Fox theaters there; booking decisions for the circuit's showcase theater, though, were left up to Roxy.[202] Selection of film programming, a hallmark of Roxy's career philosophy, remained sacrosanct.

There seemed to be few hard feelings after the buyout. It was, after all, business as usual in the film industry. Roxy and Lubin, for instance, didn't let their conflict block their plan to market Roxy Receiver radio sets in late 1927.[203] In a vertically (and increasingly horizontally) integrated business, as long as Roxy was a hired hand and not an owner, he would never have full control over his career.

Fox Theatre Circuit Expansion

In April, Roxy's dreams of running his own chain also faded to black. Fox dissolved the now superfluous Roxy Circuit (Roxy's Mansion was subsequently abandoned, while Roxy's Midway later opened as Warner's Beacon in 1929), and the Roxy Theatre became the new flagship of the much larger Fox theater chain. "Hitherto," Fox told the *New York Times*, "the Fox Corporation pictures have been in the position of a man in evening clothes who does not know what to do—is all dressed up and no place to go. Now we have a Broadway outlet for our productions. The new theatre will inspire the studio staff. It will make the work harder but much sweeter."[204] Although Warner Bros., FBO, and other distributors were able to book occasional films, the theater's independent status was gone. The Roxy might as well have been renamed the Fox-Roxy Theatre.

The Roxy acquisition, the forty-second theater in Fox's chain, was an integral part of an expansion effort that included new theaters in Newark, Brooklyn, Philadelphia, Washington, D.C., Detroit, St. Louis, San Francisco, Oakland, and Los Angeles.[205] Fox hoped to place Roxy in charge of his expanding exhibition empire to help supervise the live presentations, music, and marketing of these new movie houses.[206] Fox envisioned Roxy, like Sam Katz at Paramount's Publix division, setting exhibition standards and practices for the palatial theaters he planned to open. Fox reasoned that these theaters would "benefit through management by a man who has directed many of the large and important theatres of New York."[207]

Fox's new Washington, D.C., movie palace, constructed inside the National Press Club building, was the first one ready for Roxy's guidance. Capitalizing on Roxy's stardom and popularity with Washington audiences, Fox changed the name of the theater to the Fox-Roxy, hoping to link the building with the radio star and the famous New York theater.[208] A short time after the announcement, a capitol-area fan wrote to Roxy, "[O]ur morning papers are telling us you will have a theatre here soon—GOOD."[209]

Variety reported in April that "Los Angeles is [also] to have a Fox-Roxy Theater. The chain grows!"[210] In May, Fox announced that twenty new 5,000-seat theaters would be built "along the lines of the Roxy," according to *Variety*.[211] Fox predicted that by 1929 the company would have thirty 5,000-seat theaters across the country.[212] *Motion Picture News* predicted that the new 5,000-seat Fox in Detroit would also have Roxy in "full charge of all productions to be shown."[213]

Roxy had already begun supervising presentation at the Academy of Music in New York by May 30. *Motion Picture News* reported that this was "Roxy's initial step in the proposed supervision of leading Fox houses."[214] While there may have been a desire to rotate Roxy stage shows to other Fox houses such as the Academy, *Variety* reported that "Roxy theatre presentations could not be sent around because of special staging adaptable only to the Roxy and [were therefore] unsuitable for other houses." The smaller presentations developed at the Academy of Music, though, only two miles from the Roxy and thus able to benefit from the same New York pool of talent, would be "routed over the Fox Circuit of first run theatres" in Washington, D.C. and Philadelphia. Rather than serving as a staging site for other Fox presentations, the Roxy Theatre became something of a circuit-wide audition for other Fox theaters. New artists such as Natacha Nattova, pending the success of their appearances at the Roxy, could then be signed to appear at the Academy of Music and throughout the entire Fox circuit.[215]

THE CONVERGENCE OF STARDOM

The use of Roxy's name for other Fox theaters and initiatives came on the heels of Roxy's (and His Gang's) growing celebrity. Roxy's face and name could frequently be found in the pages of New York's newspapers, music, radio, and film trade journals, and a host of other magazines as his brand image was used to sell a growing number of products. A Carl Fischer advertisement in *The Metronome* in January 1927 featured Roxy's face and name to help sell music by Victor Herbert.[216] Roxy's name and likeness were also used to advertise a new Funk & Wagnalls–produced booklet, *Twelve Weeks to Health,* which, without a hint of irony, noted its endorsement by the overweight Babe Ruth and the increasingly cherubic Roxy, whose prolific frankfurter consumption had been widely noted by journalists and may have added to his enlarging physique.[217] (The *New Yorker* had lovingly described him at forty-two years old as "fat and short.")[218] In May, Roxy's face and signature also graced a Lucky Strike cigarettes advertisement, with the tagline, " 'Roxy' heard by millions, a favorite in Radio-land, always careful of his voice."[219] A few months later, he appeared in nationwide advertisements for FADA radios.[220]

Roxy was certainly not the only one taking advantage of the currency of fame or the new possibilities of media convergence. Roxy and His Gang whistler Margaret "Mickey" McKee appeared in an eponymous Vitaphone short,[221] and longtime Gang duo Douglas Stanbury and Maria Gambarelli, whom Roxy had linked over the air, appeared in another ten-minute Vitaphone short.[222] *Variety* commented that the short "was too obviously theatrical and lacked illusion. Gamby's dancing, of course, was okeh, and she made a graceful figure, but the lighting of the whole business hurt. Stanbury's fine, strong voice, however, saves the film subject and qualifies it as acceptable.[223] Gambarelli and Stanbury both appeared in other Vitaphone shorts with Gambarelli starring in *Gold Digging Gentlemen*[224] and *Whispering Jack Smith,*[225] while Stanbury later appeared in *Pack Up Your Troubles.*[226]

Roxy Theatre organist Lew White also found additional outlets.[227] In March 1927, he signed an exclusive agreement with music publisher Robbins Music to write organ music for the company and another contract with Brunswick-Balke-Collender to produce double-sided records of popular tunes played on the Kimball organ in White's new broadcasting studio at the Roxy.[228] The method for recording those discs demonstrated the speed with which convergence took place; while the Roxy had been built for broadcasting, Roxy had not had the foresight to outfit the studios with recording capability.[229] Brunswick decided that instead of installing costly equipment at the Roxy,

White would perform these songs on the Kimball organ and then relay the performance via WJZ to the Brunswick "laboratories some distance away" where it would be recorded.[230] In effect, then, White's earliest recordings for Brunswick are not recordings of his live performance in the studio but a recording of the relay of that performance.

Brunswick's contract with White enabled the recording company to compete with the Victor Talking Machine Company, which had previously signed a deal with Paramount Theatre organist Jesse Crawford, who had already produced "big sellers" for the company.[231] In April, White began churning out records for Brunswick such as a double-sided 78 record featuring "Blue Skies" and "Honolulu Moon." The marketing machinery that sold these discs, which included producing newspaper advertisements and coordinating store displays in the United States and Canada, prominently linked White with the Roxy Theatre, further spreading the name of the movie house (and by proxy its eponymous radio star).[232] White contributed a number of other records, including a double-sided 78 of "Charmaine," the Rapee-Pollack theme song for *What Price Glory*—in sync with its presentation at the Roxy—and "Doll Dance."[233]

The British trade journal *The Bioscope* noted the pervasive nature of White's records not only in the United States but also in England, where they were manufactured by the company's British arm, British Brunswick, Ltd. The Roxy Theatre, the journal reported, "was a household word with British exhibitors" who, after purchasing Lew White's recordings, had the "advantage, now open to the smallest hall in the country" of playing these records and "advertising 'Intermission by the organ of the "Roxy" Theatre, New York.'" *The Bioscope* added that "As rendered by the 'Panatrope,' these records are said to give a vivid impression of the scope and volume of the Roxy instrument. They are another instance of the extent to which the 'Panatrope' is levelling [*sic*] the small hall up to the large in the important matter of music." British exhibitors could now advertise, after purchasing a variety of Brunswick discs, that they had "music from the Roxy."[234]

The convergence of motion picture exhibition, broadcasting, and music recording was further exemplified by Brunswick's announcement in late March that it would build a new Chicago radio station, WCFL, for the "exploitation for its records and phonographs."[235] The station began broadcasting on May 3, 1927, and its bandwidth transmitted far outside the Chicago area, providing radio promotion for new Lew White records such as "It All Depends on You" and "Trail of Dreams," recorded from a Roxy Theatre narrowcast to the Brunswick "laboratories," and advertised in local newspapers such as the *Sheboygan*

Press in Wisconsin and in trade journals such as *Variety*.[236] White soon added "At Sundown" and "Underneath the Weeping Willow" a short time later.[237] By then, *Variety* noted, organ recordings of popular tunes had become big sellers.[238]

Movietone and Lindbergh

The year 1927 was also a crucial period for the development of synchronous sound recording, reproduction, and exhibition using some of the same patents that had made broadcasting possible. Once the Roxy Theatre became part of the Fox circuit, Roxy outfitted the theater with Movietone capability and used the venue for a Movietone demonstration in May for "a bunch of newspaper people."[239] Thus, because of its size and acclaim, it was the Roxy—not the Harris, Gaiety, or Globe—that became the lauded site of the Movietoned Charles Lindbergh newsreel that delighted six thousand patrons when it debuted on May 21, 1927. The screening of the historic flight featured a "cacophony of sound," *Variety* reported, "comprised of on location sound embedded in the newsreel, the applause of the audience," and "festive noise effects contributed by the Roxy orchestra."[240]

When Lindbergh returned to the States in June, Roxy was there to greet him in Washington, D.C., emceeing "Lindbergh Radio Day," when the famous pilot was presented with the Distinguished Flying Cross by President Coolidge and given a hero's return by the Washington Reception Committee. NBC broadcast the program nationwide on NBC-Red and NBC-Blue with Roxy formally introducing Lindbergh at the National Press Club. (The event boosted Roxy's profile and served the Fox Theatre in Washington.) After Roxy's introductions, Lindbergh spoke to the crowd about his flight across the Atlantic while the United States Marine Band supplied patriotic music. Thirty million listeners were expected to tune in midday from home, work, or gathered in public spaces.[241] Once more, film and radio placed Roxy at one of the era's more memorable moments.

Roxy Rules the Roost

Weekly preparations at the Roxy were perhaps even more frenzied than they had been at the Capitol.[242] Roxy continued to score "all the films that are shown," the *New Yorker* noted, picking his way through a card catalogue of themes in the projection room during every rehearsal. "And in the $70,000 music library once belonging to Victor Herbert, half a dozen copyists and harmonizers do the rest. A good part of each week goes into developing musical ideas—ideas for ballets, ideas for chorus numbers, ideas for illustrating and dramatizing overtures and symphonies."[243] This work was often done, of course, in concert with Rapee or one of the many others on his music staff, such as Charles Previn or Maurice Baron.

On Fridays, following the day's performances, the entire cast and crew of the theater's stage shows gathered together in the auditorium and worked until well into the next morning. "It is a violent scene then in that great bowl of an auditorium," Allene Talmey wrote, "with the little ballet dancers standing around, kimono on shoulder, the electricians, the orchestra players, the costumers all watching, listening to a stubby man down in front blazing with orders and enthusiasm, getting plaintive. 'Can't you do that little thing for me?' he pleads. 'Must you, Sol, play the piccolo right there?' "[244] The rehearsals were just as rigorous as before, but with an even larger cast and expectations.

Roxy now slept at home only three or four days out of each week due to the late hours for rehearsals and the needs of everyday management. Slumber, when it could be enjoyed, was often taken in a private apartment at the palatial theater.[245] His living quarters were not an outsized linen closet but a handsome apartment managed by a butler whose uniform, like every detail in the building, was carefully designed with "gilt buttons embossed handsomely with a red R." Rosa designed the apartment "with a complete kitchen, pantry, dining room, bathroom, and exercise room, library, bedroom and reception room."[246] The kitchen was staffed by a white-capped chef cooking food for Roxy whenever he needed it.[247] An on-site chef just to cook frankfurters (and chicken broth, hamburgers, and corned beef and cabbage) was a suitable metaphor for a man who used one hundred and ten musicians for an orchestra that could have easily eked by with *only* eighty.[248]

Roxy and his employees went back to work three hours before showtime after his brief slumber early Saturday morning. Roxy sat at a desk in the eighth row of the enormous auditorium, reviewing the show once again. When the *New Yorker* visited rehearsals in May, Roxy cut out two songs he didn't like— even though they had taken hours to rehearse—just a short time before the first performance. He also made other changes:

He tells the coloratura whistler not to keep it up so long. He raises the orchestra an extra foot to improve its tone. He rushes up on the stage and rearranges some of the ballet. He goes back to the desk and criticizes the tempo of the third movement. And all the time his voice is going out through a microphone to loud-speakers located in every departmental vantage point of this gigantic theatre. The property room hears it, and the electrician and the music library and the projection booth, and the grandfather of loud-speakers up above the proscenium sends out to everyone of the three hundred at work this metallic parody of the voice of Jehovah. And those who want to answer back must come on foot to do so.[249]

The *New Yorker* was not the only publication to notice that Roxy had outgrown his pater familias persona that he had honed to perfection at the Capitol (when his broadcasting career was still young and the stakes were lower). Roxy and his workers strove to create a finely tuned machine that gave off the appearance of unbridled efficiency, while masking the enormous human toil it took to put on this human carnival.

Roxy also took advantage of his managerial position whenever it suited him. Even though the house had three top conductors and more than a hundred musicians who could have handled the task with much more aplomb, Roxy still insisted on conducting the orchestra from time to time.[250] As long as the grosses stayed high, Fox and John Zanft ignored his early managerial and budgetary decisions. For a while, at least, it was a functional partnership. Roxy was therefore still able to slash away at any and all films that passed through his projectors. *Variety* noted in May, for instance, that Roxy had cut *Alaskan Adventures* (1926) from roughly 6,000 feet to only two reels. "[I]t still drew much comment and no doubt some business," the journal noted, but "It's commencing, however to be a question at the Roxy whether it is the picture or stage end of the program that is the heavy draw."[251] Roxy had been quite up-front about his focus on the theater's live performances and not on the so-called feature film. "I'm paying no attention to the picture end," he told *Variety* in February 1927, shortly before the theater opened. "I'll get pictures. But the drawing card here is going to be the stage show. I'm going to have 250 people on the stage between the performing end and the orchestra pit, and I want to see the person in New York who won't pay $1 to see them."[252] "This is in every sense a picture theater, and all our efforts are pointed toward the fact that everything must be pictorial," Roxy added. "Everything must be a picture, but not necessarily always on celluloid."[253] As Dudley Glass later wrote in the *Sydney Morning Herald*, "It is, perhaps, fair to add that films are also shown at this super-cinema."[254]

WHAT PRICE MUSIC

Major Bowes and Major Rothafel were not only competitors over the radio and at the box office; both also became involved in the production of scores for synchronous sound motion pictures in 1927. Roxy had worked with Rapee et al. to produce music for the short and feature films and live performances he exhibited at the Capitol and at the Roxy. Bowes was less overtly involved in this process at the Capitol, but he seemed more than willing to take equal credit.

In 1926, Warner Bros. musical director Herman Heller had hired the Capitol's William Axt and David Mendoza to score the company's first feature-length Vitaphone film, *Don Juan* (1926). Mendoza and Axt, who had been valorized for their scores for *Ben-Hur* and *The Big Parade* (1925), were each paid $3,500 for their work. According to Scott Eyman, Axt "chafed at his lowly fee and tried to hold on to the publishing rights to the music as compensation."[255] Mendoza was unhappy too, not about his pay but about Major Bowes's insistence that his name be added to the score's credits. "Finally we got contracted for [*Don Juan*] and Major Bowes' name was on it," Mendoza recalled in 1972. "We got $3,500.00 a piece for that, and Major Bowes put himself down for $3,500.00. It came to two days before the opening, and they refused to pay Bowes the money because he did nothing. So he took out an injunction against the opening, and they had to pay him."[256]

Don Juan was exhibited at the Roxy exactly one year after its August 6, 1926, premiere at Warners' Theatre with its original Vitaphone discs containing the Mendoza and Axt score.[257] Roxy was thus able to present the musical compositions of his former Capitol Theatre employees. More importantly, Roxy demonstrated that he had enough independence to show off a rival sound format even at a time when Fox was enthusiastically selling the industry on Movietone.

The exhibition of *Don Juan* at the Roxy was sandwiched between *Wolf's Clothing* (1927) and *What Price Glory*, the latter film booked for its "popular" run at the Roxy months after its 1926 release. Although the Roxy was the flagship of the Fox theater circuit, smaller legitimate houses like the Globe and Harris would typically debut new Fox feature films at roadshow prices. These films would later make their way to the Roxy and incorporated into "an evening's entertainment," blended into the unitary text where they would receive prime but not exclusive billing.[258]

What Price Glory's exhibition at the Roxy Theatre was one of the most celebrated of Roxy's career. He channeled his Marine Corps background

whether these prologues were merely inspired by the Roxy Theatre's presentation or if they were shared by Fox executives such as John Zanft. In either case, it is worth noting that the duplication of Roxy's unitary text for *Street Angel* extended his influence on Fox films and their exhibition even further.

Roxy had previously linked prologues and other stage performances with his feature films through cultural, generic, or aesthetic markers. The theme song, though, now often became the thematic and aesthetic glue that bound the live and recorded elements of the unitary text. It also reinforced the importance of music as a binding and conferring agent for Fox films. Financially, the use of the theme song in both the live performance preceding the film and in the film itself built a fan base for the tune. After hearing the tune two, six, or ten times over a given evening, audiences would be able to walk out of a Fox theater whistling or humming the tune. Erno Rapee noted that "Even in a popular picture it is often necessary to create a love theme which follows through the picture and is often heard from the lips of the audience as it is leaving the theater." This link, he later observed, between in-theater listening and post-theater humming "was responsible for three of my best-known successes[:] *Charmaine*, written for 'What Price Glory,' *Diane*, written for 'Seventh Heaven,' and *Angela Mia*, written for 'The Street Angel.' "[73] *Variety* noted, "From the picture producer[']s standpoint" as well "the song hook-up is invaluable. It gives their celluloid product a new form of plugging and exploitation over the radio, on the records and in the streets, through mass whistling and harmonizing, which no amount of paid advertising could accomplish."[74] These songs thus became emotional keepsakes of a treasured memory of an evening out or of the film itself. When the song later played over the radio in a variety of forms, it only added to consumer awareness and desire. This desire was acted out in the purchase of millions of pieces of sheet music featuring imagery from the film and phonograph recordings featuring the music. Played on home pianos or listened to on phonograph players, the tune ultimately spurred the need to see the film again—binding the music and the personal memory to the filmic image, if only for two hours. Theme songs may have served initially as a structuring device for film scorers, but they soon became imbedded in tangible, multifaceted material objects that profited from the convergence of film, broadcasting, music publishing, and recording that defined this new era.

"Angela Mia" enabled this trend as the song remained popular on local radio stations and national broadcasts over the next year. Washington, D.C., station WRC, for instance, built an entire program out of Rapee's works and dubbed the show "Rapeeana," "A symphonic sketch built on the popular success of Erno Rapee." Rapee (and Rapee-Pollack) tunes were performed by a fifty-piece concert orchestra and conducted by Rapee during the 9:00 P.M. broadcast on February 28, 1929. A bevy of Fox film theme songs were featured, such as "Charmaine," "Diane," "Little Mother," "Angela Mia," and "Marian," from F. W. Murnau's forthcoming Fox film, *4 Devils* (1928).[75]

By September 1928, after the song had infiltrated the airwaves and major urban movie houses, millions of sheet music and record buyers were snatching up copies of "Angela Mia" to take home. By then, Brunswick had already begun selling panatropes (records) of the song, which led to new moments of movie house convergence. Although the recordings were traditionally sold for consumer use, the Rochester (New York) Theatre played the record of "Angela Mia" in the lobby for four weeks before the film's exhibition there *and* during its presentation. Once again, it is important to reiterate that the unitary text of silent and early sound film exhibition was *not* confined to the auditorium but began in the lobby and linked the pre-show entertainment to the main feature.[76] The Chas. M. Stebbins Picture Supply Co., a Kansas City, Missouri, "Independent Theatre Equipment Dealer," which sold "Effects Records for All Types of Non-Synchronous Machines," offered a host of theme song records for movie houses without Movietone capability, including recordings of "Angela Mia," the Rapee-Pollack tune "Someday Somewhere" from Fox's *The Red Dance* (1928), and "Neapolitan Nights" from Fox's *Fazil* (1928)—both films scored by Roxy and Rapee.[77]

As *Street Angel* opened in cities across the country in 1928 and 1929, "Angela Mia" often became the chief attraction. In Chicago, *Street Angel* and *Sunrise* were joined together in one large advertisement for the Uptown and Tivoli theaters, respectively, with a photograph of Janet Gaynor and the headline, "MOVIETONE MARVELS—MIRACLES OF SOUND!" On the *Street Angel* side of the Balaban & Katz circuit advertisement, the ad noted that the film contained "Sound—'Angela Mia' and Other Love-Music Matchlessly Sung and Played."[78] Fox (and other film companies) had a new marketing tool: if audiences were unfamiliar or disinterested in the stars or plot of a film, they could at least be lured in by a tune heard over the radio or played live in nightclubs and dance halls. "The power of the screen to attract the music fans is thoroughly sensed by the music men in more than one way, regarding picture songs," *Variety* reported, "since film presentations are being given extraordinary attention as exploitation media."[79]

Film music, once orchestrated locally by movie theater organists, pianists, or conductor/composers, was increasingly nationalized after the success of theme songs such as "Angela Mia." Audiences, after hearing the song through their radios or in nightclubs or dance halls, came to expect film-related theme songs to be played during their exhibition in local theaters through recorded soundtracks or live by orchestras or organists. Cue sheets and sheet music aided this process, as did the growing availability of Brunswick, Columbia, Victor, and other recordings.

FOX AND FIGURES

Roxy and Rapee continued to assemble/score and record soundtracks for Fox films throughout 1928. Howard Hawks's *Fazil* (1928), which opened at the Gaiety Theatre on June 4, 1928, featured a "synchronized Movietone accompaniment arranged by S. L. Rothafel and Erno Rapee."[80] The soundtrack had one important deviation in that the film's theme song was not written by Rapee-Pollack but by John S. Zamecnik and published by Sam Fox Publishing.[81] The film's theme song was a popular hit, though it hardly matched Rapee's earlier successes.[82]

The *Los Angeles Times* was among the many newspapers that gladly reproduced Fox talking points that *Fazil*'s Movietone score was performed and recorded by "110 musicians."[83] The *Dallas Morning News* parroted the numerical claim that the "tuneful and atmospheric musical score," which the newspaper credited to Rapee alone, was "played by the Roxy Theater 110-piece orchestra."[84] *Win That Girl* (1928), another Fox film whose score was credited to Rapee alone (by *Variety*),[85] was also marketed as having "Sound Effects and Music Accompaniment by [the] 110-piece Roxy Theatre Orchestra," as noted in an October 8, 1928, advertisement for the Fox-owned Oshkosh (Wisconsin) Theatre.[86] Fox's *The Air Circus* (1928) was similarly marketed at the Oshkosh Theatre with a soundtrack "Accompanied by [the] 110-Piece Roxy Theatre Orchestra."[87] An advertisement in the *Sheboygan Press* for *Mother Knows Best* (1928) at the Majestic Theatre noted that audiences could "HEAR and SEE on Fox Movietone Synchronized with Music and Sound Effects, Musical Accompaniment by [the] Roxy 110 Piece Orchestra."[88] *Four Sons* was also advertised at the Stratford Theatre in Poughkeepsie, New York, with "A Magnificent Musical Score Rendered by the GREAT ROXY 110 Piece Orchestra."[89] Harold Franklin noted that Fox-approved taglines for the company's new part-talkies included "Gloriously set to Golden Sound, with Voices and 110-piece Roxy Theatre Orchestra on the Movietone Accompaniment!" The inflated number was not always 110, however; Franklin cited another (unnamed) Fox Movietone film ad that featured a "marvellous [*sic*] music score played by the 75 musicians of the Roxy Theatre on the Movietone!"[90] If the size of the orchestra used to record these soundtracks was indeed an embellishment, it certainly appears to have been company sanctioned.

Variety, whose "Inside Stuff" columns routinely blasted studio and exhibition hokum, had had enough. The trade journal announced in its July 18, 1928, edition that musicians had come forward to say that "Advertising matter and announcements mentioning symphony orchestras of 75 to 110 pieces in film synchronization work is baloney." Instead of 110 musicians, the number typically used for "canned accompaniment" was actually 24, "with 30 a maximum." *Variety* argued further, "Apart from the economic factor the employment of more than 30 instruments is mechanically successful. When over 30 pieces are used for recording the emulsion is unable to register the overtones, partials and harmonies thus created." In a final jab at Fox's (and others') marketing practices, the journal noted, "While the general public will accept at face value announcements of 110-piece symphony orchestras the trained ears will easily detect the exaggerations."[91] In addition to questions about the actual size of the orchestra that recorded these soundtracks and the location of their recording, it remains difficult to decipher whether some films like *Win That Girl* were truly scored by Roxy and/or Rapee or even performed by members of the Roxy orchestra.

THE RED DANCE, MOTHER KNOWS BEST, AND THE RIVER PIRATE (1928)

The Red Dance, which debuted at the Globe Theatre on June 25, 1928, with a "synchronized score by S. L. Rothafel and Erno Rapee," according to *Variety*, was a return to the previous assembly line of theme song–Movietone score–radio promotion–music publishing.[92] Rapee and Pollack wrote the film's theme song, "Someday, Somewhere (We'll Meet Again)."[93] Edwin Evans, writing in *The Bioscope* in August 1928, noted that he had just attended a Fox trade screening in London of *The Red Dance* featuring its Movietone score. "[T]he effect of the mechanically reproduced accompaniment was astonishingly good," he wrote in his column "Music and Musicians" and was "undoubtedly a very serious threat to the cinema musician." Credit for the score was given solely to Roxy, whom Evans noted had produced "a better [musical] setting than most of ours." He added that Movietone scores certainly seemed to benefit from rehearsals and the ability to rerecord any problems. "I will wager that Mr. Rothafel was not rung up at a few days' notice to provide the music, given one 'run-through' of the reel, and half a rehearsal with his band," Evans noted. "Such a setting could not be produced that way. The adaptation showed concentrated care, and the performance ample preparation."[94] The Movietone score's use of the theme song did not go unnoticed. Evans argued that the "practically all Russian" music did not fit harmoniously with the theme song, "Someday, Somewhere." "I suppose Rapee and his publishers will make a pretty penny by it, but it does the film no good, and it cheapens the otherwise excellent setting."[95] In Evans's estimation—and in a growing number of opinions—cue sheets, silent film accompaniment, and Vitaphone and Movietone scores were increasingly placing commercial considerations above artistic value.

When *Mother Knows Best* premiered at the Globe Theatre on September 16, 1928, the theme song, "Sally of My Dreams" (written by William Kernell) was "plugged" into the Roxy-Rapee score.[96] The extent to which Roxy's influence could be felt throughout the Fox circuit was found once again in the presentation of the film at the Fox Theatre in Detroit. Not only did the Movietone film feature the Roxy-Rapee score, four of Roxy's theater/radio stars were on hand for the live presentation preceding the film: Harold Van Duzee sang "Laugh, Clown, Laugh," Adelaide De Loca and Viola Philo performed "Cradle Song," and Douglas Stanbury sang "On the Road to Mandalay." Reinforcing the fluidity and complexity of the unitary texts that surrounded these films at the Roxy and other theaters of the period, the Detroit Fox noted that " 'Sally of My Dreams' closes the stage show and fades into the picture," much as Roxy had been doing since *What Price Glory*'s famous transition.[97]

Rapee Goes Universal

Scores for other films such as *The River Pirate* (1928) continued to build Erno Rapee's considerable prestige within the film and music publishing industries and led to new offers from companies other than Fox. Like Hugo Riesenfeld's journeyman work for Tiffany-Stahl and David Mendoza and William Axt's work for Warner Bros., movie theater music directors of the era were not yet constrained by the bounds of exclusive studio contracts.

Rapee and Pollack had already contributed (with Walter Hirsch) "When Love Comes Stealing" for Universal's *The Man Who Laughs* (1928).[98] Rapee's role at the Roxy Theatre offered additional marketing opportunities for companies that solicited his work on theme songs and scores. He was able, for instance, to plug "When Love Comes Stealing" into the Roxy Theatre prologue during the week of April 14, 1928, when it was performed by Gladys Rice and Douglas Stanbury.[99] Sheet music further capitalized on the song's presentation at the Roxy: an inset photograph of Gladys Rice appeared on selected covers and noted that "When Love Comes Stealing" was "Successfully Introduced by Gladys Rice at the Roxy Theatre, New York."[100]

Rapee's work for Universal was not a one-time event. Universal announced in June 1928 that the company, like Warner Bros., Fox, and United Artists, would synchronize eighteen of its films, and Fox loaned Rapee to Universal. Rapee's first Movietone score for Universal was for *Uncle Tom's Cabin* (1927), which had originally been scored by Hugo Riesenfeld in 1927.[101] A Universal advertisement in *Variety* noted that Rapee's newly Movietoned *Uncle Tom's Cabin* would feature the "world famous Dixie Jubilee Singers" and "Erno Rapee's Augmented Symphonic Orchestra."[102] The Roxy name was not present.

Instead of drawing on classical works, Rapee used a wide range of more historically relevant songs, including "Rolling Home," "Good-bye Brother," "Lead Kindly Light," "Oh, Eliza," "Glory, Glory, Hallelujah," and "Nobody Knows What Trouble I've Had" to add thematic flavor.[103] Sound effects, such as the cracking of a whip, were also added, along with a single word of dialogue. The film was also shortened to one hundred and fourteen minutes and given a "general release at popular prices" in the fall of 1928. Historian David Pierce notes that Rapee recorded the soundtrack in New York, though the exact location is, once again, unknown. The film was subsequently distributed to sound-equipped and silent theaters, with a cue sheet compiled by James C. Bradford distributed to the latter.[104] Rapee's *Uncle Tom's Cabin* soundtrack, like others of the period, offered opportunities for more convergence: when the newly Movietoned film was shown at the Lafayette Theatre in Buffalo, New York, the theater's manager broadcasted the film's soundtrack over the radio during an October midnight show to entice home audiences to see the film.[105]

Rapee's work on *Uncle Tom's Cabin* seems to have been sanctioned by William Fox, who may have hoped that Universal's use of Movietone would help spur the industry to adopt his sound-on-film system instead of Vitaphone or RCA's new Photophone system. Fox did not approve any additional work by Rapee for Universal, though, and thus it came as a shock to Fox when he discovered that when Universal had borrowed Movietone recording equipment for tests on *Show Boat* (1929) for nine days at a cost of $30,000, they had done so in part to clandestinely record "dialogue and sound" for a new motion picture and three previously canned films—*Last Warning* (1929), *Lonesome* (1929), and *It Can Be Done* (1929). As word filtered out of Universal City that the studio had used the equipment for three other films, Fox angrily recalled the loaned Movietone truck on August 28—three days before it was to be returned. Fox officials were so irate about the chicanery that rumors began circulating that Fox would file an injunction to prevent the films' distribution.[106]

Fox was furious at Universal, *Variety* reported, but he may have been even angrier at Erno Rapee, who had scored these films without asking for Fox's permission. Fox treated Rapee's side work as corporate treason, and he excoriated Roxy over his employee's behavior. Roxy reportedly went "to the mat" for Rapee, and Fox was cajoled into keeping him. Rapee may have worried about the security of his position within the company, but he was certainly not in danger of poverty or unemployment. He was earning money from Fox and Universal, and his music publishing contracts and theme songs with Pollack had already "netted both a small fortune."[107]

4 DEVILS . . . AND THE REST OF THE FOX FILMS

Roxy and Rapee had been tapped to work on F. W. Murnau's next film, *4 Devils*, before the dustup between Fox and Rapee. The film opened at the Gaiety Theatre on October 3, 1928, with a "synchronized score by S. L. Rothafel," according to a *Variety* review. The *New York Times* gave a clearer description of the division of labor: "music score arranged by S.L. Rothafel and directed by Erno Rapee."[108]

The popularity and importance of theme songs in the late 1920s had, by then, begun spurring film companies to lower their risk by not relying heavily on one tune that might or might not catch on with the public. Instead, two, three, or more affiliated songs were now being composed to tie in with a film's soundtrack. *4 Devils* had two: "Marian," the love theme, and "Destiny," the dramatic theme, which *The Metronome* noted was "used as a solid musical background throughout the dramatic action." Both songs were written by Rapee and Pollack and published by De Sylva, Brown & Henderson.[109]

Roxy and Rapee assembled another synchronized score for *Dry Martini* (1928), but their work scoring Fox films was over.[110] Days before the film's premiere, Fox opened an enormous new studio in Beverly Hills, Fox Movietone City, which was equipped with sound stages and recording halls. As Fox postproduction moved west, Rapee announced in November 1928 that he would begin scoring films for MGM and Paramount.[111] Instead of beginning work for those studios, which already employed William Axt and David Mendoza, and Nat Finston, respectively, Rapee signed a five-year contract with DeSylva, Brown & Henderson to head a new music publisher known as Sound Music Corp. for "Theme Songs, Popular Songs, Production Scores, Standard Music, Scoring, Synchronizing, [and] Recording."[112] Rapee was given a substantial amount of stock as part of his compensation.[113] *Musical Courier* announced that the Sound Music Corp. would soon be renamed the Roxy Music Corp. to reflect Rapee's day job, but this does not appear to have taken place.[114] In the end, the Roxy Music name did not stick. The company was finally renamed the Crawford Music Corporation, reflecting DBH employee Bobby Crawford's management of the new music publishing arm.

Roxy's musicians were similarly involved in other projects. In late 1928, the Studebaker Corporation of America and the Fox-Case Corporation, owners of Movietone's sound-on-film technology, threw some of the most popular figures of late-1920s American culture, including Knute Rockne, Florenz Ziegfeld, and "ROXY'S FAMOUS Radio and Stage ORCHESTRA," into a cinematic blender and churned out a film named *Champions* (1928). (This seems to be the first and only time the Roxy Theatre orchestra ever appeared on film.) Produced for $50,000, the film was described by a Lowville, New York, newspaper as "The most elaborate and unique motion picture with sound accompaniment ever made for industrial use." It was, according to press accounts, the first "commercial" Movietone film made for purely marketing purposes.[115]

Fox, Rapee, and Movietone City

William Fox had two large projects ongoing by the end of 1928: expanding his exhibition empire nationally and internationally and opening his new $10 million studio in Los Angeles on October 28, 1928. Instead of spending money on radio or music publishing, a large part of Fox's focus was on the completion of Fox Movietone City in what was then Beverly Hills and buying up theater chains (Poli, West Coast Theatres, Saxe, etc.).[116]

Fox Film's move westward was part of a general trend whereby sound motion pictures were being scored in growing numbers out west, where many studios had built new sound and scoring stages. Movie palace conductors like George Lipschultz also found new (and more lucrative) positions at southland studios like Fox, where he became musical director, following the trend away from movie theater orchestra pits and into studio scoring stages.[117] One of Lipschultz's first hires was Hugo Friedhofer, who would become one of

Hollywood's most prolific orchestrators/composers of the mid-twentieth century, working on such films as *Gone With the Wind* (1939), *Casablanca* (1943), *Mildred Pierce* (1945) and *The Best Years of Our Lives* (1946). Friedhofer's first job at Fox was orchestrating music for *Sunny Side Up* (1929).[118]

Many other prolific songwriters as well as music and movie palace composers, conductors, and musicians went west as well. "Tin Pan Alley has come to Hollywood," Muriel Babcock observed in the *Los Angeles Times* in December 1928.

> For judging from the announcements which daily roll forth from the film studios, all the song writers who ever set a note to music sheet [and] all the fair-haired lads who ever thumped a piano down in McGuire's Cafe have come west to write theme songs and hit songs for the now talking and singing pictures. Whether the available supply of baby grands and uprights in Los Angeles will prevail, whether the music stores will stand the strain, remains to be seen. Tin Pan Alley is here.

Recent émigrés from New York City included stars like Al Jolson and songwriters like Irving Berlin, who had traveled west for United Artists. William Axt, Billy Rose, Arthur Freed, and Fred Fisher all moved out of New York and arrived in Culver City by the end of 1928 to work exclusively for MGM.[119] Axt had moved laterally in the corporation. Friedhofer recalled that "it was the big exodus from the East, out to this new gold mine on the coast."[120]

The *Los Angeles Times* continued to track the emigration from New York to Los Angeles over the next several months. By then, DeSylva, Brown & Henderson, longtime publishers of Fox's (and other studios') music, had also moved west, working at Movietone City on *Fox Movietone Follies* (1929). Other songwriters who routinely gathered at the Brown Derby on Vine Street in Hollywood included Vincent Youmans, L. Wolfe Gilbert, Walter Donaldson, and Cole Porter. Harry Akst, also formerly of the Capitol Theatre in New York, moved west to work for RKO.[121]

Fox's new Movietone City was meant to attract not only the best stars, writers, and directors but also the industry's most coveted songwriters. The market for (theme) songwriters in 1928 and 1929 in Hollywood was akin to that of software and web developers seven decades later: they controlled the job market and set the price for salaries. Fox built bungalows for its stable of songwriters and paid them inordinately well to keep them happy at a time when every studio was bidding for their services.[122] Fox studio musicians in Los Angeles, though, did not get the same kind of salaries (or treatment). The dissolution and/or diminution of movie theater orchestras across the country due to the conversion to sound created scores of unemployed pianists, violinists, and other musicians. Their labor was not hard to come by; the lucky ones ended up working in film studios for music directors like Arthur Kay, who directed the 100-piece Fox orchestra on the lot.[123] Kay was another movie palace transplant, having been musical director at Grauman's Million Dollar in Los Angeles. To fill out his Fox studio orchestra, he stole eighteen of the theater's best musicians and contracted them to Fox.[124]

Erno Rapee's Divided Attention

Despite these shifts, New York was not completely abandoned, as Richard Koszarski illustrates in *Hollywood on the Hudson*. Music for Fox's latest film, *The River* (1929), for instance, reminds us that despite the activity at Movietone City, the new studio did not spell the end for East Coast film production or musical accompaniment. While much of Fox's songwriting and scoring had indeed moved west by then, selected films still received the Rapee (Rapee-Pollack) treatment, even in 1929. For *The River*, Rapee and Pollack wrote their last theme song together, "I Found Happiness," which was published by DBH even after the company's principals had moved to Los Angeles.[125]

Rapee kept up his hectic schedule throughout 1929, working for Fox, NBC, and other film companies. In addition to his work conducting the *Roxy Stroll* on Sunday mornings on NBC, Rapee began conducting the Mobiloil Hour orchestra for NBC on Wednesday evenings as well. *Movie Age* noted in April 1929 that Rapee continued to work "constantly arranging synchronized scores for Fox films and other companies."[126] Those other companies included a new commission from General Pictures Corp. to score *The Bachelor's Club* (1929) using Movietone.[127] Oscar Price, president of General Pictures, boasted, "Not only have I contracted for one of the best sound systems available today. . . . I have secured the services of Erno Rapee, one of America's leading composers, to write the complete score and to personally conduct his famous Roxy Theatre orchestra which will record it on the Movietone for the 'Bachelors Club.'" Price argued that "there is hardly a home in this country, equipped with a radio, that hasn't heard and enjoyed the Roxy Theatre orchestra conducted by Erno Rapee."[128] It is unclear whether the same musicians from the Roxy Theatre who were used for recording Fox soundtracks were also utilized for General Pictures' film. Rapee also signed a deal with Home-Talkie Productions to appear in two short films "featuring a pianolog of his most popular compositions." *Movie Age* remarked that he would "finally see and hear himself on the screen."[129]

Rapee's compromised attention from Fox, Roxy, and the Roxy Theatre might have been problematic in 1927 and 1928 when he was chiefly responsible (along with Roxy and Lew Pollack) for Fox theme songs and Movietone soundtracks. By 1929, though, Buddy DeSylva, Lew Brown, and Roy Henderson of DBH were not only publishing many of Fox's theme songs but writing music and lyrics for new Fox films as well. Rapee was no longer the company's primary choice for theme songs and scores. DBH was subsequently given an exclusive music publishing contract for the latest Fox feature films.[130] The Rapee era at Fox was effectively over.

Fox Creates Red Star

By the end of 1929, all five media conglomerates were churning out music hits, but not everyone was taking full monetary advantage. Whereas some of these companies had already created their own music publishing firms such as Famous Music (Paramount) or bought out music publishers (MGM/Robbins and Warner Bros./M. Witmark), Fox and RKO remained satisfied with music publishing partnerships rather than full ownership until November 1929.

After watching DBH pocket a healthy portion of the publishing revenue from the above-mentioned Fox films, Fox vice president and general manager Winfield Sheehan established the company's own music publishing firm, Red Star Music Company, to enable Fox to keep all of its copyrights and publishing revenue. Fox's new music publishing arm was given exclusive publishing rights to songs from all future Fox films—and would also publish music for other film companies, Broadway productions, and independent songwriters. The company quickly hired a stable of top songwriters to assure a lineup of hit songs for future films.[131]

Red Star officially opened for business on January 6, 1930, at 729 Seventh Avenue in Manhattan (one block south of the Roxy at 49th Street) with 10,000 square feet of offices, a large reception room, and nine piano studios. The opening ceremonies were attended by "music men" and filmed for Fox Movietone News distribution. Pat Flaherty immediately signed new talent Cliff Friend and dispatched him to Hollywood to team up with famed songwriter/composer Jimmy Monaco, who would go on to work on a number of 1930 Fox films. Red Star made an early splash by publishing songs from the Fox Grandeur production *Happy Days* (1930).[132]

RKO and NBC Make Radio Music Together

Radio Pictures matched Fox's efforts and leveraged its far more convergent assets later that year. In November 1929, NBC announced the formation of the Radio Music Company (RMC) for its own film *and* broadcasting units. The $6 million Radio Music Company was formed by the music publishing firms of Carl Fischer, Inc., and Leo Feist, Inc., and the National Broadcasting Company (to benefit both NBC networks and its corporate cousins, Radio Pictures and RKO). The latter company, "through its affiliation with RCA and N.B.C.," *Motion Picture News* reported, "is now in line with other film producing companies as to a source for original and copyrighted musical composition." The new organization would not only benefit from the inclusion of songs in new Radio Pictures films but also their promotion over NBC's networks and their association with Victor's phonograph and radio departments. "All the resources of Victor such as copyrighted music and services of those under Victor contract, will be at the disposal of the new company," *Motion Picture News* noted. "In addition to acting as a musical unit for Radio Pictures the organization is in a position to popularize songs and other composition through National Broadcasting [NBC]."[133] *The Metronome* viewed the merger of Feist and Fischer and its combination with RCA/NBC/RKO as a perfect union of the times, exploiting both popular and classical music through "the greatest influence of modern times in the dissemination of music of all kinds—radio broadcasting."[134]

The creation of RMC enabled NBC and Radio Pictures to have an in-house arm that would keep all of the music publishing revenue within the conglomerate and facilitate the exploitation of songs across a wide range of media. The move also consecrated RCA/NBC/RKO as the only fully convergent media conglomerate with film production, distribution, and exhibition, control of network broadcasting, and music publishing and recording. NBC president Merlyn Aylesworth later told a United States Senate committee, "It is necessary for us to be in the music business to protect ourselves" because "the movies have bought most of the music houses." He added that "[W]e have got to control the music situation. It is a simple business proposition with a little touch of sentiment in it."[135]

The formation of Red Star and the Radio Music Company consolidated the entertainment industry even more. By 1930, over 90 percent of the country's music was now being published by companies owned by the Big Five media conglomerates: Fox, Warner Bros., Loew's, Paramount, and RCA.[136] Of those five multinational, multimedia conglomerates, only Fox remained devoid of a consistent broadcasting outlet. The other four companies could produce a film knowing that any of its hit songs could be promoted over the air through national and/or local broadcasts and published and distributed through licensed sheet music. RCA, as the most convergent of the conglomerates, could also sell multiple versions of those songs on disc directly to movie patrons who, by the late 1920s, were also music buyers.

RMC's board of directors demonstrated the importance of the new company to RCA. The list included Aylesworth, president of NBC, and now chairman of the board of RMC; Hiram Abrams, president of RKO; Leo Feist, president of Leo Feist, Inc.; E. E. Shumaker, president of the Victor Corporation; David Sarnoff, executive vice president of RCA; H. P. Davis, chairman of the board of NBC; and Walter S. Fischer, president of Carl Fischer, Inc. There was another RMC board member, though, who slipped into reports by both *Motion Picture News* and *The Metronome* without any additional fanfare or surprise: S. L. Rothafel. It should have come as a surprise (or at least a noteworthy mention) that Roxy was not joining the board of Fox's new Red Star Music Company just a block away from the Roxy, but was instead joining the board of the Radio Music Company, the music publishing division of RCA (and by proxy, RKO)—one of Fox's chief rivals. Although those studying the development of Radio City Music Hall and Rockefeller Center would point to 1930 as the year when Roxy decided to jump from Fox to RCA/RKO, his exclusion from Fox's new music publishing arm, and his embrace by RCA, seems in retrospect to be a crucial marker that the Fox-Roxy union was coming to an end and that Roxy's sights had begun turning elsewhere. Erno Rapee was left out of Red Star as well; with Fox Films' production (and scoring) moving west, Roxy and Rapee's influence over the scoring of Fox films was over.

EXIT STAGE ROXY

The year 1929 had been another strong year for the Roxy Theatre. Roxy had even redoubled his efforts to produce industry-leading stage shows despite their cost. While many theaters were firing their orchestras, removing their stage producers and productions, and enjoying the enormous cost savings that came with synchronous sound films, Roxy was undeterred. W. R. Wilkerson commented in *Exhibitors Daily Review* in May 1929 that while "presentations have actually driven patrons away from houses, the Rothafel entertainment has drawn them in. Every act on every bill every week in the year is a gem. How Roxy and his crew of assistants are able to conceive, rehearse and stage these weekly changes is one of the big mysteries of the amusement business."[138] In 1929, Roxy had also been "accorded the distinction of rank as an international authority" when he was asked to contribute the "Stage Lighting" section for the latest edition of the *Encyclopedia Britannica*.[139] News that a motion picture theater director had been selected for such an honor made national headlines, with the *Dallas Morning News* reporting that Roxy's article on stage lighting would be the first on the subject for the encyclopedia.[140]

His radio show also remained popular, but the Gang, as audiences had known them for seven years, began to break apart. Gambarelli had danced for the last time at the Roxy Theatre on February 17, 1928, and had supposedly "retired from active work on the stage." Instead, she partnered with George Hale to dance and choreograph productions for vaudeville houses, motion picture theaters, and a new wave of short and feature films. The Gamby-Hale Dancers quickly grew in prestige and were featured in numerous (Paramount) Publix stage shows at the Paramount Theatre in Times Square, such as "West Point Days," "Babes on Broadway," and eleven additional shows in mid- to late 1928.[141] Gamby branched out on her own in 1929, becoming the "Creator and Trainer" of the Gamby Girls, who appeared across the Publix circuit. The Gamby Girls were also featured in a number of important early Paramount sound films shot at the Astoria studios, including the 1929 films *Glorifying the American Girl* (1929), *The Cocoanuts* (1929), and *Hole in the Wall* (1929).[142] In 1930, following her previously mentioned breakdown, she resumed her work for Paramount-Publix, producing more film prologues for the Publix Theatre circuit, such as "The Melting Pot" and "The Ballet Class," which, Richard Koszarski notes, featured Agnes de Mille and the Gamby Girls "perform[ing] routines they had originated at the Roxy."[143]

Douglas Stanbury had also profited from his earlier performances at the Roxy. In November 1929, he appeared in his second Vitaphone short, *Marching Home*, described by *Motion Picture News* as a filmed version of a performance he had given months earlier at the Roxy Theatre. "There is a male chorus of fifty voices in a corking silhouette marching finish for the picture," the *News* remarked. "Stan sings well and can be played up because of his radio rep."[144] Stanbury would later appear at RKO's famed Palace Theatre with his old radio mate Gamby.[145]

Members of the radio and stage troupe continued to make personal appearances, using the Roxy Theatre as a stepping-stone to other shows and theaters in the United States, Canada, and Europe. In April 1930, members of the Gang appeared at Shea's Hippodrome in Toronto (operated by RKO) for a week of performances.[146] In England, Beatrice Belkin, a longtime fixture of the

Roxy Theatre's prologues, began a series of European tours between 1930 and 1931, appearing first at Beckstein Hall in Berlin, singing the Zerbinetta aria from Strauss's *Ariadne auf Naxos*.[147] As these longtime Roxy and His Gang figures departed, they drained the show of its star wattage.

RAPEE AND WARNER BROS.

Of all the signs that the Roxy Theatre's nucleus was breaking apart, none was more prominent than Erno Rapee's resignation on January 1, 1930. He announced his departure from the Roxy to become the new musical director for Warner Bros., becoming the latest movie palace conductor/ music director to leave for Hollywood.[148] Like so many others, Rapee was lured to the West Coast by money, creative autonomy, and the realization that movie palaces would no longer serve as the site of musical arrangement for American feature films. Rapee's departure for California was the symbolic end of this transitional era and a fitting way to begin the 1930s.[149]

"One by one the boys are making the long trek westward," Doron Antrim of *The Metronome* wrote as Rapee left behind a movie theater and radio audience "numbering into the millions." Rapee, he argued, had been "a real factor in the musical life of this city and nation," citing his work and that of other (movie palace) conductors over the past fifteen years "through such mediums as the phonograph, motion picture theatre, radio and the latest development, sound film." Rapee, he added, "can always reflect with justifiable pride that he has done more to make good music popular in this country than any other individual." Rapee wasn't nostalgic, but hopeful:

> I am proud to say that I have had not an inconsiderable part in this program of education through my affiliation with the motion picture theatre. Before the advent of the symphony orchestra in the motion picture theatre it is safe to say that the rank and file had never seen and heard a symphony orchestra. Through my association with Roxy and particularly in the Roxy Theatre, where I directed a symphony orchestra of 110 musicians, I have kept my finger on the pulse of popular taste constantly and have seen a remarkable development. It is only a matter of years before America will be leading the world musically.[150]

In five hectic years, Rapee had moved from Philadelphia to Berlin to New York and, by 1930, Los Angeles. In that time, he had worked for Fox, Ufa,

Universal, and now Warner Bros. It would be impossible to dismiss his contribution to film music during the 1920s. The *Los Angeles Times* noted that five years after its publication, Rapee's *Encyclopedia of Music for Pictures* was still "used in every studio in the country."[151]

Antrim concluded (correctly) that for Rapee to leave the Roxy, Fox, and NBC, "There must have been unusual inducements financial and otherwise to cause him to leave all this and go into a new enterprise."[152] Rapee's three-year contract with Warner Bros. paid him $1,250 per week in the first year of his contract, $1,750 per week in the second year, and $2,000 per week in the third year, in addition to considerable royalties for original compositions.[153] Rapee was perhaps most excited, though, about the possibilities that full-time musical composition and arrangement could afford. "I look for the talking picture to be the most important development in this country during the next several years," Rapee predicted.

> It will even eclipse the radio in importance. After only one year of awkward experimentation it is certainly the most powerful influence in popular American music today. It has caused little less than a revolution among picture theatres, publishers, musicians, song writers and the rest. But out of it all I expect will come something really distinctive and American, something approaching an art. . . . We are living in an age of marvels and I look for a musical renaissance in this country, the like of which has never been witnessed in any other country in the world.[154]

Rapee added later that the one-time boom of theme songs had faded into a new desire for motion picture operettas, "a production wherein the theme is not needed," but where the soundtrack comprised multiple tunes with no organizing, single theme.[155]

The Metronome estimated Rapee's new work schedule at Warner Bros. to last from 10:00 A.M. to 5:00 P.M. each week—a half day by Roxy Theatre standards.[156] As head of music for Warners and First National, Rapee's schedule may have changed, but his theory and method of composition had remained largely the same. As Myrtle Gebhart of the *Los Angeles Times* reported, there was a much closer link between movie palace arrangement and studio music arrangement than is often discussed.[157] Rapee maintained this continuity between movie palace composition and studio composition by hiring other (former) movie house composers to augment Warner Bros.' already impressive stable of composers and songwriters. Perhaps the most celebrated signing was that of David Mendoza. Mendoza recalled that after Rapee had been in Los

Angeles only a few weeks he began calling Mendoza "every night at dinner time." Mendoza recalled that "The minute he heard I had left the Capitol—I was doing radio—he was calling me up. I was earning $2,000 a week in commercial radio and in those days there were practically no taxes. Well, anyway, after a lot of haranguing and being annoyed by these telephone calls, I said, 'All right.'" Mendoza held an important position in Warner Bros.' music department and was responsible for selecting the music, arranging the score, and conducting the Vitaphone Orchestra for films such as *The Public Enemy* (1931).[158]

Roxy Breaks Out on His Own

In 1930, theme songs, stars, films, radio programs, sheet music, records, and other properties were now seen by conglomerates like RCA (NBC-RKO-RMC), Paramount (CBS-Publix-Famous Music), and Warner Bros. (First National-Brunswick-Stanley-Witmark-Remick-Chappell-Harms) as corporate assets that could and should benefit other divisions of the company. Musicals were produced (much as they are today) because they would not only satisfy the revenue models and corporate strategies of RKO, for instance, but would feature enough music to help boost the profits of RMC and RCA-Victor through their promotion on NBC-Blue and/or NBC-Red. The growth of new technologies and their subsequent convergence has typically begun new waves of corporate acquisition and consolidation, especially as the elusive desire for synergy across divisions and brands spurs executives to dream big not only about content or artistic merit, but about technology, power, and corporate survival in a changing media landscape.

Roxy was not directly involved in the broader technological and corporate convergence of the media industries. His current position—expanding the scope of his stage shows, maintaining his radio program, and devoting most of his time to his theater—was now quaint and, despite its still apparent glitz and prestige, part of the old dynamic and not the new. While Warner Bros. and Erno Rapee were building for the future, the beginning of 1930 was quite different for Fox, Roxy, and their enormous theater. *Time* reported that despite all of the plaudits the Roxy Theatre still received, including its designation as a top New York tourist attraction, "few stockholders in Roxy Theatres Corp. are proud of their palatially gaudy enterprise." Roxy A stock had declined from its initial price of $40 in 1925 to a new post–stock market crash low of $22 by February 1930. Shares had still never been listed on any stock exchange.[159]

Investors, instead of reaping a profit, had taken a nearly 50 percent loss in their investment.

A few months after the stock market crash of October 1929, investors wanted accountability and no longer accepted empty promises—even from Roxy. Roxy had initially sold the theater's stock as a way to be "one big Gang together, running our own big theatre."[160] Now stockholders were a different kind of "gang"—or, rather, a mob. In a typical year, five or ten investors might attend the Roxy Theatres Corp. annual meeting. In February 1930, five hundred angry investors appeared, "armed with the spirit of 'We want to know why!'" *Time* reported that Roxy "confessed in a long *theme-song* [my emphasis] of woe that his stockholders have made him cry like a baby." The *Time* article was one of the very few that noted the strife behind the scenes at the Roxy Theatre and gives at least some insight into the potential heartache the situation may have given its managing director. (Stockholders were not mollified either by the annual report, which showed that the theater had actually made $643,047 net profits in 1929 compared to $607,677 in 1928, or the fact that gross box office reached $5,131,675 compared to approximately $5,000,000 in 1928.) The scene was pitiful: outraged board members, outraged stockholders, and a plaintive, bewildered Roxy sentimentalizing for his unhappy audience:

> In the first place, I want to tell you that at the beginning I was betrayed. My partner [Herbert Lubin] sold me out and left me to carry this awful load. I have received scurrilous letters from you stockholders, and some of the accusations which have been made against me have caused me to cry like a baby. After I was betrayed [by Lubin et al.] I stuck only because I felt that most of you people had bought stock because it was my project. I got nothing out of it. I have lost a larger personal fortune in sticking with you. I have nothing besides my salary, and that is nothing to what I could make for my family if I was free to accept other offers.

Roxy had left the Capitol Theatre five years earlier to gain his independence, but ended up working for thousands of unhappy bosses, a fraction of whom had come to this meeting to mete out a small pound of flesh. "Never until last week's confession would one have thought that 'Roxy' walks under the shadow he described so feelingly, interrupted only by baiting from unsympathetic stockholders," *Time* noted in its "Rocky Roxy" report on February 17, 1930. After "three hours of bickering," stockholders voted to receive a dividend, hoping to drain some of their money out of the enterprise.[161] They would have been better off selling their shares while there was still time.

Roxy's uncompromising standards may not have aided the theater's financial struggles. Even after the meeting, he did not seem to cut back much on production costs or overhead. By February 1930, eight thousand musicians had already lost their jobs during the conversion to sound but Roxy's 110-piece orchestra remained fully intact in 1930 and was even augmented to a staggering 125 musicians the following year.[162] As the Depression began, and then worsened, ticket sales at the Roxy dropped and Roxy Theatres Corp. stock slid much further. The stockholder issues were just one of the many reasons Roxy may have been looking for an exit. His troubles with Fox management and the company's overall health may have abetted his association with Radio Music Corp. and the RCA-NBC-RKO combine. By his own account, the Roxy Theatre had been a critical hit and a financial disappointment.

Rumors began circling not long after the tumultuous stockholder meeting that Roxy was set to sign a new contract with RCA. One account in the *Dallas Morning News* in May 1930 noted that with Roxy's early departure from his beloved theater, even before the settled departure date, Sid Grauman would become its new stage producer and managing director.[163] The news could only have rattled Roxy Theatre investors even more. Roxy attempted to settle their nerves and stop press phone calls by intimating three weeks later that he would fulfill the remainder of his contract that was set to expire in March 1932.[164] In June, the Associated Press reported (again) that Roxy was leaving—now linked with a proposal to possibly run a new sixty-story "Radio Centre" for RCA and NBC.[165] No one at RCA or at the Roxy would confirm it.

Roxy's name, despite the stockholder laments and the swirling rumors, was still highly marketable. In May 1930, he began appearing in nationwide advertisements for Old Gold cigarettes.[166] The following month, Roxy's name alone was enough to sell Tydol gasoline. An advertisement featuring Roxy's chauffeur, Frank Bond, asked, "Who are better judges of Gasoline . . . than the drivers of America's finest cars?"[167]

In September 1930, Roxy took a two-month "vacation" in Europe and refused to "divulge his immediate plans" to the press. Despite his silence, the *Hollywood Reporter* printed the entertainment industry's worst-kept secret: Roxy had traveled to Europe in preparation for his new role with RCA-NBC-RKO. In his absence, Marco Wolf, of Fanchon & Marco, now production head of all Fox stage musicals, took over his duties at the Roxy.[168]

The Roxy Theatre foundered along the remainder of the year as the theater's staff remained in flux. Joseph Littau, who had replaced Rapee in January, left as well on October 20, 1930, to become the new conductor of the Omaha Symphony Orchestra.[169] (One year later, Beatrice Belkin would return from

Europe and marry Littau and retire from the stage.)[170] By then, the Roxy had already lost many of its old veterans.

"That's All Folks!"

In Los Angeles, the situation for musicians, composers, and conductors was suddenly no more stable either. Sheet music sales had begun declining, record sales collapsed around the Depression, and the popularity of musicals, which had flooded theaters in the previous three years, was also waning. These developments, coupled with a deep and growing concern about the ongoing economic decline, led Warner Bros. and other studios to cut costs and slash payroll. Rapee, after arriving with boundless energy and hope for a new artistic moment in Hollywood, severed his contract with Warner Bros. on October 10, 1930, and received a severance payment of $42,900.[171] He returned to New York, took the baton back from Littau at the Roxy, and resumed his radio conducting for NBC. Oscar Strauss, who had worked for Rapee, was not far behind, leaving the following month to launch his new operetta in Vienna, *The Farmer General*.[172] The composer had gotten all he wanted out of his brief time with Warner Bros., though. The *Los Angeles Times* reported that he had left with enough money "to have kept Beethoven all his life."[173] Another Rapee employee, Sigmund Romberg, left shortly after as well. "Romberg, Erno Rapee and a few others, big in their field of popular creation and interpretation in music unquestionably left the colony sadder but wiser men," the *Times* wrote of the frustration that caused many to leave amid the constraints of the studio system. "Both came here with the idea that they might become almost Wagners of the screen, or at least bring music of high quality to the films. Rapee, especially, now shining in the capacity of conductor, I think, particularly felt that the film might permit him a greater latitude for expression than his previous associations. They were both too early."[174] (Or perhaps they were too late.) David Mendoza noted that, if anything, Rapee, Strauss, and Romberg did Warner Bros. a favor by leaving before they were axed. By 1931, "Musicals stopped, and they began getting rid of everybody on high salary."[175] A good number of Roxy's protégés remained in Los Angeles, including William Axt at MGM, Nat Finston at Paramount, and Hugo Riesenfeld, who worked for a variety of studios, and continued the movie palace aesthetic in their own work.[176]

Fox, like Warner Bros., also shed much of its high-priced staff and "cut down very drastically," according to Hugo Friedhofer.[177] Red Star Music was not a runaway success, in part perhaps because of the economic decline and the nation's theme-song fatigue. Pat Flaherty quit in October 1930 to form his own music publishing firm after feeling abandoned by Fox's continued side deals with DBH and Harms, Inc.[178] The company's decision to use songs from other music publishers in its films reflects either corporate mismanagement or a lack of belief in Flaherty and his stable of songwriters. Red Star never reached the success that Famous Music, MGM's Robbins Music Corp., and Warner Bros.' myriad publishing companies achieved in the 1930s and throughout the remainder of the twentieth century.

Exit Stage Roxy, Part II

Fox soon had another corporate departure to absorb. Roxy did not return to his post at the Roxy Theatre, or to his radio show, until early December 1930.[179] Upon his return, he announced his departure from the Roxy Theatre on January 1, 1931, exchanging his $3,000 per week salary at the Roxy for a $5,000 per week position working for RCA-NBC-RKO on their new theater-radio project at Rockefeller Center.[180] (Roxy did not officially exit the Roxy Theatre until March 29, 1931, when Marco Wolf took over as producer.)[181] Harry Arthur, general manager of Fox's eastern circuit, took over day-to-day operations of the massive theater.

Roxy did not go quietly. Like his exiting remarks when leaving the Rialto and Rivoli eleven years earlier, Roxy charged that the film industry now had a "deplorable lack of practical idealism" and an "even more deplorable oversupply of commercialism. These two things have placed the industry in the rut in which it now finds itself," he told the *Hollywood Reporter*. "There used to be men and women in the business who had ideals, who had imagination, but they are scarce now."[182] His estimation of the industry's "commercialism," though, was that its drive to produce musicals and other extravaganzas, and perhaps its stream of remakes of silent films, had laid bare the industry's appetite for money, not new material or ideas.

Roxy subsequently turned away from film and more toward radio and the new Rockefeller Center project, which promised to marry radio, music, television, live performance, and film in a new city of convergence. Fox had Movietone City, Universal had Universal City, and Radio Corporation of America and Roxy would soon have their Radio City.

For the remainder of Roxy's career, radio and the stage would capture his imagination and attention. He wouldn't abandon feature-length films, but he could no longer score, edit, or enhance their assembly. He could, however, surround them with music, dance, and other live performance. It was on the radio that Roxy found a full measure of control, artistic freedom, and inspiration. NBC Artists Service sent Roxy and a reconstituted Gang on a three-month tour around the country beginning in Brooklyn on February 4, 1931.[183] It had been more than five years since the Gang's last tour. Roxy, who had been sequestered inside his "cathedral" producing lavish stage shows and musical arrangements for his theater and for Fox's early sound films, was eager to spread his wings. He never worked for Fox (the man or the company) again.

The NBC networks also needed a new music director in 1931 and lured Rapee away from the troubled Roxy Theatre that July. Roxy and Rapee, who had been magnetized to one another for a decade and a half, were under the same corporate umbrella once again. In a few short months, they would be sharing more than office supplies at Radio City Music Hall, where Rapee would become, once again, musical director and head conductor under Roxy. "With Roxy slated for an important position in the new Radio City," Pierre Key noted in the *Los Angeles Times*, "it was a foregone conclusion that sooner or later the sprightly Erno would bob up somewhere."[184]

The five-year period between 1926 and 1931 ended as it began for Roxy and Rapee: together for an enormous new project that promised to expand the possibilities of broadcasting, film, music, and theatrical entertainment. Today, Radio City Music Hall is a landmark building, a chief attraction for live performance, and one of the city's most popular tourist destinations. But in 1931, Radio City and Rockefeller Center were more than architectural projects or the promise of a new entertainment venue. When everything else seemed to be going down, at Radio City cranes, steel, and concrete were going up. Roxy's newest project symbolized hope in a desperate era. Construction workers found jobs, out-of-work musicians gained employment, and newspapers throughout the country focused on the entertainment complex as a ray of hope when all else seemed to be collapsing.

Millions were unemployed and scrambling for work and food, but for old money like Nelson Rockefeller, and new money like Samuel Rothafel and Erno Rapee, life and art were still full of possibilities. Nestled high above the street in his new RKO office, Roxy had become tone-deaf to the times. Reality, like prosperity, though, was just around the corner . . .

8. THE PROLOGUE IS PAST
ROXY, MEDIA DIVERGENCE, AND RADIO CITY MUSIC HALL
(1931–1936)

Traditions are the best guides we have in what not to do.
—Samuel "Roxy" Rothafel, November 1931

Between 1926 and 1931, the once disparate media industries converged in the United States, creating a new entertainment industry dominated by multinational media conglomerates with film, broadcasting, music, and other media, technology, content, and intellectual property divisions. This convergence enabled companies like RCA to promote their RKO musicals by airing select songs on the company's NBC-Red and NBC-Blue networks, sell sheet music through the Radio Music Company, press phonograph recordings of these songs through RCA-Victor, and use all of these ancillary revenue streams and marketing opportunities to bring more audiences into RKO theaters nationwide. This set of industrial and technological synergies was made possible in part by the entertainment industry's ability to leverage content, technologies, intellectual property, and labor for maximum profit. By the end of 1930, all five major media companies (RCA, Paramount, Loew's, Warner Bros., and Fox) owned or were affiliated with radio programs, stations, or networks, as well as music publishing and/or recording companies.

If the late 1920s can be characterized by media convergence and the industrial and artistic changes it wrought, the period between 1931 and 1932 laid bare a lesser theorized industrial phenomenon: *media divergence*. This divergence, in which utopian technological and corporate synergies are disbanded, often occurs because of a conglomerate's inability to synergize various divisions, manage and/or alleviate corporate debt, fix faulty economic models and business practices, and, in many cases, maximize media technologies and media properties. In recent years, Time Warner's disastrous multi-billion dollar merger with America Online was finally reversed in 2009 with the spin-off of AOL into a separate entity. The *Wall Street Journal* noted that the acquisition had become a "major distraction" for management and investors, and Time Warner sought to shed the Internet-based company to become "a more efficient operation devoted to movies, TV shows and other entertainment and information."[1] In other words, too much convergence, especially with underwhelming divisions or outdated technologies, can stifle growth rather than enable it.

In 1931, a host of mergers in the entertainment industry were also decoupled because of economic difficulties and/or a lack of industrial synergies or technological convergence. In December 1931, Time Warner's ancestor, Warner Bros., divested its Brunswick records unit and the related "radio, phonograph and recording interests" it had purchased in April 1930 after abandoning its own Vitaphone sound-on-disc technology.[2] Less than six months later, Paramount, suffering from a severe decline in its own stock price, was similarly forced to sell back its 49 percent share in CBS to the network for $5.5 million.[3] In so doing, Paramount lost its ability to leverage CBS to promote its films, theaters, and its Famous Music–published songs. It is worth remembering, of course, that Paramount and CBS were later converged and diverged again by Viacom, a corporation owned by Sumner Redstone of National Amusements. Warner Bros., despite selling Brunswick, would later become one of the largest music publishing and recording companies in the world. Rather than seeing convergence and divergence as separate entities, we can more properly understand their competing logics in an interplay of technological, industrial, and cultural exchanges that ebb and flow over time.

In 1931, Harry Warner was not the only mogul feeling the urge to diverge. The same technological developments that fostered the entertainment industry's convergence in the 1920s had altered film and film exhibition in ways that now frustrated Roxy. He had always sought to converge media technologies and hybridize entertainment, but with hermetically sealed motion pictures delivered to his theaters with sound effects and music already embedded, Roxy began to see the future of entertainment diverging in two vastly different directions. During the transition to sound, the Roxy Theatre orchestra imbued those still-silent films with music. The advent of synchronous sound films created competing entertainments with both film and live performances offering sound, image, music, and songs. In Roxy's view, the future of mass entertainment would be both convergent (industrial synergies for film, radio, television, and music) and divergent (with separate venues for film and live performance).

'30 ROCK

In December 1929, as the Rockefeller Center project moved from the conceptual to the logistical, the Metropolitan Opera told John D. Rockefeller that the group would not be moving to the new Rockefeller Center complex, despite numerous negotiations between Rockefeller and the opera company. RCA chairman Owen Young began looking for an impresario who could shepherd alternative but still high-class entertainment to the proposed theaters. He immediately thought of Roxy.[4] Journalist Jack Banner would later place these events in slightly different order. In his 1934 account, Banner wrote that it was Roxy who approached David Sarnoff and RCA when he decided to exit the Roxy Theatre. "And it was Sarnoff who first planted the seed of Radio City in Roxy's brain," Banner added. "Sarnoff always had a high regard for Roxy, and when Roxy told him that he was finished with the Fox Film interests and Lubin, Sarnoff immediately offered him an advisory berth in the erection of Radio City."[5] Roxy's ascension to the board of RCA's new music publishing division, Radio Music Company, in December 1929 was the likely first step in bringing him into the RCA/Rockefeller Center fold (see Chapter 7).

The Sarnoff-Rothafel relationship went back much further. The two had known each other since at least 1924 when Sarnoff, then vice president of RCA, attempted to lure Roxy and His Gang away from WEAF, then owned by AT&T, and to RCA's burgeoning network.[6] Less than two years later, RCA purchased WEAF and made it the flagship of one of NBC's two radio networks. For the next five years, Roxy and His Gang's Monday evening broadcasts and the *Roxy Stroll* broadcasts on Sunday mornings over NBC-Blue were some of the network's most important programs and aided NBC's popularity in its struggle against the upstart CBS. Roxy's stardom and his unparalleled reputation as a showman were apparent to Radio Music Company board members Merlyn Aylesworth, president of NBC, Hiram Abrams, president of RKO, and David Sarnoff, executive vice president of RCA.[7] No other exhibitor, besides Major Bowes, then a vice president of Loew's/MGM, could manage the needs of the Rockefeller Center project in integrating performance, motion pictures, broadcasting, and music.

It was Owen Young who eventually brought Roxy together with Sarnoff, Aylesworth, Brown, and, most importantly, Nelson Rockefeller, to discuss the entertainment possibilities at Rockefeller Center after their opera house initiative failed. Roxy spoke to the group about the need to entertain "the modern American" with "diversified entertainment." Rockefeller subsequently approved Roxy's idea of replacing the proposed opera house with a 7,500-seat variety theater and four additional venues for "legitimate drama, musical comedy, concerts and talking motion pictures," all of which would be, according to the *New York Times*, "designed as the eventual base for the entertainment of the United States."[8] As the project progressed, Roxy took "a leading part in the discussions which led to the formulation of the plan."[9]

The *Christian Science Monitor* reported that television was to be "the keystone of this new enterprise," with NBC possibly televising the stage and radio entertainment Roxy produced in his five new theaters or in the numerous broadcasting studios to be built throughout the complex.

> Assuming that within three years these first units of the Rockefeller amusement center are ready for use by the Radio Corporation of America through [NBC] . . . television may have developed to the point where it can be used to distribute to a thousand theaters, simultaneously the sights and sounds of the entertainments Roxy is to assemble in his newest and biggest theater. . . . Operating in such a center, it would be possible to give concerts for the entertainment of listeners within the range of seventy-five radiocasting stations that are now frequently hooked up on single programs. The overhead of the theater proper would be met by its paid admissions, and the returns from the sale of the radiocasts to advertisers would be enormous.[10]

Paley and Zukor had imagined the possibilities of television during their 1929 Paramount-CBS union, but Roxy, Aylesworth, Sarnoff, and Brown seemed even more intent on making it a reality. The *Dallas Morning News* was fed the same spin. Television at Rockefeller Center, the *News* reported in February 1930, "would have its first tryout on a large scale and the relation between talking pictures, radio and television would be made closer."[11] Rockefeller Center would not only create a national entertainment center and studio, filling NBC radio and television and RKO theater pipelines, it would also amalgamate these disparate forms and allow stars, music, and performances to cross over from one medium to the next. Roxy later noted, "No matter what the march of progress brings—radio, television or whatnot—I am certain they will all tend to increase the public cacapity [*sic*] for aimiliating [*sic*] entertainment in general."[12]

The union of Roxy and Rockefeller, two of the most well-known names in American life, was commented upon often by North American newspapers over the next two years as journalists dreamed of what America's most celebrated showman could do with Rockefeller (and RCA/NBC/RKO) resources. The *Toronto Daily Star* observed in 1930 that

> Rockefeller and Roxy are a promising outfit. What they miss nobody else is likely to supply. On with the show. We are not living in an old world, but one so new that its very super-variety threatens to become a monotony of standardization. When the whole of America gets its music and other things distributed from a central heating system . . . controlled by Roxy and Rockefeller, the average individualistic actor and producer and musician might as well go to sleep along with Rip Van Winkle.[13]

Expectations for the Roxy Theatre had been astronomical in the mid-1920s, but few construction projects or cultural venues received more ink in the early 1930s than the theaters under development at Rockefeller Center. RCA, NBC, RKO, and the Rockefellers needed a mogul who could keep the press's attention on the positive elements of this massive project and not on the possible folly of building a multimillion-dollar business and entertainment center in Manhattan during the nadir of the Depression.

In the end, Roxy, RKO, and the Rockefellers settled on two entertainment venues—one larger venue for live performances *only*, a severe break from Roxy's past ideology, and another smaller venue for (primarily) motion pictures. Building two new theaters at Rockefeller Center would prove to be a far more colossal project than the Roxy Theatre. The times had changed, the industry had changed, and, more importantly, the coming of sound to motion pictures had altered Roxy's ability to exert as much influence over the films he presented. He may have been able to frame them with elaborate unitary texts, but sound motion pictures no longer needed (or expected) his editing or musical accompaniment. Film had been standardized through synchronous sound and arrived at the Roxy Theatre and other movie houses with dialogue, effects, and music already wedded. With his control over film narrative largely disabled, his creativity in motion picture exhibition was more limited. He was already far more passionate about music and broadcasting. "Talkies" simply encouraged Roxy to channel his efforts even more into his stage shows and broadcasts.

From 1908 to 1928, Roxy had been at the forefront of technological change and adoption in film exhibition and broadcasting. By spring 1931, though, when Roxy finally exited his contract with Fox and the Roxy Theatre, he had become a conservative nostalgist, repeating his time-worn broadcasting methods and his exhibition policies without noticing that more than the calendar had changed. His on-air variety show was no longer the only one of its kind, and, after nine years, it showed signs of age. Other exhibitors reduced their overhead and began booking headliners instead of prologues, but Roxy had stuck with much of the same stage show/film programming he had presented for well over a decade. It was, in fact, the blueprint for his new film theater.

In response to the dialogue-heavy films of the era, Roxy made up his mind to separate motion pictures—now prepackaged and largely unalterable by commercial first-run exhibitors—from live entertainment. As early as June 1930, his vision of the future of film exhibition had *not* included a mélange of live and recorded entertainment. The exhibitor who had been most responsible for promoting the creation of a blended unitary text, the balanced program in an evening's entertainment, no longer imagined film and live performance together. He told a group of Universal salesmen that

> the day of merging the so-called presentation idea with the picture is past, and that the pictures will be able to stand on their own. I think you are going to have purely a motion picture entertainment without any other form of entertainment that may go with it. I am firmly convinced that that is coming, especially as the universal thing. . . . I think the theatre of tomorrow will not be as large but more luxurious and confined entirely to motion pictures, as far as you are concerned. I think, on the other hand, that entertainment is coming back, and very strongly in another form. I think that variety, that is, vaudeville, in a much finer way will have a tremendous field in the next five years. So, there will be two distinct fields of entertainment, the motion picture on the one side, and rehabilitation of what is known as variety, but in a much greater and different form.[14]

Roxy's idea of two distinct theaters for two distinct entertainment forms would eventually come to pass. His estimation of variety, though, would be disastrously wrong.

Roxy and His Gang Tour (Again)

Roxy's departure from his eponymous theater was greeted with the same sentiments that occurred after his departure from the Lyric in Minneapolis nearly two decades earlier. He was presented with a bronze statuette titled "Romance" by the 100,000 women of the New York City Federation of Women's Clubs, awarded to "the person who has done most to advance the cause of music in the city." Roxy noted that despite the excitement of his new Rockefeller Center project, "This day has made me feel humble and a little sad for the scene I am leaving." Roxy was also feted with an elaborate breakfast in his Roxy Theatre offices by Walter Damrosch, Nathaniel Shilkret, Dimitri Tiomkin, and many other figures from the art, music, and film worlds.[15]

RCA, having filched Roxy from Fox, intended to fully market its new asset and funded an eighty-city tour for Roxy and His Gang that began with a show before three thousand fans at the Mecca Temple in Manhattan on February 9, 1931. The Gang traveled next to White Plains (New York), Providence (Rhode Island), Duluth (Minnesota), Atlanta, and a host of other venues throughout the country. The tour was, for the first time, truly national and aimed at building a larger audience for Roxy's radio and theatrical shows and reinforcing the importance of the Roxy brand.[16]

These concerts typically benefited various charities; Roxy and His Gang performed in Springfield, Massachusetts, for instance, for the Shriner's Hospital for Crippled Children on February 11. The following day, he and the Gang (a touring group of seventy) performed at two charity concerts in Hartford's Bushnell Memorial Hall.[17] After their evening performance, Roxy and His Gang were invited guests at Roxy's Night Club (no relation) in East Hartford.[18] The Gang made additional appearances in cities such as Miami, Chicago, Toronto, Washington, Dallas, and Houston.[19] Roxy and His Gang also traveled to Stillwater, Minnesota, where Roxy led the Stillwater Band and was celebrated as a local hero. A parade was held in his honor, along with a luncheon at the Lowell Inn where he was welcomed by the mayor and others.[20] The Stillwater newspaper later recalled, "Grey-haired men, whose shoes he had blacked when he was a boy looked up with admiration at this home town boy who had made good in a big way."[21]

The RKO Roxy Theatre and the Roxy Brand

Roxy and His Gang returned to New York in late March after strengthening the Roxy brand name, bringing new attention and listeners to his NBC broadcasts, and spurring a host of articles detailing the parameters of both the new International Music Hall at Rockefeller Center as a venue exclusively for variety performances and the RKO Roxy Theatre as a new motion picture theater. But Roxy's visit to Hartford, where he visited Roxy's Night Club after the show, demonstrated one of the most misunderstood aspects of his career. He may have been one of the era's most innovative marketers, but he was a generally underwhelming businessman. The problem of trademark had long been an issue with Roxy's famous nickname, but there is little evidence that he made any great effort to stop its use by a host of establishments in the years after his first radio broadcasts. In 1927, the Fox-owned Roxy Theatres Corporation—not Roxy—filed a motion to restrain Roxy Theatre, Inc., in Easton, Pennsylvania, from using the name "Roxy" for their theater. At the time, Roxy was supposedly in the process of trademarking his name and was advised to file a protest with the United States Patent Office. (A search of the patent office records has thus far turned up no such filing.) By then, several theaters not owned by or affiliated with Roxy had appropriated his name.[22] There were already many other offenders across the country, such as a Roxy Shoe Cleaning Parlor, a Roxy Delicatessen, a Roxy barber shop, and a Roxy gas station.[23] Two years later, the trademark issue was still unresolved. By then, the *Hartford Courant* noted, there were forty-five different establishments using the Roxy name, including the Roxy Radio Shop and the Roxy Song Shop—none of which paid a dime for its use.[24]

The problem extended overseas as well as the Roxy name became global and increasingly disconnected from its source. Roxy-brand cigarettes, for instance, did not pay Roxy for the use of his name, though they profited from its ubiquity. "You look for a better radio this year than last," read a 1932 Roxy Cigarettes advertisement in the *Toronto Star*, one day after the opening of the Music Hall. "You should expect a BETTER Cigarette . . . Now you have it . . . the new Roxy."[25] By 1930, there were already sixty Roxy cinemas in Europe and additional Roxys in China, Japan, Panama, Argentina, and Indonesia.[26] (A 2012 global search on the movie theater website Cinema Treasures reveals more than 250 cinemas that have used that name, including Roxy Theatres/Cinemas in Ghana, Mexico, Malta, Morocco, New Zealand, and China.)[27]

Roxy's laissez-faire attitude about the hundreds of theaters and other establishments that used his name without paying any license fees created a brand confusion that has continued to this day. The fact that he rarely litigated such cases seems strange in retrospect given his comments in 1930 about his belief in customer identification and branded "institutions." "I believe an institutional name is more valuable than anything else we have in this industry," Roxy told a Universal sales convention. "I believe that is what we need to obtain the greatest measure of success. After all, this is not a sprint, it is a marathon. You must build up the institution so that when they come and see your trademark, it will mean a certain quality, and they will go blindly to the theatre to see the picture."[28] That "quality" or "equity" in the Roxy name may have led some to "go blindly" to any theater bearing his nickname, an industrial mark that RKO and the Rockefellers hoped to exploit. Part of Roxy's exit agreement with the original Roxy Theatre was that the old theater would retain his brand name, but that he could continue to use it, according to the *Dallas Morning News*, "on any venture in which he may be interested, providing a distinguishing appendix, such as 'new' or 'own' is added."[29] The parameters of that tenuous agreement would become the subject of much consternation in the years to come.

Roxy and RKO Vaudeville

RKO president Hiram Abrams formally announced Roxy's role at Rockefeller Center on April 9, 1931. Brown noted that Roxy's management of the theatrical side of the Center was made in concert with RKO's renewed emphasis on the "increasing vogue of vaudeville and stage in-the-flesh performances." He told the *New York Times*, "R. K. O. has always maintained its belief that many of its patrons enjoy this form of entertainment and, accordingly, has maintained leadership in vaudeville production."[30]

The following month, the *Dallas Morning News* reported that RKO vaudeville in Texas had ceased for the summer as the company's vaudeville production underwent "a regeneration at the hands of Samuel Lionel Rothafel." Roxy, the *News* reported, "is now ace man with RKO" and its famed Palace Theater "will be turned over to Roxy immediately for the fashioning of vaudeville acts into a new kind of presentation" that would appear "for the Southern circuit about Aug. 15."[31] Len S. Brown, RKO's southern division manager, opposed the "restoration" of vaudeville in the chain's southern theaters, though. Brown wanted motion pictures; Roxy wanted a return to big-time vaudeville with eight acts, twice a day.[32] Instead of looking forward, Roxy and RKO were inexplicably returning to the past.

"Good Night and God Bless You" in Soviet Russia

Roxy ventured to Europe once again in fall 1931 to look for inspiration and talent to fill his forthcoming productions at the Music Hall (and perhaps throughout the RKO circuit). The trip was his most audacious yet and reflected his growing international esteem and *Zelig*-esque capabilities. His first stop was in London, where he visited the BBC studios and apparently annoyed local radio executives with his bluster and his "method of working."[33]

The next stop—in Germany to study local theaters—proved more successful and united Roxy with a man with whom he had frequently been compared, Max Reinhardt, who gave Roxy and his staff a tour of the Grosses Schauspielhaus in Berlin. Roxy also took a tour of the architecture and design of the new Witzleben studios of the German national radio (later an integral part of the Nazi propaganda machinery).[34] Roxy's name and work were well known throughout motion picture, broadcasting, and theatrical circles in Europe by 1931, and he was feted at a luncheon in Berlin on October 1 that was attended by "150 notables of the German theatre, film and radio world," including Director Wallauer of the German Actors' Guild and Dr. Walther Plugge of the film producers' organization. Roxy reasserted his passion for German films— as long as they were "dramatic enough to be understood without words."[35]

Roxy traveled next to Moscow for a five-day visit where he met with Constantin Stanislavski, no doubt discussing acting and method, and visited a number of constructivist theater clubs.[36] Roxy also visited the Kremlin where a troupe of Russian soldiers paraded in his honor. "I have never seen finer specimens of young manhood, or better equipped soldiers than those boys," Roxy remarked, always a fan of military regimen. "They sang as they marched and their singing was the equal of the best choral singing I have heard."[37] Roxy may have derived even greater pleasure when he was invited to broadcast a show to millions of Russian radio listeners (accompanied by a translator). Roxy treated the broadcast like any other and began with "Moscow—'Hello Everybody.'" When the program was finished, he gave his typical benediction to the communist nation, "Good night, Pleasant Dreams, God bless you," which, the *Newark Advocate and Tribune* reported, was translated into Russian.[38] It may seem hard to believe, even with Stalin's outreach to the West, that a United States Marine Corps reservist and former American propagandist would have been allowed to broadcast these messages in 1931 Moscow, but Roxy had a way of showing up in places one might not expect. He had known almost every American president since 1917, including Woodrow Wilson, Calvin Coolidge, and Herbert Hoover. Traveling to Moscow may have seemed routine.

Despite the generosity of his Soviet hosts, Roxy was not at all complimentary about his visit. "In Russia everything teems with propaganda and when propaganda walks in, art walks out," he observed. "It is now up to America to keep alive the ballet, because in its native land, it, too, is being ruined by

propaganda." He did praise "German and Russian movies," however, which he noted were "far superior to America's. They handle the camera better. They use less talk and more music and sound effects. Without knowing the language one can enjoy their movies."[39] But, overall, he told the *New York Times*, the Soviet Union was an artistic gulag:

> I spent only five days in Moscow, and my impressions are therefore only psychological. But I did notice in a very short time that I was beginning to suffer from the anesthesia that seemed to afflict the run of the people. I did not know what day of the week it was. Perhaps that is because there is no Sunday in Russia. I don't believe that one person in a thousand knew what day of the week it was. . . . The opera was mediocre. The ballet, the artistic shrine of Russia, was not as good as ours. . . . The people impressed me as a lot of children being led. Where, they didn't know.[40]

As always, Roxy returned to the United States more convinced of his political and artistic patriotism than ever. He told *Woman's Home Companion* after his return:

> We have been overhumble in our attitude to much that bears the stamp of antiquity; I believe that obsequiousness and a distinctly American form of ancestor worship have frequently taken the place of sound critical taste and judgment. I am not denying the debt we owe to the culture of European backgrounds but at the same time it is my opinion that we have reached the point where Europe, in the field of popular entertainment and popular presentation, at least, can learn something from us. . . . The man of little means in this country gets vastly more out of life than his brother abroad. He is not starved for good music and entertainment. For a small sum of money—no more, by comparison, than the European earns and spends—he hears the best and sees the best the world can offer.

By 1931, some European exhibitors, such as Sidney Bernstein of the (British) Granada Theatres circuit, had already replicated American methods after visiting the United States or copied the exhibition standards of American-run movie palaces like the Empire or Plaza cinemas in London, operated by Loew's/MGM and Paramount, respectively. Brazilian exhibitor/distributor Francisco Serrador had also traveled to the United States in the 1920s and was heavily influenced by Roxy's methods for the prologues, which appeared in Brazil's largest movie palaces in Rio de Janeiro.[41] Others, like Ufa, had hired

American exhibition personnel such as Erno Rapee to manage local cinemas. Roxy noted that during his trip he saw evidence of his own (and Rapee's) influences:

> I should be extremely stupid if I said they could teach us nothing but I should be even more stupid if I did not realize that we could teach them and have taught them a great deal. The lighting and stage technique that we perfected in the Roxy Theater on Broadway I found duplicated over and over again in foreign capitals. It was we who were the creators of that, they the followers. . . . Not only in this field have we taken the lead. People who want to hear good symphony music and jazz know that America today has the best orchestras; people who want to see excellent popular entertainment at prices within the reach of all know it is to be found here. . . . Radio City will be a nucleus of all the theater arts, both in development and expression, its schools and stages combining what we have learned from the past and what we can give to the future.[42]

Each of Roxy's prognostications and boastful statements merely ratcheted up the expectations of theatrical entertainers and journalists on both sides of the Atlantic for what lay ahead at Rockefeller Center. Roxy had met Reinhardt and Stanislavski, seen the Russian ballet and the German theater, and toured Russian, British, and German broadcasting operations and returned with scant praise. Surely, many reasoned, Radio City Music Hall and the RKO Roxy Theatre would be better than anything before accomplished in the United States or in Europe.

Roxy also returned from Europe even more determined than ever to include "grand opera" in Radio City's repertoire. If the Metropolitan Opera company could not be convinced to move to the new hall, then some other operatic group would do.[43] Roxy and Rockefeller continued to reach out to Otto Kahn to no avail. *Time* suggested that the directors of the Metropolitan Opera, including Kahn, were so frustrated by the "conservative, practical policies" of impresario Giulio Gatti-Casazza that they might have been waiting for his contract to expire in 1935 when they could "appoint some such character as Samuel ('Roxy') Rothafel to take his job. That meant surely a company reorganized and moved to Radio City."[44] But a move in 1935 would not solve the theater's immediate needs. Rumors soon spread that representatives of John D. Rockefeller and Roxy had tried to lure the Philadelphia Grand Opera instead. Roxy held a dinner party in his home for William C. Hammer, general manager of the Philadelphia opera, but no deal was made.[45] Radio City aspired to be a high-culture venue, but to the old cultural guard, with men like Roxy and companies like RKO, it may not have been high enough.

THE INTERNATIONAL MUSIC HALL DEVELOPS

By 1932, the Great Depression and its psychological effect on the country had worsened. After weathering the crisis reasonably well at first, the film industry had begun to feel the effects. Nicholas Schenck told *Film Daily Year Book* readers, "There is nothing in this business which good pictures cannot cure."[46] Schenck and other exhibitors reluctantly instituted lower prices, double features, giveaways, and other promotions to entice audiences. For Roxy, however, the question "How much does it cost?" was never asked, even during the Depression. Instead, he always wanted to know "How good is it going to be?" Touring Europe and spending the Rockefellers' money, Roxy was full of excitement over his latest project and entirely missed the sentiment of the times. "If you offer the best entertainment in town," he told the *New Movie Magazine* in February 1932, "you can name your own price."[47] He either didn't know or didn't care that many of his devoted fans could no longer afford a ticket to his forthcoming theaters.

The ability to "name your own price" also meant attracting a new kind of patron. Roxy had built his career on serving the lower and middle classes, but he now wanted to present his work at the International (later Radio City) Music Hall to the middle and upper classes—not the masses. It was a curious change and anathema to everything he had previously advocated. He commented not only on the decline in the quality of films but also "the change in the quality of the spectators" as well.[48] His new Music Hall, he decided, would attract a more upscale crowd, while his smaller RKO Roxy Theatre would entertain the masses with motion pictures. "During the next twelve months, motion pictures and stage shows will gradually become so separated that in 1933 few theaters will have combination programs as their policy," Roxy opined in the 1932 *Film Daily Year Book*.

> There is a tremendous future for the motion picture and a still greater outlook for "flesh" presentations, but together they are becoming a thing of the past. Radio City is to have separate theaters for both forms of entertainment. The gross business possible in our international music hall will far exceed what we thought possible for the Roxy when it was in the

course of construction. . . . Radio City is my one great thought and its out-
look for the coming year, and many years to come, is most promising.[49]

Roxy was resolute in his desire to split these once-allied forms of entertainment. "The policy of the motion picture theatre in Radio Centre [sic] is for
it to be divorced entirely from stage presentations," he told the Toronto Daily
Star. "Henceforward pictures and human entertainment have no place on the
same stage before the same audience."[50] Nor did motion pictures look like
the sure bet they had been for two decades. As Barron's later reported, the
major film companies would soon suffer "the worst summer in their history."[51]
Roxy's signature mix of live and filmed performance was no longer embraced
by one of its chief pioneers and promulgators.

Roxy's tastes also grew increasingly conservative with age, and he continued to ignore the new generation's wants and concerns. The "GI Generation,"
which would weather the Depression, fight in World War II, and colonize
America's postwar rural and suburban landscapes, had not grown up during
the heyday of variety and may not have been as attracted to "grand opera."
But Roxy wasn't catering to that group at Radio City. "The great mass of the
theater-going audience in America, perhaps in all countries, lies between the
ages of thirty-five and sixty," Roxy noted.

> It consists of mature people, solid people, men and women who have al-
> ready planted the roots of responsibility in their lives, people with homes
> and children, burdens and cares. . . . These are the people who recognize
> staleness much sooner than youth does and who at the same time are
> aware of the charm of the old and familiar. The good showman has a vast
> amount of respect for this audience.[52]

This audience, however, was the past and present of the entertainment business, not its future. This older group, full of "solid people," may have savored
their dollars more frugally, and it was their children—now teenagers and
young adults—who often sought theaters for social interaction, romantic rendezvous, or escape from long workdays or unemployment. Movie houses that
offered inexpensive entertainment proved most attractive during the Depression. Why Roxy sought this older crowd remains inexplicable, though they
were more likely to crave variety shows over motion pictures. The vaudeville
industry had suffered a fatal blow in the late 1920s, but Roxy was determined,
against all evidence, to resurrect it at Radio City Music Hall. In retrospect, this
passion for variety also made little industrial sense for RKO given its efforts at

this time to become a major film studio. Roxy was determined, though, and his supporters backed him. It was full speed ahead.

Europe and Radio Again

Roxy resumed scouting talent and looking for new ideas in 1932. He sailed on yet another trip to Europe with producer Martin Beck on May 5 in search of "variety material" for RKO and Radio City. The two men set up permanent offices in Europe for their respective productions to continue recruitment of talent even after the cessation of their tour.[53] Roxy now seemed almost entirely focused on live performance rather than film. While in England, he spoke at the First International Summer School of Dance in Buxton and upon his return to the United States presented a lecture at Columbia University on the "present-day theatre" for a course on contemporary literature.[54]

Roxy had also taken a break from broadcasting to focus on planning his new theaters. A fan, Olive Van Horn, wrote a poem to Roxy in January 1932, imploring him to come back on the air to provide comfort to his listeners, now struggling with unemployment, hunger, and uncertainty.

> Come back to us Roxy, come back to us soon;
> And give us your music that was a real boon;
> Tell us hard times are over, fair weather ahead;
> That the storm clouds are broken.
> Depression is Dead.[55]

Roxy did make sporadic radio appearances that year, directing the General Motors orchestra for a tribute to Minnesota and directing Erno Rapee's orchestra on NBC in June for a broadcast performance of the "Roxy March."[56] Otherwise, he remained largely off the air.

RKO, meanwhile, continued to tinker with its upcoming emphasis on variety. Terry Turner, in charge of national exploitation for RKO, sounded a cautionary note about Roxy's desire to bring in opera and more high-class entertainment. A poll of RKO exhibitors revealed that in New York, at least, "The general opinion seemed to be that a personal anybody, whether he told jokes or danced his head off, was the piece de resistance." In addition, circuit managers noted that rather than opera stars and ballerinas, audiences (according to a *Syracuse Herald* report) wanted "Picture stars, radio entities, musical comedy names, established vaudeville features, magicians, 'flash' acrobatic acts, noted comedians and dancers." Roxy countered Turner's report by noting that "any attempt to tailor bills to meet the demands of audiences is the bunk."[57] Turner was overruled.

Roxy's vision for RKO vaudeville was to have far greater influence on the "entire RKO circuit" and not just upon Radio City, the *Dallas Morning News* reported. Charles Koerner, southern division manager for RKO Theaters, traveled to New York in October 1932 to meet with RKO executives and with Roxy in order to better prepare "to book what Roxy will develop in the world's largest and most complete variety theater. Within six weeks after these attractions play in New York they will be available for the Majestic in Dallas and other theaters [in San Antonio and Houston] of the territory."[58] Radio City Music Hall would not only set the course for variety in New York but also curate the programming of innumerable RKO theaters. That, at least, was the plan.

GREAT EXPECTATIONS

As the opening of Radio City Music Hall and the RKO Roxy Theatre neared, pressure mounted inside the two art deco theaters. In addition to his own need to top every theater he had ever opened in New York, Roxy was also under immense public scrutiny. Critic Gilbert Seldes noted that with Roxy's decision to make Radio City Music Hall a venue for variety only, "What is done there will either energize or stultify entertainment in America for a generation."[59] Others, including Roxy, saw Radio City as a ray of hope in an otherwise dismal economic and social climate. He noted in August 1932:

> Many people have remarked that the activity and bustle about Radio City in Rockefeller Center is a definite inspiration in the center of a big metropolis—a sort of example to all the world to forge ahead and get busy. In this same sense it strikes us that Radio City, when completed, will be a beacon light to the entire industry. Even as one astounding picture from any producer serves to help the entire fraternity, so Radio City will act as a stimulus to the entire nation and will help lift [it] out of the doldrums of depression. It will automatically broadcast a sincerity of purpose—a message of faith and optimism. Radio City will be a challenge and an inspiration, not only to our industry, but to all industries, to move forward and onward.[60]

Across the city and around the nation, the Rockefeller Center project became a topic of conversation and an endless source of newspaper journalism.

Roxy and His Gang returned to the air on November 13, broadcasting for the first time from Rockefeller Center.[61] Roxy presented an hour of entertainment featuring the Music Hall's future "singers, actors and artists" along with music from Erno Rapee's new symphony orchestra.[62] The broadcast was not innovative but simply a return to form. Roxy also reached out to his growing international audience, as the show was rebroadcast in Germany and "heard around the world on a shortwave pickup."[63]

The first radio broadcast was roundly criticized by *Forum and Century* critic Cyrus Fisher, who wrote ominously, "I hope this lumbering carryall is not an example of the work of the geniuses who are going to make Radio City a place of creative delight and immortal glory. . . . Grand opera is brought down to the comprehension of the masses." Despite the criticism, Fisher still envisioned the opening of the new theaters as an opportunity to bring back the excitement of the recent past. "He is the last rose of all those worthies who flowered during the golden showers of '28 and '29," Fisher said of Roxy. "Alone he has been transplanted to the tender gardens of Radio City, where it is hoped he will start a whole new growth of beauties."[64]

In November and December, Roxy stepped up his publicity campaign. Daniel Okrent writes that as the theater took shape, "Touring journalists from the popular press were shepherded through the unfinished Music Hall and the RKO Roxy, dazzled with details of the lavish spending, enticed with glimpses of the vast auditorium spaces, regaled with assertions of grand accomplishments." As he had for the Roxy Theatre before its debut, Roxy "was now operating in three modes: publicist, producer, and construction foreman." Okrent observed:

> He was superb in the first capacity, unmatched in the second, and—well, whatever common touch he had was now long past, and his communications with the workmen were at best strained. While his friend Nelson Rockefeller, son of the world's richest man, could spend a lunch hour sharing sandwiches with carpenters or electricians sitting on a beam out in the sun, Roxy had attained a grandiosity that threatened to separate him from the very people who comprised his audience. . . . He might still know the name of everybody who worked for him, but he expected them to hold the door for him whenever he passed by. Inspecting the construction, he'd pick his way through oceans of plaster and forests of scaffolding, his chauffeur following at a "respectful distance," remembered Louis Bouche, "carrying [Roxy's] lap robe."[65]

Most of Radio City's key employees were familiar with Roxy's dual role as taskmaster and father figure. Erno Rapee, associate conductors Charles Previn and Joseph Littau, all of whom served under him at the Roxy Theatre, came to Rockefeller Center to work at one of the two new theaters.[66] Maurice Baron, who had also worked at the Roxy, served as one of Radio City's associate composers and arrangers. Lew White returned as staff organist. Leo Russotto, an integral part of the Roxy Theatre radio broadcasts, moved to Radio City to oversee Roxy's radio broadcasts there.[67] "On the creative side," Okrent writes, "almost the entire core of the Roxy Theatre's staff jumped to the Music Hall," including associate producer Leon Leonidoff, ballet mistress Florence Rogge, costume department head Hattie Rogge (Florence Rogge's sister), as well as lighting engineer Eugene Braun. "So complete was Roxy's raid on his old operation that even Anna Beckerle, the nurse who had run the Roxy infirmary, came over to the Music Hall, where she would preside over cuts and sprains and fainting spells for the next thirty-five years."[68] Many of the Roxy Theatre's accountants and Roxy's longtime secretary, Leah Klar, also migrated. Art Smith, who had been with Roxy since the Regent Theatre in 1913, was hired as chief projectionist at Radio City;[69] Charles Griswold, who had been with Roxy since the Rialto, and was according to Okrent, "the General Pershing of the usher corps," moved to Radio City from the Roxy; and former employee Sydney Goldman became assistant theater manager. The latter two also "brought a platoon of ushers with them."[70] One of the only elements from the Roxy not (yet) at Radio City by the end of November was Russell Markert and his Roxyettes. Two weeks later, they were at Radio City, expanded to forty-eight dancers, and part of the upcoming show.[71]

Some of these veterans may have desired to be part of New York's newest theatrical showcase. Some may have wanted to work for Roxy again. Others may have simply realized that the Rockefeller Center theaters were the best gig in town. The Roxy Theatre, for instance, was now more unstable than ever. Fox Film Corporation had already lost control of the Roxy Theatre Corporation by April 18, 1932, when Class A stockholders assumed control of the board of directors after failing to receive their dividends.[72] The upheaval that resulted forced many of the stage performers and musicians out of the Roxy. The new president of the Roxy Theatres Corporation, Harry G. Kosch, hired Hugo Riesenfeld in late April to assemble a smaller, eighty-piece orchestra to bring large-scale concerts back to the theater.[73] One month later, the Roxy Theatre fell into receivership after defaulting on its mortgage payment.[74] Job stability at the Roxy and other venues was precarious. Radio City and the RKO Roxy looked like much safer bets.[75]

There may have been a more talented group of musicians, dancers, art directors, stage managers, singers, conductors, and other performers in the United States, but none seemed to outmatch the array of talent assembled for Radio City Music Hall and the RKO Roxy. "If you measure an executive by the quality of the people he hires," Okrent writes, "Roxy was nonpareil."[76] Journalist Jack Banner confirmed that Roxy's talent scouting and taste were unsurpassed:

> Two of his finds have crashed the well-nigh impregnable portals of the Metropolitan Opera Company—Frederick Jaegel and Edith Fleischer. Evelyn Herbert has become a musical comedy star; Eugene Ormandy, one of his assistants, is now a noted symphony director; Billy Akst [sic], another assistant, is head man of the Metro-Goldwyn-Mayer music department, and Yasha Bunchuk and Erno Rapee are leading orchestra directors. This is an imposing list of talent discovery; a list unmatched thus far in radio annals.[77]

With so much talent still in house, Roxy began trying to cram it all into Radio City's opening night. The *New York Times* noted in late November that the first show was already overstuffed with appearances by Martha Graham and Harold Kreutzberg, "leaders in the modern dance movement; Vera Schwartz, contralto, who has sung in Berlin and Vienna; and the Tuskegee Negro Choir."[78] Even here, most of Radio City's featured attractions were not new to Roxy or his previous audiences. The Roxyettes were certainly well known by then, five years after their debut in New York and seven years after their founding by Russell Markert. Martha Graham's booking was also more of a reunion than an avant-garde selection. Graham had been part of Roxy shows at the California Theatre in Los Angeles nearly thirteen years earlier as part of the Denishawn dance company.[79] Some of the vaudeville artists he later assembled for the show were also seasoned, though fading, names.

Roxy's plans for Radio City included a permanent ballet corps and chorus, each with one hundred members or more, and a dancing troupe of forty-eight women. Roxy imagined the opening show as a "pageant of the entire theatre," that included jazz, opera, "circus numbers," and "dramatic sketches," and one that "exclude[ed] motion pictures, which will be presented at the other large theatre in the Rockefeller Center development." The cost of the show would be enormous, but Roxy planned to reduce overhead by keeping each program in place for four weeks rather than one (or more) as he had at the Roxy. Two performances daily with top prices of $2.50 would keep the theater firmly in the black—as long as audiences were steady.[80] But how many could afford to go regularly?

Roxy traveled to Washington, D.C. in early December and formally invited President Hoover to the opening of Radio City Music Hall. The two men met on the south lawn of the White House and smiled for photographers.[81] The photographs captured both key figures of the 1920s on seemingly different career trajectories. Hoover had just lost the 1932 presidential election. Hoover was on the way out, while Roxy appeared to be on the way up.

"To the Hands of Roxy!"

What those cameras may have failed to capture was the frailty of both subjects. Despite his stoic appearance, Roxy had suffered a series of ailments over the past two years and had been hospitalized in 1931 after a mild heart attack.[82] In March 1932, the *Stillwater Gazette* reported that Roxy had undergone surgery, for which he had "declined to disclose the nature of the operation."[83] Preparations and rehearsals for Radio City Music Hall and the RKO Roxy Theatre, despite his health problems, remained as grueling as ever. Weeks before opening, Roxy was diagnosed with severe exhaustion and acute prostatitis. A private nurse accompanied him throughout each day of planning and rehearsals, enabling him to suffer through the pain.[84] His urologist ordered him to go a hospital "right away," but Roxy refused.[85] As his condition worsened, he wanted to postpone the opening, "but that," he noted later, "did not prove practical."[86]

Instead, Roxy ratcheted up expectations even more with a series of dramatic advertisements. Radio City's December 21 ad in the *New York Times* featured the following debut attractions:

> Spectacular Stage Shows . . . Twice Daily Glorious parade of stage talent . . . Eminent artists from every phase of the theatre . . . Spectacle, music, dance, drama, comedy, minstrelsy, variety . . . Company of 1000 . . . Miracles of lighting and stagecraft . . . New standards of comfort and luxury . . . New thrills, beauty, glamorous splendor . . . The dazzling climax of two years of preparation. . . . Dr. Rockwell, Ray Bolger, Weber and Fields, Taylor Holmes, DeWolf Hopper, Sisters of the Skillet . . . Titta Ruffo, Vera Schwartz, Coe Glade, Caroline Andrews, Harold Van Duzee, Otto Fassell, John Pierce, Jeannie Lang . . . Orchestra of 90, Chorus of 100, famous Tuskegee Choir of 110 . . . Harold Kreutzberg and his ballet, Martha Graham and

her group, Patricia Bowman, premier danseuse; Ballet Corps of 80; Russell Markert's dancers, the 48 Roxyettes; Berry Brothers, Cherry and June Preisser . . . Frederick Lewis, the Wallenda Troupe, Four Bronetts, Kikuta Japs, countless novelties.[87]

Douglas Haskell wrote in *The Nation* that Roxy's claims over the artistic direction of the entire theater and its presentations demonstrated his disregard for reality. The famous proscenium of Radio City Music Hall, often thought to be Roxy's inspiration while sailing to Europe, was actually part of the auditorium's design six months before Roxy began working for the Rockefellers. Haskell remarked sarcastically, "Roxy has one advantage over God. He can apparently work backwards or forwards. He would not hesitate to create something that was already there."[88]

Radio City's December 23, 1932, advertisement in the *New York Times* profiled the theater's workers and their devotion "To The Hands of 'ROXY.'" Roxy wrote to his patrons:

> We believe that nothing approaching the Radio City Theatres has ever been given to the entertainment world. . . . Into this crowning work of my life I have poured the best that I have learned in 25 years of theatrical experience. With the cooperation of Mr. Aylesworth and his associates; Mr. Rockefeller and his associates; the architects, builders and artisans who aided in this vast enterprise, we have achieved a magnitude and splendor heretofore undreamed of in the theatre. . . . The same inviting atmosphere which you have come to know in other theatres directed by me—the same spirit of service and courtesy—will here be evident always. . . . In this spirit we bid you welcome to 'The Entertainment Center of the World.'[89]

In the final days leading up to Radio City's debut, the *New York Times* examined the aspirations of Roxy and his army of talent in setting the course for the 1930s. The description alone gave a sense of the ambition and the clutter of Roxy's new show:

> At the Radio City Music Hall Roxy hopes to originate a new type of variety and to build his entire bill from it without the assistance of any motion pictures whatsoever. He interprets variety not in the older sense, but much more broadly, more—if one may use the word—modernly. Variety to Roxy means not only acrobats, comic singers, blackface comedians, jazz bands, clowns, dance acts and sketches, but also classical ballet,

the modern dance in terms of Harold Kreutzberg and Martha Graham, choirs, symphonic music and opera. He believes that this material ought to be staged in the grand manner, regardless of whether it is a clown act, an oratorio or a bit of opera.[90]

This mélange of variety acts, despite the dancers, hardly conjures up the word "modernly," but it may have been in their presentation that Roxy hoped to make them all palatable and contemporary. As a list, it seems to be a taxonomy of the past.

While the acts may not have been entirely new, the venue proved enormously influential to the sound design of contemporary theaters. Emily Thompson's research on the changing soundscape after 1933 illuminates the many ways in which Radio City was at the forefront of new theater acoustic design that focused on sound absorption, rather than on sound reverberation. Mimicking more closely the aural properties of sound in new movie theaters and the sound of radio in the home, reverberation was passé in theater architecture with the dismissal of theater orchestras. Despite the fact that Radio City was designed to be a live performance theater, by 1933, Thompson notes, reverberation "now became just another kind of noise, unnecessary and best eliminated." Unlike the cavernous and reverberant Roxy Theatre of 1927, Radio City would be "clear, direct, and nonreverberant" as well as "efficient," technologically proficient in a way that "demonstrated man's technical mastery over his physical environment," and commoditized as a packaged sound that was part of a new, modern aesthetic. Although Radio City, Thompson notes, sought to become a combination symphony hall/opera house/vaudeville theater and "celebrate th[at] soundscape," it instead "signaled the end of this period of [acoustic] change" that had been developed from 1900 to 1933. Radio City Music Hall's live acts did not rely on the acoustic properties of the theater to transmit their sound, which was captured instead by stage microphones, much like synchronous sound motion pictures transmitted through speakers.[91] The lack of sound reverberation was intended to aid Roxy's efforts to create intimacy in a theater with 5,960 seats. Instead of enormous balconies, Roxy built tiers that did not obstruct the view of those below. Instead of sound reverberation, Roxy amplified the sound of his performers and aimed it at his audience. Reverberation reinforced the size of palatial theaters. Targeted, nonreverberant sound was aimed at individuals, not at a mass audience.

The RKO Roxy Theatre was similarly appointed and designed. Like the Music Hall, there was an air of spacious intimacy throughout and no overhanging balconies obscuring patrons' views. Roxy had initially planned to make the RKO Roxy the first pure movie house with "entirely cinema entertainment," but found that "conditions of the industry didn't warrant it." As with his former Roxy and Capitol theaters, "stage entertainments" would still supplement the films. Much of the staff for Radio City Music Hall served double duty and worked for the RKO Roxy as well: Robert Edmond Jones was its art director, Leon Leonidoff ran the production department, Erno Rapee was the theater's musical director, Martha Graham was "in charge of the modern dancing," and Russell Markert produced the Roxyette performances. Roxy, as always, asserted his right to refuse RKO product, continuing a career-long insistence on reviewing and approving each film. He proudly noted that "RKO will not force us to run their pictures if we don't like them."[92] From all appearances, Roxy seemed to have the free rein he desired.

Nearly every one of Roxy's elaborate openings, from the Alhambra in Milwaukee in 1911 to the Roxy Theatre in 1927, had been met with glowing approval. He *and* the entertainment world expected nothing less than perfection. Roxy's medical condition, though, had worsened and, he would later argue, limited his ability to produce effectively. "With that show, sick as I was," Roxy told the *New York Herald Tribune*, "there wasn't a chance to really get it whipped into shape, but I stuck with it night and day, with doctors and nurses in constant attendance; I wouldn't let my associates down."[93] Illness may have played a part, but it also seemed to provide a tidy excuse.

Unfortunately for Roxy, RKO, the Rockefellers, and every other party involved, Radio City's opening night on December 27, 1932, was a critical disaster. After rain and traffic delayed the start of the show by more than an hour, a restless crowd sat through one colossal bomb after another. Brooks Atkinson noted, "The opening performance lasted from 8:30 until 2:30 the next morning, and neither Roxy nor vaudeville ever recovered from that brutal avalanche of fun."[94] The *Toronto Daily Star* was equally merciless, dubbing Radio City a "gigantic" failure and noting that "Nothing quite so blasting to the show business in any country equals the supreme flop of the new Radio City enterprise."[95] The *Literary Digest* remarked that the show was "in many ways, a program of the National Broadcasting Company," but "unlike the wireless, you can't turn it off when you are bored."[96] Roxy, the *New Republic* wrote, assembled "a job lot of vaudeville turns which . . . do not add up into a vaudeville program, and they bored the first few audiences stiff. The net effect was of a series of movie 'prologues,' one after the other."[97] Unlike his shows at the Roxy and the Capitol, these attractions did not frame some large capstone entertainment nor provide any cohesive thematic flavor. They simply added scale and volume to the show. It was big, massive, gaudy—and completely wrong for the time.

The morning after Radio City's debut, Roxy returned to Rockefeller Center to oversee the following night's debut of the RKO Roxy. The second premiere was uneventful. "I stuck it out until both the Music Hall and the RKO Roxy had opened," he recalled two months later. "Then they took me out of the theater on a stretcher. I want to tell you I am a pretty sick man. I had four doctors and four nurses and they stayed up all night with me two nights. There were blood givers there ready all the time."[98] After the opening, Roxy reentered the hospital for surgery and a long recuperation.

In forty-eight hours, everything Roxy had worked for since 1930 was ripped apart by the press and slashed by RKO. The RKO Roxy Theatre would, for the moment, remain relatively unchanged, but Radio City Music Hall, as Roxy had conceived it, would only last another week. The much anticipated resurrection of vaudeville did not come to pass; if anything, the disastrous failure of Radio City Music Hall was variety's gurgling death rattle. *Motion Picture Herald* would comment two years later that after Radio City's disastrous debut "there remained nothing to do about vaudeville but write the obituary."[99] It was also, though few realized it at the time, the figurative death of Roxy's career and stature.

RADIO CITY CHANGES ITS POLICY

The public response to Radio City's entertainment was not uniformly positive, but contemporary accounts differ wildly as to the theater's actual drawing prowess. *Time*, which dubbed the entertainment enterprise "Rothafeller Center," noted that Radio City Music Hall's nut (its overhead) was $85,000 per week. This was merely the base weekly cost of running the theater. The massive production budgets, including payments for temporary acts, costumes, sets, and numerous other expenses, made this number much higher. Thus, while the *Wall Street Journal* reported on January 6, 1933, that the Music Hall had grossed $112,000 in its first week, Roxy's spending and production extravaganzas came close to matching the amount of its first week of revenue. Radio City Music Hall as a variety house was an unsustainable dream.[100] Exact figures are unknown, but the *Toronto Daily Star* noted at the time that it was "No wonder Roxy went to the hospital. . . . A loss of $100,000 in one week is enough to start any sanitarium."[101]

Days after its opening, Radio City Music Hall announced a change in policy effective Wednesday, January 11, in which the theater would become a more conventional "vaudeville-motion picture theater."[102] Roxy was apparently not consulted on the programming switch, as *The Bee* in Danville, Virginia, noted that Merlyn Aylesworth "planned to confer today [January 5, 1933] with Roxy, who has been ill for several days, on the policy changes."[103] Once more, Roxy had opened a theater only to see his position within the corporate hierarchy diminished after a few days. This latest alteration would prove far more difficult for Roxy than Fox's acquisition of the Roxy Theatre nearly six years earlier. After the change, the RKO Roxy Theatre became superfluous, a condition that only worsened in the ensuing years. There were reports that the smaller theater would be devoted to stage plays or even close, but no such move was made.[104] RKO now had two enormous theaters featuring live and filmed entertainment to program and not enough of its own films to spread around. To fill in the gaps, the two theaters began exhibiting films distributed by Fox, Universal, and Columbia as well.[105] (The ability to play Fox films was made possible by John D. Rockefeller, Jr., one of the largest shareholders in Chase National Bank that "indirectly controlled" Fox Film Corporation during its economic difficulties.)[106]

Aylesworth also reduced Radio City's admission prices, which ranged from 99 cents to $2.50 per ticket,[107] in order to "place admission within reach of every one."[108] Tickets were lowered to 35 cents from 11:30 A.M. to 1:00 P.M., 55 cents from 1:00 to 6:00, 75 cents from 6:00 to 10:30, and 55 cents for shows after 10:30 P.M.[109] "We discovered once more that entire families who had come with great anticipation were being turned away," Aylesworth told the *New York Times*.[110] Roxy, after a quarter-century of managing theaters that catered to the lower and middle classes, had inexplicably abandoned his reliance on these groups at the very moment in which they were growing. Two dollars and fifty cents may have been possible for some during the heady 1920s, but those prices were largely unaffordable during the nadir of the Depression.

Roxy's staff did not universally embrace these programmatic changes. Robert Jones resigned on January 9, 1933, arguing that the loss of much of the theater's live entertainment would cause a significant reduction in his work. Others left with him, frustrated by the changes Aylesworth and RKO had instituted without Roxy's approval. Two associate musical conductors and an associate ballet master, whose roles were now diminished with the reduction in live entertainment, also quit. Clark Robinson, whom Roxy worked with at the Capitol and Roxy Theatres, took over Jones's position.[111]

Roxy had not yet recovered from his surgery, but he was already planning the stage show that would accompany *The Bitter Tea of General Yen* (1933), working with his staff from his hospital bed.[112] The first performance of the new film and stage policy at Radio City on January 11, 1933, was a return to old practices. Mordaunt Hall of the *New York Times* remarked, unsurprisingly, that the live entertainment that accompanied *The Bitter Tea of General Yen* "cannot be said to be very different from other exhibitions of singing and dancing offered by Mr. Rothafel."[113] In the end, Roxy had worked two and a half years just to reinstitute the same Roxy Theatre–style entertainment in an auditorium with forty more seats.

There was considerable consternation between Roxy and RKO in the weeks that followed the policy change. On January 18, the *Dallas Morning News* began printing rumors that RKO and Roxy had severed their connection.[114] *New York Daily News* columnist Ben Gross asked RKO management about Roxy's health after the operation and "got quickly shushed."[115] Roxy was persona non grata at RKO and Rockefeller Center, the fall guy for one of the most debated entertainment ventures of the 1930s. He would later describe those months of professional isolation and physical recovery as "dreary" and "pain-wracked."[116]

Most devastating to Roxy was that his professional reputation was not enough to counter these attacks. Rumors that he had been fired, that he was too ill to work, and that he had made up his illness to cover his professional embarrassment wreaked havoc on his already fragile psyche (and ego). Roxy, once lauded and adored by a fawning press, was subject to the worst ridicule of his career. "If ever a man was kicked when he was down, that man was Roxy Rothafel!" Jack Jamison later wrote in *Radio Guide*. "At one moment, here was a man at the top of his trade. All the great names of Broadway flashed across his path. Famous men and beautiful women surrounded him. He created a new vogue in stage entertainment. He created star after star. . . . The next moment he was a failure and an outcast, walking in the echo of bitter, mocking laughter."[117] Roxy lashed out at his critics and the rumors that circulated throughout New York and the entertainment world in a lengthy screed to the *Herald Tribune*:

I'll be back in April, after a trip South, and go to work. That ought to settle all this stuff that is going around about me. Oh, I've heard the things they have been saying. They're all wolves, this Broadway crowd. They're glad when somebody who has always stood for something constructive in the theater stubs his toe. While I was flat on my back they were circulating

rumors that I was "out" at Radio City, that I wasn't sick at all—just stall-
ing. . . . I'm sick of it. These sophisticated, worldly wise, narrow-faced,
sharp-eyed low-lifes that hang around Broadway! I used to like to walk
down Broadway in the old days. Now I never walk there when I can help
myself. I feel like I ought to go home and take a bath when I do. The whole
street exists by shots in the arm of excitement, filthy scandals, and jealous
rumors.[118]

Roxy still felt compelled to explain the disastrous opening night, accepting
little responsibility for his role in setting expectations for the theater(s) too
high. "What did they think I was—a miracle man, a demi-god? That's silly. We
all make mistakes. I'm human. I make mistakes, too." He added that despite
all of the scorn for his initial variety show, he had "foreseen from the start that
it would be impossible to maintain a vaudeville policy at the Music Hall, but
that it would have to be run as a picture theater," conceding, finally, "The time
was not right to try to ask a $2.50 top."[119] It is impossible to know whether
Roxy was merely covering his professional backside or if he had intended all
along to lower prices and introduce films to Radio City. There is no evidence
to suggest that he intended to do either. He acknowledged that Radio City
"was a failure at the first," but he was unwilling to concede that he had grossly
miscalculated and remained convinced that vaudeville would be "revived over
the country" and would be "bigger and better vaudeville" than ever before.[120]

The theaters may have been a financial mess, another difficulty for the
beleaguered RKO, but they were exceedingly popular with audiences, with
677,000 people attending shows at Radio City Music Hall and at the RKO
Roxy in their first four weeks of operation.[121] That news was tempered, however, by RKO's filing for receivership in late January 1933.[122] The entertainment industry was suffering, with Paramount, Fox, and RKO all experiencing
severe economic and corporate issues. Roxy, meanwhile, continued his con-
valescence away from Rockefeller Center and RKO's financial difficulties for
the next two and a half months. He traveled a great deal and met with RKO
executives in Dallas in late March where Charles Koerner of RKO hosted a
dinner for him with other exhibitors.[123] A photograph of a tanned, relaxed
Roxy appeared in the *Dallas Morning News* in late March with the headline,
"Seems to Be Little Wrong With This Invalid."[124] He also appeared on local
radio station WFAA to give "a brief talk."[125] Roxy traveled next with his doctor,
Joseph McCarthy, to San Antonio, Corpus Christi, and into Mexico, playing
golf in each location, before a trip to Hot Springs, Arkansas, and a return to
New York in April.[126]

Roxy Returns to Rockefeller Center

Roxy finally returned to his managerial duties at Radio City Music Hall and the RKO Roxy Theatre on May 1, 1933.[127] Six days later, Roxy and His Gang went back on the air as well.[128] Though his reputation and professional stature had suffered, Roxy's theatrical and radio audiences still looked to him for entertainment and solace during the Depression. A listener sent the following tale of woe to Roxy:

> Sunday morn for the world, just another day for me, just another day too many! To live another day—only to die a thousand deaths. Just tired in body and sick in mind and spirit by the buffeting of the last five years and trying so hard to "keep shin up" as Roxy advises for the sake of others. . . . This morning seemed more unendurable than usual, what with hounding by collectors and lawyers and sheriffs. After a life time of what the world considers a moderate success. Fate. Bitter irony. So bitter. So hard to carry on. And then the voice of Roxy. Balm of Gilead! . . . Your music, Roxy was going to millions, but coming just to me, just to me. . . . I do want to listen again, next week, and hear, hear that still, small voice back of Roxy's music, bidding me to go on.[129]

Radio remained one of Roxy's most important activities each week, the one area of his professional life where he still had nearly unfettered control. As he had done at the Capitol and Roxy theaters, Roxy also integrated the Gang into Radio City's stage shows. The Gang's appearance on stage at Radio City in mid-July drew "thousands of their fans" who "fill[ed] the big theatre to see their favorites in person." In addition to veterans like Gladys Rice, Patricia Bowman, "Wee Willie" Robyn, Mickey McKee, Harold Van Duzee, and Frank Moulan, new members Jan Peerce and Ross Graham were also on the bill.[130]

In late June, Clark Robinson had resigned and a new art director, "Victor Menille," according to the *New York Times*, replaced him. "The strain of producing so many shows, week after week, is very great," Roxy told the newspaper, "Also we like to give all the outstanding designers a chance."[131] Robinson's twenty-seven-year-old replacement—*Vincente Minnelli*—became "the youngest man to ever hold such a responsible position in the theatre world," according to house organ *Radio City News*.[132] Minnelli began his career at the Chicago Theatre for Balaban & Katz as a costume designer. He later moved to New York and worked at the Paramount Theatre in Manhattan producing costumes for the larger Paramount theater circuit. Minnelli also began

designing sets for Paramount films shot in the nearby Astoria studios. When
Paramount cancelled its expensive national stage shows in lieu of headliners
and big bands, Minnelli was suddenly unemployed.[133] Radio City snatched
him up. Roxy and Minnelli had a contentious relationship, according to
Emanuel Levy: "The egomaniacal Roxy was notorious for his rambunctious
nature and fault-finding; nothing was good enough for him. As a result, Minnelli, his youngest and most defenseless employee, became an easy target for
Roxy's caustic barbs."[134] *The New Movie Magazine* reported in 1932, before
the theaters opened, that Roxy had already become increasingly "egotistical,"
"dominant and aggressive," but was still "a wizard at organization" who was
"fully aware of the value of man-power when properly directed."[135] It took
many months, but Roxy eventually recognized that the future film director
was a gifted member of his production team. "You know," Roxy noted in December 1933, "I've been picking on this fellow, but all that picking brought
good results. He's an artist." "From then on," Levy writes, "Minnelli's relationship with Roxy was cordial. Though it was a painful way to whip Minnelli into
shape, it had proved effective. Roxy's abrasiveness pushed Minnelli to creative
heights he didn't even know he was capable of."[136]

Health concerns did not stop Roxy's laborious rehearsals. Several hundred members of Radio City assembled each week on the top floor of the
Music Hall where Roxy sat at a table with "his chief lieutenants," Leonidoff,
in charge of productions, Rapee, head of music, and, now, Vincente Minnelli, in charge of stage design and costume creation, to design the lavish
productions for each week's performances. When the meetings and dress
rehearsals were over, Roxy comforted his "children": "That's all, kids. Keep
up the good work."[137]

Backstage, life at Radio City Music Hall, despite the appearance of normal-
ity, was increasingly difficult for everyone, especially Roxy. RKO had cut his
salary in half upon his return in May, and major decisions were now subject
to approval by a committee. Roxy had always required absolute independence
and became enormously frustrated by the constraints. Daniel Okrent writes
that Roxy "did not like this, and behaved just as one might expect, throwing
tantrums and loudly proclaiming his indispensability. He brutalized his creative team, belittled their work, and repeatedly threatened to quit."[138] Inside
Radio City, *Radio Guide* later reported, the air became choked with "quarrel-
ing and dissatisfaction."[139] The growing strain was apparent in a letter Roxy
penned to NBC president Merlyn Aylesworth protesting Radio City's new
reserved-seat policy. Roxy attacked the move as the decision of the inexperi-
enced and a reflection of his professional isolation within Rockefeller Center.

"I would like very much to get together with you some time and cry on your shoulder," Roxy wrote Aylesworth. "I need a little something to kind of 'pep' me up. You and Rex are about the only two guys that I seem to get much from, and I cannot find Rex. I guess I'm nuts! Anyway, I'm still functioning."[140] The strain only grew worse over time.

"It's the Roxy and I'm Roxy" Revisited

In 1931, the *Brisbane Courier* in Australia wrote that "The name 'Roxy' is familiar enough to every one interested in the pictures, but it is not generally known that it has no legal standing. It was adopted by Samuel L. Rothafel, who is now taking steps to have it legalized. He is going before the courts to ask that they make it his own."[141] Despite his famous nickname's notoriety on the radio and in theatrical circles, Roxy had never trademarked the name. He did not do so in 1931 either. The launch of the RKO Roxy Theatre, the old Roxy Theatre argued, complicated its efforts to retain its audience during the Depression. Despite the earlier agreement between the Roxy Theatres Corporation and RKO in which both sides could use the Roxy name for different theaters, the original Roxy Theatre sued RKO claiming that the RKO Roxy was creating brand confusion by not strictly using the "new" designation. Between 1932 and 1933, the two sides exchanged alternating victories in separate courts.[142]

In September 1933, RKO informed Roxy that it had "abandoned" their legal fight; the RKO Roxy Theatre was to be renamed the RKO Center Theatre.[143] Roxy did not give up. He took his case to the United States Supreme Court in an attempt to overturn an earlier Second Circuit of Appeals decision, but the court refused to hear the case, delivering a final win to the original Roxy Theatre.[144] It was another in a series of personal and professional losses that year. Roxy had now effectively lost the right to use his own nickname, his famous brand, on any other theatrical venture in New York City. He had spent more than a decade building an enormous amount of equity in the name "Roxy," but he had failed to protect his most important asset.

The Yom Kippur War of 1933

Despite the growing financial restrictions, Roxy did not cut back dramatically on the size of his shows, just the quantity. In early September, he presented a "spectacular entertainment of dancing, singing and thrilling features" that was, a Radio City Music Hall ad bellowed, "created by 'ROXY' and presented by a cast of 500 artists."[145] In November, Roxy told his radio listeners that a recent Leonidoff and Rogge–produced stage show was so elaborate that he was "Sorry we haven't television enough yet to show you this."[146] The unitary text was still paramount to Roxy, as a Radio City Music Hall press release noted that the "spectacular" stage show for *Little Women* (1933) "surrounds" the film with a "beautiful atmospheric prologue."[147]

Roxy's decades-old mixture of secular entertainment and religious and cultural reverence also reached its artistic height in 1933. Though the fall and winter would come and go without much fanfare, more than three-quarters of a century later one of Radio City's holiday-themed stage shows remains one of the most celebrated American theatrical spectacles and the most visible expression of secularized Christian pageantry. By contrast, Roxy's work on Jewish-themed material demonstrated the fissures that remain even today between America's secular Jewry and its still-observant members.[148]

Jan Peerce, who would become a nationally revered radio and opera singer in the decades ahead, was conscripted by Roxy to star in the theatrical observance of the Jewish High Holy Days, Yom Kippur and Rosh Hashanah. In late summer 1933, Roxy called Peerce into his office and laid out his vision for his boldest High Holy Day–themed presentation. Peerce was thrilled and Roxy promised him two full weeks of performing. There was one catch, however: Roxy wanted the Orthodox Peerce to sing *during* the holidays. Peerce refused the assignment. Roxy subsequently pounded on his desk and, as Peerce recalled four decades later, "rose from it and towered over it and me—no small feat for a rather small man." Roxy "displayed a cruel side of his nature that I'd heard about, but seldom seen," Peerce recalled. Roxy roared: "Whaddya mean, you don't work! First of all, this is *more* than work. Second of all, you'll be creating something finer than any cantor in any synagogue can do. The people who don't go to the synagogue will come to the theatre and hear you sing the *Kol Nidre* and you'll reach them in a way the synagogue couldn't." Peerce demurred once again. The two volleyed back and forth before Roxy delivered an ultimatum: "Now, what would you say if I told you that if you don't do this, you will never sing in this theatre again?" Peerce was unmoved and Roxy was speechless. After several minutes of silence, in which Roxy could apparently mount no convincing argument, Peerce asked if he could leave. "Roxy just nodded."[149] Later that day, Roxy summoned Peerce and was greeted, once again, by three minutes of silence. Finally, Roxy asked Peerce to sit down. "I owe you an apology," Roxy began. "I misbehaved. I said things I shouldn't have said. I threatened you when I shouldn't have."[150] Roxy, after all, was just as resolute about long-standing principles.

Roxy eventually commemorated the High Holy Days season with "a special arrangement of famous 'Hebrew Themes', played by Erno Rapee and the Symphony Orchestra and sung by Roxy and His Gang favorite, Willie Robyn, and the Choral Ensemble."[151] The elaborate show lasted two weeks. During a time of increasing concern for Jews in Germany, Roxy's country of origin, the show may have fulfilled a personal function for the secular Roxy and may have constituted another sign of his growing Jewish (cultural) consciousness.[152] Roxy was already keenly aware of events transpiring in Europe whose far-reaching consequences for Jews few at the time could imagine. He told a journalist from the *Toronto Daily Star*, Frank Chamberlain, that he had become gravely concerned about the increasing signs of totalitarianism and anti-Semitism in Germany. Chamberlain noted that their conversation "drifted toward Hitler":

> Roxy, a Jew himself, deplored conditions in Germany to-day. "If such a state of affairs is permitted to go on any longer, it will mean the beginning of the end of things," he said sorrowfully. "I try to understand Hitler's attitude, but I cannot condone his methods. The big nations of the world, Britain, France, the United States, must stand together to see that civilization doesn't topple over."[153]

On November 29, 1933, Roxy produced and emceed an enormous fundraising concert held on behalf of the American Jewish Joint Distribution Committee, American Jewish Congress, and the Hebrew Immigrant Aid Society, with proceeds donated "for the relief of distressed Germany Jewry." Roxy's entertainment included a mixture of the secular and the religious, with performances by George Jessel, Molly Picon, and a soloist made famous at the Roxy, James Melton. There were also "Jewish Pageant Dancers," fencing bouts, radio stars, opera singers, the Yiddish Art Quartet, and more than a dozen other acts. Roxy's flair for quantity was certainly on display. There were also four major set pieces. Two months after performing "Kol Nidre" (in place of Jan Peerce) at Radio City, Willie Robyn repeated his presentation of the hymn along with eight other performers. The show finally concluded with a "Chassedic Temple Dance and Song," featuring Jack Kurtz, and a "Dance of the Commandments." The show reflected Roxy's unique (and sometimes bizarre) melding of religious and/or biblical themes and his affection for theatrical spectacle. The entertainment committee of the relief effort noted that Roxy pulled much of its talent from Brooklyn's Fox and Paramount theaters (and not Radio City).[154] Roxy's many Jewish presentations are scarcely remembered today, but they were important moments of mass exposure to Jewish culture, even if tempered by commerce, artistry, and ego.

RADIO CITY CHRISTMAS SPECTACULAR

If the subject of Roxy and religion, or Roxy and religious celebration, is discussed today, it is most often in connection with what is known internationally as "Radio City's Christmas Spectacular," a descendant of Roxy's (and Leonidoff and Markert's) holiday-themed presentation that was featured there in December 1933. Roxy presented the RKO musical *Flying Down to Rio* (1933), the Walt Disney "Silly Symphony" *The Night Before Christmas* (1933), the return of Maria Gambarelli in Leo Delibes's ballet *Coppelia*, the Roxyettes performing "In a Christmas Tree," and the two stage extravaganzas that have been performed ever since: the "Living Nativity" and Russell Markert's "Parade of the Wooden Soldiers."[155]

The Christmas show, like many other Radio City productions that year, was largely an expansion of earlier Roxy and Leonidoff ideas. What has often been forgotten is that the "Living Nativity" and the "Parade of the Wooden Soldiers," like the staging of "Kol Nidre" during the High Holy Days, were not original to Radio City but were repeating holiday attractions developed at earlier Roxy venues. "Parade of the Wooden Soldiers" was performed at the Capitol Theatre in June 1923 and staged at the Roxy in July 1928 using the Roxyettes under the same Roxy, Leonidoff, and Markert production team.[156] The "Living Nativity" was performed at least as early as Christmas 1924 at the Capitol Theatre.[157] The nativity tradition continued on at the Roxy Theatre in December 1928 and 1929.[158] Even Roxy noted that there was little new in its presentation in 1933. He wrote in the December 28, 1933, program, "Our Christmas show, now an institution of many years standing, we hope will always please you."[159] In its corporate battle with the original Roxy Theatre (and other holiday-themed performances at theaters such as the Capitol), Radio City Music Hall had a vested interest in claiming the holiday as its own in the years that followed. By promoting these well-known spectacles as holiday classics, Radio City established an evergreen holiday tradition for families to attend that imbued secular entertainment with religious significance. *Variety* noted in April 1929 that the Roxy Theatre and Roxy's holiday shows had already become an established part of the city's annual holiday celebrations:

> However perfunctory observance of holidays may be at the average pic-
> ture palace, at this super-tabernacle they never fail to commemorate the
> occasion, whatever it is, with royal munificence. Roxy's Christmas and
> Roxy's Easter, not omitting Roxy's patriotic salaams, are peculiarly and
> distinctly a New York institution, as Peter Pan belongs to London and the
> music festivals to Berlin. In this glorification of respected traditions the
> Roxy becomes something more than just a place to kill a couple of hours.
> It enters intimately into the home life of every family where there are
> children and where holidays are markings that chart the year. It's entirely
> reasonable to guess that these Roxy pageants are already becoming an
> integral part of family routine during the school recess period. And this,
> on that phoniest of all boulevards, Broadway, is a distinction.[160]

Reinstituting these Christmas pageants at Radio City was not a revelation to audiences or critics, nor was it treated that way by the press in 1933. It was simply good business.

For nearly a decade, Roxy had already made whatever movie house he operated a perfunctory holiday destination for families where art, religion, and culture could be celebrated in a quintessentially American hodge-podge. Like Jewish songwriters Irving Berlin ("White Christmas") and Mel Tormé ("The Christmas Song: Chestnuts Roasting on an Open Fire"),[161] the Jew-ish Samuel Rothafel had a significant hand in producing one of America's most iconic Christmas celebrations. "Parade of the Wooden Soldiers" and the "Living Nativity" were certainly redesigned and redeveloped at Radio City over the next seven decades, but they did not originate there in 1933. Roxy and his staff developed these Christmas spectaculars at the Capitol and Roxy long before Nelson Rockefeller had paid Columbia University a nickel for its midtown land.

TURNING OFF THE RADIO

The year 1933 was better than many had expected after the January reor-ganization. Though both theaters had reported a loss of roughly $134,000 by August 25, 1933, September's ticket sales had generated a net profit of over $90,000 before factoring in rent.[162] Radio City had also managed to admit 6,025,000 patrons following its debut a year earlier. The opening of the Roxy in 1927, with less competition and no Depression to worry about, had admitted 6,500,000 in its inaugural year. Radio City may not have been everything Roxy had hoped for, but its assessment as a failure is overly exaggerated.[163]

As 1934 began, the Music Hall and the RKO Center Theatre seemed stable. Much had changed from Roxy's initial vision, but the theaters had found an audience and a routine. A typical Music Hall press release announced on January 6, 1934, that Roxy would present "an exceptionally colorful and glamorous group of production numbers" that week.[164] Instead, and quite unexpectedly, he quit both Radio City and the RKO Center out of frustration with the micromanagement of RKO executives, his greatly reduced pay and control, and Nelson Rockefeller's lack of support.[165] Roxy's resignation was to be effective February 16, but it became more or less immediate. The *New York Times* noted that an "RKO spokesperson explained that Roxy's withdrawal was the result of criticism by his superiors" who complained about his prodigious spending on live entertainment. Other factors included critiques that his shows were "too long and that they lacked humor." His "dislike" for supervision was another problem. Leon Leonidoff, Roxy's longtime collaborator, immediately began supervising the theater's stage shows, something he would continue to do at Radio City for the next four decades.[166]

In previous years, a Roxy resignation could clear out the top ranks of a theater's production and management team. This time, however, few of his long-standing employees went with him. Vincente Minnelli noted that, despite building so many careers, "there were no drawn out tearful goodbyes."[167] It had been a difficult year for everyone, and jobs were scarce. There is some evidence to suggest that it was Roxy who simply walked out of the building and did not say good-bye to his staff. He wrote to Leonidoff on January 11, a few days after his departure:

> I am about to go away for a much needed rest. I did not want to go thru the ordeal of saying goodbye to you, because that would have been too difficult. I simply want you to know that to have been associated with you has been a wonderful experience, and while what we have accomplished is not the work of any one individual, but rather the work of all bound together by a common cause. Had we been left alone and encouraged, it could have meant but one thing – unbounded success; but it was not to be. . . . it is the further hope that in the not too distant future, we may again be associated together.[168]

Leonidoff and Roxy never worked together again. RKO attributed Roxy's departure to "failure to keep the costs of his stage spectacles within the budget limitations prescribed by the supervisory committee" and the subsequent "friction between Mr. Rothafel and the Radio City management." Roxy, not surprisingly, adamantly defended his spending practices. "The budget was at all times adhered to," he countered. "At no time were the stage shows produced in excess of the budget allowance."[169] For Roxy, there was a more fundamental issue than merely being micromanaged; he felt that his work as an artist was being constrained by finances and corporate thinking. "I had a definite idealism," Roxy complained to *Time*, "and I couldn't go back on it."[170] He told Herbert Westen of *Radioland* nearly a year later, "the cause of his split with the Music Hall was what has been called the curse of the modern age—money."

> The explanation is simple enough. It was matter of idealism—my idealism as a showman and an artist. The things I saw, others couldn't see. The things I wanted to do, they couldn't see. Those in control couldn't see the future because they put two silver dollars before their eyes where the glasses should have been. The proof is in their financial losses and the fact that the Music Hall has never reached the artistic height of the old Roxy![171]

He gave a similar explanation to *Radio Mirror*. "Because I refused to put aside my ideals, because I felt that money was of secondary importance at the time, I could not come to an agreement with the people with whom I was working. No artist can sacrifice his ideals and remain an artist," Roxy lamented. "Money, nothing, must stand in his way." The most difficult part of his departure, he added, was having to leave his radio show.[172] He signed off after his last NBC broadcast on January 14, 1934.[173] "I had to fight a prolonged battle with myself," he told *Radio Mirror*. "Roxy, in my estimation, would soon become plain Samuel Rothafel."[174]

Roxy was still convinced that his resignation would spur the Music Hall to bring him back and restore his full salary. "While I'm out," Roxy told New York's Cheese Club in mid-January, "I'll come back."[175] Roxy sent a telegram to Nelson Rockefeller in hopes of returning: "COMMAND ME IF YOU THINK IT ADVISABLE I AM AT YOUR SERVICE."[176] Rockefeller never responded. Radio City and Roxy were finished as a mutual entity. Jack Banner of *Radio Guide* dubbed the three-year escapade the biggest disappointment in Roxy's long career: "Radio City was Roxy's Waterloo."[177] The assessment was prescient.

Roxy eventually came to terms with his departure from Radio City and NBC, though his anger lingered for some time. Bitter comments were printed on both sides. By February 23, Roxy decided it was time to move on and he closed a deal with Adolph Zukor for "Roxy's Gang" to tour Paramount's largest movie houses in Manhattan, Brooklyn, Boston, Chicago, Buffalo, and elsewhere. His tours had always been for the benefit of various charities; now they were for the benefit of Roxy and Paramount. His salary for the tour was a large and tempting increase—earning between $7,500 and $15,000 per week, depending on the venue.[178] (The *Dallas Morning News* reported that Roxy's $10,000 per week fee, for example, was too much for the state's Interstate Theatres circuit.)[179]

LONDON CALLING

The Paramount tour was not scheduled to begin until the end of March 1934. Biding his time, Roxy traveled to England in early March in hopes once again of building a massive cinema in London and, more importantly, exploring new broadcasting ventures. Though Roxy was no longer working for Radio City or the National Broadcasting Company, his long association with the RCA-NBC-RKO conglomerate and its executives was far from over. In mid-1927, NBC had hoped to link up with the British Broadcasting Corporation (BBC) to inaugurate "a service of across-the-ocean broadcasting, by which London and New York would regularly exchange feature programs."[180] Seven years later, David Sarnoff, then president of RCA and "a firm friend of Roxy," sailed with him in a joint effort to seize outright control of the BBC.[181] The *Toronto Daily Star* reported that Roxy and Sarnoff went to England to "smash the B. B. C. altogether and substitute private enterprise and commercial broadcasting in Britain." Roxy and Sarnoff hoped to "inspir[e] attacks on the general director of the B. B. C., Sir John Reith, and to 'break' the B.B.C. so that American interests could assume control." Roxy did not deny these reports.[182]

When they arrived, Roxy and Sarnoff attempted to capture the BBC's charter, which terminated at the end of 1936, through "the American-controlled British electrical combine . . . [a]ided by powerful British interests." The two were so confident of their plans, the *New York Times* noted, that Roxy "intended to build a 'Radio City' in London based on the New York original." But Roxy and Sarnoff had waded knee-deep into British politics and policy. Their attack prompted Reith to formally meet with members of Parliament to "discuss the crisis in the corporation affairs." The idea of American executives acquiring the BBC may seem far-fetched in retrospect, but in 1934 not everyone in England was convinced of the public control model. "The Laborites want more government supervision and others less officialdom and more freedom," the *New York Times* reported.[183] Their move was certainly audacious, even by Roxy's standards, but if it succeeded, NBC would have control of American and British broadcasting, a new British outlet for its American programs, and a new source of content for its American networks.

Ultimately, Sarnoff and Roxy failed to pry the BBC loose as Reith fought hard to keep the network a purely British operation. In hindsight, Roxy and Sarnoff were probably not the best choices to lead such an initiative. Given the general climate of anti-Semitism in England during the 1930s, the possibility of two prominent American Jewish executives purchasing what was considered British public property was remote at best, particularly given their well-earned reputations for their tough negotiating and work styles.

The London cinema project, following the collapse of the BBC initiative, was also a nonstarter.[184] The "scheme to build a cinema and cabaret theatre near Charing Cross," the (London) *Times* reported, would "have been the biggest in Europe," but like other recent Roxy efforts, "The negotiations came to nothing" and Roxy "was greatly disappointed to have to abandon those plans."[185] Roxy was confident, however, that "there will be a Roxy theater in London"[186] and he planned to split his time between London and New York in the months to come to ensure that one or more London ventures materialized.[187] They never did.

Back in the United States, Roxy planned to become involved in one or more theatrical ventures in Florida with "land operator" Henry Doherty. Nothing came of it. Before his trip to Europe, Roxy had also met with the original Roxy Theatre's bondholders "relative to his regaining operating control of that theatre." The plan called for United Artists and/or Loew's to operate the theater, then in receivership, if Roxy were to return to his post.[188] Once more, no deal was made. In April, Roxy told *Motion Picture Herald* that his return to the original Roxy Theatre was still imminent. Herbert Lubin, Roxy's original partner, was again associated with the move to return Roxy to the Roxy. "I cannot make any sort of statement until the 'thing' is signed," Roxy told the *Herald*. "You know as well as I that something is going on and when the final arrangements are made I will talk." Howard Cullman, operating receiver of the Roxy, denied these reports throughout the year.[189]

TOURING IS PARAMOUNT

Instead, Roxy prepared for the only job for which he had a firm contract: touring Paramount's movie houses with his Gang.[190] Much of the original Gang was gainfully employed at the Capitol or Roxy theaters or at Radio City Music Hall. Maria Gambarelli, after a brief appearance at Radio City in December 1933, had begun appearing at Grauman's Chinese Theatre in Hollywood in February.[191] Douglas Stanbury did not join the tour; he was currently headlining at the Imperial Theatre in Toronto.[192] There were some familiar faces, though. Jan Peerce left Radio City to join Gang veterans Viola Philo, Beatrice Belkin, Yasha Bunchuk, Harold Van Duzee, and Willie Robyn.[193]

The twelve-week tour began in Boston at Paramount's Metropolitan Theater on March 30.[194] The *Christian Science Monitor* remarked that Roxy and His Gang were "very likely" to be "a bigger attraction to more theatergoers than the film" and their one-hour act "was greeted with prolonged applause."[195] Over the next month and a half, the Gang toured the United States,[196] completing their final appearances on May 19, 1934.[197] Though they seemed to draw steady crowds, *News-week* reported that the tour's profits were "disappointing."[198] At the Brooklyn Paramount in April, *Variety* reported that the new Gang were "of little import at this time"[199] and also made scant impact on grosses during a May appearance at the Chicago Theatre.[200] The nostalgia tour even sputtered in Minneapolis, one of the important sites of his early life and career. The agitated Roxy "ripp[ed] into the newspaper critics" in the Twin Cities "who weren't too kind" and also spoke of the city's residents "in uncomplimentary terms."[201] The tour and Roxy's career had become a mess.

Roxy next planned to make a short film starring the Gang, but no information or prints can be found for this project.[202] In June, Roxy's London plans surfaced again as he reportedly began designing a $5,000,000 theater with 5,000 seats near Trafalgar Square. "The site is superb," the *Toronto Daily Star* noted, "probably the world's best." Paramount had faced stiff resistance in 1925 in buying and leasing British theaters and the *Star* commented that it would be "a bad sequel . . . to let the head of American exhibitors loose on the theatre of the business."[203] Once again, the London project was abandoned. In August, Roxy promised to return to producing stage shows "on a scale surpassing anything he has hitherto done."[204] The *Dallas Morning News*'s report on August 30 that Roxy would soon "buy a site at [London's] Hyde Park Corner . . . for a supermovie [sic] house" again came to nothing.[205] For the first time since 1919, Roxy was unemployed.

PALEY'S COMET

Roxy spent the summer of 1934 at home and "out in the sticks, doing a little broadcasting from independent stations."[206] The fading broadcaster and exhibitor *News-week* dubbed "radio's forgotten man" finally signed a new contract with Fletcher's Castoria and CBS in mid-July for a new forty-five-minute broadcast on Saturday nights at 8:00 beginning September 15. Auditions for his new show began in late July at CBS's Radio Playhouse. *News-week* reported that Roxy was finally "his old self" again, "praising, criticizing, and shouting at the parade of would-be talent on the stage."[207]

A smaller show on the CBS network wasn't enough for Roxy. Every new theater or radio program he pitched would have to outdo his previous efforts. Instead of installing a new Gang of artists and reusing his old format, Roxy promised that his new radio show would feature "ear pictures"—aural adaptations of his "elaborate stage presentation ideas," coupled with "musical dramatizations of songs—old and new."[208] Roxy noted that these ear pictures would "stimulat[e] pictorial images conjured through the medium of sound alone." He described the remaining banter on the show as "easy informality and pleasant intimacy," what the *New York Times* noted would be an "attempt to adhere to a relaxed pace and the intimacy of a neighborhood visit."[209]

Jack Banner of *Radio Guide* provided an in-depth assessment of Roxy's continuous disappointments on the eve of his new CBS broadcast. "The past seven months," he reported after extensive interviews, "have been bitter and lonely ones for Roxy. . . . The homes of the most celebrated citizens on two continents were open to him; distinguished men and women of the arts and letters begged his company; princes, prime ministers and other lords of the upper strata extended cordial invitations to dine and to make holiday—but still Roxy brooded over the temporary loss of his seven million fans."[210] *Radioland* noted that Roxy's departure from Radio City had served neither party. The Music Hall is "still the most pretentious theater in the world," the journal noted, "but it hasn't been the same since Roxy left."[211]

Roxy's new variety show on WABC, the CBS flagship, began on September 15, 1934, and aired throughout the network, reaching a possible listening audience of more than 65,000,000.[212] *Variety* wasn't complimentary, though, commenting that "the first installment of S. L. Rothafel's program for Fletcher's Castoria was slow to the point of tedium. . . . Show is devoid of humor. That's a weakness."[213] Still, longtime friend and NBC executive John Royal congratulated him on his first show for CBS. Roxy, ever the nostalgist, responded, "It was funny, not being on NBC, but we did the best we could, and we hope of course to do better." He added, with more than a hint of sadness, "You are the only one at NBC to send me a message, and I appreciate it very much."[214] With no theater to call home, Roxy prepared his radio scripts at his fifteen-room penthouse, Apartment 16D at the Majestic Apartments on Central Park West.[215]

By November 1934, rumors circulated again that Roxy was headed back to the Roxy Theatre. The plan called for Roxy and former partner Herbert Lubin to lease the palatial theater.[216] Roxy told Herbert Westen of *Radioland* that "the deal is on for me to go back into my first love, the Roxy, sometime late this year. That's where I brought radio up to the point where it is today, and that's where I'm going on from."[217] The theater's bondholders, however, denied their efforts.[218]

His public esteem (and his radio audience) had steadily diminished in the months since he left Radio City, and the press had also stopped genuflecting and serving as his public relations arm. Westen's article in *Radioland*, for instance, eschewed the laudatory tone of past interviews. He noted that despite being the "pioneer of radio entertainment, father of all the modern radio programs, maker of stars, the man who, after ten years, ha[d] risen to the throne as the high God of Radio City," Roxy had "mysteriously disappear[ed] down some trapdoor to oblivion early this year. To me," Westen wrote, Roxy "looked like a small boy who had been spanked."[219] Roxy, without his own theater or another theatrical venture for the first time since 1908, was lost.

ROXY RETURNS TO PENNSYLVANIA

The Stanley Company of America, by 1934 a subsidiary of Warner Bros., opened its grandest Philadelphia movie palace, the 4,378-seat Mastbaum Theatre, on February 28, 1929. The theater primarily exhibited Warner Bros. feature films and offered its opening night audience a seventy-six piece orchestra, a chorus of sixty, and a ballet corps of thirty-two.[220] *Variety* described the theater's elaborate mix of entertainment as tending "toward the Roxy style."[221] The Mastbaum, though, proved to be a difficult house to fill and, by October 1929, *The American Organist* reported that the Mastbaum had yet to turn a profit.[222] The theater closed two years later on September 12, 1931, after a musicians' strike and, after reopening that December, struggled throughout 1932 until it closed once again. Stanley brought grand opera into the venue in the summer of 1933, but this programming failed to keep the theater open past September.[223] Its success was also hindered by local legislation: the Mastbaum, like other Philadelphia theaters, could only operate six days a week as motion pictures were still prohibited on Sundays.[224]

In November 1934, after the latest Roxy Theatre deal collapsed, Harry Warner announced that Roxy would take over the dormant Mastbaum.[225] The theater was leased to the Roxy-Philadelphia Corporation and subsequently renamed the Roxy-Mastbaum. The lessor, the Warner Bros.–owned Stanley Company, held a right to terminate the lease any time after February 17, 1935.[226] Roxy had less than two months to ensure its success. He removed the decorative flashing lights on the Mastbaum roof, leaving only the Mastbaum name, took down the 20th Street marquee, and stripped the marquee on Market Street leaving only the lettering board. Inside, the theater's huge dome chandelier was taken down and, according to historian Irvin Glazer, "the entire house was relamped to a brighter intensity."[227] Many in Philadelphia hoped that Roxy's name and prestige would draw an additional 100,000 to 150,000 to the area from across metropolitan Philadelphia.[228]

Much of the Roxy-Mastbaum's entertainment was a carbon copy of his Roxy and Radio City efforts. Advertisements for the revamped theater noted that its "Fascinating Stage Program" was "Conceived by Roxy and his brilliant staff" and included a "Cosmopolitan Orchestra, New Stage-craft, Ballet Moderne, Roxy's Gang, [and] Roxyettes."[229] His new corps of forty-eight Roxyettes, reclaiming the name following Radio City's transformation of the Roxyettes into the Rockettes, inaugurated the theater on Christmas Eve with his traditional Christmas pageant that included, as before, "Parade of the Wooden Soldiers."[230] Roxy proudly noted in a *Philadelphia Inquirer* advertisement that his live entertainment included 200 artists "in a stage show novel and original beyond any Roxy has ever produced." Roxy hired a new fifty-five-member orchestra, conducted by former Roxy, Fox, and Radio City employees Adolphe Kornspan, Leon Leonardi, and Yasha Bunchuk. The orchestra was also backed by a chorus of thirty.[231] The Roxy-Mastbaum reopened on December 24, 1934, featuring the Warner Bros. film *Sweet Adeline*.[232] It was the anniversary of Roxy's first film screening in Pennsylvania at the Family Theatre twenty-six years earlier.[233] Roxy's career had come full circle.[234]

The gala premiere was vintage Roxy and attended by locals in "civic, social, artistic and industrial circles." The *Philadelphia Inquirer* noted simply that the crowd comprised a "Who's Who of What's What." Philadelphia may have been far from the media spotlight, but Roxy was determined to prove that his entertainment ideas were still viable in an age of double features and economic depression. "In short," he said, "we want to make this theatre one of the great cinema theatres of the world, if not the outstanding one."[235] His lone NBC friend, John Royal, was on hand for its debut.[236]

Roxy continued his CBS broadcasts each week, but he immediately created a new local Philadelphia program to advertise his new Gang and his new theater. On January 6, 1935, he began broadcasting weekly over WCAU from 3:00 to 3:45 on Sundays, featuring "his famous orchestra, the Roxy Glee Club, Adolph Cornspan [sic], Leon Leonardi, Yacha Bunch[uk], Aminie Deloro, Alfred Seville and many others," according to the Inquirer.[237] Variety noted that Roxy had "brought to Philly the most outstanding variety show in years."[238]

Still, the Roxy-Mastbaum proved to be even less of a success than Radio City. For reasons unknown—though it may have been his need to cover the enormous overhead—Roxy repeated the same financial mistakes he made during the opening days of Radio City. He had more than 4,000 seats to fill for each show, but instead of drawing in patrons with low prices as he had done between 1908 and 1931, he charged patrons seventy-five cents for each evening ticket. These prices not only excluded the lower classes, which had made up a significant portion of his Roxy Theatre patronage and that of his other former theaters, but also made going to the Roxy-Mastbaum for an evening show an impossibility for the unemployed—a group whose ranks were still growing. The theater's opening two weeks were "definitely under expectations," Variety reported, with a gross of $38,000 and $47,000, respectively.[239] The Roxy-Mastbaum was performing poorly enough that Warner Bros. considered shifting Roxy and his staff to Warner Bros.' Hollywood Theatre in Manhattan which, also under duress, had recently closed.[240] By January 22, 1935, Variety reported that the theater was "now definitely down beyond the danger zone" with "no indication that this week will see much of a change."[241]

On January 31, Roxy finally altered his pricing policy to "bring this entertainment to this community within the reach of everybody's purse." He added that there would be "no lowering or cheapening of the standard of this theatre." Ticket prices were subsequently lowered to sixty-five cents for orchestra seats, fifty-five cents for the balcony, and between forty and fifty-five cents for morning and afternoon shows.[242] As a result, Variety reported, "business is perking."[243] The lowered prices, plus a Jack Benny appearance, generated $37,000 in early February.[244]

In mid-February, Roxy toasted (or roasted) New York in a new stage show titled "Manhattan Madness." It is hard to fully understand what his intentions may have been, but the mélange of performances depicted a suicide in a Times

Square skyscraper, a pair of Park Avenue drunks, "an East Side hurdy gurdy," an Upper West Side synagogue, "and the motely [sic] crew to be met with on Riverside Drive."[245] Depressives, drunks, street performers, and Jews—this, after twenty-two years in New York, was Roxy's vision of Manhattan. "From back-stage," Jack Jamison writes, "I saw one of the last shows he put on [at the Roxy-Mastbaum], with the remnants of his company who were loyal to him. He was still a showman. . . . Some of the spark was still there. He made you feel that each performer was a great, glamorous, exciting discovery, and that you were going to listen to a rare treat." A stagehand nodded towards Roxy as he stood in the limelight introducing his artists and remarked, "He was a good little guy while he lasted."[246]

While the theater sputtered along, CBS renewed Roxy's radio contract in late February for another six months.[247] Roxy's career seemed diminished but stable. It was not. The next day, February 23—as if he had been holding on to the theater merely to prove his vitality to CBS—Roxy announced the closure of the Roxy-Mastbaum. He privately blamed the theater's troubles on a ban placed by Cardinal Dougherty of Philadelphia on any Catholics visiting the city's movie theaters.[248] The New York Times reported that the theater had "been losing money almost since its opening." In years past, Roxy would have worked directly with Dougherty to escape such a ban. By 1935, though, Roxy's attention to political and civic details and his abilities with public outreach had slipped considerably. He came up with a different (and vague) public reason for his decision to close the theater, announcing that he had to "give up all personal activity in Philadelphia until the Fall of the year. Certain developments in connection with prior obligations make it impossible for me to be constantly present here, and . . . I cannot success-fully supervise the theatre under my own name from a distance, even if it is only 100 miles."[249]

The last performance at the Roxy-Mastbaum was held on March 2 and Roxy seemed resolute to try it all again. "I believe I have learned to under-stand just what Philadelphia likes in the way of combined stage and screen entertainment," he told the Inquirer, "and while I leave with regret and feel distressed at having to disband the loyal, efficient and able organization which came together under my supervision, I look forward with hope and pleasure to the idea of resuming in the fall."[250] Roxy never returned to the Mastbaum and the theater withered for the next decade. (In 1942, Boxoffice reported that, "Except for a concert and a convention, the big deluxer's doors haven't been opened since Samuel L. 'Roxy' Rothafel tried to take the Mastbaum out of the red more than eight years ago.")[251] The Mastbaum, to quote Jerry Stagg, was a true "jinx house."

Rumors circulated in the press that Roxy had personally lost upwards of $200,000 in the theater, though he claimed that figure was "a lot of apple sauce." He later admitted, however, that he had lost roughly $30,000 in the venture.[252] The financial loss may have been the reason he moved from the Majestic Apartments to a suite in the Hotel Gotham a few months later and placed many of his and Rosa's belongings in storage.[253] The *Dallas Morning News* noted that with the exception of his CBS show "Roxy now has no job and has published no plans."[254]

"On the Outside Looking In"

Sometime between April and May 1935, Roxy suffered another heart attack, but word never reached the press.[255] In May, he sued RKO for more than $214,000, claiming that he had been paid only half of what he had been promised in his contract for Radio City Music Hall and the RKO Roxy Theatre.[256] He continued working on his CBS radio show and on behalf of Jewish causes, a personal interest that seemed to coincide with Hitler's rise in Germany. In June 1935, Roxy produced "special units" for the June Night Frolic at Yankee Stadium to aid the Jewish National Fund as it raised money to build a refuge in Palestine for those fleeing Europe.[257]

In August, one of the last few vestiges of the influence Roxy had once had on motion picture presentation vanished when Major Bowes announced that the Capitol Theatre had officially dropped its stage shows. The Palace and Radio City Music Hall were now the only two theaters in the Times Square area with a stage show/film policy.[258]

In September, his CBS contract ended and Roxy was even more isolated from the entertainment business. He wrote to Aylesworth shortly before his contract ended with CBS: "You know I am a sentimental sort of cuss and I know you will understand when I say to you that it hurts like hell to be on the outside looking in, and that, regardless of what anyone may say or think, the old N. B. C. and even before that the old W. E. A. F. are very near and dear to me and no-one can ever take their place."[259] Two months later, NBC began working on a Roxy radio show tie-up with Frigidaire, but no deal was concluded.[260] The *New York Times* reported that the new show would have begun airing during the winter of 1935.[261] Instead, Roxy joined an advisory

committee for WPA projects that included Walter Damrosch, George Gershwin, and Paul Whiteman.[262]

The year 1935, like 1934, had been an unrelenting string of personal, medical, and professional setbacks. Radio City Music Hall had begun to prosper
without him, and his closest professional rival, Major Bowes, had become the
new king of radio with his weekly broadcasts from the Capitol Theatre and
his new "Amateur Hour" program, which earned him a salary well in excess
of $1 million per year and was the top-rated broadcast of 1935.[263] A front-
page *Variety* headline that September dubbed Bowes show business's new
"No. 1 Money Man," with "one of the largest weekly incomes in the United
States,"[264] while the *Christian Science Monitor* observed that 1935 "would be
remembered as 'Major Bowes' year."[265] From 1908 to 1932, Roxy had experienced unparalleled success; the three years that followed were riddled with
defeats as he, unlike Bowes, failed to innovate his radio shows or his theatrical ventures.

THE NEXT CHAPTER

The start of 1936, however, provided Roxy with a new set of opportunities.
Suddenly, it seemed, he was back in demand. NBC and CBS both began eye-
ing radio projects for him, while the original Roxy Theatre finally seemed
ready to welcome him back as managing director, this time with Paramount
assuming operation of the financially troubled theater.[266] The *New York American* noted that in addition to a new radio show, Roxy was planning to take
over management of not one but possibly two Broadway theaters.[267]

On January 2, radio producer Nellie Revell sent NBC's John Royal a letter
after hearing that NBC wanted Roxy back on the network.[268] "I heard you say
you were looking for an idea for Roxy, and I have one," she wrote, outlining
her plans for a show titled *Roxy's Rendezvous,* a variety show in which Roxy
would introduce famous guests before they performed on the air. "I have
thought of little else for two days, and I believe I have a wow," Revell added.
"If it is worth anything to you, you are welcome to it. I don't even want to
work on it. I don't even want to write it, because Roxy wouldn't stick to a
script anyhow. . . . I think this is a honey."[269] The next day, NBC executive D.
S. Tuthill also wrote to John Royal regarding a tenth anniversary program at
NBC: "At this meeting I suggested the name of Roxy as a logical personality
to present these old time radio stars to the microphone, I pointed out that
no radio program going on the air, proposing to present a parade of radio

artists who had helped to make radio, would be complete without Roxy, who probably had had as much to do with early broadcast programs as anybody in the business. This suggestion met with general approval, and it was then I discussed the matter with Roxy, who has, and is, most enthusiastic about the idea."[270]

CBS also continued to pursue Roxy for a new program, *Roxy's Professionals,* which would air on Sunday evenings at 8:00, his old, coveted time slot. NBC countered with yet another show, *Roxy Comes A-Calling,* which would feature Roxy emceeing a broadcast with "stars of the stage and screen."[271] Not surprisingly, Roxy chose NBC due to his long relationship with Royal, Sarnoff, and Aylesworth and his nostalgia for the past.[272]

While Roxy waited for his new NBC and Roxy Theatre contracts to be finalized, he went golfing on January 12 and returned home with Rosa in good spirits.[273] For two very long years Roxy had pined for another opportunity at the Roxy Theatre and to return to NBC. He would finally have his chance. That evening, the future seemed bright. Roxy went to sleep in his Hotel Gotham bed and never woke up. He was only fifty-three years old.

For more than a year, Roxy's doctor, Seymour Wanderman, had told him to stop working and "live carefully." Roxy refused and responded that "he wanted to die at work."[274] Instead, he died at home of "angina pectoris" and "coronary occlusion"—a heart attack—at around 7:00 A.M. on January 13, 1936.[275] "The bad heart . . . took second place to his ambitions," the *New York Evening Post* remarked. "Chief of these ambitions was to regain control of the Roxy Theatre, which was built around his personality and according to his ideas. He wanted to prove, after two unsuccessful connections, that his old ideas were right. He wanted to do something for investors who lost their money in Roxy's."[276] Roxy had been adamant, despite Wanderman's warnings, that he would "live to be 80—and see every one of my doctors gone, no doubt, before my turn comes. I have too much work to do," he added, "I can't afford to die right now."[277] He left one more Roxy-esque quote to remember: "I would rather die with my boots on and work until I drop," he had told the *New York World-Telegram.* "Death is just a big show in itself."[278]

In 1919, Roxy revealed that his unhealthy diet—which along with smoking no doubt affected his heart and shortened his life span—was a symptom of his longing for those early days in Forest City, serving ale to the town's coal miners at the Freedman House and collecting five-cent tickets at his back-room nickelodeon. "I like to go back in my mind to the old days in that Pennsylvania town better than anything," he told the *Los Angeles Times* just before taking over the California Theatre for Samuel Goldwyn. "Sometimes today

I slip into a lunch counter and order a hamburger sandwich with onions on it just to recall the flavor of those days. My doctor says I'll kill myself . . . on those sandwiches, but I can't resist the temptation."[279] Others, however, saw a figurative element to Roxy's heart attack after Radio City and two years of failure. "The doctors," Jack Jamison writes, "when they signed 'heart trouble' to his death certificate, knew what they were doing. For heart trouble it was that killed Roxy Rothafel. His heart indeed was broken."[280]

A few hours before Roxy's final heart attack, newspaper boys began selling the morning edition of the *New York Times* featuring an advertisement for Gene Sarzen's new book, *The Secret of Keeping Fit*, featuring endorsements by the portly trio of Babe Ruth, Paul Whiteman, and a soon-to-be-deceased Samuel Rothafel. It was a testament to a different advertising age and Roxy's enduring popularity.[281] His death was made public early enough in the day to reach afternoon and evening newspapers, where front-page notices of his passing were printed nationwide.[282] The *New York Evening Journal* wrote that night that Roxy "bestrode the New York theatrical scene in a manner second only to the great Ziegfield [*sic*]."[283]

The following day, newspapers and trade journals featured extensive obituaries listing his accomplishments and his influence on film, music, broadcasting, and popular culture. *Variety*'s obituary noted Roxy's decades-long status as "Films' No. 1 Exhibitor,"[284] while Terry Ramsaye in *Motion Picture Herald* remarked that Roxy would be "remembered in the annals of the screen as one of its formative influences, such a factor in terms of exhibition as David Wark Griffith has been in production or as Adolph Zukor in distribution. Roxy, foremost, taught the screen pride and self-respect."[285] W. R. Wilkerson, founder of the *Hollywood Reporter*, opined that "The greatest motion picture showman that ever lived has gone to another world maybe to revamp its entertainment ideas."

> Samuel Rothafel was the father of present-day motion picture exhibition he was the pioneer who brought the picture business out of the store shows and 15-cent admissions. He created the presentation house, the picture stage show; he brought into movie theaters the big concert orchestras, the ballets, the concert and opera singers. Every important feature of motion picture presentation in the theater today was the inspiration of Roxy. . . . The picture business owes the better part of its existence to Sam Rothafel. He did more, individually, to bring about picture progress than anyone else. His going will be felt; his shoes will be hard to fill. His value to the industry will, probably, never be duplicated.[286]

The *Hartford Courant* spoke directly to his value as a star and a cultural tastemaker:

> Of the personalities who shaped, flavored and colored the Twenties, Roxy was among the foremost. He was probably the premier showman of the decade. Just as no visit to New York early in the century was complete without a visit to the Hippodrome, so no visit there ten years ago was complete without a visit to the theater bearing his name. The immaculate ushers, the symphony orchestra that rose playing from the pit, the ballet and the chorus on the stage, the ornate house itself all constituted a spectacle that almost completely overwhelmed the movies that were supposed to be its major attraction. His success at Roxy's provoked imitation from coast to coast, until the whole country was dotted with "movie palaces" devoted to "stage presentations" as well as the films themselves. . . . His monuments are everywhere.[287]

With film exhibition already changing dramatically around the country, as exhibitors tossed out their orchestras, organists, and live performers and replaced them with single headliners or double features, Roxy's broadcasting innovations proved more lasting, with thousands of radio and television variety shows filling the airwaves since his first broadcast in 1922. "If any one individual deserves the honor of being known as 'The First Man of Radio,'" Jack Banner had written in *Radio Guide*, "this short, florid-faced, blue-eyed genius of the theater is that man."

> His historic broadcasts revolutionized radio. He was the first man in the history of broadcasting whose programs were sent out via remote control. He was the first program director to offer symphonic music to the radio public. His farseeing vision enabled him to be the first to present musical backgrounds for sketches and dramas, and if this one contribution alone doesn't entitle him to immortality, then try to imagine listening to a modern radio dramatic sketch without the musical background. His programs are the first short-waved affairs on record, and he was the first to adopt the now universal method of split timing. Thus it can be seen that while Roxy had nothing to do with the mechanical progress of the radio industry, he contributed richly to the cultural progress of the new art. His programs served as the testing grounds and jumping-off spots.[288]

It was Aaron Stein of the *New York Post* who summed up Roxy's influence on broadcasting most succinctly. "The sudden death of Samuel Lionel Rothafel makes of radio's first major impresario a historical figure," Stein wrote on January 14, 1936.

> It is difficult to conceive any idea of what American broadcasting might be today if Roxy had not pioneered in setting a form for its entertainment. Although in the last months of his life he was not active at the microphones, it is impossible to tune in on any station for any length of time without encountering some marked trace of the design and attitude which he brought to radio. . . . It is futile to deny the importance of the part he has had in the process of transforming radio from an instrument of communication into a form of entertainment. So successful was the variety show pattern which he early imposed upon broadcasting that even today it is still the standard radio form.[289]

The *American Hebrew*'s sentimental tribute noted that Roxy's impending comeback at NBC and at the old Roxy Theatre "makes his untimely passing all the more poignant."[290]

ROXY'S EPILOGUE

Funeral services were held on January 15 at the Central Synagogue on 55th Street and Lexington Avenue—just a few avenues away from his Times Square theaters—with Rabbi Jonah Wise conducting the Reform service.[291] More than 1,500 crowded into the synagogue for the funeral. Attendees included Erno Rapee, James Melton, David Mendoza, Tommy Dowd, Douglas Stanbury, Gladys Rice, current and former Roxyettes, as well as executives of NBC and members of the Catholic Actors Guild, the Jewish Theatrical Guild, the American Federation of Actors, and the Actors Friars, Lambs, Players, and Cheese clubs.[292] Five hundred others who could not gain admittance stood outside the synagogue during the service.[293]

At 11:00 A.M., an honor guard of a dozen Marines preceded a group of pallbearers carrying Roxy's casket up the steps of the temple, down the central aisle, and up to the altar as the organist played "Ase's Death" from Roxy's favorite *Peer Gynt*. Wise then recited Psalm 23 followed by his eulogy. "In our mortal sphere," Wise told mourners, "he distinguished himself, by his great faith in new forms of art in the fields of radio and the motion picture."

He took these amusements out of the realm of the trivial, the childish and the insignificant, and with his finger now stilled in death pointed to greater possibilities than were known to those who exploited these devices. It may be that we are not here at the grave of a humble worker. It may be that we are standing at the grave of a prophet whose name in years to come may be written as that of one who gave new values, new beauty and new dignity to the fields in which he labored.

Jan Peerce sang the Jewish prayer for the dead, "El Malei Rachamim," and reportedly sobbed several times during his rendition. Roxy's casket, draped with an American flag, was then carried out of the temple, preceded by Wise and the Marine honor guard, as organist Lew White played Chopin's "Funeral March." Wise then read Psalm 91. Outside, a bugler and member of Roxy's American Legion Post played "Taps."[294] The *New York World-Telegram* noted that the service contrasted starkly with Roxy's own sense of theatrics. Lasting only thirty minutes, it was somber and without fanfare.[295] Still, it was a mixture of much of what Roxy had used as the source of his creative inspiration and moral compass: his ethnic and religious background, his love of music, and his unaltered passion for the Marines.[296]

That evening, the Loew's radio station WHN broadcasted a commemorative radio program from 8:00 to 9:30 in tribute to Roxy's thirteen years on the air. Nearly all of the Gang participated, even those who had not been in contact with him for years. Erno Rapee, David Mendoza, Eugene Ormandy, Maria Gambarelli, Douglas Stanbury, Patricia Bowman, Beatrice Belkin, Yasha Bunchuk, Willie Robyn, Gladys Rice, and Frank Moulan all gathered together for the last time.[297] Four days later, an hour-long program aired over the CBS network featuring Melton, Peerce, Belkin, Rice, Bunchuk, and Mickey McKee, among others.[298] NBC, whose NBC-Red and NBC-Blue networks were popularized in part by Roxy and his radio protégé Major Bowes, was conspicuously silent.

The *Hollywood Reporter* featured a full-page advertisement for *Major Bowes Amateur Theatre of the Air* film shorts two days after Roxy's death. By then, Bowes's top-rated "Amateur Hour" program, radio's latest convergent property, had created a bevy of new ancillary revenue streams, including a group of short films distributed by RKO that featured the program's radio winners.[299] Bowes was now the most successful radio host in the country and had taken full advantage of the entertainment industry's convergent possibilities, earning money from personal appearances, product endorsements, licensed merchandise, records, publishing, and these RKO-distributed films.[300]

A decade later, as Ted Mack took over Bowes' broadcast and brought the show to television—and when programs such as *Star Search* and *American Idol* became the sensations of their own eras—Bowes's name and influence, like Roxy's, were also forgotten. That is the inevitable price of fame and the cost of forgetting media's past.

After WHN's broadcast tribute to Roxy on January 15, Erno Rapee rejoined his colleagues Leon Leonidoff and Russell Markert at Radio City Music Hall. The entertainment industry that Roxy helped create through his leading role in converging film, broadcasting, and music publishing and recording moved on without him. Roxy was the past. The past was prologue(s).

AFTERWORD

"The story I have to tell never was written while he lived. But someone is bound to write it some day, so it may as well be written now. It is neither too late nor too soon."
—Jack Jamison, *Radio Guide* April 1936

In the months that followed Roxy's death, the entertainment industry, comprising film, broadcasting, and music publishing and recording, was focused on the trends of the moment, not the pioneers of the past. Major Bowes was riding the amateur wave and, like Roxy before him, left NBC for CBS. Movie palaces were booking headliners, not stage shows, and smaller houses were focused on giveaways and double features, not classical music and cultural uplift. Rather than reviving his methods, members of the Roxy Memorial Committee, including Edward G. Robinson, William S. Paley, M. H. Aylesworth, Erno Rapee, George S. Kaufman, and Harry M. Warner, paid tribute to his life and career by planting the Roxy Memorial Grove in Palestine "on the hills of Nazareth" in the George Washington Memorial Forest.[1]

Others thought of commemorating him through film. Musicals and biopics were staple genres of 1930s American studio production, and Roxy's life and career seemed ripe for adaptation. His tragic January, in which he passed away just at the moment of his triumphant comeback, would certainly have made for a terrific narrative climax. (Edward G. Robinson seemed ideal for the role.) The first Roxy biopic in development was reported in March 1936, just two months after his death, with a screenplay based on his life being developed at Republic Pictures by Alexander Leftwich.[2] The following month, the *Los Angeles Times* reported that "Precedent having been set by 'The Great Ziegfeld,' films glorifying the lives of Daniel Frohman and the late S. L. (Roxy) Rothafel are announced to follow in short order."[3] For reasons unknown, nothing came of the project. Nearly a decade later, Louella Parsons reported, "My old friend [Roxy] . . . is the latest to have his life filmed. . . . Joseph Tushinsky, associate producer with Charles R. Rogers of 'The Life of Chauncey Olcott,' has bought the screen rights."[4] Tushinky's project never materialized. Nearly four decades later, in March 1982, Philip Goldberg and George Feltenstein copyrighted a treatment for "a musical drama based on the life of Sam Rothafel." It, too, seems to have been unproduced.[5] Instead of being memorialized on stage and screen, his famous nickname proliferated until it became so common that most could not remember or cite its derivation. Instead of being a brand associated with Samuel Rothafel, the name "Roxy" became shorthand for entertainment, like Bijou, Palace, or Majestic. The nickname was even copied by his own son Arthur who became a (regionally) famous broadcaster in New England, providing essential ski reports each winter under the nickname "Roxy."[6]

Roxy's venerable widow, Rosa, outlived her workaholic husband by more than four decades. Arthur's son, Art Rothafel, recalls visits to Radio City Music Hall in the decades after the showman's death, in which doormen never forgot "Mrs. Roxy" and led her through the side entrance of Roxy's—and the film industry's—palatial mausoleum to the past. For more than forty-five years, Radio City Music Hall remained a monument to the mélange of live and recorded entertainment once provided by hundreds of movie houses nationwide. After the Capitol, Roxy, and other theaters had long since dropped the format, Radio City Music Hall ironically became the lasting monument to Roxy's influential style, carried forward by his old comrades Leon Leonidoff and Russell Markert, who both remained with Radio City and the Rockettes well into the 1970s.

Radio City is now one of the only theaters left from Roxy's gilded, frenzied heyday. The Family Theatre burned in the 1930s and today the site is a small grocery store. The Alhambra in Milwaukee, the Lyric in Minneapolis, and every other motion picture theater Roxy managed, with the exception of the Regent and Radio City in New York, are gone. The Strand, Knickerbocker, Rialto, Rivoli, Park, California, Capitol, RKO Roxy (Center), and Mastbaum theaters have all been demolished. The Roxy Theatre, for instance, was demolished over a half century ago. His office in Radio City Music Hall, though, is pristinely maintained, as if Roxy, Rapee, Leonidoff, and Markert might stumble in any moment for a production meeting. In the surrounding buildings, his old network, NBC, continues on. At Radio City, the Christmas Spectacular still draws in a global (and growing) crowd with shows in New York and through a national tour.

Signing Off

What started out as a project to analyze Roxy's influence on film exhibition between 1908 and 1935 transformed over time into a much larger study of the convergence of art and industry; the film industry's battles with reformers; how motion picture exhibitors attracted middle- and upper-class audiences; the ways in which movie theaters developed a generation of musicians who later performed in symphonies and opera halls; the use of film to further propaganda; the movie house as a dynamic public sphere where art was used to entertain and indoctrinate; the use of broadcasting to promote motion pictures; the utilization of movie theater orchestras and in-house composers/arrangers for synchronous sound films; the development of the theme song craze; the exploitation of theme songs through broadcasting and music publishing and recording to generate box office and ancillary revenue streams; and the consolidation and convergence of film, broadcasting, and music into a multinational, multimedia entertainment industry.

Research on Roxy is limited only by a researcher's time, focus, and proclivity. Merging an avant-garde and artistic flair with a marketer's desire for exploitation and public acclaim, these disparate qualities make him a fascinating yet elusive figure. Like most historical studies, what is not discussed here is much larger than what is contained in these many pages. Still, it is hoped that this book will inspire a rejuvenated focus on Roxy's multi-pronged career by scholars in cinema and media studies, musicology, performance studies, American studies, history, and numerous other fields. As Roxy was regularly ranked with Chaplin, Zukor, Griffith, Pickford, Loew, and Sarnoff during his lifetime, our historical forgetfulness is a current condition and certainly not reflective of his historical importance or a remotely accurate scholarly assessment.

Nearly eight decades after his untimely death, media scholars can learn much about the early development of motion pictures, broadcasting, and media convergence through his work. Today, the provenance of the name "Roxy" has drifted into historical obscurity, but for generations of American moviegoers and radio listeners before World War II, that name was as familiar as Ford, AT&T, and Metro-Goldwyn-Mayer. As silent film actor and Forest

City native Pat O'Malley remarked twenty years after Roxy's death, "Today the name means little, but a couple of decades ago almost every thing connected with that name made news."

American Showman is the first scholarly book to analyze the multidimensional work of a single American motion picture exhibitor in the silent *and* early sound film eras and one of very few accounts to focus on the career of a prominent broadcaster during this same period. Through an examination of Samuel Rothafel's multiple roles as a theatrical and motion picture producer, radio broadcaster, film exhibitor and editor, talent scout and booker, music arranger, and marketer, I hope to have suggested the many avenues for future scholars to articulate the work and influence of the showmen and women of this period who routinely worked in film, radio, music, legitimate theater, vaudeville, and other areas of the growing and increasingly convergent entertainment industry. Roxy was an exemplary showman but he was also part of a generational cohort that conceived of the movie theater as more than a venue for film—and radio as more than just a medium. The public movie theater and the private living room were, in Roxy's eyes, fertile and transformative venues that played an indispensable role in the transformation of America and American culture.

For now, as Roxy would say, "Goodnight, Pleasant Dreams, and God Bless You."

NOTES

Introduction

AC   Atlanta Constitution
CJ   Cinema Journal
FH   Film History
LAEE   Los Angeles Evening Express
LAT   Los Angeles Times
MPN   Motion Picture News
NYT   New York Times

NYPL   *New York Public Library for the Performing Arts*

1. Bergstrom, "Murnau, Movietone and Mussolini." Janet Bergstrom's essay analyzes this vitally important aspect of Roxy's career and was the first to challenge the long-accepted "fact" that Hugo Riesenfeld scored F. W. Murnau's *Sunrise* (1927).

2. Paley, *As It Happened*, 52; Socolow, "Always in Friendly Competition," in Hilmes, ed., *NBC: America's Network*, 30, 31; Gomery, *The Coming of Sound*, 123; "Find Paramount Broadcast Presents Pleasing Program but Has No Startling Feature," *MPN*, Sept. 28, 1929, 1130; "Paramount Radio Hook-Up Will Be National in Scope," *MPN*, Sept. 21, 1929, 1052.

3. *Syncopation* Advertisement, *Variety*, Feb. 27, 1929, 78, 79.

4. "Radio-Ing the Air Waves," *AC,* Sept. 17, 1928, 7; Warner Bros. Vitaphone Pictures Advertisement, *Variety,* Oct. 3, 1928, 18.

5. Whitfield, *In Search of American Jewish Culture,* 30.

6. Ross, *Working-Class Hollywood: Silent Film and the Shaping of Class in America,* 190.

7. Staiger, "The Future of the Past," 127.

8. William Uricchio, "Historicizing Media in Transition," in Thornburn and Jenkins, eds., *Rethinking Media Change: The Aesthetics of Transition,* 33, 34.

9. Hansen, *Babel and Babylon,* 93.

10. Quoted in Hansen, *Babel and Babylon,* 99.

11. Ibid., 93, 94.

12. Ibid., 98.

13. Gunning, "Now You See It, Now You Don't: The Temporality of the Cinema of Attractions," in Grieveson and Krämer, eds., *The Silent Cinema Reader,* 47.

14. Hiley, "'At the Picture Palace': The British Cinema Audience, 1895–1920," in Fullerton, ed., *Celebrating 1895: The Centenary of Cinema,* 96, 97, 102.

15. David Robinson, Preface, in Usai, *Silent Cinema: An Introduction,* xi.

16. Koszarski, *An Evening's Entertainment,* 9.

17. "Wonderful Effects at California," *LAEE,* Dec. 10, 1919, 29.

18. Henry E. Dougherty, "Something About the Future Picture House," *LAEE,* Dec. 13, 1919, 3:1.

19. "Rothapfel Arranges Elaborate Prologue," *MPN,* Sept. 13, 1919, 2217.

20. Ross, 187.

21. Altman, *Silent Film Sound,* 389. Roxy noted that in addition to aesthetics, his style of musical accompaniment was to "interpret what the director intended to convey" and "to emphasize and amplify his meaning." W. Stephen Bush, "The Art of Exhibition," *Moving Picture World,* Nov. 21, 1914, 1063.

22. Golda M. Goldman, "Story of Samuel L. Rothafel and His Career," *American Hebrew,* Feb. 16, 1921, 464.

23. "How Exhibitor Can Become a 'Producer,'" *MPN,* Dec. 28, 1918, 3873.

24. Waller, *Main Street Amusements: Movies and Commercial Entertainment in a Southern City, 1896–1930,* 217, 218.

25. Waller, "Hillbilly Music and Will Rogers: Small Town Picture Shows in the 1930s," in Stokes and Maltby, eds., *American Movie Audiences,* 164–179; Doherty, "This Is Where We Came In: The Audible Screen and the Voluble Audience of Early Sound Cinema," in Stokes and Maltby, eds., 150.

26. "Spectacular 'Roxy' Stage Show Surrounds 'Little Women' on Music Hall Stage this Week," Radio City Music Hall press release, Nov. 16, 1933, 1; "Record-Breaking 'Little Women' and 'Roxy' Stage Show in Second Week at the Music Hall," Radio City Music Hall press release, Nov. 26, 1933, 1.

27. Browne, "The Political Economy of the Television (Super) Text," 176, 177.

28. S. L. (Roxy) Rothafel, "The Architect and the Box Office," *Architectural Forum* 57:3 (Sept. 1932): 194.

29. Quoted in Edwin Schallert, "Rothapfel a Harmonist," *LAT*, Nov. 2, 1919, III1.

30. Edwin Schallert, "Films," *LAT*, Nov. 24, 1919, II12.

31. Despite the term "continuous performance," rare was the theater that never ceased programming throughout the day. During the mid to late silent era, showtimes were often printed in newspaper ads, posted on box office windows, and regulated by exhibitors to schedule personnel such as projectionists, ushers, and musicians.

32. Hansen, "Benjamin, Cinema and Experience: The Blue Flower in the Land of Technology," 186.

33. Benjamin, "The Work of Art in the Age of Mechanical Reproduction," in Durham and Kellner, *Media and Cultural Studies: Keyworks*, 26.

34. Andrew, "Film and Society: Public Rituals and Private Space," in Hark, ed., *Exhibition: The Film Reader*, 162.

35. Janet Staiger, "Writing the History of American Film Reception," in Melvyn Stokes and Richard Maltby, eds., *Hollywood Spectatorship: Changing Perceptions of Cinema Audiences* (London: BFI, 2001), 26–28.

36. "Lets Walter Heroine Live," *NYT*, Apr. 9, 1917, 13.

37. "Rothapfel Has Convictions," *Variety*, Oct. 25, 1918, 39.

38. Eric T. Clarke, "An Exhibitor's Problems in 1927," *Transactions of the Society of Motion Picture Engineers* 11:31 (1927): 450–457.

39. Roxy-Mastbaum program, Jan. 31, 1935, 3.

40. Eileen Creelman, "Feature Plays and Players," unknown newspaper, c. Jul. 1933 (NYPL); "Rothapfel Staging Elaborate Prologue for 'Passion,'" *MPN*, Dec. 25, 1920, 125.

41. "Record Gross at Capitol," *Variety*, Dec. 17, 1920, 45.

42. Prologue reprinted in "Rothafel Prologue with Lines and Business," *MPN*, Jun. 18, 1921, 3693.

43. Budd, "The Cabinet of Dr. Caligari: Conditions of Reception," 47.

44. "Rothafel Prologue with Lines and Business," 3693.

45. "The Screen," *NYT*, Oct. 9, 1922, 17.

46. "Wonderful Effects at California," *LAEE*, Dec. 10, 1919, 29.

47. Advertisement, *LAEE*, Dec. 5, 1919, 3:5.

48. Henry Dougherty, "California's Big Bill; Pickford at Kinema," *LAEE*, Dec. 8, 1919, 17.

49. Altman, *Silent Film Sound*, 274.

50. Walter Benjamin, *What Is Epic Theatre* (London: Verso, 1983), 19, quoted in Bertellini, "Restoration, Genealogy and Palimpsests," 290.

51. "Griffith Himself Stages Prologue for 'Greatest Thing in Life' in Los Angeles," *MPN*, Jan. 4, 1919, 88.

52. Grace Kingsley, "Flashes," *LAT*, Dec. 20, 1918, II3.

53. The Elinor score was played live for the next eleven weeks at the Carthay Circle. In April 1928, two months after closing at the Carthay Circle, the Movietone version of *Sunrise* opened in downtown Los Angeles at the Criterion Theatre. Bergstrom, "Murnau, Movietone and Mussolini," 196–199.

54. David Pierce, "'Carl Laemmle's Outstanding Achievement,'" *FH* 10:4 (1998): 468, 471.

55. Bertellini, "Restoration, Genealogy and Palimpsests," 284.

56. Ibid.

57. Horak, "Film History and Film Preservation: Reconstructing the Text of *The Joyless Street* (1925)."

58. Usai, Silent Cinema, 160.

1. A New Art for a New Art Form (1908–1913)

LAT	Los Angeles Times
MFP	Milwaukee Free Press
MPN	Motion Picture News
MPW	Moving Picture World
NYC	New York Clipper
NYT	New York Times
FCN	Forest City News (*Forest City, PA*)
MDN	Milwaukee Daily News
MJ	Minneapolis Journal
MMT	Minneapolis Morning Tribune
MST	Minneapolis Sunday Tribune
MS	Milwaukee Sentinel
MT	Minneapolis Tribune

AMPAS	*Margaret Herrick Library, Academy of Motion Picture Arts and Sciences*
MCNY	*Museum of the City of New York*
NYPL	*New York Public Library for the Performing Arts*

1. Musser in collaboration with Nelson, *High-Class Moving Pictures*, 4.

2. "'Roxy' and His 'Gang' Are Coming Soon," *Springfield News*, Apr. 11, 1925, n.p. (NYPL – MWEZ + NC 18, 311).

3. S. L. Rothafel, "A Bit About Myself," *Radio Broadcast*, Oct. 1923, 458.

4. Twelfth Census of the United States, 1900 Census, vol. 98, Enumeration District No. 540, sheet 15. Cecilia's father was Markus Schwersons [Schwersenz?] and her mother's maiden name was Jacobosky (a Polish-Jewish name). Her father (and mother) may have originally come from the Swarzedz area, between Poland and Berlin. The area was one of many that were alternately part of Prussia and Poland, thus the changing nature of her country of origin (sometimes labeled as Prussia, other times labeled as Poland, depending on the year of the census report or birth or death certificate). "Cellia Rothapfel," Certificate and Record of Death, State of New York, Dec. 8, 1901. Certificate No. 36168.

5. Roxy's brother Max claimed to have been born in Bromberg on his 1904 United States passport application. "Rothapfel, Max," *U.S. Passport Application*, Jun. 28, 1904. Ancestry.com. *U.S. Passport Applications, 1795–1925* [database online]. Provo, UT: Ancestry.com Operations, Inc., 2007 (accessed Jul. 8, 2011).

6. Talmey, *Doug and Mary and Others*, 178.

7. On his 1899 naturalization application, Gustav claimed to have arrived in New York on September 26, 1884. Max's June 28, 1904 United States passport application, however, lists his father's date of entry as September 1885 aboard the steamship *Katie*, roughly three months after Max was born (according to 1886 immigration records). The *Katie* was cleared for entry in New York on September 24, 1885. The eight-month separation—not twenty months—between Gustav's arrival in September 1885 and the rest of the family in May 1886, as well as the timing of Max's birth (roughly June 1885 according to 1886 immigration records) and Gustav's departure, lends credence to 1885 as the actual date. (Max always listed November 23 as his birthday, though, with various years depending on the passport application.) "Rothapfel, Max," *U.S. Passport Application*, Jun. 28, 1904; "Rothapfel, Gustav," *Petitions for Naturalization*, Dec. 8, 1899. Ancestry.com. *Index to Petitions for Naturalization Filed in New York City, 1792–1989* [database online]. Provo, UT: Ancestry.com Operations, Inc., 2007 (accessed Jul. 8, 2011); "Marine Intelligence," *NYT*, Sep. 25, 1885, 8; "Marine Intelligence," *NYT*, Sep. 17, 1884, 8; Ancestry.com, *New York Passenger Lists, 1820–1957* [database online]. Provo, UT: The Generations Network, 2006 (accessed Dec. 26, 2006).

8. "Marine Intelligence," *NYT*, May 12, 1886, 8; Hamburg Passenger Lists, Jan.–Jun. 1886, Family History Center, Los Angeles.

9. Ancestry.com, *New York Passenger Lists, 1820–1957* [database online]. Provo, UT: The Generations Network, 2006 (accessed Dec. 26, 2006); Ira A. Glazier and P. William Filby, *Germans to America: List of Passengers Arriving at U.S. Ports* (Wilmington, DE: Scholarly Resources, Inc., 1996), 61; "Germans to America, 1875–1888," Genealogy.com (accessed Jul. 10, 2003); "Entries into New York, 1886," Family History Center, Los Angeles.

10. Johnson, *Stillwater: Minnesota's Birthplace*, 33, 68, 73; Brent Peterson, "The Grand Opera House," *Historical Whisperings*, Jul. 1995, 3.

11. "Mike-roscopes," *Radio News*, Jan. 1931, 669.

12. The other two were Mankato and Hastings. Jewish communities were just developing in "river towns" like St. Anthony and Minneapolis. Plaut, *The Jews in Minnesota*, 50; Johnson, 33, 68, 73.

13. Johnson, 68.

14. Edwin F. Barrett, *Stillwater City Directory* (Stillwater, MN: E. F. Barrett, 1887), 189.

15. "Gustav Rothapfel," Declaration of Intention, State of Minnesota, Washington County, Oct. 18, 1886. Reel 2, vol. D, Code 4, p. 259 (Iron Range Research Center). For reasons unknown, Gustav reapplied for naturalization thirteen years later in Brooklyn. Thus, the Rothapfels were not American citizens, it seems, until at least 1899.

"Rothapfel, Gustav," U.S. Naturalization Record Indexes, Dec. 8, 1899, R314, vol. 301, p. 175.

16. "Rothapel [*sic*]," Certificate of Birth, Stillwater, Minnesota, Feb. 13, 1887. Certificate No. B-157-30.

17. "Rothapfel," Certificate of Birth, Stillwater, Minnesota, Jul. 15, 1888. Certificate No. B-174-27.

18. "Minnesotan, Thought Failure, Builds Largest Movie House," *Saint Paul Pioneer Press*, Jun. 21, 1925, 10.

19. "'Roxy' Dies on Eve of Big Comeback," *New York American*, Jan. 14, 1936 (NYPL).

20. Rothafel, "A Bit About Myself," 458.

21. "Home Town Greets Roxy in Minnesota," *NYT*, Mar. 14, 1931, 22.

22. "S. L. Rothapfel, 'Roxy,' Found Dead in Room in New York Hotel," unknown Stillwater newspaper, Jan. 13, 1936, 6 (Washington County Historical Society, Stillwater, MN).

23. Johnson, 68.

24. *Stillwater City Directory* (St. Paul, MN: R. L. Polk, 1891), 228.

25. This untitled article offers the first evidence that Rosalie was not a well woman. *The Messenger* (Stillwater, MN), May 17, 1890, n.p. (Washington County Historical Society).

26. *Stillwater City Directory*, 241.

27. Untitled, *Stillwater Daily Gazette*, May 31, 1893, reprinted in "Looking Backward," *Stillwater Daily Gazette*, May 31, 1919, 4.

28. Twelfth Census of the United States, 1900 Census, vol. 98, Enumeration District No. 540, sheet 15.

29. "Rothapel [*sic*]," Certificate of Birth, Stillwater, Minnesota, Apr. 30, 1894. Certificate No. B-237-14; Mortuary Register of the City of Stillwater, Health Office, May 1894; *Stillwater City Directory*, 213.

30. The move to 40 Vernon Avenue in Brooklyn was certainly prescient. Two years later, the lumber industry began a serious decline. By 1914, the pine forests had been stripped and the timber industry in Stillwater was dead. The city would not soon recover. By 1927, there were only twenty-two Jews left in Stillwater. Johnson, 73, 74; *Stillwater City Directory*, 221; *Lain & Healy's Brooklyn Directory for the Year Ending May 1st, 1896* (Brooklyn: Lain & Healy, 1896), 1263; Plaut, 50.

31. Louis Sobol with Samuel L. Rothafel, "'Roxy,' The Voice of Broadway," *New York American*, ca. 1935, n.p. (Marine Corps History Center).

32. Rothafel, "A Bit About Myself," 458–464.

33. *Rialto Theatre Program-Magazine*, Rialto Theatre, ca. Apr. 1916, 3.

34. Rothafel, "A Bit About Myself," 458–464.

35. Mary Jacobs, "They Never Told Till Now," *Radioland*, May 1935, 30.

36. Mary B. Mullett, "Roxy and His Gang," *American Magazine*, Mar. 1925, 34.

37. Twelfth Census of the United States, 1900 Census, vol. 98, Enumeration District No. 540, sheet 15.

38. "Cellia Rothapfel," Certificate and Record of Death, State of New York, Dec. 8, 1901, Certificate No. 36168; "Deaths Reported Dec. 8," *NYT*, Dec. 9, 1901, 9; M.D., "Hospitals and Students," *NYT*, Apr. 2, 1905, 11; Morris Kaplan, "4 Hospitals Here Agree on Merger," *NYT*, Dec. 23, 1964, 24. A quarter century later, Rudolph Valentino would die at the same hospital (then located at 47th Street).

39. "Just 'Roxy'—That's All," *Unknown*, ca. Dec. 25, 1925, n.p. (MCNY).

40. Rothafel, "A Bit About Myself," 458–464.

41. In one of two U.S. Marine Corps muster rolls from May 1902, Roxy's middle name is listed as Loeser. "Muster Roll," May 1902, Marine Barracks, New York, New York (Records of the U.S. Marine Corps, Record Group 127, National Archives, Washington, DC); Tom Sterrett, "What D'Ye Know," *The Leatherneck*, Nov. 1927, 40; "Muster Roll," May 1902, Recruiting Service at New York, New York (Records of the U.S. Marine Corps, Record Group 127, National Archives, Washington, DC).

42. "Muster Roll," Oct. 1902, Marine Barracks, Boston, Massachusetts (Records of the U.S. Marine Corps, Record Group 127, National Archives, Washington, DC); "Muster Roll," Nov. 1902, USS *Bancroft* (Records of the U.S. Marine Corps, Record Group 127, National Archives, Washington, DC); *Dictionary of American Naval Fighting Ships* (Washington, DC: Navy Dept., Office of the Chief of Naval Operations, Naval History Division, 1959), 90; K. Jack Bauer, *Ships of the Navy* (Troy, NY: Rensselaer Polytechnic Institute, 1970), 150. Paul H. Silverstone, *The New Navy, 1883–1922* (New York: Routledge, 2006), 68.

43. Sobol with Rothafel, "'Roxy,' The Voice of Broadway."

44. "Muster Roll," Dec. 1903, USS *Bancroft* (Records of the U.S. Marine Corps, Record Group 127, National Archives, Washington, DC).

45. "Muster Roll," Mar. 1904, USS *Bancroft* (Records of the U.S. Marine Corps, Record Group 127, National Archives, Washington, DC).

46. "Muster Roll," Apr. 1904, USS *Bancroft* (Records of the U.S. Marine Corps, Record Group 127, National Archives, Washington, DC); "Muster Roll," May 1904, USS *Bancroft* (Records of the U.S. Marine Corps, Record Group 127, National Archives, Washington, DC).

47. "Roxy Succumbs to Heart Attack While Asleep," *Brooklyn Daily Eagle*, Jan. 13, 1936, n.p. (NYPL).

48. "Muster Roll," Jul. 1904, USS *Bancroft* (Records of the U.S. Marine Corps, Record Group 127, National Archives, Washington, DC).

49. *Upington's General Directory of Brooklyn, New York City* (Brooklyn: George Upington, 1903), 816.

50. "Van Buren Homestead (picture)/New York Historical Society," Brooklyn Public Library catalog record. Photograph was taken on November 1, 1903. Available at http://iii.brooklynpubliclibrary.org/record=b10753103 (accessed Jun. 12, 2011).

51. "Rothapfel, Max," *U.S. Passport Application*, Jun. 28, 1904; "List or Manifest of Alien Passengers for U.S. Immigration Officer at Port of Arrival," Apr. 10, 1904, Ancestry.com (accessed Dec. 26, 2006).

52. "Muster Roll," Mar. 1905, USS *Bancroft* (Records of the U.S. Marine Corps, Record Group 127, National Archives, Washington, DC); "Muster Roll," Mar. 1905, Marine Barracks, Fort Jefferson, Dry Tortugas, Florida (Records of the U.S. Marine Corps, Record Group 127, National Archives, Washington, DC).

53. "Contents Noted," *The Leatherneck*, Nov. 1931, 53; "Muster Roll," Jul. 1905, Marine Barracks, Navy Yard, Norfolk, Virginia (Records of the U.S. Marine Corps, Record Group 127, National Archives, Washington, DC); "Muster Roll," Aug. 1905, Recruiting District, Pittsburg, Pennsylvania (Records of the U.S. Marine Corps, Record Group 127, National Archives, Washington, DC); "Muster Roll," Sept. 1905, Marine Barracks, Navy Yard, Norfolk, Virginia (Records of the U.S. Marine Corps, Record Group 127, National Archives, Washington, DC).

54. Ibid.

55. "Muster Roll," Oct. 1905, Marine Barracks, Navy Yard, Norfolk, Virginia (Records of the U.S. Marine Corps, Record Group 127, National Archives, Washington, DC).

56. James S. McQuade, "The Belasco of Motion Picture Presentations," *MPW*, Dec. 9, 1911, 798.

57. Quoted in "A Daily Sports Writer Says—," *The Leatherneck*, Mar. 21, 1925, 5. The Boxer Rebellion was a frequent tidbit in Roxy biographies, as demonstrated by an October 1915 article in the *New York Clipper* and numerous others. "Rothapfel Lecture Tour Embraces Wide Territory," *NYC*, Oct. 30, 1915, 42. As a recent example, the American National Biography entry for "Roxy Rothafel" notes that he "saw action in China's Boxer Rebellion . . ." William Stephenson, "Rothafel, Roxy," *American National Biography Online* (Feb. 2000; www.anb.org/articles/18/18-01009.html; accessed Apr. 24, 2009).

58. Sobol with Rothafel, n.p.

59. S. L. Rothapfel, "Roxey Broadcasting from the Capitol Theatre," *The Leatherneck*, Jul. 11, 1925, 8.

60. Rothafel, "A Bit About Myself," 458–464.

61. "Another of Roxy's Dreams Realized in Opening of His New Giant Theater," *Kansas City Star*, Jan. 6, 1933, C.

62. Both teams reportedly objected to Roxy's refereeing. "The Great Game," *Daily Hampshire Gazette*, Aug. 18, 1906, 6; "Hampshire County," *Springfield Daily Republican*, Jun. 15, 1906, 10; "Hampshire County," *Springfield Daily Republican*, Aug. 17, 1906, 8. Roxy was listed as a boarder at The Hampton in the *Northampton and Easthampton Directory* (Northampton, MA: Price and Lee, 1907), 157.

63. Rothafel, "A Bit About Myself," 458–464; McQuade, "The Belasco of Motion Picture Presentations," 798.

64. S. L. Rothapfel Commemorative Tribute, presented to Samuel L. Rothapfel in New York, Jun. 24, 1916 (NYPL).

65. William Henry Feeney, "Impressions of Carbondale," *Carbondale Leader*, Sept. 21, 1907, 4.

66. "Corner Stone of Jewish Synagogue Laid Yesterday," *Carbondale Leader*, Sept. 16, 1907, 5; "Newsy Notes for Rapid Reading," *FCN*, Sept. 19, 1907.

67. McQuade, "The Belasco of Motion Picture Presentations," 798.

68. Quoted in Roxy, "Roxy's 'Hello Everybody,'" *Boston Traveler*, Mar. 23, 1925, n.p. (NYPL – MWEZ + NC 18, 311).

69. The other Carbondale pitcher listed (Boyd) appears to have played more of the game, judging by the number of assists and strikeouts recorded. Boyd was also listed first in the box score. "Badly Beaten by Honesdale," *Carbondale Leader*, Jul. 25, 1907, 5.

70. "Base Ball," *FCN*, Sept. 5, 1907.

71. "How It Happened," *FCN*, Sept. 12, 1907. Roxy later claimed that he received the nickname from "a foreigner, with whom he first did business, [who] couldn't pronounce his name." "Yes, Roxy Looks and Smiles Just as He Sounds, Folks," *Detroit News*, Jul. 23, 1925, n.p. (NYPL – MNN: **ZZ-38679). Eight years later, though, he recalled that the nickname was developed when playing baseball. "One day I was rounding third base and started home," he told Nellie Revell, "'Slide, Roxy, slide!' shouted the coach, and I've been Roxy ever since." Nellie Revell, "Nellie Revell Interviews Roxy," *Radio Digest*, Jan. 1933, 10. A year later, he corroborated this latter version. "Once when I was eleven years old," he told *Radio Guide* in September 1934, "I was playing ball with a group of my pals on the sandlots of my old home town. Along about the eighth inning I came to bat. My team was behind by one run. There was a man on base, and I hit the first ball for a home run. I streaked around the bases and was just rounding third base when one of my teammates, in a burst of excitement, hollered 'Come on, Roxy, come on and slide!' That was the first time I had ever heard the name, and it stuck . . ." Jack Banner, "'ROXY,'" *Radio Guide*, Sept. 22, 1934, 8.

72. "How It Happened."

73. "Topics of the Town," *FCN*, Sept. 19, 1907, 1.

74. "Topics of the Town," *FCN*, Feb. 5, 1908, 1.

75. "'Roxy' Summoned by Grim Reaper," *FCN*, Jan. 16, 1936, 1.

76. Sobol with Rothafel, n.p.

77. Jacobs, "They Never Told Till Now," 30, 64.

78. Ibid.; "Topics of the Town," *FCN*, May 28, 1908, 1.

79. Obelenus, *Highlights of Forest City Borough History*, n.p.

80. Cooper, *Forest City Centennial*, 14.

81. Obelenus, n.p.

82. Twelfth Census of the United States, 1900 Census, Supervisor's District No. 5, Enumeration District No. 82, sheet 17.

83. Thirteenth Census of the United States: 1910-Population, Enumeration District No. 65, sheets 36–37. Pennsylvania, Susquehanna County.

84. Obelenus, n.p.

85. Ibid.; Kenneth J. Cooper, *Forest City Centennial* (Forest City, PA: The Forest City Centennial Association, Inc., 1964), 14, 19, 21.

86. Obelenus, n.p.

87. Muchitz Hotel advertisement, *FCN*, Jan. 24, 1907; Obelenus, n.p.

88. Freedman House advertisement, *FCN*, Sept. 5, 1907. Martin and Theresa Muchitz had also emigrated from Austria in 1890. Thirteenth Census of the United States: 1910-Population, Emuneration District No. 65, sheet 37, Pennsylvania, Susquehanna County.

89. "Republican Club," *FCN*, Oct. 15, 1908, 1.

90. "The 'Greatest Ever!' " *Daily Express*, Feb. 11, 1923, 6.

91. Obelenus, n.p.

92. "Topics of the Town," *FCN*, Sept. 17, 1914, n.p.

93. "Topics of the Town," *FCN*, Jun. 13, 1907, 1; "Topics of the Town," *FCN*, Aug. 1, 1907, 1; "Topics of the Town," *FCN*, Aug. 22, 1907, 1; "Topics of the Town," *FCN*, Sept. 17, 1908, 1; "Topics of the Town," *FCN*, Jun. 24, 1909, 1; "Topics of the Town," *FCN*, Jun. 16, 1910, 1.

94. "Topics of the Town," *FCN*, Sept. 12, 1907, 1.

95. Pat O'Malley, "Roxy Story," Aug. 26, 1957, 2. (Unpublished article submitted to *FCN* and provided by *Forest City News*/John Kameen.)

96. Jacobs, 30, 64.

97. Roxy, "Don't Be Afraid to Fail!" *Radio Mirror*, Dec. 1934, 64.

98. "Broadway's Wizard of the Screen," *The Sun*, ca. Jun. 19, 1924, n.p. (NYPL – MNN: *ZZ-38713).

99. Sobol with Rothafel, n.p.

100. "A Few Things We Need," *The Shoppers' Guide* (Forest City, PA), May 28, 1907, 1.

101. "Just a Word in Passing," *FCN*, Dec. 19, 1907.

102. " 'Roxy' Summoned by Grim Reaper."

103. "The Music that Is in Every Man," *The Etude*, Dec. 1927, 903.

104. Roxy, "Don't Be Afraid to Fail!"

105. "A New Theatre," *FCN*, Nov. 9, 1908.

106. "How an Exhibitor Made Good," *MPN*, Jan. 3, 1914, 15, 16.

107. Family Theatre (Carbondale) advertisement, *Carbondale Leader*, Dec. 26, 1908, 3; Family Theatre (Forest City) advertisement, *FCN*, Jun. 30, 1910.

108. "How an Exhibitor Made Good," *MPN*, Jan. 3, 1914, 15.

109. "The New 'Family Theatre,'" *FCN*, Dec. 17, 1908.

110. Ibid.; Family Theatre advertisement, *FCN*, Dec. 24, 1908.

111. "Topics of the Town," *FCN*, Dec. 24, 1908, 1.

112. Ibid.

113. Rothapfel, "From a Pennsy Barroom to the Rialto," *MPW*, Mar. 10, 1917, n.p. (MCNY).

114. Family Theatre advertisement, *FCN*, Dec. 24, 1908.

115. " 'Madam Butterfly' Christmas Attraction at the Grand," *FCN*, Dec. 17, 1908; Grand Opera House advertisement, *FCN*, Dec. 24, 1908; Grand Opera House advertisement, *Carbondale Leader*, Dec. 14, 1908, 3.

116. "Topics of the Town," *FCN*, Dec. 31, 1908, 1.

117. Family Theatre advertisement, *FCN*, Dec. 31, 1908.

118. "The Music that Is in Every Man," 903.

119. Rothapfel, "From a Pennsy Barroom to the Rialto."

120. Jack Jamison, "The Man Who Dreamed Too Much," Radio Guide, Apr. 18, 1936, 3.

121. Golda M. Goldman, "Story of Samuel L. Rothapfel and His Career," *American Hebrew*, Feb. 16, 1921, 463.

122. "How an Exhibitor Made Good," *MPN*, Jan. 3, 1914, 15, 16.

123. Rothapfel, "From a Pennsy Barroom to the Rialto."

124. "How an Exhibitor Made Good," *MPN*, Jan. 3, 1914, 15.

125. "How an Exhibitor Made Good," *MPN*, Jan. 10, 1914, 19.

126. Family Theatre advertisement, *FCN*, Jan. 14, 1909; "The Family," *FCN*, Jan. 14, 1909, 1.

127. Jacobs, 30, 64.

128. In their application, Roxy once again asserted that he was born in Stillwater, Minnesota, on July 9, 1882, while Rosa listed her birth in Austria on August 5, 1883. "Samuel Rothapfel and Rosa Freedman," Affidavit of Applicant for Marriage License, No. 18, Susquehanna County, filed Jan. 26, 1909. Roxy continued to assert that he was born in Minnesota for the 1910 census as well. Thirteenth Census of the United States: 1910-Population, Emuneration District No. 64, sheet 7, Pennsylvania, Susquehanna County, Roll 1421, Book 2, p. 89.

129. "Topics of the Town," *FCN*, Feb. 11, 1909, 1.

130. "How an Exhibitor Made Good," *MPN*, Jan. 3, 1914, 16.

131. "Topics of the Town," *FCN*, Feb. 11, 1909, 1.

132. "The Trial of the White Man"; "The Half Breed." AFI Catalog Online (accessed Dec. 21, 2006).

133. Family Theatre advertisement, *FCN*, Mar. 18, 1909.

134. Family Theatre advertisement, *FCN*, Mar. 25, 1909.

135. Family Theatre advertisement, *FCN*, Apr. 8, 1909; Family Theatre advertisement, *FCN*, Apr. 22, 1909.

136. Roxy, "Don't Be Afraid to Fail!" 64.

137. Samuel Rothapfel, quoted in W. Stephen Bush, "The Art of Exhibition," *MPW*, Nov. 11, 1914, 1064.

138. Roxy, "Don't Be Afraid to Fail!" 64.

139. "The Music that Is in Every Man," 903.

140. Hall, *The Best Remaining Seats*, 28.

141. W. Stephen Bush, "The Art of Exhibition," *MPW*, Oct. 31, 1914, 627.

142. "Watch It Grow," *FCN*, Apr. 29, 1909.

143. Family Theatre advertisement, *FCN*, May 20, 1909.

144. Family Theatre advertisement, *FCN*, May 6, 1909.

145. "Topics of the Town," Jun. 24, 1909.

146. "Topics of the Town," May 13, 1909, 1.

147. "Topics of the Town," *FCN*, Jul. 1, 1909.

148. Thirteenth Census of the United States: 1910-Population, Emuneration District No. 64, sheet 7, Pennsylvania, Susquehanna County, Roll 1421, Book 2, p. 89.

149. Family Theatre advertisement, *FCN*, Jul. 8, 1909.

150. "Topics of the Town," *FCN*, Jul. 22, 1909.

151. Family Theatre advertisement, *FCN*, Jul. 29, 1909.

152. "Topics of the Town," *FCN*, Jul. 29, 1909, 1.

153. Letter, Richard A. Rowland to Wm. H. Selig, May 13, 1906. (Charles Clarke Collection, AMPAS).

154. Family Theatre advertisement, *FCN*, Sept. 16, 1909.

155. Family Theatre advertisement, *FCN*, Aug. 26, 1909.

156. Family Theatre advertisement, *FCN*, Aug. 12, 1909.

157. Family Theatre advertisement, *FCN*, Sept. 2, 1909.

158. "Topics of the Town," *FCN*, Sept. 2, 1909, 1.

159. "How an Exhibitor Made Good," Jan. 10, 1914, 19, 20.

160. Family Theatre advertisement, *FCN*, Sept. 9, 1909.

161. Family Theatre advertisement, *FCN*, Oct. 21, 1909; "Passion Play at Family a Big Success," *FCN*, Oct. 28, 1909.

162. "Passion Play at Family a Big Success."

163. "How an Exhibitor Made Good," Jan. 10, 1914, 19, 20.

164. "Topics of the Town," *FCN*, Nov. 4, 1909.

165. Family Theatre advertisement, *FCN*, Nov. 4, 1909.

166. "At the Family," *FCN*, Nov. 11, 1909.

167. "At the Family," *FCN*, Dec. 9, 1909; "At the Family," *FCN*, Dec. 23, 1909.

168. Ibid.

169. "At the Family," *FCN*, Dec. 16, 1909.

170. "At the Family," *FCN*, Dec. 23, 1909.

171. Ibid.

172. Advertisement, *FCN*, Dec. 30, 1909.

173. Obelenus, n.p.

174. "Spring Time at Cohens'," *FCN*, Mar. 4, 1909, 1; Family Theatre advertisement, *FCN*, Jan. 13, 1910.

175. "Topics of the Town," *FCN*, Oct. 6, 1910, 1.

176. "Exhibiting as a Fine Art," *MPW*, Feb. 10, 1910, 202, 203.

177. "Attractions at the Family," *FCN*, Jan. 13, 1910.

178. "Topics of the Town," *FCN*, Jan. 20, 1910, 1.

179. "Topics of the Town," *FCN*, Feb. 3, 1910, 1. Edward McCrew, who operated the theater, lived at the hotel. Thirteenth Census of the United States: 1910-Population, Emuneration District No. 65, sheet 37, Pennsylvania, Susquehanna County.

180. "Topics of the Town," *FCN*, Feb. 3, 1910, 1.

181. Ibid.; Rothapfel, "From a Pennsy Barroom to the Rialto."

182. Family Theatre advertisement, *FCN*, Feb. 3, 1910.

183. S. L. Rothapfel, "Exhibiting as a Fine Art," *MPW*, Feb. 10, 1910, 202, 203.

184. Family Theatre advertisement, *FCN*, Feb. 3, 1910; Rothapfel, "From a Pennsy Barroom to the Rialto."

185. S. L. Rothapfel, "Dignity of the Exhibitor's Profession," *MPW*, Feb. 26, 1910, 289.

186. "Exhibiting as a Fine Art," *FCN*, Feb. 17, 1910.

187. Family Theatre advertisement, *FCN*, Mar. 10, 1910; Family Theatre advertisement, *FCN*, Mar. 31, 1910.

188. "Topics of the Town," *FCN*, Mar. 24, 1910.

189. Family Theatre advertisement, *FCN*, Mar. 31, 1910.

190. Grand Theatre advertisement, *FCN*, Apr. 14, 1910; Family Theatre advertisement, *FCN*, Apr. 14, 1910; "Topics of the Town," *FCN*, Apr. 21, 1910; Family Theatre advertisement, *FCN*, Apr. 28, 1910; Family Theatre advertisement, *FCN*, May 5, 1910.

191. Grand Theatre advertisement, *FCN*, Apr. 7, 1910; Family Theatre advertisement, *FCN*, Apr. 7, 1910.

192. Family Theatre advertisement, *FCN*, Apr. 7, 1910; "Scranton's Population Is Only 129,867," *Carbondale Leader*, Aug. 16, 1910, 3.

193. S. L. Rothapfel, "Management of the Theater," *MPW*, Apr. 9, 1910, 548.

194. "The New Family," *FCN*, May 12, 1910. Roxy also received a visitor that month, his brother Max, whose flourishing cocoa import business now had offices in Brazil and Hamburg, Germany, the city they had both left twenty-three years earlier. "Topics of the Town," *FCN*, May 26, 1910, 1. There is no evidence, though, that Gustav or Annie, who had since left her father's house, ever traveled to Forest City to visit Roxy. It is possible that they may have been reunited during Roxy's trip to Manhattan earlier that year, but the cigar store owner may not have seen his new grandson until much later. Gustav's life had become busier, as well, with his recent marriage to a woman twenty years his junior. Thirteenth Census of the United States: 1910-Population, Emuneration District No. 1013, sheet 8. New York, Kings County, Roll 983, Book 1, p. 247.

195. Quoted in Family Theatre advertisement, *FCN*, Jun. 30, 1910.

196. "Topics of the Town," *FCN*, Aug. 18, 1910, 1. J. Adam Puffer, surveying the local theater scene at the time of Roxy's management in Carbondale, reported that all of the city's theatrical establishments were now presenting material "of a high order." "Puffer Roasts Newspapers, Finds Good in Picture Shows," *Carbondale Leader*, Aug. 31, 1910, 2.

197. Family Theatre advertisement, *FCN*, Oct. 13, 1910.

198. "Topics of the Town," *FCN*, Oct. 27, 1910, 1.

199. "Topics of the Town," *FCN*, Nov. 10, 1910, 1; Keith and Proctor's Fifth Avenue advertisement, *NYT*, Nov. 20, 1910, X3. In another version of events, Roxy supposedly

offered his services to Keith for free—and they were accepted at that price. "Broadway's Wizard of the Screen."

200. "Moving Pictures Shown in the Full Stage Light," Variety, Nov. 19, 1910, 1; "Daylight Picture" Advertisement, Variety, Jan. 1, 1911, 39.

201. "Topics of the Town," FCN, Nov. 10, 1910, 1.

202. "Moving Pictures Shown in the Full Stage Light," Variety, Nov. 19, 1910, 1; "Daylight Picture" Advertisement, Variety, Jan. 1, 1911, 39.

203. Family Theatre advertisement, FCN, Nov. 24, 1910.

204. "Topics of the Town," FCN, Dec. 1, 1910, 1. By December, Rosa turned over the management of the Family Theatre to W. H. Hill, who was now operating the Grand Theatre as well. "Topics of the Town," FCN, Dec. 8, 1910, 1.

205. Family Theatre advertisement, FCN, Dec. 1, 1910; "'Light House' Films Are Shown," MPW, Dec. 17, 1910, 1401.

206. McQuade, "The Belasco of Motion Picture Presentations," MPW, Dec. 9, 1911, 798.

207. "Daylight Pictures," Hartford Courant, Feb. 3, 1911, 15.

208. "Out of Town News," NYC, Feb. 11, 1911, 1296.

209. "Topics of the Town," FCN, Feb. 23, 1911; "Topics of the Town," FCN, Mar. 2, 1911, 1.

210. Family Theatre advertisement, FCN, Mar. 2, 1911.

211. "Topics of the Town," FCN, Mar. 23, 1911.

212. "Vaudeville Begins at New York," NYT, Mar. 28, 1911, 13; "New Sight on a Famous Old Site," NYT, Sept. 5, 1937, 120.

213. Photograph, Marcus Loews Herald Square, Margaret Herrick Library. (AMPAS).

214. "'Light House' Films Are Shown."

215. Orpheum Theater advertisement, LAT, Mar. 28, 1911, I2.

216. "See These by Daylight," LAT, Mar. 6, 1911, I11; "Daylight Pictures," MPW, Mar. 25, 1911, 645.

217. "'Daylight' Shows Compulsory in California, Motography, Apr. 1911, 45. "California Legislature: Past and Present – 1911." Available at www.capitolmuseum.ca.gov/english/legislature/history/year1911.html (accessed Jun. 12, 2011).

218. Julian Johnson, "New Orpheum's Bright Birth in Sudden Blaze of Tungsten Glory," LAT, Jun. 27, 1911, I2.

219. Orpheum Theatre advertisement, LAT, Jul. 5, 1911, I2; Orpheum Theatre advertisement, LAT, Jul. 26, 1911, I2

220. "Motion Pictures in Madison Garden," NYT, May 23, 1911, 11. Twelve years later, the Trans-Lux Daylight Picture Screen would be launched to far more success for that company. "Daylight Screen Made for Movies," Wall Street Journal, Jul. 17, 1923, 11.

221. Henry, "Boston: B. F. Keith's Theater," MPW, Apr. 15, 1911, 829.

222. Charles E. Schneider, "The So Called Daylight Screens," MPW, Apr. 15, 1911, 824.

223. Widen and Anderson, *Milwaukee Movie Palaces*, 43, 44. There is evidence to suggest that Fehr either still had little faith in the idea or that Roxy had made backup plans. The *New York Clipper* reported that Roxy would manage the summer season of the B. F. Keith's Columbia Theatre in Cincinnati after his work at the Alhambra. "Out of Town News," *NYC*, May 27, 1911, 17.

224. "Topics of the Town," *FCN*, Jul. 6, 1911.

225. Alhambra Theatre advertisement, *MDN*, May 27, 1911, 3; "Bernhardt Comes to Alhambra for Two Performances," *MDN*, May 27, 1911, 7.

226. "Bringing the Classics to Motion Picture Audiences," *Musical America*, ca. Jun. 1923, 5.

227. Widen and Anderson, 43, 44.

228. Alhambra Theatre advertisement, *MS*, Jun. 10, 1911, 4; James S. McQuade, "Chicago Letter," *MPW*, Jul. 22, 1911, 107.

229. "At the Theater," *MDN*, Jun. 5, 1911, 6; "At the Theater," *MDN*, Jun. 6, 1911, 6; "Week at the Theaters," *MDN*, Jun. 10, 1911, 7.

230. "Summer Amusements," *MFP*, Jun. 11, 1911, 6; "Attractions at the Milwaukee Theaters," *TSS*, Jun. 11, 1911, Special Features, part 4, p. 3.

231. "Summer Amusements," *MFP*, Jun. 11, 1911, 6.

232. Alhambra Theatre advertisement, *MDN*, Jun. 24, 1911, 3.

233. "At the Theater," *MDN*, Jun. 14, 1911, 6.

234. "At the Theater," *MDN*, Jun. 13, 1911, 6.

235. "At the Theater," *MDN*, Jun. 16, 1911, 6.

236. "Week at the Theaters," *MDN*, Jun. 17, 1911, 7.

237. "Attractions at the Milwaukee Theaters," *TSS*, Jun. 18, 1911, part 4, p. 3.

238. "Attractions at the Milwaukee Theaters," *TSS*, Jun. 25, 1911, part 4, p. 3.

239. McQuade, "The Belasco of Motion Picture Presentations," 798; "Don't Give the People What They Want," *The Green Book Magazine*, Aug. 1914, 226.

240. "A Progressive Exhibitor," *MPW*, Sept. 2, 1911, 618.

241. James S. McQuade, "Chicago Letter," *MPW*, Aug. 12, 1911, 366; "Brevities of the Business," *Motography*, Aug. 1911, 100.

242. The agreement included an additional $1,320 dollars annually for the required rental of the "so-called Kimball lease"—an adjoining property—and the lease of the emergency exit on the east side of the theater. "Lease Fehr, Lyric," Aug. 1911, Shubert Archive, Contracts, Group II, 239.

243. "Topics of the Town," *FCN*, Jul. 20, 1911; "Topics of the Town," *FCN*, Aug. 24, 1911; "Topics of the Town," *FCN*, Aug. 31, 1911.

244. Email conversation with Jana Armstead, Ramsey County Historical Society, Jul. 23, 2007; "Crystal Theatre 446 Wabasha, St. Paul," Minnesota Historical Society Photograph Collection, Location no. MR2.9 SP3.1C p106, Negative no. 55158. Available at http://collections.mnhs.org/visualresources/image.cfm?imageid=62646 (accessed Jun. 12, 2011).

245. The matter was "Adopted by the assembly Aug. 31 1911" and approved. "A'y F No. 13286," in *Proceedings of the Common Council of the City of St. Paul Ramsey County, Minnesota 1911*, St. Paul, Minnesota, 284 (available on Google Books).

246. "Brevities of the Business," *Motography*, Sept. 1911, 149.

247. Colonial Theatre advertisement, *St. Paul Pioneer-Press*, Sept. 3, 1911.

248. Marks, *Music and the Silent Film*, 92.

249. "This Week at the Local Theaters," *MT*, Sept. 24, 1911, 19.

250. "How an Exhibitor Made Good," *MPN*, Jan. 10, 1914, 20.

251. "The Week at Local Theaters," *MST*, Sept. 17, 1911, 18; Lyric Theatre advertisement, *MJ*, Sept. 17, 1911, 9; "Amusements," *MJ*, Sept. 17, 1911, 10; "On Vaudeville Stages," *MJ*, Oct. 17, 1911, 12.

252. "At the Playhouses Last Night," *MMT*, Sept. 19, 1911, 5.

253. "Promissory Notes About Local Bills of the Week," *MJ*, Sept. 24, 1911, 9.

254. "Pictures de Luxe Open at Lyric Next Week," *MT*, Sept. 10, 1911, 18.

255. Ibid., 797.

256. "The New Grand Draws a Throng," *MJ*, Sept. 19, 1911, 12.

257. "The Week at Local Theaters," *MST*, Sept. 17, 1911, 18; Lyric Theatre advertisement, *MJ*, Sept. 17, 1911, 9; "Amusements," *MJ*, Sept. 17, 1911, 10; "On Vaudeville Stages," *MJ*, Oct. 17, 1911, 12.

258. McQuade, "The Belasco of Motion Picture Presentations," 797.

259. "This Week at the Local Theater," *MST*, Oct. 15, 1911, 26.

260. Lyric Theatre advertisement, *MJ*, Sept. 24, 1911, 9.

261. McQuade, "The Belasco of Motion Picture Presentations," 798.

262. Ibid.

263. Ibid., 797.

264. "Sheehans in 'Bo, Girl," *MJ*, Sept. 28, 1911, 12.

265. "This Week at the Local Theaters," *MST*, Oct. 1, 1911, 21.

266. "Elsie Janis as a Slim Princess," *MJ*, Oct. 13, 1911, 20.

267. "'Busy Izzy' Comes Back," *MJ*, Oct. 31, 1911, 16.

268. James S. McQuade, "Staging the Passion Play," *MPW*, Dec. 30, 1911, 1055.

269. "This Week at the Local Theaters," *MST*, Nov. 5, 1911, 28.

270. "How an Exhibitor Made Good," *MPN*, Jan. 10, 1914, 20, 21.

271. Letter quoted in W. Stephen Bush, "The Art of Exhibition," *MPW*, Dec. 12, 1914, 1512.

272. Untitled, *MJ*, Nov. 23, 1911, 16; "A Few Moments with the Truthful Press Agents," *MJ*, Dec. 10, 1911, 14.

273. McQuade, "Staging the Passion Play," 1055.

274. Grau, *The Theatre of Science*, 290, 291.

275. McQuade, "Staging the Passion Play," 1055.

276. "This Week at the Local Theaters," *MT*, Dec. 17, 1911, 30.

277. James S. McQuade, "Minneapolis Situation," *MPW*, Nov. 25, 1911, 631.

278. "Diva as a Bootblack," *MJ*, Dec. 28, 1911, 4.

279. "Minneapolis Houses Officially Approved," *Motography*, Feb. 1912, 60.

280. "How an Exhibitor Made Good," 20, 21.

281. McQuade, "The Belasco of Motion Picture Presentations," 798.

282. Ibid., 797; Robert Sobel and John Raimo, eds., "Adolph O. Eberhart," *Biographical Directory of the Governors of the United States, 1789–1978,* vol. 2 (Westport, CT: Meckler Books, 1978), 785, 786.

283. S. L. Rothapfel to Gov. A. O. Eberhardt [*sic*], Jan. 6, 1912, Box 63, A. O. Eberhart Papers, Minnesota Historical Society.

284. "Diva as a Bootblack"; "Governor at Lyric Tonight," *MJ*, Jan. 12, 1912, 16.

285. S. L. Rothapfel, "The League and the Exhibitor," *MPN*, Aug. 22, 1914, 23.

286. "Minnesota Organized in Convention," *Motography*, Sept. 14, 1912, 193.

287. Letter from Mrs. J.K., *Minneapolis Tribune*, reprinted in James S. McQuade, "Chicago Letter," *MPW*, Mar. 2, 1912, 761.

288. "Rothapfel Resigns Management of Lyric," *MPW*, May 11, 1912, 612.

289. Ibid.

290. "Topics of the Town," *FCN*, May 9, 1912; James S. McQuade, "The Coming of Columbus," *MPW*, May 4, 1912, 409; "Publicity Matter on Selig's 'Columbus,'" *Motography*, May 1912, 231; "Topics of the Town," *FCN*, Aug. 15, 1912.

291. *The Coming of Columbus* advertisement, *MPW*, May 4, 1912, 451.

292. "Chicago Film Brevities," *MPW*, May 11, 1912, 612; James S. McQuade, "Chicago Letter," *MPW*, Jun. 1, 1912, 809. At the city's Parkway Theatre, Martha Butler of the Minneapolis Lyric was booked for a two-week engagement, perhaps on Roxy's suggestion. James S. McQuade, "Chicago Letter," *MPW*, Jun. 15, 1912, 1012.

293. "Topics of the Town," *FCN*, Aug. 15, 1912; "Publicity Matter on Selig's 'Columbus,'" 231.

294. "Chicago Film Brevities," 612; James S. McQuade, "Chicago Letter," *MPW*, Jun. 1, 1912, 809. In Roxy's absence at Minneapolis's Lyric, Herman Fehr either gave up on the theater or was given a sweetheart deal by Saxe to vacate the premises. Although Fehr's original lease allowed him to continue operating the theater until at least 1919, by June 1912, Fehr was out. On June 1, 1912, Saxe signed a two-year lease with the Shubert Theatrical Company at $16,000 per year, with an option to extend their contract to 1919. Herman Fehr telegrammed J. J. Shubert that Saxe wanted "immediate possession" of the theater. Fehr waived his rights to the theater and even paid the rent for June, July, and August (and was quite possibly paid back). Once again a Shubert house that had been gentrified by Roxy had been scooped up by Saxe and tossed Herman Fehr. "Saxe Bros., Lyric," Jun. 1, 1912; letter from Herman Fehr to J. J. Shubert, Jun. 3, 1912; telegram from Herman Fehr to J. J. Shubert, Jun. 6, 1912. (Shubert Archive, Contracts, Group II, 239)

295. James S. McQuade, "Chicago Letter," *MPW*, Jun. 15, 1912, 1012.

296. James S. McQuade, "Chicago Letter," *MPW*, Jun. 22, 1912, 1107.

297. "Brevities of the Business," *Motography*, Jun. 1912, 284.

298. Stagg, *The Brothers Shubert*, 104, 105.

299. "Drama and Music of the Week," *Sunday Record-Herald* (Chicago), Jun. 2, 1912, 5:5.

300. Stagg, 104, 105.

301. Jerry Stagg noted that J. J. Shubert never forgave Roxy, and when his spectacular, eponymous theater opened in New York in 1927, J. J. is said to have angrily commented that "the son of a bitch is still crazy about palms! In Florida he should have theaters!" Stagg, 104, 105.

302. "Boyd," *Sunday World-Herald* (Omaha, NE), Jun. 23, 1912, 6-E; James S. McQuade, "Chicago Letter," *MPW*, Jul. 6, 1912, 27. Roxy's influence with daylight pictures continued that summer as well. "The management of the Idle Hour is always on the lookout for some improvement," the *Aberdeen Daily News* in South Dakota reported in July 1912. "This time it is the daylight screen. The man that made motion pictures famous in old New York, Chicago, Milwaukee, and Minneapolis was S. L. Rothapfel, and if you ever get a chance to visit the latter place go to the Lyric and see the system used." The owners of Aberdeen's Idle Hour theater installed daylight pictures in both their Aberdeen and Watertown theaters to "great success." "Something New," *Aberdeen* (SD) *Daily News*, Jul. 5, 1912, 5.

303. Boyd's advertisement, *Sunday World-Herald* (Omaha, NE), Jul. 14, 1912, E:6.

304. Stagg 104, 105.

305. "Chicago Film Brevities," *MPW*, Jul. 20, 1912, 230.

306. By mid-December, the Shuberts would also cease operating Boyd's altogether, subleasing the house to the Burgess Woodward Theatre Company. "The Sam S. Shubert Booking Agency, Lee Shubert, and Burgess Woodward Theatre Company Agreement," Dec. 3, 1912, Shubert Archive, Contracts, Group II, 236.

307. "Chicago Film Brevities," *MPW*, Jul. 20, 1912, 230.

308. Hough noted Roxy's influence elsewhere as well. During his travel to Milwaukee, he observed that the Alhambra, a year and a half after Roxy's makeover, was still the hottest ticket in town. Despite the "oppressive" summer heat, long lines of patrons waiting to enter were still utterly routine. James S. McQuade, "Chicago Letter," *MPW*, Aug. 3, 1912, 424.

309. "This Week's Diversions in Theater and Park," *MJ*, Jul. 7, 1912, 8:7.

310. Saxe's Lyric advertisement, *MJ*, Jul. 14, 1912, 8:8; Boyd's advertisement, *Sunday World-Herald* (Omaha, NE), Jul. 14, 1912, E:6.

311. Saxe's Lyric advertisement, *MJ*, Jul. 28, 1912, 8:8; "What the Showmen Offer in Theaters and Parks," *MJ*, Jul. 28, 1912, 8:8.

312. "Bernhardt as Elizabeth," *MJ*, Nov. 17, 1912, 8:9; "New Faces in Vaudeville, Stock and Burlesque," *MJ*, Nov. 24, 1912, 8:9; Saxe's Lyric advertisement, *MJ*, Nov. 24, 1912, 8:9.

313. Rothafel, "A Bit About Myself," 459.

314. "Statistics from Minneapolis," *MPW*, Feb. 28, 1913, 771.

315. "Vaudeville, Stock and Burlesque," *MJ*, Jan. 12, 1913, 8:9.

316. James S. McQuade, "Chicago Letter," *MPW*, Feb. 8, 1913, 555; Saxe's Lyric advertisement, *MJ*, Feb. 16, 1913, 8:9. The slogan was accompanied by "as Clean as Your

Own Home" in the theater's March 2, 1913 advertisement. Saxe's Lyric advertisement, *MJ*, Mar. 2 1913, 8:9.

317. "Story of Christ in Moving Pictures," *MJ*, Apr. 27, 1913, 8:10.

318. James S. McQuade, "Chicago Letter," *MPW*, May 31, 1913, 906.

319. He had similarly told his Forest City patrons years earlier that "we will close the doors and keep them closed until the performance is over. Absolute quiet is imperative." James S. McQuade, "Chicago Letter," *MPW*, May 24, 1913, 796; "Topics of the Town," *FCN*, Oct. 14, 1909, 1; Family Theatre advertisement, *FCN*, Oct. 21, 1909; "Passion Play at Family a Big Success," *FCN*, Oct. 28, 1909.

320. Saxe's Lyric advertisement, *MJ*, Apr. 20, 1913, 8:9.

321. James S. McQuade, "Chicago Letter," *MPW*, May 24, 1913, 796.

322. Ibid.; "Lyric," *MJ*, May 11, 1913, 8:10.

323. "'From Manger to Cross' to Be Given Again," *MJ*, May 11, 1913, 8:9.

324. James S. McQuade, "Chicago Letter," *MPW*, May 24, 1913, 796; Saxe's Lyric advertisement, *MJ*, Apr. 27, 1913, 8:10.

325. James S. McQuade, "Chicago Letter," *MPW*, Jun. 14, 1913, 1121. For his encore presentation of Selig's 1911 production of *Cinderella* between June 9 and 11, Roxy costumed his chorus as well. "The Stage," *MJ*, Jun. 6, 1913, 8:8.

326. "Minnesota Exhibitors' League," *MPW*, Jul. 12, 1913, 157.

327. Ashkenazic (Central and Eastern European) Jewish custom dictated that children were traditionally named for the dead. Roxy gave the newest Rothapfel the middle name of his deceased mother, Cecelia. "Beta Cecelia Rothapfel," Record of Birth, Minneapolis, Minnesota, Jun. 26, 1913. Certificate No. 26711.

328. "The Stage," *MJ*, Aug. 17, 1913, 8:7; "Moving Pictures," *MJ*, Sept. 14, 1913, 8:10.

329. "How an Exhibitor Made Good," *MPN*, Jan. 10, 1914, 20, 21.

2. BROADWAY MELODY (1913–1917)

AC	Atlanta Constitution
CDT	Chicago Daily Tribune
CSM	Christian Science Monitor
FCN	Forest City News (*Forest City, PA*)
IS	Indianapolis Star
ISS	Indianapolis Sunday Star
LAT	Los Angeles Times
MPN	Motion Picture News
MvPN	Moving Picture News
MPW	Moving Picture World
NYC	New York Clipper
NYDM	New York Dramatic Mirror
NYT	New York Times

NYTB   New York Tribune
RTWR   Roxy Theatre Weekly Review

MCNY   *Museum of the City of New York*
NYPL   *New York Public Library for the Performing Arts*

1. Charlie Keil and Shelly Stamp, "Introduction," in Keil and Stamp, eds., *American Cinema's Transitional Era*, 1, 7–9.

2. "Biggest Picture Theater," *NYDM*, Feb. 5, 1913, 26.

3. David Robinson, "The Year 1913," *Griffithiana* 50 (1994), 9.

4. "Film Flashes," *Variety*, Nov. 7, 1913, 14.

5. "Biggest Picture Theater," *NYDM*, Feb. 5, 1913, 26; "The Regent Theatre," *MvPN*, Apr. 5, 1913, 11.

6. "Two New Picture Houses," *Variety*, Feb. 7, 1913, 14.

7. "The 'Skydome' Moving Picture House," *MvPN*, Sept. 23, 1911, 18.

8. "Where Is the Keith Dividend? Keith's Admissions Reduced," *Variety*, Aug. 22, 1913, 3.

9. "Alhambra," *Variety*, Sept. 5, 1913, 20.

10. "Keith Calling for Help," *Variety*, Oct. 10, 1913, 3.

11. "Shows at the Box Office in the New York Theatres," *Variety*, Nov. 7, 1913, 10.

12. Roxy and Rosa would not see each other again for months. "Topics of the Town," *FCN*, Aug. 21, 1913.

13. "The Finest Motion Picture Theatre in United States to Be at Minneapolis," *Waterloo* (IA) *Reporter*, Sept. 6, 1913, 11.

14. "New Amusement Place," *FCN*, Oct. 16, 1913, 1.

15. Terry Ramsaye, *A Million and One Nights* (New York: Simon & Schuster, 1986), 676.

16. Loew's Inc., "Marcus Loew Entertainer of a Nation," ca. 1920, 5 (NYPL); John D. Thompson, "Elgin-Winter Garden Theatres Reborn," *Marquee*, 24:3 (1992), 5; Hilary Russell, "An Architect's Progress," *Marquee*, 21:1 (1989), 6; Christopher Hume, "The Elgin Winter Garden Reopens," *Toronto Star*, Dec. 3, 1989, C1; Michael R. Miller, "Theatres of the Bronx," *Marquee*, 4:3 (1972), n.p; Morrison, *Broadway Theatres*, 9; "The Real Estate Field," *NYT*, Apr. 11, 1913, 15.

17. Ramsaye, 676.

18. "Movies or Beer?" *New York Evening Post*, Jun. 7, 1924, n.p. (NYPL – MNN: *ZZ-38713).

19. "Bringing the Classics to Motion Picture Audiences," *Musical America*, ca. Jun. 1923, 5.

20. "New Amusement Place," *FCN*, Oct. 16, 1913, 1; "Regent Changes Hands," *Variety*, Oct. 17, 1913, 14.

21. Jeffrey Gurock, *When Harlem Was Jewish* (New York: Columbia University Press, 1979), 106.

22. Therese Rose Nagel, "Movie Magnate, Began Career as _____; Now Owns Largest Picture Theater," unknown publication, Apr. 28, 1923, n.p. (NYPL – 1526).

23. Gurock, 106–109.

24. "New York and the Moving Picture Theatre," *MPW*, Dec. 31, 1910, 1522, 1523.

25. Kathryn Fuller, "'You Can Have the Strand in Your Own Town,'" in Waller, ed., *Moviegoing in America*, 88.

26. J. A. A., "Regent Theatre, New York City," *MPW*, Dec. 20, 1913, 1401, 1402.

27. W. Stephen Bush, "The Theatre of Realization," *MPW*, Nov. 15, 1913, 714, 715.

28. "Advertising the Picture," *MPN*, Dec. 13, 1913, 28.

29. Bush, "The Theatre of Realization," 714, 715; J. A. A., "Regent Theatre, New York City," 1401, 1402.

30. J. A. A., "Regent Theatre, New York City," 1401, 1402.

31. "Prominent Exhibitors," *Motography*, Nov. 29, 1913, 394.

32. Naylor, *American Picture Palaces*, 41.

33. Gordon Whyte, "Carl Edouarde," *The Metronome*, Feb. 1928, 27.

34. "Extended Tour for First Regiment Band," *Binghamton Press and Leader*, Jul. 10, 1908, 1; "Panama Canal Model at Show," *Post-Standard* (Binghamton, NY), Mar. 24, 1913, 7.

35. "Knapp's Band at the Belasco," *NYTB*, Feb. 22, 1909, 7; Whyte, "Carl Edouarde," 27; "Panama Canal Model at Show," 7; untitled article, *Syracuse Journal*, Apr. 26, 1913, 7.

36. Whyte, "Carl Edouarde," 27.

37. "Film Flashes," *Variety*, Nov. 14, 1913, 14.

38. "'Don't Give the People What They Want,'" *Green Book Magazine*, Aug. 1914, 230.

39. J. A. A., "Regent Theatre, New York City," 1401, 1402.

40. Bush, "The Theatre of Realization," 714, 715.

41. Ibid.

42. "Exhibiting the Picture," *NYDM*, Jan. 14, 1914, 54.

43. Bush, "The Theatre of Realization," 714, 715.

44. J. A. A., "Regent Theatre, New York City," 1401, 1402.

45. Bush, "The Theatre of Realization," 714, 715.

46. "'Don't Give the People What They Want,'" 226.

47. *Motography* was quick to point out that their arrival had turned Roxy's head from the Regent, if only briefly. "Since the bringing of his family to New York," the trade paper noted, Roxy "devotes all his spare moments to furthering his acquaintance with his five-months-old daughter, Beta, and his four-year-old son." *Motography* also repeated a humorous story about Arthur Rothapfel's clockwatching on behalf of his father. "The other night, having come home from the Regent for dinner and to don full dress for the evening's greeting of patrons, he over-stayed his usual hour in coming back at Beta and was reminded of the fact by his small son, who warned, 'Say, pop! you'll lose your job if you don't hurry!'" "Topics of the Town," *FCN*, Nov. 27, 1913; "Brevities of the Business," *Motography*, Dec. 13, 1913, 449.

48. W. A. J., "A De Luxe Presentation," *MPN*, Dec. 6, 1913, 16.

49. J. A. A., "Regent Theatre, New York City," 1401, 1402.

50. Rothafel, quoted in W. Stephen Bush, "The Art of Exhibition," *MPW*, Nov. 11, 1914, 1064.

51. J. A. A., "Regent Theatre, New York City," 1401, 1402.

52. W. A. J., "A De Luxe Presentation," 16.

53. "Regent Theatre, New York City" *MPW*, Dec. 20, 1913, 1401.

54. W. A. J., "A De Luxe Presentation," 16.

55. Quoted in W. A. J., "A De Luxe Presentation," 16.

56. A. D. M., "Belasco Sees 'The Good Little Devil' Film, *MPN*, Dec. 27, 1913, 23.

57. "Another Movie Miracle," *NYT*, Apr. 3, 1927.

58. "Crowds at Rothapfel's Regent," 394.

59. Jas. S. McQuade, "Chicago Letter," *MPW*, May 17, 1913, 689.

60. Horace Fuld, "Exhibiting the Picture," *NYDM*, Jan. 14, 1914, 54.

61. W. Stephen Bush, "Rothapfel Rehearsing," *MPW*, Feb. 14, 1914, 787.

62. Ibid.

63. J. A. A., " 'Quo Vadis' at the Regent," *MPW*, Feb. 7, 1914, 680; Bush, "Rothapfel Rehearsing," 787.

64. J. A. A., " 'Quo Vadis' at the Regent," 680.

65. Ibid.; Bush, "Rothapfel Rehearsing," 787.

66. J. A. A., " 'Quo Vadis' at the Regent," 680.

67. Rothafel, quoted in Bush, "The Art of Exhibition," 1064.

68. J. A. A., " 'Quo Vadis' at the Regent," 680.

69. Ibid.

70. Marks, 93, 94.

71. Altman, *Silent Film Sound*, 274, 275.

72. "New York Movie Manipulation," *The Metronome*, Jun. 1916, 16.

73. W. A. J., "A De Luxe Presentation," 16.

74. The Strand Inaugural Program, Apr. 1914, 3; "Million-Dollar Theatre Opens," *MPN*, Apr. 18, 1914, 23.

75. "New Strand Opens; Biggest of Movies," *NYT*, Apr. 12, 1914, 15.

76. "Strand's Big Start," *Variety*, Apr. 17, 1914, 20.

77. Hugo Münsterberg, "Why We Go to the Movies," *The Cosmopolitan*, Dec. 15, 1915, reprinted in Allan Langdale, ed. *Hugo Münsterberg on Film* (New York: Routledge, 2002), 172.

78. Fuld, 54.

79. "How an Exhibitor Made Good," Jan. 10, 1914, 21.

80. "Million-Dollar Theatre Opens," *MPN*, Apr. 18, 1914, 23.

81. "Rothapfel Back from Europe," *MPW*, Mar. 21, 1914, 1526; "Elaborate Picture Policy," *Variety*, Feb. 6, 1914, 22.

82. "Rothapfel Sails for Europe," *MPW*, Jan. 24, 1914, 398; "Rothapfel Will Sail," *MPW*, Jan. 31, 1914, 557; Ancestry.com., "New York Passenger Lists, 1820–1957,"

2006; EllisIsland.org., "List of United States Citizens, Ellis Island Immigration Records, Mar. 4, 1914"; "America First in Picture Theatres," *MPN*, Mar. 21, 1914, 25.

83. Ancestry.com, "New York Passenger Lists, 1820–1957"; EllisIsland.org, "List of United States Citizens."

84. "Rothapfel Back from Europe," 1526.

85. "America First in Picture Theatres," *MPN*, Mar. 21, 1914, 25.

86. "Rothapfel Back from Europe," 1526.

87. "America First in Picture Theatres," 25.

88. "Rothapfel Back from Europe," 1526.

89. "The Rapid Evolution of the Modern Theatre Type," *American Architect*, Sept. 23, 1914, 186.

90. W. Stephen Bush, "Opening of the Strand," *MPW*, Apr. 18, 1914, 371.

91. "Strand's Big Start," *Variety*, Apr. 17, 1914, 20.

92. "Strand Theater Opens," *NYDM*, Apr. 15, 1914, 31.

93. "New Strand Opens; Biggest of Movies," *NYT*, Apr. 12, 1914, 15.

94. Bush, "Opening of the Strand," 371; "Million-Dollar Theatre Opens," 23.

95. The Strand inaugural program, Apr. 1914, 10.

96. "Million-Dollar Theatre Opens," 23.

97. Ibid.

98. Bush, "Opening of the Strand," 371.

99. The Strand inaugural program, 10.

100. "Million-Dollar Theatre Opens," 23; Bush, "Opening of the Strand," 371.

101. The Strand inaugural program, 10, 11.

102. "A $1,000,000 Picture Theatre on Broadway," *Blue Book*, Aug. 1914, 699 (NYPL).

103. "A Theatre with Four Million Patrons a Year," *Photoplay Magazine*, Apr. 1915, 84.

104. Rothafel, quoted in W. Stephen Bush, "The Art of Exhibition," *MPW*, Dec. 12, 1914, 1512.

105. "Million-Dollar Theatre Opens," 23; Bush, "Opening of the Strand," Apr. 18, 1914, 371.

106. Bush, "Opening of the Strand," Apr. 18, 1914, 371.

107. Quoted in Richard Alleman, *The Movie Lover's Guide to New York* (New York: Harper & Row, 1988), 90, 91.

108. Bush, "Opening of the Strand," Apr. 25, 1914, 502.

109. Ibid.

110. "Mrs. Maude Sails Home an American Favorite," *NYT*, Apr. 26, 1914, X6.

111. Bush, "Opening of the Strand," Apr. 25, 1914, 502; "Strand Theater Opens," 31.

112. Unlike his previous openings, there was no mention of the use of "daylight pictures." Four years after marketing the technique, it was no longer a central part of his repertoire. The Strand inaugural program, Apr. 1914, 10, 12.

113. Bush, "Opening of the Strand," Apr. 25, 1914, 502.

114. "Strand's Big Start," *Variety*, Apr. 17, 1914, 20.

115. "Brewster's Millions," *Fort Wayne* (IN) *Journal-Gazette*, May 11, 1914, 9.

116. "New Strand Opens in Newark," *MPN*, May 16, 1914, 26.

117. "Theatre Burglary Like a Melodrama," *NYT*, May 19, 1914, 9.

118. "The World of the Movies," *NYT*, May 24, 1914, 68.

119. For his part, Loew was becoming one of the most powerful impresarios. Loew's Theatrical Enterprises purchased the Sullivan and Considine Theatrical Syndicate in late March for roughly $5 million, giving the once impoverished Lower East Side boy a circuit of 80 theaters and control of up to 120 other houses following the purchase. "Loew in $4,000,000 Vaudeville Deal," *NYT*, Mar. 27, 1914, 11; "Loew Buys Circuit," *LAT*, Mar. 28, 1914, II6.

120. "A $1,000,000 Picture Theatre on Broadway," *Blue Book*, Aug. 1914, 698 (NYPL).

121. "Banquet Tendered to Visiting Exhibitors and Guests at the Hotel Biltmore New York City June 12," photograph and caption, *MPN*, Jun. 30, 1914, 28.

122. "A $1,000,000 Picture Theatre on Broadway," 698 (NYPL).

123. " 'Don't Give the People What They Want," 230.

124. "A $1,000,000 Picture Theatre on Broadway," 698 (NYPL).

125. Rothafel, quoted in W. Stephen Bush, "The Art of Exhibition," *MPW*, Oct. 17, 1914, 323.

126. "The 'Educational' Picture," *MPN*, Jul. 11, 1914, 65.

127. Grau, 290, 291.

128. " 'Don't Give the People What They Want," 230.

129. Rothafel, quoted in W. Stephen Bush, "The Art of Exhibition," *MPW*, Nov. 21, 1914, 1063.

130. Frank A. Edson, "The Movies: A New Department; Samuel L. Rothapfel," *The Metronome*, Aug. 1915, 18.

131. Ibid., 19.

132. Grau, 290, 291.

133. "Don't Give the People What They Want," 226, 230.

134. W. Stephen Bush, "The Art of Exhibition," *MPW*, Oct. 31, 1914, 628.

135. Roxy could be paradoxical, though; despite his carefully manicured rehearsals and scores, he also argued that "The best results are obtained spontaneously." S. L. Rothapfel, "Dramatizing Music for the Picture," *Reel Life*, Sept. 5, 1914, 23.

136. Ibid.

137. "Notes Written on the Screen," *NYT*, Aug. 9, 1914, X7.

138. Strand Theatre program, ca. Sept. 1914 (NYPL).

139. Rothafel, quoted in W. Stephen Bush, "The Art of Exhibition," *MPW*, Oct. 31, 1914, 628.

140. W. Stephen Bush, "The Art of Exhibition," *MPW*, Jun. 5, 1915, 1613

141. William A. Johnston, "Pictures and Publications," *MPN*, Jun. 19, 1915.

142. "The Strand Theatre in New York," unknown publication, Jun. 1916, n.p. (NYPL).

143. Golda M. Goldman, "Story of Samuel L. Rothafel and His Career," *American Hebrew*, Feb. 16, 1921, 463.

144. Nasaw, *Going Out*, 202.

145. Grau, 290, 291.

146. Rothafel, quoted in Bush, "The Art of Exhibition," Dec. 12, 1914, 1511.

147. Ibid.

148. Rothafel, quoted in Bush, "The Art of Exhibition," Nov. 11, 1914, 1063.

149. "'Use Your Heads' Says Movie Genius," *Salt Lake Tribune*, Nov. 11, 1915, 14.

150. "Improvement of Motion Pictures Is Constant Cry," *CSM*, Oct. 2, 1915, 2.

151. Rothafel, quoted in Bush, "The Art of Exhibition," Nov. 11, 1914, 1063.

152. Allan Langdale, "S(t)imulation of Mind: The Film Theory of Hugo Münsterberg," in Langdale, 6.

153. Rothafel, "The Heart Is the Target," 13.

154. Frank Landy, quoted in Langdale, 6.

155. Langdale, 3.

156. Jack Banner, "'ROXY,'" *Radio Guide*, Sept. 29, 1934, 7.

157. Lynne Denig, "The Rialto—A Theatre Without a Stage," *The Theatre*, May 1916, n.p. (MoMA). Roxy would continue to espouse the use of psychology and audience surveillance throughout his career. In 1920, for instance, he noted, "My theory is that one must be a natural psychologist, a practical psychologist," in order to be a successful exhibitor. Raymond Blythwayt, "Rothapfel as a Cinema Reformer," *LAT*, Jan. 18, 1920, III19.

158. "Special Showing of 'The Rose of the Rancho,'" *MPW*, Nov. 28, 1914, 1241.

159. "3 More Theatres Join Movie Field," *NYT*, Nov. 30, 1914, 9.

160. "Notable Showing of 'The Eternal City,'" *MPW*, Jan. 9, 1915, 199.

161. Rothafel, quoted in Bush, "The Art of Exhibition," Dec. 12, 1914, 1512.

162. "1915, as Seen from 1914," *MPN*, Dec. 19, 1914, 26.

163. "The Strand Theatre in New York," unknown publication, Jun. 1916, n.p. (NYPL); "A Theatre with Four Million Patrons a Year."

164. "Times Square the Theatrical Centre," *NYT*, Jan. 1, 1915, 13.

165. "A Theatre with Four Million Patrons a Year," 84.

166. "Theatrical Notes," *NYT*, Mar. 18, 1915, 11.

167. To celebrate the theater's efficiency and create some visual recognition for his staff and artists, Roxy and his "forces" found time enough to travel across the river to Fort Lee, New Jersey, and the World Film studios on March 22 to shoot a "fire drill" of the Strand employees for use in the "Strand Topical Review." "Timely Picture Topics," *NYC*, Apr. 2, 1915, 18.

168. "The Strand Theatre in New York," n.p. (NYPL); "A Theatre with Four Million Patrons a Year," 84.

169. Edson, 18.

170. Rothafel, quoted in W. Stephen Bush, "The Art of Exhibition," *MPW*, Jan. 16, 1915, 355.

171. John B. Gorgan, "A Moving Picture Maestro," *The National Magazine*, ca. 1915, 301. (Google Books).

172. "Photoplay Amusements," *Eau Claire* (WI) *Sunday Leader*, Jul. 11, 1915, 7.

173. "Great Film Plays for Long Runs," *MPW*, Feb. 13, 1915, 958.

174. World Film Corporation advertisement, *MPN*, Apr. 3, 1915, 5.

175. "Hippodrome a Film House," *San Antonio* (TX) *Light*, Mar. 7, 1915, 23.

176. Rothafel, quoted in Bush, Jan. 16, 1915, 356.

177. Bush, Jan. 16, 1915, 355, 356.

178. Rothafel, quoted in Bush, 356.

179. Despite their contentious relationship, Arthur Rothafel had a lot in common with his father and not just their love of broadcasting. Arthur admitted that as much as he had issues with his father, he "probably wasn't the light of his life either. I was probably [a] pretty bad kid actually. . . . I was probably a bit flighty. . . . I wasn't very stable." Like his father, Arthur also sought discipline through the military. "[I d]idn't get stable until I went into the army in 1940. I was flighty as hell and did strange things. I was a good example or a bad example of a rich man's son. I think that's the size of it." Undated Arthur Rothafel interview, ca. 1990. (Audiotape)

180. "A Theatre with Four Million Patrons a Year," 84.

181. *Tikkun Olam* is a Hebrew phrase meaning "repairing the world." For Roxy, the function was social and cultural, not religious.

182. Rothafel, quoted in Bush, Jan. 16, 1915, 355.

183. Gorgan, 301 (Google Books).

184. Ibid., 355, 356.

185. "Theatrical Notes," *NYT*, Feb. 27, 1915, 11.

186. Brett Page, "In Gotham's Playhouses—The Reform of Vaudeville," *ISS*, May 30, 1915.

187. O. O. McIntyre, "Sketches of Little New York," *Portsmouth* (OH) *Daily Times*, Jun. 11, 1915, 3.

188. Hammerstein's Victoria Program, Mar. 15, 1915, n.p. (NYPL).

189. "The Strand Employes [*sic*] Pay Tribute to Rothapfel," *MPN*, Jun. 12, 1915, 64; "Five Silver Vases for Rothapfel," *NYT*, May 30, 1915, 13.

190. "Written on the Screen," *NYT*, Jun. 6, 1915, X9.

191. "Insure Rialto's Director," *NYT*, Jun. 11, 1915, 15; "New Incorporations," *NYT*, Jun. 19, 1915, 14; "Great Movie Theatre on Old Victoria Site," *Lincoln* (Nebraska) *Daily Star*, Apr. 2, 1916, 8.

192. "Exit Hammerstein's Victoria; Enter the Rialto Theatre," *MPN*, Jun. 5, 1915, 61.

193. Edson, 18.

194. "'Cavalleria' Packs Manhattan," *NYTB*, Feb. 24, 1908, 7.

195. "Thurber Scholarships," *Hopkinsville Kentuckian*, Dec. 22, 1908, 4.

196. "Theatrical," *Anaconda* (MT) *Standard*, May 21, 1911, 11.

197. Roxy envisioned future college students with the following schedules: "History, 10 reels a week, Economics 6 reels, Latin and Greek 1 reel each—and the rest of

the courses in proportion." "Five Dollar 'Jit Show' in Future?" *Lincoln* (NE) *Daily Star*, Jul. 5, 1915, 1.

198. "Tribute to Rothapfel," 288, 289.

199. "Notes," *NYC*, Jul. 3, 1915, 4.

200. "'Trilby,'" *MPN*, Sept. 18, 1915, 85.

201. "'Trilby' at the Star Today," *Ogdensburg News*, Oct. 23, 1915, n.p.; "New 'Coast Defender' Arrives," *WP*, Nov. 21, 1915, 5; "Lyric-Christmas Day," *Lima* (OH) *Sunday News*, Dec. 24, 1915, 12; "St. Regis Theatre 'Trilby' Pictures," *Trenton* (NJ) *Evening Times*, Jan. 13, 1916, 15.

202. "'Battle Cry of Peace' at Vitagraph," *NYT*, Sept. 1, 1915, 9; Untitled, *NYT*, Sept. 5, 1915, X2.

203. "'The Battle Cry of Peace,' The Only Photoplay with an All-Star Cast," *Sandusky* (OH) *Star-Journal*, Jan. 13, 1916, 13; "'The Battle Cry of Peace,' The Only Photoplay with an All-Star Cast," *Sheboygan* (WI) *Press*, Feb. 11, 1916, 7.

204. "Carmen," *AFI Catalog Online*. Available at www.afi.com/members/catalog/DetailView.aspx?s=&Movie=16484 (accessed Jul. 19, 2011).

205. "First Showing Made of 'Carmen' Motion Picture," *CSM*, Oct. 2, 1915, 2.

206. "New Times Square Theatre this Fall on Site of the Long Popular Victoria," *NYT*, Sept. 26, 1915, XX1.

207. "Rush Work on Rialto," *NYT*, Aug. 14, 1915, 7.

208. Terry Ramsaye, "'Roxy,'" *Motion Picture Herald*, Jan. 18, 1936, 13.

209. "Rothapfel Lecture Tour Embraces Wide Territory," *NYC*, Oct. 30, 1915, 42; "Rothapfel Will Speak to Local Picture Men," *AC*, Oct. 19, 1915, 8.

210. "Rothapfel Lecture Tour Embraces Wide Territory," 42; "S. L. Rothapfel Guest at Dinner," *Dallas Morning News*, Oct. 27, 1915, 13.

211. "The City and Environs," *LAT*, Nov. 1, 1915, I8.

212. "Unique Banquet Being Arranged," *Salt Lake Tribune*, Oct. 30, 1915, 8.

213. "'Use Your Heads' Says Movie Genius," *Salt Lake Tribune*, Nov. 11, 1915, 14.

214. "The Public Not So Gullible," *Kansas City* (MO) *Times*, Nov. 15, 1915, 1.

215. "Persons and Things," *Daily Northwestern* (Oshkosh, WI), Nov. 18, 1915, 6.

216. "Coming to Give Lecture," *ISS*, Oct. 24, 1915, 15; "New York Manager Heard by Indiana Film Show Men," *ISS*, Nov. 21, 1915, 51.

217. "Rothapfel Lecture Tour Embraces Wide Territory," 42.

218. Ramsaye, "'Roxy,'" 13.

219. Bob Lee, "This Is Easy When Press Agents Are Handy," *CDT*, Jul. 13, 1916, 13.

220. King, "'Made for the Masses with an Appeal to the Classes': The Triangle Film Corporation and the Failure of Highbrow Film Culture," 15.

221. "Rothapfel Goes to the Knickerbocker," *NYT*, Jan. 6, 1916, 13; "Written on the Screen," *NYT*, Jan. 9, 1916, X4.

222. "Rothapfel Takes Hold of Knickerbocker Theatre," *MPN*, Jan. 22, 1916, 347.

223. Quoted in Lahue, *Dreams for Sale: The Rise and Fall of the Triangle Film Corporation*, 79.

224. "Rothapfel Takes Hold of Knickerbocker Theatre," 347; Knickerbocker Theatre advertisement, *NYT*, Jan. 23, 1916, X8.

225. "Rothapfel Goes to the Knickerbocker," 13; "Written on the Screen," Jan. 9, 1916, X4.

226. "Rothapfel Takes Hold of Knickerbocker Theatre," 347; Knickerbocker Theatre advertisement, Jan. 23, 1916, X8.

227. "Rothapfel Organizes News Service for Knickerbocker Theatre," *MPN*, Feb. 25, 1916, 1205; "Written on the Screen," *NYT*, Feb. 13, 1916, X9.

228. W. Stephen Bush, "Exhibition Wins," *MPW*, Feb. 26, 1916, 1278.

229. "Knickerbocker Theatre Opens under Rothapfel," *MPN*, Jan. 29, 1916, 549.

230. Knickerbocker Theatre advertisement, *NYT*, Jan. 16, 1916, X6.

231. "Hearing in Knickerbocker Theatre Suit Postponed," *MPN*, Feb. 19, 1916, 974.

232. "Written on the Screen," *NYT*, Feb. 6, 1916, X8.

233. King, 16.

234. "Written on the Screen," Feb. 6, 1916, X8.

235. "Films Stay at Knickerbocker," *NYT*, Feb. 22, 1916, 11.

236. King, 16.

237. "Rothapfel Opens Chicago's Colonial for Triangle," *MPN*, Mar. 18, 1916, 1582; "Triangle to Take Over the Colonial," *CDT*, Feb. 3, 1916, 14.

238. Colonial Theatre advertisement, *CDT*, Feb. 25, 1916, 8.

239. All of this training was put to good effect during a performance on February 26 when smoke from a fire two blocks away billowed softly into the theater. Some patrons, recalling the horrific Iroquois Theater fire thirteen years earlier, "became visibly disturbed." Roxy's staff, without missing a beat, walked up and down the theater and in "an assuring tone" lied to the Colonial's new patrons: "There is no danger," they repeated. "The odor is caused by the new projection machines." "Rothapfel Opens Chicago's Colonial for Triangle," 1582.

240. Alfred De Manby Advertisment, *Variety*, Mar. 17, 1916, 30. The early use of the "Roxy" nickname here is notable.

241. "The Rialto Policy," *Middletown* (NY) *Daily Times-Press*, Mar. 6, 1916, 2.

242. Kitty Kelly, "Lots of Dying in 'The Feast of Life,'" *CDT*, Apr. 24, 1916, 20.

243. Lee, 13.

244. Quoted in Thomas P. Riggio, ed., *Theodore Dreiser: American Diaries 1902–1926* (Philadelphia: University of Pennsylvania Press: 1982), 233.

245. "Great Movie Theatre on Old Victoria Site," *Lincoln* (NE) *Daily Star*, Apr. 2, 1916, 8.

246. "New Million Dollar Picture Palace Projected for B'Way," *Variety*, Nov. 3, 1916, 21.

247. S. L. Rothapfel to George Kleine, Mar. 21, 1916 (George Kleine Papers, Library of Congress, Box 51).

248. "Films and Film Folk," *Wid's*, Apr. 20, 1916, 515.

249. *Rialto Theatre Program-Magazine*, Rialto Theatre, ca. Apr. 1916, 17.

250. "Two Triangles for Opening of Rialto, New York," *MPN*, Apr. 29, 1916, 2544.

251. *Rialto Theatre Program-Magazine*, 16.

252. M. Norden shared the other half. United States Patent Office. Patent No. 49, 491. Filed Jun. 16, 1916, Serial No. 104,116. Patented Aug. 8, 1916.

253. "Rothapfel Opens His Rialto, Film Wonder Palace," *MPN*, May 6, 1916, 2675.

254. James McKenzie, "Rialto Marks New Era in Theatre Construction," *MPN*, May 6, 1916, 2770.

255. Ibid., 1916, 2733, 2734, 2742.

256. "Rothapfel Opens His Rialto, Film Wonder Palace," 2675.

257. Lynne Denig, "The Rialto—A Theatre Without a Stage," *The Theatre*, May 1916, n.p. (MoMA).

258. "Films and Film Folk," 530.

259. "'Police!' for Rialto Theatre," *MPN*, May 27, 1916, 3235.

260. "Seeing the Rialto with Rothapfel," *MPN*, Oct. 20, 1917, 2714.

261. For the scenic, *Niagara Falls*, "The music did not fit the picture as it was originally arranged, so Rothapfel did what few exhibitors would think of doing—[he] rearranged the scenic to fit the picture," *Motion Picture News* remarked. "The result was so perfect an accompaniment that the notes might have been written for the film by one of the world's masters. The audience burst into wild applause at the end of it." "Seeing the Rialto with Rothapfel," *MPN*, Nov. 3, 1917, 3086.

262. "Seeing the Rialto with Rothapfel," *MPN*, Oct. 27, 1917, 2891.

263. The Knickerbocker had already been subleased by the Charles Frohman Estate and Klaw and Erlanger earlier in the month for musical and dramatic live productions beginning in September 1916. Roxy, though, could hardly wait that long to be rid of it. His eyes were squarely on making the Rialto an even bigger success than the Strand, his neighbor five blocks to the north. "Knickerbocker Leased," *NYT*, Apr. 8, 1916, 13.

264. "Movies," *NYT*, Apr. 30, 1916, X8; "Triangle Leaves Knickerbocker House," *MPN*, May 13, 1916, 2908.

265. "Circle Theater Is Real Model," *IS*, Aug. 30, 1916, 14.

266. "Director Rothapfel Back from Indiana," *MPW*, Jul. 15, 1916, 461; "Circle Theater to Open on Aug. 30," *IS*, Aug. 13, 1916, 33.

267. "Circle Theater to Open on Aug. 30," 33.

268. The Circle Theatre advertisement, *ISS*, Aug. 27, 1916, 17.

269. "Circle Theater Is Real Model," 14.

270. The Circle Theatre advertisement, Aug. 27, 1916, 17.

271. "Circle Theater to Open on Aug. 30," 33.

272. "Circle Theater Is Real Model," 14.

273. "Circle Theater Seat Sale Establishes Mark for City," *IS*, Aug. 29, 1917, 6.

274. "Circle Theater Is Real Model," 14; The Circle Theatre advertisement, *IS*, Aug. 30, 1916, 14.

275. "Circle Theater Is Real Model," 14.

276. "Motion Pictures," *ISS*, Aug. 27, 1916, 33.

277. "Circle Theater Is Real Model," 14.

278. "Circle Theater Seat Sale Establishes Mark for City," 6.

279. "Circle Theater Is Real Model," 6, 14.

280. "Throng Attends Circle Opening," *IS*, Aug. 31, 1916, 8.

281. Rialto program, Sept. 10, 1916, 3.

282. Edwin Schallert, "Rothapfel a Harmonist," *LAT*, Nov. 2, 1919, III1.

283. Family Theatre handbill, Sept. 17, 1916.

284. "New Picture Theatre for Broadway," *NYT*, Nov. 2, 1916, 11.

285. "New Million Dollar Picture Palace Projected for B'Way," 21. According to *Variety*, Roxy resigned from the Rialto in December as soon as the deal for the Rivoli was completed. Instead, he remained at the Rialto and eventually managed both theaters. "Rothapfel Resigns," *Variety*, Dec. 29, 1916, 17.

286. "Rothapfel Goes in for Open Booking at Rialto," *MPN*, Dec. 23, 1916, 3983.

287. "Notes Written on the Screen," *NYT*, Dec. 17, 1916, X8.

288. "Amusements," *Brownsville Daily Herald*, Apr. 6, 1917, 3.

289. "The Stage," *TMJ*, Jul. 27, 1913, 8:6.

290. "Lets Walter Heroine Live," *NYT*, Apr. 9, 1917, 13.

291. "Editors Note," in Lieutenant Samuel Rothapfel, "Let's Get Together—*Everybody!*" *Photoplay*, Oct. 1918, 35.

292. "Rothapfel Has Convictions," *Variety*, Oct. 25, 1918, 39.

293. "New Incorporations," *NYT*, Apr. 25, 1917, 17; "Charley Chaplin May Get $1,000,000 a Year," *NYT*, Jul. 1, 1917, 5.

294. O'Malley, "Roxy Story," 3.

295. "Putting New Orleans on the Moving Picture Map," *MPW*, Jul. 21, 1917, 475–478; "Strand's Opening the Picture Event in South," *MPW*, Jul. 28, 1917, 673. Thank you to Bob Dickson for the references.

296. Quoted in *New Orleans Times-Picayune*, Jul. 6, 1917. Available at www.saengeramusements.com/theatres/nawlins/strand/nostrand.htm (accessed Jun. 12, 2011).

297. "Putting New Orleans on the Moving Picture Map"; "Strand's Opening the Picture Event in South."

298. Harriette Underhill, "Samuel Rothapfel Diagnosed," *NYTB*, Feb. 17, 1918, C7.

299. George Jean Nathan, "The Philosopher in the Rothapfel Orchard," *Vanity Fair*, Apr. 1917, 45.

300. "The Musical World," *Lincoln* (NE) *Sunday Star*, Sept. 2, 1917, 5.

301. "Seeing the Rialto with Rothapfel," *MPN*, Nov. 3, 1917, 3086.

302. "Music Notes," *NYT*, Aug. 2, 1917, 7; Rialto advertisement, *NYT*, Aug. 5, 1917, X5.

303. "Seeing the Rialto with Rothapfel," *MPN*, Oct. 27, 1917, 2891.

304. Underhill, "Samuel Rothapfel Diagnosed," C7.

305. "Various Musical Events," *NYT*, Dec. 16, 1917, X8.

306. "Bringing the Classics to Motion Picture Audiences," *Musical America*, ca. Jun. 1923, 5; Eric Beheim, "Rapee, Erno," *American National Biography Online* (Feb. 2000;

www.anb.org/articles/18/18-02660.html; accessed Jul. 1, 2008); Gordon Whyte, "The Little Man with the Big Orchestra," *The Metronome*, Oct. 15, 1926, 18, 19.

307. Whyte, "The Little Man with the Big Orchestra," 18, 19.

308. George Seilo, "Erno Rapee—An Appreciation," *The Metronome*, Jan. 1929, 33, 45.

309. "A New Era in Picture Music," *Dance Review*, Mar. 1923, n.p. (NYPL – 1526).

310. Thomas Stewart, "The Meeting Place of Radio Fans," *RTWR*, Jul. 2, 1927, 6; Whyte, "The Little Man with the Big Orchestra," 18, 19; "At the Theatres," *Lincoln* (NE) *Sunday Star*, Oct. 25, 1914, 2; "At the Majestic," *Fort Wayne* (IN) *Sentinel*, Nov. 2, 1914, 15.

311. "Elmer Hoelzle, Tenor, Makes Debut," *NYT*, Dec. 29, 1916, 7.

312. "A New Era in Picture Music," *Dance Review*, Mar. 1923, n.p. (NYPL – 1526).

313. "About You! And You!! And You!!!" *NYC*, Jan. 16, 1918, 15.

314. "Seeing the Rialto with Rothapfel," *MPN*, Oct. 13, 1917, 2528.

315. Ibid.

316. "Japanese Exhibitor 'Sees the Rialto with Rothapfel,'" *MPN*, Dec. 1, 1917, 3805. Roxy's name had spread north as well, with his advice reprinted in newspapers such as Winnipeg's *Manitoba Free Press*. "Here's a Suggestion for Real Music in Small House," *Manitoba Free Press*, Dec. 1, 1917, 33.

317. "'Some' Letter," the Rivoli program, Dec. 28, 1917, n.p.

318. "How to Get Rothapfel's Advice," advertisement, *MPN*, Dec. 22, 1917, 4343.

319. "The Rivoli Most Palatial of Picture Playhouses," *Theatre Magazine*, Dec. 1917, 403.

320. "Seeing the Rialto with Rothapfel," *MPN*, Dec. 22, 1917, 4388.

321. "The Rivoli Most Palatial of Picture Playhouses," 403.

322. The Rivoli advertisement, *Theatre Magazine*, Dec. 1917, 406.

323. "The Rivoli Most Palatial of Picture Playhouses," 403.

324. Roxy, quoted in Underhill, "Samuel Rothapfel Diagnosed," C7.

3. The Movie House as Recruiting Center (1917–1918)

CDT	Chicago Daily Tribune
LAT	Los Angeles Times
MC	Musical Courier
MPN	Motion Picture News
MPW	Moving Picture World
NYC	New York Clipper
NYDM	New York Dramatic Mirror
NYT	New York Times
NYTB	New York Tribune
RTWR	Roxy Theatre Weekly Review

CPI   *National Archives, Record Group 63, Records of the Committee on Public Information, Entry 1, General Correspondence of George Creel*
MCHC   *Marine Corps History Center*
MCNY   *Museum of the City of New York*
NYPL   *New York Public Library for the Performing Arts*

1. Kelly, *Cinema and the Great War*, 15, 17, 18.

2. Michael McCarthy, "Committee on Public Information," in Venzon, ed., *The United States in the First World War: An Encyclopedia*, 162.

3. Ibid.

4. Mock and Larson, *Words that Won the War*, vii.

5. Creel, *Rebel at Large: Recollections of Fifty Crowded Years*, 157.

6. McCarthy, 163.

7. Kelly, 15.

8. Creel, *Rebel at Large*, 157.

9. Woodrow Wilson to Secretaries of State, War, and Navy, Apr. 13, 1917, reprinted in Wood, ed., *Film and Propaganda in America: A Documentary History*, n.p.

10. McCarthy, in Venzon, 162.

11. Doenecke, "Creel, George Edward."

12. Quoted in Mock and Larson, 134.

13. Quoted in DeBauche, *Reel Patriotism: The Movies and World War I*, 75.

14. United States Committee on Public Information, *The Creel Report: Complete Report of the Chairman of the Committee on Public Information*, 22, 23. Ryerson later resigned from the Four Minute Men to enter the training school in Annapolis, and another Chicago resident, William McCormick Blair, became the group's national director on June 16, 1917.

15. United States Committee on Public Information, 22, 26.

16. Ibid., 22, 30.

17. This, of course, did not include African-Americans, who in the Jim Crow era were seldom welcomed by white audiences and, even if they could gain admittance, were rarely treated as equal patrons, even in many northern theaters during this time.

18. The use of film by the government was not new, of course. In 1911, the Bureau of Reclamation, for instance, had produced a film about agriculture to demonstrate problems in the West. The next year, the Civil Service Commission produced another film, *Won Through Merit.* Training films, too, had been made by the military for internal purposes, while the Signal Corps began overseeing the production of sixty-two training films made by private producers under their supervision. Isenberg, *War on Film: the American Cinema and World War I, 1914–1941*, 70, 71.

19. Mock and Larson, 136; "Division of Films Shows a Profit," *MPN*, Jan. 11, 1919, 233.

20. Creel, *How We Advertised America*, 120, 121.

21. United States Committee on Public Information, 51.

22. "Uplifters Boss War Films," *MPW*, Jan. 26, 1918, 483.

23. Quoted in Kelly, 27.

24. "Movies Mobilized to Aid in War Work," *NYT*, Jul. 29, 1917, 8; "Movie Industry Now Mobilized to Do Its Bit," *Chicago Daily Tribune*, Jul. 29, 1917, 12; "About You! And You!! And You!!!" *NYC*, Aug. 22, 1917, 17.

25. Debauche, "Film in the First World War," in Venzon, ed., *The United States in the First World War: An Encyclopedia*, 223.

26. DeBauche, *Reel Patriotism*, 89.

27. Letters to Creel, reprinted in advertisement, "Don't Hamper the Screen," *MPN*, Jun. 22, 1918, reprinted in Wood, ed., *Film and Propaganda in America: A Documentary History*, n.p.

28. "Marine Intelligence," *NYT*, May 12, 1886, 8; "Hamburg passenger lists, Jan.–Jun. 1886," Family History Center, Los Angeles; "New York Passenger Lists, 1820–1957," Ancestry.com, (accessed Dec. 26, 2006); Ira A. Glazier and P. William Filby, *Germans to America: List of Passengers Arriving at U.S. Ports* (Wilmington, DE: Scholarly Resources, 1996), 61; "Germans to America, 1875–1888," Genealogy.com (accessed Jul. 10, 2003); "Entries into New York, 1886," Family History Center, Los Angeles.

29. Roxy was, of course, not alone in casting off his Germanic background. Milwaukee's Germania Bank and German-American Bank, for instance, became the National Bank of Commerce and the American National Bank, while the city's Deutscher Club became the Wisconsin Club, and many German residents also chose to Americanize their name. Curiously, Roxy would wait until 1920 to drop the "p" from his name, reluctant perhaps to shed the "Rothapfel" name and brand he had built in roughly a decade in trade journals and New York newspapers. DeBauche, *Reel Patriotism*, 91. *The Battle Cry of Peace*, AFI Catalog Online.

30. Mould, 269.

31. "Rothapfel Tells of Advance on Weeklies," *MPN*, Aug. 31, 1918, 1374.

32. Ibid., 1374, 1377.

33. Samuel L. Rothapfel, "Rothapfel Gives Some Hints on Weeklies," *MPN*, Aug. 24, 1918, 1220.

34. Mould, 270.

35. Rothapfel, "Rothapfel Gives Some Hints on Weeklies," 1220.

36. Mould, 270.

37. DeBauche, *Reel Patriotism*, 80.

38. "Seeing the Rialto with Rothapfel," *MPN*, Dec. 1, 1917, 3804. The theater's patriotic fervor swept up six Rialto ushers who enlisted in the United States Navy by early June 1917 with Roxy's promise that they could have their jobs again upon their return from the war. "Six Rialto Ushers Enlist," *NYC*, Jun. 13, 1917, 5.

39. "War-Time Antagonism Halts Wagner Operas," *MC*, Nov. 8, 1917, 5; Editor-in-Chief, "Variations," *MC*, Nov. 8, 1917, 21; "More Patriotic Agitation Against Alien

Musicians," *MC*, Dec. 6, 1917, 19; Barbara L. Tischler, "Music," in Venzon, ed., *The United States in the First World War: An Encyclopedia*, 394.

40. "Patriotic Fury Directed at Boston Orchestra," *MC*, Nov. 8, 1917, 5, 19.

41. Rialto Revue (Rialto Theatre Program), Feb. 10, 1918, 7. In popular music, Russian-Jewish immigrant Israel Isidore Baline, better known as Irving Berlin, joined the cause by penning "Let's All Be Americans Now." (It was first recorded in June 1917 shortly after the American entrance into the war.) According to Barbara Tischler, the song "expressed a spirit of consensus that was intended to cross the ethnic and class lines that George Creel and the CPI considered to be major barriers to consensus building in the new wartime climate." Tischler, in Venzon, ed., *The United States in the First World War: An Encyclopedia*, 393.

42. "Seeing the Rialto with Rothapfel," *MPN*, Oct. 20, 1917, 2714.

43. "Seeing the Rialto with Rothapfel," *MPN*, Oct. 27, 1917, 2891.

44. "Rothapfel Leads Exhibitors in Thanksgiving Week Smoke Fund Drive," *MPN*, Nov. 24, 1917, 3602; Rothafel letter, reprinted in *MPN*, Dec. 1, 1917, 3762.

45. In addition to selling Liberty bonds at theaters, recruiters also set up tables and held "peach-stone matinees" where part of the cost of admission was a peach pit which would then be used in the construction of gas masks. "First National Exhibitors Get Behind 'Some Smoke' Campaign," *MPN*, Dec. 1, 1917, 3794.

46. "Seeing the Rialto with Rothapfel," *MPN*, Dec. 8, 1917, 3987.

47. "Seeing the Rialto with Rothapfel," *MPN*, Oct. 20, 1917, 2714.

48. "Seeing the Rialto with Rothapfel," *MPN*, Dec. 1, 1917, 3804.

49. "More Exhibitors Join Drive to Get Smokes for Soldiers," *MPN*, Dec. 8, 1917, 3971.

50. Campbell, 76.

51. Keil and Stamp, eds., *American Cinema's Transitional Era: Audiences, Institutions, Practices*.

52. "Rivoli," *Variety*, Jan. 4, 1918, 41.

53. Ibid.; "Rivoli Fills Promises of Triumph," *MPN*, Jan. 12, 1918, 221.

54. Rivoli Theatre Program, Dec. 28, 1917, n.p; "Rivoli Fills Promises of Triumph," 221; "Rivoli Another Triumph for Rothapfel," *NYC*, Jan. 2, 1918, 32.

55. "Rivoli Fills Promises of Triumph," 221.

56. Rivoli theatre program, Dec. 28, 1917, n.p.

57. "Rivoli, Rothapfel's New Theatre, Has Gala Opening—Remarkably Good Program Offered," *Exhibitor's Trade Review*, Jan. 12, 1918, 514.

58. Telegram, S. L. Rothapfel to George R. Creel, Dec. 17, 1917 (National Archives, Record Group 63, Records of the Committee on Public Information, Entry 1, General Correspondence of George Creel, CPI 1-A1, Box 20, Folder Rothapfel, S. L.).

59. "Rivoli, Rothapfel's New Theatre, Has Gala Opening—Remarkably Good Program Offered," 514. House was not actually a colonel but was given the sobriquet by Texas governor James Hogg in gratitude for his electioneering. Charles E. Neu,

"House, Edward Mandell," *American National Biography Online* (Feb. 2000; www.anb.org/articles/06/06-00291.html; accessed Aug. 2, 2011).

60. Advertisement, *Milwaukee Journal*, Jun. 2, 1918, in DeBauche, *Reel Patriotism*, 99.

61. J. H. Hecht to Thomas A. Edison, Co., Jun. 22, 1918; L. W. McChesney to George Kleine, Jun. 24, 1918 (George Kleine Papers, Subject File, Box 51, Library of Congress, Manuscript Division).

62. S. L. Rothapfel to George Kleine, Jun. 22, 1918; George Kleine to S. L. Rothapfel, Jul. 1, 1918; S. L. Rothapfel to George Kleine, Jul. 5, 1918 (George Kleine Papers, Subject File, Box 51, Library of Congress, Manuscript Division).

63. Roxy wrote to George Kleine: "THE UNBELIEVER was presented at this theatre with the specific understanding that I was to receive $1,000 for editing and rewriting the titles which I did and which was very satisfactory from all points of view as far as I know." S. L. Rothapfel to George Kleine, Jun. 22, 1918; S. L. Rothapfel to George Kleine, Jul. 5, 1918 (George Kleine Papers, Subject File, Box 51, Library of Congress, Manuscript Division).

64. "Editorial: 'Sam' Rothapfel, U. S. Marine," *The Recruiters' Bulletin*, Feb. 1918, 16.

65. "Patriotic Film at Rivoli Next Week," *NYT*, Feb. 9, 1918, 13.

66. "New Patriotic Film," *NYT*, Feb. 12, 1918, 9.

67. " 'Biggest Patriotic Punch' on Record Shown in Rivoli Presentation of 'The Unbeliever,'" *MPN*, Mar. 2, 1918, 1280.

68. "Rothapfel's Answers to Exhibitors," *MPN*, Mar. 2, 1918, 1279.

69. DeBauche, *Reel Patriotism*, 126.

70. Harriette Underhill, "Samuel Rothapfel Diagnosed," *NYTB*, Feb. 17, 1918, C7.

71. "Publicity Bureau Notes," *The Recruiters' Bulletin*, Apr. 1918, 29; "Rothapfel Becomes a Marine," *NYC*, Mar. 20, 1918, 31.

72. "Publicity Bureau Notes," 29.

73. "About You! And You!! And You!!!" *NYC*, ca. 1918, n.p.

74. "United War Work Publicity Plans," *War Libraries*, Sept. 9, 1918, 4.

75. "Films and Concerts in the Metropolitan," *NYT*, Mar. 21, 1918.

76. "U.S. Haste Costs Rothapfel the Metropolitan," *NYC*, Mar. 27, 1918, 5.

77. "Rothapfel Leaves for Duty," *NYC*, Apr. 10, 1918, 33; "Marines Get Thrilling Air Pictures," *MPW*, Jul. 6, 1918, 42.

78. "U-Boat Spied Off Carolina May 3," *Middletown* (NY) *Times-Press*, Jun. 4, 1918, 8.

79. "Marines Get Thrilling Air Pictures," 42.

80. Pendo, *Aviation in the Cinema*, 240; "Written on the Screen," *NYT*, May 19, 1918, 53.

81. "Written on the Screen," *NYT*, Jun. 23, 1918, 36.

82. "Relayed Releases," *NYT*, Jun. 9, 1918, 46.

83. Pendo, 240; "Written on the Screen," NYT, May 19, 1918, 53.

84. "Show 'Devil Dogs' in Training Camp," *NYT*, Jun. 10, 1918, 9.

85. "Failed to Obtain Permit," *NYT*, Jun. 25, 1918, 24.

86. Heywood Broun, "On the Screen," *NYTB*, Jun. 24, 1918, 9.

87. Rivoli Advertisement, *NYTB*, Jun. 23, 1918, C5.

88. "Written on the Screen," Jun. 23, 1918, 36.

89. Heywood Broun, "On the Screen," *NYTB*, Jun. 24, 1918, 9.

90. Heywood Broun, "Nothing in Particular," *NYTB*, Jul. 21, 1918, C2.

91. "Marines Get Thrilling Air Pictures," 42.

92. "What the Camera Can Do," *NYT*, Aug. 25, 1918, 33.

93. Pendo, 240.

94. "Relayed Releases," 46.

95. "Written on the Screen," *NYT*, Jul. 21, 1918, 33.

96. "Movie Man Invades Home of Cannibals," *NYT*, Jul. 22, 1918, 9.

97. "The Job of Selling Government Films," *NYTB*, Dec. 1, 1918, C5.

98. Joseph B. Thomas to Samuel L. Rothapfel, Jun. 5, 1918 (CPI 1-A1, Box 20, Folder Rothapfel, S. L.).

99. In April 1917, Roxy had already "place[d] a ban" on war lecturers at the Rialto because they had "turned out disastrously for the house." "War Lecturers A Failure," *Variety*, Apr. 27, 1917, 20.

100. Joseph B. Thomas to Samuel L. Rothapfel, Jun. 11, 1918 (CPI 1-A1, Box 20, Folder Rothapfel, S. L.).

101. Roxy is hardly mentioned in Creel's multiple memoirs and reports, though, and in Creel's 1920 survey of the CPI's propaganda efforts, *How We Advertised America*, Roxy's initials are given as "L. S." Rothapfel instead of "S. L." Despite their professional relationship, their personal contact seems to have been little in quantity and even less after the war was over.

102. Samuel L. Rothapfel to Joseph B. Thomas, Jun. 11, 1918 (CPI 1-A1, Box 20, Folder Rothapfel, S. L.).

103. Ibid.

104. Ibid.

105. George Creel to Samuel L. Rothapfel, Jun. 26, 1918 (CPI 1-A1, Box 20, Folder Rothapfel, S. L.).

106. Bringing media companies and personalities together with American military and foreign policy efforts would of course continue in the Cold War, with Edward R. Murrow's documentary work for the U.S. Information Agency.

107. Isenberg, 72; *Pershing's Crusaders*, AFI Catalog Online.

108. "Written on the Screen," *NYT*, May 5, 1918, 57; advertisement, *NYT*, May 21, 1918, 11; *Pershing's Crusaders*, AFI Catalog Online.

109. Isenberg, 72.

110. *Pershing's Crusaders* advertisement, *NYT*, May 25, 1918, 11.

111. *Pershing's Crusaders* advertisement, *NYT*, May 18, 1918, 11.

112. United States Committee on Public Information, 49, 52.

113. Campbell, 79.

114. Isenberg, 73.

115. Campbell, 79

116. Quoted in Mock and Larson, 141.

117. "America's Answer; Following the Fleet to France," *AFI Catalog Online*; "Film Our Men in Trenches," *NYT*, Jul. 13, 1918, 9.

118. "Clippings and Comments," *NYT*, Jul. 7, 1918, 35.

119. By mid-July, Roxy had been transferred to the inactive list of the Marine Corps. He retained his commission and was "subject to call at any time," despite receiving no pay for his service. "Lieut. Rothapfel on Inactive List," *NYT*, Jul. 16, 1918, 11; "Rothapfel to Stage War Film," *NYC*, Jul. 17, 1918, 32.

120. Creel, *How We Advertised America*, 122.

121. "Written on the Screen," *NYT*, Jul. 21, 1918, 33; "'America's Answer' Opens Tonight," *NYT*, Jul. 29, 1918, 9

122. "'America's Answer' Stirs War Spirit," *NYT*, Jul. 30, 1918, 9; "'America's Answer' Opens Tonight," *NYT*, Jul. 29, 1918, 9.

123. Undated telegram, Samuel L. Rothapfel to George Creel (CPI 1-A1, Box 20, Folder Rothapfel, S. L.).

124. *America's Answer* advertisement, *MPN*, Sept. 21, 1918, 1818.

125. United States Committee on Public Information, 49, 52.

126. "Loan Films Shown," *Variety*, Sept. 20, 1918, 49.

127. "Under Four Flags," *Variety*, Nov. 22, 1918, 45.

128. "Written on the Screen," *NYT*, Nov. 17, 1918, 46.

129. Mould, 266, 267.

130. "Under Four Flags," *Variety*, Nov. 22, 1918, 45.

131. "'Under Four Flags,'" *MPN*, Nov. 30, 1918, 3269.

132. Harriette Underhill, "On the Screen," *NYTB*, Nov. 18, 1918, 9.

133. Isenberg, 72; "'Under Four Flags,'" *MPW*, Nov. 30, 1918, 988.

134. "Official Film Tells How War Was Won," *NYT*, Nov. 18, 1918, 13.

135. "Official Film Tells How War Was Won," 13. Despite those and other accolades, *Variety*, which took a harder line than most other trade journals of the period, commented that while "It is all very interesting . . . there is really too much picture, the scenes being extended more than is necessary to give one a comprehensive view of what is intended to be conveyed. Most could be cut in half and the same result achieved in a trifle over an hour." "Under Four Flags," *Variety*, 45.

136. "Written on the Screen," *NYT*, Nov. 24, 1918, 48.

137. *Under Four Flags* advertisement, *MPW*, Jan. 11, 1919, 174.

138. "Airplanes to Advertise Movie," *NYT*, Nov. 16, 1918, 18.

139. "'Under Four Flags' Shown at Both Rivoli and Rialto," *MPW*, Nov. 30, 1918, 928.

140. "Written on the Screen," Nov. 17, 1918, 46. The afternoon benefit would commence a lifelong campaign by Roxy to raise funds for wounded soldiers.

141. "At Two Extremes," *MPN*, Dec. 14, 1918, 3510; "Too Fat to Fight," *Variety*, Nov. 25, 1918, 38; "Written on the Screen," *NYT*, Dec. 1, 1918, 76; "Too Fat to Fight," *AFI Catalog Online*.

142. 142. "At Two Extremes," 3510; "Too Fat to Fight," 38.

143. Ibid.

144. "Rothapfel Leads the Orchestra," *NYT*, Aug. 12, 1918, 7.

145. "Rivoli a Year Old," *MPN*, Jan. 4, 1919, 82.

146. Creel, *How We Advertised America*, 122.

147. United States Committee on Public Information, 55.

148. Campbell, 78.

149. *Under Four Flags* advertisement, *MPN*, Jan. 18, 1919, 343.

150. "Tribute to 'Under Four Flags,'" *MPN*, Feb. 1, 1919, 721.

151. "'Under Four Flags' Third Official War Picture," *MPW*, Nov. 16, 1918, 747.

152. *Under Four Flags* advertisement, *MPN*, Jan. 18, 1919, 343.

153. "Taste for Entertainment, Happy and Quiet Themes," *Variety*, Nov. 22, 1918, 3.

154. "Too Fat to Fight," 38.

155. United States Committee on Public Information, 49, 52. Outside of those three states, distribution of all three feature films had been handled by the Division of Films' George Bowles, who "had made a name for himself in exploiting 'The Birth of a Nation,'" Creel proudly noted in 1920. Creel, *How We Advertised America*, 121.

156. The Division of Films was closed by Apr. 1919. "U.S. to Drop Films," *NYC*, Feb. 19, 1919, 33.

157. "Foreign Propaganda Ban May Close Div. of Films," *Variety*, Dec. 13, 1918, 45.

158. "Shadows on the Screen," *NYTB*, Feb. 2, 1919, D4.

159. Louis Sobol with Samuel L. Rothafel, "'Roxy,' the Voice of Broadway," unknown, ca. 1935, n.p. (MCHC).

160. Roxy remained an enlisted man until April 5, 1922, when he was honorably discharged from the Marine Corps Reserve. "Marine Corps Orders," *The Leatherneck*, Apr. 8, 1922, 7.

161. "Marine Barracks, Navy Yard," *The Leatherneck*, Jan. 24, 1925, 2.

162. "Soldier of Fortune, Whose Voice Is Known to Millions, Outlines Enterprise at Fort Orange Club Dinner," unknown clipping, ca. 1927 (MCNY).

4. "The Man Who Gave the Movies a College Education" (1919–1922)

CSM	Christian Science Monitor
CDT	Chicago Daily Tribune
EH	Exhibitors Herald
EHM	Exhibitors Herald and Motography
LAE	Los Angeles Examiner
LAEE	Los Angeles Evening Express
LAT	Los Angeles Times
MC	Musical Courier

MPN	Motion Picture News
MPW	Moving Picture World
NYC	New York Clipper
NYDM	New York Dramatic Mirror
NYMT	New York Morning Telegraph
NYT	New York Times

MCHC	*Marine Corps History Center*
MCNY	*Museum of the City of New York*
NYPL	*New York Public Library for the Performing Arts*

1. Kendall, *Never Let Weather Interfere*, 275.

2. "Expansion of Tivoli Planned," *San Francisco Chronicle*, Dec. 17, 1918, 9.

3. "California's Opening Is Brilliant," *MPW*, Jan. 11, 1919, 195.

4. "Film News Condensed," *NYC*, ca. Jan. 1919, n.p.

5. "Owners Dine Rothapfel and Goldwyn," *MPN*, Jan. 4, 1919, 69.

6. Grace Kingsley, "Flashes," *LAT*, Dec. 16, 1918, II4.

7. "Rialto Rattles," *NYC*, Jan. 15, 1919, 11.

8. "Rothapfel Leaves the Rialto and Rivoli," *MPN*, Jan. 18, 1919, 363.

9. "Rothapfel Became Excited," *NYC*, Aug. 28, 1918, 1.

10. "Owners Dine Rothapfel and Goldwyn," 69.

11. "Movies Mobilized to Aid War Work," *NYT*, Jul. 29, 1917, 8; "Movie Industry Now Mobilized to Do Its Bit," *CDT*, Jul. 29, 1917, 12; "About You! And You!! And You!!!" *NYC*, Aug. 22, 1917, 17.

12. "Sherrill Feast Was Lively Affair," *NYC*, Oct. 30, 1918, 4.

13. Terry Ramsaye, "'Roxy,'" *Motion Picture Herald*, Jan. 18, 1936, 13, 14.

14. "Editorial," *NYT*, Jan. 12, 1919, reprinted in advertisement, *MPW*, Apr. 5, 1919, 18.

15. "Rothapfel Leaves the Rialto and Rivoli," 363.

16. "Rothapfel Reports," *Variety*, Jan. 17, 1919, 57.

17. "Rothapfel Leaves the Rialto and Rivoli," 363.

18. Roxy had visited the set of the film at Vitagraph Studios and criticized William P. S. Earle's directing, arguing that the scene being shot that day "did not convey a sense of sincerity." Blackton brushed Earle aside and suggested that Roxy take over, "whereupon," the *New York Times* reported, "he showed the actors how he thought it should be done." Blackton was either impressed enough by the results or knew the inclusion of the scene would guarantee its exhibition at the important Rialto Theatre, as he kept Roxy's version of the scene in the final cut of the film. "Notes Written on the Screen," *NYT*, Feb. 4, 1917, X8.

19. "Editors Note," in Lieutenant Samuel Rothapfel, "Let's Get Together—*Everybody!*" *Photoplay*, Oct. 1918, 36.

20. "Rothapfel Reports," 57.

21. "Rothapfel Leaves the Rialto and Rivoli," 363.

22. "Samuel Rothapfel, Program Producer," *MPW*, Feb. 22, 1919, 1048.

23. "Rothapfel Incorporates Co.," *NYC*, Feb. 19, 1919, 33; "Rothapfel Forms New Company," *EHM*, Mar. 1, 1919, 27.

24. "Rothapfel Initial Unit Program," *MPW*, May 24, 1919, 1147.

25. "Samuel Rothapfel, Program Producer," *MPW*, Feb. 22, 1919, 1048.

26. "Written on the Screen," *NYT*, Feb. 23, 1919, 40.

27. "Samuel Rothapfel, Program Producer," 1048.

28. "Rothapfel Forms New Company to Furnish Complete Programs," *EHM*, Mar. 1, 1919, 27.

29. *Rothapfel Unit Programme* advertisement, *MPN*, Apr. 12, 1919, 2248.

30. "Rothapfel for Forty-Five Cities," *MPN*, Apr. 26, 1919, 2646.

31. *Rothapfel Unit Programme* advertisement, *MPN*, Apr. 19, 1919, 2409.

32. This early blockbuster strategy would be used by successive films in the decades to follow before its wide-scale adoption more than half a century later.

33. "Rothapfel's Jump from the Camp Chair," *MPN*, May 3, 1919, 2875.

34. "Rothapfel Unit Proves Successful," *MPN*, May 24, 1919, 3441; "Rothapfel Unit Scores Success in First Showing," *Atlanta Constitution*, May 25, 1919, D7.

35. Roxy also traded on his postwar esteem with Major T. C. Sterrett and Colonel A. S. McLemore of the United States Marine Corps toasting Roxy as their brothers in arms. "Rothapfel Unit Scores Success in First Showing," D7.

36. "Rothapfel Sells Foreign Rights," *MPN*, May 24, 1919, 3433.

37. *Rothapfel Unit Programme* advertisement, *MPN*, May 24, 1919, 3345–3348.

38. "Park Theatre" clipping, *New Rochelle* (NY) *Daily Star*, May 26, 1919, n.p. (MCNY).

39. S. Jay Kaufman, "Round the Town," *New York Globe and Commercial*, May 29, 1919, n.p. (MCNY).

40. Quoted in *Rothapfel Unit Programme* advertisement, *MPN*, May 31, 1919, 3519.

41. "Rothapfel Initial Unit Program," *MPW*, May 24, 1919, 1147.

42. "In the News Net," *NYT*, May 25, 1919, 47.

43. "Notes of Motion Picture Plays and Players," *Evening Sun*, May 31, 1919. n.p. (MCNY).

44. Park Theatre advertisement, *NYT*, May 25, 1919, 48; "Along Broadway Snap Shot of Local Affairs," *Broadway Evening News*, May 30, 1919, n.p. (MCNY).

45. "The Rothapfel Program," *NYT*, Jun. 8, 1919, 50.

46. "Movies," *CDT*, Jun. 6, 1919, 22.

47. "Country Takes Kindly to Rothapfel Unit," *MPN*, Jun. 28, 1919, 186.

48. Loew's Metropolitan advertisement, *NYT*, Jul. 20, 1919, 40. The film would continue to appear around the country for the next year, playing at least as late as April 1920 in Clearfield, Pennsylvania, at the Driggs Theatre. Driggs Theatre advertisement, *Clearfield* (PA) *Progress*, Mar. 27, 1920, 5.

49. Mae Tinee, "Right Off the Reel," *CDT*, Aug. 3, 1919, G4.

50. Daisy Dean, "News Notes from Movieland," *Olean* (NY) *Evening Herald*, Oct. 1, 1919, 7.

51. Harold Franklin, "'De Luxe' the Foundation of the Industry," *MPN*, Sept. 27, 1919, 2583.

52. "Grauman Makes Prologue and Stage Setting the Talk of Los Angeles," *MPN*, Sept. 27, 1919, 2588.

53. "The Screen," *NYT*, Sept. 1, 1919, 14.

54. "Rothapfel Stages Elaborate Prologue," *MPN*, Sept. 13, 1919, 2217.

55. *False Gods* caption, *Middletown* (NY) *Times-Press*, Sept. 26, 1919, 7; "In the Local Theatres," *Olean* (NY) *Evening Herald*, Oct. 4, 1919, 7; the Auditorium advertisement, *Kingston* (NY) *Daily Freeman*, Oct. 1, 1919, 10; "New Incorporations," *NYT*, Oct. 2, 1919, 26. Roxy stopped in Milwaukee along the way in late September 1919 and was greeted warmly by the *Daily Northwestern*, which noted that he had returned to the Midwestern city he once called home with "dignity and éclat." "Persons and Things," *Daily Northwestern*, Sept. 26, 1919, 6.

56. Edwin Schallert, "Rothapfel a Harmonist," *LAT*, Nov. 2, 1919, III1. As Roxy was traveling west for Goldwyn, Sid Grauman was in New York. The rising exhibitor "invade[d]" the city, according to the *Motion Picture News*, where a dinner was given in his honor. The *News* had found a new star to champion, and Louella Parsons and Adolph Zukor were among the invited guests there to toast him. While Grauman enjoyed talking about the film business and his theater, he and Roxy differed in one important way—at least in the estimation of the *News*. "Grauman is about the last person that Syd. Grauman, himself wants to talk about," the *News* reported. He and Roxy may have shared their love of prologues and elaborate stage settings, but they were inherently different personalities. "Grauman of Coast Invades New York," *MPN*, Oct. 4, 1919, 2767.

57. Berg, *Goldwyn*, 93, 94.

58. Jas. S. McQuade, "Rothapfel Predicts Big Advance in Picture Presentation During the Year," *MPW*, Feb. 14, 1920, 1065.

59. "Los Angeles Welcomes Newest Theatre," *MPN*, Jan. 18, 1919, 421.

60. Elinor had just returned to Los Angeles after a seventeen-month absence during which he had served as a military interpreter in World War I and then worked for D. W. Griffith as "general music director-composer and arranger" for *Broken Blossoms'* "staging" on the East coast. In early October 1919, *MPN* particularly commended Elinor's accompaniment and Miller's presentation of *His Majesty, the American*, for instance, as part of a new "epoch in the presentation of pictures." "California Theatre Is Again to the Front," *MPN*, Oct. 4, 1919, 2777.

61. "California Theatre Is Again to the Front," 2777.

62. "California Deal Complete," *LAT*, Oct. 29, 1919, III4.

63. "California Theater Open Again Tonight," *LAEE*, Nov. 7, 1919, 16. Roxy's friend, Forest City native and prolific silent-film actor Pat O'Malley, recalled that in October 1919, "Sid Grauman[']s 'Million Dollar Theatre' was still holding the crowd's

[*sic*] so the directors of the California decided that the only way to make the theatre pay was to get some one who knew more than Sid Grauman. There was only one in the Country [*sic*], Samuel L. Rothafel." Pat O'Malley, "Roxy Story," Aug. 26, 1957, 2 (Unpublished article submitted to the *Forest City News*).

64. Edwin Schallert, "Musical," *LAT*, Oct. 29, 1919, III4; "Holy Carpet Is Seen in New Farrar Play," *LAEE*, Nov. 1, 1919, II:2; "Moving Pictures," *LAEE*, Nov. 2, 1919, IX:3; Schallert, "Rothapfel a Harmonist," III1.

65. "Flame of the Desert," *AFI Catalog Online*. Available at www.afi.com/members/catalog/DetailView.aspx?s=&Movie=15320 (accessed Aug. 13, 2011); "California to Reopen Tonight," *LAT*, Nov. 7, 1919, III4.

66. Grace Kinglsey, "California Reopens," *LAT*, Nov. 8, 1919, II7.

67. "'California' Flooded by Goldenrays," *LAE*, Nov. 8, 1919, 1:5.

68. Henry E. Dougherty, "The California Opening Gala Event Celebrated," *LAEE*, Nov. 8, 1919, 2:1.

69. "California Play Draws Big Crowds," *LAE*, Nov. 10, 1919, 1:10.

70. "Rothapfel Is Receiving Praise," *LAEE*, Dec. 6, 1919, 3:6.

71. "The 'Tour Through Grauman's' Stunt Complete," *MPN*, Dec. 6, 1919, 4082.

72. "Sid Grauman Tells How He Will Present Bills," *LAEE*, Dec. 13, 1919, 3:4

73. Henry E. Dougherty, "Sid Grauman Believes in Democracy," *LAEE*, Dec. 27, 1919, 21.

74. "East versus West," *Atlanta Constitution*, Nov. 23, 1919, D5.

75. "Wonderful Effects at California," *LAEE*, Dec. 10, 1919, 29.

76. California Theatre advertisement, *LAEE*, Dec. 5, 1919, 3:5.

77. Henry E. Dougherty, "California's Big Bill; Pickford at Kinema," *LAEE*, Dec. 8, 1919, 17.

78. Henry E. Dougherty, "Something About the Future Picture House," *LAEE*, Dec. 13, 1919, 3:1.

79. Quoted in California Theatre advertisement, *LAT*, Dec. 24, 1919, III4.

80. Dougherty, "Something About the Future Picture House," 3:1.

81. "Rothapfel Returns Today," *LAT*, Jan. 3, 1930, H9; "S.L. Rothapfel Back from San Francisco," *LAEE*, Jan. 7, 1920, 19.

82. California Theatre advertisement, *LAE*, Jan. 4, 1920, 9:3; California Theatre advertisement, *LAEE*, Jan. 5, 1920, 10.

83. "Rothapfel's Unusual Bill," *LAEE*, Jan. 3, 1920, 3:5.

84. "Drama," *LAT*, Jan. 5, 1920, II12.

85. California Theatre advertisement, Jan. 10, 1920, 3:2.

86. "Douglas Fairbanks at the California," *LAEE*, Jan. 12, 1920.

87. "Rothapfel in Chicago," *Wid's Daily*, January 31, 1920, 2.

88. Jas. S. McQuade, "Chicago News Letter," *MPW*, Feb. 14, 1920, 1065.

89. "Messmore Kendall Dies at 86; a Leader in Patriotic Societies," *NYT*, May 2, 1959, 23; Kendall, 264.

90. Kendall, 264, 265.

91. "Two Theatres on Wendel Property," *NYT*, Jan. 10, 1917, 5. In his book, Kendall notes that the lease was for $50,000, not $100,000, but I am using the more contemporary account because of the 30-year time span and the allowance for personal embellishment. Either way, it was a terrific deal. Kendall, 265.

92. Kendall, 266; "New Broadway Theatre," *NYT*, Jan. 28, 1917, XX5.

93. Kendall, 266, 270.

94. When Roxy left the Rialto and Rivoli, there was speculation that he would become the Capitol's managing director, but this did not happen. "Rothapfel Rumors," *Variety*, Jan. 10, 1919, 49.

95. The latter's connection to the Capitol would eventually be phased out in exchange for a $200,000 loan by Kendall to Selwyn and Company for the construction of two other theaters on 42nd Street, as they had originally wanted for the 50th Street property. "Capitol Theatre to Open," *NYT*, Aug. 28, 1919, 8; Kendall, 268, 269.

96. Kendall, 269, 270.

97. Capitol Theatre advertisement, *NYT*, Oct. 16, 1919, 17.

98. Kendall, 266, 267.

99. Quoted in Kendall, 270.

100. "Rothapfel in Charge of Capitol Presentations," *MPN*, Jun. 5, 1920, 4608; "Capitol Gets 'Lone Wolf's Daughter,'" *LAE*, Jan. 8, 1920, 1:14.

101. "Staff of Capitol Theatre Is Announced; Opening Soon," *MPN*, Oct. 25, 1919, 3129.

102. Kendall, 269, 270; Ewen, *George Gershwin, His Journey to Greatness*, 236.

103. "Goldwyn Buys into Capitol," *NYT*, May 16, 1920, 14; Kevin Lewis and Arnold Lewis, "Include Me Out: Samuel Goldwyn and Joe Godsol," *Film History* 2:2 (Jun.-Jul. 1988): 141–143. Messmore Kendall remembers these events differently. According to his autobiography, all of the studios wanted a piece of the Capitol and were bidding against one another to obtain control. Kevin and Arnold Lewis's research refutes this. Kendall, 271.

104. "Goldwyn Buys into Capitol," 14; Lewis and Lewis, 141–143.

105. Ibid.

106. Jobes, *Motion Picture Empire*, 198, 271; "Rothapfel Re-Opens Capitol," *NYC*, Jun. 9, 1920, 28.

107. Kendall, 275.

108. "Try for Every Ball," *Magazine of Business*, Jan. 1928, 11.

109. Capitol Theatre advertisement, *NYT*, May 30, 1930, X2.

110. "Broadway Welcomes Back S. L. Rothapfel," *MPN*, Jun. 13, 1920, 4924.

111. Capitol Theatre program, Jun. 13, 1920, 3, 6, 8.

112. "Production Manager," *LAT*, Feb. 9, 1924, A9; "Bringing the Classics to Motion Picture Audiences," *Musical America*, ca. Jun. 1923, 5; untitled clipping, *National Police Gazette*, Jun. 16, 1923, n.p. (NYPL – 1526).

113. Untitled, *NYC*, Jun. 16, 1920, 34.

114. "Gambarelli Likes to Dance," *Evening Post*, May 10, 1924, n.p. (NYPL – MNN: *ZZ-38713); "Wants His $180 Back," *NYC*, Jun. 4, 1919, 10; Empire Theatre advertisement, *NYC*, Dec. 13, 1919, n.p.

115. "Show Reviews," *NYC*, Jul. 4, 1917, 7; "New Acts," *NYC*, Jul. 4, 1917, 9; Temple Theatre advertisement, *Syracuse Herald*, ca. Mar. 25, 1918, 10.

116. "Gambarelli Likes to Dance"; "Bringing the Classics to Motion Picture Audiences," 5; untitled clipping, *National Police Gazette*, Jun. 16, 1923, n.p. (NYPL-1526); "Old Capitol to Die in Blaze of Glory," *Oakland Tribune*, Aug. 17, 1968, 9-B; Barbara Delatiner, "Reflections on a Stagestruck Life," *NYT*, Apr. 24, 1988, L125.

117. Quoted in Jennifer Dunning, "Maria Gambarelli Fenton, 89, a Metropolitan Opera Ballerina," *NYT*, Feb. 9, 1990, D18.

118. Koszarski, *An Evening's Entertainment*, 51.

119. "The Screen," *NYT*, Jun. 5, 1920, 24.

120. "Broadway Welcomes Back S. L. Rothapfel," *MPN*, Jun. 13, 1920, 4924.

121. Kendall, 275.

122. "Their Beginnings," *Photoplay*, Sept. 1920, 34, 35.

123. "Just a Year," *Wid's Daily*, undated clipping (MCNY).

124. The New York–born Axt was trained in New York and Berlin and began his conducting career as an assistant conductor under Oscar Hammerstein at the Philadelphia Opera House. He later worked as a conductor for a traveling show of Hammerstein's light opera "Naughty Marrietta," and then as a conductor for Victor Herbert (a Roxy favorite) before serving in that same role for Capitol Theatre skeptic Morris Gest at the Century Theatre. "Bringing the Classics to Motion Picture Audiences," *Musical America*, ca. Jun. 1923, 5 (NYPL).

125. "Rapee Leaves Rivoli," *NYC*, Nov. 19, 1919, 33; "Lassie," *Internet Broadway Database*. Available at http://ibdb.com/production.php?id=6795 (accessed Jul. 13, 2011); Nora Bayes Theatre advertisement, *NYT*, Apr. 10, 1920, 20; Alexander Woolcott, "The Play," *NYT*, Apr. 7, 1920, 9; Capitol Theatre program, Jun. 13, 1920, 6; "Screen," *NYT*, Oct. 24, 1919, X2.

126. "'Motion Picture Night' at the Friars," *NYT*, Nov. 11, 1920, 12; Friar's 2nd Annual Motion Picture Night advertisement, undated clipping (MCNY).

127. George Kleine to S. L. Rothapfel, May 5, 1921 (George Kleine Papers, Library of Congress, Box 51).

128. "'Passion' Has Big Premier," *MPN*, Dec. 4, 1920, 4278; Pratt, "Passion, the German Invasion & the Emergence of the Name 'Lubitsch,'" 42–44.

129. "Screen," *NYT*, Oct. 24, 1919, X2.

130. "'Passion' Booked for Capitol," *MPN*, Dec. 11, 1920, 4459.

131. "'Passion' Has Big Premier," *MPN*, Dec. 4, 1920, 4278; Pratt, 42–44.

132. "Consensus of Published Reviews," *MPW*, Dec. 11, 1920, 714; "'Passion,' First National Film, to Have Premiere at Capitol Theatre December 12," *MPW*, Dec. 11, 1920, 750.

133. Eileen Creelman, "Feature Plays and Players," unknown newspaper, c. Jul. 1933 (NYPL); "Rothapfel Staging Elaborate Prologue for 'Passion,'" *MPN*, Dec. 25, 1920, 125.

134. "Germany Puts Ban on American Movies," *NYT*, Dec. 12, 1920, E1.

135. "He has since done his public a kindness by dropping the troublesome letter," Carl Helm wrote in *Personality* magazine. Carl Heim, "Introducing Roxy—in Person," *Personality*, Jul. 1928, 96.

136. One notable exception to the ubiquity of his cut was a special nine-reel performance at Carnegie Hall two weeks after the Capitol debuted the film.

137. "The Screen," *NYT*, Dec. 13, 1920, 21.

138. "Rothapfel Staging Elaborate Prologue for 'Passion,'" 125.

139. "Record Gross at Capitol," *Variety*, Dec. 17, 1920, 45.

140. "Rothapfel Staging Elaborate Prologue for 'Passion,'" 125.

141. "Capitol Theatre Attendance Record Is Again Smashed, this Time by 'Passion,'" *MPW*, Dec. 25, 1920, 1055.

142. "Record Gross at Capitol," 45.

143. "Passion," *Variety*, Dec. 17, 1920, 40.

144. "Douglas Fairbanks' Latest Production Smashes All Capitol Theatre Records," *MPW*, Dec. 18, 1920, 898; "175,000 See 'Passion' During Week's Showing at Capitol, New York," *The Atlanta Constitution*, Feb. 6, 1921, D6; S. L. Rothafel, "Making The Program," *The Mentor*, Jul. 1921, 33.

145. Eyman, *Ernst Lubitsch: Laughter in Paradise*, 74. Roxy's postwar focus on Europe was not only on its films. A month after Roxy's exhibition of *Passion*, Herbert Hoover, chairman of the Motion Picture Committee, announced that Roxy had been appointed to "aid the suffering children of Europe." Roxy planned to allow speakers for the drive at the Capitol and he pledged to raise $5,000 for the effort. "Screen," *NYT*, Jan. 16, 1921, X2.

146. David P. Howells, "German Film Competition an Inspiration to Producers Here Rather than a Menace," *MPW*, Jan. 8, 1921, 161.

147. "Du Barry Picture," *LAT*, Feb. 20, 1921, III40.

148. First National Pictures advertisement, *EH*, Apr. 2, 1921, 25.

149. Eileen Creelman, "Feature Plays and Players," unknown newspaper, ca. Jul. 1933 (NYPL).

150. "Amusements," *West Australian* (Perth), Aug. 9, 1935, 2.

151. Hubbert, "Modernism at the Movies: *The Cabinet of Dr. Caligari* and a Film Score Revisited," 64.

152. "Rothafel to Present Foreign Feature at Capitol this Spring," *EH*, Mar. 19, 1921, 34.

153. Capitol Theatre advertisement, *NYT*, Mar. 21, 1921, 25.

154. "Unusual Program at the Capitol," *The Metronome*, Apr. 1921, 84, quoted in Hubbert, 75.

155. Capitol Theatre advertisement, *NYT*, Apr. 3, 1921, 88.

156. Prologue reprinted in "Rothafel Prologue with Lines and Business," *MPN*, Jun. 18, 1921, 3693; "Rothafel to Present Foreign Feature at Capitol This Spring," 34; "The Screen," *NYT*, Apr. 4, 1921, 22.

157. Budd, "The Cabinet of Dr. Caligari: Conditions of Reception," 47.

158. "Rothafel Prologue with Lines and Business," 3693; Kristin Thompson, "Dr. Caligari at the Folies-Bergère," in Budd, ed., *The Cabinet of Dr. Caligari: Texts, Contexts, Histories*, 147–148.

159. Kristin Thompson, 147–148.

160. "A significant and previously unacknowledged part of this film score's history," Hubbert notes, "is that its content was something of a mystery even to contemporary critics." Hubbert, 65, 78.

161. "Comes Stravinsky to the Film Theatres," *Musical America*, Apr. 16, 1921, 5.

162. Ibid. Roxy may have felt even more confident about his scoring abilities after speaking at "the first national conference of motion picture and musical interests" in late January 1921 at the Hotel Astor "under the auspices of the *Motion Picture News*." "Music and Picture Men Convene," *NYC*, Jan. 26, 1921, 16.

163. Hubbert, 80–82.

164. Ibid., 85, 86.

165. The *Times* credited the score's adaptation to Roxy, but the arrangement to Rapee, William Axt, and Hermann Hand. "The Screen," *NYT*, May 2, 1921, 20.

166. Hubbert, 64.

167. "Hello Everybody!" *RTWR*, Apr. 30, 1927, 3.

168. Kenneth Macgowan, "The Artistic Future of the Movies," *North American Review* CCXIII:783 (Feb. 1921): 260.

169. Paul Steinhart, "S. L. Rothafel's Got First Idea for Film Presentation While Working as Bartender," *Zit's Weekly Newspaper*, May 21, 1921, 14.

170. Golda M. Goldman, "Story of Samuel L. Rothafel and His Career," *American Hebrew*, Feb. 16, 1921, 463.

171. Capitol Theatre advertisement, *NYT*, May 3, 1921, 26.

172. Capitol Theatre advertisement, *NYT*, May 8, 1921, 74.

173. Stokes, *D. W. Griffith's The Birth of a Nation*, 235–237.

174. "Mental Photo of Samuel Rothafel," *American Pictorial*, Apr. 3, 1922, n.p. (NYPL). The successful re-release of *Birth* prompted George Kleine to send a letter to Roxy imploring him to bring back *Quo Vadis?* "I have held QUO VADIS out of New York ever since you and I discussed it in your office one evening several years ago," Kleine wrote. "You may recall that Mr. [Felix] Kahn was present and doubted the wisdom of showing a reissue. I suppose that the success of the BIRTH OF A NATION this week at your theatre is bringing many propositions to revive old successes before you, but I believe that QUO VADIS is so exceptional a film." Roxy, however, did not agree. George Kleine to S. L. Rothapfel, May 5, 1921 (George Kleine Papers, Subject File, Box 51, Library of Congress, Manuscript Division).

175. Walter F. Eberhardt, "Back Stage in the Movies," *Filmplay Journal*, Jan. 1922, 20.

176. Avery Strakosch, "And They Thought *He* Was the BLACK SHEEP of the Family!" *Brain Power*, May 1923, n.p.

177. Eberhardt, 20, 21. Another backstage visit was afforded to columnist James W. Dean, who observed Roxy and Rapee synchronizing *Hungry Hearts* with "stirring music." James W. Dean, "James W. Dean's Film Reviews," *Ogden* (UT) *Standard-Examiner*, Dec. 17, 1922, 36.

178. Capitol Theatre program, Aug. 27, 1922, 1.

179. Ibid.

180. Ibid.; Robert P. Undegraff, "'Hand-Ball Gives Me 'Second Wind' for Work,' Says Rothafel," *Physical Culture*, Aug. 1922, 31.

181. Undegraff, 31.

182. Ibid.

183. Undegraff, 31. Roxy's efforts with lighting would become so well known that he would later be asked by professional lighting engineers and students of stage lighting to give a "demonstration of his theories and methods." The invited guests included "lighting engineers from the Westinghouse Lamp Company, the Western Electric Company, the Society for Electrical Development and students of engineering and stage lighting at Columbia University, and the Polytechnic Institute of Brooklyn." "Rothafel to Demonstrate Theatre Lighting Methods," *Exhibitor's Herald*, ca. May 12, 1923, n.p. (NYPL – 1526). Roxy would later be asked to write a seminal article on stage lighting for the *Encyclopedia Britannica*. Rothafel, "Stage Lighting," in *The Theatre and Motion Pictures: A Selection of Articles from the New 14th Edition of the Encyclopedia Britannica*, 46–48.

184. Undegraff, 76, 78; Curtis Mitchell from *Edison Lamp Works News* noted that lighting rehearsals were conducted at midnight Saturday for up to three hours. Curtis Mitchell, "Lighting the World's Largest Moving Picture Theatre," *Edison Lamp Works News*, Nov. 1923, 1, 2 (NYPL-MNN: *ZZ-38750).

185. Eberhardt, 21, 54.

186. Hubbert, 71.

187. Dr. Frank Crane, "Work an Obsession," *The Globe*, Apr. 12, 1923, n.p. (NYPL).

188. Undegraff, 30.

189. "Inside Stuff on Music," *Variety*, Jun. 8, 1927, 46.

190. Untitled clipping, *Evening Mail*, ca. Jun. 16, 1922, n.p. (NYPL).

191. Ewen, *Dictators of the Baton*, 198–201.

192. "New School Teaches Picture Presentation," *Lima* (OH) *News*, Sept. 8, 1922, 21.

193. "Starring in New York Hit," *LAT*, Jun. 4, 1922, III32.

194. "Rothafel Celebrating His Second Anniversary," *NYMT*, ca. Jun. 1922, n.p. (NYPL).

195. Capitol Theatre advertisement, *NYT*, Jun. 4, 1922, 80; "S. L. Rothafel on a Fishing Trip to Vermont," *Daily Hotel Reporter*, Jun. 8, 1922, n.p. (NYPL); untitled clipping, *Brooklyn Standard Union*, Jun. 7, 1922, n.p. (NYPL).

196. "Thinks Future Culture Is in the Films," unknown clipping, ca. Jun. 8, 1922, n.p. (NYPL).

197. "S. L. Rothafel on a Fishing Trip to Vermont," n.p.; untitled clipping, *Brooklyn Standard Union*, n.p.

198. Rotha, *Robert J. Flaherty: A Biography*, 43.

199. Robert Flaherty, quoted in Rotha, *Robert J. Flaherty: A Biography*.

200. Unknown clipping, ca. Jun. 7, 1922, n.p. (NYPL).

201. Unknown clipping, ca. Jun. 20, 1922, n.p. (NYPL).

202. "Eskimo Lobby Display," *Film Daily*, Jun. 10, 1922, n.p. (NYPL).

203. "'Nanook of the North' to Open at the Capitol," *EH*, Jun. 17, 1922, n.p. (NYPL).

204. "Summer Enterprise Shows Strength of American Theatre," unknown clipping, ca. Jun. 1922, n.p. (NYPL).

205. "How 'Nanook' Reached B'dway," *New York American*, Aug. 1, 1922, n.p. (NYPL).

206. "'Nanook of the North' to Open at the Capitol," n.p.

207. "Eskimo Starred at the Capitol," *NYMT*, ca. Jun. 12, 1922, n.p. (NYPL).

208. "'Nanook of the North,' Real Life Film at the Capitol," unknown clipping, ca. Jun. 1922, n.p. (NYPL).

209. Sherwood, *The Best Moving Pictures of 1922–3*, 8.

210. "Low Business Records in Broadway Film Houses," unknown clipping, Jun. 16, 1922, n.p. (NYPL). Flaherty's arrival in New York and Roxy's presentation of the film were celebrated by the Dutch Treat Club, who made Flaherty and Roxy honorary members that June. At a luncheon at the Hotel Martinique in their honor, Flaherty projected three reels of the film for the one hundred and eight members gathered. "Treats Dutch Treaties," *NYMT*, June 16, 1922, n.p. (NYPL).

211. "How 'Nanook' Reached B'dway," n.p. (NYPL).

5. A Capitol Idea (1922–1925)

AC	Atlanta Constitution
BT	Boston Traveler
LAT	Los Angeles Times
MPN	Motion Picture News
MPW	Moving Picture World
NYC	New York Clipper
NYM	New York Morning Telegraph
NYT	New York Times
RG	Radio Guide
TDS	Toronto Daily Star
WP	Washington Post

MCNY   *Museum of the City of New York*
NYPL   *New York Public Library for the Performing Arts*
WHS   *Wisconsin Historical Society*

1. "Broadcasting," *Encyclopædia Britannica. Encyclopædia Britannica Online.* Encyclopædia Britannica, 2011.

2. MacDonald, *Don't Touch that Dial!*, 19.

3. "Radio," *NYT*, Nov. 19, 1922, 99.

4. Halper, *Invisible Stars*, 15.

5. "Broadcasting," *Encyclopædia Britannica.*

6. "20 Years on the Radio," *Newsweek*, Aug. 24, 1942, 67.

7. MacDonald, 18.

8. Jack Banner, "'Roxy,'" *RG*, Sept. 29, 1934, 7.

9. "Music by Radio Heard at Banquet," *LAT*, Feb. 21, 1922, II12.

10. Banning, *Commercial Broadcasting Pioneer*, 113, 114.

11. Jack Banner, "'ROXY,'" *RG*, Sept. 15, 1934, 8. Ben Hall writes (without citation) that Major Bowes scoffed at the idea at first. "Comfort the enemy?" Hall quotes Bowes as saying, "Never!" Hall, 68. Whether Bowes truly objected, though, is unknown.

12. Capitol Theatre program, Nov. 12, 1922, 1.

13. Jack Banner, "'ROXY,'" *RG*, Sept. 15, 1934, 8.

14. Ibid.

15. "Frederick W. M'Kown," *NYT*, Mar. 1, 1935, 19.

16. Banner, "'ROXY,'" Sept. 15, 1934, 8.

17. "Frederick W. M'Kown," 19.

18. "Music Notes," *NYT*, Nov. 24, 1922, 23.

19. Banner, "'ROXY,'" Sept. 15, 1934, 8.

20. Carl Helm, "Introducing Roxy—in Person," *Personality*, Jul. 1928, 97, 98.

21. Isabel Leighton, "ROXY," *Good Housekeeping*, Jan. 1931, 60.

22. "Radio," *News-week*, Jul. 28, 1934, 22.

23. Banning, 114.

24. Okrent, 208; "Here's 'Roxey' and 'The Gang,'" *Evening World*, Jun. 9, 1923, 9.

25. "Screen," *NYT*, Dec. 31, 1922, 74.

26. "Robin Hood in Radio Debut," *LAT*, Nov. 22, 1922, II3.

27. In December 1922, Roxy turned up at a radio convention held at Grand Central Palace and impressed at least one journalist with "the colors and stage settings" he had produced for the musical portion of the day's events. "Radio Show Is Glow of Color," *Manitoba* (Canada) *Free Press*, Jan. 13, 1923, 23.

28. Kendall, 275.

29. "Today's Radio Program," *NYT*, Jan. 14, 1923, XX5.

30. "Today's Program," *NYT*, Jan. 28, 1923, X11.

31. Jack Banner, "'ROXY,'" *RG*, Sept. 22, 1934, 8.

32. Kendall, 275.

33. Ibid., 115.

34. "Mr. Rothafel's Trip to England," *The Sun*, Feb. 28, 1923, n.p. (NYPL – 1526).

35. Clipping, *Photoplay Magazine*, date unknown, n.p. (NYPL – MFL+ n.c. 1526); untitled clipping, *Pensacola* (FL) *Journal*, Apr. 8, 1923, n.p. (NYPL – 1526); "Here's 'Roxey' and 'The Gang,'" 9.

36. Clipping, *Evening Standard*, Jan. 29, 1923, n.p. (MCNY).

37. "A Welcome Visitor," *The Bioscope*, Feb. 2, 1923, n.p.; "Go Thou and Do Likewise," *The Film Renter & Moving Picture News*, Feb. 17, 1923, n.p. (MCNY).

38. "U.S. Film King," *South Wales Echo*, Feb. 3, 1923, n.p. (MCNY).

39. "Mystery Man of the Movies," *Liverpool Courier*, Feb. 1, 1923, n.p. (MCNY).

40. Untitled clipping, *Kinematograph Weekly*, Feb. 1, 1923, n.p. (MCNY).

41. "Rothafel Forecasts in England," *Exhibitors Trade Review*, Apr. 28, 1923, 1110.

42. Ibid.; quoted in Quinn Martin, "The Screen," *The World*, Mar. 18, 1923, n.p. (MCNY).

43. "Go Thou and Do Likewise," n.p.

44. "Letters of Fire Wanted," *The Motion Picture Studio*, Feb. 24, 1923, n.p. (MCNY).

45. Untitled clipping, *MPN*, Mar. 17, 1923, n.p. (NYPL – 1526).

46. Unknown clipping, Feb. 9, 1923, n.p. (MCNY); Bernstein, *Walter Wanger, Hollywood Independent*, 50–53.

47. "Mr. Rothafel's Trip to England."

48. Unknown clipping, Feb. 9, 1923, n.p. (MCNY); Bernstein, 50–53.

49. "Mr. Rothafel's Trip to England."

50. "List of United States Citizens," SS *Berengaria*, Feb. 18, 1923, 41. Available at http://ellisisland.org/ (accessed July 17, 2011).

51. "Cinematograph Developments," *Western Argus* (Kalgoorlie, WA, Australia), Apr. 10, 1923, 11. Some of Roxy's employees, on the other hand, appraised him in more realistic terms. Capitol Theatre tenor Willie Robyn later noted that "Roxy knew nothing about music, but he had an awful lot of nerve, and was a marvelous showman. None better. (He) had a great feel for production. He was a genius in his own way, but music-no. He would get up and conduct an opera, or anything that was popular like *Tannhauser* and make a blunder at some most inopportune time. But after all, he was Roxy, and the concert was over, and that was it." Willie Robyn, quoted in Tim Brooks, "Willie Robyn: A Recording Artist in the 1920s," *ARSC Journal* 23:1 (1992): 46.

52. Capitol Theatre program, Apr. 15, 1923, 3.

53. "Famous Movie Exhibitor Here," *Rochester Herald*, Feb. 28, 1923, n.p. (NYPL – 1526).

54. "Big Job for Rothafel," *NYC*, ca. Apr. 1, 1923, n.p. (NYPL – 1526).

55. "Notables of New York," *Atlantic City Gazette Review*, Apr. 18, 1923, n.p. (NYPL – 1526).

56. "Capitol Tokens Are Ready Now," *Evening Mail*, May 26, 1923, n.p. (NYPL – MFL+ n.c. 1526).

57. Evelyn Lanzius, "Roxie, Lil, Bert and Louis of WEAF," *Radio Digest*, Jun. 2, 1923, 5.

58. Clipping, *Colorado Springs Telegram*, Apr. 15, 1923, n.p. (NYPL – MFL+ n.c. 1526).

59. "Likes Broadcasting," *MPW*, Feb. 16, 1924; Gladys Hall, "He Makes the World at Home," *Classic*, Aug. 1923, 25.

60. Untitled clipping, *Exhibitor's Trade Review*, ca. May 15, 1924, n.p. (NYPL – MNN: *ZZ-38713).

61. Hilmes, *Radio Voices*, xviii.

62. "Radio—Will It Help the Theatre Problem Industry Wants Settled," *Exhibitors Trade Review*, May 8, 1923, 1122. (NYPL – MNN: *ZZ-38713).

63. "Here's 'Roxey' and 'The Gang.'"

64. Another letter sent to *The Billboard* in 1925 noted Roxy's and the Capitol's immense appeal (and the training of the ushers therein): "I am the actress who suffered a broken neck and fractured skull more than three years ago. As a result I was temporarily crippled. The first time I was out alone was when I sneaked away one day when my dear, dear mother and father were out together. They are so devoted to me and would have been afraid for me to go out but I got a taxi to take me to the Capitol Theatre. I bought my ticket and started to walk through the lobby, holding my hand against the wall. A page, who had been standing beside the ticket taker, observed my effort and instantly came to my aid. He offered his arm and escorted me to a seat, assisted me to remove my coat, and when I mentioned the time I had to leave he said he would be back at that hour to assist me. He was showing me every courtesy and helped me to a taxi, warning the chauffeur to drive very carefully. My first day out in nearly three years! It was a happy one and such courtesy and attention deserves broadcasting." Unknown letter, *The Billboard*, Mar. 14, 1925, quoted in Capitol Theatre program, Mar. 29, 1925, 1.

65. "Roxie" (S. L. Rothafel), "A Bit About Myself," *Radio Broadcast*, Oct. 1923, 463.

66. "Radio—Will It Help the Theatre Problem Industry Wants Settled," 1122.

67. Mr. and Mrs. Brown-Jones, "Making a Party Call on S.L. Rothafel," *The Wireless Age*, Jun. 1923, 33.

68. Capitol Theatre program, Jul. 15, 1923, 3.

69. Capitol Theatre program, Mar. 29, 1925, 3; Capitol Theatre program, Jun. 14, 1925, 3.

70. "Radio—Will It Help the Theatre Problem Industry Wants Settled," 1122.

71. Mr. and Mrs. Brown-Jones, 33.

72. Untitled clipping, *Brooklyn Citizen*, Apr. 28, 1923, n.p. (NYPL – 1526).

73. Lanzius, 5.

74. Untitled clipping, *Brooklyn Citizen*, Apr. 28, 1923, n.p. An early-May 1923 example featured introductory remarks at 7:30, followed by "Dance of the Hours"

performed by the Capitol Grand Orchestra. At 7:40, incidental music for the "Capitol Magazine" (a selection of newsreels and other short films) could be heard, followed by Verdi's "Impressions of Rigoletto" performed by the orchestra under Rapee. From 8:05 to 9:00, the Gang performed in the studio. Untitled clipping, *Radio Globe*, May 5, 1923, n.p. (NYPL – 1526). The June 10, 1923, broadcast revealed a similar schedule, which included an overture from the Capitol Grand Orchestra, a "Japanese Chant" sung by the "Male Chorus of the Capitol Grand Ensemble," a "musical interpretation to 'A Dream of the Sea,'" "Indian Love Lyrics" and "a series of tableaux by William Robyn, and Capitol Mixed Quartet, interpreted by the Capitol Ballet Corp [*sic*]." After the musical accompaniment for the "Capitol Magazine" aired, the one-hundred-minute broadcast concluded with Roxy and His Gang performing live in the studio for the remaining fifty minutes. Untitled clipping, *Daily Times*, Jun. 10, 1923 (NYPL – 1526).

75. "Capitol Tokens Are Ready Now," *Evening Mail*, May 26, 1923, n.p. (NYPL – 1526).

76. Vandy Cape, "The World of Music," *Hostess Magazine*, ca. Jan. 1924, n.p. (NYPL – MNN: *ZZ-38750).

77. Lanzius, 5.

78. Mary Radcliffe, "Roxy-Radio's 'Biggest Personality,'" unknown clipping, n.p. (NYPL – MNN: *ZZ-38750).

79. Untitled clipping, Jan. 31, 1924, n.p. (NYPL – MNN: *ZZ-38750).

80. Phillips & Crew Piano Co. advertisement, *AC*, Feb. 1, 1920, 3A; Duo-Art advertisement, *Kansas City Times*, Feb. 20, 1920, 6.

81. "Queen of Sheba to Visit Mexia," *Mexia* (TX) *Evening News*, Feb. 20, 1922, 3.

82. Kalinak, *How the West Was Sung: Music in the Westerns of John Ford*, 29, 30.

83. Garden Theatre advertisement, *Davenport* (IA) *Democrat and Leader*, Nov. 14, 1923, 12.

84. "A New Era in Picture Music," *Dance Review*, Mar. 1923, n.p. (NYPL – 1526).

85. Brunswick Records advertisement, *LAT*, Jan. 24, 1923, II7; Brunswick Records advertisement, *Evening World*, Apr. 13, 1923, n.p. (NYPL – MFL+ n.c. 1526).

86. "Good Orchestral Music Recorded," *LAT*, Feb. 18, 1923, III42; Brunswick Records advertisement, *Chicago Heights Star*, Apr. 12, 1923, 3; Brunswick Records advertisement, *Hartford Courant*, Apr. 14, 1923, 5.

87. Brunswick Records advertisement, *LAT*, Jan. 24, 1923, II7.

88. "Strand Radio Shows," *Variety*, Jun. 16, 1923; Crowther, *The Lion's Share*, 129.

89. Philadelphia Fox Theatre program, Dec. 10, 1923, 3; Whyte, "The Little Man with the Big Orchestra," 18, 19. At the Fox, Rapee duplicated Roxy's presentation efforts with thematic prologues and other live accompaniment. Untitled clipping, *NYMT*, Feb. 17, 1924, n.p. (NYPL – MNN: *ZZ-38750); Fox Theatre (Philadelphia) program, Dec. 10, 1923, 5.

90. "Radio Program," *Watertown* (NY) *Daily Times*, Feb. 2, 1924, 4.

91. "Likes Broadcasting," *MPW*, Feb. 16, 1924; Crafton, *The Talkies*, 42.

92. "Radio and Screen," *N.Y. Exhibitor's Trade Review*, Mar. 9, 1924, n.p. (NYPL – MNN: *ZZ-38713).

93. "Radio Is Box Office Danger," *Variety*, Mar. 5, 1924, n.p. (NYPL – MNN: *ZZ-38750).

94. "A Manager's Anniversary," *NYT*, Jun. 15, 1924, n.p. (NYPL – MNN: *ZZ-38713).

95. "Capitol Theatre to Celebrate First Anniversary of Its Broadcasting Service this Evening," *Brooklyn Citizen*, Nov. 18, 1923, n.p. (NYPL – MNN: *ZZ-38750).

96. "Rothafel Praises Radio in Theatre," *NYMT*, Feb. 22, 1924, n.p. (NYPL – MNN: *ZZ-38750); Mr. and Mrs. Brown-Jones, 33; Lanzius, 5.

97. "Filmland," *Evening Mail*, Oct. 24, 1923, n.p. (MCNY).

98. "Radio and Screen," *N.Y. Exhibitor's Trade Review*, 9 Mar. 1924, n.p. (NYPL – MNN: *ZZ-38713).

99. "Radio Injuring Neighborhood Patronage Says Sydney B. Lust," unknown clipping, n.p. (NYPL – MNN: *ZZ-38713).

100. "'Roxy,'" *Zit's Weekly Newspaper*, Feb. 22, 1924, n.p. (NYPL – MNN: *ZZ-38750).

101. Thos. B. Hanly, "Many *and* Various," *NYMT*, Mar. 2, 1924, n.p. (NYPL – MNN: *ZZ-38750).

102. "Radio Is Box Office Danger," n.p.

103. "Rothafel Raps Radio Raillery," *Zit's Weekly Newspaper*, Feb. 29, 1924, n.p. (NYPL – MNN: *ZZ-38750).

104. Lanzius, 5.

105. "'Black Cyclone' Hit," *Exhibitor's Trade Review*, ca. 1925, clipping (NYPL).

106. "What Are the Wild Tubes Saying," *TDS*, Nov. 13, 1923, 19.

107. "Betsy Ayres of Capitol and Radio Fame, Praises Joseph Regneas and S. L. Rothafel," *Musical Courier*, Jan. 24, 1924, n.p. (NYPL – MNN: *ZZ-38750).

108. Cape, n.p.

109. "Here's 'Roxey' [*sic*] and 'The Gang,'" *Evening World's Radio Section*, Jun. 9, 1923.

110. "Show Stopping," [. . .]*ington Daily News*, Apr. 2, 1924, n.p. (NYPL – MNN: *ZZ-38713).

111. Overland Radio Store advertisement, unknown source, ca. Nov. 1923, n.p. (NYPL – MNN: *ZZ-38750).

112. Rothafel, "A Bit About Myself," 458–464.

113. Overland Radio Store advertisement, ca. Dec. 1923, *The Sun and The Globe*, n.p. (MCNY).

114. "Production Manager," *LAT*, Feb. 9, 1924, A9; "Oumansky of Grauman Houses," unknown clipping, Feb. 17, 1924, n.p. (NYPL – MNN: *ZZ-38750).

115. "Broadway's Preparing for Buyers," *Utica* (NY) *Observer Dispatch*, Mar. 3, 1923, 4D.

116. "[S]he works out her own choreography," Dorothy Day observed, "arranges all of the dances and invents new combinations of steps all the time." Like any good Capitol foot soldier, Gamby also began to think and talk like Roxy. "I cannot have

time to see my friends because friends, like anything beautiful, have to be cultivated and I spend practically all my time in the theatre," she noted, expressing the same workaholic nature as her employer. Dorothy Day, "Here Is the World's Youngest Ballet Mistress," *NYMT*, Mar. 9, 1924, n.p. (NYPL – MNN: *ZZ-38750).

117. Photographs and articles about Gambarelli, including the following article, appear in numerous clippings in a Capitol Theatre scrapbook from this period. "Mlle. Gambarelli Becomes Radio Star," *New York Review*, Jan. 19, 1924, n.p. (NYPL – MNN: *ZZ-38750). Roxy also drummed up further publicity by dressing up her friendship with Douglas Stanbury as an on-air romance—a fiction he kept up for years. (He tried the same tactic with Gang members Vee Lawnhurst and Bill Langon.) In a 1984 interview with Peter Mintun, Lawnhurst noted that Gambarelli was more than just Roxy's most popular stage and, later, radio attraction, "she was Roxy's girlfriend." If her account is to be believed, the fabricated romance between Gambarelli and Stanbury may have served as ideal cover for his own relationship with the dancer. Unpublished interview transcript with Vee Lawnhurst, Jan. 26, 1984. Special thank you to Galen Wilkes for providing copies of the interview and a letter Lawnhurst wrote him on April 29, 1985, about the crafted "Billy and Vee" on-air romance. Vee Lawnhurst to Galen Wilkes, Apr. 22, 1985.

118. "Movie Music," unknown clipping, ca. Mar. 9, 1924, n.p. (NYPL – MNN: *ZZ-38750).

119. "Capitol Theatre Artists to Tour," *Review*, Jan. 12, 1924, n.p. (NYPL – MNN: *ZZ-38750).

120. "Betsy Ayres of Capitol and Radio Fame, Praises Joseph Regneas and S. L. Rothafel," *Musical Courier*, Jan. 24, 1924, n.p. (NYPL – MNN: *ZZ-38750).

121. Banner, Sept. 22, 1934, 26.

122. "Great Roxie Gang Works Hackensack," unknown clipping, ca. Feb. 9, 1924, n.p. (NYPL – MNN: *ZZ-38750).

123. "Capitol Artists to Sing for Cabinet Members," *New York Review*, Feb. 16, 1924, n.p. (NYPL – MNN: *ZZ-38750).

124. "On the Shadow Stage," *WP*, Feb. 17, 1924, 8.

125. Untitled clipping, *NYMT*, Feb. 17, 1924, n.p. (NYPL – MNN: *ZZ-38750).

126. "Capitol of Sing Sing," *Telegraph*, Mar. 8, 1924, n.p. (NYPL – MNN: *ZZ-38750).

127. Untitled clipping, *New York American*, Mar. 8, 1924, n.p. (NYPL – MNN: *ZZ-38750).

128. "When Roxy Rothafel and His Gang Went Roaming," *NYMT*, May 25, 1924, n.p. (NYPL – MNN: *ZZ-38713).

129. "Capitol's Radio Outfit Will Tour," *Times Square Daily*, ca. Mar. 8, 1924, n.p; "Treat for Sing Sing," *NYMT*, Mar. 9, 1924, n.p. (NYPL – MNN: *ZZ-38750).

130. "Treat for Sing Sing," n.p.; unknown clipping, Mar. 14, 1924, n.p. (NYPL – MNN: *ZZ-38750).

131. "Roxie's Gang Draws $8,600," *NYC*, Mar. 20, 1924, n.p. (NYPL – MNN: *ZZ-38750); Mary B. Mullett, "Roxy and His Gang," *American Magazine*, Mar. 1925, 34.

132. "Capitol's Radio Outfit Will Tour," n.p., "When Roxy Rothafel and His Gang Went Roaming," n.p.

133. James C. Young, "Broadcasting Personality," *Radio Broadcast*, Jul. 1924, 249.

134. "'Roxy's' Radio Tour Sellout in R.I.," *Times Square Daily*, Mar. 11, 1924, n.p. (NYPL – MNN: *ZZ-38750); "Capitol Theatre Co. on Tour," *New York Star*, ca. Mar. 18, 1924, n.p. (NYPL – MNN: *ZZ-38750).

135. Memorandum to J. A. Holman, ca. Mar. 17, 1924 (WHS, 93, Box 5, Folder 1).

136. "'Roxy' and 'His Gang' Will Attend First Annual Radio Show," *WP*, Feb. 24, 1924; A. V. Llufrio, memo to S. L. Ross, Mar. 22, 1924 (WHS, 93, Box 5, Folder 1); Catherine Kenny, "What's Best on the Radio," *WP*, Jan. 25, 1925, SM10; "Capitol Theatre Company to Tour," _____ *City Review*, Mar. 13, 1924, unknown clipping, n.p. (NYPL – MNN: *ZZ-38713); "'Roxy' and 'His Gang' Will Attend First Annual Radio Show," *WP*, Feb. 24, 1924, 15.

137. Unknown clipping, ca. Mar. 30, 1924, n.p. (NYPL – MNN: *ZZ-38750).

138. "Rothafel's Tour a Sell Out," *NYMT*, Mar. 14, 1924, n.p. (NYPL – MNN: *ZZ-38750).

139. "Soldier of Fortune, Whose Voice Is Known to Millions, Outlines Enterprise at Fort Orange Club Dinner," unknown clipping (MCNY).

140. Banner, Sept. 22, 1934, 26.

141. "Capitol Artists to Go on Tour," *New York Herald*, Mar. 16, 1924, n.p. (NYPL – MNN: *ZZ-38750).

142. "Roxy's $8,600 in Two Shows," *Times Square Daily*, ca. Mar. 20, 1924, n.p. (NYPL – MNN: *ZZ-38750); "Capitol Theatre Company to Tour."

143. "'Roxy' and 'His Gang' Will Attend First Annual Radio Show," 15; Llufrio to Ross, Mar. 22, 1924; Kenny, SM10; "Capitol Theatre Company to Tour," n.p.; untitled clipping, *Journal of Commerce*, Mar. 22, 1924, n.p. (NYPL – MNN: *ZZ-38750).

144. Llufrio to Ross, Mar. 22, 1924.

145. "Show Stopping," _____ington Daily News*, Apr. 2, 1924, n.p. (NYPL – MNN: *ZZ-38713).

146. "Roxy's Gang Moves to Larger Quarters," *Telegram and Evening Mail*, Apr. 26, 1924, n.p. (NYPL – MNN: *ZZ-38713).

147. "Service Hospital Radio Fund, Started by 'Roxie,' $4,500 Short," *Washington Star*, Apr. 6, 1924, n.p. (NYPL – MNN: *ZZ-38713).

148. Kenny, n.p.

149. Untitled clipping, *Brooklyn Daily Eagle*, Apr. 21, 1924, n.p. (NYPL – MNN: *ZZ-38713).

150. Kenny, n.p.

151. Untitled clipping, *Brooklyn Daily Eagle*, Apr. 21, 1924, n.p.; "Roxie Touring," *Evening World*, Apr. 23, 1924, n.p.; "New Bedford the Only 'Town' He Was In," unknown clipping, ca. Apr. 26, 1924, n.p.; untitled clipping, *Evening Post*, Apr. 29, 1924, n.p.; untitled clipping, *Musical Courier*, ca. Apr. 30, 1924, n.p. (NYPL – MNN: *ZZ-38713).

152. "'Roxie' and Gang and Kiddie Fund," *Elizabeth Daily Journal*, Apr. 30, 1924, n.p.

153. Untitled clipping, *New York American*, Jun. 13, 1924, n.p. (NYPL – MNN: *ZZ-38713).

154. "65,000,000 Movie Merger Completed," *NYT*, Apr. 18, 1924, 21; Gomery, *The Hollywood Studio System* (1986), 54; Altman, *Hollywood East*, 94.

155. "Edward Bowes Returns Home; Harold Lloyd Nearing Big City," *Telegraph*, ca. Jan. 1924, n.p. (NYPL – MNN: *ZZ-38750).

156. "Movies or Beer?" *New York Evening Post*, Jun. 7, 1924, n.p. (NYPL – MNN: *ZZ-38713).

157. "Newburgh Sees 'Hearts Aflame,'" *Kingston Daily Freeman*, Jan. 4, 1923.

158. "'Scaramouche at Capitol," *Globe and Evening Mail*, Feb. 25, 1924, n.p. (NYPL – MNN: *ZZ-38750). Roxy was still working for other companies as well, such as First National, during the early to mid-1920s. In March 1924, he prepared a prologue for the premiere exhibition of Frank Borzage's film *Secrets* at the Astor Theatre. "Rothafel Preparing Prologue," *NYMT*, Mar. 13, 1924, n.p. (NYPL – MNN: *ZZ-38750). One journalist told Roxy that the score he wrote for *Secrets* was "one of the best you ever wrote" and noted that "Miss Talmadge owes you a debt of gratitude," unknown clipping, ca. Mar. 30, 1924, n.p. (NYPL – MNN: *ZZ-38750).

159. "'Roxy' and His Gang Coming to Lafayette," *Ramapo Valley Independent*, Apr. 11, 1924, n.p.; "'Roxie' and His Gang at Rivoli May 8," *Rutherford* (NJ) *Republican*, ca. Apr. 9, 1924, n.p. (NYPL – MNN: *ZZ-38713).

160. L-S-N-R, "On the Radio Last Night," *Brooklyn Daily Eagle*, Jun. 16, 1924, n.p. (MCNY).

161. Banner, Sept. 22, 1934, 26.

162. "The Capitol," *American Organist*, Nov. 1924, 642.

163. James C. Young, "Broadcasting Personality," *Radio Broadcast*, Jul. 1924, 250.

164. "Fans Welcome 'Roxie' Home," *Caldwell News*, unknown clipping, n.p. (NYPL – MNN: *ZZ-38713).

165. Warren Susman, *Culture as History: The Transformation of American Society in the Twentieth Century* (New York: Pantheon Books, 1984), 271–285.

166. Revell, "Nellie Revell Interviews Roxy," *Radio Digest*, Jan. 1933, 10.

167. "Roxy, Who Caused Recent Radio Controversy, Began as $2-a-Week Cash-Boy," *Boston Sunday Post*, n.p.

168. "Roxy Himself Again," unknown clipping, Feb. 10, 1925, n.p. (NYPL – MWEZ + NC 18, 311).

169. "'Roxie' ---- And His Gang," *New Bedford* ____, Apr. 25, 1924, n.p. (NYPL – MNN: *ZZ-38713).

170. Bunchuk had been a protégé of famous Russian composer Alexander Glazounoff and had also made a name for himself in Europe. Several U.S. Navy officials eventually arranged for his emigration to the United States. Roxy, "Hello Everybody," unknown clipping, Mar. 16, 1925, n.p. (MCNY); "Roxy and His Gang

Coming Next Week," *Baltimore Post*, ca. Feb. 28, 1925, n.p. (NYPL – MWEZ + NC 18, 311); Brooks, 36.

171. Untitled clipping, *New York Tribune*, Mar. 11, 1924, n.p. (NYPL – MNN: *ZZ-38750).

172. "Warner 'Throttled' While Broadcasting," *Baltimore Evening Sun*, ca. Feb. 4, 1925, n.p. (NYPL – MWEZ + NC 18, 311).

173. Untitled clipping, *New York Tribune*, Mar. 14, 1924, n.p. (NYPL – MNN: *ZZ-38750). A month later, the *Tribune* was at it again, this time hammering away at Roxy's use of the phrase "Let's go." The phrase "belongs to the most abused section of the vernacular of the day," the newspaper noted. One of Roxy's fans called up the *Tribune* and went on so long about the newspaper's treatment of Roxy that the journalist "finally gave up" and began "listening with our eyes fixed on the ceiling. Defense for our riddled feelings was out of the question." Untitled clipping, *New York Herald Tribune*, ca. Apr. 18, 1924, n.p. (NYPL – MNN: *ZZ-38713). Scouring hundreds of pages of the Capitol Theatre's scrapbooks of the 1920s also reveals another, albeit short, criticism aimed this time at Gamby, America's new radio darling. She "finally 'tumbled into the soup,'" one writer noted in the *Brooklyn Daily Eagle* in April 1924. "This little giggly creature has tried our patience many a time." L-S-N-R, "On the Radio _____," *Brooklyn Daily Eagle*, ca. Apr. 26, 1924, n.p. (NYPL – MNN: *ZZ-38713).

174. Mary Radcliffe, "Roxy-Radio's 'Biggest Personality,'" unknown clipping, n.p. (NYPL – MNN: *ZZ-38750).

175. J. A. Holman, memo to W. E. Harkness, Dec. 27, 1924 (WHS, 93, Box 5, Folder 1).

176. Jere J. O'Connor to Walter S. Gifford, Jan. 26, 1925 (WHS, 93, Box 5, Folder 1).

177. J. A. Holman to W. E. Harkness, Jan. 29, 1925 (WHS, 93, Box 5, Folder 1).

178. J. A. Holman to Jere J. O'Connor, Jan. 28, 1925 (WHS, 93, Box 5, Folder 1).

179. Jere J. O'Connor to Walter S. Gifford, Jan. 29, 1925 (WHS, 93, Box 5, Folder 1).

180. Lewis, *Empire of the Air*, 178.

181. Eyman, *The Speed of Sound*, 73, 74. According to Lina Warner, AT&T/Western Electric would never have signed their deal with Warner Bros. to create Vitaphone if Sam Warner, whose last name was an Ellis Island creation, had not passed for 100 percent gentile. Lina Warner even wore a crucifix to a dinner with executives from AT&T, Western Electric, and Bell Labs to supposedly seal the deal. Sperling, Millner, and Warner, *Hollywood Be Thy Name: The Warner Brothers Story*, 99.

182. Schwartz, *The Last Lone Inventor: A Tale of Genius, Deceit, and the Birth of Television*, 98.

183. Okrent, 138, 139.

184. Hilmes, *Radio Voices*, 62, 63.

185. Roger Batchelder, "'Roxy' and the 'Gang' to Return Uncensored to Air Tonight," *Boston Sunday Globe*, Feb. 8, 1925, n.p. (NYPL – MWEZ + NC 18, 311).

186. J. J. Frish to WEAF, Jan. 29, 1925 (WHS, 93, Box 5, Folder 1).

187. "Gagging of Roxy by WEAF Brings Storm of Protests; Not Dignified, Company Says," *Brooklyn Daily Eagle,* Feb. 3, 1925, n.p. (NYPL – MWEZ + NC 18, 311).

188. J. A. Holman to Major Edward Bowes, Feb. 2, 1925 (WHS, 93, Box 5, Folder 1).

189. "Gagging of Roxy by WEAF Brings Storm of Protests; Not Dignified, Company Says," n.p.

190. Ibid.

191. "Ministers in Sympathy with Roxy's Jollity," *Worcester Evening Gazette*, Feb. 4, 1925, n.p. (NYPL – MWEZ + NC 18, 311).

192. Aunt Enna, "News Radio Column," unknown clipping, Feb. 3, 1925, n.p. (NYPL – MWEZ + NC 18, 311).

193. "Give 'Roxy' His Freedom!," *Providence News*, Feb. 3, 1925, n.p. (NYPL – MWEZ + NC 18, 311).

194. "'Roxy' and 'Gang' Plan Concert Tour," *Arctic* (RI) *Times*, Feb. 21, 1925, n.p. (NYPL – MWEZ + NC 18, 311).

195. "Roxie to Be Himself Again," *Baltimore News*, Feb. 3, 1925, n.p. (NYPL – MWEZ + NC 18, 311).

196. "Notables to Attend Dinner for Harry Cooper," *Sun and the Globe*, Jan. 9, 1924, n.p.; "Cooper to be Feted on Retirement from Stage," *New York American*, Jan. 10, 1924, n.p.; untitled clipping, *NYMT*, Jan. 10, 1924, n.p. (NYPL – MNN: *ZZ-38750).

197. Robert T. Small, "WEAF Narrowly Escapes Probe for Attempt to Curb 'Roxie,'" *Evening Star*, n.p. (NYPL – MWEZ + NC 18, 311).

198. "The Case of Roxy," *Hackensack Republican,* Feb. 5, 1925, n.p. (NYPL – MWEZ + NC 18, 311).

199. "Roxy Himself Again," unknown clipping, Feb. 10, 1925, n.p. (NYPL – MWEZ + NC 18, 311).

200. "The 'Roxy' of Old Greets Radio Fans," *NYT*, Feb. 9, 1925, 15.

201. "'Roxy,' Idol of Radio Fans, Freed from Theatened Censorship," *Woonsocket* (RI) *Call-Republican*, Feb. 1, 1925, n.p. (NYPL – MWEZ + NC 18, 311).

202. Untitled clipping, ca. Mar. 15, 1925, n.p. (NYPL – MWEZ + NC 18, 311).

203. J. M. Purnas, "Dear Editor," *Washington Star*, Feb. 27, 1925, n.p. (NYPL – MWEZ + NC 18, 311).

204. "Roxy Denounced," unknown clipping, c. Mar. 1925, n.p. (NYPL – MWEZ + NC 18, 311).

205. Clipping, *Popular Radio*, Aug. 1925, n.p. (NYPL – ** ZZ-38679).

206. "Pastor Holds Listening to Roxy on Sunday No Sin; He Does It Himself," *Worcester Telegram*, Mar. 9, 1925, n.p. (NYPL – MWEZ + NC 18, 311).

207. Mary B. Mullett, "'Roxy and His Gang," *American Magazine,* Mar. 1925, 102. Instead of hurting church attendance, the radio had been (and would soon become) a boon to organized religion. "In uplift work score one for radio," the *Waltham*

News Tribune reported, "for here comes the report of the Evangelical Church of America which shows that church attendance during the past year increased over one million souls. This marked increased of men and women attending Divine services is credited to radio." "Static," *Waltham News-Tribune*, Mar. 20, 1925, n.p. (NYPL – MWEZ + NC 18, 311).

208. "Radio Announcers Organize a Club," *Jacksonville* (FL) *Times-Union*, Mar. 1, 1925, n.p. (NYPL – MWEZ + NC 18, 311).

209. "Town Criers Hold Souvenir Dinner," *Providence Journal*, Mar. 3, 1925, n.p. (NYPL – MWEZ + NC 18, 311).

210. "'Roxy' at Manhattan Opera House," *Evening Graphic*, Mar. 4, 1925, n.p. (NYPL – MWEZ + NC 18, 311).

211. "Roxy and Gang at Lyric Next Week," *Baltimore News*, ca. Mar. 1, 1925, n.p. (NYPL – MWEZ + NC 18, 311).

212. "Watching 'Em Strut," *Baltimore Post*, Mar. 6, 1925, n.p. (NYPL – MWEZ + NC 18, 311).

213. "'Announces' in Baltimore for First Time," unknown clipping, ca. Mar. 6, 1925, n.p. (NYPL – MWEZ + NC 18, 311).

214. "'Roxy' and the Whole Gang Coming," *Washington Times*, Feb. 20, 1925, n.p; "'Roxy and Gang' Will Perform for Coolidge," *Jersey City Journal*, ca. Mar. 1, 1925, n.p. (NYPL – MWEZ + NC 18, 311).

215. "Press Club Show Seats to Go on Sale Tomorrow," *Washington Star*, Feb. 25, 1925, n.p. (NYPL – MWEZ + NC 18, 311).

216. "Large Seat Demand for 'Roxie' Program," *WP*, ca. Mar. 6, 1925, n.p. (NYPL – MWEZ + NC 18, 311).

217. "President Enjoys 'Roxie' Concert," *Washington Star*, Mar. 10, 1925, n.p. (NYPL – MWEZ + NC 18, 311).

218. "The Presidency: The White House Week: Mar. 16, 1925," *Time*, Mar. 16, 1925. Available at www.time.com/time/magazine/article/0,9171,719996,00.html (accessed July 17, 2011).

219. The *Atlanta Constitution* noted that it was "wonderfully written." "Broadcasting," *AC*, Jul. 19, 1925, B6. Rothafel and Yates, *Broadcasting: Its New Day*; "Radio Notes," *Brockton* (MA) *Enterprise*, Mar. 2, 1925, n.p. (NYPL – MWEZ + NC 18, 311); "Books Just Arrived from the Publishers," *Dallas Morning News*, Mar. 29, 1925, 3:5. In July 1925, Erno Rapee published his first collection of music as well, *Erno Rapee's Encyclopedia of Music for Pictures*, with the subtitle "As Essential as the Picture." *American Organist* noted, "The Encyclopedia embodies an idea so unique and yet so simple that it is astonishing that such a publication should have been so long delayed." "Encyclopedia of Music for Pictures," *American Organist*, 8:7 (Jul. 1925): 282.

220. "Meet 'Roxy' in the Traveler," *Boston Herald*, Mar. 20, 1925, n.p. (NYPL – MWEZ + NC 18, 311); Samuel Rothafel, "Roxy's Hello Everybody," *Chicago Daily Tribune*, Mar. 22, 1925, D11.

221. Roxy, "Roxy's 'Hello Everybody,'" *BT*, Mar. 23, 1925, n.p. (NYPL – MWEZ + NC 18, 311).

222. "I'll Broadcast Every Week Day in the News Says Inimitable Roxy," *Providence News*, Mar. 14, 1925, n.p. (NYPL – MWEZ + NC 18, 311).

223. Roxy, "Roxy's 'Hello Everybody,'" *BT,* Mar. 23, 1925, n.p. (NYPL – MWEZ + NC 18, 311).

224. Roxy, "Hello Everybody," *WP*, Mar. 30, 1925, n.p. (NYPL – MWEZ + NC 18, 311).

225. Untitled clipping, *Newsburyport News-Herald*, Mar. 19, 1925, n.p. (NYPL – MWEZ + NC 18, 311).

226. "Special Police Squad to Handle Roxy Crowd," *BT*, Apr. 18. 1925, n.p. (NYPL – MWEZ + NC 18, 311).

227. "Boston Roars Splendid Welcome as Roxy Reaches South Station," *BT*, Apr. 21, 1925, n.p. (NYPL – MWEZ + NC 18, 311).

228. "Plan Welcome for 'Roxy' and His Gang," *Worcester* (MA) *Post*, Mar. 13, 1925, n.p.; "'Roxy' and 'Gang' Plan Concert Tour," *Arctic* (RI) *Times*, Feb. 21, 1925, n.p.; untitled clipping, *Waterbury* (CT) *Democrat*, Apr. 20, 1925, n.p. (NYPL – MWEZ + NC 18, 311); "Roxy and His Gang," *NYT*, Apr. 25, 1925, 13; "'Roxy's Gang' Aids Camp Fund," *NYT*, May 1, 1925, 12.

229. Roxy and His Gang advertisement, *Hartford Courant*, Apr. 26, 1925, A5.

230. "Radio First in Roxy's Heart," *Radio World*, Apr. 18, 1925, n.p. (NYPL – MWEZ + NC 18, 311).

231. "Doc" Clifford, "Around Galley Fires," *The Leatherneck*, May 9, 1925, 7.

232. "Testimonial Dinner to Major Rothafel," *Syracuse Herald*, May 10, 1925, III:5.

233. "Dinner to S. L. Rothafel," *NYT*, May 10, 1925, 18; "News from the News," *The Leatherneck*, May 23, 1925, 8.

234. "Radio First in Roxy's Heart."

235. "Broadway's Wizard of the Screen," *The Sun*, c. Jun. 19, 1924, n.p. (NYPL – MNN: *ZZ-38713).

236. "What of the Radio," *Exhibitors Trade Review,* Mar. 22, 1924, n.p. (MCNY); Hilmes, *Hollywood and Broadcasting*, 36.

237. Gomery, *The Coming of Sound*, 16.

238. "Latest News from the Radio Studios," *NYT*, May 31, 1925, XX14; Hilmes, *Hollywood and Broadcasting*, 35.

239. "New Radio Station to Open Wednesday," *LAT*, Mar. 1, 1925, B11; Warner, quoted in Hilmes, *Hollywood and Broadcasting*, 33–35. "Their model was undoubtedly S.L. Rothafel," Eyman writes. Eyman, 67.

240. Loew's State advertisement, *LAT*, Mar. 10, 1925, A11.

241. Warner, quoted in Hilmes, *Hollywood and Broadcasting*, 33–35.

242. "Broadcasting Boost to Picture Industry," *St. Louis Globe*, Apr. 19, 1925, n.p. (NYPL – MWEZ + NC 18, 311).

243. Hilmes, *Hollywood and Broadcasting*, 34, 35, Eyman, 67. WBPI was located at the same venue where *The Jazz Singer* (1927) would open the following year, further merging the developing technologies of radio broadcasting and motion picture sound exhibition.

244. "Broadcasting Record Challenged," *The Bioscope*, Sept. 22, 1927, 26.

245. "Broadcasting by Cinemas," *The Bioscope*, Dec. 23, 1926, 23.

246. "Broadcasting Record Challenged," 26.

247. "Two Wise Men of Gotham Who Came Out of the West," *New York Herald Tribune*, Jun. 15, 1924.

248. "Roxy of the Radio to Have Own Movie Theatre with Seats for 6,000 at 7th Av. and 50th St.," *NYT*, Jun. 3, 1925, 1.

249. Ibid.

250. "$6,000,000 Movie Theatre to Be Built," *Lima* (OH) *News*, Jun. 3, 1925, 1.

251. "Chicagoan to Design Biggest Movie for N.Y.," *Chicago Tribune*, Jun. 7, 1925, F24.

252. The *Los Angeles Times* argued at the time that his career was now the answer to anyone who doubted the impact of radio and its growing list of stars. "They say also that many a man has been made by the radio," the *Times* noted. "Then you say 'who?' and after a minute they announce in earnest unison, 'Roxy.' " "Cyril Maude to Brighten Arlen Play," *LAT*, Aug. 2, 1925, D17.

253. "Profiles: Deux Ex Cinema," *New Yorker*, May 28, 1927, 20.

254. Lucille Husting, " 'Hello, Everybody!' " *Radio News*, Dec. 1927, 604; "A Perfect Personnel at Your Service," Alicoate, ed., *Roxy: A History*, 27.

255. "Radio's Intimate in Its Appeal to Church," *TDS*, Jul. 2, 1925, 1; "Roxy's Rollicking Songs Make Depot Arches Ring," *TDS*, Jul. 2, 1925, 15.

256. "To Bring Radio Home to Disabled Veterans," *TDS*, Jul. 3, 1925, 3.

257. " 'Roxy and His Gang' from Toronto," *TDS*, Jul. 3, 1925, 12.

258. "What Are the Wild Tubes Saying?," *TDS*, Jul. 20, 1925, 10.

259. "Yes, Roxy Looks and Smiles Just as He Sounds, Folks," *Detroit News*, Jul. 23, 1925, n.p. (NYPL – MNN: **ZZ-38679).

260. "6 N.E. Governors Sign Roxy Card," *Boston Herald*, Jul. 27, 1925, n.p. (NYPL – *ZZ-38679).

261. "Roxy Bids Adieu to His Gang and Radio Audience," *Herald Tribune*, Jul. 27, 1925, n.p. (NYPL – *ZZ-38679).

262. " 'Roxy' Says Au Revoir," *Woonsocket* (RI) *Call-Republican*, Jul. 28, 1925, n.p. (NYPL – *ZZ-38679).

263. J.A.R., untitled clipping, *Brooklyn Daily Times*, Jul. 27, 1925, n.p. (NYPL – *ZZ-38679).

264. Eavesdropper, untitled clipping, ca. Sept. 26, 1925, n.p. (NYPL – *ZZ-38679).

6. "It's the Roxy and I'm Roxy" (1925-1927)

AC	Atlanta Constitution
DMN	Dallas Morning News
EH	Exhibitors Herald
HC	Hartford Courant
LAT	Los Angeles Times
MC	Musical Courier
MPN	Motion Picture News
MPW	Moving Picture World
NYT	New York Times
NY	New Yorker
RG	Radio Guide
RTWR	Roxy Theatre Weekly Review
TDS	Toronto Daily Star
WP	Washington Post
MCNY	*Museum of the City of New York*
NYPL	*New York Public Library for the Performing Arts*
WHS	*Wisconsin Historical Society*

1. Jack Jamison, "The Man Who Dreamed Too Much," *Radio Guide*, Apr. 18, 1936, 18.

2. "$3,000 Subscribed for Radios for Veterans," *TDS*, Jul. 31, 1925, 25.

3. "Yes, Roxy Looks and Smiles Just as He Sounds, Folks," *Detroit News*, Jul. 23, 1925, n.p. (NYPL-MNN: **ZZ-38679).

4. "'Roxy' Says Au Revoir," *Woonsocket* (RI) *Call-Republican*, Jul. 28, 1925, n.p. (NYPL-MNN: **ZZ-38679).

5. S. L. Rothafel, "*Speed* Makes the Show Go but Profits Start with *Control*," *Magazine of Business*, Jun. 1928, 721, 769.

6. "Rothafel to Have 6 Big Film Houses," NYT, Jul. 20, 1925, 19. Rumors of Roxy's departure from the Capitol trickled in throughout July 1925. "Roxie's Own Is as Good," *TDS*, Jul. 18, 1925, n.p. (NYPL-MNN: **ZZ-38679).

7. "Capitol," *American Organist*, Aug. 1925, 316.

8. "Rothafel to Have 6 Big Film Houses," 19; "Roxie's Own Is as Good," n.p.

9. "Capitol," 316.

10. Red, "News Flashes from U.S.A.," *The Bioscope*, Sept. 10, 1925, 64.

11. Gordon Whyte, "The Little Man with the Big Orchestra," *The Metronome*, October 15, 1926, 19.

12. Ibid.; Red, "News Flashes from U.S.A.," *The Bioscope*, Sept. 3, 1925, 35; Red, "News Flashes from U.S.A.," *The Bioscope*, Sept. 24, 1925, 41.

13. "Capitol," 316; Red, "News Flashes from U.S.A.," *The Bioscope*, Sept. 10, 1925, 64.

14. Red, "News Flashes from U.S.A.," Sept. 3, 1925, 35

15. Red, "News Flashes from U.S.A.," Sept. 24, 1925, 41.

16. "Berlin Movie Palace Like One on Broadway," *NYT*, Sept. 26, 1925, 17.

17. Red, "News Flashes from U.S.A.," *The Bioscope*, Oct. 22, 1925, 27.

18. Kreimeier, *The UFA Story*, 136; "Erno Rapee Wins Ovation in Berlin," *NYT*, Jul. 28, 1926, 18.

19. Whyte, "The Little Man with the Big Orchestra," 19.

20. "UFA Palace to Be Popular House," *The Bioscope*, Aug. 12, 1926, 18; "Erno Rapee Off," *NYT*, Aug. 5, 1926, 23. When Ufa opened a 950-seat cinema in Konigsberg, Germany, in 1927, they named it the Capitol after the New York site of Rapee's (and Roxy's) rise to international prominence. "UFA Erecting New Theatre in Konigsberg," *MPN*, Sept. 2, 1927, 704.

21. Kracauer, "Cult of Distraction: On Berlin's Picture Palaces," 91, 92.

22. "The Theatre," *Wall Street Journal*, Jan. 10, 1929, 4.

23. Erno Rapee, "What Price Music," *Variety*, Jun. 8, 1927, 12. In the years that followed, Rapee remained something of a celebrity in Germany. He would receive numerous solicitations to tour Germany's cinemas, including a lucrative offer from Sam Rachman to tour the country for $1,500 per week. Rapee considered but ultimately rejected these offers. In each case, *Variety* noted, "The phenomenal growth of picture house business in Germany" enabled these solicitations. "Germans Want Rapee to Tour at $1,500," *Variety*, Mar. 14, 1928, 13.

24. J. A. Holman to Edgar S. Bloom, Aug. 24, 1925 (WHS, 93, Box 5, Folder 1).

25. "Ten Outstanding Events this Week," *NYT*, Oct. 25, 1925, XX17. Roxy also became a freelance showman again. Samuel Goldwyn hired him to stage the premiere of *Stella Dallas* at New York's Apollo Theater days before going back on the air. "Radical Film Great Success," *LAT*, Oct. 25, 1925, 29. He also continued his work for the military, becoming a major in the 7th Regiment of the Marines—the first Marine Corps Reserves unit in the military branch's history. "Marines Form First Reserve Regiment in Their History," *Indiana Evening Gazette*, Nov. 20, 1925, n.p.; "Marine Corps Reserve to the Front," *The Leatherneck*, Nov. 25, 1925, 9.

26. "Roxey's New Gang Goes on Air Oct. 30," *Brooklyn Daily Times*, Oct. 22, 1925, n.p. (NYPL-MNN: **ZZ-38679); "Roxy's New 'Gang' Hailed by Admirers," *New York Telegram*, ca. Oct. 24, 1925, 8 (NYPL-MNN: **ZZ-38679).

27. "Radio's Famous Family," *New York American*, Dec. 6, 1925, n.p. (NYPL-MNN: **ZZ-38679).

28. "Mary Lewis to Sing Today with Symphony Orchestra," *NYT*, Nov. 22, 1925, XX16.

29. Roxy Theatres Corporation advertisement, *NYT*, Nov. 12, 1925, 23.

30. Roxy Theatres Corporation advertisement, *HC*, Nov. 13, 1925, 19; Roxy Theatres Corporation advertisement, *Utica* (NY) *Press*, Nov. 13, 1925, 24.

31. Roxy Theatres Corporation advertisement, *NYT*, Nov. 29, 1925, E15; " 'Roxy' Insured for $2,000,000," *Boston Evening Globe*, Dec. 12, 1925, n.p. (MCNY).

32. " 'Roxy and His Gang' to Build a Theater," *HC*, Nov. 15, 1925, D9.

33. "The Talk of the Town," *NY*, Mar. 19, 1927, 17.

34. Sinclair, *Upton Sinclair Presents William Fox*, 342.

35. "Roxy Gang Promotion," *Variety*, ca. Dec. 25, 1925, n.p. (MCNY).

36. Samuel Rothafel, "Foreword," in *The Roxy Theatre, The Largest Theatre in the World* (New York: Bennett, Bolster & Coghill, 1927), 1 (stock pamphlet).

37. "'Roxy and His Gang' Personal Appearance Under the Auspices of the Y. M. H. A. Community Home, Trenton, New Jersey at the Crescent Temple" program, Jan. 25, 1926 (Rutgers University Library); "Capital Committee Unable to Pay 'Roxy,'" *NYT*, Jan. 26, 1926, 5; "Roxy's Life Story Reads like a Page from a Book of Romance," unknown clipping, Jan. 22, 1926, n.p. (MCNY).

38. "Plans Already Launched for A.M.P.A. 'Naked Truth Dinner,'" *Atlanta Film Review*, Dec. 26, 1925, n.p. (MCNY).

39. "Roxy," *Radio World*, ca. Mar. 1926, n.p.; "Roxy Gets Popularity Medal; Spurs Him to Greater Work," unknown clipping (MCNY).

40. "'Roxy' Signs for Fox News," *MPW*, Feb. 20, 1926, n.p. (MCNY).

41. Handbook of Projection advertisement, *MPW*, Feb. 6, 1926, 556; Arch Preserver Shoes advertisement, *NYT*, Mar. 24, 1926, 14.

42. Arcadia Ball Room advertisement, *Bridgeport* (CT) *Telegram*, Mar. 11, 1926, 10; "Did You Ever Bring a Big Time Show to a Small Time Town?," *EH*, Mar. 20, 1926, n.p. (MCNY).

43. "Roxie and Mrs. Roxie Sail for Coast," _____ *Mirror*, Mar. 19, 1926, n.p.; "'Roxy,' Famous Showman Here," *Los Angeles Evening-Express*, Apr. 7, 1926, n.p.; untitled clipping, *Washington Times*, ca. Apr. 7, 1926, n.p. (MCNY).

44. "McClure's Magazine Now Has Radio Department," *Columbus Dispatch*, May 10, 1926, n.p. (MCNY).

45. "Roxy's Gang One Reelers," *Motion Pictures Today*, May 29, 1926, n.p.; untitled clipping, New York Telegraph, ca. May 1926, n.p. (MCNY).

46. "Previn Will Be Roxy's Musical Conductor," *Motion Pictures Today*, Oct. 16, 1926, n.p. (MCNY).

47. "Presentation News and Reviews," *The Metronome*, Oct. 15, 1926, 27.

48. Charles Previn photograph, *Theatre Magazine*, Sept. 1928, 47.

49. Among the highly trained musicians in the orchestra was trumpeter Cy Feuer. Feuer would later produce musicals such as *Guys and Dolls* and *How to Succeed in Business Without Really Trying*—just one of the many people who used their work with Roxy as a stepping-stone. Richard Severo and Jesse McKinley, "Cy Feuer, Producer of 'Guys and Dolls' and Other Broadway Musicals, Is Dead at 95," *NYT*, May 18, 2006, n.p.

50. Whyte, "The Little Man with the Big Orchestra," 19.

51. Ibid.

52. "New Fox Academy of Music, New York City Opened; Seating Capacity 3,873," *MPN*, Oct. 23, 1926, 1578.

53. "Fox Academy Opens with Elaborate Bill," *MPN*, Oct. 23, 1926, 1605.

54. "New Fox Academy of Music, New York City Opened, Seating Capacity 3,873," 1578.

55. Academy of Music program, Nov. 21, 1926, reprinted in Shire, ed., *Nellé*, 23.

56. Doherty, *Hollywood's Censor: Joseph I. Breen and the Production Code Administration*, 24, 25.

57. "'America's Answer' Stirs War Spirit," *NYT*, Jul. 30, 1918, 9.

58. Ray L. Hall, "Seeing Is Believing," *The Independent*, Sept. 18, 1926, 325; Morrison, *Broadway Theatres*, 120, 121.

59. Doherty, *Hollywood's Censor*, 25.

60. Allene Talmey notes that Roxy "arranged the presentation of the Eucharistic Congress film by request from a Cardinal," though George Cardinal Mundelein was an archbishop. Talmey, *Doug and Mary and Others*, 178; Doherty, *Hollywood's Censor*, 22.

61. "That Man 'Roxy'—and the Y.M.C.A.," *Elizabeth Times*, Apr. 24, 1926, n.p. (MCNY).

62. Doherty, *Hollywood's Censor*, 26; "Roadshowed," *MPN*, Nov. 13, 1926, 1854.

63. "Eucharistic Film Has Premiere," *MPN*, Nov. 20, 1926, 1938; Doherty, *Hollywood's Censor*, 26, 27.

64. "Eucharistic Film Has Premiere," 1938.

65. Doherty, *Hollywood's Censor*, 27.

66. Ibid.

67. The film had previously been shown at the Carthay Circle Theatre in Los Angeles with a different score. William A. Johnston, "An Editor on Broadway," *MPN*, Dec. 4, 1926, 2129; *What Price Glory* program, ca. 1926, 8.

68. Johnston, "An Editor on Broadway," 2129.

69. George Seilo, "Erno Rapee—an Appreciation," *The Metronome*, Jan. 1929, 33, 45.

70. "What Theme Song Was Most Popular?" *MPN*, May 11, 1929, 1571.

71. Josephine Vila, "Notes," *MC*, Mar. 3, 1927, 49.

72. Jacobs, *The Decline of Sentiment: American Film in the 1920s*, 152.

73. "What Theme Song Was Most Popular?" 1571.

74. He told the *Los Angeles Times* in 1930, for instance, that "In developing the theme song, I think I have not only lifted the standard of the motion picture, but indirectly I have made a lot of fortunes for many otherwise struggling composers." "Theme Song Writer Arrives," *LAT*, Feb. 9, 1930, A8. Other trade and popular journals later backed the claim as well. "What Erno Rapee Thinks of Hollywood," *The Metronome*, Jul. 1930, 30; Lee Shippey, "Lee Side o' LA," *LAT*, Mar. 19, 1930, A4.

75. Johnston, "An Editor on Broadway," 2129.

76. "'What Price Glory' Premiere," 2149.

77. Ibid.

78. "4 Conductors Preside over Roxy Orchestra," *MPN*, Dec. 31, 1926, 2542. Stahlberg had previously been associated with Victor Herbert and was not only a conductor but a composer as well. "Roxy's $8,000,000 Theatre to Open March 11," *Morning*

Telegraph, Feb. 27, 1927, 4. Stahlberg had replaced Rapee at the Rivoli in November 1919. "Rapee Leaves Rivoli," *New York Clipper*, Nov. 19, 1919, 33.

79. "S. L. Rothafel Completes Staff of Conductors," *The Metronome*, Jan. 1, 1927, 33.

80. Fox Pictures advertisement, *MPN*, Oct. 16, 1926, n.p. Rapee was given one additional honor in December 1926 when he was asked by *The Metronome* to contribute to a new section dedicated to music and motion pictures. (The journal also announced the commencement of a new radio section.) "New Features for the New Year," *The Metronome*, Dec. 15, 1926, 17.

81. "Roxy Stock for Houses," *Variety*, Dec. 22, 1926, 10.

82. Roxy wired Paramount executive Harold B. Franklin, who would later play a significant and obtrusive role in his career, to congratulate him upon the theater's opening. Roxy to Harold B. Franklin, Nov. 19, 1926. (Harold Franklin Collection, Academy of Motion Picture Arts and Sciences.)

83. "Roxy Circuit Plans Chain of Theatres," *NYT*, Dec. 17, 1926, 27.

84. "S. L. Rothafel Now Located at His 'Roxy' Theatre," *MPN*, Jan. 21, 1927, 221.

85. Talmey, 179.

86. "S. L. Rothafel Now Located at His 'Roxy' Theatre," 221.

87. "A Perfect Personnel at Your Service," in Alicoate, ed., *Roxy: A History*, 27.

88. Talmey, 180.

89. "Points of Interest in the Roxy Theatre," Roxy Theatre publicity materials, ca. 1927, 1 (author's collection).

90. Gordon Whyte, "Roxy," *The Metronome*, Feb. 1, 1927, 18.

91. Carl Helm, "Introducing Roxy—in Person," *Personality*, Jul. 1928, 95.

92. Samuel Rothafel, quoted in Helm, 95, 96.

93. "A Perfect Personnel at Your Service," 27.

94. "Former Marine 'Music' Opens World's Largest Theatre," *The Leatherneck*, Apr. 1927, 36.

95. "Roxy Outlines His Theatre," *NYT*, Aug. 13, 1925, 19.

96. "Straight Noses," *Variety*, Feb. 2, 1927, 11.

97. Clipping, *Sioux City* (IA) *Citizen*, Feb. 13, 1927 (MCNY).

98. Rothafel, quoted in W. Stephen Bush, "Exhibition Wins," *MPW*, Feb. 26, 1916, 1278.

99. "A Perfect Personnel at Your Service," 27.

100. "A Trip Through the New Roxy Theatre," *NYT*, Feb. 27, 1927, 4; Helm, "Introducing Roxy—in Person," 98.

101. "A Perfect Personnel at Your Service," 27.

102. "Roxy's $8,000,000 Theatre to Open March 11," *New York Morning Telegraph*, Feb. 27, 1927, 4.

103. "A Perfect Personnel at Your Service," 27.

104. Timothy Noah, "A Skeleton Key to 'You're the Top,'" *Slate*, Jun. 9, 2005. Available at www.slate.com/id/2120550/ (accessed Jul. 22, 2011).

105. "A Trip Through the New Roxy Theatre," 1.

106. "Ballet Genius en Route," *MPN*, Feb. 4, 1927, 376.

107. "Can Chaplin Come Back? Expert Opinions Differ," *TDS*, Jan. 22, 1927, 11.

108. Advertisement, *NYT*, Mar. 7, 1927, 16.

109. Samuel Rothafel, "Foreword," 1.

110. "Roxy's $8,000,000 Theatre to Open March 11," 4.

111. "Arthur Smith with Roxy," *MPN*, Feb. 18, 1927, 606.

112. This figure was lowered to ten by October. "The Changing Picture," *The Bioscope*, Oct. 27, 1927, xi.

113. "Arthur Smith with Roxy," 606.

114. "A Trip Through the New Roxy Theatre," 4.

115. "Roxy Switchboard Claimed Largest," *MPN*, Jan. 21, 1927, 253.

116. "A Trip Through the New Roxy Theatre," 4.

117. Roxy Theatre advertisement, *NYT*, Mar. 7, 1927, 16.

118. "Former Marine 'Music' Opens World's Largest Theatre," 36.

119. "Music Library at the New 'Roxy,'" *The Metronome*, Mar. 1, 1927, 23.

120. "Keynotes: An Interview with Erno Rapee," *RTWR*, Apr. 30, 1927, 17.

121. "A Trip Through the New Roxy Theatre," 4.

122. "Roxy Theatre Opening Set for March 11," *MPN*, Mar. 11, 1927, 865.

123. "Former Marine 'Music' Opens World's Largest Theatre," 36.

124. "The Builders of the Roxy," in Alicoate, ed., *Roxy: A History*, 19.

125. Thomas C. Kennedy, "Seeing 'the Roxy' with Roxy," *MPN*, Feb. 4, 1927, 379.

126. S. Jay Kaufman, "Herbert Lubin," in Alicoate, ed., *Roxy: A History*, 7.

127. Josephine Vila, "Music and the Movies," *MC*, Jun. 2, 1927, 40.

128. MacDonald, *Don't Touch that Dial!: Radio Programming in American Life,* 25; "'Roxy and His Gang' Return to the Microphone Tomorrow Night Over Nine Stations," *NYT*, Mar. 6, 1927; "Capitol and Roxy Sew Up WEAF and WJZ," *Variety*, Mar. 6, 1927.

129. Jack Banner, "'ROXY,'" *Radio Guide*, Sept. 29, 1934, 7.

130. Gordon Whyte, "'You're on the Air,'" *The Metronome*, Mar. 1, 1927, 38; "'Roxy' Announces Program Soloists," *AC*, Mar. 6, 1927, B4.

131. Banner, Sept. 29, 1934, 7. Jack Alicoate noted that "tests have revealed that the acoustical conditions" for these studios were "ideal for broadcasting purposes, surpassing even the expectations of the architects." "The Gang," in Alicoate, ed., *Roxy: A History*, 29.

132. "The Gang," 29.

133. "'Roxy' to Be Heard Again from New Moorish Theater," *HC*, Mar. 6, 1927, 9D.

134. "'Roxy and His Gang' Return to the Microphone Tomorrow Night over Nine Stations," *NYT*, Mar. 6, 1927, X19.

135. Ralph L. Power, "Long-Distance Tales Abound," *LAT*, Mar. 7, 1927, A7.

136. "'Hello Everybody'; Roxy Back on the Air," *NYT*, Mar. 8, 1927, 22.

137. Will H. Smith, "Radio-Ing the Air Waves," *AC*, Mar. 8, 1927, 16.

138. "Maestro, Jumping About Like a Grasshopper, Holds the Baton During Most of the Concert—Nervous Tension Among the 'Gang,'" *NYT*, Mar. 13, 1927, X22.

139. "Famous Players' New York Studios Go to Hollywood," *TDS*, Mar. 12 1927, 9.

140. "Radio and Showmanship," *MPN*, Jun. 3, 1927, 2177.

141. Roxy Theatre advertisement, *American Hebrew*, Mar. 11, 1927, n.p.

142. "Roxy's," *MC*, May 12, 1927, 45.

143. Banner, Sept. 29, 1934, 7.

144. Hilmes, *Hollywood and Broadcasting*, 36.

145. Merritt Crawford, "Broadcasting War Looms to Offset Roxy's Competition," *MPW*, Mar. 19, 1927, 1.

146. "Chicago Radio Station to Broadcast Warner News," *MPN*, Apr. 22, 1927, 1451. Warner Bros. also remained active through Los Angeles and New York stations KFWB and WBPI, respectively.

147. "Late Chicago News," *MPW*, Mar. 19, 1927, 1.

148. "B. & K.'s Radio Station," *Variety*, Mar. 16, 1927, 7.

149. "Inside Stuff on Pictures," *Variety*, Mar. 9, 1927, 13.

150. A photograph of Roxy on the set of Metropolis is featured in "'Metropolis' and More DVDs; 'Marlene' and More Events," *Notebook*, Nov. 23, 2010. Available at http://mubi.com/notebook/posts/metropolis-and-more-dvds-marlene-and-more-events (accessed Sep. 3, 2011).

151. "Inside Stuff on Pictures," Mar. 9, 1927, 13.

152. Poli's Majestic advertisement, *Bridgeport Telegram*, Apr. 8, 1927, 19.

153. Uptown Theatre advertisement, *TDS*, May 31, 1927, 13.

154. "Broadway Bows to Roxy," *MPW*, Mar. 19, 1927, 169.

155. Helm, 98.

156. "Roxy's 'Cathedral' Is Opened," *MPN*, Mar. 25, 1927, 1031.

157. "Roxy Theater with Galaxy of Stars Opens To-Night," *New York Herald Tribune*, Mar. 11, 1927, n.p. (NYPL); "Goings on About Town," *NY*, Mar. 5, 1927, 12.

158. "Broadway Bows to Roxy," *MPW*, Mar. 19, 1927, 169.

159. "Former Marine 'Music' Opens World's Largest Theatre," 36.

160. "Roxy's 'Cathedral' Is Opened," 1031.

161. "'Roxy' Announces Program Soloists," *AC*, Mar. 6, 1927, B4.; "Stahlberg Walks on Roxy," *Variety*, Mar. 16, 1927, 9.

162. "Broadway Bows to Roxy," 169.

163. Roxy Theatre dedicatory program, Mar. 11, 1927, 1, 2.

164. Ibid.

165. "Broadway Bows to Roxy," 169.

166. Roxy Theatre dedicatory program, 1, 2.

167. "Notes," *MC*, Mar. 17, 1927, 45.

168. Roxy Theatre dedicatory program, 1, 2.

169. Ibid.

170. "Prologue Passes from Special Showing," *MPN*, Jun. 3, 1927, 2197.

171. "The Talk of the Town," *NY*, Mar. 19, 1927, 17.

172. "Former Marine 'Music' Opens World's Largest Theatre," 36.

173. "Broadway Bows to Roxy," 169.

174. "Heard on Broadway," *Theatre Magazine*, Aug. 1928, 32.

175. "At the World's Crossroads," *MPW*, Mar. 19, 1927, 170.

176. "Profiles: Deux Ex Cinema," *NY*, 22.

177. "Presentation News and Reviews," *The Metronome*, Aug. 15, 1926, 17.

178. "Broadway Bows to Roxy," 169.

179. Talmey, 181.

180. "Roxy Open; Broadway Off," *MPN*, Apr. 1, 1927, 1168.

181. F. A. Enders, " 'The Cathedral of Motion Pictures,' " *The Bioscope*, Apr. 7, 1927, 31.

182. The 5,920-seat figure comes from a variety of sources, including David Naylor's *American Picture Palaces*, Anthony Slide's *The New Historical Dictionary of the American Film Industry*, as well as the May 9, 1927, New York City Certificate of Occupancy. Naylor, *American Picture Palaces*, 110; Anthony Slide, *The New Historical Dictionary of the American Film Industry* (Lanham, MD: Scarecrow Press, 1998), 176; Bureau of Buildings, City of New York, Borough of Manhattan, Certificate of Occupancy No. 12283. Mar. 9, 1927 (NYC Department of Buildings). As William Savoy notes in *Marquee*'s 1979 tribute to the Roxy Theatre and its 5,920 seats: "Rothafel, never opposed to a little healthy exaggeration, continued to advertise the 'over 6,000 seats' figure and instructed staff, if questioned, to answer, 'There are over 6,000 seats in the theatre . . . not necessarily all in the auditorium!' " (Roxy had counted every chair in the building.) Savoy, "Introductory Notes," 1.

183. Quoted in Samuel Rothafel, "Hello Everybody!" *RTWR*, Apr. 14, 1928, 3.

184. Allvine, *The Greatest Fox of Them All*, 114, 115.

185. "The Roxy Lesson," *MPN*, Apr. 1, 1927, 1.

186. "Another Movie Miracle," *NYT*, Apr. 3, 1927, X7.

187. "Fox Films Buy Roxy Theaters," *DMN*, Mar. 26, 1927, I:4; "Fox Purchases Roxy Chain; Rothafel Stays as Manager," *EH*, ca. Mar. 25, 1927, n.p. (MCNY).

188. "Behind the Screens," *New York World*, ca. Mar. 27, 1927, n.p. (MCNY).

189. "The Layman Tries His Hand Making Motion Pictures," *TDS*, Apr. 2, 1927, 9.

190. "William Fox Buys Roxy Theater," unknown clipping, ca. Mar. 25, 1927, n.p. (NYPL).

191. William Fox, quoted in Sinclair, *Upton Sinclair Presents William Fox*, 332.

192. "Fox Purchases Roxy Chain; Rothafel Stays as Manager"; "$20,000,000 Paid for Roxy Theater in New York City," *Miami Herald*, Mar. 26, 1927, n.p. (MCNY).

193. "$408,152 Glory Record at New York Roxy," *MPN*, Sept. 16, 1927, 842.

194. "Another Movie Miracle," *NYT*, Apr. 3, 1927.

195. "Roxy Theatre Added to Fox Chain," *MPN*, Apr. 8, 1927, 1254.

196. "Behind the Screens," *New York World*, ca. Mar. 27, 1927, n.p. (MCNY).

197. "New Roxy Theatre Purchased by Fox," *NYT*, Mar. 26, 1927, 21.

198. "Fox to Roxy?" *Variety*, Apr. 6, 1927, 4.

199. "Inside Stuff," *Variety*, Apr. 6, 1927, 22.

200. "Roxy Theatre Added to Fox Chain," *MPN*, Apr. 8, 1927, 1254.

201. "Roxy Speaking," *Variety*, Apr. 13, 1927, 1.

202. "Zanft Booker of Films for 28 Fox Houses," *Variety*, Apr. 13, 1927, 9.

203. "Lubin's Radio Sets," *Variety*, Dec. 7, 1927, 12.

204. "Another Movie Miracle," X7.

205. "5000-Seat Fox Theater for Oakland," *Oakland Tribune*, Mar. 26, 1927, 1; "Fox Purchases Roxy Chain; Rothafel Stays as Manager."

206. "Roxy Theatre Added to Fox Chain," 1254.

207. "Fox Purchases Roxy Chain; Rothafel Stays as Manager."

208. "New Theatre to Be Named Fox-Roxy," *NYT*, Apr. 5, 1927, 30; "Fox Erecting Theatres in Washington, New York," *MPN*, Apr. 15, 1927, 1359.

209. "Radio and Showmanship," *MPN*, Jun. 3, 1927, 2177.

210. "Notes," *MC*, Apr. 21, 1927, 45. Fox eventually abandoned those plans and instead secured a year and a half lease of the Carthay Circle Theatre, where the company's *What Price Glory* was already playing its nineteenth week, assuring Fox film premieres in New York and Los Angeles at dedicated shop-window theaters throughout 1927 and in the years to come. "Fox's £4,000,000 Deal," *The Bioscope*, Apr. 14, 1927, 24.

211. "Fox Building 20 De Luxe Houses, Bringing Circuit Around 50," *Variety*, May 6, 1927, 12.

212. "We are not seeking battle," Fox noted. "Our theatre plans are not to be construed as an invasion of the exhibition field, because they are not. Where we have had ample representation, we will not build. Where our friends are to be found, we will not build." "Thirty Fox First Runs by 1929," *MPN*, May 27, 1927, 2063.

213. "Fox Detroit Theatre of Massive Design," *MPN*, Jul. 1, 1927, 2512.

214. "Roxy Will Supervise Fox' Academy, N.Y.," *MPN*, May 27, 1927, 2082; "Do You Know That—," *MC*, May 26, 1927, 45.

215. "Touring Roxy Shows into M.P. Houses," *Variety*, Jun. 6, 1927, 10.

216. Rapee, of course, also had a contract with Fischer. Carl Fischer, Inc., advertisement, *The Metronome*, Jan. 15, 1927, 8.

217. Funk & Wagnalls Company advertisement, *NYT*, Jan. 20, 1927, 2.

218. "The Talk of the Town," *NY*, Mar. 19, 1927, 18.

219. Lucky Strike cigarettes advertisement, *NYT*, May 10, 1927, B3.

220. FADA radio advertisement, *NYT*, Sept. 25, 1927, XX18; FADA radio advertisement, *Sheboygan* (WI) *Press*, Oct. 27, 1927, 7.

221. Eyman, 120.

222. Majestic Theatre advertisement, *NYT*, Jun. 9, 1927, 21.

223. Unfortunately, no location was given for the filming. "Vitaphone," *Variety*, Jun. 20, 1927, 22.

224. "New Warner Program: Restore 100 Shorts a Year!," *The Vitaphone Project*, 4:2 (Fall 1998). Available at www.picking.com/vitaphone42.html (accessed Jul. 22, 2011).

225. Barrios, *A Song in the Dark*, 30.

226. The Vitaphone Project, "Complete List of Restorable Shorts!!" Available at www.picking.com/vitaphone-complete-list.html (accessed Jul. 22, 2011).

227. White, who had studied in Germany and graduated from the Philadelphia Music Academy, spent eight previous seasons with the Stanley Company of America, including five at Philadelphia's Stanley Theatre. "New York's Situation," *American Organist*, Feb. 1928, 67; advertisement, *Variety*, Mar. 30, 1927, 18.

228. "White and Brunswick Vs. Crawford and Victor," *Variety*, Apr. 6, 1927, 53. By the following year, White had established his own theater organ training school, the White Institute of Organ, and begun weekly broadcasts through WJZ and the NBC Blue network. Lew White advertisement, *American Organist*, Jul. 1928, 270.

229. There are, unfortunately, no known recordings of any of the thirteen years of Roxy and His Gang radio programs.

230. "Inside Stuff on Music," *Variety*, Jun. 8, 1927, 46.

231. "White and Brunswick vs. Crawford and Victor," *Variety*, Apr. 6, 1927, 53.

232. Brunswick Record advertisement, *TDS*, Apr. 8, 1927, 20.

233. Brunswick Record No. 3581.

234. "Roxy's Music for British Cinemas," *The Bioscope*, Aug. 25, 1927, 43.

235. "Brunswick's Own," *Variety*, Mar. 23, 1927, 47.

236. "WEAF Satisfied with Radioing Disk Records," *Variety*, Aug. 31, 1927, 53; "Brunswick's WCFL," *Variety*, Apr. 27, 1927, 50; Brunswick Record advertisement, *Sheboygan* (WI) *Press*, May 31, 1927, 4; Lew White advertisement, *Variety*, Jun. 8, 1927, 16.

237. Brunswick advertisement, *Atlanta Constitution*, Oct. 27, 1927, 9.

238. "Inside Stuff on Music," *Variety*, Aug. 3, 1927, 34.

239. "Press Attend Fox Movietone Show at Roxy Theater," *EH*, May 7, 1927, n.p. (MCNY).

240. "Roxy," *Variety*, Jun. 15, 1927, 26; Koszarski, *Hollywood on the Hudson*, 152.

241. "_A Will _ Story of _o's Arrival," *DMN*, Jun. 10, 1927, I:7.

242. Talmey, 173–181.

243. "Profiles: Deux Ex Cinema," 21.

244. Talmey, 175.

245. "Profiles: Deux Ex Cinema," 22.

246. Helm, 98.

247. Talmey, 175.

248. Roxy didn't just spend his employers' money—his own closets at his Riverside Drive apartment and at the Roxy were full of "clothes he seldom wears." He reportedly bought "suits and shirts and neckties by the dozen, and gets 20 pairs of shoes at a time—all alike. If a collar strikes his fancy he buys 50." His appetite for cars was apparently no different. "Any salesman of imported motor cars can sell him one by proving that it will go faster than the one he has." Like his prodigious collection of overcoats, his appetite for new automobiles was similarly foolhardy: Roxy had little time to go

outside and even less to go driving. Deming Seymour, "A New Yorker at Large," *Rochester Democrat and Chronicle*, Apr. 19, 1930, n.p.

249. "Profiles: Deux Ex Cinema," 22.

250. "Do You Know That—," *MC*, May 26, 1927, 45.

251. "Inside Stuff on Pictures," *Variety*, May 18, 1927, 12.

252. "Roxy," *Variety*, Jun. 22, 1927, 37.

253. Rothafel, quoted in "Leaders See Prosperity for 1928," *1928 Film Daily Yearbook* (New York: Film Daily, 1928), 509.

254. Dudley Glass, "New York Talkies," *Sydney Morning Herald* (Australia), Aug. 15, 1931, 9.

255. Eyman, 88.

256. Quoted in Slide, *Silent Topics*, 73. Mendoza noted that most of his early work for synchronous sound films occurred in Camden, New Jersey, not at the Capitol or in its broadcasting studio, but at the Victor Talking Machine Company "plant." The music was scored in segments after viewing the film and then recorded on disc.

257. Mordaunt Hall, "Vitaphone Stirs as Talking Movie," *NYT*, Aug. 7, 1926, 6; "Program," *RTWR*, Aug. 6, 1927, 13.

258. The Sam H. Harris Theatre, where the film was still showing in mid-May 1927, was used as a shop-window theater for Fox branch managers in the New York area for a sales convention. Fox was so enthusiastic about his new films, including *What Price Glory*, *7th Heaven*, and *Sunrise*, that he prolonged the convention by three days to make sure all of his company's branch managers could go back to their territories and begin selling the films. The managers were also given a Movietone demonstration on Sunday, May 15, and then made a group visit to the Roxy Theatre on Monday, May 16. "Thirty Fox First Runs by 1929," *MPN*, May 27, 1927, 2063.

259. Roxy Theatre advertisement, *NYT*, Aug. 13, 1927, 11.

260. "World's Record for 'Glory,'" *MPN*, Sept. 2, 1927, 699.

261. "Presentation News and Reviews," *The Metronome*, Sept. 1, 1927, 57.

262. "Roxy's Prolog," *Variety*, Aug. 31, 1927, 41.

263. "'Over There,'" *Variety*, Aug. 7, 1927, 27.

264. Ibid.; "'Charmaine' Again," *Newsweek*, Dec. 24, 1951, n.p. (NYPL); *RTWR*, Aug. 20, 1927, 12, 13.

265. "'Over There,'" 27.

266. Joe Bigelow, "Roxy, Films' No. 1 Exhibitor, Pioneer in Cinema Standards, Dies at 53," *Variety*, Jan. 15, 1936, 4, 31.

267. "Movietone Music for Fox Specials," *Variety*, Aug. 10, 1927, 11.

268. "Keynotes: An Interview with Erno Rapee," *RTWR*, Apr. 30, 1927, 16. Rapee added, "Suppose your picture has its setting in China. You must go to Chinese music to find all your themes, even those you use for the characters. But do not forget that Oriental music, particularly, becomes very monotonous, and that you must vary it by the introduction of contrasting bits." Roxy's influence upon Rapee's style was apparently long lasting. Nearly two decades earlier, Roxy had told *Moving Picture World*

that theater musicians should have a "good repertoire of the classics, semi-classics, patriotic and popular selections, and should be careful to learn the national airs of the different countries." S. L. Rothapfel, "Music and Motion Pictures," *MPW*, Apr. 16, 1910, 593.

269. "'Charmaine' Again," *Newsweek*, Dec. 24, 1951, n.p. (NYPL); "Film Theme Song Near Monopoly of Publishing Trade," *Variety*, Oct. 17, 1928, 73; "Film Houses Working for Song Selling," *Variety*, Nov. 21, 1928, 57.

270. Eric T. Clarke, "An Exhibitor's Problems in 1927," *Transactions of the Society of Motion Picture Engineers* 11:31 (1927): 450–457.

271. Quoted in "The Kinema," *West Australian* (Perth, Australia), Dec. 24, 1927, 7.

272. "Pictures and People," *MPN*, Sept. 2, 1927, 643; "Roxy Record Net Will Benefit Fox," *Wall Street Journal*, Sept. 1, 1927, 7; "$408,152 Glory Record at New York Roxy," 842.

273. "World's Record for 'Glory,'" *MPN*, Sept. 2, 1927, 699.

274. "$408,152 Glory Record at New York Roxy," 842.

275. "The Hits of the Season," *The Metronome*, Sept. 1, 1927, 54.

276. Sherman, Clay & Co. advertisement, *The Metronome*, Oct. 1, 1927, 17.

277. "Fox Installs Movietone," 921.

278. "Owner Spends Money to Provide Air," *LAT*, Nov. 21, 1927, A7.

279. Edwin Schallert, "Coast Movietone Opening in Los Angeles Theatre Creates Sensation," *MPN*, Nov. 18, 1927, 1558.

280. Josephine Vila, "Music and the Movies," *MC*, Apr. 7, 1927, 44.

281. "'Charmaine' Will Be Feature of Program," *DMN*, Jan. 15, 1928, Radio News:1.

282. "Louis Levy's Stage Production," *The Bioscope,* Jan. 12, 1928, 55.

283. Roxy had worked with Hilliker seven years earlier on the Americanized *Passion*. "'Seventh Heaven' a Winner,' News' Man Reports After Coast Premiere," *MPN*, May 20, 1927, 1951.

284. The staggered release of Frank Borzage's film serves as an important reminder that feature films during this period did not always premiere in New York before expanding westward but were often capable of reversing the order of our retrospective conventional wisdom. "Movietone," *Variety*, Jun. 1, 1927, 25; *7th Heaven* advertisement, *NYT*, May 21, 1927, 25; "'Glory' at Roxy in August," *Variety*, Apr. 13, 1927, 14.

285. Mordaunt Hall, "The Screen," *NYT*, Sept. 24, 1927, 15.

286. "Movietone Music for Fox Specials," 11; "7th Heaven," *RTWR*, Sept. 10, 1927, 13.

287. "Movietone Accompanies 'Seventh Heaven,'" *MPN*, Sept. 16, 1927, 847.

288. *7th Heaven* advertisement, *NYT*, Sept. 8, 1927, 25.

289. "7th Heaven," *RTWR*, Sept. 10, 1927, 13.

290. "Program," *RTWR*, Sept. 10, 1927, 12.

291. *7th Heaven*'s cue sheet was compiled by Erno Rapee, not Michael Krueger, and did not feature "Diane," suggesting a lack of integration between the Rapee-Pollack

theme song and the plug it could have provided the song's publishers. It is hard to account for its exclusion from the printed cue sheet but again emphasizes the importance in analyzing each film's music theater by theater. *Seventh Heaven* cue sheet (Collection of Thematic Music Cue Sheets for Silent Films, 1915–1928, Box 10, Folder 5, UCLA Performing Arts Special Collections).

292. James Melton, "Diane/An Old Guitar and an Old Refrain," Columbia, 1206-D (author's collection).

293. M. D. Kann, ed., *Film Daily Year Book* (New York: Film Daily, 1928), 848.

294. "Fox Installs Movietone," 921.

295. Glazer, *Philadelphia Theatres, A–Z,* 156; "Fox Installs Movietone," 921. Roxy also added to his list of responsibilities by supervising the Fox Theatre in Philadelphia (Rapee's former venue) with the "installation of a Roxy show" that, according to the *Wall Street Journal*, "set up a new high record for admissions in this house." "Roxy Record Net Will Benefit Fox," *Wall Street Journal*, Sept. 1, 1927, 7.

296. "Fox Installs Movietone," 921.

297. Five years before *The Last Laugh*, Roxy envisioned a film almost completely devoid of intertitles. "I believe that the day will come when all that is supplied by artificial means in pictures will be taken care of by the music," Roxy noted in 1919. "By this I mean the subtitles. It may not be possible to completely abolish the written word, but everything will make way for the idea picture, which is the supreme." Edwin Schallert, "Rothapfel a Harmonist," *LAT*, Nov. 2, 1919, III1.

298. Dunham Thorp, "Roxy Builds His Dream," *Motion Picture Classic*, Dec. 1926, 73.

299. "Hello Everybody!" *RTWR*, Apr. 30, 1927, 3.

300. Bergstrom, 193.

301. "Hello Everybody!" *RTWR*, Jun. 25, 1927, 3.

302. "Movietone Music for Fox Specials," 11; Mordaunt Hall, "The Screen," *NYT*, Sept. 24, 1927, 15; "7th Heaven," *RTWR*, Sept. 10, 1927, 13. Janet Bergstrom adds that "*Film Daily* reported the same thing on 7 September." "Murnau, Movietone, and Mussolini," 197. Janet Bergstrom notes that Hugo Riesenfeld, for reasons unknown, had long been credited with this film's score before her 2005 article "Murnau, Movietone, and Mussolini" appeared in *Film History*. Bergstrom, 195.

303. Times Square Theatre program, reprinted in Bergstrom, 198.

304. "William Farnum Is Stage Host," *LAT*, Nov. 23, 1927, A9; Edwin Schallert, "'Sunrise' Rare Art Feature," *LAT*, Dec. 1, 1927, A9.

305. Now able to book synchronous sound short and feature films, the Criterion changed its presentation methods and "inaugurated the new continuous policy of the house." Audiences could now drop in whenever without fear of interrupting the now-scarce live entertainment. "Film Is Enhanced by Roxy's Music," *LAT*, Apr. 26, 1928, A9. The *Los Angeles Times* reiterated that Roxy wrote the score for *Sunrise* in a May 13 article: "George O'Brien Keeps Diary on Old Trunk Lid," *LAT*, May 13, 1928, B17.

306. Bergstrom, 197.

307. "George Bancroft Showing in a Great Thriller at Imperial," *Zanesville* (OH) *Signal*, Jan. 18, 1929, 15.

308. "'Sunrise' Shows Moral Contrasts," (Reno) *Nevada State Journal*, Aug. 11, 1929, 14.

309. "Davis for Fox's, Wash.," *Variety*, Aug. 24, 1927, 53; "Fox's, Washington, Brilliant Opening," *Variety*, Sept. 21, 1927, 16.

310. "Roxy Opens Fox Theater on Tuesday," *WP*, Sept. 18, 1927, 2; Fox Theatre advertisement, *WP*, Sept. 21, 1927, 8.

311. "President Attends Fox Washington Opening," *MPN*, Sept. 30, 1927, 984.

312. "Brilliant Audience Attends Opening of New Fox Theatre," *EH*, Oct. 1, 1927, 29.

313. "New Fox Theatre in Washington," *The Bioscope*, Dec. 8, 1927, ix.

314. "The Presidency: The Coolidge Week: Oct. 3, 1927," *Time*, Oct. 3, 1927. Available at www.time.com/time/magazine/article/0,9171,730997,00.html (accessed Jul. 22, 2011).

315. Unknown clipping, _____ *Herald*, ca. Sept. 21, 1927, n.p. (MCNY).

316. Fox Theatre (Washington, DC) program, Sept. 25, 1927, 5.

317. Fox Theatre (Washington, DC) program, Oct. 2, 1927, 3.

318. "Fox's Wash. House Adopts Philly Policy," *Variety*, Oct. 26, 1927, 5.

319. Fox Theatre (Washington, DC) program, Sept. 19, 1927, 5.

320. "Fox Interests Plan to Spread Theater Holdings to Northwest, Reports Say," unknown clipping, ca. Oct. 1927, n.p. (MCNY).

321. "New Fox Baltimore House for Roxy Shows," *MPN*, Nov. 4, 1927, 1438.

322. "Roxy Determined to Hold Leadership," *Variety*, Nov. 9, 1927, 5.

323. "Fox's Policy Change Hurts Gross, $27,000," *Variety*, Nov. 2, 1927, 7.

324. "Fox," *Variety*, Oct. 26, 1927, 27.

325. "Fox's Wash. House Adopts Philly Policy," 5.

326. "Fox, Wash., Going Now to Stage Band and M. C.," *Variety*, Jan. 4, 1928, 6; Fox Theatre advertisement, *Variety*, Jan. 4, 1928, 138.

327. "Fox," *Variety*, Dec. 14, 1927, 37. Roxy rehired Wenger in the fall of 1928. "Hello Everybody!" *RTWR*, Nov. 3, 1928, 1.

328. Advertisement, *The Bioscope*, Dec. 5, 1928.

329. FADA advertisement, *NYT*, Sept. 25, 1927, XX18; Lucky Strike advertisement, *LAT*, May 10, 1927, B3.

330. Banner, Sept. 29, 1934, 7.

331. Information taken from original photographs owned by the author.

332. "A Pledge to Stevens Point," *Stevens Point* (WI) *Daily Journal*, Apr. 1, 1929, Fox Theatre section: 11.

333. S. L. Rothafel, "The Music That Is in Every Man," *The Etude*, Dec. 1927, 904; S. L. Rothafel ("Roxy"), "Ten Million Listeners Guide the Gang," *RTWR*, Oct. 6, 1928, 3; "A Theatre Anniversary," *Wall Street Journal*, Mar. 9, 1928.

334. Hilmes, *Radio Voices: American Broadcasting 1922–1934*, 63.

335. Dudley Glass, "New York Talkies," *Sydney Morning Herald* (Australia), Aug. 15, 1931, 9.

336. "Roxy-Fox Film Prices," *Variety*, Dec. 28, 1927, 5.

337. Kann, ed., *Film Daily Year Book*, 848.

338. Ibid.

339. William A. Johnston, "Back to the Movies," *MPN*, Nov. 18, 1927, 1556. The *New Yorker* argued in May that the theater's overhead was roughly $70,000 per week, noting that Roxy "knows the radio helps bring into the box-office the $110,000 that has to be counted every week before $40,000 or so is put away in profit." "Profiles: Deux Ex Cinema," May 28, 1927, 21.

340. Jack Jamison, "The Man Who Dreamed Too Much," *Radio Guide*, Apr. 18, 1936, 18.

341. "Roxy Starts New Sunday A.M. Shows," *Motion Pictures Today*, Oct. 8, 1927, n.p. (MCNY); "A Helping Hand," *RTWR*, Oct. 22, 1927, 3; "Leading Radio Programs," *Cass City* (MI) *Chronicle*, Oct. 26, 1928, 5.

342. "Ten Million Listeners Guide the Gang," *RTWR*, Oct. 6, 1928, 3.

343. Mary Jordan, "Radio Has Made 'High-Brow' Music Popular," *Radio News*, Feb. 1928, 884.

344. Gustav Saenger, "Training New Audiences for Symphonic Music," *Musical Observer*, Aug. 11, 1928, 1.

345. Erno Rapee, quoted in Ewen, *Dictators of the Baton*, 283.

346. Josephine Vila, "Music and the Movies," *MC*, Jun. 9, 1927, 28.

347. Gordon Whyte, "Roxy and Erno Rapee," *The Metronome*, Dec. 1927, 53.

348. Carl Fischer, Inc., advertisement, *The Metronome*, Dec. 1927, 27.

349. Whyte, "Roxy and Erno Rapee," 53, 54.

350. "Rockettes to Paris," *Time*, Jun. 21, 1927. Available at www.time.com/time/magazine/article/0,9171,757977,00.html (accessed Jul. 22, 2011); Porto, *The Radio City Rockettes: A Dance through Time*, 31, 33.

351. "The Screen," *NYT*, Oct. 31, 1927, 22.

352. "Christmas Numbers on Roxy's Program," *DMN*, Dec. 25, 1927, Amusement: 9; Roxy Theatre advertisement, *NYT*, Dec. 18, 1927, X6; "Presentation News and Reviews," *The Metronome*, Jan. 1928, 36.

353. "Jews Who's Who," *Time*, Dec. 12, 1927. Available at www.time.com/time/magazine/article/0,9171,737054,00.html (accessed Jul. 22, 2011).

7. It's All Playing in Sheboygan (1928–1931)

AC   Atlanta Constitution
CSM   Christian Science Monitor
DMN   Dallas Morning News
EH   Exhibitors Herald

HC	Hartford Courant
LAT	Los Angeles Times
MC	Musical Courier
MPN	Motion Picture News
MPW	Moving Picture World
NYT	New York Times
RG	Radio Guide
RTWR	Roxy Theatre Weekly Review
TDS	Toronto Daily Star
WP	Washington Post
WSJ	Wall Street Journal
AMPAS	*Academy of Motion Picture Arts and Sciences*
MCNY	*Museum of the City of New York*
NYPL	*New York Public Library for the Performing Arts*
USC-WB	*University of Southern California - Warner Bros. Archive*

1. "U. A. Names Riesenfeld," *MPN*, Dec. 16, 1927, 1892-D.

2. "Fox Films Buys 250 Theaters," *LAT*, Jan. 26, 1928, A1; "Fox Buys West Coast Theatres and Interest in First Nat'l," *MPN*, Jan. 28, 1928, 265.

3. "Fox Films Buys 250 Theaters," A1; "Fox Buys West Coast Theatres and Interest in First Nat'l," 265.

4. "Fox-West Coast Hook-Up," *Variety*, Jan. 25, 1928, 5.

5. "$2,000,000 Shrine Mosque to House Huge Theater," *AC*, Jan. 29, 1928, 1.

6. "Cinemagnification," *Time*, Feb. 6, 1928. Available at www.time.com/time/magazine/article/0,9171,731517,00.html (accessed Jul. 25, 2011).

7. "Fox Buys $25,000,000 Poli Theatre Chain; Talking Films for 20 New England Houses," *NYT*, 1.

8. Fox also built a new orchestra pit at the Hartford theater to accommodate a thirty-piece orchestra. "Alterations to Capitol Theater, Plan," *HC*, Sept. 20, 1928, 7.

9. "Roxy's Production Cost," *Variety*, Mar. 7, 1928, 16.

10. "Rockets at Roxy's Indef.," *Variety*, Mar. 21, 1928, 15; "Hello Everybody!" *RTWR*, Apr. 21, 1928, 2.

11. Russell E. Markert advertisement, *Variety*, Dec. 5, 1928, 46.

12. "New Irving Berlin Song at Roxy," *The Metronome*, Mar. 1928, 42.

13. Untitled, *The Metronome*, Aug. 1928, 25.

14. John Grierson, "The Industry at a Parting of the Ways," *MPN*, Nov. 13, 1926, 1842.

15. "The Theatre," *WSJ*, Mar. 9, 1928, 4; "Pictures and People," *MPN*, Mar. 10, 1928, 799.

16. "From the Far Corners," *RTWR*, Mar. 10, 1928, 4.

17. "Hello Everybody!" *RTWR*, Jun. 2, 1928, 2.

18. Karen Bramson quoted in "Roxy's in Viking Eyes," *NYT*, Mar. 18, 1928, 124.

19. *The Jazz Singer* advertisement, *MPN*, Mar. 17, 1928, 760, 761.

20. "Key City Reports," *MPN*, Apr. 11, 1928, 1207.

21. "Program," *RTWR*, Mar. 31, 1928; Roxy Theatre advertisement, *NYT*, 122.

22. H.Z.T., "The Theatre," *WSJ*, Apr. 11, 1928, 4. Janet Bergstrom makes a similar argument about the "incongruousness" of the 1927 exhibition of a Movietone recording of Benito Mussolini with *Sunrise* at the Times Square Theatre in Manhattan. Bergstrom, "Murnau, Movietone and Mussolini," 188.

23. S. L. Rothafel, "Speed and Business," *The Magazine of Business*, May 1928, 567.

24. S. L. Rothafel, "*Speed* Makes the Show Go but Profits Start with *Control*," *The Magazine of Business*, Jun. 1928, 721, 769.

25. "Hours with ROXY," *The Bioscope*, Mar. 1, 1928, 30.

26. Paramount executive Al Kaufman, in charge of much of the company's European exhibition, had a nervous breakdown in mid-May 1928 in Paris, and Jesse Lasky was forced to sail to Europe to oversee the company's operation there. "Kaufman's Breakdown," *Variety*, May 23, 1928, 9.

27. He was briefly replaced by Pedro Rubin as the new ballet master and dance producer at the Roxy. "Leon Stages 2100 Numbers for 'Roxy,'" *Radio City News*, Sept. 7, 1933, 1; "Rubin at Roxy," *Variety*, Jun. 6, 1928, 10.

28. Okrent, *Great Fortune*, 347, 348.

29. "Maria Gambarelli Has Breakdown," *NYT*, Jun. 15, 1929, 20. After recuperating in Colorado, Gamby resumed her dancing career with appearances through RKO's fading vaudeville circuit. "The Dance: Rhythms of Sight and Sound," *NYT*, Sept. 15, 1929, X9.

30. "Roxy Will Stick," *Variety*, May 30, 1928, 7.

31. "Fox's Musical Programs and Chorus in New Fox's," *Variety*, Aug. 29, 1928, 19.

32. Charles Griswold, who had worked for Roxy since his days at the Rialto Theatre, also opened the new Fox theaters in Brooklyn, Washington, D.C., and St. Louis. "'Roxy' Aides Are Service Veterans," *Radio City News*, Aug. 24, 1933, 3.

33. "From the Boxoffice Files . . . Twenty Years Ago," *Boxoffice*, Feb. 26, 1929, 56; Miles Krueger, "Introduction," in Shire, ed., *Nellé*, 22, 24.

34. "Four Sons," *Variety*, Feb. 15, 1928, 24. Credit for these Movietoned scores remains difficult to discern. While *Musical Courier* noted that *Four Sons* was scored by Roxy, *Motion Picture News* noted that Rapee was the creator. "Music and the Movies," *MC*, Feb. 16, 1928, 42; "'4 Sons,' Fox Special, at Gaiety, Feb. 13," *MPN*, Jan. 28, 1928, 265.

35. "The Screen," *NYT*, Feb. 14, 1928, 27.

36. "'4 Sons,' Fox Special, at Gaiety, Feb. 13," 265.

37. "A New Mother Song," *The Metronome*, Apr. 1928, 54.

38. "Mrs. Coolidge Requests Little Mother," *The Metronome*, Jun. 1928, 53.

39. Abel, "Radio Ramblings," *Variety*, Jun. 20, 1928, 56.

40. "Presentation News and Review," *The Metronome*, Sept. 1928, 100; *RTWR*, Aug. 11, 1928, 11.

41. "Roxy," *Variety*, Aug. 22, 1928, 44.

42. "Hello Everybody!" *RTWR*, Sept. 1, 1928, 2; "Roxy, New York City," in M. D. Kann, ed. *Film Daily Year Book* (New York: Film Daily, 1929), 879.

43. Fox Theatre (Brooklyn, NY) program, ca. Sept. 15, 1928. In Los Angeles, the film played the Metropolitan Theater and featured a "symphonic Movietone accompaniment, recorded by the Roxy orchestra." "Movietone Score Used with Film," *LAT*, Sept. 10, 1928, A7; "Roxy, New York City," 879.

44. Mordaunt Hall, "The Screen," *NYT*, Mar. 6, 1928, 20. *Variety*, like the *Times*, noted that "Rothafel and Erno Rapee are credited with the orchestration." "Mother Machree," *Variety*, Mar. 7, 1928, 23.

45. "'Mother Machree' and Other New Films," *CSM*, Mar. 13, 1928, 12.

46. "Pictures and People," *MPN*, Mar. 10, 1928, 799.

47. "Fox's Big Music Saving by Movietone," *Variety*, Mar. 21, 1928, 13.

48. Untitled, *The Metronome*, Aug. 1928, 25.

49. "Fox's Big Music Saving by Movietone," 13.

50. "Roxy Gives Views on Sound Picture," *MPN*, Aug. 18, 1928, 537.

51. "Musicians Plan Opposition to Sound Devices," *DMN*, Jul. 8, 1928, n.p.

52. The film's score was credited to Roxy, according to *Variety*, and "assisted" once again by Erno Rapee. "Street Angel," *Variety*, Apr. 11, 1928, n.p. (AMPAS). Even the trade journal was inconsistent on this point. Another article in the same issue noted that the film "carried an excellent Roxy-Rapee score, with a pleasant theme song," giving each equal credit. "Movietone," *Variety*, Apr. 11, 1928, 34. *The Metronome* confirmed that Roxy and Rapee were working in collaboration to produce these scores. Contrary to their previous arrangement at the Capitol, in which Roxy suggested themes and specific pieces to Rapee who then arranged the score according to these inspirations, Fox Movietone scores seemed, according to press accounts at least, to have been far more collaborative in nature, melding Rapee's and Pollack's theme songs with Roxy's and Rapee's predilections for standard movie palace–approved selections. Untitled, *The Metronome*, Aug. 1928, 25.

53. Mordaunt Hall, "The Screen," *NYT*, Apr. 10, 1928, 33.

54. "'My Angel' Descends on Country," *The Metronome*, May 1928, 45.

55. Ibid.

56. "Street Angel" cue sheet (Museum of the Moving Image).

57. "House's War Veterans Are to Radio Program," *WP*, May 18, 1928, 16.

58. *RTWR*, Jun. 16, 1928, 7, 9.

59. "Music and the Movies," *MC*, Jun. 21, 1928, 28.

60. "Presentation News and Review," Sept. 1928, 99.

61. Ibid., 99, 100.

62. Untitled, *The Metronome*, Aug. 1928, 25.

63. "Presentation News and Review," Sept. 1928, 99.

64. "Roxy, New York City," 879.

65. "Presentation News and Review," Sept. 1928, 99.

66. "Roxy Plans Mess with Celebrities," *Musical America*, Aug. 11, 1928, 13.

67. The third week of *Street Angel* (when Roxy was absent from the theater) proved to be the film's financial apex, earning $144,000 at the box office, $18,000 more than its first week. *The Metronome* noted, "S. L. Rothafel found a fourth week the only way of taking care of the thousands who failed to see the film during the first three weeks of its engagement." "Presentation News and Review," Sept. 1928, 99. "Roxy, New York City," 879.

68. "At the Theaters," *AC*, Aug. 8, 1928, 10.

69. "New York & New Jersey," *MPN*, Sept. 8, 1928, 811.

70. "Inside Stuff—Music," *Variety*, Sept. 12, 1928, 56.

71. Fox Theatre (Brooklyn, NY) program, ca. Aug. 31, 1928.

72. "This Week's Screen Plays," *WP*, Sept. 2, 1928, A1.

73. Erno Rapee, "The Future of Music in Moviedom," *The Etude*, Sept. 1929, 650.

74. "Picture Song Working for Pub. and Screen," *Variety*, Oct. 31, 1928, 56.

75. "'Rapeeana' to Be Given over WRC," *WP*, Feb. 28, 1929, 14.

76. "Selling Sound to Rochester," *MPN*, Sept. 29, 1928, 1003.

77. Chas. M. Stebbins Picture Supply Co. advertisement, *Movie Age*, Jun. 1, 1929, 12.

78. Uptown and Tivoli Theaters advertisement, *Chicago Daily Tribune*, Sept. 10, 1928, 34.

79. "'Picture Songs' Now Most Important to Publishers—Big Hits Among Them," *Variety*, Jun. 13, 1928, 55.

80. Mordaunt Hall, "The Screen," *NYT*, Jun. 5, 1928, 21.

81. Sam Fox Publishing Co. advertisement, *Variety*, Oct. 24, 1928, 32.

82. In Los Angeles, after its debut at the Carthay Circle Theatre, the Sam Fox Publishing Co. received an order for 25,000 copies of "Neapolitan Nights." "'Picture Songs' Now Most Important To Publishers—Big Hits Among Them," 55. As a lost film, it is hard to ascertain how Zamecnik's song may or may not have infiltrated the score.

83. "'Fazil' to End Stay at Carthay," *LAT*, Sept. 6, 1928, A9.

84. "Arabian Film Wins Favor at the Majestic," *Sheboygan Press*, Sept. 6, 1928, 19; P. H., Jr., "'Fazil,'" *DMN*, Oct. 8, 1928, I:4. The *Dallas Morning News* commented, though, that while "It is an excellent score . . . no 'Diane' nor 'Angela Mia' are likely to come out of it."

85. "Roxy," *Variety*, Oct. 3, 1928, 39.

86. Oshkosh Theatre advertisement, *Daily Northwestern* (Oshkosh, WI), Oct. 8, 1928, 7.

87. Ibid., Oct. 29, 1928, 6.

88. Majestic Theatre advertisement, *Sheboygan* (WI) *Press*, Oct. 27, 1928, 14.

89. Stratford Theatre advertisement, *Poughkeepsie* (NY) *Eagle-News*, Oct. 11, 1928, 2.

90. Franklin, *Sound Motion Pictures, from the Laboratory to Their Presentation*, 267, 268.

91. "Inside Stuff—Music," *Variety*, Jul. 18, 1928, 54.

92. "The Red Dance," *Variety*, Jun. 27, 1928, 14; Fox advertisement, *NYT*, Jun. 26, 1928, 29. When the film later screened at the State Theatre in Uniontown, Pennsylvania, an advertisement in the *Morning Herald* noted its "Synchronized musical score arranged by S. L. Rothafel and Erno Rapee, played by the 110-piece Roxy Theatre orchestra." State Theatre advertisement, *Morning Herald*, Jan. 17, 1929, 13.

93. "Music and the Movies," *MC*, Nov. 22, 1928, 42.

94. Edwin Evans, "'Movietone' Setting to a Featured Film; Impressions of Mechanical Process; The Result Analyzed," *The Bioscope*, Aug. 15, 1928, service supplement: v.

95. Ibid., v, vi.

96. "Mother Knows Best," *Variety*, Sept. 19, 1928, 12.

97. Fox Theatre advertisement, reprinted in Shire, ed., *Nellé*, 29.

98. Rapee's original melody had been used in the Capitol Theatre's exhibition of United Artists' *Robin Hood* in 1923. It was reworked with lyrics by Pollack and Hirsch as "When Love Comes Stealing" for the Universal film. Capitol Theatre program, Jan. 28, 1923, 2, 3; Robbins Music Corporation advertisement, *Variety*, Jan. 4, 1929, 42.

99. "Roxy," *Variety*, Apr. 18, 1928, 38; "Presentation News and Reviews," *The Metronome*, May 1928, 43; *RTWR*, Apr. 21, 1928, 9.

100. Erno Rapee, Lew Pollack, and Walter Hirsch, "When Love Comes Stealing," Robbins Music Corporation, 1928 (author's collection).

101. "'Uncle Tom's Cabin' to Be Synchronized," *MPN*, Jun. 23, 1928, 2104.

102. Universal advertisement, *Variety*, Jun. 27, 1928, 17.

103. Letter, E.W. Kramer, general manager, Universal Pictures, to New York State Censorship Commission, Aug. 9, 1928 (New York State Archives), quoted in David Pierce, "'Carl Laemmle's Outstanding Achievement,'" *Film History* 10:4 (1998): 476.

104. Ibid., 471.

105. "Broadcasting Midnite Show," *Variety*, Oct. 3, 1928, 28.

106. "Fox Recalls Tone Truck upon Finding U Has Secretly Made Sound Picture," *Variety*, Sept. 5, 1928, 5.

107. "Rapee Sticks at Roxy," *Variety*, Oct. 3, 1928, 57.

108. "4 Devils," *Variety*, Oct. 10, 1928, 15; Mordaunt Hall, "The Screen," *NYT*, Oct. 4, 1928, 26. When the film played the Fox Locust Theatre in Philadelphia, the theater's program noted that it featured a "Synchronized Movietone Accompaniment" with "Musical score by S. L. Rothafel (Roxy) Directed by Erno Rapee." Undated Fox Locust (Philadelphia) Theatre program, 1.

109. "Two Theme Songs in '4 Devils,'" *The Metronome*, Nov. 1928, 62.

110. "Dry Martini," *Variety*, Nov. 7, 1928, 24.

111. "Rapee's Scores," *Variety*, Nov. 7, 1928, 57.

112. "Rapee Takes Charge of Firm's Sound Music," *Variety*, Nov. 14, 1928, 57; De Sylva, Brown & Henderson advertisement, *Variety*, Nov. 21, 1928, 31.

113. "Rapee Takes Charge of Firm's Sound Music," 57.

114. "New Roxy Music Corp.," *Variety*, Nov. 28, 1928, 56.

115. *Champions* advertisement, *Syracuse Herald*, Jan. 20, 1929, 1:9; Rex Theatre advertisement, *Ironwood* (MI) *Daily Globe*, Apr. 12, 1929, 8; "The Studebaker Film," *Journal and Republican and Lowville* (NY) *Times*, Jan. 24, 1929, 1. There is some evidence that the film may have had a modular construction, able to be reassembled for other car manufacturers' use. The *Dallas Morning News* noted, for instance, that a month before the film's wide release in January 1929, a Movietone film made by the Graham-Paige Motors Company was exhibited at an automobile conference in Dallas in December 1928. Like *Champions*, this film also included "incidental music by the Roxy Theater orchestra." "First Commercial Movietone Ever Made Shown at Motor Car Conference in Dallas," *DMN*, Dec. 9, 1928, Automobile: 4.

116. Gomery, *The Coming of Sound*, 53.

117. Over the years, more and more movie theater conductors and band leaders moved to Hollywood, including George Stoll, an orchestra leader at Portland, Oregon's Broadway Theatre in the late 1920s who, after working in radio, became a central figure in MGM's music department. Clar and Melnick, *Lollipop*, 79; "Mme. Secrets in Mystic Song," *LAT*, Sept. 30, 1924, A3.

118. The following year, as a music arranger for the studio, he made enough money to buy his family a house at 854 Kenneth Road in Glendale. Danly, ed., *Hugo Friedhofer: The Best Years of His Life,* 7, 8, 32.

119. Muriel Babcock, "Tin Pan Alley Invades Town," *LAT*, Dec. 9, 1928, C13, C24.

120. "The American Film Institute's Hugo Friedhofer Oral History," ca. 1974, reprinted in Danly, ed., 32.

121. John C. Flinn, "Hollywood's Dernier Cri," *LAT*, Jun. 9, 1929, X6.

122. "Bungalows for Fox Writers," *Variety*, Feb. 13, 1929, 58.

123. "Hall of Music Is Dedicated to Fox," *MPN*, Oct. 5, 1929, 1198.

124. "The American Film Institute's Hugo Friedhofer Oral History," reprinted in Danly, ed., 34, 35.

125. "Theme Song Composers Repeat," *The Metronome*, Feb. 1929, 43; Erno Rapee, "The Future of Music in Moviedom," *The Etude*, Sept. 1929, 650.

126. "Erno Rapee, a Symbol of Wide Versatility," *Movie Age*, Apr. 13, 1929, 22.

127. *The Bachelors Club* advertisement, *Movie Age*, Feb. 2, 1929, 4.

128. "Oscar Price Synchronizes Richard Talmadge Picture," *Movie Age*, Feb. 2, 1929, 13.

129. "Erno Rapee Signed for Home-Talkies," *Movie Age*, May 4, 1929, 7.

130. "Regarding 'Fox Movietone Follies,'" *The Metronome*, May 1929, 53. John Flinn noted in the *Los Angeles Times* that in their work for Fox "these young men in Hollywood have gained an importance second only to the most popular screen stars." Flinn, "Hollywood's Dernier Cri," X6.

131. "Red Star Music Company Under Way," *The Metronome*, Dec. 1929, 43.

132. "Fox Music Unit, Red Star, Ready," *MPN*, Dec. 21, 1929, 23; William Stull, "Seventy Millimetres" [*sic*], *American Cinematographer*, Feb. 1930, n.p. Reprinted by Widescreen Museum. Available at www.widescreenmuseum.com/Widescreen/70mm-feb1930.htm (accessed Jul. 25, 2011).

133. "Radio Closes Music Deal with Carl Fischer, Feist and N.B.C.," *MPN*, Dec. 7, 1929, 22.

134. "Two Publishers Merge with R. C. A.," *The Metronome*, Jan. 1930, 42.

135. Merlyn Aylesworth, quoted in Barnouw, *A Tower in Babel*, 232.

136. Gomery, *The Coming of Sound*, 152, 153.

137. "Two Publishers Merge with R. C. A.," 42; "Radio Closes Music Deal with Carl Fischer, Feist And N.B.C.," 22.

138. Quoted in *RTWR*, May 18, 1929, 2.

139. "New Recognition for Roxy as Authority on Stage Design," *MPN*, Oct. 5, 1929, 1238.

140. "Roxy Writes Encyclopedic Chapter on Theater Lights," *DMN*, Oct. 27, 1929, Amusements:3. Roxy's contribution focused on the psychological dimensions of light and color and how each could be used to conjure emotions and an audience's imagination. "In this use," he wrote, "it is parallel to the function of music." Still, Roxy argued that it was best not to create themes through light, as he did with music, but to embrace the creativity in a field that has "no specific rules for the director to follow. He may use his ingenuity and his imagination to the full extent." Rothafel, "Stage Lighting," in *The Theatre and Motion Pictures: A Selection of Articles from the New 14th Edition of the Encyclopedia Britannica*, 46–48.

141. Dorris, "Leo Staats at the Roxy," 96; Bernard N. Beck, "Presenting the Picture," *The Metronome*, Aug. 1928, 23.

142. Gamby Girls advertisement, in J. W. Alicoate, ed., *Film Daily Year Book* (New York: Film Daily, 1930), 187.

143. Koszarski, *Hollywood on the Hudson,* 203.

144. "Spotlight, Douglas Stanbury and Hamilton Comedy Shorts Highlights," *MPN*, Nov. 16, 1929, 30.

145. B. F. Keith's Palace Theatre photograph (author's collection).

146. "What Press Agents Say About Coming Events," *Toronto Daily Star*, Apr. 24, 1930, 4.

147. "Makes Debut in Berlin," *NYT*, May 1, 1930, 37; "Joseph Littau Weds," *NYT*, Oct. 21, 1931, 26.

148. "Erno Rapee to Leave Roxy's," *NYT*, Jan. 2, 1930, 35.

149. Joseph Littau, who had worked with Rapee over a decade earlier at the Rivoli, where they shared conducting duties, replaced him. "Written on the Screen," *NYT*, Aug. 10, 1919, XX6.

150. Doron K. Antrim, "American Opera Coming," *The Metronome*, Feb. 1930, 14.

151. "Hollywood Gets Rapee," *LAT*, Mar. 16, 1930, B11.

152. Ibid.; Alma Whitaker, "High C of Finance Scored by Golden Note Musician," *LAT*, Apr. 6, 1930, B9; Myrtle Gebhart, "Tin Pan Alley Says Good Bye," *LAT*, May 10, 1931, K9.

153. Erno Rapee, Musical Director, Warner Bros. Contract, Dec. 31, 1929, 1 (USC-WB, Folder 12634A).

154. Antrim, "American Opera Coming," 14.

155. "What Erno Rapee Thinks of Hollywood," *The Metronome*, Jul. 1930, 30.

156. "Among the Cinemakers," *The Metronome*, May 1930, 25.

157. Gebhart, "Tin Pan Alley Says Good Bye," K9.

158. Slide, *Silent Topics*, 73, 76.

159. "Rocky Roxy," *Time*, Feb. 17, 1930. Available at www.time.com/time/magazine/article/0,9171,738704,00.html (accessed Jul. 25, 2011).

160. Roxy Theatres Corporation advertisement, *NYT*, Nov. 12, 1925, 23.

161. "Rocky Roxy."

162. "Theme Song Writer Arrives," *LAT*, Feb. 9, 1930, A8; "Roxy Orchestra Adds 31," *NYT*, Jan. 2, 1931, 29.

163. "Notes on the Passing Show," *DMN*, May 7, 1930, I:14.

164. "Notes on the Passing Show," *DMN*, May 30, 1930, I:10.

165. "Huge 60-Storey Radio Centre Planned by NBC and RCA," *Toronto Daily Star*, Jun. 19, 1930, 26.

166. Old Gold advertisement, *News-Palladium* (Benton Harbor, MI), May 28, 1930, 5.

167. Tydol advertisement, *NYT*, Jun. 24, 1930, 34.

168. "Is 'Roxy' Quitting," *Toronto Daily News*, Oct. 9, 1930, 1; "Gloomy Dean of St. Paul's Speaks on Air Sunday Noon," *Toronto Daily Star*, Dec. 6, 1930, 20; "Marco at Roxy in Roxy's Place," *Hollywood Reporter*, Sept. 19, 1930, 1.

169. "Littau Will Head Omaha Orchestra," *NYT*, Sept. 30, 1930, 34.

170. "Joseph Littau Weds," 26.

171. Erno Rapee to Warner Bros. Pictures, Inc., Oct. 10, 1930, 1, 2 (USC-WB, Folder 12634A).

172. "Two Others Depart Hollywood," *LAT*, Oct. 24, 1930, A9.

173. Whitaker, "High C of Finance Scored by Golden Note Musician," B9; "Styles in Music Vary," *LAT*, Jun. 8, 1930, B17.

174. Edwin Schallert, "Romberg Spell Floats Away," *LAT*, Jul. 31, 1931, A9.

175. Quoted in Slide, *Silent Topics*, 73, 76.

176. Riesenfeld, too, dabbled in other projects, co-producing film shorts for United Artists, including *Glorious Vamps, Overture of 1812, Irish Rhapsody, Manhattan Serenade,* and *The Wizard's Apprentice* (1930), which were "presented by" Joseph M. Schenck and distributed by Artcinema Associates. "United Artists Co. Making Short Group," *Movie Age*, Sept. 28, 1929, 19; "Hollywood Melody Makers," *MPN*, Oct. 12, 1929, 32-B.

177. Danly, ed., 33.

178. "Song of the Big Trail," *The Metronome*, Oct. 1930, 39; "Flaherty Resigns," *The Metronome*, Nov. 1930, 49.

179. "Is 'Roxy' Quitting," 1; "Gloomy Dean of St. Paul's Speaks on Air Sunday Noon," 20; "Marco at Roxy in Roxy's Place," 1.

180. "Roxy Leaving by Jan. 1st for NBC at $5,000 Per," *Variety*, Dec. 12, 1930, 4.

181. "Marco Succeeds Roxy March 29," *Exhibitors Forum*, Feb. 3, 1931, 10.

182. "Roxy Raps Money Chase," *Hollywood Reporter*, Dec. 12, 1930, 1, 3.

183. "Roxy and Gang to Make Tour of Provinces," *DMN*, Dec. 29, 1930, I:6.

184. Pierre V. R. Key, "Pierre Key's Music Article," *LAT*, Jul. 19, 1931, B15.

8. THE PROLOGUE IS PAST (1931–1936)

AC	Atlanta Constitution
CSM	Christian Science Monitor
DMN	Dallas Morning News
HC	Hartford Courant
LAT	Los Angeles Times
MC	Musical Courier
MPN	Motion Picture News
NYT	New York Times
PI	Philadelphia Inquirer
RCN	Radio City News
RG	Radio Guide
RTWR	Roxy Theatre Weekly Review
TDS	Toronto Daily Star
WP	Washington Post
WSJ	Wall Street Journal
AMPAS	*Academy of Motion Picture Arts and Sciences*
MCNY	*Museum of the City of New York*
NYPL	*New York Public Library for the Performing Arts*
WHS	*Wisconsin Historical Society*

1. Shira Ovide and Emily Steel, "It's Now Official: AOL, Time Warner to Split," *WSJ*, May 29, 2009, B1.

2. "Warner Bros. Acquire," *WSJ*, Apr. 10, 1930, 13; "Consolidated Film Industries," *WSJ*, Dec. 12, 1931, 11.

3. "Paramount Out of Radio Chain," *LAT*, Mar. 9, 1932, 12.

4. "Two Publishers Merge with R. C. A.," *The Metronome*, Jan. 1930, 42; "Radio Closes Music Deal with Carl Fischer, Feist and N.B.C.," *MPN*, Dec. 7, 1929, 22.

5. Jack Banner, "'ROXY,'" *RG*, Oct. 6, 1934, 8.

6. J. A. Holman to W. E. Harkness, Dec. 27, 1924 (WHS, 93, Box 5, Folder 1).

7. "Two Publishers Merge with R. C. A.," 42; "Radio Closes Music Deal with Carl Fischer, Feist and N.B.C.," 22.

8. "Rockefeller Opens New Epoch for Radio," *NYT*, Jun. 16, 1930, 1, 5.

9. "Rockefeller Begins Work in the Fall on 5th Av, Radio City," *NYT*, Jun. 17, 1930, 1.

10. "A National Entertainment Center," *CSM*, Jun. 18, 1930, 16. Eight decades later, the Metropolitan Opera and its high-definition broadcasts have fulfilled a version of this plan by selling tickets to live audiences and tickets to movie theaters projecting those performances.

11. "Television Theater Soon," *DMN*, Feb. 23, 1930, Society, Arts, Music, Amusement, Radio: 9.

12. "Entertainment Taste Improves," *Decatur* (IL) *Daily Review*, Jun. 21, 1931, 6.

13. "New Gotham Music Mecca Appears to Be a Certainty," *TDS*, Mar. 29, 1930, 9.

14. "Roxy Turns Universal Sales Convention into Open Forum," *Universal Weekly*, Jun. 7, 1930, 19.

15. "100,000 Clubwomen Pay Roxy Honor," *NYT*, Feb. 2, 1931, 23.

16. "Roxy and His Gang Give Merry Show," *NYT*, Feb. 9, 1931, 25.

17. "Roxy and His Gang Coming for Benefit," *HC*, Jan. 19, 1931, 22; Bushnell Memorial advertisement, *HC*, Feb. 12, 1931, 9.

18. "Night Club to Entertain Roxy and His Gang," *HC*, Feb. 12, 1931, 11.

19. "Notes on the Passing Show," *DMN*, Mar. 6, 1931, I:14; "Roxy's Gang Will Appear Locally in Red Cross Benefit," *DMN*, Feb. 7, 1931, I:4; "Radio Troupe to Show Here," *Port Arthur* (TX) *News*, Feb. 15, 1931, 19; "Opera Singer Added to Show," *DMN*, Feb. 15, 1931, I:8; "Roxy's Gang Stage Great Joy Carnival," *TDS*, Feb. 17, 1931, 8; John Rosenfield, Jr., "Reviewing the Reviews," *DMN*, Feb. 22, 1931, Society, Music, Amusements, Art: 8; "The Great Roxy Will Bring His Gang to Kansas City," *Kansas City Star*, Feb. 22, 1931, n.p.

20. "Home Town Greets Roxy in Minnesota," *NYT*, Mar. 14, 1931, 22. "Hello, Sam," a resident of the city supposedly told Roxy, "I hear you've been out of town." O. O. McIntyre, "New York Day by Day," *Chronicle Telegram* (Elyria, OH), May 18, 1931, 8.

21. "S. L. Rothapfel, 'Roxy,' Found Dead in Room in New York Hotel," unknown Stillwater newspaper, Jan. 13, 1936, 6 (Washington Historical Society, Stillwater, MN).

22. "Expect Legal Jam in 'Roxy's' Suit over Trade Name," *MPW*, Sept. 24, 1927, 215; "Flashes of Static," *HC*, Sept. 25, 1927, E11.

23. Untitled clipping, ca. Sept. 24, 1927, n.p. (MCNY).

24. "Lights of New York," *HC*, May 26, 1929, E2.

25. Roxy Cigarettes advertisement, *TDS*, Dec. 28, 1932, 9. The cigarettes were just as popular in 1933 when they sponsored the "Secret Service Thriller" radio show; Roxy "Secret Service Thriller" advertisement, *TDS*, Feb. 1, 1933, 20.

26. "After Long Career Before Public, Samuel L. Rothafel Secludes Self Behind Mike," *Utica Observer-Dispatch*, Aug. 10, 1930, A:7.

27. Web search for "Roxy" theaters, Cinema Treasures. Available at www. cinematreasures.org (accessed Jan. 6, 2012).

28. "Roxy Turns Universal Sales Convention into Open Forum," *Universal Weekly*, Jun. 7, 1930, 19.

29. "Roxy's New Job Brings Salary of $5,000 Per Week," *DMN*, Dec. 15, 1930, I:6.

30. "Post in Radio City Accepted by Roxy," *NYT*, Apr. 10, 1931, 26.

31. "Notes on the Passing Show," *DMN*, May 11, 1931, I:4.

32. "Notes on the Passing Show," *DMN*, Aug. 10, 1931, I:4.

33. Elwood to S. L. Rothafel, Oct. 15, 1931 (WHS, U.S. MSS 17A4, Box 4, Folder 127).

34. "Roxy Feted in Berlin," *NYT*, Oct. 1, 1931, 35; Anthony Rudel, *Hello Everybody!: The Dawn of American Radio*, 314; Okrent, *Great Fortune*, 215.

35. "Roxy Feted in Berlin," 35.

36. Rudel, 314; Okrent, 215.

37. "Moscow Made Roxy Long for America," *NYT*, Nov. 20, 1931, 29.

38. "Wire Briefs," *Newark Advocate and American Tribune*, Oct. 7, 1931, 2.

39. "Roxy Returns with Praise for America," *HC*, Oct. 30, 1931, 5.

40. "Moscow Made Roxy Long for America," 29.

41. Luciana Corrêa de Araújo, "Movie Prologues in Rio de Janeiro (1926–1927)," paper presented at "Cinema Across Media" conference, Berkeley, California, Feb. 24–26, 2011.

42. "The Heart Is the Target," *Woman's Home Companion*, Jul. 1932, 14.

43. "Opera in Radio City Promised by Roxy," *NYT*, Dec. 5, 1931, 19; "Roxy Will Not Mix Pictures and Plays," *TDS*, Dec. 12, 1931, 5.

44. "Speech from the Throne," *Time*, Dec. 28, 1931. Available at www.time.com/time/magazine/article/0,9171,753245,00.html (accessed Jul. 25, 2011).

45. "No Philly Opera," *DMN*, Jan. 3, 1932, 9.

46. Nicholas Schenck, quoted in "Forecast for 1932 by Industry Leaders," in Jack Alicoate, ed., *The 1932 Film Daily Year Book of Motion Pictures* (New York: The Film Daily, 1932), 39, 45.

47. Lynde Denig, "Millions in a Name," *The New Movie Magazine*, Feb. 1932, 70.

48. "What the Exchanges Say," *DMN*, Dec. 14, 1931, II:2.

49. Samuel Rothafel in "Forecast for 1932 by Industry Leaders," in Alicoate, ed., 39, 45.

50. "Roxy Will Not Mix Pictures and Plays," 5.

51. "Sharp Turn-Up in Movie Receipts," *Barron's*, Sep. 26, 1932, 5.

52. "The Heart Is the Target," 13.

53. "Notes of the Passing Show," *DMN*, Apr. 26, 1932, I:10; "Rothafel, Beck in Search of Talent," *New England Film News*, Apr. 28, 1932, 10.

54. "Plan Summer Dance School," *Chronicle Telegram*, Jun. 13, 1932, 7; "Books and Authors," *NYT*, Jun. 19, 1932, BR12.

55. Olive A. Van Horn to Roxy, Jan. 5, 1932 (WHS, U.S. MSS 17A4, Box 13, Folder 67).

56. "Theater-of-the-Air," *DMN*, Jun. 27, 1932, I:5.

57. Chester B. Bahn, "Speaking Very Candidly—," *Syracuse Herald*, Jul. 17, 1932, III:9.

58. "RKO Majestic to Institute Stage Policy," *DMN*, Oct. 18, 1932, I:14.

59. Gilbert Seldes, "An Open Letter to Roxy," *Modern Music*, Nov.–Dec. 1932, 4.

60. "Industry Leaders Hail the New Era," *New England Film News*, Aug. 25, 1932, 13.

61. "Broadcast from Radio City Is Listed on NBC," *Mansfield* (OH) *News*, Nov. 11, 1932, 14.

62. "Roxy to Broadcast Nov. 13," *NYT*, Oct. 27, 1932, 22.

63. "First Broadcast from Radio City," *NYT*, Nov. 14, 1932, 21.

64. Cyrus Fisher, "Radio Reviews," *Forum and Century*, Feb. 1933, 126.

65. Okrent, 232, 233.

66. In mid-June 1931, Erno Rapee was named general music director of the National Broadcasting Company, reporting to John Royal, director of programs for NBC. "Erne [*sic*] Rapee to N. B. C. Chain," *Kansas City Star*, Jun. 21, 1931, n.p.

67. "Radio City Town Crier," *RCN*, Jul. 27, 1933, 13.

68. Okrent, 233.

69. "'Roxy' Aides Are Service Veterans," *RCN*, Aug. 24, 1933, 3.

70. Okrent, 233; "'Roxy' Aides Are Service Veterans," 3.

71. Okrent, 235.

72. "Fox Film Loses Grip on Roxy Theatres," *NYT*, Apr. 19, 1932, 29.

73. "Big Orchestra Back at the Roxy Soon," *NYT*, Apr. 29, 1932, 13.

74. "Roxy Theatre Goes into Receivership," *NYT*, May 19, 1932, 25.

75. Three weeks before Radio City opened, RKO leased Roxy's first New York theater, the Regent. The timing was cruelly coincidental. Carl Edouarde, who had been such an integral part of Roxy's success at the Regent, and who had been badly injured in the famous Pathé studio fire, passed away days later. "Theatre in Harlem Is Leaded to R. K. O.," *NYT*, Dec. 7, 1932, 42; "Plan Funeral Today for Theatrical Man," *Rochester Democrat and Chronicle*, Dec. 10, 1932.

76. Okrent, 234.

77. Jack Banner, "Roxy," *RG*, Sep. 29, 1934, 7.

78. "First Radio City Show Is Announced in Part," *NYT*, Nov. 22, 1932, 24. Roxy remained an active patron of the Tuskegee Choir. William Dawson's 1934 song "Oh! What a Beautiful City" was "Dedicated to the Tuskegee Choir and their patron, Mr. S.L. Rothafel at Radio City." William L. Dawson, "Oh! What a Beautiful City" sheet music, 2 (author's collection).

79. California Theatre advertisement, *LAE*, Jan. 4, 1920, 9:3; California Theatre advertisement, *LAEE*, Jan. 5, 1920, 10; "Drama," *LAT*, Jan. 5, 1920, II12.

80. "First Radio City Show Is Announced in Part," 24.

81. "Roxy Invites Hoover," *Charleston* (WV) *Daily Mail*, Dec. 1, 1932, 2; "'Roxy' Invites Hoover to Opening," *NYT*, Dec. 2, 1932, 26.

82. Okrent, 233.

83. "'Roxy' Undergoes Operation Condition Is Reported Good," *Stillwater* (MN) *Gazette*, Mar. 16, 1932, 1.

84. Okrent, 233.

85. "Roxy Lets Fly at 'The Wolves' on Broadway," *New York Herald Tribune*, Feb. 15, 1933, 15.

86. Walter Trumbull, "'Roxy' Full of Big Plans for Future," *HC*, Mar. 5, 1933, A4.

87. Radio City Music Hall advertisement, *NYT*, Dec. 21, 1932, 23.

88. Douglas Haskell, "Roxy's Advantage over God," *The Nation*, Jan. 4, 1933, 11.

89. Radio City Music Hall advertisement, *NYT*, Dec. 23, 1932, 20.

90. "Back Comes the Music Hall," *NYT*, Dec. 25, 1932, X1.

91. Thompson, *The Soundscape of Modernity*, 3, 4, 231.

92. "New Roxy Theatre Plans Its Opening," *NYT*, Nov. 23, 1932, 15.

93. "Roxy Lets Fly at 'The Wolves' on Broadway," 15.

94. Atkinson, *Broadway*, 183.

95. "Roxy's Newest Flop Is a Gigantic One," *TDS*, Jan. 14, 1933, 25.

96. Untitled clipping, *Literary Digest*, Jan. 14, 1933, 17.

97. B.B., "Roxy and His Patron," *New Republic*, Jan. 11, 1933, 242.

98. "Roxy Lets Fly at 'The Wolves' on Broadway," 15.

99. "The Variety Bill," *Motion Picture Herald*, Sept. 28, 1935, 7.

100. "Radio City Theatres," *WSJ*, Jan. 6, 1933, 3. *Barron's* confirms these figures, noting that income was estimated to be $110,000 for the Music Hall and $70,000 at the RKO Roxy with overhead for the "ultra-expensive show and ballet in both houses" costing $80-100,000 for the Music Hall and $50-60,000 for the RKO Roxy. "Rockefellers' Large Interest in the 'Movies,'" *Barron's*, Jan. 16, 1933, 10.

101. "Roxy's Newest Flop Is a Gigantic One," 25.

102. "Radio City Theatres," 3.

103. "Deny Reports New 'Roxy' Is to Be Closed," *The Bee* (Danville, VA), Jan. 5, 1933, 6.

104. "Radio City Theatres," *WSJ*, Jan. 6, 1933, 3. Months later, the RKO Roxy would drop its competitive stage shows and begin showing second-run films at reduced prices, reducing its overhead and its possibility for profit. "Newspaper Specials," *WSJ*, May 25, 1933, 3; "Sunday Morning Fire Destroys Freedman Home," *Forest City* (PA) *News*, May 25, 1933, 1.

105. "Radio Music Hall to Be Movie House," *NYT*, Jan. 6, 1933, 23.

106. "Rockefeller Now World's Showman," *Ironwood* (MI) *Daily Globe*, Apr. 8, 1933, 3.

107. "All Men Dream," *New Yorker*, Jan. 7, 1933, n.p. (NYPL).

108. "Radio Music Hall to Be Movie House," 23.

109. "Rockefellers' Large Interest in the 'Movies,'" *Barron's*, Jan. 16, 1933, 10.

110. "Radio Music Hall to Be Movie House," 23.

111. "Radio City Loses Jones, Art Chief," *NYT*, Jan. 10, 1933, 26.

112. "Radio Music Hall to Be Movie House," 23.

113. Mordaunt Hall, "The Screen," *NYT*, Jan. 12, 1933, 20.

114. "'Scarlet Dawn' Old Mill Film," *DMN*, Jan. 18, 1933, I:6.

115. Jay Maeder, "Change in Plans Roxy's Wondrous Music Hall, 1932," *New York Daily News*, Nov. 22, 2004.

116. Roxy, "Don't Be Afraid to Fail!" *Radio Mirror*, Dec. 1934, 22.

117. Jack Jamison, "The Man Who Dreamed Too Much," *RG*, Apr. 18, 1936, 18.

118. "Roxy Lets Fly at 'The Wolves' on Broadway," 15.

119. Ibid.

120. "Roxy Himself to Tarry Here for Four Days," *DMN*, Mar. 21, 1933, I:8.

121. Untitled, *Barron's*, Feb. 6, 1933, 18.

122. "R-K-O in Receivership," *Barron's*, Jan. 30, 1933, 25.

123. "Dallas Exhibitors Will Entertain Mr. Rothafel," *DMN*, Mar. 21, 1933, I:8.

124. "Seems to Be Little Wrong with this Invalid," *DMN*, Mar. 22, 1933, I:12.

125. "Talk by Roxy WFAA Event for Thursday," *DMN*, Mar. 23, 1933, I:11.

126. "Roxy Himself to Tarry Here for Four Days," I:8.

127. "'Roxy' Returns to His Work at Radio City," *RCN*, May 15, 1933, 1; "Radio City Personalities," *RCN*, May 29, 1933, 2.

128. "Radio Programs," *Mansfield News-Journal* (OH), May 5, 1933, 22.

129. Unknown to Roxy, ca. Jun. 1933 (WHS, U.S. MSS 17A4, Box 21, Folder 36).

130. "'Roxy' and His Radio 'Gang' Attracting Thousands of Fans to Radio City Music Hall," RKO Radio City Theatres press release, Jul. 15, 1933. (NYPL).

131. "Clark Robinson Quits," *NYT*, Jun. 29, 1933, 22.

132. "Personalities in Radio City," *RCN*, Jul. 27, 1933, 5; "Rothafel Out of RKO and Music Hall, Breach Reported over High Show Costs," *Variety*, Jan. 9, 1934, 5.

133. Levy, *Vincente Minnelli: Hollywood's Dark Dreamer*, 22–31.

134. Ibid., 31, 32.

135. Denig, 70.

136. Levy, 31, 32.

137. "Amusement Row," *DMN*, Aug. 19, 1933, 1:6.

138. Okrent, 345. Okrent does not cite his sources for this assessment.

139. Jamison, 18.

140. S. L. Rothafel to M. H. Aylesworth, Aug. 18, 1933 (WHS, U.S. MSS 17A4, Box 21, Folder 36).

141. "The World of Pictures," *Brisbane Courier* (Brisbane, Queensland), Jul. 4, 1931, 19.

142. "7th Av. Movie Loses Use of Name 'Roxy,'" *NYT*, Dec. 6, 1932, 27. While Roxy was recovering from surgery in the winter and spring of 1933, the original Roxy Theatre posted an advertisement in the *New York Times* that was at once benevolent and ingenious: "Hello Mr. Rothafel! We're glad you're well again," the February 24

advertisement noted. "Everybody is glad that you're back on your feet, Roxy. And here's some more news that will cheer you up. The original Roxy Theatre has staged a comeback, too. It would do your heart good, Mr. Rothafel, to hear the laughter and applause that rings thru the original Roxy, week after week, as the audience revels in our great show. And you ought to see the crowds . . . just like the old days!" The gesture did not inspire détente. Roxy Theatre advertisement, *NYT*, Feb. 24, 1933, 13.

143. "Rothafel Ends Fight over the Name 'Roxy,'" *NYT*, Sept. 6, 1933, 24.

144. "Appeals in Roxy Case," *NYT*, Sept. 7, 1933, 17; "'Roxy' Loses to Roxy Theatre," *WSJ*, Oct. 10, 1933, 3; "'Roxy' Name Hearing Refused to Rothafel," *NYT*, Oct. 10, 1933, 24.

145. Radio City Music Hall advertisement, *NYT*, Sept. 6, 1933, 24.

146. "Three Canadians in Roxy Spectacle," *TDS*, Nov. 11, 1933, 6.

147. "Spectacular 'Roxy' Stage Show Surrounds 'Little Women' on Music Hall Stage this Week," Radio City Music Hall press release, Nov. 16, 1933, 1; "Record-Breaking 'Little Women' and 'Roxy' Stage Show in Second Week at the Music Hall," Radio City Music Hall press release, Nov. 26, 1933, 1 (NYPL).

148. Roxy was cited by the *American Hebrew* and *Jewish Tribune*, along with over 200 others, in the nation's "Jewish Who's Who." Roxy was not cited in the motion picture category with Katz, Laemmle, et al., but in "Theatre." "210 Cited for Work in Jewish Who's Who," *NYT*, Dec. 2, 1932, 18.

149. Jan Peerce, quoted in Levy, *The Bluebird of Happiness*, 101, 102.

150. Ibid., 102, 103.

151. "'Roxy' Is Offering One of His Famous Variegated Bills at Music Hall this Week," Radio City Music Hall press release, Sept. 23, 1933, 1 (NYPL).

152. Roxy had contributed to a number of Jewish causes over the years. In October 1932, for instance, he produced "Federation—a Pageant" for the Jewish Federation, utilizing "unique lighting and sound effects" and "numerous stage and radio luminaries" to give "spectators a graphic survey of the Federation's work among the poor and needy." "Full Support of Private Philanthropies Urged at Federation Drive Opening," *Jewish Telegraphic Agency*, Oct. 18, 1932.

153. Frank Chamberlain, "Are You Listening?" *TDS*, Sept. 25, 1933, 18.

154. "Brooklyn's Greatest Benefit Performance for the Relief of Distressed German Jewry" program, Nov. 29, 1933, 8, 9 (author's collection).

155. Vincente Minnelli designed the famous pants for the Roxyettes' "Parade". "'Roxy's' Great Christmas Show Is in Second Big Week at Radio City Music Hall," Radio City Music Hall press release, Dec. 30, 1933 (NYPL); Gia Kourlas, "A Little Respect, Please for a High-Kicking New York Institution," *NYT*, Dec. 24, 2005, B9.

156. Capitol Theatre program, Jun. 17, 1923, 4; *RTWR*, Jul. 7, 1928, 9.

157. Capitol Theatre program, Dec. 21, 1924, 2.

158. *RTWR*, Dec. 29, 1928, 9; *RTWR*, Dec. 20, 1929, 11;

159. Roxy, "A Message from 'Roxy,'" *Radio City Program Magazine*, Dec. 28, 1933, 3.

160. Quoted in "Hello Everybody!" *RTWR*, Apr. 6, 1929, 2.

161. Critic/columnist Frank Rich once wrote that "White Christmas" was "Jewish music." Frank Rich, "Jewish Yuletide," *NYT*, Dec. 1, 1994, A33; Stephanie Rosenbloom, "A Happy Hipster Hanukkah," *NYT*, Dec. 15, 2005, G1.

162. "Among the Industrials," *Barron's*, Nov. 13, 1933, 13.

163. The RKO Center Theatre trailed far behind, with just over two million tickets sold in 1933. "Projection Jottings," *NYT*, Dec. 31, 1933, X5.

164. "Tamara Geva, Modern Dance Star, in 'Roxy's' Stage Show at the Radio City Music Hall," Radio City Music Hall press release, Jan. 6, 1934 (NYPL).

165. Jack Banner, " 'Roxy,' " *RG*, Oct. 6, 1934, 8; "Roxy Rothafel Goes to Florida for Rest," *LAT*, Jan. 8, 1934, 2. "Roxy Sues R.-K.-O. Corp.," *NYT*, May 24, 1935, 25.

166. Rumors had been circulating about his departure—including a possible return to the original Roxy—for months. "Roxy Quits in Row over Stage Costs," *NYT*, Jan. 9, 1934, 18; "Rothafel Out of RKO and Music Hall, Breach Reported over High Show Costs," *Variety*, Jan. 9, 1934, 5.

167. Vincente Minnelli, quoted in Okrent, 347. Still, Minnelli wasn't pleased with the constraints that pushed Roxy out either. "Minnelli didn't mind the numerous sleepless nights and endless work," Levy writes, but "he did mind the budgetary cuts." Levy, *Vincente Minnelli: Hollywood's Dark Dreamer*, 32.

168. S. L. Rothafel to Leon Leonidoff, Jan. 11, 1936 (author's collection).

169. "Roxy Quits in Row over Stage Costs," 18.

170. "Milestones: Jan. 15, 1934," *Time*, Jan. 15, 1934. Available at www.time.com/time/magazine/article/0,9171,746827,00.html (accessed Jul. 28, 2011).

171. Herbert Westen, "Rebellious Roxy Returns," *Radioland*, Nov. 1934, 54.

172. Roxy, "Don't Be Afraid to Fail!" *Radio Mirror*, Dec. 1934, 22, 23.

173. C. E. Butterfield, "Radio Day by Day," *Frederick* (MD) *Post*, Jan. 11, 1934, 4.

174. Roxy, "Don't Be Afraid to Fail!" 22, 23.

175. "Inside Stuff—Pictures," *Variety*, Jan. 23, 1934, 44.

176. Samuel Rothafel to Nelson Rockefeller, quoted in Okrent, 346.

177. Roxy kept a bust of Napoleon in his office. Banner, Oct. 6, 1934, 8.

178. "Rothafel Takes Job on Paramount Stage," *NYT*, Feb. 2, 1934, 21; "Roxy Sues R,-K,-O. Corp," 25.

179. "Offered for Dallas," *DMN*, Mar. 21, 1934, II:3.

180. "Music on the Air," *MC*, Jul. 14, 1927, 12.

181. Banner, Oct. 6, 1934, 8. Although Roxy was no longer involved with the American Radio City Music Hall, executives like Sarnoff, NBC president Aylesworth, and NBC publicity manager John Royal remained in close contact. "Biggest British Cinema Will Be Built by Roxy," *NYT*, Mar. 14, 1934, 1.

182. "Are You Listening," *TDS*, Apr. 7, 1934, 24.

183. "Says Roxy Sought British Air Control," *NYT*, Mar. 18, 1934, N15.

184. The London Radio City project, now the third reported effort of this kind over a seven-year stretch, would have been the "biggest motion-picture house in the

British Isles" with 6,000 seats and was planned to open near Piccadilly Circus in London. "Biggest British Cinema Will Be Built by Roxy," 1.

185. "Death of Mr. Samuel L. Rothafel," *The Times* (London), Jan. 14, 1936, 13.

186. "Fairbanks Denies He'll Build British Radio City with Roxy," *Syracuse Herald*, Mar. 14, 1934, X; "2 Fairbanks Deny Part in 'Roxy's' Plans," *HC*, Mar. 15, 1934, 9.

187. "Boston Snapshots," *CSM*, Apr. 3, 1934, 4.

188. "Rothafel Sails for London to Discuss Theatre Proposition; Accepts Doherty Florida Deal," *Variety*, Mar. 6, 1934, 3.

189. "Rothafel Return to Roxy Seen," *Motion Picture Herald*, Apr. 14, 1934, 16.

190. "Biggest British Cinema Will Be Built by Radio City," 1.

191. Grauman's Chinese advertisement, *LAT*, Feb. 9, 1934, 13; "Gambarelli 'Rescued' from Metropolitan Opera Ballet," *LAT*, Feb. 18, 1934, A8.

192. "Stanbury Is Good Baritone at Imperial," *TDS*, Mar. 17, 1934, 26.

193. Mordaunt Hall, "W.C. Fields, Adrienne Ames and Joan Marsh in the Paramount's Latest Pictorial Farce," *NYT*, Apr. 7, 1934, 19.

194. "Roxy's Gang to Tour Paramount Houses," *NYT*, Mar. 15, 1934, 27; "Roxy's Theater Tour to Start in Boston," *DMN*, Mar. 21, 1934, II:3. Roxy wrote to Zukor shortly before leaving New York, reminiscing about their memories together before taking "this final cruise into the seas of show business." Roxy may have known that his final years were at hand. Roxy to Adolph Zukor, Mar. 28, 1934 (AMPAS).

195. "Melody in Spring," *CSM*, Apr. 2, 1934, 11.

196. In mid-May, Roxy performed with the Gang in Minneapolis. They stopped in Stillwater, Minnesota, as well for a hometown welcome. " 'Roxy' Coming to Town, Welcome Planned for City's Favorite Son," *Stillwater Gazette*, May 3, 1934, n.p. (Washington Historical Society, Stillwater, MN).

197. "Roxy's Gang Here en Route to N. Y. City," *Syracuse Herald*, May 19, 1934, 12.

198. "Radio," *News-week*, Jul. 28, 1934, 22.

199. "Roxy Gang, 'Trumpet,' $18,000, Poor," *Variety*, Apr. 17, 1934, 9.

200. "Roxy Gang with Flapper Film N.S.G.," *Variety*, May 8, 1934, 9.

201. "Roxy Pulls an Eva Le Gallienne; Pans Crix and Audience in Mpls.," *Variety*, May 22, 1934, 1.

202. "Are You Listening," *TDS*, Jun. 5, 1934, 20.

203. "London to Have Theatre Along Radio City Lines," *TDS*, Jun. 9, 1934, 22.

204. "Roxy to Return to a Stage Career," *NYT*, Aug. 5, 1934, N3.

205. "Notes on—The Passing Show," *DMN*, Aug. 30, 1934, I:4.

206. Herbert Westen, "Rebellious Roxy Returns," *Radioland*, Nov. 1934, 54.

207. By then, Roxy had already amassed seven million fan letters. "Radio," *News-week*, 22; C.E. Butterfield, "Radio Day by Day," *Frederick* (MD) *Post*, Jul. 17, 1934, 4; Carroll Nye, "Southlanders Win Dial Triumph," *LAT*, Jul. 18, 1934, 16; "Broadcasters Busy Mapping Elaborate Plans for Fall Programs—Many Old Favorites to Return," *NYT*, Aug. 12, 1934, XX15.

208. Carroll Nye, "Rudy Vallee Offers Radio Dialers Another Headline Bill Today," *LAT*, Aug. 30, 1934, 19.

209. Orrin E. Dunlap, Jr., "Up Goes the Curtain," *NYT*, Sept. 2, 1934, XX11.

210. Banner, "'ROXY,'" *RG*, Sept. 15, 1934, 5.

211. Westen, 54.

212. "Roxy's Return," *NYT*, Aug. 12, 1934, XX15; "'Roxy' Returns to Radio Scene," *Jewish Telegraphic Agency*, Aug. 8, 1934.

213. "Radio Reports," *Variety*, Sept. 18, 1934, 40.

214. Samuel Rothafel to John Royal, Sept. 17, 1934 (WHS, U.S. MSS 17AF, Box 31, Folder 61).

215. Westen, 16; "Radio," *News-Week*, 22.

216. "Again Nix Roxy, Lubin Offer for the 7th Av. Roxy," *Variety*, Nov. 6, 1934, 5.

217. Westen, 54.

218. "Again Nix Roxy, Lubin Offer for the 7th Av. Roxy," 5.

219. Ibid., 16, 55.

220. Glazer, *Philadelphia Theatres, A-Z*, 163–166.

221. "Mastbaum," *Variety*, Mar. 6, 1929, 39.

222. "Unsound Sound Business," *The American Organist*, Oct. 1929, 616.

223. Glazer, 163–166.

224. The ban was lifted in November 1935. Joan McGettigan, "Facing the Depression: Movie Exhibition in the Philadelphia Area, 1931," *Journal of American and Comparative Cultures* 24:1/2 (Spring 2001): 21.

225. "Roxy to Operate Mastbaum, Large Philadelphia House," *MPH*, Nov. 24, 1934, 33. Contemporary accounts note that the Mastbaum seated 4,800. Martin Lewis, "Along the Airialto," *RG*, Nov. 24, 1934, 6; "Rothafel to Direct Philadelphia House," *NYT*, Nov. 15, 1934, 25.

226. Irvin Glazer, "The Philadelphia Mastbaum," *Marquee* 7:1 (1975): 6.

227. Ibid.

228. "Roxy Will Manage Mastbaum Theatre," *PI*, Nov. 15, 1934, 3.

229. Roxy-Mastbaum advertisement, *PI*, Dec. 22, 1934, 13.

230. "What's Showing on Local Screens this Week," *PI*, Dec. 23, 1934, 10; "Roxy-Mastbaum in Gala Opening," *PI*, Dec. 24, 1934, 4.

231. Roxy-Mastbaum advertisement, *PI*, Dec. 24, 1924, 10.

232. Ibid.

233. "Roxy Will Manage Mastbaum Theatre," 3.

234. Glazer claims that "Roxy never showed up for the opening!" He does not cite his source for this information. Glazer, "The Philadelphia Mastbaum," 6.

235. "Roxy-Mastbaum in Gala Opening," 4.

236. John Royal to Hope Williams, Dec. 16, 1934 (WHS, U.S. MSS 17AF, Box 31, Folder 61).

237. "'Roxy's' Gang to Return," *PI*, Dec. 23, 1934, 17.

238. "Radio Reports," *Variety*, Jan. 8, 1935, 44.

239. "Roxy Mastbaum Disappointing, 'Forsaking' 1G, Town on Whole NSG," *Variety*, Jan. 8, 1935, 8.

240. "Talk Roxy for B'Way H'Wood," *Variety*, Jan. 15, 1935, 20.

241. "'Bengal' and 'Pres. Vanishes' Alone OK in Philly; Roxy-Mastbaum N.S.G.," *Variety*, Jan. 22, 1935, 11.

242. Roxy-Mastbaum advertisement, *PI*, Jan. 30, 1924, 13.

243. "Variety House Reviews," *Variety*, Feb. 5, 1935, 17.

244. "Jack Benny Scores at Roxy-Mastbaum," *PI*, Feb. 9, 1935, 10; "Benny Personal Gets Roxy-Mastbaum $37,000, Best Gross Since 1st Week," *Variety*, Feb. 12, 1935, 9.

245. Mildred Martin, "'The Good Fairy' at Roxy-Mastbaum," *PI*, Feb. 16, 1935.

246. Jamison, 18.

247. Carroll Nye, "Radio Bills Turf Event," *LAT*, Feb. 23, 1935, 4.

248. "S.L. Rothafel Dies; 'Roxy' of Theater," *NYT*, Jan. 14, 1936, 21.

249. "Roxy Project to Close," *NYT*, Feb. 24, 1935, N8.

250. "Roxy-Mastbaum to Close Doors Next Saturday," *PI*, Feb. 24, 1935, 11.

251. "5,000-Seat Mastbaum to Reopen in Philly," *Boxoffice*, Aug. 29, 1942, 58.

252. "S.L. Rothafel Dies; 'Roxy' of Theater," 21.

253. "Roxy Dies in Sleep in His Suite in Hotel," *New York World-Telegram*, Jan. 13, 1936, n.p. (NYPL); "S. L. Rothafel, Theater's Roxy Dies in Sleep," *New York Sun*, Jan. 13, 1936, n.p. (NYPL); "S. L. Rothafel Dies; 'Roxy' of Theater," 21. The Hotel Gotham is now known as the Peninsula. Christopher Gray, "Streetscapes / The Old Gotham Hotel, Now the Peninsula New York; A History Shaped, in Part, by State Liquor Laws," *NYT*, Jan. 3, 1999, RE7.

254. "Notes on—The Passing Show," *DMN*, Feb. 26, 1935, II:2.

255. "'Roxy' Stricken in Hotel Rooms," *Ironwood* (MI) *Daily Globe*, Jan. 13, 1936, 1; "S.L. Rothafel Dies; 'Roxy' of Theater," 21. Since 1933, *TDS* would later note, his health had been bad. "'Roxy' of Theatrical Fame Dies Suddenly in Sleep," *TDS*, Jan. 13, 1936, 17.

256. "Roxy Sues R.-K.-O. Corp.," 25.

257. Untitled, *NYT*, Jun. 12, 1935, 18.

258. "Broadway Capitol Drops Stage Show," *Motion Picture Herald*, Aug. 3, 1935, 54.

259. Samuel Rothafel to M. H. "Deac" Aylesworth, Sept. 5, 1935 (WHS, 17AF, Box 41, Folder 21).

260. Niles Trammell to Bertha Brainerd, Nov. 18, 1935 (WHS, 17AF, Box 41, Folder 21).

261. "Merry-Go-Round of the Air," *NYT*, Nov. 3, 1935, XX7.

262. Isabel Morse Jones, "'Artist's Career Lasts Just as Long As Public Wants Him'—Lawrence Tibbett," *NYT*, Nov. 3, 1935, A1.

263. "Radiography," *LAT*, Sept. 29, 1935, A8.

264. "Bowes No. 1 Money Man," *Variety*, Sept. 18, 1935, 1, 35.

265. "Man with Magic Wand: 1935 Model," *CSM*, Aug. 23, 1935, 2.

266. Joe Bigelow, "Roxy, Films' No. 1 Exhibitor, Pioneer in Cinema Standards, Dies at 53," *Variety*, Jan. 15, 1936, 4, 31; "Roxy Re-organizing Declared Nearer," *MPH*, Feb. 15, 1936, 21.

267. "'Roxy' Dies on Eve of Big Comeback," *New York American*, Jan. 14, 1936, n.p. (NYPL).

268. Revell had known Roxy for at least three years. Nellie Revell, "Nellie Revell Interviews Roxy," *Radio Digest*, Jan. 1933, 10.

269. Nellie Revell to John Royal, Jan. 2, 1936 (WHS, 19AF, Box 49, Folder 46).

270. D. S. Tuthill to John Royal, Jan. 3, 1936 (WHS, 17AF, Box 44, Folder 44).

271. It is not clear whether or not this was Revell's radio idea with a new title.

272. "Roxy Succumbs to Heart Attack While Asleep," *Brooklyn Daily Eagle*, Jan. 13, 1936, n.p. (NYPL); Alton Cook, "Roxy Death Scraps Programs," *New York World-Telegram*, Jan. 14, 1936, n.p. (NYPL); "'Roxy' Dies in Sleep," *Daily Mirror*, Jan. 14, 1936, n.p. (NYPL); "'Roxy' Dies on Eve of Big Comeback," n.p.

273. "'Roxy' Stricken in Hotel Rooms," 1; "'Roxy' Summoned by Grim Reaper," *Forest City News*, Jan. 16, 1936, 1.

274. "Movie Palace Creator Had Defied Doctor," *New York Evening Post*, Jan. 13, 1936, n.p. (NYPL).

275. "Samuel L. Rothafel," Department of Health of the City of New York Bureau of Records, Certificate of Death, No. 1361, Jan. 13, 1936, 1; "Roxy Succumbs to Heart Attack While Asleep," n.p.

276. "Movie Palace Creator Had Defied Doctor," n.p.

277. Louis Sobel, "The Voice of Broadway," *New York American*, n.p. (NYPL).

278. "Roxy Dies in Sleep in His Suite in Hotel," n.p.

279. Quoted in Edwin Schallert, "Rothapfel a Harmonist," *LAT*, Nov. 2, 1919, III1.

280. Jamison, 3.

281. *The Secret of Keeping Fit* advertisement, *NYT*, Jan. 13, 1936, 36.

282. "'Roxy' Called by Death," *Arcadia* (CA) *Daily Tribune*, Jan. 13, 1936, 1; "'Roxy' Stricken in Hotel Rooms," 1; "S. L. Rothapfel, 'Roxy,' Found Dead in Room in New York Hotel," unknown clipping, Jan. 13, 1936, 1 (Washington Historical Society, Stillwater, MN).

283. "'Roxy' Rothafel Dies in Hotel at 53," *New York Evening Journal*, Jan. 13, 1936, n.p. (NYPL).

284. Bigelow, 4.

285. Terry Ramsaye, "'Roxy,'" *MPH*, Jan. 18, 1936, 13.

286. W. R. Wilkerson, "Tradeviews," *Hollywood Reporter*, Jan. 14, 1936, n.p. (NYPL).

287. "Roxy," *HC*, Jan. 15, 1936, 12.

288. Jack Banner, "'ROXY,'" *RG*, Sept. 15, 1934, 5.

289. Aaron Stein, "Roxy Leaves His Mark on Radio's Broadcasting Style," *New York Post*, Jan. 14, 1936, n.p. (NYPL).

290. "The Passing of 'Roxy,'" *American Hebrew*, Jan. 17, 1936, n.p. (NYPL); Bigelow, n.p.

291. "Roxy Dies in Sleep in His Suite in Hotel," n.p.

292. "Roxy Is Buried; Pomp He Loved Absent at Rites," *New York World Telegram*, Jan. 15, 1936, n.p. (NYPL); "Final Tribute Paid to Roxy," *New York Sun*, Jan. 15, 1936, n.p. (NYPL); "'Roxy' Buried, Mourned by Afflicted," unknown clipping, ca. Jan. 15, 1936, n.p. (NYPL).

293. "Final Tribute Paid to Roxy," n.p. (NYPL); "Roxy's Funeral Is Shorn of Splendor He Exploited," unknown clipping, ca. Jan. 15, 1936, n.p. (NYPL).

294. Unknown clipping, ca. Jan. 15, 1936, n.p. (NYPL).

295. "Roxy Is Buried; Pomp He Loved Absent at Rites," n.p.

296. When his casket reached the Linden Hills Cemetery in Brooklyn, the honor guard fired a ceremonial volley of shots. "Roxy Is Buried; Pomp He Loved Absent at Rites," n.p. The Roxy Memorial Grove was later planted in the George Washington Forest in Palestine, not far from the Roxy Theatre in Jerusalem. "Answers to Questions," *Sheboygan* (WI) *Press*, Apr. 27, 1936, 9; "A "Roxy" Theatre Opened by Palestine Entrepreneurs," *Jewish Telegraphic Agency*, Jan. 14, 1934. Roxy left an estate worth $215,560—not enormous, but a still significant sum. "S. L. Rothafel Left Estate of $215,560," *NYT*, Jan. 1, 1938, 10.

297. "Roxy's Rites this Morning," *New York American,* Jan. 15, 1936, n.p. (NYPL).

298. "Sparks from the Antennae," *LAT*, Jan. 19, 1936, C10.

299. *Major Bowes Amateur Theatre of the Air* advertisement, *Hollywood Reporter*, Jan. 15, 1936, 15.

300. "The Wheel of Major Bowes Gave Opportunity to Many Americans," *Kansas City Times*, Apr. 27, 1956.

AFTERWORD

| LAT | Los Angeles Times |
| MPH | Motion Picture News |

NYPL   *New York Public Library for the Performing Arts*

1. "Roxy Memorial Grove Planned for Palestine," *MPH*, Mar. 21, 1936, 60.

2. "To Film Roxy's Life," *Variety*, Mar. 25, 1936, 1.

3. Philip K. Scheuer, "A Town Called Hollywood," *LAT*, Apr. 26, 1936, B1.

4. Louella G. Parsons, "Peggy Ann Garner Gets Plum in 'Junior Made,'" unknown clipping, Oct. 16, 1945 (NYPL).

5. Philip S. Goldberg and George Feltenstein, "Roxy: A Musical Drama Based upon the Life of Sam Rothafel: Treatment/Book by Philip Goldberg and George Feltenstein." United States Copyright Office. PAu000387315. Mar. 30, 1982.

6. Like his father, Arthur Rothafel also produced articles and a book: Roxy Rothafel, *Roxy's Ski Guide to New England* (Charlotte, NC: East Woods Press, 1978).

BIBLIOGRAPHY

BOOKS

Abel, Richard. *The Red Rooster Scare: Making Cinema American, 1900–1910*. Berkeley: University of California Press, 1999.

——. *Americanizing the Movies and "Movie-Mad" Audiences, 1910–1914*. Berkeley: University of California Press, 2006.

Abel, Richard and Rick Altman. *The Sounds of Early Cinema*. Bloomington: Indiana University Press, 2001.

Acland, Charles R. *Screen Traffic: Movies, Multiplexes, and Global Culture*. Durham, NC: Duke University Press, 2003.

Alexander, Michael. *Jazz Age Jews*. Princeton, NJ: Princeton University Press, 2001.

Alicoate, Jack, ed. *Roxy: A History*. New York: The Film Daily, 1927.

Alleman, Richard. *The Movie Lover's Guide to New York*. New York: Harper & Row, 1988.

Allen, Robert C. and Douglas Gomery. *Film History: Theory and Practice*. New York: McGraw-Hill, 1985.

Allvine, Glendon. *The Greatest Fox of Them All*. New York: Lyle Stuart, 1969.

Altman, Diana. *Hollywood East*. New York: Birch Lane, 1992.

Altman, Rick. *Silent Film Sound*. New York: Columbia University Press, 2004.

Altman, Rick, ed. *Sound Theory, Sound Practice*. New York: Routledge, 1992.

Atkinson, Brooks. *Broadway*. New York: Macmillan, 1970.

Balio, Tino, ed. *The American Film Industry*. Madison: University of Wisconsin Press, 1985.

——. *Grand Design: Hollywood as a Modern Business Enterprise, 1930–1939*. New York: Scribner, 1993.

Banning, William Peck. *Commercial Broadcasting Pioneer*. Cambridge, MA: Harvard University Press, 1946.

Barnouw, Erik. *A History of Broadcasting in the United States, Volume I – to 1933*. New York: Oxford University Press, 1966.

Barnouw, Erik et al. *Conglomerates and the Media*. New York: The New Press, 1997.

Barrios, Richard. *A Song in the Dark*. New York: Oxford University Press, 1995.

Beardsley, Charles. *Hollywood's Master Showman: The Legendary Sid Grauman*. New York: Cornwall Books, 1983.

Berg, A. Scott. *Goldwyn*. New York: Riverhead Books, 1989.

Bernstein, Matthew. *Walter Wanger, Hollywood Independent*. Minneapolis: University of Minnesota Press, 2000.

Besse, Kirk J. *Show Houses: Twin Cities Style*. Minneapolis, MN: Victoria Publications, 1997.

Bolter, Jay David and Richard Grusin. *Remediation*. Cambridge, MA: MIT Press, 1999.

Bordwell, David, Janet Staiger, and Kristin Thompson. *The Classical Hollywood System: Film Style & Mode of Production to 1960*. New York: Columbia University Press, 1985.

Bowser, Eileen. *History of the American Cinema 2: Transformation of the Screen, 1907–1915*. New York: Scribner, 1990.

Bradley, Edwin M. *The First Hollywood Sound Shorts, 1926–1931*. Jefferson, NC: McFarland, 2005.

Brodkin, Karen. *How Jews Became White Folks and What That Says About Race in America*. New Brunswick, NJ: Rutgers University Press, 1998.

Budd, Mike, ed. *The Cabinet of Dr. Caligari: Texts, Contexts, Histories*. New Brunswick, NJ: Rutgers University Press, 1990.

Buhle, Paul. *From the Lower East Side to Hollywood: Jews in American Popular Culture*. New York: Verso, 2004.

Butler, Jeremy G., ed. *Star Texts: Image and Performance in Film and Television*. Detroit: Wayne State University Press, 1991.

Butsch, Richard, ed. *For Fun and Profit: The Transformation of Leisure into Consumption*. Philadelphia: Temple University Press, 1990.

Caldwell, John T. *Production Cultures: Industrial Reflexivity and Critical Practice in Film and Television*. Durham, NC: Duke University Press, 2008.

Campbell, Craig W. *Reel America and World War I: Film in the U.S., 1914–1920*. Jefferson, NC: McFarland, 1985.

Carr, Steven Alan. *Hollywood and Anti-Semitism: A Cultural History Up to World War II*. New York: Cambridge University Press, 2001.

Clar, Reva Howitt and Mimi Melnick, ed. *Lollipop: Vaudeville Turns with a Fanchon and Marco Dancer*. Lanham, MD: Scarecrow Press, 2002.

Conant, Michael. *Antitrust in the Motion Picture Industry.* Berkeley: University of California Press, 1960.

Cooper, Kenneth J. *Forest City Centennial.* Forest City, PA: Forest City Centennial Association, 1964.

Crafton, Donald. *The Talkies.* Berkeley, CA: University of California Press, 1997.

Creel, George. *How We Advertised America.* New York: Harper, 1920.

——. *Rebel at Large: Recollections of Fifty Crowded Years.* New York: Putnam, 1947.

Crowther, Bosley. *The Lion's Share.* New York: Dutton, 1957.

Danly, Linda, ed., *Hugo Friedhofer: The Best Years of His Life.* Lanham, MD: Scarecrow Press, 1999.

Debauche, Leslie Midkiff. *Reel Patriotism: The Movies and World War I.* Madison, WI: University of Wisconsin Press, 1997.

Diner, Hasia. *Lower East Side Memories: A Jewish Place in America.* Princeton, NJ: Princeton University Press, 2000.

——. *A New Promised Land: A History of Jews in America.* New York: Oxford University Press, 2003.

Doerksen, Clifford. *American Babel.* Philadelphia: University of Pennsylvania Press, 2005.

Doherty, Thomas. *Projections of War: Hollywood, American Culture, and World War II.* New York: Columbia University Press, 1999.

——. *Hollywood's Censor: Joseph I. Breen & the Production Code Administration.* New York: Columbia University Press, 2007.

Douglas, Susan J. *Inventing American Broadcasting, 1899–1922.* Baltimore: Johns Hopkins University Press, 1987.

——. *Listening In: Radio and the American Imagination.* Minneapolis: University of Minnesota Press, 2004.

Dragonette, Jessica. *Faith Is a Song: The Odyssey of an American Artist.* New York: D. McKay, 1951.

Eisler, Hanns and Theodor W Adorno. *Composing for the Films.* Atlantic Highlands, NJ: Athlone Press, 1947.

Ewen, David. *Dictators of the Baton.* Chicago: Alliance Book, 1943.

——. *George Gershwin, His Journey to Greatness.* Englewood Cliffs, NJ: Prentice Hall, 1970.

Eyles, Allen. *The Granada Theatres.* London: BFI, 1998.

——. *Gaumont British Cinemas.* London: BFI, 1999.

Eyman, Scott. *Ernst Lubitsch: Laughter in Paradise.* New York: Simon & Schuster, 1993.

——. *The Speed of Sound.* Baltimore: Johns Hopkins University Press, 1997.

Feingold, Henry. *A Time for Searching: Entering the Mainstream, 1920–1945.* Baltimore, MD: Johns Hopkins University Press, 1992.

Forsher, James. *The Community of Cinema: How Cinema and Spectacle Transformed the American Downtown.* Westport, CT: Preager, 2003.

Francisco, Charles. *The Radio City Music Hall.* New York: Dutton, 1979.

Franklin, Harold Brooks. *Sound Motion Pictures: From the Laboratory to Their Presentation*. Garden City, NY: Doubleday, Doran, 1929.

Fullerton, John, ed. *Screen Culture: History and Textuality*. Eastleigh, England: John Libbey, 2004.

—— and Jan Olsson, eds. *Allegories of Communication: Intermedial Concerns from Cinema to the Digital*. Eastleigh, England: John Libbey, 2004.

Gabler, Neal. *An Empire of Their Own*. New York: Crown, 1988.

Glazer, Irvin R. *Philadelphia Theatres, A–Z*. New York: Greenwood Press, 1986.

Goldstein, Eric. *The Price of Whiteness: Jews, Race, and American Identity*. Princeton, NJ: Princeton University Press, 2006.

Gomery, Douglas. *The Hollywood Studio System*. New York: St. Martins Press, 1986.

——. *Shared Pleasures: A History of Movie Presentation in the United States*. Madison: University of Wisconsin Press, 1992.

——. *The Coming of Sound*. London: Routledge, 2005.

——. *The Hollywood Studio System: A History*. London: BFI, 2005.

Gomery, J. Douglas. *The Coming of Sound to the American Cinema: A History of the Transformation of an Industry*. Dissertation. University of Wisconsin, Madison, 1975.

Goren, Arthur. *New York Jews and the Quest for Community; The Kehillah Experiment, 1908–1922*. New York: Columbia University Press, 1970.

——. *The Politics and Public Culture of American Jews*. Bloomington: Indiana University Press, 1999.

Gottlieb, Jack. *Funny, It Doesn't Sound Jewish: How Yiddish Songs and Synagogue Melodies Influenced Tin Pan Alley, Broadway, and Hollywood*. Albany: State University of New York, 2004.

Grau, Robert. *The Theatre of Science*. New York: Broadway, 1914.

Green, Fitzhugh. *The Film Finds Its Tongue*. New York: Putnam, 1929.

Gross, Ben. *I Looked and I Listened; Informal Recollections of Radio and TV*. New York: Random House, 1954.

Gurock, Jeffrey. *When Harlem Was Jewish*. New York: Columbia University Press, 1979.

Hall, Ben. *The Best Remaining Seats: The Story of the Golden Age of the Movie Palace*. New York: Bramhall House, 1961.

Halper, Donna L. *Invisible Stars: A Social History of Women in American Broadcasting*. Armonk, NY: Sharpe, 2001.

Hansen, Miriam. *Babel and Babylon: Spectatorship in American Silent Film*. Cambridge, MA: Harvard University Press, 1991.

Hark, Ina Rae, ed. *Exhibition: The Film Reader*. London: Routledge, 2002.

Heinze, Andrew. *Adapting to Abundance: Jewish Immigrants, Mass Consumption, and the Search for American Identity*. New York: Columbia University Press, 1990.

Hemenez, Richard L. *The United States Marine Corps in Books and the Performing Arts*. Jefferson, NC: McFarland, 2001.

Hilmes, Michele. *Radio Voices: American Broadcasting 1922–1934*. Minneapolis. University of Minnesota Press, 1997.

——. *Hollywood and Broadcasting*. Urbana: University of Illinois Press, 1999.

——. *Only Connect: A Cultural History of Broadcasting in the United States*. Belmont, CA: Thomson Higher Education, 2002.

——, ed. *NBC: America's Network*. Berkeley: University of California Press, 2007.

—— and Jason Loviglio, eds. *Radio Reader: Essays in the Cultural History of Radio*. New York: Routledge, 2002.

Hoberman, J. and Jeffrey Shandler, eds. *Entertaining America: Jews, Movies, and Broadcasting*. Princeton, NJ: Princeton University Press, 2003.

Isenberg, Michael T. *War on Film: The American Cinema and World War I, 1914–1941*. Rutherford, NJ: Fairleigh Dickinson University Press, 1981.

Jacobs, Lea. *The Decline of Sentiment: American Film in the 1920s*. Berkeley: University of California Press, 2008.

Jancovich, Mark and Lucy Faier with Sarah Stubbings. *The Place of the Audience: Cultural Geographies of Film Consumption*. London: BFI Publishing, 2003.

Jenkins, Henry. *What Made Pistachio Nuts? Early Sound Comedy and the Vaudeville Aesthetic*. New York: Columbia University Press, 1992.

——. *Convergence Culture*. New York: New York University Press, 2006.

Jobes, Gertrude. *Motion Picture Empire*. Hamden, CT: Archon Books, 1966.

Johnson, Patricia Condon. *Stillwater: Minnesota's Birthplace*. Afton, MN: Afton Historical Society Press, 1982.

Joselit, Jenna. *The Wonders of America: Reinventing Jewish Culture 1880–1950*. New York: Hill and Wang, 1994.

Kalinak, Kathryn. *How the West Was Sung: Music in the Westerns of John Ford*. Berkeley: University of California Press, 2007.

Keil, Charlie and Shelley Stamp, eds. *American Cinema's Transitional Era*. Berkeley: University of California Press, 2004.

Kelly, Andrew. *Cinema and the Great War*. New York: Routledge, 1997.

Kendall, Messmore. *Never Let Weather Interfere*. New York: Farrar, Straus, 1946.

Kenney, Dave. *Twin Cities Picture Show: A Century of Moviegoing*. St. Paul: Minnesota Historical Society Press, 2007.

Kozarski, Richard. *An Evening's Entertainment: The Age of the Silent Feature Picture, 1915–1928*. New York: Scribner, 1990.

——. *Hollywood on the Hudson*. Piscataway, NJ: Rutgers University Press, 2008.

Kraft, James P. *Stage to Studio: Musicians and the Sound Revolution, 1890–1950*. Baltimore: Johns Hopkins University Press, 1996.

Kreimeier, Klaus. *The UFA Story*. Berkeley: University of California Press, 1996.

Lahue, Kalton C. *Dreams for Sale: The Rise and Fall of the Triangle Film Corporation*. South Brunswick, NJ: Barnes, 1971.

Landon, John W. *Behold the Mighty Wurlitzer: The History of the Theatre Pipe Organ*. Westport, CT: Greenwood Press, 1983.

Langdale, Allan, ed. *Hugo Münsterberg on Film*. New York: Routledge, 2002.

Lastra, James. *Sound Technology and the American Cinema: Perception, Representation, Modernity*. New York: Columbia University Press, 2000.

Lee, Gypsy Rose. *Gypsy, a Memoir*. New York: Harper, 1957.

Leslie, Serge. *The Seven Leagues of a Dancer*. London: Beaumont, 1958.

——. *A Dancer's Scrapbook with Doris Niles: A Chronicle, 1919–1929*. Princeton, NJ: Princeton Book, 1987.

Leinwand, Gerald. *1927: High Tide of the Twenties*. New York: Four Walls Eight Windows, 2001.

Levy, Alan. *The Bluebird of Happiness: The Memoirs of Jan Peerce*. New York: Harper & Row, 1976.

Levy, Emanuel. *Vincente Minnelli: Hollywood's Dark Dreamer*. New York: St. Martin's Press, 2009.

Lewis, Tom. *Empire of the Air*. New York: Edward Burlingame Books, 1991.

Liebman, Roy. *Vitaphone Films: A Catalogue of the Features and Shorts*. Jefferson, NC: McFarland, 2003.

Loviglio, Jason. *Radio's Intimate Public*. Minneapolis: University of Minneapolis Press, 2005.

MacDonald, J. Fred. *Don't Touch that Dial!: Radio Programming in American Life, 1920–1960*. Chicago: Nelson-Hall, 1979.

Marks, Martin Miller. *Music and the Silent Film*. New York: Oxford University Press, 1997.

May, Lary. *The Big Tomorrow: Hollywood and the Politics of the American Way*. Chicago: University of Chicago Press, 2000.

McChesney, Robert W. *Telecommunications, Mass Media, and Democracy: The Battle for the Control of U.S. Broadcasting, 1928–1935*. New York: Oxford University Press, 1993.

Melnick, Ross and Andreas Fuchs. *Cinema Treasures: A New Look at Classic Movie Theatres*. St. Paul, MN: MBI, 2004.

Mock, James R. and Cedric Larson. *Words that Won the War*. Princeton, NJ: Princeton University Press, 1939.

Morrison, William. *Broadway Theatres*. Toronto: Dover Publications, 1999.

Mould, David H. *American Newsfilm 1914–1919: The Underexposed War*. New York: Garland, 1983.

Murray, Susan. *Hitch Your Antenna to the Stars: Early Television and Broadcast Stardom*. New York: Routledge, 2005.

Musser, Charles. *The Emergence of Cinema: the American Screen to 1907*. Berkeley: University of California Press, 1994.

—— with Carol Nelson. *High-Class Moving Pictures: Lyman H. Howe and the Forgotten Era of Traveling Exhibition, 1880–1920*. Princeton, NJ: Princeton University Press, 1991.

Nasaw, David. *Going Out*. Cambridge, MA: Harvard University Press, 1993.

Naylor, David. *American Picture Palaces*. New York: Prentice Hall, 1981.

O'Brien, Charles. *Cinema's Conversion to Sound: Technology and Film Style in France and the U.S.* Bloomington: Indiana University Press, 2005.

Obelenus, John S. *Highlights of Forest City Borough History*. Forest City, PA: *Forest City News*, 1938.

Okrent, Daniel. *Great Fortune*. New York: Viking, 2003.

Paley, William S. *As It Happened*. New York: Doubleday, 1979.

Pease, Edward C. and Everette E. Dennis, eds. *Radio: The Forgotten Medium*. New Brunswick, NJ: Transaction, 1995.

Pendo, Stephen. *Aviation in the Cinema*. Metuchen, NJ: Scarecrow Press, 1985.

Plaut, W. Gunther. *The Jews in Minnesota*. New York: American Jewish Historical Society, 1959.

Porto, James. *The Radio City Rockettes: A Dance Through Time*. New York: Harper Collins, 2006.

Reay, Pauline. *Music in Film: Soundtracks and Synergy*. New York: Wallflower, 2004.

Rennie, Karen. *Gail Grant: A Life in Ballet*. M.F.A. Thesis. Toronto: York University, 1992.

Robinson, David. *From Peep Show to Palace*. New York: Columbia University Press, 1996.

Ross, Steven J. *Working-Class Hollywood: Silent Film and the Shaping of Class in America*. Princeton, NJ: Princeton University Press, 1998.

Roth, Joseph. *What I Saw: Reports from Berlin, 1920–1933*. New York: Horton, 2003.

Rotha, Paul. *Robert J. Flaherty: A Biography*. Philadelphia: University of Pennsylvania Press, 1983.

Rothafel, Samuel Lionel and Raymond Francis Yates. *Broadcasting: Its New Day*. New York: Century, 1925.

Rudel, Anthony J. *Hello, Everybody!: The Dawn of American Radio*. Orlando, FL: Harcourt, 2008.

Schwartz, Evan I. *The Last Lone Inventor: A Tale of Genius, Deceit, and the Birth of Television*. New York: HarperCollins, 2002.

Segrave, Kerry. *Foreign Films in America: A History*. Jefferson, NC: McFarland, 2004.

Seldes, Gilbert. *The Movies Come from America*. New York: Scribner, 1937.

Sharp, Dennis. *Picture Palaces*. New York: Praeger, 1969.

Sherwood, Robert E. *The Best Moving Pictures of 1922–3*. Boston: Small, Maynard, 1923.

Shire, Sanford, ed. *Nellé*. New York: Rizzoli, 1981.

Sinclair, Upton. *Upton Sinclair Presents William Fox*. Los Angeles: Upton Sinclair, 1933.

Slide, Anthony. *Silent Topics*. Lanham, MD: Scarecrow Press, 2005.

Smith, Sally Bedell. *In All His Glory: The Life of William S. Paley*. New York: Simon & Schuster, 1990.

Smulyan, Susan. *Selling Radio: The Commercialization of American Broadcasting, 1920–1934*. Washington, DC: Smithsonian Institution Press, 1994.

Sperling, Cass Warner, Cork Millner, and Jack Warner. *Hollywood Be Thy Name: The Warner Brothers Story*. Lexington: University Press of Kentucky, 1998.

Spigel, Lynn and Jan Olsson, eds. *Television After TV: Essays on a Medium in Transition*. Durham, NC: Duke University Press, 2004.

Stagg, Jerry. *The Brothers Shubert*. New York: Random House, 1968.

Staiger, Janet. *Interpreting Films: Studies in the Historical Reception of American Cinema*. Princeton, NJ: Princeton University Press, 1992.

—— and Sabine Hake. *Convergence Media History*. New York: Routledge, 2009.

Stokes, Melvyn. *D. W. Griffith's The Birth of a Nation: A History of "The Most Controversial Motion Picture of All Time."* New York: Oxford University Press, 2007.

—— and Richard Maltby, eds. *American Movie Audiences: From the Turn of the Century to the Early Sound Era*. London: BFI, 1999.

Stones, Barbara. *America Goes to the Movies: 100 Years of Motion Picture Exhibition*. North Hollywood, CA: National Association of Theatre Owners, 1993.

Talmey, Allene. *Doug and Mary and Others*. New York: Macy-Masius, 1927.

Thompson, Emily. *The Soundscape of Modernity*. Cambridge, MA: MIT Press, 2002.

Thornburn, David and Henry Jenkins, eds. *Rethinking Media Change: The Aesthetics of Transition*. Cambridge, MA: MIT Press, 2004.

Umbrecht, Hans Ulrich. *In 1926: Living at the Edge of Time*. Cambridge, MA: Harvard University Press, 1997.

United States Committee on Public Information. *The Creel Report: Complete Report of the Chairman of the Committee on Public Information* (1919). New York: Da Capo Press, 1972.

Usai, Paolo Cherchi. *Silent Cinema: An Introduction*. London: BFI, 2000.

Valentine, Maggie. *The Show Starts on the Sidewalk*. New Haven, CT: Yale University Press, 1994.

Venzon, Anne Cipriano, ed. *The United States in the First World War: An Encyclopedia*. New York: Garland, 1995.

Waller, Gregory A. *Main Street Amusements: Movies and Commercial Entertainment in a Southern City, 1896–1930*. Washington, DC: Smithsonian Institution Press, 1995.

——. *Moviegoing in America*. Malden, MA: Blackwell, 2002.

Ware, Walter. *Ballet Is Magic; A Triple Monograph: Harriet Hoctor, Paul Haakon, Patricia Bowman*. New York: Ihra, 1936.

Weis, Elisabeth and John Belton, eds. *Film Sound: Theory and Practice*. New York: Columbia University Press, 1985.

Wenger, Beth. *New York Jews and the Great Depression: Uncertain Promise*. New Haven, CT: Yale University Press, 1996.

Whitfield, Stephen J. *Paradoxes of American Jewish Culture*. Ann Arbor: University of Michigan, 1993.

——. *In Search of American Jewish Culture*. Hanover, NH: University Press of New England, 1999.

Widen, Larry and Judi Anderson. *Milwaukee Movie Palaces*. Milwaukee: Milwaukee County Historical Society, 1986.

Wilinsky, Barbara. *Sure Seaters: The Emergence of Art House Cinema*. Minneapolis: University of Minnesota Press, 2000.

Winston, Brian. *Media Technology and Society; A History: From the Telegraph to the Internet*. New York: Routledge, 1998.

Wojtowicz, Robert, ed. *Sidewalk Critic: Lewis Mumford's Writings on New York*. New York: Princeton Architectural Press, 1998.

Wood, Richard, ed. *Film and Propaganda in America: A Documentary History*. Westport, CT: Greenwood Press, 1990.

Wurtzler, Steve J. *Electric Sounds*. New York: Columbia University Press, 2007.

Wyatt, Justin. *High Concept: Movies and Marketing in Hollywood*. Austin: University of Texas Press, 1994.

Zukor, Adolph. *The Public Is Never Wrong*. New York: Putnam, 1953.

Articles from Scholarly Journals or Anthologies

Abel, Richard. "'Don't Know Much about History,' or the (In)vested Interests of Doing Cinema History." *Film History* 6:2 (Summer 1994): 110–115.

Allen, Richard C. "From Exhibition to Reception: Reflections on the Audience in Film History." *Screen* 31:4 (Winter 1990): 347–356.

Anderson, Gillian B. "The Presentation of Silent Films, or, Music as Anaesthesia." *Journal of Musicology* 5:2 (Spring 1987): 257–295.

Andrew, Dudley. "Film and Society: Public Rituals and Private Space." In *Exhibition: The Film Reader*, edited by Ina Rae Hark, 161–171. New York: Routledge, 2002.

Bannerman, Henrietta. "An Overview of the Development of Martha Graham's Movement System (1926–1991)." *Dance Research* 17:2 (Winter 1999): 9–46.

Belton, John. "Awkward Transitions: Hitchcock's 'Blackmail' and the Dynamics of Early Film Sound." *Musical Quarterly* 83:2 (Summer 1999): 227–246.

Benjamin, Walter. "The Work of Art in the Age of Mechanical Reproduction." In *Media and Cultural Studies: Keywords*, edited by Meenakshi Gigi Durham and Douglas M. Kellner, 18–40. Malden, MA: Blackwell, 2006.

Bergstrom, Janet. "Murnau, Movietone and Mussolini." *Film History* 27:2/3 (2005): 187–204.

Bertellini, Giorgio. "Restoration, Genealogy and Palimpsests. On Some Historiographical Questions." *Film History* 7:3 (Autumn 1995): 277–290.

Brewster, Ben. "Periodization of Early Cinema." In *American Cinema's Transitional Era*, edited by Charlie Keil and Shelley Stamp, 66–75. Berkeley: University of California Press, 2004.

Browne, Nick. "The Political Economy of the Television (Super) Text." *Quarterly Review of Film Studies* 9:3 (Summer 1984).

Budd, Mike. "The Cabinet of Dr. Caligari: Conditions of Reception." *Cine-Tracts* 3:4 (Winter 1981).

Caldwell, John T. "Convergence Television: Aggregating Form and Repurposing Content in the Culture of Conglomeration." In *Television After TV*, edited by Lynn Spigel and Jan Olsson, 41–74. Durham, NC: Duke University Press, 2004.

——. "Welcome to the Viral Future of Cinema (Television)." *Cinema Journal* 45:1 (Fall 2005): 90–97.

——. "Critical Industrial Practice: Branding, Repurposing and the Migratory Patterns of Industrial Texts." *Television and New Media* 7:2 (May 2006): 99–134.

Clarke, Eric T. "An Exhibitor's Problems in 1927." *Transactions of the Society of Motion Picture Engineers* 11:31 (1927): 450–457.

Corbett, Kevin J. "The Big Picture: Theatrical Moviegoing, Digital Television, and Beyond the Substitution Effect." *Cinema Journal* 40:2 (Winter 2001): 17–34.

Crafton, Donald. "Mindshare: Telephone and Radio Compete for the Talkies." In *Allegories of Communication*, edited by John Fullerton and Jan Olsson, 141–156. Rome: John Libbey, 2004.

Debauche, Leslie Midkiff. "Film in the First World War." In *The United States in the First World War: An Encyclopedia*, edited by Anne Cipriano Venzon, 223. New York: Garland, 1995.

Doherty, Thomas. "The Playhouse Is the Thing." *Chronicle of Higher Education* 51:27 (March 11, 2005): B15.

——. "Return with Us Now to Those Thrilling Days of Yesteryear: Radio Studies Rise Again." *Chronicle of Higher Education* 50:37 (May 21, 2004): B12.

——. "This Is Where We Came In: The Audible Screen and the Voluble Audience of Early Sound Cinema." In *American Movie Audiences: From the Turn of the Century to the Early Sound Era*, edited by Melvyn Stokes and Richard Maltby, 143–163. London: BFI, 1999.

Dorris, George. "Leo Staats at the Roxy, 1926–1928." *Dance Research* 13:1 (Summer 1995): 84–99.

Fuller, Kathryn. "'You Can Have the Strand in Your Own Town.'" In *Moviegoing in America*, edited by Gregory A. Waller, 88–99. Malden, MA: Blackwell, 2002.

Gomery, Douglas. "What Was Adolph Zukor Doing in 1927?" *Film History* 17:2/3 (2005): 205–216.

Gunning, Tom. "Now You See It, Now You Don't: The Temporality of the Cinema of Attractions." In *The Silent Cinema Reader*, edited by Lee Grieveson and Peter Kramer, 41–50. New York: Routledge, 2004.

Hansen, Miriam. "Benjamin, Cinema and Experience: The Blue Flower in the Land of Technology." *New German Critique* 40 (Winter 1987): 179–224.

Herzog, Catherine. "The Movie Palace and the Theatrical Source of Its Architectural Style." *Cinema Journal* (Spring 1981): 15–37.

Higashi, Sumiko. "In Focus: Film History, or a Baedeker Guide to the Historical Turn." *Cinema Journal* 44:1 (Fall 2004): 94–100.

Hiley, Nicholas. "'At the Picture Palace': The British Cinema Audience, 1895–1920." In *Celebrating 1895: The Centenary of Cinema*, edited by John Fullerton. Sydney, Australia: Libbey, 1998.

Horak, Jan-Christopher. "Film History and Film Preservation: Reconstructing the Text of *The Joyless Street* (1925)." *Screening the Past* 5 (December 1998), available at www.latrobe.edu.au/screeningthepast/firstrelease/fir1298/jhfr5b.html (accessed August 4, 2011).

Hubbard, Preston J. "Synchronized Sound and Movie-House Musicians, 1926–29." *American Music* 3:4 (Winter 1985): 429–441.

Hubbert, Julie. "Modernism at the Movies: *The Cabinet of Dr. Caligari* and a Film Score Revisited." *Musical Quarterly* 88:1 (2005): 63–94.

Jenkins, Henry. "'Shall We Make It for New York or for Distribution?': Eddie Cantor, 'Whoopee,' and Regional Resistance to the Talkies." *Cinema Journal* 29:3 (Spring 1990): 32–52.

——. "Convergence? I Diverge." *Technology Review* (June 2001): 93.

——. "Convergence Is Reality." *Technology Review* (June 6, 2003): 1–2, available at www.technologyreview.com/biomedicine/13223/page1/ (accessed August 4, 2011).

——. "The Cultural Logic of Media Convergence," *International Journal of Cultural Studies* 7:1 (March 2004): 33–43.

——. "Quentin Tarantino's 'Star Wars'?: Digital Cinema, Media Convergence, and Popular Culture." In *Media and Cultural Studies: Keyworks*, edited by Durham and Kellner, 549–576.

Jones, Janna. "Channeling Hollywood: Picture Palace Employees and Celebrity Culture." *Journal of Popular Film & Television* 31:3 (Fall 2003): 109–124.

Jones, Steve. "Music and the Internet." *Popular Music* 19:2 (April 2000): 217–230.

Kepley, Vance, Jr., "Whose Apparatus? Problems of Film Exhibition and History." In *Post-Theory: Reconstructing Film Studies*, edited by David Bordwell and Noel Carroll, 533–549. Madison: University of Wisconsin Press, 1996.

King, Rob. "'Made for the Masses with an Appeal to the Classes': The Triangle Film Corporation and the Failure of Highbrow Film Culture." *Cinema Journal* 44:2 (Winter 2005): 3–33.

Kracauer, Siegfried. "Cult of Distraction: On Berlin's Picture Palaces." Reprinted in *New German Critique*, 40 (Winter, 1987): 91–96.

Kraft, James P. "Musicians in Hollywood: Work and Technological Change in Entertainment Industries, 1926–1940." *Technology and Culture* 35:2 (April 1994): 289–314.

Lagny, Michele. "Film History: Or History Expropriated." *Film History* (Spring 1994): 26–44.

Lagos, Taso. "Film Exhibition in Seattle, 1897–1912: Leisure Activity in a Scraggly, Smelly Frontier Town." *Historical Journal of Film, Radio and Television* 23:2 (June 2003): 101–115.

Langdale, Allan. "S(t)imulation of Mind: The Film Theory of Hugo Münsterberg." In *Hugo Münsterberg on Film*, edited by Allan Langdale, 1–41. New York: Routledge, 2002.

Lewis, Kevin and Arnold Lewis. "Include Me Out: Samuel Goldwyn and Joe Godsol." *Film History* 2:2 (June–July 1988): 133–153.

Macgowan, Kenneth. "The Artistic Future of the Movies." *North American Review* CCXIII:783 (February 1921): 260–265.

——. "The Coming of Sound to the Screen." *Quarterly of Film Radio and Television* 10:2 (Winter 1955): 136–145.

Mann, Denise. "The Spectacularization of Everyday Life: Recycling Hollywood Stars and Fans in Early Television Shows." In *Private Screenings*, edited by Lynn Spigel and Denise Mann, 41–69. Minneapolis: University of Minnesota Press.

Melnick, Ross. "Rethinking Rothafel: Roxy's Forgotten Legacy." *The Moving Image* 3:2 (Fall 2003): 62–95.

——. "Station R-O-X-Y: Roxy and the Radio." *Film History* 17:2/3 (2005): 217–233.

——. "Reality Radio: Remediating the Radio Contest Genre in Major Bowes' Amateur Hour Films." *Film History* 23:3 (Fall 2011): 331–347.

Mould, David H. "Washington's War on Film: Government Film Production and Distribution 1917–1918." *Journal of the University Film Association* (Summer 1980).

Musser, Charles. "Historiographic Method and the Study of Early Cinema." *Cinema Journal* 44:1 (Fall 2004): 101–107.

Potamkin, Harry Alan. "Music and the Movies." *Musical Quarterly* 15:2 (April 1929): 281–296.

Pratley, Gerald. "Furthering Motion Picture Appreciation by Radio." *Hollywood Quarterly* 5:2 (Winter 1950): 127–131.

Pratt, David. "*Passion*, the German Invasion & the Emergence of the Name 'Lubitsch.'" *Wide Angle* 13 (January 1991): 34–70.

Ross, Steven J. "Jargon and the Crisis of Readability." *Cinema Journal* 44:1 (Fall 2004): 130–133.

Rothafel, S. L. "Stage Lighting." In *The Theatre and Motion Pictures: A Selection of Articles from the New 14th Edition of the Encyclopedia Britannica*, 46–48. New York: Encyclopedia Britannica, 1933.

Ruggill, Judd Ethan. "Convergence: Always Already, Already." *Cinema Journal* 48:3 (Spring 2009): 105–110.

Russo, Alexander. "Defensive Transcriptions: Radio Networks, Sound-on-Disc Recording, and the Meaning of Live Broadcasting." *Velvet Light Trap* 54 (2004): 4–17.

Sagoff, Mark. "On Restoring and Reproducing Art." *Journal of Philosophy* 75:9 (September 1978): 453–470.

Savoy, William, ed. "Roxy Theatre Issue." *Marquee* (First Quarter, 1979): 1.

Sharrett, Christopher. "9/11, the Useful Incident, and the Legacy of the Creel Committee." *Cinema Journal* 43:4 (Summer 2004): 125–131.

Sklar, Robert. "Does Film History Need a Crisis?" *Cinema Journal*, 44:1 (Fall 2004): 134–138.

Sobchack, Vivian. "What Is Film History? or the Riddle of the Sphinxes." In *Reinventing Film Studies*, edited by Christine Gledhill and Linda Williams, 300–315. New York: Oxford University Press, 2000.

Socolow, Michael J. "Always in Friendly Competition." In *NBC: America's Network*, edited by Michele Hilmes, 25–43. Berkeley: University of California Press, 2007.

Spadoni, Robert. "Geniuses of the Systems: Authorship & Evidence in Classical Hollywood Cinema." *Film History* 7:4 (Winter 1995): 362–385.

Spigel, Lynn. "TV's Next Season?" *Cinema Journal* 45:1 (Fall 2005): 83–90.

Staiger, Janet. "The Future of the Past." *Cinema Journal* 44:1 (Fall 2004): 126–129.

Taylor, Timothy D. "Music and the Rise of Radio in 1920s America." *Historical Journal of Film, Radio and Television* 22:4 (October 2002): 425–443.

Thissen, Judith. "Charlie Steiner's Houston Hippodrome; Moviegoing on New York's Lower East Side, 1909–1913." In *American Silent Film: Discovering Marginalized Voices*, edited by Gregg Bachmann and Thomas J. Slater, 27–47. Carbondale: Southern Illinois University Press, 2002.

——. "Jewish Immigrant Audiences in New York City, 1905–1914." In *American Movie Audiences*, edited by Stokes and Maltby, 15–28.

Uricchio, William. "Re-discovering the Challenge of Textual Instability: New Media's Lessons for Old Media Historians." In *Screen Culture: History and Textuality*, edited by John Fullerton, 161–168. Eastleigh, England: Libbey, 2004.

Waller, Gregory A. "Hillbilly Music and Will Rogers: Small Town Picture Shows in the 1930s." In *American Movie Audiences*, edited by Stokes and Maltby, 164–179.

Selected Trade, Academic, and Popular Journals Cited

For specific articles, please see the notes for each chapter.

American Hebrew

American Organist

Atlanta Constitution

The Bioscope

Boston Traveler

Boxoffice

Brooklyn (Daily) Eagle

Carbondale Leader (Carbondale, PA)

Chicago Daily Tribune

Christian Science Monitor

Cinema Journal

Dallas Morning News

Detroit News

The Etude

Exhibitors Herald / Exhibitors Herald and Motography

Exhibitor's Trade Review

Film Daily

Film History

Forest City News (Forest City, PA)
Hartford Courant
Historical Journal of Film, Radio and Television
Hollywood Reporter
Indianapolis Star
Indianapolis Sunday Star
The Leatherneck
Los Angeles Examiner
Los Angeles Evening Express
Los Angeles Times
The Metronome
Milwaukee Daily News
Milwaukee Free Press
Milwaukee Sentinel
Minneapolis Journal
Minneapolis Morning Tribune
Minneapolis Sunday Tribune
Minneapolis Tribune
Motion Picture Classic
Motion Picture Herald
Motion Picture News
Motography
Movie Age
Moving Picture World
Musical America
Musical Courier
New York American
New York Clipper
New York Dramatic Mirror
New York Morning Telegraph
New York Times
New York Tribune/New York Herald Tribune
New Yorker
News-week/Newsweek
Philadelphia Inquirer
Photoplay
Radio Broadcast
Radio City News
Radio Digest
Radio Guide
Radio Mirror
Radio News

Radioland
Roxy Theatre Weekly Review
Syracuse Herald
The Theatre
Theatre Magazine
Time
Toronto Daily Star
Variety
Wall Street Journal
Washington Post
Zit's Weekly Newspaper

INDEX

Italicized names with dates indicate short and feature-length motion picture titles unless otherwise noted. Radio stations, performing arts centers, hotels, theaters, and other establishments are indexed with locations.

FILM AND CULTURE   A SERIES OF COLUMBIA UNIVERSITY PRESS

Edited by **John Belton**